Harley Granville Barker

1877 - 1946

the plays of

Harley Granville Barker

as performed at
the *edinburgh international festival* 1992

edinburgh festival society

Caution: This play is protected by copyright throughout the world and all the rights are strictly reserved. Application for performance etc. must be made before rehearsal to the Society of Authors, 84 Drayton Gardens, London, SW10 9SB. No performance may be given unless a licence has been obtained.

This edition of the plays performed at the Edinburgh International Festival 1992 published by the Edinburgh Festival Society, 21 Market Street, Edinburgh, EH1 1BW.

ISBN 0 903605 05 8

Designed and produced by **Paradigm Design Ltd.** Oxford.

Printed in Great Britain.

The Voysey Inheritance

1903-5

ACT I

The Office of Voysey and Son is in the best part of Lincoln's Inn. Its panelled rooms give out a sense of grandmotherly comfort and security, very grateful at first to the hesitating investor, the dubious litigant. MR VOYSEY'S own room into which he walks about twenty past ten of a morning radiates enterprise besides. There is polish on everything; on the windows, on the mahogany of the tidily packed writing-table that stands between them, on the brasswork of the fireplace in the other wall, on the glass of the firescreen which preserves only the pleasantness of a sparkling fire, even on MR VOYSEY'S hat as he takes it off to place it on the little red curtained shelf behind the door. MR VOYSEY is sixty or more and masterful; would obviously be master anywhere from his own home outwards, or wreck the situation in his attempt. Indeed there is a buccaneering air sometimes in the twist of his glance, not altogether suitable to a family solicitor. On this bright October morning, PEACEY, the head clerk, follows just too late to help him off with his coat, but in time to take it and hang it up with a quite unnecessary subservience. MR VOYSEY is evidently not capable enough to like capable men about him. PEACEY, not quite removed from Nature, has made some attempts to acquire protective colouring. A very drunken client might mistake him for his master. His voice very easily became a toneless echo of MR VOYSEY'S; later his features caught a line or two from that mirror of all the necessary virtues into which he was so constantly gazing; but how his clothes even when new contrive to look like old ones of MR VOYSEY'S is a mystery, and to his tailor a most annoying one. And PEACEY is just a respectful number of years his master's junior. Relieved of his coat, MR VOYSEY carries to his table the bunch of beautiful roses he is accustomed to bring to the office three times a week and places them for a moment only near the bowl of water there ready to receive them while he takes up his letters. These lie ready too, opened mostly, one or two private ones left closed and discreetly separate. By this time the usual salutations have passed, PEACEY'S 'Good morning, sir'; MR VOYSEY'S 'Morning, Peacey'. Then as he gets his letters MR VOYSEY starts his day's work.

MR VOYSEY: Any news for me?

PEACEY: I hear bad accounts of Alguazils preferred, sir.

MR VOYSEY: Oh..who from?

PEACEY: Merrit and James's head clerk in the train this morning.

MR VOYSEY: They looked all right on...Give me the Times. *(PEACEY goes to the fireplace for the Times; it is warming there. MR VOYSEY waves a letter, then places it on the table.)* Here, that's for you..Gerrard's Cross business. Anything else?

PEACEY: *(as he turns the Times to its Finance page)* I've made the usual notes.

MR VOYSEY: Thank'ee.

PEACEY: Young Benham isn't back yet.

MR VOYSEY: Mr Edward must do as he thinks fit about that. Alguazils,

Alg - oh, yes.

(He is running his eye down the columns. PEACEY leans over the letters.)

PEACEY: This is from Mr Leader about the codicil..You'll answer that?

MR VOYSEY: Mr Leader. Yes. Alguazils. Mr Edward's here, I suppose.

PEACEY: No, sir.

MR VOYSEY: *(his eye twisting with some sharpness)* What!

PEACEY: *(almost alarmed)* I beg pardon, sir.

MR VOYSEY: Mr Edward.

PEACEY: Oh, yes, sir, been in his room some time. I thought you said Headley: he's not due back till Thursday.

(MR VOYSEY discards the Times and sits to his desk and his letters.)

MR VOYSEY: Tell Mr Edward I've come.

PEACEY: Yes, sir. Anything else?

MR VOYSEY: Not for the moment. Cold morning, isn't it?

PEACEY: Quite surprising, sir.

MR VOYSEY: We had a touch of frost down at Chislehurst.

PEACEY: So early!

MR VOYSEY: I want it for the celery. All right, I'll call through about the rest of the letters.

(PEACEY goes, having secured a letter or two, and MR VOYSEY having sorted the rest [a proportion into the waste-paper basket] takes up the forgotten roses and starts setting them into a bowl with an artistic hand. Then his son EDWARD comes in. MR VOYSEY gives him one glance and goes on arranging the roses but says cheerily.)

MR VOYSEY: Good morning, my dear boy.

(EDWARD has little of his father in him and that little is undermost. It is a refined face but self-consciousness takes the place in it of imagination, and in suppressing traits of brutality in his character it looks as if the young man had suppressed his sense of humour too. But whether or no, that would not be much in evidence now, for EDWARD is obviously going through some experience which is scaring him [there is no better word]. He looks not to have slept for a night or two, and his standing there, clutching and unclutching the bundle of papers he carries, his eyes on his father, half appealingly but half accusingly too, his whole being altogether so unstrung and desperate, makes MR VOYSEY'S uninterrupted arranging of the flowers seem very calculated indeed. At last the little tension of silence is broken.)

EDWARD: Father..

MR VOYSEY: Well?

EDWARD: I'm glad to see you.

(This is a statement of fact. He doesn't know that the commonplace phrase sounds ridiculous at such a moment.)

MR VOYSEY: I see you've the papers there.

EDWARD: Yes.

MR VOYSEY: You've been through them?

EDWARD: As you wished me..

MR VOYSEY: Well? *(EDWARD doesn't answer. Reference to the papers seems to overwhelm him with shame. MR VOYSEY goes on with cheerful impatience.)* Come, come, my dear boy, don't take it like this. You're puzzled and worried, of course. But why didn't you come down to me on Saturday night? I expected you..I told you to come. Then your mother was wondering why you weren't with us for dinner yesterday.

EDWARD: I went through all the papers twice. I wanted to make quite sure.

MR VOYSEY: Sure of what? I told you to come to me.

EDWARD: *(He is very near crying.)* Oh, father.

MR VOYSEY: Now look here, Edward, I'm going to ring and dispose of these letters. Please pull yourself together. *(He pushes the little button on his table.)*

EDWARD: I didn't leave my rooms all day yesterday.

MR VOYSEY: A pleasant Sunday! You must learn, whatever the business may be, to leave it behind you at the Office. Why, life's not worth living else.

(PEACEY comes in to find MR VOYSEY before the fire ostentatiously warming and rubbing his hands.) Oh, there isn't much else, Peacey. Tell Simmons that if he satisfies you about the details of this lease it'll be all right. Make a note for me of Mr Grainger's address at Menton. I shall have several things to dictate to Atkinson. I'll whistle for him.

PEACEY: Mr Burnett..Burnett and Marks has just come in, Mr Edward.

EDWARD: *(without turning)* It's only fresh instructions. Will you take them?

PEACEY: All right.

(PEACEY goes, lifting his eyebrows at the queerness of EDWARD'S manner. This MR VOYSEY sees, returning to his table with a little scowl.)

MR VOYSEY: Now sit down. I've given you a bad forty-eight hours, have I? Well, I've been anxious about you. Never mind, we'll thresh the thing out now. Go through the two accounts. Mrs Murberry's first..how do you find it stands?

EDWARD: *(his feelings choking him)* I hoped you were playing off some joke on me.

MR VOYSEY: Come now.

(EDWARD separates the papers precisely and starts to detail them; his voice quite toneless. Now and then his father's sharp comments ring out in contrast.)

EDWARD: We've got the lease of her present house, several agreements.. and here's her will. Here's also a power of attorney expired some time over her securities and her property generally..it was made out for six months.

MR VOYSEY: She was in South Africa.

EDWARD: Here's the Sheffield mortgage and the Henry Smith mortgage with Banker's receipts..her Banker's to us for the interest up to date..four and a half and five per cent. Then..Fretworthy Bonds. There's a note scribbled in your writing that they are at the Bank; but you don't say what Bank.

MR VOYSEY: My own..Stukeley's.

EDWARD: *(just dwelling on the words)* Your own. I queried that. There's eight thousand five hundred in three and a half India Stock. And there are her Banker's receipts for cheques on account of those dividends. I presume for those dividends.

MR VOYSEY: Why not?

EDWARD: *(gravely)* Because then, father, there are her Banker's half yearly receipts for other sums amounting to an average of four hundred and twenty pounds a year. But I find no record of any capital to produce this.

MR VOYSEY: Go on. What do you find?

EDWARD: Till about three years back there seems to have been eleven thousand in Queenslands which would produce—did produce exactly the same sum. But after January of that year I find no record of 'em.

MR VOYSEY: In fact the Queenslands are missing, vanished?

EDWARD: *(hardly uttering the word)* Yes.

MR VOYSEY: From which you conclude?

EDWARD: I supposed at first that you had not handed me all the papers.

MR VOYSEY: Since Mrs Murberry evidently still gets that four twenty a year, somehow; lucky woman.

EDWARD: *(in agony)* Oh!

MR VOYSEY: Well, we'll return to the good lady later. Now let's take the other.

EDWARD: The Hatherley Trust.

MR VOYSEY: Quite so.

EDWARD: *(with one accusing glance)* Trust.

MR VOYSEY: Go on.

EDWARD: Father ..

(His grief comes uppermost again and MR VOYSEY meets it kindly.)

MR VOYSEY: I know, my dear boy. I shall have lots to say to you. But let's get quietly through with these details first.

EDWARD: *(bitterly now)* Oh, this is simple enough. We're young Hatherley's only trustees till his coming of age in about five years' time. The property was eighteen thousand invested in Consols. Certain sums were to be allowed for his education; we seem to be paying them.

MR VOYSEY: Regularly.

EDWARD: Quite. But where's the capital?

MR VOYSEY: No record?

EDWARD: Yes..A note by you on a half sheet..Refer to the Bletchley Land Scheme.

MR VOYSEY: That was ten years ago. Haven't I credited him with the interest on his capital?

EDWARD: The balance ought to be re-invested. There's this *(a sheet of figures)* in your hand-writing. You credit him with the Consol interest.

MR VOYSEY: Quite so.

EDWARD: But I think I've heard you say that the Bletchley scheme paid seven and a half.

MR VOYSEY: At one time. Have you also taken the trouble to calculate what will be due from us to the lad?

EDWARD: Yes..even on the Consol basis..capital and compound interest.. about twenty six thousand pounds.

MR VOYSEY: A respectable sum. In five years' time?

EDWARD: When he comes of age.

MR VOYSEY: That gives us, say, four years and six months in which to think about it.

(EDWARD waits, hopelessly, for his father to speak again; then says)

EDWARD: Thank you for showing me these, sir. Shall I put them back in your safe now?

MR VOYSEY: Yes, you'd better. There's the key. *(EDWARD reaches for the bunch, his face hidden.)* Put them down. Your hand shakes..why, you might have been drinking..I'll put them away later. It's no use having hysterics, Edward. Look your trouble in the face.

(EDWARD'S only answer is to go to the fire, as far from his father as the room allows. And there he leans on the mantelpiece, his shoulders heaving .)

MR VOYSEY: I'm sorry, my dear boy. I wouldn't tell you if I could help it.

EDWARD: I can't believe it. And that you should be telling me..such a thing.

MR VOYSEY: Let yourself go..have your cry out, as the women say. It isn't pleasant, I know. It isn't pleasant to inflict it on you.

EDWARD: How I got through that outer office this morning, I don't know. I came early but some of them were here. Peacey came into my room; he must have seen that there was something up.

MR VOYSEY: That's no matter.

EDWARD: *(able to turn to his father again; won round by the kind voice)* How long has it been going on? Why didn't you tell me before? Oh, I know you thought you'd pull through; but I'm your partner..I'm responsible too. Oh, I don't want to shirk that..don't think I mean to shirk that, father. Perhaps I ought to have discovered, but those affairs were always in your hands. I trusted..I beg your pardon. Oh, it's us..not you. Everyone has trusted us.

MR VOYSEY: *(calmly and kindly still)* You don't seem to notice that I'm not breaking my heart like this.

EDWARD: What's the extent of the mischief? When did it begin? Father, what made you begin it?

MR VOYSEY: I didn't begin it.

EDWARD: You didn't. Who then?

MR VOYSEY: My father before me. *(EDWARD stares.)* That calms you a little.

EDWARD: I'm glad..my dear father! *(And he puts out his hand. Then just a doubt enters his mind.)* But I..it's amazing.

MR VOYSEY: *(shaking his head)* My inheritance, Edward.

EDWARD: My dear father!

MR VOYSEY: I had hoped it wasn't to be yours.

EDWARD: D'you mean to tell me that this sort of thing has been going on here for years? For more than thirty years!

MR VOYSEY: Yes.

EDWARD: That's a little hard to understand just at first, sir.

MR VOYSEY: *(sententiously)* We do what we must in this world, Edward; I have done what I had to do.

EDWARD: *(his emotion well cooled by now)* Perhaps I'd better just listen quietly while you explain.

MR VOYSEY: *(concentrating)* You know that I'm heavily into Northern Electrics.

EDWARD: Yes.

MR VOYSEY: But you don't know how heavily. When I got the tip the Municipalities were organising the purchase, I saw of course the stock must be up a hundred and forty five—a hundred and fifty in no time. Now Leeds will keep up her silly quarrel with the other place..they won't apply for powers for another ten years. I bought at ninety five. What are they today?

EDWARD: Seventy two.

MR VOYSEY: Seventy one and a half. And in ten years I may be..I'm getting on for seventy, Edward. That's mainly why you've had to be told.

EDWARD: With whose money are you so heavily into Northern Electrics?

MR VOYSEY: The firm's money.

EDWARD: Clients' money?

MR VOYSEY: Yes.

EDWARD: *(coldly)* Well..I'm waiting for your explanation, sir.

MR VOYSEY: You seem to have recovered pretty much.

EDWARD: No, sir, I'm trying to understand, that's all.

MR VOYSEY: *(with a shrug)* Children always think the worst of their parents, I suppose. I did of mine. It's a pity.

EDWARD: Go on, sir, go on. Let me know the worst.

MR VOYSEY: There's no immediate danger. I should think anyone could see that from the figures there. There's no real risk at all.

EDWARD: Is that the worst?

MR VOYSEY: *(his anger rising)* Have you studied these two accounts or have you not?

EDWARD: Yes, sir.

MR VOYSEY: Well, where's the deficiency in Mrs Murberry's income..has she ever gone without a shilling? What has young Hatherley lost?

EDWARD: He stands to lose—

MR VOYSEY: He stands to lose nothing if I'm spared for a little, and you will only bring a little common sense to bear and try to understand the difficulties of my position.

EDWARD: Father, I'm not thinking ill of you..that is, I'm trying not to. But won't you explain how you're justified..?

MR VOYSEY: In putting our affairs in order?

EDWARD: Are you doing that?

MR VOYSEY: What else?

EDWARD: *(starting patiently to examine the matter)* How bad were things when you first came to control them?

MR VOYSEY: Oh, I forget.

EDWARD: You can't forget.

MR VOYSEY: Well..pretty bad.

EDWARD: Do you know how it was my grandfather began to—

MR VOYSEY: Muddlement, muddlement! Fooled away hundreds and thousands on safe things..well, then, what was he to do? He'd no capital, no credit, and was in terror of his life. My dear Edward, if I hadn't found it out in time, he'd have confessed to the first man who came and asked for a balance sheet.

EDWARD: Well, what exact sum was he to the bad then?

MR VOYSEY: I forget. Several thousands.

EDWARD: But surely it has not taken all these years to pay off—

MR VOYSEY: Oh, hasn't it!

EDWARD: *(making his point)* Then how does it happen, sir, that such a comparatively recent trust as young Hatherley's has been broken into?

MR VOYSEY: Well, what could be safer than to use that money? There's a Consol investment and not a sight wanted of either capital or interest for five years.

EDWARD: *(utterly beaten)* Father, are you mad?

MR VOYSEY: On the contrary, when my clients' money is entirely under my control, I sometimes re-invest it. The difference between the income this money was bringing to them and the profits it then actually brings to me, I..I utilise in my endeavour to fill up the deficit in the firm's accounts..I use it to put things straight. Doesn't it follow that the more low-interest-bearing capital I can use the better..the less risky things I have to put it into. Most of the young Hatherley's Consol capital..the Trust gives me full discretion..is now out on mortgage at four and a half and five..safe as safe can be.

EDWARD: But he should have the benefit.

MR VOYSEY: He has the amount of his Consol interest.

EDWARD: Where are the mortgages? Are they in his name?

MR VOYSEY: Some of them..some of them. That really doesn't matter. With regard to Mrs Murberry..those Fretworthy Bonds at my bank..I've raised five thousand on them. But I can release her Bonds tomorrow if she wants them.

EDWARD: Where's the five thousand?

MR VOYSEY: I'm not sure..it was paid into my own account. Yes, I do remember. Some of it went to complete a purchase..that and two thousand more out of the Skipworth fund.

EDWARD: But, my dear father—

MR VOYSEY: Well?

EDWARD: (summing it all up very simply) It's not right.

(MR VOYSEY considers his son for a moment with a pitying shake of the head .)

MR VOYSEY: Why?..why is it so hard for a man to see beyond the letter of the law! Will you consider, Edward, the position in which I found myself at that moment? Was I to see my father ruined and disgraced without lifting a finger to help him?..quite apart from the interest of our clients. I paid back to the man who would have lost most by my father's mistakes every penny of his money. And he never knew the danger he'd been in..never passed an uneasy moment about it. It was I that lay awake. I have now somewhere a letter from that man to my father thanking him effusively for the way in which he'd conducted some matter. It comforted my poor father. Well, Edward, I stepped outside the letter of the law to do that service. Was I right or wrong?

EDWARD: In the result, sir, right.

MR VOYSEY: Judge me by the result. I took the risk of failure..I should have suffered. I could have kept clear of the danger if I'd liked.

EDWARD: But that's all past. The thing that concerns me is what you are doing now.

MR VOYSEY: (gently reproachful now) My boy, can't you trust me a little? It's all very well for you to come in at the end of the day and criticise. But I who have done the day's work know how that work had to be done. And here's our firm, prosperous, respected and without a stain on its honour. That's the main point, isn't it?

EDWARD: (quite irresponsive to this pathetic appeal) Very well, sir. Let's dismiss from our minds all prejudices about speaking the truth..acting upon one's instructions, behaving as any honest firm of solicitors must behave..

MR VOYSEY: Nonsense, I tell no unnecessary lies. If a man of any business ability gives me definite instructions about his property, I follow them.

EDWARD: Father, no unnecessary lies!

MR VOYSEY: Well, my friend, go and knock it into Mrs Murberry's head, if you can, that four hundred and twenty pounds of her income hasn't, for the last eight years, come from the place she thinks it's come from, and see how happy you'll make her.

EDWARD: But is that four hundred and twenty a year as safe to come to her as it was before you meddled with the capital?

MR VOYSEY: I see no reason why—

EDWARD: What's the security?

MR VOYSEY: *(putting his coping stone on the argument)* My financial ability.

EDWARD: *(really not knowing whether to laugh or cry)* Why, one'd think you were satisfied with this state of things.

MR VOYSEY: Edward, you really are most unsympathetic and unreasonable. I give all I have to the firm's work..my brain..my energies..my whole life. I can't turn my abilities into hard cash at par..I wish I could. Do you suppose that if I could establish every one of these people with a separate and consistent bank balance tomorrow that I shouldn't do it?

EDWARD: *(thankfully able to meet anger with anger)* Do you mean to tell me that you couldn't somehow have put things right by this?

MR VOYSEY: Somehow? How?

EDWARD: If thirty years of this sort of thing hasn't brought you hopelessly to grief..during that time there must have been opportunities..

MR VOYSEY: Must there! Well, I hope that when I'm under ground, you may find them.

EDWARD: I!

MR VOYSEY: Put everything right with the stroke of your pen, if it's so easy!

EDWARD: I!

MR VOYSEY: You're my partner and my son; you'll inherit the business.

EDWARD: *(realising at last that he has been led to the edge of this abyss)* Oh no, father.

MR VOYSEY: Why else have I had to tell you all this?

EDWARD: *(very simply)* Father, I can't. I can't possibly. I don't think you've any right to ask me.

MR VOYSEY: Why not, pray?

EDWARD: It's perpetuating the dishonesty.

(MR VOYSEY hardens at the unpleasant word.)

MR VOYSEY: You don't believe that I've told you the truth.

EDWARD: I want to believe it.

MR VOYSEY: It's no proof...my earning these twenty or thirty people their rightful incomes for the last—how many years?

EDWARD: Whether what you have done and are doing is wrong or right..I can't meddle in it.

(For the moment MR VOYSEY looks a little dangerous.)

MR VOYSEY: Very well. Forget all I've said. Go back to your room. Get back to your own mean drudgery. My life work—my splendid life work—ruined! What does that matter?

EDWARD: Whatever did you expect of me?

MR VOYSEY: *(making a feint at his papers)* Oh, nothing, nothing. *(Then he slams them down with great effect.)* Here's a great edifice built up by years of labour and devotion and self-sacrifice..a great arch you may call it..a bridge which is to carry our firm to safety with honour. *(This variation of Disraeli passes unnoticed.)* My work! And now, as I near the end of my life, it still lacks the key-stone. Perhaps I am to die with my work just incomplete. Then is there nothing that a son might do? Do you think I shouldn't be proud of you, Edward..that I shouldn't bless you from—wherever I may be, when you completed my life's work ..with perhaps just one kindly thought of your father?

(In spite of this oratory, the situation is gradually impressing EDWARD .)

EDWARD: What will happen if I desert you?

MR VOYSEY: I'll protect you as best I can.

EDWARD: I wasn't thinking of myself, sir.

MR VOYSEY: *(with great nonchalance)* Well, I shan't mind the exposure, you know. It won't make me blush in my coffin..and you're not so quixotic, I hope, as to be thinking of the feelings of your brothers and sisters. Considering how simple it would have been for me to have gone to my grave in peace and quiet and let you discover the whole thing afterwards, the fact that I didn't, that I have taken thought for the future of all of you might perhaps have convinced you that I..! But there..consult your own safety.

(EDWARD has begun to pace the room; indecision growing upon him.)

EDWARD: This is a queer thing to have to make up one's mind about, isn't it, father?

MR VOYSEY: *(watching him closely and modulating his voice)* My dear boy, I understand the shock to your feelings that this disclosure must have been.

EDWARD: Yes, I came this morning thinking that next week would see us in the dock together.

MR VOYSEY: And I suppose if I'd broken down and begged your pardon for my folly, you'd have done anything for me, gone to prison smiling, eh?

EDWARD: I suppose so.

MR VOYSEY: Yes, it's easy enough to forgive. I'm sorry I can't go in sack-cloth and ashes to oblige you. *(Now he begins to rally his son; easy in his strength.)* My dear Edward, you've lived a quiet humdrum life up to now, with your poetry and your sociology and your agnosticism and your ethics of this and your ethics of that..dear me, these are the sort of garden oats which young men seem to sow nowadays!..and you've never before been brought face to face with any really vital question. Now don't make a fool of yourself just through inexperience. Try and give your mind without prejudice to the consideration of a very serious matter. I'm not angry at what you've said to me. I'm quite willing to forget it. And it's for your own sake and not for mine, Edward, that I do beg you to—to—to be a man and take a practical common-sense view of the position you find yourself in. It's not a pleasant position, I know, but it's unavoidable.

EDWARD: You should have told me before you took me into partnership.

(Oddly enough it is this last flicker of rebellion which breaks down MR VOYSEY'S caution. Now he lets fly with a vengeance.)

MR VOYSEY: Should I be telling you at all if I could possibly help it? Don't I know that you're all about as fit for the job as a babe unborn? Haven't I been worrying over that for these last three years? But I'm in a corner...and am I to see my firm come to smash simply because of your scruples? If you're a son of mine you'll do as I tell you. Hadn't I the same choice to make?..and it's a safer game for you now than it was for me then. D'you suppose I didn't have scruples? If you run away from this, Edward, you're a coward. My father was a coward and he suffered for it to the end of his days. I was sick-nurse to him here more than partner. Good lord!..of course it's pleasant and comfortable to keep within the law..then the law will look after you. Otherwise you have to look pretty sharp after yourself. You have to cultivate your own sense of right and wrong; deal your own justice. But that makes a bigger man of you, let me tell you. How easily..how easily could I have walked out of my father's office and left him to his fate; no one would have blamed me! But I didn't. I thought it my better duty to stay and..yes, I say it with all reverence..to take up my cross. Well, I've carried that cross pretty successfully. And what's more, it's made a happy man of me..a better, stronger man than skulking about in shame and in fear of his life ever made of my poor dear father. *(Relieved at having let out the truth, but doubtful of his wisdom in doing so, he changes his tone.)* I don't want what I've been saying to influence you, Edward. You are a free agent..and you must decide upon your own course of action. Now don't let's discuss the matter any more for the moment.

(EDWARD looks at his father with clear eyes.)

EDWARD: Don't forget to put these papers away.

(He restores them to their bundles and hands them back: it is his only comment. MR VOYSEY takes them and his meaning in silence.)

MR VOYSEY: Are you coming down to Chislehurst soon? We've got Hugh and his wife, and Booth and Emily, and Christopher for two or three days, till he goe back to school.

EDWARD: How is Chris?

MR VOYSEY: All right again now..grows more like his father. Booth's very proud of him. So am I.

EDWARD: I think I can't face them all just at present.

MR VOYSEY: Nonsense.

EDWARD: *(a little wave of emotion going through him)* I feel as if this thing were written on my face. How I shall get through business I don't know!

MR VOYSEY: You're weaker than I thought, Edward.

EDWARD: *(a little ironically)* A disappointment to you, father?

MR VOYSEY: No, no.

EDWARD: You should have brought one of the others into the firm.. Trenchard or Booth.

MR VOYSEY: *(hardening)* Trenchard! *(He dismisses that.)* Well, you're a better man than Booth. Edward, you mustn't imagine that the whole world is standing on its head merely because you've had an unpleasant piece of news. Come down to Chislehurst tonight..well, say tomorrow night. It'll be good for you..stop your brooding..that's your worst vice, Edward. You'll find the household as if nothing had happened. Then you'll remember that nothing really has happened. And presently you'll get to see that nothing need happen if you keep your head. I remember times, when things have seemed at their worst, what a relief it's been to me..my romp with you all in the nursery just before your bedtime. Do you remember?

EDWARD: Yes. And cutting your head open once with that gun.

MR VOYSEY: *(in a full glow of fine feeling)* And, my dear boy, if I knew that you were going to inform the next client you met of what I've just told you..

EDWARD: *(with a shudder)* Oh, father!

MR VOYSEY: ..And that I should find myself in prison tomorrow, I wouldn't wish a single thing I've ever done undone. I have never wilfully harmed man or woman. My life's been a happy one. Your dear mother has been spared to me. You're most of you good children and a credit to what I've done for you.

EDWARD: *(the deadly humour of this too much for him)* Father!

MR VOYSEY: Run along now, run along. I must finish my letters and get into the City.

(He might be scolding a schoolboy for some trifling fault. EDWARD turns to have a look at the keen unembarrassed face. MR VOYSEY smiles at him and proceeds to select from the bowl a rose for his buttonhole.)

EDWARD: I'll think it over, sir.

MR VOYSEY: Of course, you will. And don't brood, Edward, don't brood.

(So EDWARD leaves him; and having fixed the rose to his satisfaction, he rings his table telephone and calls through it to the listening clerk.) Send Atkinson to me, please.

(Then he gets up, keys in hand, to lock away Mrs Murberry's and the Hatherley Trust papers.)

ACT II

The VOYSEY dining-room at Chislehurst, when children and grandchildren are visiting, is dining-table and very little else. And at this moment in the evening when five or six men are sprawling back in their chairs, and the air is clouded with smoke, it is a very typical specimen of the middle-class English domestic temple; the daily sacrifice consummated, the acolytes dismissed, the women safely in the drawing-room and the chief priests of it taking their surfeited ease round the dessert-piled altar. It has the usual red-papered walls (like a reflection, they are, of the underdone beef so much consumed within them), the usual varnished woodwork which is known as grained oak; there is the usual, hot, mahogany furniture; and, commanding point of the whole room, there is the usual black-marble sarcophagus of a fireplace. Above this hangs one of the two or three oil paintings, which are all that break the red pattern of the walls, the portrait painted in 1880 of an undistinguished looking gentleman aged sixty; he is shown sitting in a more graceful attitude than it could ever have been comfortable for him to assume. MR VOYSEY'S father it is, and the brass plate at the bottom of the frame tells us that the portrait was a presentation one. On the mantlepiece stands of course, a clock; at either end a china vase filled with paper spills. And in front of the fire—since that is the post of vantage, stands at this moment MAJOR BOOTH VOYSEY. He is the second son, of the age that it is necessary for a Major to be, and of an appearance that many ordinary Majors in ordinary regiments are. He went in the army because he thought it would be like a schoolboy's idea of it; and, being there he does his little all to keep it so. He stands astride, hands in pockets, coat-tails through his arms, cigar in mouth, moustache bristling. On either side of him sits at the table an old gentleman; the one is MR EVAN COLPUS, the vicar of their parish, the other MR GEORGE BOOTH, a friend of long standing, and the Major's godfather. MR COLPUS is a harmless enough anachronism, except for the waste of £400 a year in which his stipend involves the community. Leaving most of his parochial work to an energetic curate, he devotes his serious attention to the composition of two sermons a week. They deal with the difficulties of living the Christian life as experienced by people who have nothing else to do. Published in series from time to time, these form suitable presents for bedridden parishioners. MR GEORGE BOOTH, on the contrary, is as gay an old gentleman as can be found in Chislehurst. An only son, his father left him at the age of twenty-five a fortune of a hundred thousand pounds (a plum, as he called it). At the same time he had the good sense to dispose of his father's business, into which he had been most unwillingly introduced five years earlier, for a like sum before he was able to depreciate its value. It was MR VOYSEY'S invaluable assistance in this transaction which first bound the two together in great friendship. Since that time MR BOOTH has been bent on nothing but enjoying himself. He has even remained a bachelor with that object. Money has given him all he wants, therefore he loves and reverences money; while his imagination may be estimated by the fact that he has now reached the age of sixty-five, still possessing more of it than he knows what to *do with. At the head of the table, meditatively cracking walnuts, sits MR VOYSEY. He has his back there to the conservatory door—you know it is the conservatory door because there is a curtain to pull over it, and because half of it is frosted glass with a purple key pattern round the edge. On MR VOYSEY'S left is DENIS TREG-ONING, a nice enough young man. And at the other end of the table sits EDWARD, not smoking, not talking, hardly listening, very depressed. Behind him is the ordinary door of the room, which leads out into the dismal draughty hall. The MAJOR'S voice is like the sound of a cannon through the tobacco smoke.*

MAJOR: Of course I'm hot and strong for conscription..

MR BOOTH: My dear boy, the country'd never stand it. No Englishman—

MAJOR: *(dropping the phrase heavily upon the poor old gentleman)* I beg your pardon. If we..the Army..say to the country..upon our honour conscription is necessary for your safety..what answer has the country? What? *(He pauses defiantly.)* There you are..none!

TREGONING: Booth will imagine because one doesn't argue that one has nothing to say. You ask the country.

MAJOR: Perhaps I will. Perhaps I'll chuck the Service and go into the House. *(then falling into the sing-song of a favourite phrase)* I'm not a conceited man..but I believe that if I speak out upon a subject I understand and only upon that subject the House will listen..and if others followed my example we should be a far more business-like and go-ahead community.

(He pauses for breath and MR BOOTH seizes the opportunity.)

MR BOOTH: If you think the gentlemen of England will allow themselves to be herded with a lot of low fellers and made to carry guns!

MAJOR: *(obliterating him once more)* Just one moment. Have you thought of the physical improvement which conscription would bring about in the manhood of the country? What England wants is Chest! *(He generously inflates his own.)* Chest and Discipline. Never mind how it's obtained. Don't we suffer from a lack of it in our homes? The servant question now...

MR VOYSEY: *(with a crack of a nut)* Your godson talks a deal, don't he? You know, when our Major gets into a club, he gets on the committee..gets on any committee to enquire into anything..and then goes on at 'em just like this. Don't you, Booth?

(MAJOR knuckles under easily enough to his father's sarcasm.)

MAJOR: Well, sir, people tell me I'm a useful man on committees.

MR VOYSEY: I don't doubt it...your voice must drown all discussion.

MAJOR: You can't say I don't listen to you, sir.

MR VOYSEY: I don't..and I'm not blaming you. But I must say I often think what a devil of a time the family will have with you when I'm gone. Fortunately for your poor mother, she's deaf.

MAJOR: And wouldn't you wish me, sir, as eldest son..Trenchard not counting..

MR VOYSEY: *(with a crack of another nut)* Trenchard not counting. By all means, bully them. Never mind whether you're right or wrong..bully them. I do manage things that way myself, but I think it's your best chance..if there weren't other people present I might say your only chance, Booth.

MAJOR: *(with some discomfort)* Ha! If I were a conceited man, sir, I could trust you to take it out of me.

MR VOYSEY: *(as he taps MR BOOTH with the nut crackers)* Help yourself, George, and drink to your godson's health. Long may he keep his chest notes! Never heard him on parade, have you?

TREGONING: I notice military men must display themselves..that's why Booth acts as a firescreen. I believe that after mess that position is positively rushed.

MAJOR: *(cheering to find an opponent he can tackle)* If you want a bit of fire, say so, you sucking Lord Chancellor. Because I mean to allow you to be my brother-in-law, you think you can be impertinent.

(So TREGONING moves to the fire and that changes the conversation.)

MR VOYSEY: By the bye, Vicar, you were at Lady Mary's yesterday. Is she giving us anything towards that window?

COLPUS: Five pounds more; she has promised me five pounds.

MR VOYSEY: Then how will the debt stand?

COLPUS: Thirty-three..no, thirty-two pounds.

VOYSEY: We're a long time clearing it off.

COLPUS: *(gently querulous)* Yes, now that the window is up, people don't seem ready to contribute as they were.

TREGONING: We must mention that to Hugh!

COLPUS: *(tactful at once)* Not that the work is not universally admired. I have heard Hugh's design praised by quite competent judges. But certainly I feel now it might have been wiser to have delayed the unveiling until the money was forthcoming.

TREGONING: Never deliver goods to the Church on credit.

COLPUS: Eh? *(TREGONING knows that he is a little hard of hearing.)*

VOYSEY: Well, as it was my wish that my son should do the design, I suppose the end I shall have to send you a cheque.

MAJOR: Anonymously.

COLPUS: Oh, that would be—

VOYSEY: No, why should I? Here, George Booth, you shall halve it with me.

MR BOOTH: I'm damned if I do.

COLPUS: *(proceeding, conveniently deaf)* You remember that at the meeting we had of the parents and friends to decide on the positions of the names of the poor fellows and the regiments and coats of arms and so on..when Hugh said so violently that he disapproved of the war and made all those remarks about landlords and Bibles and said he thought of putting in a figure of Britannia blushing for shame or something..I'm beginning to fear that may have created a bad impression.

MAJOR: Why should they mind..what on earth does Hugh know about war? He couldn't tell a battery horse from a bandsman. I don't pretend to criticise art. I think the window'd be very pretty if it wasn't so broken up into bits.

MR BOOTH: *(fortified by his 'damned' and his last glass of port)* These young men are so ready with their disapproval. When I was young, people weren't always questioning this and questioning that.

MAJOR: Lack of discipline.

MR BOOTH: *(hurrying on)* The way a man now even stops to think what he's eating and drinking. And in religious matters..Vicar, I put it to you..there's no uniformity at all.

COLPUS: Ah..I try to keep myself free from the disturbing influences of modern thought.

MR BOOTH: You know, Edward, you're worse even than Hugh is.

EDWARD: *(glancing up mildly at this sudden attack)* What have I done, Mr Booth?

MR BOOTH: *(not the readiest of men)* Well..aren't you another of those young men who go about the world making difficulties?

EDWARD: What sort of difficulties?

MR BOOTH: *(triumphantly)* Just so..I never can make out..Surely when you're young you can ask the advice of your elders and when you grow up you find Laws..lots of laws divine and human laid down for our guidance. *(Well in possession of the conversation he spreads his little self.)* I look back over a fairly long life and..perhaps I should say by Heaven's help..I find nothing that I can honestly reproach myself with. And yet I don't think I ever took more than five minutes to come to a decision upon any important point. One's private life is, I think, one's own affair..I should allow no one to pry into that. But as to worldly things..well, I have come into several sums of money and my capital is still intact ..ask your father. *(MR VOYSEY nods gravely.)* I've never robbed any man. I've never lied over anything that mattered. As a citizen I pay my taxes without grumbling very much. Yes, and I sent conscience money too upon one occasion. I consider that any man who takes the trouble can live the life of a gentleman. *(And he finds that his cigar is out.)*

MAJOR: *(not to be outdone by this display of virtue)* Well, I'm not a conceited man, but—

TREGONING: Are you sure, Booth?

MAJOR: Shut up. I was going to say when my young cub of a brother-in-law-to-be interrupted me, that Training, for which we all have to be thankful to you, Sir, has much to do with it. *(Suddenly he pulls his trousers against his legs.)*

I say, I'm scorching! D'you want another cigar, Denis?

TREGONING: No, thank you.

MAJOR: I do. (*And he glances round, but TREGONING sees a box on the table and reaches it. The Vicar gets up.*)

COLPUS: M-m-m-must be taking my departure.

MR VOYSEY: Already!

MAJOR: (*frowning upon the cigar box*) No, not those. Where are the Ramon Allones? What on earth has Honor done with them?

MR VOYSEY: Spare time for a chat with Mrs Voysey before you go. She has ideas about a children's tea fight.

COLPUS: Certainly I will.

MAJOR: (*scowling helplessly around*) My goodness!..one can never find anything in this house.

COLPUS: I won't say good-bye then.

(*He is sliding through the half opened door when ETHEL meets him flinging it wide. She is the younger daughter, the baby of the family but twenty-three now.*)

MR VOYSEY: I say, it's cold again tonight! An ass of an architect who built this place..such a draught between these two doors.

(*He gets up to draw the curtain. When he turns COLPUS has disappeared, while ETHEL has been followed into the room by ALICE MAITLAND, who shuts the door after her. MISS ALICE MAITLAND is a young lady of any age to thirty. Nor need her appearance alter for the next fifteen years; since her nature is healthy and well-balanced. She possesses indeed the sort of athletic chastity which is a characteristic charm of Northern spinsterhood. It mayn't be a pretty face, but it has alertness and humour; and the resolute eyes and eyebrows are a more innocent edition of MR VOYSEY'S, who is her uncle. ETHEL goes straight to her father [though her glance is on DENIS and his on her] and chirps, birdlike, in her spoiled-child way*).

ETHEL: We think you've stayed in here quite long enough.

MR VOYSEY: That's to say, Ethel thinks Denis has been kept out of her pocket much too long.

ETHEL: Ethel wants billiards..not proper billiards..snooker or something. Oh Papa, what a dessert you've eaten. Greedy pig!

(*ALICE is standing behind EDWARD, considering his hair-parting, apparently.*)

ALICE: Crack me a filbert, please, Edward..I had none.

EDWARD: (*jumping up, rather formally, well-mannered*) I beg your pardon, Alice Won't you sit down?

ALICE: No.

MR VOYSEY: (*taking ETHEL on his knee*) Come here, puss. Have you made up your mind yet what you want for a wedding present?

ETHEL: (*rectifying a stray hair in his beard*) After mature consideration, I decide a cheque.

MR VOYSEY: Do you!

ETHEL: Yes, I think that a cheque will give most scope to your generosity. If you desire to add any trimmings in the shape of a piano or a Turkey carpet you may..and Denis and I will be very grateful. But I think I'd let yourself go over a cheque.

MR VOYSEY: You're a minx.

ETHEL: What's the use of having money if you don't spend it on me?

MAJOR: *(giving up the cigar search)* Here, who's going to play?

MR BOOTH: *(pathetically as he gets up)* Well, if my wrist will hold out..

MAJOR: *(to TREGONING)* No, don't you bother to look for them. *(He strides from the room, his voice echoing through the hall.)* Honor, where are those Ramon Allones?

ALICE: *(calling after)* She's in the drawing-room with Auntie and Mr Colpus.

MR VOYSEY: Now I should suggest that you and Denis go and take off the billiard table cover. You'll find folding it up a very excellent amusement. *(He illustrates his meaning with his table napkin and by putting together the tips of his forefingers, roguishly.)*

ETHEL: I am not going to blush. I do kiss Denis..occasionally..when he asks me.

MR BOOTH: *(teasing her)* You are blushing.

ETHEL: I am not. If you think we're ashamed of being in love, we're not, we're very proud of it. We will go and take off the billiard table cover and fold it up..and then you can come in and play. Denis, my dear, come along solemnly and if you flinch I'll never forgive you. *(She marches off and reaches the door before her defiant dignity breaks down; then suddenly—)* Denis, I'll race you. *(And she flashes out. TREGONING loyal, but with no histrionic instincts, follows her rather sheepishly.)*

TREGONING: Ethel, I can't after dinner.

MR VOYSEY: Women play that game better than men. A man shuffles through courtship with one eye on her relations.

(The MAJOR comes stalking back, followed in a fearful flurry by his elder sister, HONOR. Poor HONOR [her female friends are apt to refer to her as Poor HONOR] is a phenomenon common to most large families. From her earliest years she has been bottle-washer to her brothers. While they were expensively educated she was grudged schooling; her highest accomplishment was meant to be mending their clothes. Her fate is a curious survival of the intolerance of parents towards her sex until the vanity of their hunger for sons had been satisfied. In a less humane society she would have been exposed at birth. But if a very general though patronising affection, accompanied by no consideration at all, can bestow happiness, HONOR is not unhappy in her survival. At this moment, however, her life is a burden.)

MAJOR: Honor, they are not in the dining-room.

HONOR: But they must be!—Where else can they be? *(She has the habit of accentuating one word in each sentence and often the wrong one.)*

MAJOR: That's what you ought to know.

MR VOYSEY: *(as he moves towards the door)* Well..will you have a game?

MR BOOTH: I'll play you fifty up, not more. I'm getting old.

MR VOYSEY: *(stopping at a dessert dish)* Yes, these are good apples of Bearman's. I think six of my trees are spoilt this year.

HONOR: Here you are, Booth.

(She triumphantly discovers the discarded box, at which the MAJOR becomes pathetic with indignation.)

MAJOR: Oh, Honor, don't be such a fool. These are what we've been smoking. I want the Ramon Allones.

HONOR: I don't know the difference.

MAJOR: No, you don't, but you might learn.

MR VOYSEY: *(in a voice like the crack of a very fine whip)* Booth.

MAJOR: *(subduedly)* What is it, sir?

MR VOYSEY: Look for your cigars yourself. Honor, go back to your reading or sewing or whatever you were fiddling at, and fiddle in peace.

(MR VOYSEY departs, leaving the room rather hushed. MR BOOTH has not waited for this parental display. Then ALICE insinuates a remark very softly.)

ALICE: Have you looked in the Library?

MAJOR: *(relapsing to an injured mutter)* Where's Emily?

HONOR: Upstairs with little Henry, he woke up and cried.

MAJOR: Letting her wear herself to rags over the child..!

HONOR: Well, she won't let me go.

MAJOR: Why don't you stop looking for those cigars?

HONOR: If you don't mind, I want a reel of blue silk now I'm here.

MAJOR: I daresay they are in the Library. What a house! *(He departs.)*

HONOR: Booth is so trying.

ALICE: Honor, why do you put up with it?

HONOR: Someone has to.

ALICE: *(discreetly nibbling a nut, which EDWARD has cracked for her)* I'm afraid that I think Master Major Booth ought to have been taken in hand early.. with a cane.

HONOR: *(as she vaguely burrows into corners)* Papa did. But it's never prevented him booming at us..oh, ever since he was a baby. Now he's flustered me so I simply can't think where this blue silk is.

ALICE: All the Pettifers desired to be remembered to you, Edward.

HONOR: I must do without it. *(But she goes on looking.)* I sometimes think, Alice that we're a very difficult family..except perhaps Edward.

EDWARD: Why except me?

HONOR: *(who has only excepted out of politeness to present company)* And you were always difficult..to yourself. *(Then she starts to go, threading her way through the disarranged chairs.)* Mr Colpus will shout so loud at Mother and she hates people to think she's so very deaf. I thought Mary Pettifer looking old.. *(and she talks herself out of the room)*

ALICE: *(after her)* She's getting old.

(Now ALICE does sit down; as if she'd be glad of her tête-a-tête.)

ALICE: I was glad not to spend August abroad for once. We drove into Cheltenham to a dance..carpet. I golfed a lot.

EDWARD: How long were you with them?

ALICE: Not a fortnight. It doesn't seem three months since I was here, does it?

EDWARD: I'm down so very little.

ALICE: I'm here a disgraceful deal.

EDWARD: You know they're always pleased.

ALICE: Well, being a homeless person! But what a cart-load to descend all at once.. yesterday and today. The Major and Emily..Emily's not at all well. Hugh and Mrs Hugh. And me. Are you staying?

EDWARD: No. I must get a word with my father..

ALICE: Edward, a business life is not healthy for you. You look more like half-baked pie-crust than usual.

EDWARD: *(a little enviously)* You're very well.

ALICE: I'm always well and nearly always happy.

(MAJOR returns. He has the right sort of cigar in his mouth and is considerably mollified.)

ALICE: You found them?

MAJOR: Of course, they were there. Thank you very much, Alice. Now I want a knife.

ALICE: I must get you a cigar-cutter for Christmas, Booth.

MAJOR: Beastly things, I hate 'em, thank you. *(He eyes the dessert disparagingly.)* Nothing but silver ones.

(EDWARD hands him a carefully opened pocket knife.)

MAJOR: Thank you, Edward. And I must take one of the candles. Something's gone wrong with the library ventilator and you never can see a thing in that room.

ALICE: Is Mrs Hugh there?

MAJOR: Writing letters. Things are neglected, Edward, unless one is constantly on the look out. The Pater only cares for his garden. I must speak seriously to Honor.

(He has returned the knife, still open, and now having lit his cigar at the candle he carries this off.)

ALICE: Honor has the patience of a..of an old maid.

EDWARD: Yes, I suppose her mission in life isn't a very pleasant one. *(He gives her a nut, about the fifteenth.)* Here; 'scuse fingers.

ALICE: Thank you. *(looking at him, with her head on one side and her face more humorous than ever)* Edward, why have you given up proposing to me?

(He starts, flushes; then won't be outdone in humour.)

EDWARD: One can't go on proposing for ever.

ALICE: *(reasonably)* Why not? Have you seen anyone you like better?

EDWARD: No.

ALICE: Well..I miss it.

EDWARD: What satisfaction did you find in refusing me?

ALICE: *(as she weighs the matter)* I find satisfaction in feeling that I'm wanted.

EDWARD: Without any intention of giving yourself..throwing yourself away.

ALICE: *(teasing his sudden earnestness)* Ah, now you come from mere vanity to serious questions.

EDWARD: Mine was a very serious question to you.

ALICE: But, Edward, all questions are serious to you. I call you a perfect little pocket-guide to life..all questions and answers; what to eat, drink, and avoid, what to believe and what to say..

EDWARD: *(sententiously)* Well..everything matters.

ALICE: *(making a face)* D'you plan out every detail of your life..every step you take..every mouthful?

EDWARD: That would be waste of thought. One must lay down principles.

ALICE: I prefer my plan, I always do what I know I want to do. Crack me another nut.

EDWARD: Haven't you had enough?

ALICE: I know I want one more.

(He cracks another, with a sigh which sounds ridiculous in that connection.)

ALICE: I know it just as I knew I didn't want to marry you..each time.

EDWARD: Oh, you didn't make a rule of saying no.

ALICE: As you proposed..on principle? No, I always gave you a fair chance. I'l give you one now if you like. Courage, I might say yes..all in a flash. Oh, you'd never get over it.

EDWARD: I think we won't run the risk.

ALICE: Edward, how rude you are. *(She eats her nut contentedly.)* There's nothing wrong, is there?

EDWARD: Nothing at all.

(They are interrupted by the sudden appearance of MRS HUGH VOYSEY, a brisk, bright little woman, in an evening gown, which she has bullied a cheap dressmaker into making look exceedingly smart. BEATRICE is as hard as nails and as clever as paint. But if she keeps her feelings buried pretty deep it is because they are precious to her; and if she is impatient with fools it is because her own brains have had to

win her everything in the world, so perhaps she does overvalue them a little. She speaks always with great decision and little effort.)

BEATRICE: I believe I could write important business letters upon an island in the middle of Fleet Street. But while Booth is poking at a ventilator with a billiard cue..no, I can't.

(She goes to the fireplace, waving her half finished letter.)

ALICE: *(soothingly)* Didn't you expect Hugh back to dinner?

BEATRICE: Not specially . . He went to rout out some things from his studio. He'll come back in a filthy mess.

ALICE: Ssh! Now if you listen..Booth doesn't enjoy making a fuss by himself..you'll hear him put up Honor.

(They listen. But what happens is that The MAJOR appears at the door, billiard cue in hand, and says solemnly..)

MAJOR: Edward, I wish you'd come and have a look at this ventilator, like a good fellow.

(Then he turns and goes again, obviously with the weight of an important matter on his shoulders. With the ghost of a smile EDWARD gets up and follows him.)

ALICE: If I belonged to this family I should hate Booth. *(With which comment she joins BEATRICE at the fireplace.)*

BEATRICE: A good day's shopping? .

ALICE: 'M. The baby bride and I bought clothes all the morning. Then we had lunch with Denis and bought furniture.

BEATRICE: Nice furniture?

ALICE: Very good and very new. They neither of them know what they want. *(Then suddenly throwing up her chin and exclaiming.)* When it's a question of money I can understand it..but if one can provide for oneself or is independent why get married! Especially having been brought up on the sheltered life principle..one may as well make the most of its advantages..one doesn't go falling in love all over the place as men seem to..most of them. Of course with Ethel and Denis it's different. They've both been caught young. They're two little birds building their nest and it's all ideal. They'll soon forget they've ever been apart.

(Now HONOR flutters into the room, patient but wild-eyed.)

HONOR: Mother wants last week's Notes and Queries. Have you seen it?

BEATRICE: *(exasperated at the interruption)* No.

HONOR: It ought not to be in here. *(So she proceeds to look for it.)* She's having a long argument with Mr Colpus over Oliver Cromwell's relations.

ALICE: *(her eyes twinkling)* I thought Auntie didn't approve of Oliver Cromwell.

HONOR: She doesn't, and she's trying to prove that he was a brewer or something. I suppose someone has taken it away.

(So she gives up the search and flutters out again.)

ALICE: This is a most unrestful house.

BEATRICE: I once thought of putting the Voyseys into a book of mine. Then I concluded they'd be as dull there as they are anywhere else.

ALICE: They're not duller than most people.

BEATRICE: But how very dull that is!

ALICE: They're a little nosier and perhaps not quite so well mannered. But I love them.

BEATRICE: I don't. I should have thought love was just what they couldn't inspire.

ALICE: Of course, Hugh is unlike any of the others.

BEATRICE: He has most of their bad points. But I don't love Hugh.

ALICE: *(her eyebrows up, though she smiles)* Beatrice, you shouldn't say so.

BEATRICE: Sounds affected, doesn't it? Never mind; when he dies I'll wear mourning..but not weeds; I bargained against that when we were engaged.

ALICE: *(her face growing a little thoughtful)* Beatrice, I'm going to ask questions. You were in love with Hugh when you married him?

BEATRICE: Well..I married him for his money..

ALICE: He hadn't much.

BEATRICE: I had none..and I wanted to write books. Yes, I loved him.

ALICE: And you thought you'd be happy?

BEATRICE: *(considering carefully)* No, I didn't. I hoped he'd be happy.

ALICE: *(a little ironical)* Did you think your writing books would make him so?

BEATRICE: My dear Alice, shouldn't a man..or a woman feel it a very degrading thing to have their happiness depend upon somebody else?

ALICE: *(after pausing to find her phrase)* There's a joy of service. Is that very womanly of me?

BEATRICE: *(ironically herself now)* Ah, but you've four hundred a year.

ALICE: What has that to do with it?

BEATRICE: *(putting her case very precisely)* Fine feelings, my dear, are as much a luxury as clean gloves. Now, I've had to earn my own living; consequently there isn't one thing in my life that I have ever done quite genuinely for its own sake..but always with an eye towards bread-and-butter, pandering to the people who were to give me that. I warned Hugh..he took the risk.

ALICE: What risk?

BEATRICE: That one day I'd be able to get on without him.

ALICE: By the time he'd learnt how not to without you?

BEATRICE: Well, women must have the courage to be brutal.

(The conservatory door opens and through it come MR VOYSEY and MR BOOTH in the midst of a discussion.)

MR VOYSEY: My dear man, stick to the shares and risk it.

MR BOOTH: No, of course, if you seriously advise me—

MR VOYSEY: I never advise greedy children; I let 'em overeat 'emselves and take the consequences—

ALICE: *(shaking a finger)* Uncle Trench, you've been in the garden without a hat after playing billiards in that hot room.

MR BOOTH: We had to give up..my wrist was bad. They've started pool.

BEATRICE: Is Booth going to play?

MR VOYSEY: We left him instructing Ethel how to hold a cue.

BEATRICE: Ah! I can finish my letter.

(Off she goes. ALICE is idly following with a little paper her hand has fallen on behind the clock.)

MR VOYSEY: Don't run away, my dear.

ALICE: I'm taking this to Auntie..Notes and Queries..she wants it.

MR BOOTH: Damn..this gravel's stuck to my shoe.

MR VOYSEY: That's a new made path.

MR BOOTH: Now don't you think it's too early to have put in those plants?

MR VOYSEY: No, we've had a frost or two already.

MR BOOTH: I should have kept the bed a good ten feet further from that tree.

MR VOYSEY: Nonsense, the tree's to the north of it. This room's cold. Why don't they keep the fire up! *(He proceeds to put coals on it.)*

MR BOOTH: You were too hot in that billiard room. You know, Voysey.. about those Alguazils?

MR VOYSEY: *(through the rattling of the coals)* What?

MR BOOTH: *(trying to pierce the din)* Those Alguazils.

(MR VOYSEY with surprising inconsequence points a finger at the silk handkerchief across MR BOOTH'S shirt front.)

MR VOYSEY: What d'you put your handkerchief there for?

MR BOOTH: Measure of precau- *(at that moment he sneezes)* Damn it..if you've given me a chill dragging me through your infernal garden..

MR VOYSEY: *(slapping him on the back)* You're an old crock.

MR BOOTH: Well, I'll be glad of this winter in Egypt. *(He returns to his subject.)* And if you think seriously, that I ought to sell out of the Alguazils before I go..? *(He looks with childlike enquiry at his friend, who is apparently yawning slightly.)* Why can't you take them in charge?..and I'll give you a power of attorney..or whatever it is..and you can sell out if things look bad.

(At this moment PHOEBE, the middle aged parlour maid, comes in, tray in hand. Like an expert fisherman MR VOYSEY once more lets loose the thread of the conversation.)

MR VOYSEY: D'you want to clear?

PHOEBE: It doesn't matter, sir.

MR VOYSEY: No, go on..go on.

So MARY, the young housemaid, comes in as well, and the two start to clear the table. All of which fidgets poor MR BOOTH considerably. He sits shrivelled up in the armchair by the fire; and now MR VOYSEY attends to him.)

MR VOYSEY: What d'you want with high interest at all..you never spend half your income?

MR BOOTH: I like to feel that my money is doing some good in the world. Mines are very useful things and forty-two per cent is pleasing.

MR VOYSEY: You're an old gambler.

MR BOOTH: *(propitiatingly)* Ah, but then I've you to advise me. I always do as you tell me in the end, now you can't deny that..

MR VOYSEY: The man who don't know must trust in the man who do! *(He yawns again.)*

MR BOOTH: *(modestly insisting)* There's five thousand in Alguazils—what else could we put it into?

MR VOYSEY: I can get you something at four and a half.

MR BOOTH: Oh, Lord..that's nothing.

MR VOYSEY: *(with a sudden serious friendliness)* I wish, my dear George, you'd invest more on your own account. You know-what with one thing and the other—I've got control of practically all you have in the world. I might be playing old Harry with it for all you know.

MR BOOTH: *(overflowing with confidence)* My dear feller..if I'm satisfied! Ah, my friend, what'll happen to your firm when you depart this life!..not before my time, I hope, though.

MR VOYSEY: *(with a little frown)* What d'ye mean?

MR BOOTH: Edward's no use.

MR VOYSEY: I beg your pardon..very sound in business.

MR BOOTH: May be..but I tell you he's no use. Too many principles, as I told him just now. Men have confidence in a personality, not in principles. Where would you be without the confidence of your clients?

MR VOYSEY: *(candidly)* True!

MR BOOTH: He'll never gain that.

MR VOYSEY: I fear you dislike Edward.

MR BOOTH: *(with pleasant frankness)* Yes, I do.

MR VOYSEY: That's a pity. That's a very great pity.

MR BOOTH: *(with a flattering smile)* He's not his father and never will be. What's the time?

MR VOYSEY: *(with inappropriate thoughtfulness)* Twenty to ten.

MR BOOTH: I must be trotting.

MR VOYSEY: It's early.

MR BOOTH: Oh, and I've not said a word to Mrs Voysey..*(As he goes to the door he meets EDWARD, who comes in apparently looking for his father; at any rate catches his eye immediately, while MR BOOTH obliviously continues.)*

MR BOOTH: Will you stroll round home with me?

MR VOYSEY: I can't.

MR BOOTH: *(mildly surprised at the short reply)* Well, good-night. Good-night, Edward.

(He trots away.)

MR VOYSEY: Leave the rest of the table, Phoebe.

PHOEBE: Yes, sir.

MR VOYSEY: You can come back in ten minutes.

(PHOEBE and MARY depart and the door is closed. Alone with his son MR VOYSEY does not move; his face grows a little keener, that's all.)

MR VOYSEY: Well, Edward?

(EDWARD starts to move restlessly about, like a cowed animal in a cage; silently for a moment or two. Then when he speaks, his voice is toneless and he doesn't look at his father.)

EDWARD: Would you mind, sir, dropping with me for the future all these protestations about putting the firm's affairs straight..about all your anxieties and sacrifices. I see now, of course..a cleverer man than I could have seen it yesterday..that for some time, ever since, I suppose, you recovered from the first shock and got used to the double dealing, this hasn't been your object at all. You've used your clients' capital to produce your own income..to bring us up and endow us with. Booth's ten thousand pounds; what you are giving Ethel on her marriage..It's odd it never struck me yesterday that my own pocket money as a boy must have been quite simply withdrawn from some client's account. You've been very generous to us all, Father. I suppose about half the sum you've spent on us first and last would have put things right.

MR VOYSEY: No, it would not.

EDWARD: *(appealing for the truth)* Yes, yes..at some time or other!

MR VOYSEY: Well, if there have been good times there have been bad times. At present the three hundred a year I'm to allow your sister is going to be rather a pull.

EDWARD: Three hundred a year..while you don't attempt to make a single client safe. Since it isn't lunacy, sir..I can only conclude that you enjoy such a position.

MR VOYSEY: Safe? Three trusts—two of them big ones—have been wound up within this last eighteen months, and the accounts have been above suspicion. What's the object of all this rodomontade, Edward?

EDWARD: If I'm to remain in the firm, it had better be with a very clear understanding of things as they are.

MR VOYSEY: *(firmly, not too anxiously)* Then you do remain?

EDWARD: *(in a very low voice)* I must remain.

MR VOYSEY: *(quite gravely)* That's wise of you..I'm very glad. *(And he is silent for a moment.)* And now we needn't discuss the unpractical side of it any more.

EDWARD: But I want to make one condition. And I want some information.

MR VOYSEY: *(his sudden cheerfulness relapsing again)* Well?

EDWARD: Of course no one has ever discovered..and no one suspects this state of things?

MR VOYSEY: Peacey knows.

EDWARD: Peacey!

MR VOYSEY: His father found out.

EDWARD: Oh. Does he draw hush money?

MR VOYSEY: *(curling a little at the word)* It is my custom to make him a little present every Christmas. *(He becomes benevolent.)* I don't grudge the money .. Peacey's a devoted fellow.

EDWARD: Certainly this should be a heavily taxed industry. *(Then he smiles at his vision of the mild old clerk.)* Peacey! There's another thing I want to ask, sir. Have you ever under stress of circumstances done worse than just make this temporary use of a client's capital? You boasted to me yesterday that no one had ever suffered in pocket in the end because of you. Is that absolutely true?
(MR VOYSEY draws himself up, dignified and magniloquent.)

MR VOYSEY: My dear Edward, for the future my mind is open to you; you can discover for yourself how matters stand today. But I decline to gratify your curiosity as to what is over and done with.

EDWARD: *(with entire comprehension)* Thank you, sir. The condition of my remaining is that we should really try as unobtrusively as you like and put things straight.

MR VOYSEY: *(with a little polite shrug)* I've no doubt you'll prove an abler man of business than I.

EDWARD: We can begin by halving the salary I draw from the firm; that leaves me enough.

MR VOYSEY: I see..Retrenchment and Reform.

EDWARD: And it seems to me that you can't give Ethel this five thousand pounds dowry.

MR VOYSEY: *(shortly, with one of the quick twists of his eye)* I have given my word to Denis..

EDWARD: Because the money isn't yours to give.

MR VOYSEY: *(in an indignant crescendo)* I should not dream of depriving Ethel of what, as my daughter, she has every right to expect. I am surprised at your suggesting such a thing.

EDWARD: *(pale and firm)* I'm set on this, Father.

MR VOYSEY: Don't be such a fool, Edward. What would it look like.. suddenly to refuse without rhyme or reason? What would old Tregoning think?

EDWARD: Oh, can't you see it's my duty to prevent this?

MR VOYSEY: You can prevent it by telling the nearest policeman. It is my duty to pay no more attention to these scruples of yours than a nurse pays to her child's tantrums. Understand, Edward, I don't want to force you to continue my partner. Come with me gladly or don't come at all.

EDWARD: *(dully)* It is my duty to be of what use I can to you, sir. Father, I want to save you if I can.

(He flashes into this exclamation of almost broken-hearted affection. MR VOYSEY looks at his son for a moment and his lip quivers. Then he steels himself.)

MR VOYSEY: Thank you! I have saved myself quite satisfactorily for the last thirty years, and you must please believe that by this time I know my own business best.

EDWARD: *(hopelessly)* Can't we find the money some other way? How do manage now about your own income?

MR VOYSEY: I have a bank balance and a cheque book, haven't I? I spend what I think well to spend. What's the use of earmarking this or that as my own? You say none of it is my own. I might say it's all my own. I think I've earned it..

EDWARD: *(anger coming on him)* That's what I can't forgive. If you'd lived poor..if you'd really done all you could for your clients and not thought only of your own aggrandisement..then, even though things were no better than they are now, I could have been proud of you. But, Father, own the truth to me least.. that's my due from you, considering how I'm placed by all you've done. Didn't you simply seize this opportunity as a means to your own ends, to your own enriching?

MR VOYSEY: *(with a sledge hammer irony)* Certainly. I sat that morning in father's office, studying the helmet of the policeman in the street below thinking what a glorious path I had happened on to wealth and honour and renown. *(Then he begins to bully EDWARD in the kindliest way.)* My boy, you evidently haven't begun to grasp the A.B.C. of my position. What has carried me to victory? The confidence of my clients. What has earned that confidence? A decent life, my integrity, my brains? No, my reputation for wealth..that, and nothing else. Business nowadays is run on the lines of the confidence trick. What makes old George Booth so glad to trust me with every penny he possesses? Not affection.. he's never cared for anything in his life but his collection of prints.

EDWARD: *(stupefied, helpless)* Is he involved?

MR VOYSEY: Of course he's involved, and he's always after high interest too...it's little one makes out of him. But there's a further question here, Edward. Should I have had confidence in myself, if I'd remained a poor man? No, I should not. You must either be the master of money or its servant. And if one is not opulent in one's daily life one loses that wonderful..financier's touch. One must be confident oneself..and I saw from the first that I must at any cost inspire confidence. My whole public and private life has tended to that. All my surroundings..you and your brothers and sisters that I have brought into, and up, and put out in the world so worthily...you in your turn inspire confidence.

EDWARD: Not our worth, not our abilities, nor our virtues, but the fact that we travel first class and take cabs when we want to.

MR VOYSEY: *(impatiently)* Well, I haven't organised Society upon a basis of wealth.

EDWARD: I sat down yesterday to make a list of the people who are good enough to trust their money to us. It'll be a pretty long one..and it's an interesting one, from George Booth with his big income to old Nursie with her savings which she brought you so proudly to invest. But you've let those be, at least.

MR VOYSEY: I just..took the money..

EDWARD: Father!

MR VOYSEY: Five hundred pounds. Not worth worrying about.

EDWARD: That's damnable.

MR VOYSEY: Indeed. I give her seventy-five pounds a year for it. Would you like to take charge of that account, Edward? I'll give you five hundred to invest tomorrow.

(EDWARD, hopelessly beaten, falls into an almost comic state of despair.)

EDWARD: My dear Father, putting every moral question aside..it's all very well your playing Robin Hood in this magnificent manner; but have you given a moment's thought to the sort of inheritance you'll be leaving me?

MR VOYSEY: *(pleased for the first time)* Ah! That is a question you have every right to ask.

EDWARD: If you died tomorrow could we pay eight shillings in the pound ..or seventeen..or five? Do you know?

MR VOYSEY: And the answer is, that by your help I have every intention, when I die, of leaving a will behind me of property to you all running into six figures. D'you think I've given my life and my talents for a less result than that? I'm fond of you all..and I want you to be proud of me..and I mean that the name of Voysey shall be carried high in the world by my children and grandchildren. Don't you be afraid, Edward. Ah, you lack experience, my boy..you're not full grown yet..your impulses are a bit chaotic. You emotionalise over your work, and you reason about your emotions. You must sort yourself. You must realise that money making is one thing, and religion another, and family life a third.. and that if we apply our energies whole-heartedly to each of these in turn, and realise that different laws govern each, that there is a different end to be served, a different ideal to be striven for in each..

(His coherence is saved by the sudden appearance of his wife, who comes round the door smiling benignly. Not in the least put out, in fact a little relieved, he greets her with an affectionate shout, for she is very deaf.)

MR VOYSEY: Hullo, Mother!

MRS VOYSEY: Oh, there you are, Trench. I've been deserted.

MR VOYSEY: George Booth gone?

MRS VOYSEY: Are you talking business? Perhaps you don't want me.

MR VOYSEY: No, no..no business.

MRS VOYSEY: *(who has not looked for his answer)* I suppose the others are in the billiard room.

MR VOYSEY: *(vociferously)* We're not talking business, old lady.

EDWARD: I'll be off, sir.

MR VOYSEY: *(genial as usual)* Why don't you stay? I'll come up with you in the morning.

EDWARD: No, thank you, sir.

MR VOYSEY: Then I shall be up about noon tomorrow.

EDWARD: Good-night, Mother.

(MRS VOYSEY places a plump kindly hand on his arm and looks up affectionately.)

MRS VOYSEY: You look tired.

EDWARD: No, I'm not.

MRS VOYSEY: What did you say?

EDWARD: (too weary to repeat himself) Nothing, Mother dear.

(He kisses her cheek, while she kisses the air.)

MR VOYSEY: Good night, my boy.

(Then he goes. MRS VOYSEY is carrying her Notes and Queries. This is a dear old lady, looking older too than probably she is. Placid describes her. She has had a life of little joys and cares, has never measured herself against the world, never even questioned the shape and size of the little corner of it in which she lives. She has loved an indulgent husband and borne eight children, six of them surviving, healthy. That is her history.)

MRS VOYSEY: George Booth went some time ago. He said he thought you'd taken a chill walking round the garden.

MR VOYSEY: I'm all right.

MRS VOYSEY: D'you think you have?

MR VOYSEY: *(in her ear)* No.

MRS VOYSEY: You should be careful, Trench. What did you put on?

MR VOYSEY: Nothing.

MRS VOYSEY: How very foolish! Let me feel your hand. You are quite feverish.

MR VOYSEY: *(affectionately)* You're a fuss-box, old lady.

MRS VOYSEY: *(coquetting with him)* Don't be rude, Trench.

(HONOR descends upon them. She is well into that nightly turmoil of putting everything and everybody to rights which always precedes her bedtime. She carries a shawl which she clasps round her mother's shoulders, her mind and gaze already on the next thing to be done.)

HONOR: Mother, you left your shawl in the drawing-room. Can they finish clearing?

MR VOYSEY: *(arranging the folds of the shawl with real tenderness)* Now who's careless!

(PHOEBE comes into the room.)

HONOR: Phoebe, finish here and then you must bring in the tray for Mr Hugh.

MRS VOYSEY: *(having looked at the shawl, and HONOR, and connected the matter in her mind)* Thank you, Honor. You'd better look after your father; he's been walking round the garden without his cape.

HONOR: Papa!

MR VOYSEY: Phoebe, you get that little kettle and boil it, and brew me some whiskey and water. I shall be all right.

HONOR: *(fluttering more than ever)* I'll get it. Where's the whiskey? And Hugh coming back at ten o'clock with no dinner. No wonder his work goes wrong. Here it is! Papa, you do deserve to be ill.

(Clasping the whiskey decanter, she is off again. MRS VOYSEY sits at the dinner table and adjusts her spectacles. She returns to Notes and Queries, one elbow firmly planted and her plump hand against her plump cheek. This is her favourite attitude; and she is apt, when reading, to soliloquise in her deaf woman's voice. At least, whether she considers it soliloquy or conversation is not easy to discover. MR VOYSEY stands with his back to the fire, grumbling and pulling faces.)

MRS VOYSEY: This is a very perplexing correspondence about the Cromwell family. One can't deny the man had good blood in him..his grandfather Sir Henry, his uncle Sir Oliver..

MR VOYSEY: There's a pain in my back.

MRS VOYSEY: ..and it's difficult to discover where the taint crept in.

MR VOYSEY: I believe I strained myself putting in all those strawberry plants.

(MARY, the house parlour maid, carries in a tray of warmed-up dinner for HUGH and plants it on the table.)

MRS VOYSEY: Yes, but then how was it he came to disgrace himself so? I believe the family disappeared. Regicide is a root and branch curse. You must read this letter signed C.W.A...it's quite interesting. There's a misprint in mine about the first umbrella maker..now where was it..*(and so the dear lady will ramble on indefinitely).*

ACT III

The dining-room looks very different in the white light of a July noon. Moreover on this particular day, it isn't even its normal self. There is a peculiar luncheon spread on the table. The embroidered cloth is placed cornerwise and on it are decanters of port and sherry; sandwiches, biscuits and an uncut cake; two little piles of plates and one little pile of napkins. There are no table decorations, and indeed the whole room has been made as bare and as tidy as possible. Such preparations denote one of the recognised English festivities, and the appearance of PHOEBE, the maid, who has just completed them, the set solemnity of her face and the added touches of black to her dress and cap, suggest that this is probably a funeral. When MARY comes in, the fact that she has evidently been crying and that she decorously does not raise her voice above an unpleasant whisper makes it quite certain.

MARY: Phoebe, they're coming back..and I forgot one of the blinds in the drawing-room.

PHOEBE: Well, pull it up quick and make yourself scarce. I'll open the door.

(MARY got rid of, PHOEBE composes her face still more rigorously into the aspect of formal grief and with a touch to her apron as well goes to admit the funeral party. The first to enter are MRS VOYSEY and MR BOOTH, she on his arm; and the fact that she is in widow's weeds makes the occasion clear. The little old man leads his old friend very tenderly.)

MR BOOTH: Will you come in here?

MRS VOYSEY: Thank you.

(With great solicitude he puts her in a chair; then takes her hand.)

MR BOOTH: Now I'll intrude no longer.

MRS VOYSEY: You'll take some lunch?

MR BOOTH: No.

MRS VOYSEY: Not a glass of wine?

MR BOOTH: If there's anything I can do just send round.

MRS VOYSEY: Thank you.

(He reaches the door, only to be met by the MAJOR and his wife. He shakes hands with them both.)

MR BOOTH: My dear Emily! My dear Booth!

(EMILY is a homely, patient, pale little woman of about thirty-five. She looks smaller than usual in her heavy black dress and is meeker than usual on an occasion of this kind. The MAJOR, on the other hand, though his grief is most sincere, has an irresistible air of being responsible for, and indeed rather proud of, the whole affair.)

MAJOR: I think it all went off as he would have wished.

MR BOOTH: *(feeling that he is called on for praise)* Great credit..great credit.

(He makes another attempt to escape and is stopped this time by TRENCHARD VOYSEY, to whom he is extending a hand and beginning his formula. But

TRENCHARD speaks first.)

TRENCHARD: Have you the right time?

MR BOOTH: *(taken aback and fumbling for his watch)* I think so..I make it fourteen minutes to one. *(He seizes the occasion.)* Trenchard, as a very old and dear friend of your father's, you won't mind me saying how glad I was that you were present today. Death closes all. Indeed..it must be a great regret to you that you did not see him before..before..

TRENCHARD: *(his cold eye freezing this little gush)* I don't think he asked for me.

MR BOOTH: *(stoppered)* No? No! Well..well..*(At this third attempt to depart he actually collides with someone in the doorway. It is HUGH VOYSEY.)*

MR BOOTH: My dear Hugh..I won't intrude.

(Quite determined to escape he grasps his hand, gasps out his formula and is off. TRENCHARD and HUGH, eldest and youngest son, are as unlike each other as it is possible for VOYSEYS to be, but that isn't very unlike. TRENCHARD has in excelsis the cocksure manner of the successful barrister; HUGH the rather sweet though querulous air of diffidence and scepticism belonging to the unsuccessful man of letters or artist. The self-respect of TRENCHARD'S appearance is immense, and he cultivates that air of concentration upon any trivial matter, or even upon nothing at all, which will some day make him an impressive figure upon the Bench. HUGH is always vague, searching Heaven or the corners of the room for inspiration, and even on this occasion his tie is abominably crooked. The inspissated gloom of this assembly, to which each member of the family as he arrives adds his share, is unbelievable. Instinct apparently leads them to reproduce as nearly as possible the appearance and conduct of the corpse on which their minds are fixed. HUGH is depressed partly at the inadequacy of his grief: TRENCHARD conscientiously preserves an air of the indifference which he feels; the MAJOR stands statuesque at the mantelpiece; while EMILY is by MRS VOYSEY, whose face in its quiet grief is nevertheless a mirror of many happy memories of her husband .)

MAJOR: I wouldn't hang over her, Emily.

EMILY: No, of course not.

(Apologetically, she sits by the table.)

TRENCHARD: I hope your wife is well, Hugh?

HUGH: Thank you, Trench: I think so. Beatrice is in America..doing some work there.

TRENCHARD: Really!

(There comes in a small, well-groomed, bullet-headed boy in Etons. This is the MAJOR'S eldest son. Looking scared and solemn he goes straight to his mother.)

EMILY: Now be very quiet, Christopher..

(Then DENIS TREGONING appears.)

TRENCHARD: Oh, Tregoning, did you bring Honor back?

TREGONING: Yes.

MAJOR: *(at the table)* A glass of wine, Mother.

MRS VOYSEY: What?

(The MAJOR hardly knows how to turn his whisper decorously into enough of a shout for his mother to hear. But he manages it.)

MAJOR: Have a glass of wine?

MRS VOYSEY: Sherry, please.

(While he pours it out with an air of its being medicine on this occasion and not wine at all, EDWARD comes quickly into the room, his face very set, his mind obviously on other matters than the funeral. No one speaks to him for the moment and he has time to observe them all. TRENCHARD is continuing his talk to TREGONING.)

TRENCHARD: Give my love to Ethel. Is she ill that—

TREGONING: Not exactly, but she couldn't very well be with us. I thought perhaps you might have heard. We're expecting..

(He hesitates with the bashfulness of a young husband. TRENCHARD helps him out with a citizen's bow of respect for a citizen's duty).

TRENCHARD Indeed. I congratulate you hope all will be well. Please give my best love to Ethel.

MAJOR: *(in an awful voice)* Lunch, Emily?

EMILY: *(scared)* I suppose so, Booth, thank you.

MAJOR: I think the boy had better run away and play..(He checks himself on the word.) Well, take a book and keep quiet; d'ye hear me, Christopher? (CHRIST-OPHER, who looks incapable of a sound, gazes at his father with round eyes. EMILY whispers 'Library' to him and adds a kiss in acknowledgement of his good behaviour. After a moment he slips out, thankfully.)

EDWARD: How's Ethel, Denis?

TREGONING: A little smashed, of course, but no harm done..I hope.

(ALICE MAITLAND comes in, brisk and businesslike; a little impatient of this universal cloud of mourning.)

ALICE: Edward, Honor has gone to her room; I must take her some food and make her eat it. She's very upset.

EDWARD: Make her drink a glass of wine, and say it is necessary she should come down here. And d'you mind not coming back yourself, Alice?

ALICE: *(her eyebrows up)* Certainly, if you wish.

MAJOR: *(overhearing)* What's this? What's this?

(ALICE gets her glass of wine and goes. The MAJOR is suddenly full of importance.)

MAJOR: What is this, Edward?

EDWARD: I have something to say to you all.

MAJOR: What?

EDWARD: Well, Booth, you'll hear when I say it.

MAJOR: Is it business?..because I think this is scarcely the time for business.

EDWARD. Why?

MAJOR. Do you find it easy and reverent to descend from your natural grief to the consideration of money?...I do not. *(He finds TRENCHARD at his elbow.)* I hope you are getting some lunch, Trenchard.

EDWARD: This is business and rather more than business, Booth. I choose now, because it is something I wish to say to the family, not write to each individually.and it will be difficult to get us all together again.

MAJOR: *(determined at any rate to give his sanction)* Well, Trenchard, as Edward is in the position of trustee-executor..I don't know your terms..I suppose ..

TRENCHARD: I don't see what your objection is.

MAJOR: *(with some superiority)* Don't you? I should not have called myself a sentimental man, but..

EDWARD: You had better stay, Denis; you represent Ethel.

TREGONING: *(who has not heard the beginning of this)* Why?

(HONOR has obediently come down from her room. She is pale and thin, shaken with grief and worn out besides; for needless to say the brunt of her father's illness, the brunt of everything has been on her. Six weeks' nursing, part of it hopeless, will exhaust anyone. Her handkerchief is to her eyes and every minute or two she cascades tears. EDWARD goes and affectionately puts his arm round her.)

EDWARD: My dear Honor, I am sorry to be so..so merciless. There!..there! *(He hands her into the room; then turns and once more surveys the family, who at this time mostly return the compliment. Then he says shortly)* I think you might all sit down. *(and then)* Shut the door, Booth.

MAJOR: Shut the door!

(EDWARD goes close to his mother and speaks very distinctly, very kindly)

EDWARD: Mother, we're all going to have a little necessary talk over matters..now, because it's most convenient. I hope it won't..I hope you don't mind. Will you come to the table?

(MRS VOYSEY looks up as if understanding more than he says.)

MRS VOYSEY: Edward..

EDWARD: Yes, Mother dear?

MAJOR: *(commandingly)* You'll sit here, Mother, of course.

(He places her in her accustomed chair at the foot of the table. One by one the others sit down, EDWARD apparently last. But then he discovers that HUGH has lost himself in a corner of the room and is gazing into vacancy.)

EDWARD: Hugh, would you mind attending?

HUGH: What is it?

EDWARD: There's a chair.

(HUGH takes it. Then for a minute-while EDWARD is trying to frame in coherent

sentences what he must say to them—for a minute there is silence, broken only by HONOR'S sniffs, which culminate at last in a noisy little cascade of tears.)

MAJOR: Honor, control yourself.

(And to emphasise his own perfect control he helps himself majestically to a glass of sherry. Then says..)

MAJOR: Well, Edward?

EDWARD: I'll come straight to the point which concerns you. Our father's will gives certain sums to you all..the gross amount would be something over a hundred thousand pounds. There will be no money.

(He can get no further than the bare statement, which is received only with varying looks of bewilderment, until MRS VOYSEY, discovering nothing from their faces, breaks this second silence.)

MRS VOYSEY: I didn't hear.

HUGH: *(in his mother's ear)* Edward says there's no money.

TRENCHARD: *(precisely)* I think you said.. 'will be.'

MAJOR: *(in a tone of mitigated thunder)* Why will there be no money?

EDWARD: *(letting himself go)* Because every penny by right belongs to the clients father spent his life in defrauding. I mean that in its worst sense.. swindling..thieving. I have been in the swim of it, for the past year..oh, you don't know the sink of iniquity. And now I must collect every penny, any money that you can give me; put the firm into bankruptcy; pay back all we can. I'll stand my trial..it'll come to that with me..and as soon as possible. *(He pauses, partly for breath, and glares at them all.)* Are none of you going to speak? Quite right, what is there to be said? *(then with a gentle afterthought)* I'm sorry to hurt you, Mother.

(The VOYSEY family is simply buried deep by this avalanche of horror. MRS VOYSEY, though, who has been watching EDWARD closely, says very calmly..)

MRS VOYSEY: I can't hear quite all you say, but I guess what it is. You don't hurt me, Edward..I have known of this for a long time.

EDWARD: *(with almost a cry)* Oh, Mother, did he know you knew?

MRS VOYSEY: What do you say?

TRENCHARD: *(collected and dry)* I may as well tell you, Edward, I suspected everything wasn't right about the time of the last quarrel with my father. I took care not to pursue my suspicions. Was father aware that you knew, Mother?

MRS VOYSEY: We never discussed it. There was once a great danger, I believe..when you were all younger..of his being found out. But we never discussed it.

EDWARD: *(swallowing a fresh bitterness)* I'm glad it isn't such a shock to all of you.

HUGH: *(alive to a dramatic aspect of the matter)* My God..before the earth has settled on his grave!

EDWARD: I thought it wrong to put off telling you.

(HONOR, the word swindling having spelt itself out in her mind, at last gives way to a burst of piteous grief..)

HONOR: Oh, poor papa!..poor papa!

EDWARD: *(comforting her kindly)* Honor, we shall want your help and advice.

(The MAJOR has recovered from the shock, to swell with importance. It being necessary to make an impression he instinctively turns first to his wife.)

MAJOR: I think, Emily, there was no need for you to have been present at this exposure, and that now you had better retire.

EMILY: Very well, Booth.

(She gets up to go, conscious of her misdemeanour. But as she reaches the door, an awful thought strikes the MAJOR.)

MAJOR: Good Heavens..I hope the servants haven't been listening! See where they are, Emily..and keep them away..distract them. Open the door suddenly. (She does so, more or less, and there is no one behind it.) That's all right.

(Having watched his wife's departure, he turns with gravity to his brother.)

MAJOR: I have said nothing as yet, Edward. I am thinking.

TRENCHARD: *(a little impatient at this exhibition)* That's the worst of these family practices..a lot of money knocking around and no audit ever required. The wonder to me is to find an honest solicitor at all.

MAJOR: Really, Trenchard!

TRENCHARD: Well, do think of the temptation.

EDWARD: Why are one's clients such fools?

TRENCHARD: The world's getting more and more into the hands of its experts, and it certainly does require a particular sort of honesty.

EDWARD: Here were all these funds simply a lucky bag into which he dipped.

TRENCHARD: Did he keep no accounts of any sort?

EDWARD: Scraps of paper. Most of the original investments I can't even trace. The money doesn't exist.

MAJOR: Where's it gone?

EDWARD: (very directly) You've been living on it.

MAJOR: Good God!

TRENCHARD: What can you pay in the pound?

EDWARD: As we stand?..six or seven shillings, I daresay. But we must do better than that. *(To which there is no response.)*

MAJOR: All this is very dreadful. Does it mean beggary for the whole family?

EDWARD: Yes, it should.

TRENCHARD: *(sharply)* Nonsense.

EDWARD: *(joining issue at once)* What right have we to a thing we possess?

TRENCHARD: He didn't make you an allowance, Booth..your capital's your own, isn't it?

MAJOR: *(awkwardly placed between the two of them)* Really..I—I suppose so.

TRENCHARD: Then that's all right.

EDWARD: *(vehemently)* It was stolen money, most likely.

TRENCHARD: Ah, most likely. But Booth took it in good faith.

MAJOR: I should hope so.

EDWARD: *(dwelling on the words)* It's stolen money.

MAJOR: *(bubbling with distress)* I say, what ought I to do?

TRENCHARD: Do..my dear Booth? Nothing.

EDWARD: *(with great indignation)* Trenchard, we owe reparation—

TRENCHARD: (readily) Quite so, but to whom? From which client or client's account was Booth's money taken? You say yourself you don't know. Very well then!

EDWARD: *(grieved)* Trenchard!

TRENCHARD: No, my dear Edward. The law will take anything it has a right to and all it can get; you needn't be afraid. There's no obligation, legal or moral, for any of us to throw our pounds into the wreck that they may become pence.

EDWARD: That's just what he would have said.

TRENCHARD: It's what I say. But what about your own position..can we get you clear?

EDWARD: That doesn't matter.

(The MAJOR'S head has been turning incessantly from one to another and by this he is just a bristle of alarm.)

MAJOR: But I say, you know, this is awful! Will this have to be made public?

TRENCHARD: No help for it.

(The MAJOR'S jaw drops; he is speechless. MRS VOYSEY'S dead voice steals in.)

MRS VOYSEY: What is all this?

TRENCHARD: Edward suggests that the family should beggar itself in order to pay back to every client to whom father owed a pound perhaps ten shillings instead of seven.

MRS VOYSEY: He will find that my estate has been kept quite separate.

(EDWARD hides his face in his hands.)

TRENCHARD: I'm very glad to hear it, Mother.

MRS VOYSEY: When Mr Barnes died, your father agreed to appointing another trustee.

TREGONING: *(diffidently)* I suppose, Edward, I'm involved?

EDWARD: *(lifting his head quickly)* Denis, I hope not. I didn't know that anything of yours—

TREGONING: Yes..all I got under my aunt's will.

EDWARD: See how things are..I've not found a trace of that yet. We'll hope for the best.

TREGONING: *(setting his teeth)* It can't be helped.

(MAJOR BOOTH leans over the table and speaks in the loudest of whispers.)

MAJOR: Let me advise you to say nothing of this to Ethel at such a critical time.

TREGONING: Thank you, Booth, naturally I shan't.

(HUGH, by a series of contortions, has lately been giving evidence of a desire or intention to say something.)

EDWARD: Well, what is it, Hugh?

HUGH: I have been wondering..if he can hear this conversation.

(Up to now it has all been meaningless to HONOR, in her nervous dilapidation, but this remark brings a fresh burst of tears.)

HONOR: Oh, poor papa..poor papa!

MRS VOYSEY: I think I'll go to my room. I can't hear what any of you are saying. Edward can tell me afterwards.

EDWARD: Would you like to go too, Honor?

HONOR: *(through her sobs)* Yes, please, I would.

TREGONING: I'll get out, Edward. Whatever you think fit to do...Oh, well, I suppose there's only one thing to be done.

EDWARD: Only that.

TREGONING: I wish I were in a better position as to work, for Ethel's sake and and the child's.

EDWARD: Shall I speak to Trenchard?

TREGONING: No..he knows I exist in a wig and gown. If I can be useful to him he'll be useful to me, I daresay. Good-bye, Hugh. Good-bye, Booth.

(By this time MRS VOYSEY and HONOR have been got out of the room: TREGONING follows them. So the four brothers are left together. HUGH is vacant, EDWARD does not speak, the MAJOR looks at TRENCHARD, who settles himself to acquire information).

TRENCHARD: How long have things been wrong?

EDWARD: He told me the trouble began in his father's time and that he'd been battling with it ever since.

TRENCHARD: *(smiling)* Oh, come now..that's impossible.

EDWARD: I believed him! Now I look through the papers, such as they are, I can only find one irregularity that's more than ten years old, and that's only to with old George Booth's business.

MAJOR: But the Pater never touched his money..why, he was a personal friend.

EDWARD: Did you hear what Denis said?

TRENCHARD: Very curious his evolving that fiction about his father..I wonder why. I remember the old man. He was honest as the day.

EDWARD: To get my sympathy, I suppose.

TRENCHARD: I think one can trace the psychology of it deeper than that. It would give a finish to the situation..his handing on to you an inheritance he had received. You know every criminal has a touch of the artist in him.

HUGH: (suddenly roused) That's true.

TRENCHARD: What position did you take up when he told you?

EDWARD: (shrugging) You know what the Pater was.

TRENCHARD: Well ..what did you attempt to do?

EDWARD: I urged him at least to put some of the smaller people right. He said..he said that would be penny wise and pound foolish. So I've done what I could myself..since he's been ill..Nothing to count..

TRENCHARD: With your own money?

EDWARD: The little I had. He kept tight hold to the end.

TRENCHARD: Can you prove that you did that?

EDWARD: I suppose I could.

TRENCHARD: It's a good point.

MAJOR: (not to be quite left out) Yes, I must say—

TRENCHARD: You ought to have written him a letter, and left the firm the moment you found out. Even then, legally..! But as he was your father..What was his object in telling you? He didn't think you'd take a hand?

EDWARD: I've thought of every reason..and now I really believe it was that he might have someone to boast to of his financial exploits.

TRENCHARD: (appreciatively) I daresay.

MAJOR: Scarcely a thing to boast of!

TRENCHARD: Depends on the point of view.

EDWARD: Then, of course, he always protested that things would come right..that he'd clear the firm and have a hundred thousand to the good. Or that if he were not spared I might do it. But he must have known that was impossible.

TRENCHARD: But there's the gambler all over.

EDWARD: Drawing up his will!

TRENCHARD: Childish!

EDWARD: I'm the sole executor.

TRENCHARD: So I should think! Was I down for anything?

EDWARD: No.

TRENCHARD: (without resentment) How he did hate me!

EDWARD: You're safe from the results of his affection anyway.

TRENCHARD: What on earth made you stay in the firm once you knew?

(EDWARD does not answer for a moment.)

EDWARD: I thought I might prevent things from getting any worse. I think I did..

TRENCHARD: You knew the personal risk you were running?

EDWARD: (bowing his head) Yes.

(TRENCHARD, the only one of the three who comprehends, looks at his brother for a moment with something that might almost be admiration. Then he stirs himself.)

TRENCHARD: I must be off. Work waiting...end of term, you know.

MAJOR: Shall I walk to the station with you?

TRENCHARD: I'll spend a few minutes with mother. (he says, at the door, very respectfully) You'll count on my professional assistance, please, Edward.

EDWARD: (simply) Thank you, Trenchard.

(So TRENCHARD goes. And the MAJOR, who has been endeavouring to fathom his final attitude, then comments—)

MAJOR: No heart, y'know! Great brain! If it hadn't been for that distressing quarrel he might have saved our poor father. Don't you think so, Edward?

EDWARD: Perhaps.

HUGH: (giving vent to his thoughts at last with something of a relish) The more I think this out, the more devilishly humorous it gets. Old Booth breaking down by the grave..Colpus reading the service..

EDWARD: Yes, the Vicar's badly hit.

HUGH: Oh, the Pater had managed his business for years.

MAJOR: Good God..how shall we ever look old Booth in the face again?

EDWARD: I don't worry about him; he can die quite comfortably enough on our six shillings in the pound. It's only one or two of the smaller fry who will suffer.

MAJOR: Now, just explain to me...I didn't interrupt while Trenchard was talking..of what exactly did this defrauding consist?

EDWARD: Speculating with a client's capital..pocketing the gains..you cut the losses; and you keep paying the client his ordinary income.

MAJOR: So that he doesn't find it out?

EDWARD: Quite so.

MAJOR: In point of fact, he doesn't suffer?

EDWARD: He doesn't suffer till he finds it out.

MAJOR: And all that's wrong now is that some of their capital is missing.

EDWARD: (half amused, half amazed at this process of reasoning) Yes, that's all that's wrong.

MAJOR: What is the—ah—deficit? (The word rolls from his tongue.)

EDWARD: Anything between two and three hundred thousand pounds.

MAJOR: (very impressed and not unfavourably) Dear me..this is a big affair!

HUGH: (following his own line of thought) Quite apart from the rights and wrongs of this, only a very able man could have kept a straight face to the world all these years, as the Pater did.

MAJOR: I suppose he sometimes made money by these speculations.

EDWARD: Very often. His own expenditure was heavy, as you know.

MAJOR: *(with gratitude for favours received)* He was a very generous man.

HUGH: Did nobody ever suspect?

EDWARD: You see, Hugh, when there was any pressing danger..if a big trust had to be wound up..he'd make a great effort and put the accounts straight.

MAJOR: Then he did put some accounts straight?

EDWARD: Yes, when he couldn't help himself.

(The MAJOR looks very enquiring and then squares himself up to the subject.)

MAJOR: Now look here, Edward. You told us that he told you that it was the object of his life to put these accounts straight. Then you laughed at that. Now you tell me that he did put some accounts straight.

EDWARD: *(wearily)* My dear Booth, you don't understand.

MAJOR: Well, let me understand..I am anxious to understand.

EDWARD: We can't pay ten shillings in the pound.

MAJOR: That's very dreadful. But do you know that there wasn't a time when we couldn't have paid five?

EDWARD: *(acquiescent)* Perhaps.

MAJOR: Very well then! If it was true about his father and all that..and why shouldn't we believe him if we can?..and he did effect an improvement, that's to his credit, isn't it? Let us at least be just, Edward.

EDWARD: *(patiently polite)* I am sorry if I seem unjust. But he has left me in a rather unfortunate position.

MAJOR: Yes, his death was a tragedy. It seems to me that if he had been spared he might have succeeded at length in this tremendous task and restored to us our family honour.

EDWARD: Yes, Booth, he spoke very feelingly of that.

MAJOR: *(Irony lost upon him.)* I can well believe it. And I can tell you that now..I may be right or I may be wrong..I am feeling far less concerned about the clients' money than I am at the terrible blow to the Family which this exposure will strike. Money, after all, can to a certain extent be done without..but Honour—

(This is too much for EDWARD.)

EDWARD: Our honour! Does any one of you mean to give me a single penny towards undoing all the wrong that has been done?

MAJOR: I take Trenchard's word for it that that would be illegal.

EDWARD: Well..don't talk to me of honour.

MAJOR: *(somewhat nettled at this outburst)* I am speaking of the public exposure. Edward, can't that be prevented?

EDWARD: *(with quick suspicion)* How?

MAJOR: Well..how was it being prevented before he died—before we knew anything about it?

EDWARD: *(appealing to the spirits that watch over him)* Oh, listen to this! First Trenchard..and now you! You've the poison in your blood, every one of you. Who am I to talk? I daresay so have I.

MAJOR: *(reprovingly)* I am beginning to think that you have worked yourself into rather an hysterical state over this unhappy business.

EDWARD: *(rating him)* Perhaps you'd have been glad..glad if I'd held my tongue and gone on lying and cheating..and married and begotten a son to go on lying and cheating after me..and to pay you your interest in the lie and the cheat.

MAJOR: *(with statesman-like calm)* Look here, Edward, this rhetoric is exceedingly out of place. The simple question before us is..What is the best course to pursue?

EDWARD: There is no question before us. There's only one course to pursue.

MAJOR: *(crushingly)* You will let me speak, please. In so far as our poor father was dishonest to his clients, I pray that he may be forgiven. In so far as he spent his life honestly endeavouring to right a wrong which he had found already committed..I forgive him. I admire him, Edward. And I feel it my duty to er—reprobate most strongly the—er—gusto with which you have been holding him up in memory to us..ten minutes after we have stood round his grave..as a monster of wickedness. I think I may say I knew him as well as you..better. And ..thank God!..there was not between him and me this—this unhappy business to warp my judgement of him. *(He warms to his subject.)* Did you ever know a more charitable man..a larger-hearted? He was a faithful husband..and what a father to all of us, putting us out into the world and fully intending to leave us comfortably settled there. Further..as I see this matter, Edward..when as a young man he was told this terrible secret and entrusted with such a frightful task.. did he turn his back on it like a coward? No. He went through it heroically to the end of his life. And as he died I imagine there was no more torturing thought than that he had left his work unfinished. (He is very satisfied with this peroration.) And now if all these clients can be kept receiving their natural incomes and if father's plan could be carried out of gradually replacing the capital—

(EDWARD at this raises his head and stares with horror.)

EDWARD: You're asking me to carry on this..Oh, you don't know what you're talking about !

(The MAJOR, having talked himself back to a proper eminence, remains good-tempered.)

MAJOR: Well, I'm not a conceited man..but I do think that I can understand a simple financial problem when it has been explained to me.

EDWARD: You don't know the nerve..the unscrupulous daring it requires to—

MAJOR: Of course, if you're going to argue round your own incompetence—

EDWARD: *(very straight)* D'you want your legacy?

MAJOR: *(with dignity)* In one moment I shall get very angry. Here am I doing my best to help you and your clients..and there you sit imputing to me the most sordid motives. Do you suppose I should touch, or allow to be touched, the money which father has left us till every client's claim was satisfied?

EDWARD: My dear Booth, I know you mean well—

MAJOR: I'll come down to your office and work with you.

(At this cheerful prospect even poor EDWARD can't help smiling.)

EDWARD: I'm sure you would.

MAJOR: *(feeling that it is a chance lost)* If the Pater had ever consulted me..

(At this point TRENCHARD looks round the door to say..)

TRENCHARD: Are you coming, Booth?

MAJOR: Yes, certainly. I'll talk this over with Trenchard. *(As he gets up and automatically stiffens, he is reminded of the occasion and his voice drops.)* I say..we've been speaking very loud. You must do nothing rash. I've no doubt he and I can devise something which will obviate..and then I'm sure I shall convince you..(glancing into the hall he apparently catches TRENCHARD'S impatient eye, for he departs abruptly saying..)* All right, Trenchard, you've eight minutes.

(The MAJOR'S departure leaves HUGH, at any rate, really at his ease.)

HUGH: This is an experience for you, Edward!

EDWARD: *(bitterly)* And I feared what the shock might be to you all! Booth has made a good recovery.

HUGH: You wouldn't have him miss such a chance of booming at us.

EDWARD: It's strange that people will believe you can do right by means which they know to be wrong.

HUGH: *(taking great interest in this)* Come, what do we know about right and wrong? Let's say legal and illegal. You're so down on the governor because he has trespassed against the etiquette of your own profession. But now he's dead...and if there weren't the scandal to think of..it's no use the rest of us pretending to feel him a criminal, because we don't. Which just shows that money..and property *(At this point he becomes conscious that ALICE MAITLAND is standing behind him; her eyes fixed on his brother. So he interrupts himself to ask..)*

HUGH: D'you want to speak to Edward?

ALICE: Please, Hugh.

HUGH: I'll go. *(He goes, a little martyrlike, to conclude the evolution of his theory in soliloquy; his usual fate. ALICE still looks at EDWARD with soft eyes, and he at her rather appealingly.)*

ALICE: Auntie has told me.

EDWARD: He was fond of you. Don't think worse of him than you can help.

ALICE: I'm thinking of you.

EDWARD: I may just escape.

ALICE: So Trenchard says.

EDWARD: My hands are clean, Alice.

ALICE: *(her voice falling lovingly)* I know that.

EDWARD: Mother's not very upset.

ALICE: She had expected a smash in his lifetime.

EDWARD: I'm glad that didn't happen.

ALICE: Yes. I've put Honor to bed. It was a mercy to tell her just at this moment. She can grieve for his death and his disgrace at the same time and the one grief will soften the other perhaps.

EDWARD: Oh, they're all shocked enough at the disgrace..but will they open their purses to lessen the disgrace?

ALICE: Will it seem less disgraceful to have stolen ten thousand pounds than twenty?

EDWARD: I should think so.

ALICE: I should think so, but I wonder if that's the Law. If it isn't, Trenchard wouldn't consider the point. I'm sure Public Opinion doesn't say so.. and that's what Booth is considering.

EDWARD: *(with contempt)* Yes.

ALICE: *(ever so gently ironical)* Well, he's in the Army..he's almost in Society..and he has to get on in both; one mustn't blame him. Of course if the money could have been given back with a flourish of trumpets..! But even then doubt whether the advertisement would bring in what it cost.

EDWARD: *(very serious)* But when one thinks how the money was obtained!

ALICE: When one thinks how most money is obtained!

EDWARD: They've not earned it!

ALICE: *(her eyes humorous)* If they had they might have given it you and earned more. Did I ever tell you what my guardian said to me when I came of age?

EDWARD: I'm thankful that your money's out of the mess.

ALICE: It wouldn't have been, but I was made to look after it myself.. much against my will. My guardian was a person of great character and no principles, the best and most loveable man I've ever met ..I'm sorry you never knew him, Edward..and he said once to me. You've no particular right to your money. You've not earned it or deserved it in any way. And don't be either surprised or annoyed when any enterprising person tries to get it from you. He has at least as much right to it as you have..if he can use it better perhaps he has more right. Shocking sentiments, aren't they? But perhaps that's why I've less patience with some of these clients than you have, Edward.

(EDWARD shakes his head, treating these paradoxes as they deserve.)

EDWARD: Alice..one or two of them will be beggared.

ALICE: *(sincerely)* Yes, that is bad. What's to be done?

EDWARD: There's old nurse..with her poor little savings gone!

ALICE: Surely that can be helped?

EDWARD: The Law's no respecter of persons..that's its boast. Old Booth with more than he wants will keep enough and to spare. My old nurse, with just enough, may starve. But it'll be a relief to clear out this nest of lies, even though one suffers one's self. I've been ashamed to walk into that office, Alice. I'll hold my head high in prison though.

(He shakes himself stiffly erect, his chin high. ALICE quizzes him.)

ALICE: Edward, I'm afraid you're feeling heroic.

EDWARD: I!

ALICE: You looked quite like Booth for the moment. *(This effectually removes the starch.)* Please don't glory in your martyrdom. It would be very stupid to send you to prison and you must do your best to keep out. *(She goes on very practically.)* We were thinking if anything could be done for these people who'll be beggared.

EDWARD: It isn't that I'm not sorry for them all..

ALICE: Of course not.

EDWARD: I suppose I was feeling heroic. I didn't mean to.

(He has become a little like a child with her.)

ALICE: It's the worst of acting on principle..one is so apt to think more of one's attitude than of the use of what one is doing.

EDWARD: Fraud must be exposed.

ALICE: And people must be ruined..!

EDWARD: What else is there to be done?

ALICE: Well..have you thought?

EDWARD: There's nothing else to be done.

ALICE: No. When on principle there's nothing to be done I'm afraid I've no use for that principle.

(He looks at her; she is smiling, it is true, but smiling quite gravely. EDWARD is puzzled. Then the yeast of her suggestion begins to work, in his mind slowly, perversely at first.)

EDWARD: Unless you expect me to take Booth's advice..go on with the game as an honest cheat..plunge, I suppose, just twice as wildly as my father did on the chance that things might come right..which he never bothered his head about. Booth offers to come to the office and assist me.

ALICE: There's something attractive about Booth at the right distance.

EDWARD: Oh..give him the money..send him to the City or Monte Carlo..he might bring it off. He's like my father..believes in himself.

ALICE: These credulous men!

EDWARD: *(ignoring her little joke)* But don't think I've any talents that way, principles or no. What have I done so far? Sat in the shame of it for a year. I did take a hand..if you knew what it felt like..I managed to stop one affair going from bad to worse.

ALICE: If that was the best you could do wasn't it worth doing? Never mind your feelings.

EDWARD: And that may cost me..at the best I'll be struck off..one's livelihood gone.

ALICE: The cost is your own affair.

(She is watching him, stilly and closely. Suddenly his face lights a little and he turns to her.)

EDWARD: I'll tell you what I could do.

ALICE: Yes.

EDWARD: It's just as irregular.

ALICE: That doesn't shock me..I'm lawless by birthright, being a woman.

EDWARD: There are four or five accounts I believe I could get quite square. Mrs. Travers..well, she'd never starve, but I'd like to see those two young Lyndhursts safe. There's money to play with, Heaven knows. It'd take a year or more to get it right and cover the tracks. Cover the tracks..sounds well doesn't it?

ALICE: Then you'd give yourself up as you'd meant to do now?

EDWARD: Go bankrupt.

ALICE: It'd be worse for you then at the trial?

EDWARD: (with a touch of another sort of pride) You said that it was my affair.

ALICE: (pain in her voice and eyes) Oh, Edward!

EDWARD: Shall I do it?

ALICE: (turning away) Why must you ask me?

EDWARD: If you've taken my principles from me, give me advice in exchange.

ALICE: (after a moment) No..you must decide for yourself.

(He jumps up and begins to pace about, doubtful, distressed.)

EDWARD: Ah, but..it means still lying and shuffling! And I'd sworn to be free of that. And..it wouldn't be easy. I'm no good at that sort of devilment. I should muddle it and fail.

ALICE: Would you?

(He catches a look from her.)

EDWARD: I might not.

ALICE: And do you need success for a lure...like a common man?

EDWARD: You want me to try?

(For answer she dares only put out her hand, and he takes it.)

ALICE: Oh, my dear..cousin!

EDWARD: (excitedly) My people must hold their tongues. I needn't have told them.

ALICE: Don't tell them this! They won't understand. I shall be jealous if you tell them.

EDWARD: *(looking at her as she at him)* You'll have the right to be. If I bring it off the glory shall be yours.

ALICE: Thank you. I've always wanted to have something useful to my credit..and I'd almost given up hoping.

(Then suddenly his face changes, his voice changes and he grips the hand he is holding so tightly as to hurt her.)

EDWARD: Ah, no, no, no, no, if my father's story were true..perhaps he began like this. Doing the right thing in the wrong way..then doing the wrong thing..then bringing himself to what he was..and so me to this. *(He flings away from her.)* No, Alice, I won't..I won't do it. I daren't take that first step down. There's a worse risk than failure..I might succeed.

(ALICE stands very still, looking at him.)

ALICE: Yes, that's the big risk. Well..I'll take it. *(He turns to her, in wonder.)*

EDWARD: You?

ALICE: I'll risk your becoming a bad man. That's a big risk for me.

(He understands, and is calmed and made happy.)

EDWARD: Then there's no more to be said, is there?

ALICE: Not now. *(As she drops this gentle hint she hears something—the hall door opening.)* Here's Booth back again.

EDWARD: *(with a really mischievous grin)* He'll be so glad he's convinced me.

ALICE: I must go back to Honor, poor girl. I wonder she has a tear left.

(She leaves him, briskly, brightly; leaves her cousin with his mouth set and a light in his eyes.)

ACT IV

MR VOYSEY'S room at the office is EDWARD'S now. It has somehow lost that brilliancy which the old man's occupation seemed to give it. Perhaps it is only because this December morning is dull and depressing, but the fire isn't bright and the panels and windows don't shine as they did. There are no roses on the table either. EDWARD, walking in as his father did, hanging his hat and coat where his father's used to hang, is certainly the palest shadow of that other masterful presence. A depressed, drooping shadow too. This may be what PEACEY feels, if no more, for he looks very surly as he obeys the old routine of following his chief to this room on his arrival. Nor has EDWARD so much as a glance for his clerk. They exchange the formalest of greetings. EDWARD sits joylessly to his desk, on which the morning's pile of letters lies, unopened now.

PEACEY: Good morning, sir.

EDWARD: Good morning, Peacey. Any notes for me?

PEACEY: Well, I've hardly been through the letters yet, sir.

EDWARD: *(his eyebrows meeting)* Oh...and I'm half an hour late myself this morning.

PEACEY: I'm very sorry, sir.

EDWARD: If Mr Bullen calls you had better show him those papers I gave you. Write to Metcalfe as soon as possible; say I've seen Mr Vickery myself this morning and the houses will not be proceeded with. Better show me the letter.

PEACEY: Very good, sir.

EDWARD: That's all, thank you.

(PEACEY gets to the door, where he stops, looking not only surly but nervous now.)

PEACEY: May I speak to you a moment, sir?

EDWARD: Certainly.

(PEACEY, after a moment, makes an effort, purses his mouth and begins.)

PEACEY: Bills are beginning to come in upon me as is usual at this season, sir. My son's allowance at Cambridge is now rather a heavy item of my expenditure. I hope that the custom of the firm isn't to be neglected now that you are the head of it, Mr Edward..Two hundred your father always made it at Christmas..in notes if you please.

(Towards the end of this EDWARD begins to pay great attention. When he answers his voice is harsh.)

EDWARD: Oh, to be sure.. your hush money.

PEACEY: *(bridling)* That's not a very pleasant word.

EDWARD: This is an unpleasant subject.

PEACEY: Well, it's not one I wish to discuss. Your father always gave me the notes in an envelope when he shook hands with me at Christmas.

EDWARD: Why notes now? Why not a rise in salary?

PEACEY: Mr Voysey's custom, sir, from before my time..my father..

EDWARD: Yes. It's an hereditary pull you have over the firm, isn't it?

PEACEY: I remember my father only saying to me when he retired..been dead twenty-six years, Mr Edward..I have told the governor you know what I know; then Mr Voysey saying..I treat you as I did your father, Peacey. We'd never another word with him on the subject.

EDWARD: A decent arrangement..and the cheapest, no doubt. Of the raising of salaries there might have been no end.

PEACEY: Mr Edward, that's uncalled for. We have served you and yours most faithfully. I know my father would sooner have cut off his hand than do anything to embarrass the firm.

EDWARD: But business is business, Peacey. Surely he could have had a partnership for the asking.

PEACEY: Ah, that's another matter, sir.

EDWARD: Well..

PEACEY: A matter of principle, if you'll excuse me. I must not be taken to approve of the firm's conduct. Nor did my dear father approve. And at anything like partnership he would have drawn the line.

EDWARD: I beg your pardon.

PEACEY: Well, that's all right, sir. Always a bit of friction in coming to an understanding about anything, isn't there, sir?

(He is going when EDWARD's question stops him.)

EDWARD: Why didn't you speak about this last Christmas?

PEACEY: You were so upset at your father's death.

EDWARD: My father died the August before that.

PEACEY: Well..truthfully, Mr Edward?

EDWARD: As truthfully as you think suitable.

(The irony of this is wasted on PEACEY, who becomes pleasantly candid.)

PEACEY: Well, I'd always thought there must be a smash when your father died..but it didn't come. I couldn't make you out. But then again by Christmas you seemed all on edge and I thought anything might happen. So I kept quiet and said nothing.

EDWARD: I see. Your son's at Cambridge?

PEACEY: Yes.

EDWARD: I wonder you didn't bring him into the firm.

PEACEY: *(taking this very kind)* Thank you. But I hope James may go to the bar. Our only son..I didn't grudge him my small savings to help him wait for his chance..ten years if need be.

EDWARD: I hope he'll make his mark before then. I'm glad to have had this talk with you, Peacey. I'm sorry you can't have the money you want.

(He returns to his letters, a little steely-eyed. PEACEY, quite at his ease, makes for the door yet again, saying..)

PEACEY: Oh, any time will do, sir.

EDWARD: You can't have it at all.

PEACEY: *(brought up short)* Can't I?

EDWARD: *(very decidedly indeed)* No..I made up my mind about this eighteen months ago. My father had warned me, but since his death the trust business of the firm is not conducted as it used to be. We no longer make illicit profits out of our clients. There are none for you to share.

(Having thus given the explanation he considers due, he goes on with his work. But PEACEY has flushed up.)

PEACEY: Look here, Mr Edward, I'm sorry we began this discussion. You'll give me my two hundred as usual, please, and we'll drop the subject.

EDWARD: You can drop the subject.

PEACEY: *(his voice rising sharply)* I want the money. I think it's not gentlemanly in you, Mr Edward, to try like this and get out of paying it me. Your father would never have made such an excuse.

EDWARD: *(flabbergasted)* Do you think I'm lying to you?

PEACEY: *(with a deprecating swallow)* I've no wish to criticise your statements or your actions at all, sir. It was no concern of mine how your father treated his clients.

EDWARD: And now it's not to concern you how honest I am. You want your money just the same.

PEACEY: Well, don't be sarcastic..a man does get used to a state of affairs whatever it may be.

EDWARD: *(with considerable force)* My friend, if I drop sarcasm I shall have to tell you very candidly what I think of you.

PEACEY: That I'm a thief because I've taken money from a thief?

EDWARD: Worse than a thief. You're content that others should steal for you.

PEACEY: And who isn't?

(EDWARD is really pleased with the aptness of this. He at once changes his tone, which indeed had become rather bullying.)

EDWARD: What, my dear Peacey, you study sociology? Well, it's too big a question to discuss now. But I'm afraid the application of this bit of it is that I have for the moment, at some inconvenience to myself, ceased to receive stolen goods, so I am in a position to throw a stone at you. I have thrown it.

(PEACEY, who would far sooner be bullied than talked to like this, turns very sulky.)

PEACEY: Then I resign my position here.

EDWARD: Very well.

PEACEY: And I happen to think the secret's worth its price.

EDWARD: Perhaps someone will pay it you.

PEACEY: *(feebly threatening)* Don't presume upon it's not being worth my while to make use of what I know.

EDWARD: *(not unkindly)* My good Peacey, it happens to be the truth I told you just now. Well, how on earth do you suppose you can successfully blackmail a man who has so much to gain by exposure and so little to lose as I?

PEACEY: *(peeving)* I don't want to ruin you, sir, and I have a great regard for the firm..but you must see that I can't have my income reduced in this way without a struggle.

EDWARD: *(with great cheerfulness)* Very well, my friend, struggle away.

PEACEY: *(his voice rising high and thin)* Well, is it fair dealing on your part to dock the money suddenly like this? I have been counting on it most of the year, and I have been led into heavy expenses. Why couldn't you have warned me?

EDWARD: Yes, that's true, Peacey, it was stupid of me. I'm sorry.

(PEACEY is a little comforted by this quite candid acknowledgement.)

PEACEY: Things may get easier for you by and bye.

EDWARD: I hope so.

PEACEY: Will you reconsider the matter then?

(At this gentle insinuation EDWARD looks up exasperated.)

EDWARD: Then you don't believe what I told you?

PEACEY: Yes, I do.

EDWARD: But you think that the fascination of swindling one's clients will ultimately prove irresistible?

PEACEY: That's what your father found, I suppose you know.

(This gives EDWARD such pause that he drops his masterful tone.)

EDWARD: I didn't.

PEACEY: He got things as right as rain once.

EDWARD: Did he?

PEACEY: So my father told me. But he started again.

EDWARD: Are you sure of this?

PEACEY: *(expanding pleasantly)* Well, sir, I knew your father pretty well. When I first came into the firm, now, I simply hated him. He was that sour; so snappy with everyone..as if he had a grievance against the whole world.

EDWARD: *(pensively)* It seems he had in those days.

PEACEY: His dealings with his clients were no business of mine. I speak as I find. After a bit he was very kind to me, thoughtful and considerate. He got to be so pleasant and generous to everyone—

EDWARD: That you have great hopes of me yet?

PEACEY: *(who has a simple mind)* No, Mr Edward, no. You're different from your father..one must make up one's mind to that. And you may believe me or not, but I should be very glad to know that the firm was solvent and going straight. I'm getting on in years myself now. I'm not much longer for the business, and there have been times when I have sincerely regretted my connection with it. If you'll let me say so, I think it's very noble of you to have undertaken the work you have. *(then, as everything seems smooth again)* And, Mr

Edward, if you'll give me enough to cover this year's extra expense I think I may promise you that I shan't expect money again.

EDWARD: *(good-tempered, as he would speak to an importunate child)* No, Peacey, no!

PEACEY: *(fretful again)* Well, sir, you make things very difficult for me.

EDWARD: Here's a letter from Mr Cartwright which you might attend to. If he wants an appointment with me, don't make one till the New Year. His case can't come on before February.

PEACEY: *(taking the letter)* I show myself anxious to meet you in every way —*(He is handed another.)*

EDWARD: 'Percival Building Estate'..that's yours too.

PEACEY: *(putting them both down resolutely)* But I refuse to be ignored. I must consider my whole position. I hope I may not be tempted to make use of the power I possess. But if I am driven to proceed to extremities..

EDWARD: *(breaking in upon this bunch of tags)* My dear Peacey, don't talk nonsense..you couldn't proceed to an extremity to save your life. You've taken this money irresponsibly for all these years. You'll find you're no longer capable even of such a responsible act as tripping up your neighbour. *(This does completely upset the gentle blackmailer. He loses one grievance in another.)*

PEACEY: Really, Mr Edward, I am a considerably older man than you, and I think that whatever our positions-

EDWARD: Don't let us argue, Peacey. You're quite at liberty to do whatever you think worth your while.

PEACEY: It's not the money, I can do without that, but these personalities—

EDWARD: I apologise for them. Don't forget the letters.

PEACEY: I will not, sir. *(He takes them with great dignity and is leaving the room.)*

PEACEY: Here's Mr Hugh waiting.

EDWARD: To see me? Ask him in.

PEACEY: Come in, Mr Hugh, please.

(HUGH comes in, PEACEY holding the door for him with a frigid politeness of which he is quite oblivious. At this final slight PEACEY goes out in dudgeon.)

EDWARD: How are you, Hugh?

HUGH: Good Lord!

(And he throws himself into the chair by the fire. EDWARD, quite used to this sort of thing, goes quietly on with his work, adding encouragingly after a moment..)

EDWARD: How's Beatrice?

HUGH: She's very busy.

(He studies his boots with the gloomiest expression. And indeed, they are very dirty and his turned-up trousers are muddy at the edge. They are dark trousers and well cut, but he wears with them a loose coat and waistcoat of a peculiar light brown

check. Add to this the roughest of overcoats and a very soft hat. Add also the fact that he doesn't shave well or regularly and that his hair wants cutting, and HUGH'S appearance this morning is described. As he is quite capable of sitting silently by the fire for a whole morning EDWARD asks him at last...)

EDWARD: What d'you want?

HUGH: *(with vehemence)* I want a machine gun planted in Regent Street.. and one in the Haymarket..and one in Leicester Squre and one in the Strand... and a dozen in the City. An earthquake would be simpler. Or why not a nice clean tidal wave? It's no good preaching and patching up any longer, Edward. We must begin afresh. Don't you feel, even in your calmer moments, that this whole country is simply hideous? The other nations must look after themselves. I'm patriotic..I only ask that we should be destroyed.

EDWARD: It has been promised.

HUGH: I'm sick of waiting. *(then as EDWARD says nothing)* You say this is the cry of the weak man in despair! I wouldn't be anything but a weak man in this world. I wouldn't be a king, I wouldn't be rich..I wouldn't be a Borough Councillor..I should be so ashamed. I've walked here this morning from Hampstead. I started to curse because the streets were dirty. You'd think an Empire could keep its streets clean! But then I saw that the children were dirty too.

EDWARD: That's because of the streets.

HUGH: Yes, it's holiday time. Those that can cross a road safely are doing some work now..earning some money. You'd think a governing race, grabbing responsibilities, might care for its children.

EDWARD: Come, we educate them now. And I don't think many work in holiday time.

HUGH: *(encouraged by contradiction)* Education! What's that? Joining the great conspiracy which we call our civilization. But one mustn't. One must stand aside and give the show away. By the bye, that's what I've come for.

EDWARD: *(pleasantly)* What? I thought you'd only come to talk.

HUGH: Take that money of mine for your clients. You ought to have had it when you asked for it. It has never belonged to me, in any real..in any spiritual sense, so it has been just a clog to my life.

EDWARD: *(surprised)* My dear Hugh..this is very generous of you.

HUGH: Not a bit. I only want to start fresh and free.

EDWARD: *(sitting back from his work)* Hugh, do you really think our money carries a curse with it?

HUGH: *(with great violence)* Think! I'm the proof of it! Look at me! I felt I must create or die. I said I'd be an artist. The governor gave me a hundred and fifty a year..the rent of a studio and the price of a velvet coat he thought it; that was all he knew about art. But my respectable training got me engaged and married. Marriage in a studio puzzled the governor, so he guessed it at two hundred and fifty a year..and looked for lay-figure babies, I suppose. Ha, ha! Well, I've learnt my job. I work in a sort of way, Edward, though you mightn't think it. Well, what have I really learnt..about myself..that's the only learning.. that there's nothing I can do or be but reflects our drawing-room at Chislehurst.

EDWARD: *(considering)* What do you earn in a year? I doubt if you can afford to give this up.

HUGH: Oh, Edward..you clank the chain with the best of them. Afford! If I can't get free from these crippling advantages..Unless I find out what I'm worth in myself..whether I even exist or not? Am I only a pretence of a man animated by an income?

EDWARD: But you can't return to nature on the London pavements.

HUGH: No. Nor in England at all..it's nothing but a big back garden. *(Now he collects himself for a final outburst.)* Is there no place on this earth where a man can prove his right to live by some other means than robbing his neighbour? Put me there naked and penniless. Put me to that test. If I can't answer it, then turn down your thumb..Oh God..and I won't complain.

(EDWARD waits till the effects of this explosion are over.)

EDWARD: And what does Beatrice say to your emigrating to the backwoods..if that is exactly what you mean?

HUGH: Now that we're separating—

EDWARD: *(taken aback)* What?

HUGH: We mean to separate.

EDWARD: The first I've heard of it.

HUGH: Beatrice is making some money by her books, so it has become possible.

EDWARD: *(humorously)* Have you told anyone yet?

HUGH: We must now, I suppose.

EDWARD: Say nothing at home until after Christmas.

HUGH: They'll insist on discussing it solemnly. Ar-r-r. *(then he whistles)* Emily knows!

EDWARD: *(having considered)* I shan't take your money..there's no need. All the good has been done that I wanted to do. No one will be quite beggared now. So why should you be?

HUGH: *(with clumsy affection)* We've taken a fine lot of interest in your labours, haven't we, Hercules?

EDWARD: You hold your tongue about the office affairs, don't you? It's not through one of us it should come out, and I've told you more than Booth and the others.

HUGH: When will you be quit of the beastly business?

EDWARD: *(becoming reserved and cold at once)* Some day.

HUGH: What do you gain by hanging on now?

EDWARD: Occupation.

HUGH: But, Edward, it must be an awfully wearying state of things. I suppose any moment a policeman may knock at the door..so to speak?

EDWARD: *(appreciating the figure of speech)* Any moment. I take no precautions. I made up my mind that at least I wouldn't lower myself to that. And perhaps it's why the policeman doesn't come. At first I listened for him, day by day. Then I said to myself..next week. But a year has gone by and more. I've ceased expecting to hear the knock at all.

HUGH: But look here..is all this worth while, and have you the right to make a mean thing of your life like this?

EDWARD: Does my life matter?

HUGH: Well..of course!

EDWARD: It's so much easier to believe not. The world that you kick against is using me up. A little wantonly..a little needlessly, I do think. But let her. As I sit here now drudging honestly, I declare I begin to understand my father. But no doubt, it's all I'm fit for..to nurse fools' money.

HUGH: *(responding at once to this vein)* Nonsense. We all want a lesson in values. We're never taught what is worth having and what isn't. Why should your real happiness be sacrificed to the sham happiness which people have invested in the firm? I've never believed that money was valuable. I remember once giving a crossing-sweeper a sovereign. The sovereign was nothing. But the sensation I gave him was an intrinsically valuable thing.

(He is fearfully pleased with his essay in philosophy.)

EDWARD: And he could buy other sensations with the sovereign.

HUGH: But none like the first. You mean to stay here till something happens?

EDWARD: I do. This is what I'm brought to. No more good to be done. And I haven't the faith in myself to do wrong. And it's only your incurable optimist who has enterprise enough for suicide..even business suicide.

HUGH: Ah..I'm that. But I can't boast. Heaven knows when I shall really get out of it either. *(Then the realities of life overwhelm him again.)* Beatrice won't let me go until we're each certain of two hundred a year. And she's quite right ..I should only get into debt. You know that two fifty a year of mine is a hundred and eighty now.

EDWARD: *(mischievous)* Why would you invest sensationally?

HUGH: *(with great seriousness)* I put money into things which I knew ought to succeed

(The telephone rings. EDWARD speaks through it.)

EDWARD: Certainly..bring him in. *(Then to his brother who sits on the table idly disarranging everything.)* You'll have to go now, Hugh.

HUGH: *(shaking his head gloomily)* You're one of the few people I can talk to, Edward.

EDWARD: I like listening.

HUGH: *(as much cheered as surprised)* Do you? I believe talking does stir up the world's atoms a bit.

(In comes old MR GEORGE BOOTH, older too in looks than he was eighteen months back. Very dandyishly dressed, he still seems by no means so happy as his clothes might be making him.)

MR BOOTH: 'Ullo, Hugh! I thought I should find you, Edward.

EDWARD: *(formally)* Good morning, Mr Booth.

HUGH: *(as he collects his hat, his coat, his various properties)* Well.. Beatrice and I go down to Chislehurst tomorrow. I say..d'you know that old Nursie is furious with you about something?

EDWARD: *(shortly)* Yes, I know. Good-bye.

HUGH: How are you?

(He launches this enquiry at MR BOOTH with great suddenness just as he leaves the room. The old gentleman jumps; then jumps again at the slam of the door. And then he frowns at EDWARD in a frightened sort of way.)

EDWARD: Will you come here..or will you sit by the fire?

MR BOOTH: This'll do. I shan't detain you long.

(He takes the chair by the table and occupies the next minute or two carefully disposing of his hat and gloves.)

EDWARD: Are you feeling all right again?

MR BOOTH: A bit dyspeptic. How are you?

EDWARD: Quite well, thanks.

MR BOOTH: I'm glad..I'm glad. *(He now proceeds to cough a little, hesitating painfully.)* I'm afraid this isn't very pleasant business I've come upon.

EDWARD: D'you want to go to Law with anyone?

MR BOOTH: No..oh, no. I'm getting too old to quarrel.

EDWARD: A pleasant symptom.

MR BOOTH: *(with a final effort)* I mean to withdraw my securities from the custody of your firm..*(and he adds apologetically)* with the usual notice, of course.

(It would be difficult to describe what EDWARD feels at this moment. Perhaps something of the shock that the relief of death may be as an end to pain so long endured that it has been half forgotten. He answers very quietly, without a sign of emotion.)

EDWARD: Thank you..May one ask why?

MR BOOTH: *(relieved that the worst is over)* Certainly..certainly. I think you must know, Edward, I have never been able to feel that implicit confidence in your ability which I had in your father's. Well, it is hardly to be expected, is it?

EDWARD: *(with a grim smile)* No.

MR BOOTH: I can say that without unduly depreciating you. Men like your father are few and far between. No doubt things go on here as they have always done, but..since his death I have not been happy about my affairs.

EDWARD: *(speaking as it is his duty to)* I think you need be under no apprehension..

MR BOOTH: I daresay not. But for the first time in my long life to be worried about money affairs..I don't like the feeling. The possession of money has always been a pleasure to me..and for what are perhaps my last years I don't wish it to be otherwise. Remember you have practically my entire property unreservedly in your control.

EDWARD: Perhaps we can arrange to hand you over the reins to an extent which will ease your mind, and at the same time not..

MR BOOTH: I thought of that. I am very sorry to seem to be slighting your father' son. I have not moved in the matter for eighteen months. Really, one feels a little helpless..and the transaction of business requires more energy than..But I saw my doctor yesterday, Edward, and he told me..well, it was a warning. And so I felt it my duty..especially as I made up my mind to it some time ago. *(He comes to the end of this havering at last and adds..)* In point of fact, Edward, more than a year before your father died I had quite decided that I could never trust my affairs to you as I had to him.

(EDWARD starts almost out of his chair; his face pale, his eyes black.)

EDWARD: Did he know that?

MR BOOTH: *(resenting this new attitude)* I think I never said it in so many words. But I fancy he guessed.

EDWARD: *(as he relaxes and turns, almost shuddering, from the possibility of dreadful knowledge)* Don't say so..he never guessed. *(then, with a sudden fresh impulse)* I hope you won't do this, Mr Booth.

MR BOOTH: I have quite made up my mind.

EDWARD: Let me persuade you—

MR BOOTH: *(conciliatory)* I shall make a point of telling the family that you are in no way to blame. And in the event of any personal legal difficulties I shall always be delighted to come to you. My idea is for the future to employ merely a financial agent—

EDWARD: *(still quite unstrung really, and his nerves betraying him)* Why didn't you tell my father..why didn't you?

MR BOOTH: I did not choose to distress him by—

EDWARD: *(pulling himself together; speaking half to himself)* Well..well.. this is one way out. And it's not my fault.

MR BOOTH: You're making a fearful fuss about a very simple matter, Edward. The loss of one client, however important he may be..Why, this is one of the best family practices in London. I am surprised at your lack of dignity. *(EDWARD yields smilingly to this assertiveness.)*

EDWARD: Yes..I have no dignity. Will you walk off with your papers now?

MR BOOTH: What notice is usual?

EDWARD: To a good solicitor, five minutes. Ten to a poor one.

MR BOOTH: You'll have to explain matters a bit to me.

(Now EDWARD settles to his desk again; really with a certain grim enjoyment of the prospect.)

EDWARD: I will. Mr Booth, how much do you think you're worth?

MR BOOTH: *(easily)* Do you know, I actually couldn't say off-hand.

EDWARD: But you've a rough idea?

MR BOOTH: To be sure.

EDWARD: You'll get not quite half that out of us.

MR BOOTH: *(precisely)* I think I said I had made up my mind to withdraw the whole amount.

EDWARD: You should have made up your mind sooner.

MR BOOTH: I don't in the least understand you, Edward.

EDWARD: The greater part of your capital doesn't exist.

MR BOOTH: *(with some irritation)* Nonsense, it must exist. *(He scans EDWARD'S set face in vain.)* You mean that it won't be prudent to realise? You can hand over the securities. I don't want to reinvest simply because—

EDWARD: I can't hand over what I haven't got. *(This sentence falls on the old man's ears like a knell.)*

MR BOOTH: Is anything..wrong?

EDWARD: *(grim and patient)* How many more times am I to say that we have robbed you of half your property?

MR BOOTH: *(his senses failing him)* Say that again.

EDWARD: It's quite true.

MR BOOTH: My money..gone?

EDWARD: Yes.

MR BOOTH: *(clutching at a straw of anger)* You've been the thief..you.. you..?

EDWARD: I wouldn't tell you if I could help it..my father.

(That actually calls the old man back to something like dignity and self-possession. He thumps on EDWARD'S table furiously.)

MR BOOTH: I'll make you prove that.

(And now EDWARD buries his face in his arms and just goes off into hysterics.)

EDWARD: Oh, you've fired a mine!

MR BOOTH: *(scolding him well)* Slandering your dead father..and lying to me, revenging yourself by frightening me..because I detest you.

EDWARD: Why..haven't I thanked you for putting an end to my troubles? I do..I promise you I do.

MR BOOTH: *(shouting, and his sudden courage failing as he shouts)* Prove it..prove it to me! You don't frighten me so easily. One can't lose half of all one has and then be told of it in two minutes..sitting at a table. *(His voice tails off to a piteous whimper.)*

EDWARD: *(quietly now and kindly)* If my father had told you in plain words you'd have believed him.

MR BOOTH: *(bowing his head)* Yes.

(EDWARD looks at the poor old thing with great pity.)

EDWARD: What on earth did you want to do this for? You need never have known..you could have died happy. Settling with all those charities in your will would certainly have smashed us up. But proving your will is many years off yet, we'll hope.

MR BOOTH: *(pathetic and bewildered)* I don't understand. No, I don't understand..because your father..But I must understand, Edward.

EDWARD: Don't shock yourself trying to understand my father, for you never will. Pull yourself together, Mr Booth. After all, this isn't a vital matter to you. It's not even as if you had a family to consider..like some of the others.

MR BOOTH: *(vaguely)* What others?

EDWARD: Don't imagine your money has been specially selected for pilfering.

MR BOOTH: *(with solemn incredulity)* One has read of this sort of thing but..I thought people always got found out.

EDWARD: *(brutally humorous)* Well..you've found us out.

MR BOOTH: (rising to the full appreciation of his wrongs) Oh..I've been foully cheated !

EDWARD: *(patiently)* I've told you so.

MR BOOTH: *(his voice breaks, he appeals pitifully)* But by you, Edward.. say it's by you.

EDWARD: *(unable to resist his quiet revenge)* I've not the ability or the personality for such work, Mr Booth..nothing but principles, which forbid me even to lie to you.

(The old gentleman draws a long breath and then speaks with great awe, blending into grief.)

MR BOOTH: I think your father is in Hell..I'd have gone there myself to save him from it. I loved him very truly. How he could have had the heart! We were friends for nearly fifty years. Am I to think now he only cared for me to cheat me?

EDWARD: *(venturing the comfort of an explanation)* No..he didn't value money quite as you do.

MR BOOTH: *(with sudden shrill logic)* But he took it. What d'you mean by that?

(EDWARD leans back in his chair and changes the tenor of their talk.)

EDWARD: Well, you're master of the situation now. What are you going to do?

MR BOOTH: To get my money back?

EDWARD: No, that's gone.

MR BOOTH: Then give me what's left and—

EDWARD: Are you going to prosecute?

MR BOOTH: *(shifting uneasily in his chair)* Oh, dear..is that necessary? Can't somebody else do that? I thought the Law..What'll happen if I don't?

EDWARD: What do you suppose I'm doing here still?

MR BOOTH: *(as if he were being asked a riddle)* I don't know.

EDWARD: *(earnestly)* As soon as my father died, I began of course to try and put things straight..doing as I thought best..that is..as best I could. Then I made up my accounts showing who has lost and who hasn't..they can criticise those as they please and that's all done with. And now I've set myself to a duller sort of work. I throw penny after penny hardly earned into the half-filled pit of our deficit. But I've been doing that for what it's worth in the time that was left to me..till this should happen. If you choose to let things alone—which won't hurt you, will it?—and hold your tongue, I can go on with the job till the next smash comes, and I'll beg that off too if I can. This is my duty, and it's my duty to ask you to let me go on with it. *(He searches MR BOOTH'S face and finds there only disbelief and fear. He bursts out.)* Oh, you might at least believe me. It can't hurt you to believe me.

MR BOOTH: You must admit, Edward, it isn't easy to believe anything in this office..just for the moment.

EDWARD: *(bowing to the extreme reasonableness of this)* I suppose not..I can prove it to you. I'll take you through the books..you won't understand them.. but I can boast of this much.

MR BOOTH: I think I'd rather not. D'you think I ought to hold any further communication with you at all? *(And at this he takes his hat.)*

EDWARD: *(with a little explosion of contemptuous anger)* Certainly not. Prosecute..prosecute!

MR BOOTH: *(with dignity)* Don't lose your temper. You know it's my place to be angry with you.

EDWARD: But..*(then he is elaborately explanatory)* I shall be grateful if you'll prosecute.

MR BOOTH: *(more puzzled than ever)* There's something in this which I don't understand.

EDWARD: *(with deliberate unconcern)* Think it over.

MR BOOTH: *(hesitatingly, fidgeting)* Surely I oughtn't to have to make up my mind! There must be a right or a wrong thing to do. Edward, can't you tell me?

EDWARD: I'm prejudiced, you see.

MR BOOTH: *(angrily)* I believe you're simply trying to practise upon my goodness of heart. Certainly I ought to prosecute at once..Oughtn't I? *(then at the nadir of helplessness)* Can't I consult another solicitor?

EDWARD: *(his chin in the air)* You can write to the Times about it!

MR BOOTH: *(shocked and grieved at his attitude)* Edward, how can you be so cool and heartless?

EDWARD: *(changing his tone)* D'you think I shan't be glad to sleep at nights?

MR BOOTH: Perhaps you'll be put in prison?

EDWARD: I am in prison..a less pleasant one than Wormwood Scrubbs. But we're all prisoners, Mr Booth.

MR BOOTH: *(wagging his head)* Yes, this is what comes of your philosophy. Why aren't you on your knees?

EDWARD: To you?

(This was not what MR BOOTH meant, but as he gets up from his chair he feels all but mighty.)

MR BOOTH: And why should you expect me to shrink from vindicating the Law?

EDWARD: *(shortly)* I don't. I've explained you'll be doing me a kindness. When I'm wanted you'll find me here at my desk. *(then as an afterthought)* If you take long to decide..don't alter your behaviour to my family in the meantime. They know the main points of the business and—

MR BOOTH: *(knocked right off his balance)* Do they! Good God!..I'm invited to dinner the day after tomorrow..that's Christmas Eve. The hypocrites!

EDWARD: *(unmoved)* I shall be there..that will have given you two days. Will you tell me then?

MR BOOTH: *(protesting violently)* I can't go..I can't have dinner with them. I must be ill.

EDWARD: *(with a half smile)* I remember I went to dine at Chislehurst to tell my father of my decision.

MR BOOTH: *(testily)* What decision?

EDWARD: To remain in the firm when I first knew what was happening.

MR BOOTH: *(interested)* Was I there?

EDWARD: I daresay.

(MR BOOTH stands there, hat, stick and gloves in hand, shaken by this experience, helpless, at his wits' end. He falls into a sort of fretful reverie, speaking half to himself but yet as if he hoped that EDWARD, who is wrapped in his own thoughts, would have the decency to answer, or at least listen, to what he is saying.)

MR BOOTH: Yes, how often I dined with him. Oh, it was monstrous! *(His eyes fall on the clock.)* It's nearly lunch time now. Do you know I still can hardly believe it all? I wish I hadn't found it out. If he hadn't died I should never have found it out. I hate to have to be vindictive..it's not my nature. Indeed I'm sure I'm more grieved than angry. But it isn't as if it were a small sum. And I don't see that one is called upon to forgive crimes..or why does the Law exist? I feel that this will go near to killing me. I'm too old to have such troubles..it isn't right. And now if I have to prosecute—

EDWARD: *(at last throwing in a word)* Well..you need not.

MR BOOTH: *(thankful for the provocation)* Don't you attempt to influence me, sir .

(He turns to go.)

EDWARD: And what's more, with the money you have left..

(EDWARD follows him politely. MR BOOTH flings the door open.)

MR BOOTH: You'll make out a cheque for that at once, sir, and send it me.

EDWARD: You might..

MR BOOTH: *(clapping his hat on, stamping his stick)* I shall do the right thing, sir never fear.

(So he marches off in fine style, having, he thinks, had the last word and all. But EDWARD, closing the door after him, mutters..)

EDWARD:...Save your soul!..I'm afraid I was going to say.

ACT V

Naturally it is the dining-room—consecrated as it is to the distinguishing orgy of the season-which bears the brunt of what an English household knows as Christmas decorations. They consist chiefly of the branches of holly (that unyielding tree), stuck, cock-eyed behind the top edges of the pictures. The one picture conspicuously not decorated is that which now hangs over the fireplace, a portrait of MR VOYSEY, with its new gilt frame and its brassplate marking it also as a presentation. HONOR, hastily and at some bodily peril, pulled down the large bunch of mistletoe, which a callous housemaid had suspended above it, in time to obviate the shock to family feelings which such impropriety would cause. Otherwise the only difference between the dining-room's appearance at half-past nine on Christmas Eve and on any other evening in the year is that little piles of queer shaped envelopes seem to be lying about while there is quite a lot of tissue paper and string to be seen peeping from odd corners. The electric light is reduced to one bulb, but when the maid opens the door showing in MR GEORGE BOOTH she switches on the rest.

PHOEBE: This room is empty, sir. I'll tell Mr Edward.

(She leaves him to fidget towards the fireplace and back, not removing his comforter or his coat, scarcely turning down the collar, screwing his cap in his hands. In a very short time EDWARD comes in, shutting the door and taking stock of the visitor before he speaks.)

EDWARD: Well?

MR BOOTH: *(feebly)* I hope my excuse for not coming to dinner was acceptable. I did have..I have a very bad headache.

EDWARD: I daresay they believed it.

MR BOOTH: I have come immediately to tell you my decision..perhaps this trouble will then be a little more off my mind.

EDWARD: What is it?

MR BOOTH: I couldn't think the matter out alone. I went this afternoon to talk it over with my old friend Colpus. *(At this news EDWARD'S eyebrows contract and then rise.)* What a terrible shock to him!

EDWARD: Oh, nearly three of his four thousand pounds are quite safe.

MR BOOTH: That you and your father..you, whom he baptised..should have robbed him! I never saw a man so utterly prostrate with grief. That it should have been your father! And his poor wife!..though she never got on with your father.

EDWARD: *(with a cheerful irony)* Oh, Mrs Colpus knows too, does she?

MR BOOTH: Of course he told Mrs Colpus. This is an unfortunate time for the storm to break on him. What with Christmas Day and Sunday following so close they're as busy as can be. He has resolved that during this season of peace and goodwill he must put the matter from him if he can. But once Christmas is over..! *(He envisages the Christian old vicar giving EDWARD a hell of a time then.)*

EDWARD: *(coolly)* So you mean to prosecute. If you don't, you've inflicted on the Colpuses a lot of unnecessary pain and a certain amount of loss by telling them.

MR BOOTH: *(naïvely)* I never thought of that. No, Edward, I have decided not to prosecute.

(EDWARD hides his face for a moment.)

EDWARD: And I've been hoping to escape! Well..it can't be helped *(and he sets his teeth).*

MR BOOTH: *(with touching solemnity)* I think I could not bear to see the family I have loved brought to such disgrace. And I want to ask your pardon, Edward, for some of the hard thoughts I have had of you. I consider this effort of yours to restore to the firm the credit which your father lost a very striking one. You sacrifice your profits, I understand, to replacing the capital that has been misappropriated. Very proper..more than proper.

EDWARD: No. No. To pay interest on the money that doesn't exist but ought to..and the profits don't cover that or anything like it.

MR BOOTH: Patience..I shouldn't be surprised if you worked up the business very well.

EDWARD: *(again laying the case before MR BOOTH, leaning forward to him)* Mr Booth, you were fond of my father. You see the help you could give us, don't you?

MR BOOTH: By not prosecuting?

EDWARD: *(earnestly)* Beyond that. If you'd cut your losses..for the moment, and take only what's yours by right..why, that would relieve me of four thousand three hundred a year..and I could do so much with it. There are one or two bad cases still. One woman—I believe you know her—it's not that she's so poor ..and perhaps I'm not justified now in doing anything special..but she's got children..and if you'd help..

MR BOOTH: Stop, Edward..stop at once. If you attempt to confuse me I must take professional advice. Colpus and I have discussed this and quite made up our minds. And I've made a note or two. *(He produces a bit of paper and a pencil. EDWARD stiffens.)* May we understand that in straightening affairs you can show a proper preference for one client over another?

EDWARD: *(pulled up, draws back in his chair)* No..you had better not understand that.

MR BOOTH: Why can't you?

EDWARD: Well..suppose if I want to, I can?

MR BOOTH: Edward, do please be straightforward.

EDWARD: Why should I?

MR BOOTH: You certainly should. Do you mean to compare your father's ordinary business transactions—the hundreds of them—with his black treachery to ..to the Vicar?

EDWARD: Or to you?

MR BOOTH: Or to me.

EDWARD: Besides that, holding your tongue should be worth something extra now, shouldn't it?

MR BOOTH: I don't want to argue. My own position morally—and otherwise—is a strong one..so Colpus impresses on me..and he has some head for business.

EDWARD: Well, what are your terms?

MR BOOTH: This is my note of them. *(He takes refuge in his slip of paper.)* I make these conditions, if you please, Edward, on the Vicar's behalf and my own. They are..*(Now the pencil comes into play, ticking off each item.)* that you return to us the balance of any capital there is left..

EDWARD: *(cold again)* I am providing for that.

MR BOOTH: Good. That you should continue, of course, to pay us the usual interest upon the rest of our capital, which ought to exist and does not. And that you should, year by year, pay us back by degrees out of the earnings of the firm as much of that capital as you can afford. We will agree upon the sum.. say a thousand a year. I doubt if you can ever restore us all we have lost, but do your best and I shan't complain. There, I think that is fair dealing!

(EDWARD does not take his eyes off MR BOOTH until the whole meaning of this proposition has settled in his brain. Then, without warning, he goes off into peals of laughter, much to the alarm of MR BOOTH, who has never thought him over-sane.)

EDWARD: How funny! How very funny!

MR BOOTH: Edward, don't laugh.

EDWARD: I never heard anything quite so funny!

MR BOOTH: Edward, stop laughing.

EDWARD: Oh, you Christian gentlemen!

MR BOOTH: Don't be hysterical. The money's ours.

(EDWARD'S laughter gives way to the deepest anger of which he is capable.)

EDWARD: I'm giving my soul and body to restoring you and the rest of you to your precious money bags..and you'll wring me dry. Won't you? Won't you?

MR BOOTH: Now be reasonable. Argue the point quietly.

EDWARD: Go to the devil, sir. *(And with that he turns away from the flabbergasted old gentleman.)*

MR BOOTH: Don't be rude.

EDWARD: *(his anger vanishing)* I beg your pardon.

MR BOOTH: You're just excited. If you take time to think of it, I'm reasonable.

EDWARD: *(his sense of humour returning)* Most! Most! *(There is a knock at the door.)* Come in. Come in.

(HONOR intrudes an apologetic head.)

HONOR: Am I interrupting business? I'm so sorry.

EDWARD: *(crowing in a mirthless enjoyment of his own joke)* No! Business is over..quite over. Come in, Honor.

(HONOR puts on the table a market basket bulging with little paper parcels, and, oblivious of MR BOOTH'S distracted face, tries to fix his attention.)

HONOR: I thought, dear Mr Booth, perhaps you wouldn't mind carrying round this basket of things yourself. It's so very damp underfoot that I don't want to send one of the maids out tonight if I can possibly avoid it..and if one doesn't get Christmas presents the very first thing on Christmas morning quite half the pleasure in them is lost, don't you think?

MR BOOTH: Yes..yes.

HONOR: *(fishing out the parcels one by one)* This is a bell for Mrs Williams ..something she said she wanted so that you can ring for her, which saves the maids: cap and apron for Mary: cap and apron for Ellen: shawl for Davis when she goes out to the larder—all useful presents—and that's something for you, but you're not to look at it till the morning.

(Having shaken each of these at the old gentleman, she proceeds to re-pack them. He is now trembling with anxiety to escape before any more of the family find him there.)

MR BOOTH: Thank you...thank you! I hope my lot has arrived. I left instructions..

HONOR: Quite safely..and I have hidden them. Presents are put on the breakfast table tomorrow.

EDWARD: *(with an inconsequence that still further alarms MR BOOTH)* When we were all children our Christmas breakfast was mostly made off chocolates.

(Before the basket is packed, MRS VOYSEY sails slowly into the room, as smiling and as deaf as ever. MR BOOTH does his best not to scowl at her.)

MRS VOYSEY: Are you feeling better, George Booth?

MR BOOTH: No. *(Then he elevates his voice with a show of politeness.)* No, thank you..I can't say I am.

MRS VOYSEY: You don't look better.

MR BOOTH: I still have my headache. *(with a distracted shout)* Headache.

MRS VOYSEY: Bilious, perhaps! I quite understood you didn't care to dine. But why not have taken your coat off? How foolish in this warm room!

MR BOOTH: Thank you. I'm—er—just off.

(He seizes the market basket. At that moment BEATRICE appears.)

BEATRICE: Your shawl, mother. *(And she clasps it round MRS VOYSEY'S shoulders.)*

MRS VOYSEY: Thank you, Beatrice. I thought I had it on. *(then to MR BOOTH who is now entangled in his comforter)* A merry Christmas to you.

BEATRICE: Good evening, Mr Booth.

MR BOOTH: I beg your pardon. Good evening, Mrs Hugh.

HONOR: *(with sudden inspiration, to the company in general)* Why shouldn't I write in here..now the table's cleared!

MR BOOTH: *(sternly, now he is safe by the door)* Will you see me out, Edward?

EDWARD: Yes.

(He follows the old man and his basket, leaving the others to distribute themselves about the room. It is a custom of the female members of the VOYSEY family, especially about Christmas time, to return to the dining room, when the table has been cleared, and occupy themselves in various ways which require space and untidiness. Sometimes as the evening wears on they partake of cocoa, sometimes they abstain. BEATRICE has a little work-basket, containing a buttonless glove and such things, which she is rectifying. HONOR'S writing is done with the aid of an enormous blotting book, which bulges with apparently a year's correspondence. She sheds its contents upon the end of the dining table and spreads them abroad. MRS VOYSEY settles to the fire, opens the Nineteenth Century and is instantly absorbed in it.)

BEATRICE: Where's Emily?

HONOR: *(mysteriously)* Well, Beatrice, she's in the library talking to Booth.

BEATRICE: Talking to her husband; good Heavens! I know she has taken my scissors.

HONOR: I think she's telling him about you.

BEATRICE: What about me?

HONOR: You and Hugh.

BEATRICE: *(with a little movement of annoyance)* I suppose this is Hugh's fault. It was carefully arranged no one was to be told till after Christmas.

HONOR: Emily told me..and Edward knows..and Mother knows..

BEATRICE: I warned Mother a year ago.

HONOR: Everyone seems to know but Booth..so I thought he'd better be told. I suggested one night so that he might have time to think it over..but Emily said that'd wake Alfred. Besides she's nearly always asleep herself when he comes to bed.

BEATRICE: Why do they still have that baby in their room?

HONOR: Emily thinks it her duty.

(At this moment EMILY comes in, looking rather trodden upon. HONOR concludes in the most audible of whispers..)

HONOR: Don't say anything..it's my fault.

BEATRICE: *(fixing her with a severe forefinger)* Emily..have you taken my best scissors?

EMILY: *(timidly)* No, Beatrice.

HONOR: *(who is diving into the recesses of the blotting book)* Oh, here they are! I must have taken them. I do apologise!

EMILY: *(more timidly still)* I'm afraid Booth's rather cross..he's gone to look for Hugh.

BEATRICE: *(with a shake of her head)* Honor..I've a good mind to make you do this sewing for me.

(In comes the MAJOR, strepitant. He takes, so to speak, just time enough to train himself on BEATRICE and then fires.)

MAJOR: Beatrice, what on earth is this Emily has been telling me?

BEATRICE: *(with elaborate calm)* Emily, what have you been telling Booth?

MAJOR: Please..please do not prevaricate. Where is Hugh?

MRS VOYSEY: *(looking over her spectacles)* What did you say, Booth?

MAJOR: I want Hugh, Mother.

MRS VOYSEY: I thought you were playing billiards together.

(EDWARD strolls back from despatching MR BOOTH, his face thoughtful.)

MAJOR: *(insistently)* Edward, where is Hugh?

EDWARD: *(with complete indifference)* I don't know.

MAJOR: *(in trumpet tones)* Honor, will you oblige me by finding Hugh and saying I wish to speak to him, here, immediately?

(HONOR, who has leapt at the sound of her name, flies from the room without a word.)

BEATRICE: I know quite well what you want to talk about, Booth. Discuss the matter by all means if it amuses you..but don't shout.

MAJOR: I use the voice Nature has gifted me with, Beatrice.

BEATRICE: *(as she searches for a glove button)* Certainly Nature did let herself go over your lungs.

MAJOR: *(glaring round with indignation)* This is a family matter, otherwise I should not feel it my duty to interfere..as I do. Any member of the family has a right to express an opinion. I want Mother's. Mother, what do you think?

MRS VOYSEY: *(amicably)* What about?

MAJOR: Hugh and Beatrice separating.

MRS VOYSEY: They haven't separated.

MAJOR: But they mean to.

MRS VOYSEY: Fiddle-de-dee!

MAJOR: I quite agree with you.

BEATRICE: *(with a charming smile)* Such reaoning would convert a stone.

MAJOR: Why have I not been told?

BEATRICE: You have just been told.

MAJOR: *(thunderously)* Before.

BEATRICE: The truth is, dear Booth, we're all so afraid of you.

MAJOR: *(a little mollified)* Ha..I should be glad to think that.

BEATRICE: *(sweetly)* Don't you?

MAJOR: *(intensely serious)* Beatrice, your callousness shocks me! That you can dream of deserting Hugh..a man of all others who requires constant care and attention.

BEATRICE: May I remark that the separation is as much Hugh's wish as mine?

MAJOR: I don't believe that.

BEATRICE: *(her eyebrows up)* Really!

MAJOR: I don't imply that you're lying. But you must know that it's Hugh's nature to wish to do anything that he thinks anybody wishes him to do. All my life I've had to stand up for him..and by Jove, I'll continue to do so.

EDWARD: *(from the depths of his armchair)* If you'd taught him to stand up for himself—

(The door is flung almost off its hinges by HUGH who then stands, stamping and pale green with rage.)

HUGH: Look here, Booth..I will not have you interfering with my private affairs. Is one never to be free from your bullying?

MAJOR: You ought to be grateful.

HUGH: Well, I'm not.

MAJOR: This is a family affair.

HUGH: It is not!

MAJOR: *(at the top of his voice)* If all you can do is contradict me, you'd better listen to what I've got to say..quietly.

(HUGH, quite shouted down, flings himself petulantly into a chair. A hush falls.)

EMILY: *(in a still small voice)* Would you like me to go, Booth?

MAJOR: *(severely)* No, Emily. Unless anything has been going on which cannot discussed before you..*(then more severely still)* and I hope that is not so.

HUGH: *(muttering rebelliously)* Oh, you have the mind of a..an official flunkey!

MAJOR: Why do you wish to separate?

HUGH: What's the use of telling you? You won't understand.

BEATRICE: *(who sews on undisturbed)* We don't get on well together.

MAJOR: *(amazedly)* Is that all?

HUGH: *(snapping at him)* Yes, that's all. Can you find a better reason?

MAJOR: *(with brotherly contempt)* I have given up expecting common sense from you. But Beatrice! *(His tone implores her to be reasonable.)*

BEATRICE: It doesn't seem to me any sort of sense that people should live together for purposes of mutual irritation.

MAJOR: *(protesting)* My dear girl!..that sounds like a quotation from your last book.

BEATRICE: It isn't. I do think, Booth, you might read that book..for the honour of the Family.

MAJOR: *(successfully side-tracked.)* I have bought it, Beatrice, and—

BEATRICE: That's the principal thing, of course—

MAJOR: *(..and discovering it)* But do let us keep to the subject.

BEATRICE: *(with flattering sincerity)* Certainly, Booth. And there is hardly any subject that I wouldn't ask your advice about. But upon this..please let me know better. Hugh and I will be happier apart.

MAJOR: *(obstinately)* Why?

BEATRICE: *(with resolute patience, having vented a little sigh)* Hugh finds that my opinions distress him. And I have at last lost patience with Hugh.

MRS VOYSEY: *(who has been trying to follow this through her spectacles)* What does Beatrice say?

MAJOR: *(translating into a loud sing-song)* That she wishes to leave her husband because she has lost patience!

MRS VOYSEY: *(with considerable acrimony)* Then you must be a very ill-tempered woman. Hugh has a sweet nature.

HUGH: *(shouting self-consciously)* Nonsense, Mother.

BEATRICE: *(shouting good-humouredly)* I quite agree with you, Mother. *(She continues to her husband in an even just tone.)* You have a sweet nature, Hugh, and it is most difficult to get angry with you. I have been seven years working up to it. But now that I'm angry, I shall never get pleased again.

(The MAJOR returns to his subject, refreshed by a moment's repose.)

MAJOR: How has he failed in his duty? Tell us. I'm not bigoted in his favour. I know your faults, Hugh.

(He wags his head at HUGH, who writhes with irritation.)

HUGH: Why can't you leave them alone..leave us alone?

BEATRICE: I'd state my case against Hugh, if I thought he'd retaliate.

HUGH: *(desperately rounding on his brother)* If I tell you, you won't understand. You understand nothing! Beatrice is angry with me because I won't prostitute my art to make money.

MAJOR: *(glancing at his wife)* Please don't use metaphors of that sort.

BEATRICE: *(reasonably)* Yes, I think Hugh ought to earn more money.

MAJOR: *(quite pleased to be getting along at last)* Well, why doesn't he?

HUGH: I don't want money.

MAJOR: You can't say that you don't want money any more than you can say you don't want bread.

BEATRICE: *(as she breaks off her cotton)* It's when one has known what it is to be a little short of both..

(Now the MAJOR spreads himself and begins to be very wise, while HUGH, to whom this is more intolerable than all, can only clutch his hair.)

MAJOR: You know I never considered Art a very good profession for you, Hugh. And you won't even stick to one department of it. It's a profession that gets people into very bad habits, I consider. Couldn't you take up something else? You could still do those wood-cuts in your spare time to amuse yourself.

HUGH: *(commenting on this with two deliberate shouts of simulated mirth)* Ha! Ha!

MAJOR: *(sublimely superior)* Well, it wouldn't much matter if you didn't do them at all!

BEATRICE: *(subtly)* Booth, there speaks the true critic.

MAJOR: *(deprecating any title to omniscience)* Well, I don't pretend to know much about Art but—

HUGH: It would matter to me. There speaks the artist.

BEATRICE: The arrogance of the artist!

HUGH: We have a right to be arrogant.

BEATRICE: Good workmen are humble.

HUGH: And look to their wages.

BEATRICE: Well, I'm only a workman.

(With that she breaks the contact of this quiet deadly hopeless quarrel by turning her head away. The MAJOR, who has give friendly attention, comments.)

MAJOR: Of course! Quite so! I'm sure all that is a very interesting difference of opinion. But it's nothing to separate about.

(MRS VOYSEY leaves her armchair for her favourite station at the dining-table.)

MRS VOYSEY: Booth is the only one of you that I can hear at all distinctly. But if you two foolish young people think you want to separate..try it. You'll soon come back to each other and be glad to. People can't fight against Nature for long. And marriage is a natural state..once you're married.

MAJOR: *(with intense approval)* Quite right, Mother.

MRS VOYSEY: I know.

(She resumes the Nineteenth Century. The MAJOR, to the despair of everybody, makes yet another start; trying oratory this time.)

MAJOR: My own opinion is, Beatrice and Hugh, that you don't realise the meaning of the word marriage. I don't call myself a religious man..but dash it all, you were married in Church!..And you then entered upon an awful compact...! Surely..as a woman, Beatrice..the religious point of it ought to appeal to you. Good Lord, suppose everybody were to carry on like this! And I considered, Beatrice, that..whether you're right or whether you're wrong..if you desert Hugh, you cut yourself off from the Family.

BEATRICE: *(with the sweetest of smiles)* That will distress me terribly.

MAJOR: *(not doubting her for a moment)* Of course.

(HUGH flings up his head and finds relief at last in many last words.)

HUGH: I wish to Heaven I'd ever been able to cut myself off from the family! Look at Trenchard.

MAJOR: *(gobbling a little at this unexpected attack)* I do not forgive Trenchard for quarrelling with and deserting our father.

HUGH: Trenchard quarrelled because that was his only way of escape.

MAJOR: Escape from what?

HUGH: From tyranny!..from hypocrisy!..from boredom!..from his Happy English Home!

BEATRICE: *(kindly)* Hugh..Hugh..it's no use.

MAJOR: *(attempting sarcasm)* Speak so that Mother can hear you!

(But HUGH isn't to be stopped now.)

HUGH: Why are we all dull, cubbish, uneducated..that is hopelessly middle-class.

MAJOR: *(taking this as very personal)* Cubbish!

HUGH:..Because it's the middle-class ideal that you should respect your parents...live with them..think with them..grow like them. Natural affection and gratitude! That's what's expected, isn't it?

MAJOR: *(not to be obliterated)* Certainly.

HUGH: Keep your children ignorant of all that you don't know, penniless except for your good pleasure, dependent on you for permission to breathe freely ..and be sure that their gratitude will be most disinterested, and their affection very natural. If your father's a drunkard or poor, then perhaps you get free and can form an opinion of your own..and can love him or hate him as he deserves. But our father and mother were models. They did their duty by us..and taught us ours. Trenchard escaped, as I say. You took to the Army..so of course you've never discovered how behind the times you are. *(The MAJOR is stupent.)* I tried to express myself in art..and found there was nothing to express..I'd been so well brought up. D'you blame me if I wander about in search of a soul of some sort? And Honor—

MAJOR: *(disputing savagely)* Honor is very happy at home. Everyone loves her.

HUGH: *(with fierce sarcasm)* Yes..what do we call her? Mother's right hand! I wonder they bothered to give her a name. By the time little Ethel came they were tired of training children..*(His voice loses its sting; he doesn't complete this sentence.)*

BEATRICE: Poor little Ethel..

MAJOR: Poor Ethel!

(They speak as one speaks of the dead, and so the wrangling stops. Then EDWARD interposes quietly.)

EDWARD: Ah, my dear Hugh..

HUGH: I haven't spoken of your fate, Edward. That's too shameful.

EDWARD: Not at all. I sit at my desk daily as the servant of men whose ideal of life is to have a thousand a year..or two thousand..or three..

MAJOR: Well?

EDWARD: That's all.

MAJOR: What's the point? One must live.

HUGH: And if Booth can be said to think, he honestly thinks that's living.

MAJOR: We will return, if you please, to the original subject of discussion. Hugh, this question of a separation—

(Past all patience, HUGH jumps up and flings his chair back to its place.)

HUGH: Beatrice and I mean to separate. And nothing you may say will prevent us. The only difficulty in the way is money. Can we command enough to live apart comfortably?

MAJOR: Well?

HUGH: Well..we can't.

MAJOR: Well?

HUGH: So we can't separate.

MAJOR: *(speaking with bewilderment)* Then what in Heaven's name have we been discussing it for?

HUGH: I haven't discussed it! I don't want to discuss it! Mind—can't you mind your own business? Now I'll go back to the billiard room and my book.

(He is gone before the poor MAJOR can recover his lost breath.)

MAJOR: *(as he does recover it)* I am not an impatient man..but really.. *(and then words fail him).*

BEATRICE: *(commenting calmly)* Hugh, I am told, was a spoilt child. They grow to hate their parents sooner than others. You taught him to cry for what he wanted. Now that he's older and doesn't get it, that makes him a wearisome companion.

MAJOR: *(very sulky now)* You married him with your eyes open, I suppose?

BEATRICE: How few women marry with their eyes open!

MAJOR: You have never made the best of Hugh.

BEATRICE: I have spared him that indignity.

MAJOR: *(vindictively)* I am very glad that you can't separate.

BEATRICE: As soon as I'm reasonably sure of earning an income I shall walk off from him.

(The MAJOR revives.)

MAJOR: You will do nothing of the sort. Beatrice.

BEATRICE: *(unruffled)* How will you stop me, Booth?

MAJOR: I shall tell Hugh he must command you to stay.

BEATRICE: *(with a little smile)* I wonder would that still make a difference. It was one of the illusions of my girlhood that I should love a man who would master me.

MAJOR: Hugh must assert himself.

(He begins to walk about, giving some indication of how it should be done. BEATRICE'S smile has vanished.)

BEATRICE: Don't think I've enjoyed taking the lead in everything through-out married life. But someone had to plan and scheme and be foreseeing ..we weren't sparro ws or lilies of the field..someone had to get up and do something, if not for money, at least for the honour of it. *(She becomes conscious of his strutting and smiles rather mischievously.)* Ah..if I'd married you, Booth!

(The MAJOR'S face grows beatific.)

MAJOR: Well, I must own to thinking that I am a masterful man..that it's the duty of every man to be so. *(he adds forgivingly)* Poor old Hugh!

BEATRICE: *(unable to resist temptation)* If I'd tried to leave you, Booth, you'd have whipped me..wouldn't you?

MAJOR: *(ecstatically complacent)* Ha..well..!

BEATRICE: Do say yes. Think how it'll frighten Emily.

(The MAJOR strokes his moustache and is most friendly.)

MAJOR: Hugh's been a worry to me all my life. And now as Head of the Family...Well, I suppose I'd better go and give the dear chap another talking to. I quite see your point of view, Beatrice.

BEATRICE: Why disturb him at his book?

(MAJOR BOOTH leaves them, squaring his shoulders as becomes a lord of creation. The two sisters-in-law go on with their work silently for a moment; then BEATRICE adds..)

BEATRICE: Do you find Booth difficult to manage, Emily?

EMILY: *(putting down her knitting to consider the matter)* No. It's best to allow him to talk himself out. When he's done that he'll often come to me for advice. I let him get his own way as much as possible..or think he's getting it. Otherwise he becomes so depressed.

BEATRICE: *(quietly amused)* Edward shouldn't hear this. What has he to do with women's secrets?

EDWARD: I won't tell..and I'm a bachelor.

EMILY: *(solemnly as she takes up her knitting again)* Do you really mean to leave Hugh?

BEATRICE: *(slightly impatient)* Emily, I've said so.

(They are joined by ALICE MAITLAND, who comes in gaily.)

ALICE: What's Booth shouting about in the billiard room?

EMILY: *(pained)* Oh..on Christmas Eve, too!

BEATRICE: Don't you take any interest in my matrimonial affairs?

(MRS VOYSEY shuts up the Nineteenth Century and removes her spectacles.)

MRS VOYSEY: That's a very interesting article. The Chinese Empire must be in a shocking state! Is it ten o'clock yet?

EDWARD: Past.

MRS VOYSEY: *(as EDWARD is behind her)* Can anyone see the clock?

ALICE: It's past ten, Auntie.

MRS VOYSEY: Then I think I'll go to my room.

EMILY: Shall I come and look after you, Mother?

MRS VOYSEY: If you'd find Honor for me, Emily. *(EMILY goes in search of the harmless necessary HONOR and MRS VOYSEY begins her nightly chant of departure.)*

MRS VOYSEY: Good-night, Alice. Good-night, Edward.

EDWARD: Good-night, Mother.

MRS VOYSEY: *(with sudden severity)* I'm not pleased with you, Beatrice.

BEATRICE: I'm sorry, Mother.

(*But without waiting to be answered the old lady has sailed out of the room. BEATRICE, EDWARD, and ALICE are attuned to each other enough to be able to talk with ease.*)

BEATRICE: Hugh is right about his family. It'll never make any new life for itself.

EDWARD: There are Booth's children.

BEATRICE: Poor little devils!

ALICE: (*judicially*) Emily is an excellent mother.

BEATRICE: Yes..they'll grow up good men and women. And one will go into the Army and one into the Navy and one into the Church..and perhaps one to the Devil and the Colonies. They'll serve their country and govern it and help to keep it like themselves..dull and respectable..hopelessly middle-class. (*She puts down her work now and elevates an oratorical fist.*) Genius and Poverty may exist in England, if they'll hide their heads. For show days we've our aristocracy. But never let us forget, gentlemen, that it is the plain solid middle-class man who has made us..what we are.

EDWARD: (*in sympathetic derision*) Hear hear..! and cries of bravo!

BEATRICE: Now, that is out of my book..the next one. (*She takes up her work again.*) You know, Edward..however scandalous it was, your father left you a man's work to do.

EDWARD: (*his face cloudy*) An outlaw's!

BEATRICE: (*whimsical after a moment*) I mean that. At all events you've not had to be your father's right arm..or the instrument of justice..or a representative of the people..or anything second-hand of that sort, have you?

EDWARD: (*with sudden excitement*) Do you know what I found out the other day about (*he nods at the portrait*)..him?

BEATRICE: (*enquiring calmly*) What?

EDWARD: He saved his firm once. That was true. A pretty capable piece of heroism. Then, fifteen years afterwards..he started again.

BEATRICE: (*greatly interested*) Did he now?

EDWARD: It can't have been merely through weakness...

BEATRICE: (*with artistic enthusiasm*) Of course not. He was a man of imagination and a great financier. He had to find scope for his abilities or die. He despised these fat little clients living so snugly on their fattening little incomes..and put them and their money to the best use he could.

EDWARD: (*shaking his head solemnly*). Fine phrases for robbery.

(*BEATRICE turns her clever face to him and begins to follow up her subject keenly.*)

BEATRICE: But didn't Hugh tell me that your golden deed has been robbing your rich clients for the benefit of the poor ones?

ALICE: (*who hasn't missed a word*) That's true.

EDWARD: *(gently)* Well..we're all a bit in debt to the poor, aren't we?

BEATRICE: Quite so. And you don't possess and your father didn't possess that innate sense of the sacredness of property..*(she enjoys that phrase)* which mostly makes your merely honest man. Nor did the man possess it who picked my pocket last Friday week..nor does the tax-gatherer..nor do I. And whether we can boast of our opinions depends on such a silly lot of prejudices and cowardices that—

EDWARD: *(a little pained by as much of this as he takes to be serious)* Why wouldn't he own the truth to me about himself?

BEATRICE: He was a bit of a genius. Perhaps he took care not to know it. Would you have understood?

EDWARD: Perhaps not. But I loved him.

(BEATRICE looks again at the gentle, earnest face.)

BEATRICE: Through it all?

EDWARD: Yes. And not from mere force of habit either.

BEATRICE: *(with reverence in her voice now)* That might silence a bench of judges. Well..well..

(Her sewing finished, she stuffs the things into her basket, gets up in her abrupt unconventional way and goes without another word. Her brain is busy with the Voysey Inheritance. EDWARD and ALICE are left in chairs by the fire, facing each other like an old domestic couple.)

EDWARD: Stay and talk to me.

ALICE: I want to. Something has happened..since dinner.

EDWARD: Can you see that?

ALICE: What is it?

EDWARD: *(with sudden exultation)* The smash has come..and not by my fault. Old George Booth—

ALICE: Has he been here?

EDWARD: Can you imagine it? He got at the truth. I told him to take his money..what there was of it..and prosecute. He won't prosecute, but he bargains to take the money..and then to bleed us, sovereign by sovereign, as I earn sovereign by sovereign with the sweat of my soul. I'll see him in his Christian Heaven first..the Jew!

ALICE: *(keeping her head)* You can't reason with him?

EDWARD: No. He thinks he has the whip hand, and the Vicar has been told..who has told his wife. She knows how not to keep a secret. It has come at last.

ALICE: So you're glad?

EDWARD: So thankful—my conscience is clear. I've done my best. *(Then as usual with him, his fervour collapses.)* And oh, Alice..has it been worth doing?

ALICE: *(encouragingly)* Half a dozen poor devils pulled safe out of the fire.

EDWARD: But I'm wondering now if that won't be found out, or if I shan't just confess to the pious fraud when the time comes. Somehow I don't seem to have the conviction to carry any job through. A weak nature, my father said. He knew.

ALICE: You have a religious nature.

EDWARD: *(surprised)* Oh, no!

ALICE: *(proceeding to explain)* Which means, of course, that you don't cling to creeds and ceremonies. And the good things and the well-done jobs of this worldly world don't satisfy you..so you shirk contact with it all you can.

EDWARD: *(his eyes far away)* Yes. Do you never feel that there aren't enough windows in a house?

ALICE: *(prosaically)* In this weather..too many.

EDWARD: In my office then—I feel it when I'm at work—one is out of all hearing of all the music of the world. And when one does get back to Nature, instead of being curves to her roundness, one is all corners.

ALICE: *(smiling at him)* And you love to think prettily, don't you..just as Hugh does. You do it quite well, too. *(then briskly)* But, Edward, may I scold you?

EDWARD: For that?

ALICE: Why have you grown to be more of a sloven than ever lately? Yes, a spiritual sloven, I call it—deliberately letting yourself be unhappy.

EDWARD: Is happiness under one's control?

ALICE: My friend, you shouldn't neglect your happiness any more than you neglect to wash your face. I was desperate about you..so I came down to your office.

EDWARD: Yes, you did.

ALICE: But I found you master there, and I thanked God. Because with us, Edward, for these last eighteen months you've been more like a moral portent than a man—without a smile to throw to a friend..or an opinion upon any subject. Why did you throw up your boys' club? Why didn't you vote last November? —too out of keeping with your unhappy fate?

EDWARD: *(contrite at this)* I was wrong not to vote.

ALICE: You don't even eat properly.

(With that she completes the accusation and EDWARD searches round for a defence.)

EDWARD: But, Alice, it was always an effort to do all these things..and lately every effort has had to go to my work, hasn't it?

ALICE: Oh..if you only did them on principle..I retract..far better not to do them at all.

EDWARD: Don't laugh at me.

ALICE: Edward, is there nothing you want from life..want for its own sake? That's the only test.

EDWARD: I daren't ask.

ALICE: Yes, you dare. It's all so long past that awful time when you were.. more than a bit of a prig.

EDWARD: *(with enough sense of humour to whisper back)* Was I?

ALICE: I'm afraid so! He still stalks through my dreams sometimes..and I wake in a sweat. But I think he's nearly done with. *(Then her voice rises stirringly.)* Oh, don't you see what a blessing this cursed burden of disgrace and work was meant to be to you?

EDWARD: *(without a smile now)* But lately, Alice, I've hardly known myself. Sometimes I've lost my temper..I've been brutal.

ALICE: I knew it. I knew that would happen. It's your own wicked nature coming out at last. That's what we've been waiting for..that's what we want. That's you.

EDWARD: *(Still serious)* I'm sorry for it.

ALICE: Oh, Edward, be a little proud of poor humanity..take your own share in it gladly. It so discourages the rest of us if you don't.

(Suddenly he breaks down completely.)

EDWARD: I can't let myself be glad and live. There's the future to think of, and I'm so afraid of that. I must pretend I don't care..even to myself..even to you.

ALICE: *(her mocking at an end)* What is it you fear most about the future.. not just the obviously unpleasant things?

EDWARD: They'll put me in prison.

ALICE: Even then?

EDWARD: Who'll be the man who comes out?

ALICE: Yourself, and more than ever yourself.

EDWARD: No, no! I'm a coward. I can't stand alone, and after that I shall have to. I need affection..I need friends. I cling to people that I don't care for deeply..just for the comfort of it. I've no real home of my own. Every house that welcomes me now I like to think of as something of a home. And this disgrace in store will leave me..homeless.

(There he sits shaken. ALICE waits a moment, not taking her eyes from him; then speaks.)

ALICE: Edward, there's something else I want to scold you for. You've still given up proposing to me. Certainly that shows a lack of courage..and of perseverance. Or is it the loss of what I always considered a very laudable ambition?

(EDWARD is hardly able to trust his ears. Then he looks into her face, and his thankfulness frames itself into a single sentence.)

EDWARD: Will you marry me?

ALICE: Yes, Edward.

(For a minute he just holds his breath with happiness. But he shakes himself free of it, almost savagely.)

EDWARD: No, no, no, we mustn't be stupid. I'm sorry I asked you that.

ALICE: *(with serene strength)* I'm glad that you want me. While I live..

where I am will be Home.

EDWARD: *(struggling with himself)* No, it's too late. And if you'd said Yes before I came into my inheritance..perhaps I shouldn't have given myself to the work. So be glad that it's too late. I am.

ALICE: *(happily)* Marry you when you were only a well-principled prig.. Thanks! I didn't want you..and I don't believe you really wanted me. But now you do, and you must always take what you want.

EDWARD: *(turning to her again)* My dear, what have we to start life upon.. to build our house upon? Poverty..and prison.

ALICE: *(mischievous)* Edward, you seem to think that all the money in the world was invested in your precious firm. I have four hundred a year of my own. At least let that tempt you.

(EDWARD catches her in his arms with a momentary little burst of passion.)

EDWARD: You're tempting me.

(She did not resist, but nevertheless he breaks away from her, disappointed with himself. She goes on, quietly, serenely.)

ALICE: Am I? Unworthily? Oh, my dear, don't be afraid of wanting me. Shall we be less than friends by being more? If I thought that, should I ever have let it come to this? But now you must..look at me and make your choice..to refuse me my work and happiness in life and to cripple your own nature..or to take my hand.

(She puts out her hand frankly, as a friend should. With only a second's thought he, happy too now, takes it as frankly. Then she sits beside him and quite cheerfully changes the subject.)

ALICE: Now, about old Mr George Booth. What will he do?

EDWARD: *(responsive though impatient)* Nothing. I shall be before him.

ALICE: Can we bargain with him to keep the firm going somehow?..for if we can, I'm afraid we must.

(At this EDWARD makes a last attempt to abandon himself to his troubles.)

EDWARD: No, no..let it end here, it'll be so useless. They'll all be round in a day or two after their money like wasps after honey. And now they know I won't lift a finger in my own defence.. what sort of mercy will they have?

ALICE: *(triumphantly completing her case)* Edward, I have a faith by which I hope to live, not humbly, but defying the world to be my master. Dare to surrender yourself entirely, and you'll find them powerless against you. You see, you had something to hope or fear from Mr Booth, for you hoped in your heart he'd end your trouble. But conquer that last little atom of fear which we call selfishness, and you'll find you are doing what you wish with selfish men. *(and she adds fervently)* Yes, the man who is able, and cares deeply, and yet has nothing to hope or fear is all powerful..even in little things.

EDWARD: But will nothing ever happen to set me free? Shall I never be able to rest for a moment..turn round and say I've succeeded or I've failed?

ALICE: That's asking too much, and it isn't what matters..one must have faith to go on.

EDWARD: Suppose they all meet and agree and syndicate themselves and keep me at it for life.

ALICE: Yes, I daresay they will, but what else could you wish for?

EDWARD: Than that dreary round!

ALICE: But the world must be put tidy. And it's the work which splendid criminals leave for poor commonplace people to do.

EDWARD: *(with a little laugh)* And I don't believe in Heaven either.

ALICE: *(close to him)* But there's to be our life. What's wrong with that?

EDWARD: My dear, when they put me in prison for swindling—*(He makes the word sound its worst.)*

ALICE: I think they won't, for it wouldn't pay them. But if they are so stupid...I must be very careful.

EDWARD: Of what?

ALICE: To avoid false pride. I shall be foolishly proud of you.

EDWARD: It's good to be praised sometimes..by you.

ALICE: My heart praises you. Good-night.

EDWARD: Good-night.

(She kisses his forehead. But he puts up his face like a child, so she bends down and for the first time their lips meet. Then she from him, adding happily, with perhaps just a touch of shyness.)

ALICE: Till tomorrow.

EDWARD: *(echoing in gratitude the hope and promise in her voice)* Till tomorrow.

(She leaves him to sit there by the table for a few moments looking into his future, streaked as it is to be with trouble and joy. As whose is not? From above ..from above the mantelpiece, that is to say..the face of the late MR VOYSEY seems to look down upon his son not unkindly, though with that curious buccaneering twist of the eyebrows which distinguished his countenance in life.)

THE END

Rococo

1912

Do you know how ugly the drawing-room of an English vicarage can be? Yes, I am aware of all that there should be about it; the old-world grace and charm of Jane Austenism. One should sit upon Chippendale and glimpse the grey Norman church-tower through the casement. But what of the pious foundations of a more industrial age, churches built in mid-nineteenth century and rather scamped in the building, dedicated to the Glory of God and the soul's health of some sweating and sweated urban district ? The Bishop would have a vicarage added, grumbled the church-donor. Well, then, consider his comfort a little, but to the glory of the Vicar nothing need be done. And nothing was. The architect (this an added labour of but little love to him) would give an ecclesiastical touch to the front porch, a pointed top to the front door, add some stained glass to the staircase window. But a mean house, a stufffy house, and the Vicar must indeed have fresh air in his soul if mean and stuffy doctrine was not to be generated there. The drawing-room would be the best room, and not a bad room in its way, if it weren't that its proportions were vile, as though it felt it wanted to be larger than it was, and if the window and the fireplace and the door didn't seem to be quarrelling as to which should be the most conspicuous. The fireplace wins.

This particular one in this particular drawing-room is of yellow wood, stained and grained. It reaches not quite to the ceiling. It has a West Front air, if looking-glass may stand for windows; it is fretted, moreover, here and there, with little trefoil holes. It bears a full assault of the Vicar's wife's ideas of how to make the place "look nice". There is the clock, of course, which won't keep time; there are the vases which won't hold water; framed photographs, as many as can be crowded on the shelves; in every other crevice, knickknacks. Then, if you stand, as the Vicar often stands, at this point of vantage you are conscious of the wall-paper of amber and blue with a frieze above it measuring off yard by yard a sort of desert scene; a mountain, a lake, three palm-trees, two camels; and again; and again; until by the corner a camel and a palm-tree are cut out. On the walls there are pictures, of course. Two of them convey to you in a vague and water-colour sort of way that an English countryside is pretty. There is "Christ among the Doctors", with a presentation brass plate on its frame; there is "Simply to Thy Cross I Cling." And there is an illuminated testimonial to the Vicar, a mark of affection and esteem from thc flock he ministered to as senior curate.

The furniture is either very heavy, stuffed, sprung, and tapestry-covered, or very light. There are quite a number of small tables (occasional tables they are called), which should have four legs but have only three. There are several chairs, too, on which it would be unwise to sit down.

In the centre of the room, beneath the hanging, pink-shaded, electric chandelier, is a mahogany monument, a large round table of the "pedestal" variety, and on it tower to a climax the vicarage symbols of gentility and culture. In the centre of this table, beneath a glass shade, an elaborate reproduction of some sixteenth-century Pieta (a little High Church, it is thought; but art, for some reason, runs that way). It stands on a Chinese silk mat, sent home by some exiled uncle. It is symmetrically surrounded by gift-books, a photograph album, a tray of painted Indian figures (very jolly! another gift from the exciled uncle), and a whale's tooth. The whole affair is draped with a red embroidered cloth.

The window of the room, with so many sorts of curtains and blinds to it that one would think the Vicar hatched conspiracies here by night, admits but a blurring light, which the carpet (Brussels) reflects, toned to an ugly yellow.

You really would not expect such a thing to be happening in such a place, but this carpet is at the moment the base of an apparently mortal struggle. The Vicar is undermost; his baldish head, when he tries to raise it, falls back and bumps. Kneeling on him, throttling his collar, is a hefty young man conscientiously out of temper, with scarlet face glowing against carroty hair. His name is Reginald and he is (one regrets to add) the Vicar's nephew, though it be only by marriage. The Vicar's wife, fragile and fifty, is making pathetic attempts to pull him off.

"Have you had enough?" asks Reginald and grips the Vicar hard.

"Oh, Reginald...be good" is all the Vicar's wife's appeal.

Not two yards off a minor battle rages. Mrs. Reginald, coming up to reinforce, was intercepted by Miss Underwood, the Vicar's sister, on the same errand. The elder lady now has the younger pinned by the elbows and she emphasizes this very handsome control of the situation by teeth-rattling shakes.

"Cat...cat...cat" gasps Mrs. Reginald, who is plump and flaxen and easily disarranged.

Miss Underwood only shakes her again. " *I'll teach you manners, Miss.*"

"Oh, Reginald...do drop him," moans poor Mrs. Underwood. For this is really very bad for the Vicar.

"Stick a pin into him, Mary" advises her sister-in-law. Whereat Mrs. Reginald yelps in her iron grasp.

"Don't you dare...it's poisonous," and then, *"Oh...if you weren't an old woman I'd have boxed your ears."*

Three violent shakes. " *Would you? Would you? Would you?*"

"I haven't got a pin, Carinthia," says Mrs. Underwood. *She has conscientiously searched.* "Pull his hair, then," commands Carinthia.

At intervals, like a signal gun, Reginald repeats his query: "Have you had enough?" And the Vicar, though it is evident that he has, still, with some unsurrendering school-days' echo answering in his mind, will only gasp, " Most undignified...clergyman of the Church of England...your host, sir...ashamed of you...let me up at once."

Mrs. Underwood has failed at the hair; she flaps her hands in despair. "It's too short, Carinthia," she moans.

Mrs. Reginald begins to sob pitifully. It is very painful to be tightly held by the elbows from behind. So Miss Underwood, with the neatest of twists and pushes, lodges her in a chair, and thus released herself, folds her arms and surveys the situation. "Box my ears, would you?" is her postscript.

MRS. REGINALD. Well...you boxed father's.

MISS UNDERWOOD. Where is your wretched father-in-law?

Her hawklike eye surveys the room for this unknown in vain.

REGINALD *(The proper interval having apparently elapsed.)* Have you had enough?

Dignified he cannot look, thus outstretched. THE VICAR, therefore, assumes a mixed expression of saintliness and obstinacy, his next best resource. His poor wife moans again....

MRS. UNDERWOOD. Oh, please, Reginald...the floor's so hard for him!

REGINALD. *(A little anxious to have done with it himself.)* Have you had enough?

THE VICAR. *(Quite supine.)* Do you consider this conduct becoming a gentleman?

MRS. UNDERWOOD. And...Simon!...if the servants have heard...they must have heard! ...what will they think?

No, even this heart-breaking appeal falls flat.

REGINALD. Say you've had enough and I'll let you up.

THE VICAR *(Reduced to casuistry.)* It's not at all the sort of thing I ought to say.

MRS. UNDERWOOD. *(So helpless.)* Oh...I think you might say it, Simon, just for once.

MISS UNDERWOOD. *(Grim with the pride of her own victory.)* Say nothing of the sort, Simon!

THE VICAR has a burst of exasperation; for after all he is on the floor and being knelt on.

THE VICAR. Confound it all, then, Carinthia, why don't you do something?

CARINTHIA casts a tactical eye over Reginald. THE VICAR adds in parenthesis...a human touch!...

THE VICAR. Don't kneel there, you young fool, you'll break my watch!

MISS UNDERWOOD. Wait till I get my breath.

But this prospect raises in MRS. UNDERWOOD a perfect dithyramb of despair.

MRS. UNDERWOOD. Oh, please, Carinthia....No...don't start again. Such a scandal I wonder everything's not broken. *(So coaxingly to REGINALD.)* Shall I say it for him?

MRS REGINALD. *(Fat little bantam, as she smooths her feathers in the armchair.)* You make him say it, Reggie.

But now the servants are on poor MRS. UNDERWOOD'S brain. Almost down to her knees she goes.

MRS. UNDERWOOD. They'll be coming up to see what the noise is. Oh... Simon!

It does strike THE VICAR that this would occasion considerable scandal in the parish. There are so few good excuses for being found lying on the carpet, your nephew kneeling threateningly on the top of you. So he makes up his mind to it and enunciates with musical charm; it might be a benediction....

THE VICAR. I have had enough.

REGINALD *(In some relief.)* That's all right.

He rises from the prostrate church militant; he even helps it rise. This pleasant family party then look at each other, and, truth to tell, they are all a little ashamed.

MRS. UNDERWOOD. *(walking round the re-erected pillar of righteousness)* Oh, how dusty you are!

MISS UNDERWOOD. Yes! *(The normal self uprising.)* Room's not been swept this morning.

THE VICAR, dusted, feels that a reign of moral law can now be resumed. He draws himself up to fully five foot six.

THE VICAR. Now, sir, you will please apologize.

REGINALD. *(looking very muscular.)* I shall not.

THE VICAR drops the subject. MRS. REGINALD mutters and crows from the armchair.

MRS. REGINALD. Ha...who began it? Black and blue I am! Miss Underwood can apologize...your precious sister can apologize.

MISS UNDERWOOD. *(Crushing if inconsequent.)* You're running to fat, Gladys. Where's my embroidery?

MRS. UNDERWOOD I put it safe, Carinthia. (She discloses it and then begins to pat and smooth thc dishevelled room.) Among relations too! One expects to quarrel sometimes...it can't be helped. But not fighting! Oh, I never did...I feel so ashamed!

MISS UNDERWOOD. *(Britannia-like.)* Nonsense.

MRS. REGINALD. Nobody touched you, Aunt Mary.

THE VICAR *(After his eyes have wandered vaguely round.)* Where's your father, Reginald?

REGINALD. *(Quite uninterested. He is straightening his own tie and collar.)* I don't know.

In the little silence that follows there comes a voice from under the mahogany monument. It is a voice at once dignified and pained, and the property of Reginald's father, whose name is Mortimer Uglow. And it says...

THE VOICE. I am here.

MRS. UNDERWOOD. *(Who may be forgiven nerves.)* Oh, how uncanny!

REGINALD. *(Still at his tie.)* Well, you can come out, father, it's quite safe.

THE VOICE. *(Most unexpectedly.)* I shall not. *(And then more unexpectedly still.)* You can all leave the room.

THE VICAR. *(Who is generally resentful.)* Leave the room! Whose room is it, mine or yours? Come out, Mortimer, and don't be a fool.

But there is only silence. Why will not Mr. Uglow come out? Must he be ratted for? Then Mrs. Underwood sees why. She points to an object on the floor.

MRS. UNDERWOOD. Simon!

THE VICAR. What is it?

Again, and this time as if to indicate some mystery, MRS. UNDERWOOD points.
THE VICAR picks up the object, some disjection of the fight he thinks, and waves it
mildly.

THE VICAR. Well, where does it go? I wonder everything in the room's not
been upset!

MRS. UNDERWOOD. No, Simon, it's not a mat, it's his...

She concludes with an undeniable gesture, even a smile. The Vicar, smiling a little,
hands over the trophy.

REGINALD. *(As he views it.)* Oh, of course.

MRS. REGINALD. Reggie, am I tidy at the back?

He tidies her at the back; a meticulous matter of hooks and eyes and, oh, his fingers
are so big. MRS. UNDERWOOD has taken a little hand-painted mirror from the
mantelpiece, and this and the thing in question she places just without the screen
of the falling tablecloth much as a devotee might place an offering at a shrine. But
in MISS UNDERWOOD dwells no respect for persons.

MISS UNDERWOOD. Now, sir, for Heaven's sake put on your wig and
come out.

There emerges a hand that trembles with wrath; it retrieves the offerings; there
follow bumpings into the tablecloth as of a head and elbows.

THE VICAR. I must go and brush myself.

MRS. UNDERWOOD. Simon, d'you think you could tell the maids that
something fell over...they are such tattlers. It wouldn't be untrue. *(It wouldn't!)*

THE VICAR. I should scorn to do so, Mary. If they ask me, I must make
the best explanation I can.

THE VICAR swims out. MR. MORTIMER UGLOW, his wig assumed and hardly
awry at all, emerges from beneath thc table. He is a vindictive-looking little man.

MRS. UNDERWOOD. You're not hurt, Mortimer, are you?

MR. UGLOW's only wound is in the dignity. That he cures by taking the situation
oratorically in hand.

MR. UGLOW. If we are to continue this family discussion and if Miss
Underwood, whom it does not in the least concern, has not the decency to leave
the room and if you, Mary, cannot request your sister-in-law to leave it, I must at
least demand that she does not speak to me again.

Whoever else might be impressed, MISS UNDERWOOD is not. She does not even
glance up from her embroidery.

MISS UNDERWOOD. A good thing for you I hadn't my thimble on when I
did it.

MRS. UNDERWOOD. Carinthia, I don't think you should have boxed
Mortimer's ears...you know him so slightly.

MISS UNDERWOOD. He called me a Futile Female. I considered it a
suitable reply.

The echo of that epigram brings compensation to MR UGLOW. He puffs his chest.

MR. UGLOW. Your wife rallied to me, Reginald. I am much obliged to her ...which is more than can be said of you.

REGINALD. Well, you can't hit a woman.

MR. UGLOW. *(Bitingly.)* And she knows it.

MISS UNDERWOOD. Pf!

The sound conveys that she would tackle a regiment of men with her umbrella: and she would.

REGINALD. *(Apoplectic, but he has worked down to the waist.)* There's a hook gone.

MRS. REGINALD. I thought so! Lace torn?

REGINALD. It doesn't show much. But I tackled Uncle Simon the minute he touched Gladys...that got my blood up all right. Don't you worry. We won.

This callously sporting summary is too much for MRS. UNDERWOOD: she dissolves!

MRS. UNDERWOOD. Oh, that such a thing should ever have happened in our house!... in my drawing room!!..real blows!!!...

MRS. REGINALD. Don't cry, Aunt Mary...it wasn't your fault.

THE VICAR returns, his hair and his countenance smoother. He adds his patting consolations to his poor wife's comfort.

MRS. UNDERWOOD. And I was kicked on the shin.

MRS. REGINALD. Say you're sorry, Reggie.

THE VICAR. My dear Mary...don't cry.

MRS. UNDERWOOD. *(Clasping her beloved's arm.)* Simon did it...Reggie was throttling him black...he couldn't help it.

THE VICAR. I suggest that we show a more or less Christian spirit in letting bygones be bygones and endeavour to resume the discussion at the point where it ceased to be an amicable one. *(His wife, her clasp on his coat, through her drying tears has found more trouble.)* Yes, there is a slight rent...never mind.

The family party now settles itself into what may have been more or less the situations from which they were roused to physical combat. MR. UGLOW secures a central place. There is silence a moment.

MR. UGLOW. My sister-in-law Jane had no right to bequeath the vase...it was not hers to bequeath.

That is the gage of battle. A legacy! What English family has not at some time shattered its mutual regard upon this siren rock? One notices now that these good people are all in deep mourning, on which the dust of combat shows up the more distinctly, as it should.

MRS. UNDERWOOD. Oh, Mortimer, think if you'd been able to come to the funeral and this had all happened then...it might have done!

MISS UNDERWOOD. But it didn't, Mary...control yourself.

MR. UGLOW. My brother George wrote to me on his death-bed...*(And then fiercely to the Vicar, as if this concerned his calling.)*...on his death-bed, sir. I have the letter here....

THE VICAR. Yes, we've heard it.

REGINALD. And you sent them a copy.

MR. UGLOW's hand always seems to tremble; this time it is with excitement as he has pulled the letter from his pocket-book.

MR. UGLOW. Quiet, Reginald! Hear it again and pay attention. *(They settle to a strained boredom.)* "The Rococo Vase presented to me by the Emperor of Germany" ...Now there he's wrong. (The sound of his own reading has uplifted him: he condescends to them.) They're German Emperors, not Emperors of Germany. But George was an inaccurate fellow. Reggie has the same trick...it's in the family. I haven't it.

He is returning to the letter. But THE VICAR interposes, lamblike, ominous though.

THE VICAR. I have not suggested on Mary's behalf...I wish you would remember, Mortimer, that the position I take up in this matter I take up purely on my wife's behalf. What have I to gain?

REGINALD. *(Clodhopping.)* Well, you're her husband, aren't you? She'll leave things to you. And she's older than you are.

THE VICAR. Reginald, you are most indelicate. *(And then, really thinking it is true...)* I have forborne to demand an apology from you....

REGINALD. Because you wouldn't get it.

MRS. UNDERWOOD. *(Genuinely and generously accommodating.)* Oh, I don't want the vase...I don't want anything !

THE VICAR. *(He is gradually mounting the pulpit.)* Don't think of the vase, Mary. Think of the principle involved.

MRS. UNDERWOOD. And you may die first, Simon. You're not strong, though you look it...all the colds you get...and nothing's ever the matter with me.

MR. UGLOW. *(Ignored...ignored!)* Mary, how much longer am I to wait to read this letter?

THE VICAR. *(Ominously, ironically lamblike now.)* Quite so. Your brother is waiting patiently...and politely. Come, come; a Christian and a businesslike spirit!

MR UGLOW's breath has been taken to resume the reading of the letter when on him...worse, on that tender top-knot of his...he finds MISS UNDERWOOD's hawklike eye. Its look passes through him, piercing Infinity as she says . . .

MISS UNDERWOOD. Why not a skull-cap...a sanitary skull-cap?

MR. UGLOW. *(With a minatory though fearful gasp.)* What's that?

THE VICAR. Nothing, Mortimer.

REGINALD. Some people look for trouble!

MISS UNDERWOOD. *(Addressing the Infinite still.)* And those that it fits can wear it.

THE VICAR. *(A little fearful himself. He is terrifed of his sister, that's the* *truth; and well he may be.)* Let's have the letter, Mortimer.

MISS UNDERWOOD. Or at least a little gum...little glue...a little stickphast for decency's sake.

She swings it to a beautiful rhythm. No, on the whole, MR UGLOW will not join issue.

MR. UGLOW. I trust that my dignity requires no vindication. Never mind...I say nothing. *(And with a forgiving air he returns at last to the letter.)* "The Rococo Vase presented to me by the Emperor of Germany",...or German Emperor.

THE VICAR. Agreed. Don't cry, Mary. Well, here's a clean one. *(Benevolently he hands her a handkerchief.)*

MR. UGLOW. "On the occasion of my accompanying the mission."

MISS UNDERWOOD. Mission!

The word has touched a spot.

THE VICAR. Not a real mission, Carinthia.

MR UGLOW. A perfectly real mission. A mission from the Chamber of Commerce at...Don't go on as if the world were made up of low-church parsons and...and...their sisters!

As a convinced secularist behold him a perfect fighting cock.

REGINALD. *(Bored; oh, so bored!)* Do get ahead, father.

MR. UGLOW. *(With a flourish.)* "Mission et cetera." Here we are. "My dear wife must have the enjoyment"... *(Again he condescends to them.)* Why he called her his dear wife I don't know. They hated each other like poison. But that was George all over...soft...never would face the truth. It's a family trait. You show signs of it, Mary.

THE VICAR. *(Soft and low.)* He was on his death-bed.

REGINALD. Get on...father.

MR. UGLOW. "My wife" ...She wasn't his dear wife. What's the good of pretending it?...must have the enjoyment of it while she lives. At her death I desire it to be an heirloom for the family." *(And he makes the last sentence tell, every word.)* There you are!

THE VICAR. *(Lamblike, ominous, ironic, persistent.)* You sit looking at Mary. His sister and yours. Is she a member of the family or not?

MR. UGLOW. *(Cocksure.)* Boys before girls...men before women. Don't argue that...it's the law. Titles and heirlooms...all the same thing.

MRS. UNDERWOOD. *(Worm-womanlike, turning ever so little.)* Mortimer, it isn't as if we weren't giving you all the family things...the miniature and the bust of John Bright and grandmother's china and the big Shakespeare.

MR. UGLOW. Giving them, Mary, giving them?

THE VICAR. Surrendering them willingly, Mortimer. They have ornamented our house for years.

MRS. REGINALD. It isn't as if you hadn't done pretty well out of Aunt

Jane while she was alive!

THE VICAR. Oh, delicacy, Gladys! And some regard for the truth!

MRS. REGINALD. *(No nonsense about her.)* No, if we're talking business let's talk business. Her fifty pounds a year more than paid you for keeping her, didn't it? Did it or didn't it?

REGINALD. *(Gloomily.)* She never eat anything that I could see.

THE VICAR. She had a delicate appetite. It needed teasing...I mean coaxing. Oh, dear, this is most unpleasant!

REGINALD. Fifty pound a year is nearly a pound a week, you know,

THE VICAR. What about her clothes...what about her little holidays... what about the doctor...what about her temper to the last? *(He summons the classics to clear this sordid air.)* Oh..."De mortuis nil nisi bonum."

MRS. UNDERWOOD. She was a great trouble with her meals, Reginald.

MR. UGLOW. *(Letting rip.)* She was a horrible woman. I disliked her more than any woman I've ever met. She brought George to bankruptcy. When he was trying to arrange with his creditors and she came into the room, her face would sour them...I tell you, sour them.

MRS. REGINALD. *(She sums it up.)* Well, Uncle Simon's a clergyman and can put up with unpleasant people. It suited them well enough to have her. You had the room, Aunt Mary, you can't deny that. And anyway she's dead now... poor Aunt Jane! *(She throws this conventional verbal bone to Cerberus.)* And what with the things she has left you...! What's to be done with her clothes?

GLADYS and MRS. UNDERWOOD suddenly face each other like two ladylike ghouls.

MRS. UNDERWOOD. Well, you remember the mauve silk...

THE VICAR. Mary, pray allow me. *(Somehow his delicacy is shocked.)* The Poor.

MRS. REGINALD. *(In violent protest.)* Not the mauve silk! Nor her black lace shawl!

MISS UNDERWOOD. *(Shooting it out.)* They will make soup.

It makes MR. UGLOW jump, physically and mentally too.

MR. UGLOW. What !

MISS UNDERWOOD. The proceeds of their sale will make much needed soup...and blankets. *(Again her gaze transfixes that wig and she addresses Eternity.)* No brain under it!...No wonder it's loose! No brain.

MR. UGLOW just manages to ignore this.

REGINALD. Where is the beastly vase? I don't know that I want to inherit it.

MR. UGLOW. Yes, may I ask for the second or third time to-day?...

MISS UNDERWOOD. The third.

MR. UGLOW. *(He screws a baleful glance at her.)* May I ask for the second or third time...

REGINALD. It is the third time, father.

MR. UGLOW. *(His own son, too!)* Reginald, you have no tact. May I ask why the vase is not to be seen?

MISS UNDERWOOD. *(Sharply.)* It's put away.

MRS. REGINALD. *(As sharp as she. Never any nonsense about Gladys.)* Why?

MR. UGLOW. Gladys...ignore that, please. Mary?

MRS. UNDERWOOD. Yes, Mortimer.

MR. UGLOW. It has been chipped.

THE VICAR. It has not been chipped.

MR. UGLOW. If it has been chipped...

THE VICAR. I say it has not been chipped.

MR. UGLOW. If it had been chipped, sir...I should have held you responsible! Produce it.

He is indeed very much of a man. A little more and he'll slap his chest. But THE VICAR, lamblike, etc....we can now add dangerous....

THE VICAR. Oh, no, we must not be ordered to produce it.

MR. UGLOW. *(Trumpet-toned.)* Produce it, Simon.

THE VICAR. Neither must we be shouted at.

MISS UNDERWOOD...or bawled at. Bald at! Ha, ha!

And she taps her grey-haired parting with a thimbled finger to emphasize the pun. MR. UGLOW rises, too intent on his next impressive stroke even to notice it, or seem to.

MR. UGLOW. Simon, if you do not instantly produce the vase I shall refuse to treat this any longer in a friendly way. I shall place the matter in the hands of my solicitors.

This, in any family—is it not the final threat? MRS. UNDERWOOD is genuinely shocked.

MRS. UNDERWOOD. Oh, Simon!

THE VICAR. As a matter of principle, Mary....

REGINALD. *(Impartially.)* What rot!

MRS. UNDERWOOD. It was put away, I think, so that the sight of it might not rouse discussion...wasn't it, Simon?

REGINALD Well, we've had the discussion. Now get it out.

THE VICAR *(Lamblike...etc.; add obstinate now.)* It is my principle not to submit to dictation. If I were asked politely to produce it.

REGINALD. Ask him politely, father.

MR. UGLOW. *(Why shouldn't he have principles, too?)* I don't think I can. To ask politely might be an admission of some right of his to detain the property. This matter will go further. I shall commit myself in nothing without legal advice.

MRS. REGINALD. You get it out, Aunt Mary.

MRS. UNDERWOOD. *(Almost thankful to be helpless in the matter.)* I can't. I don't know where it is.

MR. UGLOW. *(All the instinct for law in him blazing.)* You don't...! This is important. He has no right to keep it from you, Mary. I venture to think...

THE VICAR. Husband and wife are one, Mortimer.

MR. UGLOW. Not in law. Don't you cram your religion down my throat. Not in law any longer. We've improved all that. The Married Woman's Property Act! I venture to think....

MISS UNDERWOOD has disappeared. Her comment is to slam the door.

MRS. UNDERWOOD. I think perhaps Carinthia has gone for it, Mortimer.

MR. UGLOW. *(The case given him, he asks for costs, as it were.)* Then I object...I object most strongly to this woman knowing the whereabouts of a vase which you, Mary...

THE VICAR. *(A little of the mere layman peeping now.)* Mortimer, do not refer to my sister as "this woman."

MR. UGLOW. Then treat my sister with the respect that is due to her, Simon.

They are face to face.

THE VICAR. I hope I do, Mortimer.

MR. UGLOW. And will you request Miss Underwood not to return to this room with or without the vase?

THE VICAR Why should I?

MR. UGLOW. What has she to do with a family matter of mine? I make no comment, Mary, upon the way you allow yourself to be ousted from authority in your own house. It is not my place to comment upon it, and I make none. I make no reference to the insults...the unwomanly insults that have been hurled at me by this Futile Female...

REGINALD. *(A remembered schoolmaster joke. He feels not unlike one as he watches his two elders squared to each other.)* "Apt alliteration's artful aid" ... what?

MR. UGLOW. Don't interrupt.

MRS. REGINALD. You're getting excited again, father.

MR. UGLOW. I am not.

MRS. REGINALD. Father!

There is one sure way to touch MR. UGLOW. She takes it. She points to his wig.

MR. UGLOW. What? Well...where's a glass...where's a glass?

He goes to the mantelpiece mirror. His sister follows him.

MRS. UNDERWOOD. We talked it over this morning, Mortimer, and we agreed that I am of a yielding disposition and I said I should feel much safer if I did not even know where it was while you were in the house.

MR. UGLOW. *(With very appropriate bitterness.)* And I your loving brother!

THE VICAR *(Not to be outdone by REGINALD in quotations.)* "A little more than kin and less than kind."

MR. UGLOW. *(His wig is straight.)* How dare you, Simon? A little more than ten minutes ago and I was struck...here in your house. How dare you quote poetry at me?

THE VICAR feels he must pronounce on this.

THE VICAR. I regret that Carinthia has a masterful nature. She is apt to take the law into her own hands. And I fear there is something about you, Mortimer, that invites violence. I can usually tell when she is going to be unruly; there's a peculiar twitching of her hands. If you had not been aggravating us all with your so-called arguments, I should have noticed it in time and...taken steps.

MRS. UNDERWOOD. We're really very sorry, Mortimer. We can always... take steps. But...dear me!...I was never so surprised in my life. You all seemed to go mad at once. It makes me hot now to think of it.

The truth about CARINTHIA is that she is sometimes thought to be a little off her head. It's a form of genius.

THE VICAR. I shall have a headache to-morrow...my sermon day.

MR. UGLOW now begins to glow with a sense of coming victory. And he's not bad-natured, give him what he wants.

MR. UGLOW. Oh, no, you won't. More frightened than hurt! These things happen...the normal gross-feeding man sees red, you know, sees red. Reggie as a small boy...quite uncontrollable!

REGINALD. Well, I like that! You howled out for help.

THE VICAR. *(Lamblike and only lamblike.)* I am willing to obliterate the memory.

MRS. REGINALD. I'm sure I'm black and blue...and more torn than I can see.

MR. UGLOW But what can you do when a woman forgets herself? I simply stepped aside...I happen to value my dignity.

The door opens. MISS UNDERWOOD with the vase. She deposits it on the mahogany table. It is two feet in height. It is lavishly blotched with gold and white and red. It has curves and crinkles. Its handles are bossy. My God, it is a vase!!!

MISS UNDERWOOD. There it is.

MR. UGLOW *(With a victor's dignity.)* Thank you, Miss Underwood. *(He puts up gold-rimmed glasses.)* Ah...pure Rococo!

REGINALD. The Vi-Cocoa vase!

MR. UGLOW. That's not funny, Reginald.

REGINALD. Well...I think it is.

The trophy before him, MR. UGLOW mellows.

MR. UGLOW. Mary, you've often heard George tell us. The Emperor welcoming 'em...fine old fellow...speech in German...none of them understood it. Then at the end..."Gentlemen, I raise my glass. Hock...hock...hock!"

REGINALD. *(Who knows a German accent when he hears it.)* A little more spit in it.

MR. UGLOW. Reginald, you're very vulgar.

REGINALD. Is that Potsdam?

The monstrosity has coloured views on it, one back, one front.

MR. UGLOW. Yes...home of Friedrich der Grosse! *(he calls it grocer).* A great nation. We can learn a lot from 'em!

This was before the war. What he says of them now is unprintable.

REGINALD. Yes. I suppose it's a jolly handsome piece of goods. Cost a lot.

MR. UGLOW. Royal factory...built to imitate Sevres!

Apparently he would contemplate it for hours. But THE VICAR, lamblike, etc....
Add insinuating now.

THE VICAR. Well, Mortimer, here is the vase. Now where are we?

MRS. REGINALD. *(Really protesting for the first time.)* Oh...are we going to begin all over again? Why don't you sell it and share up?

MRS. UNDERWOOD. Gladys, I don't think that would be quite nice.

MRS. REGINALD. I can't see why not.

MR. UGLOW. Sell an heirloom!...it can't be done.

REGINALD. Oh, yes, it can. You and I together...cut off the entail...that's what it's called. It'd fetch twenty pounds at Christie's.

MR. UGLOW. *(The sight of it has exalted him beyond reason.)* More...more! First-class rococo. I shouldn't dream of it.

MISS UNDERWOOD has resumed her embroidery. She pulls a determined needle as she says....

MISS UNDERWOOD. I think Mary would have a share in the proceeds, wouldn't she?

MR. UGLOW. I think not.

THE VICAR. Why not, Mortimer?

MR. UGLOW. *(With fine detachment.)* Well, it's a point of law. I'm not quite sure...but let's consider it in equity. *(Not that he knows what on earth he means!)* If I died...and Reginald died childless and Mary survived us...and it came to her? Then there would be our cousins the Bamfords as next inheritors. Could she by arrangement with them sell and...?

MRS. UNDERWOOD. I shouldn't like to sell it. It would seem like a slight on George...because he went bankrupt perhaps. And Jane always had it in her bedroom.

MISS UNDERWOOD. *(Thimbling the determined needle through.)* Most unsuitable for a bedroom.

MRS. UNDERWOOD. *(Anxious to please.)* Didn't you suggest, Simon, that I might undertake not to leave it out of the family?

THE VICAR. *(Covering a weak spot.)* In private conversation with you, Mary....

MR. UGLOW. *(Most high and mighty, oh most!)* I don't accept the suggestion. I don't accept it at all.

THE VICAR. *(And now taking the legal line in his turn.)* Let me point out to you, Mortimer, that there is nothing to prevent Mary's selling the vase for her own exclusive benefit.

MR. UGLOW. *(His guard down.)* Simon!

THE VICAR. *(Satisfied to have touched him.)* Once again, I merely insist upon a point of principle.

MR. UGLOW. *(But now flourishing a verbal sword.)* And I insist...let everybody understand it...I insist that all thought of selling an heirloom is given up! Reginald...Gladys, you are letting me be exceedingly upset.

REGINALD. Well...shall I walk off with it? They couldn't stop me.

He lifts it up; and this simplest of solutions strikes them all stupent; except MISS UNDERWOOD, who glances under her bushy eyebrows.

MISS UNDERWOOD. You'll drop it if you're not careful.

MRS. UNDERWOOD. Oh, Reggie, you couldn t carry that to the station... everyone would stare at you.

THE VICAR. I hope you would not be guilty of such an unprincipled act.

MRS. REGINALD. I won't have it at home, Reg, so I tell you. One of the servants'd be sure to...! *(She sighs desperately.)* Why not sell the thing?

MR. UGLOW. Gladys, be silent.

REGINALD. (As he puts the vase down, a little nearer the edge of the table.) It is a weight.

So they have argued high and argued low and also argued round about it; they have argued in a full circle. And now there is a deadly calm. MR. UGLOW breaks it; his voice trembles a little, as does his hand with its signet ring rattling on the table.

MR. UGLOW. Then we are just where we started half an hour ago...are we, Simon?

THE VICAR. *(Lamblike in excelsis.)* Precisely, Mortimer.

MR. UGLOW. I'm sorry. I'm very sorry. *(He gazes at them with cool ferocity.)* Now let us all keep our tempers.

THE VICAR. I hope I shall have no occasion to lose mine.

MR. UGLOW. Nor I mine.

He seems not to move a muscle, but in some mysterious way his wig shifts: a sure sign.

MRS. UNDERWOOD. Oh, Mortimer, you're going to get excited.

MR. UGLOW. I think not, Mary. I trust not.

REGINALD. *(Proffering real temptation.)* Father...come away and write a letter about it.

MR. UGLOW. *(As his wrath swells.)* If I write a letter...if my solicitors have to write a letter...there are people here who will regret this day.

MRS. UNDERWOOD. *(Trembling at the coming storm.)* Simon, I'd much sooner he took it...I'd much rather he took everything Jane left me.

MR. UGLOW. Jane did not leave it to you, Mary.

MRS. UNDERWOOD. Oh, Mortimer, she did try to leave it to me.

MR. UGLOW. (*Running up the scale of indignation.*) She may have tried... but she did not succeed...because she could not...because she had no right to do so. (*And reaching the summit.*) I am not in the least excited.

Suddenly MISS UNDERWOOD takes a shrewd hand in the game.

MISS UNDERWOOD. Have you been to your lawyer?

MR. UGLOW. (Swivelling round.) What's that?

MRS. REGINALD. Have you asked your lawyer?

He has not.

MR. UGLOW. Gladys, I will not answer her. I refuse to answer the...the... the female. (*But he has funked the "futile."*)

MRS. REGINALD. (*Soothing him.*) All right, father.

MISS UNDERWOOD. He hasn't because he knows what his lawyer would say. Rot's what his lawyer would say!

MR. UGLOW. (*Calling on the gods to protect this woman from him.*) Heaven knows I wish to discuss this calmly!

REGINALD. Aunt Mary, might I smoke?

MISS UNDERWOOD. Not in the drawing-room.

MRS. UNDERWOOD. No...not in the drawing-room, please, Reginald.

MR. UGLOW. You're not to go away, Reginald.

REGINALD. Oh, well...hurry up.

MR UGLOW looks at THE VICAR. The Vicar is actually smiling. Can this mean defeat for the house of Uglow? Never.

MR. UGLOW. Do I understand that on your wife's behalf you entirely refuse to own the validity of my brother George's letter...where is it?...I read you the passage written on his death-bed.

THE VICAR. (*Measured and comforted. Victory gleams for him now.*) Why did he not mention the vase in his will?

MR. UGLOW. There were a great many things he did not mention in his will.

THE VICAR. Was his widow aware of the letter?

MR. UGLOW. You know she was.

THE VICAR. Why did she not carry out what you think to have been her husband's intention?

MR. UGLOW. Because she was a beast of a woman.

MR. UGLOW is getting the worst of it; his temper is slipping.

MRS. UNDERWOOD. Mortimer, what language about the newly dead!

THE VICAR. An heirloom in the family?

MR. UGLOW. Quite so.

THE VICAR. On what grounds do you maintain that George's intentions are not carried out when it is left to my wife?

And indeed MR. UGLOW is "against the ropes," so to speak.

MISS UNDERWOOD. The man hasn't a wig to stand on....I mean a leg.

MR. UGLOW. *(Pale with fury, hoarse with it, even pathetic in it.)* Don't you speak to me...I request you not to speak to me.

REGINALD and GLADYS quite seriously think this is bad for him.

REGINALD. Look here, father, Aunt Mary will undertake not to let it go out of the family. Leave it at that.

MRS. REGINALD. We don't want the thing, father...the drawing-room's full already.

MR. UGLOW. *(The pathos in him growing; he might flood the best Brussels with tears at any moment.)* It's not the vase. It's no longer the vase. It's the principle.

MRS. UNDERWOOD. Oh, don't, Mortimer...don't be like Simon. That's why I mustn't give in. It'll make it much more difficult if you start thinking of it like that.

MISS UNDERWOOD. *(Pulling and pushing that embroidery needle more grimly than ever.)* It's a principle in our family not to be bullied.

MRS. REGINALD. *(In almost a vulgar tone, really.)* If she'd go and mind her own family's business!

THE VICAR knows that he has his Uglows on the run. Suavely he presses the advantage.

THE VICAR. I am sorry to repeat myself, Mortimer, but the vase was left to Jane absolutely. It has been specifically left to Mary. She is under no obligation to keep it in the family.

MR. UGLOW. *(Control breaking.)* You'll get it, will you...you and your precious female sister?

THE VICAR. *(Quieter and quieter; that superior quietude.)* Oh, this is so unpleasant.

MR. UGLOW. *(Control broken.)* Never! Never!!...not if I beggar myself in law-suits.

MISS UNDERWOOD. *(A sudden and vicious jab.)* Who wants the hideous thing?

MR. UGLOW. *(Broken, all of him...in sheer hysterics...tears starting from his eyes.)* Hideous! You hear her? They'd sell it for what it would fetch. My brother George's rococo vase! An objet d'art et vertu...an heirloom...a family record of public service! Have you no feelings, Mary?

MRS. UNDERWOOD. *(Dissolved.)* Oh, I'm very unhappy.

Again are MR. UGLOW and THE VICAR breast to breast.

THE VICAR. Don't make your sister cry, sir.

MR. UGLOW. Make your sister hold her tongue, sir. She has no right in this discussion at all. Am I to be provoked and badgered by a Futile Female?

THE VICAR and MR. UGLOW are intent on each other, the others are intent on them. No one notices that Miss Underwood's embroidery is very decidedly laid down and that her fngers begin to twitch.

THE VICAR. How dare you suppose, Mortimer, that Mary and I would not respect the wishes of the dead?

MR. UGLOW. It's nothing to do with you, either.

MISS UNDERWOOD has risen from her chair. This Gladys does notice.

MRS. REGINALD. I say...Uncle Simon.

THE VICAR. What is it?

REGINALD. Look here, Uncle Simon, let Aunt Mary write a letter undertaking...there's no need for all this row....

MRS. UNDERWOOD. I will! I'll undertake anything!

THE VICAR. *(The Church on its militant dignity now.)* Keep calm, Mary. I am being much provoked, too. Keep calm.

MR. UGLOW. *(Stamping it out.)* He won't let her...he and his sister...he won't give way in anything. Why should I be reasonable?

REGINALD. If she will undertake it, will you...?

MRS. REGINALD. Oh, Aunt Mary, stop her!

In the precisest manner possible, judging her distance with care, aiming well and true, MISS UNDERWOOD has, for the second time to-day, soundly boxed MR. UGLOWs ear. He yells.

MR. UGLOW. I say...I'm hurt.

REGINALD. Look here now...not again!

THE VICAR. *(He gets flustered. No wonder.)* Carinthia! I should have taken steps! It is almost excusable.

MR. UGLOW. I'm seriously hurt.

MRS. REGINALD. You ought to be ashamed of yourself.

MISS UNDERWOOD. Did you feel the thimble?

MRS. UNDERWOOD. Oh, Carinthia, this is dreadful!

MR. UGLOW. I wish to preserve my dignity.

He backs out of her reach that he may the better do so.

MISS UNDERWOOD. Your wig's crooked.

MRS. REGINALD *(Rousing: though her well-pinched arms have lively recollections of half an hour ago.)* Don't you insult my father.

MISS UNDERWOOD. Shall I put it straight? It'll be off again.

She advances, her eyes gleaming. To do...Heaven knows what!

MR. UGLOW. *(Still backing)* Go away.

REGINALD. *(Who really doesn't fancy tackling the lady either).* Why don't you keep her in hand?

MR. UGLOW *(Backed as far as he can, and in terror).* Simon, you're a cad and your sister's a mad cad. Take her away.

But this THE VICAR will not endure. He has been called a cad, and that no English gentleman will stand, and a clergyman is a gentleman, sir. In ringing tones and with his finest gesture your hear him. "Get out of my house!" MR. UGLOW doubtless could reply more fittingly were it not that MISS UNDERWOOD still approaches. He is feebly forcible merely. "Don't you order me about," he quavers. What is he but a fascinated rabbit before the terrible woman? The gentlemanly VICAR advances—"Get out before I put you out," he vociferates—Englishman to the backbone. But that is Reginald's waited-for excuse. "Oh, no, you don't," he says and bears down on the Vicar. MRS. UNDERWOOD yelps in soft but agonized apprehension: "Oh, Simon, be careful." MR. UGLOW has his hands up, not indeed in token of surrender,—though surrender to the virago poised at him he would,— but to shield his precious wig.

"Mind my head, do," he yells; he will have it that it is his head. "Come away from my father," calls out Mrs. Reginald, stoutly clasping Miss Underwood from behind round that iron-corseted waist. MISS UNDERWOOD swivels round. "Don't you touch me, Miss," she snaps. But Gladys has weight and the two are toppling groundward while Reginald, one hand on the Vicar, one grabbing at Miss Underwood, to protect his wife ("Stop it, do!" he shouts), is outbalanced. And the Vicar making still determinedly for Mr. Uglow, and Mr. Uglow, his wig securer, preparing to defy the Vicar, the melee is joined once more. Only Mrs. Underwood is so far safe.

The fighters breathe hard and sway. They sway against the great mahogany table. The Rococo Vase totters; it falls; it is smashed to pieces. By a supreme effort the immediate authors of its destruction—linked together—contrive not to sit down among them. MRS. UNDERWOOD is heard to breathe, "Oh... thank goodness!"

THE END

Farewell To TheTheatre

1916

This talk took place in Edward's office. He is a London solicitor and his office reflects his standing. It is, that is to say, a musty dusty room in a house two hundred years old or so, now mercilessly chopped into offices. The woodwork is so old and cracked that new paint looks old on it and fresh paper on the walls looks dingy in a day. You may clean the windows (and it is sometimes done), but nothing will make them shine. The floor has been polished and stained and painted and scraped and painted again till it hardly looks like wood at all. And the furniture is old, not old enough to be interesting, old enough to be very respectable. There are some pictures on the wall. One is a good print of Lord Mansfield, one represents a naval battle, the third a nondescript piece of mountain scenery. How the battle and the nondescript came there nobody knows. One pictures some distracted client arriving with them under his arm. They were left to lean against the wall ten years or so; then a clerk hung them up. The newest thing in the room and quite the strangest—seeming there is a photograph on the mantelpiece of Edward's daughter, and that has been here nine years or so, ever since she died. A pretty child.

Well, the papers renew themselves and the room is full of them, bundles and bundles and bundles. They spread about poor Edward like the leaves of a forest; they lie packed close like last year's leaves, and in time are buried deep like leaves of the year before last. His clerk knows what they all are and where everything is. He flicks a feather duster over them occasionally and has been observed to put some—very reluctantly—away. Very reluctantly. For, after all, these are the fabric of a first-class practice, and it is his instinct to have them in evidence. Edward has never thought about it. Thus was the room when his uncle walked out of it and he walked in, and thus he will leave it in a few years for some junior partner.

Note the signs then by which a lawyer marks himself above reproach. Beware the businesslike well-polished office, clicking with machinery. There works a man who does not practise law so much as make a practice of it. Beware!

Edward is at his desk. Wherever else is he, unless he rises wearily to stretch his long limbs before the fire? Thin, humorous, and rather more than middle-aged, a sensitive, distinguished face. One likes Edward. His clerk shows in Dorothy

Taverner. Everybody knows Miss Dorothy Taverner. The clerk beams at her with forgetful joy—shamelessly at her while he tried to say to Edward "Miss Taverner, sir." Then he departs.

EDWARD. How punctual!

DOROTHY. Twelve ten by the clock out there. Your note said eleven thirty.

EDWARD. And I said: How punctual!

They shake hands like the oldest friends. He bends a little over her pretty hand.

DOROTHY. You have no right to send for me at all when I'm rehearsing... and you know it.

EDWARD. It was urgent. Sit down.

DOROTHY. My dear Edward, nothing is more urgent than that my rehearsals should go well...and if I leave the company to the mercy of my understudy and this author-boy...though he's a nice author-boy...they don't.

EDWARD. I'm sure they don't.

DOROTHY. His beating heart tells him that we must all be bad actors because we don't live and move just like the creatures as he began thinking them into being. He almost weeps. Then I tell him God called him into collaboration fifty-three flying years too late as far as I'm concerned.

EDWARD. Oh...oh!

DOROTHY. Fifty-four will have flown on November the next eighteenth. And that cheers us all up and we start again. Well, dear friend, you are fifty-seven and you...look it.

Having made point, pause for effect. EDWARD carefully places legal documents on one side.

EDWARD. My dear Dorothy...

DOROTHY. That tone means that a little business talk has now begun. Where's the rickety paperknife that I play with? Thank you.

EDWARD. Vernon Dix and...Boothby, is that the name of your treasurer? ...paid me a formal visit yesterday afternoon.

DOROTHY. Behind my back! What about?

EDWARD. They complain you won't look at your balance-sheets....

DOROTHY. *(With cheerful charm.)* But they're liars. I look at them every week.

EDWARD. ...That you won't study them.

DOROTHY. I'm studying a new part.

EDWARD. They brought me a pretty full statement. I spent some hours over it.

DOROTHY. More money wanted?

EDWARD. They also brought me the estimate for this new play.

DOROTHY. It'll be exceeded.

EDWARD. Can more money be found?

DOROTHY. We can search. You remember the last search. The rent's paid till Christmas.

EDWARD. Trust your landlord!

DOROTHY. This play may do well.

EDWARD. It may not.

DOROTHY gives a sigh. With an impatient gesture or two she takes off her hat and puts it obliviously on Edward's inkstand. She runs her fingers through her front hair, takes out a hair-pin and viciously replaces it. Signs, these are, that she is worried.

DOROTHY. Yes, I remember the last search. Nearly kissed by old James Levison for Dear Art's sake. At my age! I wonder did he guess what an even choice it was between five thousand pounds and boxing his flat white ears.

EDWARD. There was Shelburne's five thousand and Mrs. Minto's....

DOROTHY. Well, I did kiss Lord Shelburne...he's a dear. Blue-eyed and over seventy or under twenty...then I always want to kiss them. Why?

EDWARD. My eyes...alas...were never blue and never will be now.

DOROTHY. Because I suppose then they don't care whether I do or not. All that money gone? I'm sorry. Mrs. Minto can't afford it.

EDWARD. No, it's not all gone. And another five thousand will make you safe through this season. Another ten thousand unless you've very bad luck should carry you to Christmas...otherwise, if this new play isn't an instant success, you must close.

DOROTHY sits upright in her chair.

DOROTHY. I have been in management for sixteen years. I have paid some dividends. "Dividends" is correct, I think.

EDWARD. I keep a sort of abstract which reminds me of the fearful and wonderful way you have been financed.

DOROTHY. Dear Edward, I should have cheated everybody but for you.

EDWARD. I have also managed mostly to stop you from cheating yourself. Dorothy, it is odd that the people who put money in only to make some did often manage to make it out of you, while the people who stumped up for art's sake and yours never got anything at all.

DOROTHY. I don't see anything odd in that. They got what they wanted. People always do. Some of them got the art...and one of them nearly got me.

EDWARD. Why didn't you marry him, Dorothy? A good fellow...a good match.

DOROTHY. Oh, my dear! Marry him? Marry! Confound him...why did he ask me? Now I can't ever ask him for a penny again. Yes...on that bright Sunday morning the manageress was tempted I won't deny.

EDWARD. But the record of the past five years does not warrant your promising more dividends...and that's the truth.

DOROTHY. Well...shall we hide the balance sheets away and shall I gird myself with boastfulness once more...once weary more? What is our record for

Dear Art's Sake? Shakespeare...without scenery. Moliere, Holberg, Ibsen, Strindberg, Maeterlinck, Shaw, Hauptmann, d'Annunzio, Benevente, Giacosa, Parraval, Ostrowsky, Lavalliere, Tchekoff, Galsworthy, Masefield, Henniker, Borghese, Brieux, Yeats, van Arpent and Claudel. Some of it sounds quite old-fashioned already...and some has begun to pay. When a Knight of the Garter dies, you know, they proclaim his title over his tomb. You'll have to come to my burning, Edward, and through a trumpet of rolled-up balance-sheets proclaim my titles to fame. " She, here deceased, did her duty by them, Shakespeare, Ibsen...." How I hate boasting! And boasting to millionaires to get money out of them. I'm as vain as a peacock still...but boasting I hate.

EDWARD. Then consider. You can see through the production of this... what's it called?

DOROTHY. "The Salamander." Good title!

EDWARD. If it fails...shut up...finally.

DOROTHY. Yes...I've been thinking of doing that, Edward. "The Salamander" won't succed in the fine full business sense...though now I'm whispered that for the first time it most perversely may.

EDWARD. Then what on earth are you putting it up for?

DOROTHY. Because it's good enough...and then the next can be better. It won't succeed because I've only a small part in it. Say Egoist...say Actress.

EDWARD. Wiser to keep out altogether.

DOROTHY. And then it wouldn't succeed because the dear Public would think I didn't believe in it enough. Queer silly children the dear Public are, aren't they? For ten years now my acting is held to have grown steadily worse, so quite rightly they won't rush to plays with me in them. But then they won't have my plays with me out of them either. So what's a poor body to do?

EDWARD. I don't hold that your acting has grown steadily worse.

DOROTHY. Well...not steadily perhaps. But I never was steady, was I? And you don't like the parts I choose?

EDWARD. Not when you hide yourself behind them.

DOROTHY. I never do.

EDWARD. Your old self! But I want you to finish with it all, anyway.

DOROTHY. Why?

EDWARD. Because I fear I see heart-break ahead.

DOROTHY. That you need never look to see...for the best of reasons.

EDWARD. You still do care...far too much.

DOROTHY. Do I hanker for the old thrill...like wine bubbling in one's heart...and then the stir in the audience when...on I came. Dear friend, you now prefer my acting...off the stage. My well-known enthusiasm...it seems to me it rings more tinny every day...but I'm glad it takes you in. Still, even that's only an echo...growing fainter since I died.

EDWARD. My dear Dorothy.

DOROTHY. Oh...but you knew I was dead. You own now to mourning me. You know the day and hour I died. Hypocrite...I remember how you congratulated me on the tragic occasion...kissing my hand...you're the only man that does it naturally. Doesn't that abstract remind you when we produced "The Flight of the Duchess"?

EDWARD. Many of us thought you very good.

DOROTHY. Because I was far, far better than many a bad actress would have been. It is the queerest sensation, Edward, to be dead...though after a while you get quite used to it. Are you still alive, by the way?

EDWARD. There is the same feeble flicker there has ever been.

DOROTHY. Burn on, dear Edward, burn on that I may warm my poor hands sometimes at the flame you are.

EDWARD. It can serve no better purpose.

DOROTHY. No...So I'm sure I think.

There falls a little silence. Then Edward speaks the more bitterly that it is without anger.

EDWARD. Damn them! I'd damn their souls, if they had any. They've helped themselves to you at so much a time for...how many years? Dorothy... what have they ever given you in return?

DOROTHY. Oh, if that were all my grievance I'd be a happy ghost this day. If I'd a thousand souls and they wanted them, the dear Public...as they need them...God knows they do...they should have everyone, for me. What does the law say, Edward? Is a soul private property?

EDWARD. There are decisions against it.

DOROTHY. Then I prefer your law to your religion. It's more public-spirited.

EDWARD. My ancestral brand of religion, my dear, taught me to disapprove very strongly of the theatre.

DOROTHY. And after watching my career you've found out why. How long have you been in this office, Edward?

EDWARD. Thirty years, nearly.

DOROTHY. The weight of them! Do you remember having tea at Richmond...at The Roebuck at Richmond...when they'd offered you this billet and we talked wisely of the future?

EDWARD. I do.

DOROTHY. And I made you take it, didn't I?

EDWARD. You did.

DOROTHY. And I wouldn't marry you.

EDWARD looks at her. One side of his mouth twitches a little. You might charitably call it a smile. But his eyes are smiling.

DOROTHY. Don't say you didn't ask me to marry you.

EDWARD. On that occasion?

DOROTHY. Yes...on that occasion, too. That's what one calls the Past, isn't it? How right I was...and what successes we've both been!

EDWARD. My son Charles tells me that I have done very well. Do you know, I was moved to ask him the other night as we sat in the box whether he wasn't in love with you?

DOROTHY. Do you think it's hereditary?

EDWARD. He said he had been as a boy.

DOROTHY. How old is he?

EDWARD. Twenty-three.

DOROTHY. Bless him! If young things love you, be quite sure that you're alive. I do regret sometimes.

EDWARD. What did happen...so suddenly?

DOROTHY. What happens to the summer? You go walking one day and you feel that it has gone.

EDWARD. You've been that to the Theatre.

DOROTHY. A summer day...a long, long summer day. Thank you. I prefer the sonnet which calls me a breath of spring. But truly he died...oh, that lion's head of his!...before I was full blown.

EDWARD. I know it by heart.

DOROTHY. It's a good sonnet.

EDWARD. It makes history of you.

DOROTHY. And it never made me vain a bit because indeed I knew it was true. Yes, I like to be standard literature.

EDWARD. Easy enough for a poet to be public spirited over you.

DOROTHY. But from the time I was born, Edward, I believe I knew my destiny. And I've never quarrelled with it...never. I can't imagine how people get along if they don't know by sheer instinct what they're meant to be and do. What muddles they must make of life!

EDWARD. They do...and then come to me for advice. It's how you told me to earn my living.

DOROTHY. You only tell them what the law says and what two and two make. That's all you ever tell me. But what I was alive for I have always known. So of course I knew when I died.

EDWARD. Dorothy, my dear, it hurts me to hear you say it.

DOROTHY. Why? We must all die and be born again...how many times in our lives? I went home that night and sent poor old Sarah to bed. And I didn't curse and break things...I'd always let myself do that a little on occasions...it seemed so much more human...when I was alone...oh, only when I was quite alone. But that night it had all been different...and I sat still in the dark....and wondered...wondered what was to happen now. It's a frightening thing at best to lose your old and well-trained trusted self...and not know what the new one's going to be. I was angry. I had rehearsed the wretched play so well, too. Why do people think I've no brains, Edward?

EDWARD. I suppose because you're so pretty.

DOROTHY. Or perhaps because I don't use them for the things they were never meant to be used for. I've sometimes thought, since I can't act any longer, I might show the dear Public my rehearsing. That'd teach them! But there...I've come down to wanting to teach them. Time to retire. For you see after that night I wasn't born again. Something...didn't happen. And a weary business it has been finding out what. With the dear Public helping me to discover...hard on them they've thought it. And you sopatient with my passion to keep on failing...hard on you. For you've not understood. I've disappointed you these later years. Own up.

EDWARD. If it's admitted that all my heart is your most humble servant, I'll own up again to disapproving of the Theatre...to disapproving most thoroughly of acting and of actors too, and to doubly disapproving when any new nonsense about them is added to life's difficulties.

DOROTHY. Yes...if the life you call life's so important! Well...I have four hundred a year...safe...to retire on, haven't I, Edward?

EDWARD. As safe as money can be.

DOROTHY. I do think that money ought to learn to be safe. It has no other virtues. And I've got my Abbey.

EDWARD. Milford Abbey is safe for you from everything but earthquake.

DOROTHY. How utterly right that I should end my days in a shanty built out of the stones of that great Abbey and buttressed up in its shell!

EDWARD. Is it?

DOROTHY. Oh! Edward, if you had but the artist's sense of the eternal fitness of things, you'd find it such a help....

EDWARD.....To imagining Miss Dorothy leading the Milford monks a dance.

DOROTHY. Well...their religion was not of this world, nor is mine. But yours is, dear Edward. Therefore the follies of art and saintliness must seem to you two sorts of folly and not one. St. Francis would have understood me. I should have been his dear sister Happiness. But you and the railway trains running on time would have puzzled him no end.

EDWARD. What foolishness makes you say you're dead, my dear?

DOROTHY. While...if I'd lived the cautious life, I shouldn't be. If I'd sold my fancies for a little learning, virginity for a gold ring, likings for good manners, hate for silence...if I ever could have learnt the world's way...to measure out gifts for money and thanks...well, I'd have been married to you perhaps, Edward. And then you never could have enjoyed my Imogen as you used to enjoy it. You used to say it was a perfect tonic.

EDWARD. So it was!

DOROTHY. Yes, dear, you never had a gift for subtle expression, had you?

EDWARD. From the beginning I suppose you expected more of life than ever I could find in it.

DOROTHY. Whatever I expected, my friend, I bargained for nothing at all.

EDWARD I'd like you to know this, Dorothy, that for all my rectangular soul, as you used to call it...when I asked you to marry me...

DOROTHY. On which of those great occasions?

EDWARD On the various occasions I did ask you before I did...otherwise ...marry.

DOROTHY. I think there were five...or six. I recall them with pride.

EDWARD. But not with enough of it to ensure accuracy.

DOROTHY. And was it never just for the sake of repeating yourself?

EDWARD. No. When I was most ridiculously in love I used to think three times before I faced a life with you in that...

DOROTHY. Well?

EDWARD. That flowery wilderness which was your life. I knew there were no safe roads for me there. And yet I asked you...knowing that very well.

DOROTHY. I'm glad...for your sake...that you risked it.

EDWARD Glad, for your own, you didn't?

DOROTHY. Did you really only marry her because I told you to?

EDWARD. I fear so.

DOROTHY That was a wrong reason for doing the right thing. But I could not have one of the ablest men of his set in everything else said at his club to be sentimentalizing his life away about an actress...I really couldn't. They told me she was desperately in love with you. And I never would have spoken to you again if you hadn't. Edward, it was never hard on her, was it?

EDWARD No, Dorothy, I hope and think it never was. I made her happy in every ordinary sense...at least I felt she felt so.

DOROTHY. And you did love her, didn't you, Edward?

EDWARD I shouldn't put this into words perhaps. I thought through those twenty-five years I gave her all the love that her love asked for. But the world of ...folly, one calls it...into which your laugh had once lifted me....

DOROTHY. Or was it wisdom?

EDWARD. That, my dear Dorothy, was the problem you would never consent to try and solve.

DOROTHY. She never could have liked me, Edward.

EDWARD. She thought you a great artist. She had judgment and taste, you know.

DOROTHY. Yes...she thought me an attack of scarlet fever, let us say...and that it was a very beautiful scarlet.

EDWARD. Dorothy . . . somehow that hurts.

DOROTHY. I'm sorry.

EDWARD She wasn't witty enough, you see, to say such things. But some years before she died, her nature seemed to take a fresh start, as it were. It shot out in the oddest ways...over a home for horses and cooking reforms...and a most romantic scheme for sending strayed servant girls to Australia to get married. If there had been any genius in my love for her...would she have had to wait till forty-five and then find only those crabbed half-futile shoots of inner life begin to show? While her children were amused...and I was tolerant! For quite incurably middle-aged she was by then.

DOROTHY. Had she dreaded that?

EDWARD. Not a bit. Not even in fun...as we made such a fuss of doing.

DOROTHY. Admirable Ethel. Clear-eyed and so firm-footed on this spinning earth. And Life her duty...to be punctually and cheerfully done. But over-trained a little, don't you think...just for her own happiness' sake.

EDWARD. She didn't count her happiness.

DOROTHY She should have.

EDWARD She shouldn't have died when she did.

DOROTHY. The doctors were fools.

EDWARD. Well, it was a while after...remembering my love for you...I suddenly saw how perhaps, after all, I had wronged her.

DOROTHY. It was just three years after that you asked me to marry you yet again.

EDWARD. You forgave me. Let's forget it. It was good to feel I was still a bit of a fool.

DOROTHY. Folly for certain it was then?

EDWARD. And not so old at heart as you thought.

DOROTHY. I like your declarations, Edward. They're different. But never from the beginning have you been like the others.

EDWARD. And I was never jealous of any of the three.

DOROTHY. Four.

EDWARD. Four?

DOROTHY. One that you never knew about. I told you though I should never marry...and I never have. Perhaps I'm as frightened at the meaning I might find in it...as you ought to have been.

EDWARD. They made you just as miserable at times, Dorothy, as if you had married them.

DOROTHY. Poor dears.

EDWARD. And two out of the three were really perfect fools.

DOROTHY. Three out of the four, my friend, were perfect fools...helpless fools.

EDWARD Then which wasn't?

DOROTHY. The one you never guessed about. Don't try to even now. He never really cared for me, you see...and I knew he didn't...and so I was ashamed to tell you.

EDWARD Now when was that?

DOROTHY. You're trying to guess.

EDWARD. No, honestly....

DOROTHY. Do you remember a time when I was very cross with life and wouldn't act for a whole year...in the days when I still could. I went down to Grayshott and started a garden...a failure of a garden. And you came down to see me...and we talked into the dark. And I said I ought to have married father's scrubby-headed assistant and had ten children....

EDWARD. I vaguely remember.

DOROTHY. Well, it wasn't then . . . but shortly after.

EDWARD. You wanted that experience....

DOROTHY. No...no! How dare you? Am I that sort of a creature...collecting sensations? Sometimes, Edward, I find you the biggest fool of the lot ...a fool at heart, which is worse than a fool at head...and wickeder.

EDWARD. I'm sorry!

DOROTHY. Never mind, it's not your fault now if fresh air disagrees with you. And you can't open the window here, for only dust comes in.

EDWARD. Is the room stuffy?

DOROTHY. Yes...but so's London...and so's life.

EDWARD. I do remember there was a time when I thought you were hardening a little.

DOROTHY. Well, it wasn't from that bruising. No man or woman in this world shall make me hard.

EDWARD. Dorothy, will you marry me?

DOROTHY. *(Her voice pealing out.)* Oh, my dear!

EDWARD. That's what you said to Blackthorpe when he offered you his millions on a bright Sunday morning. Don't say it to me.

DOROTHY. I never called him My dear...I was much too proper...and so is he! But you are the dear of one corner of my heart...it is the same old corner always kept for you. No, no...that sort of love doesn't live in it. So for the... seventh?...let's make it the seventh time...oh, yes, I wear them on my memory's breast like medals... no, I won't.

EDWARD. Very well. If you don't want to raise five thousand pounds you'd better close the theatre after this next play's produced.

DOROTHY. Heavens above...that's what we started to discuss. What have we been talking of since?

EDWARD. Dear Dorothy...I never do know what we talk of. I only know that by the time I've got it round to business it's time for you to go.

DOROTHY. Yes, I said I'd be back at the theatre by half-past twelve.

EDWARD. It's long after.

DOROTHY. I'm so glad. They'll finish the act without me and lunch. I never want food. Isn't it odd?

EDWARD. Do you decide to close the theatre after this next play?

DOROTHY. I decide not to ask man, woman, or devil for another penny.

EDWARD. Then you close.

DOROTHY. But if it's a success?

EDWARD. Then, when it's finished you may have a few pounds more than four hundred a year.

DOROTHY. I don't want 'em.

EDWARD. But you'll close?

DOROTHY. I will. This time I really will and never, never open again. I want my Abbey. I want to sit in the sun and spoil my complexion and acquire virtue. Do you know I can have fourteen volumes at a time from the London Library?

EDWARD. Yes...don't spoil your complexion.

DOROTHY. Well...when it is really my complexion and no longer the dear Public's I may get to like it better. To acquire knowledge for its own sake! Do you never have that hunger on you? To sit and read long books about Byzantium. Not frothy foolish blank-verse plays...but nice thick meaty books. To wonder where the Goths went when they vanished out of Italy. Knowledge and Beauty! It's only when you love them for their own sake that they yield their full virtue to you. And you can't deceive them...they always know.

EDWARD. I'm told that the secret of moneymaking's something like that.

DOROTHY. Oh, a deadlier one. Money's alive and strong. And when money loves you...look out.

EDWARD. It has never wooed me with real passion. Six and eightpences add up slowly.

DOROTHY throws herself back in her chair and her eyes up to the ceiling.

DOROTHY. You've never seen me asking for money and boasting about my art, have you?

EDWARD. That has been spared me.

DOROTHY. I'm sorry you've missed it for ever. It is just as if the millionaire and I....

EDWARD. Though they weren't always millionaires.

DOROTHY. They were at heart. I always felt we were striking some weird bargain. For all I'd see at his desk was a rather apologetic little man...though the Giant Money was outlined round him like an aura. And he'd seem to be begging me as humbly as he dared to help save his little soul...though all the while the Giant that enveloped him was business-like and jovial and stern. I shouldn't like to be only the marrow of a shadowy giant, Edward...with no heart's blood in me at all.

EDWARD. That's why our modern offices are built so high, perhaps.

DOROTHY. Yes, he reaches to the ceiling.

EDWARD. And are very airless, as you say.

DOROTHY. Ah...it's he that breathes up all the air. You have made rather a poor and arid world of it, haven't you, Edward...you and Henry and John and Samuel and William and Thomas.

EDWARD. Will Mary Jane do much better?

DOROTHY. Not when you've made a bloodless woman of her. And you used to bite your pipe and talk nonsense to me about acting...about its necessarily debilitating effect, my dear Dorothy, upon the moral character. Edward, would I cast for a king or a judge or a duchess actors that couldn't believe more in reigning or judging or duchessing than you wretched amateurs do?

EDWARD. We "put it over," as you vulgar professionals say.

DOROTHY. Do you think so? Because the public can't tell the difference ...as the voice of my business manager drones. I've fancied sometimes that actors, playing parts...but with real faith in that unreal...yet live those lives of yours more truly. Why...swiftly and keenly I've lived a hundred lives.

EDWARD. No... the trouble with my patients....

DOROTHY. Of course they are! That's why I've to be brought here by force. I never feel ill.

EDWARD Never a pain in the pocket!

DOROTHY. I never feel it.

EDWARD. The trouble when most people do is that it's all they can feel or believe in. And I have to patch them up.

DOROTHY. Put a patch on the pocket...tonic the poor reputation.

EDWARD. Though, after all, what can I say to them? If they found out that the world as they've made it doesn't exist...or perhaps their next world as they've invented it either.

DOROTHY. Oh, but I'm sure that exists...just about as much. And that you'll all be there...bustling among the clouds...making the best of things... beating your harps into coin...bargaining for eternity...and saying that of course what you go so wearily on in hope of is another and a better world.

EDWARD. Shall we meet?

DOROTHY. I think not. I flung my soul over the footlights before ever I was sure that I had one...well, I was never uncomfortably sure. As you warned me I should...biting your pipe. No, thanks, I don't want another....I have been given happier dreams. Do you remember that letter of your father's that I would read?

EDWARD. No....

DOROTHY. Oh yes! Think twice, my dear boy, think twice before you throw yourself away on this woman.

EDWARD. Old innocent! You were the cautious one.

DOROTHY. But you never knew, Edward, how tempted I was.

EDWARD. Dorothy, don't! The years haven't taught me to take that calmly.

DOROTHY. Every woman is what I was more or less....

EDWARD. Less.

DOROTHY. So they seem. And you won't pay the price of more.

EDWARD. What was it? I was ready...and ready to pay.

DOROTHY. The price to you of my freedom when you love me! Why... dear Edward...your jaw sets even now. And so...for your happiness...that your minds may be easy as you bustle through the world's work...so we must seem to choose the cat-like comfort of the fireside, the shelter of your cheque-book and our well-mannered world. And, perhaps I should have chosen that if I could have had my choice.

EDWARD. Dorothy!

DOROTHY. Had not some ruthless windy power from beyond me...blown me free.

EDWARD. Dorothy...I've loved you...and I do...with a love I've never understood. But sometimes I've been glad you didn't marry me...prouder of you as you were. Because my love would seem a very little thing.

DOROTHY. It is.

EDWARD. I never boasted...never of that.

DOROTHY. But the more precious...a jewel. And if we're to choose and possess things...nothing finer. My dear...what woman wouldn't love you? You've not been flattered enough. Never mind...you lost no dignity on your knees. I had no choice though but to be possessed...of seven angels. Oh, my dear friend... could you ever have cast them out?

EDWARD. I've watched them wear you through...the seven angels of your art that kept you from me.

DOROTHY. Yes...I'm a weary woman. For a moment there is silence.

EDWARD. But sometimes I've wondered...what we two together might have done. Oh, Dorothy, why didn't you try?

DOROTHY Not with these silly self-conscious selves. Poor prisoners... born to an evil time. But visions do come...of better beings than we are...of a theatre not tinselled...and an office not dusty with law...all rustling with quarrelsome papers. How wrong to tie up good lively quarrels with your inky tape! Oh, shut your eyes...it's easier to see then. Are they shut?

EDWARD. Close. And the grip of your hand is wonderful for the eyesight.

DOROTHY. Aren't you an artist, too, Edward...our fault if we forget it. For Law is a living thing. It must be, mustn't it?

EDWARD. Yes...I had forgotten.

DOROTHY My dreams and the stories of them are worthless unless I've a living world to dream of. What are words and rules and names for men to live by? Armour with nothing inside it. So our dreams are empty, too.

EDWARD Oh...Dorothy, my dear, it may sound as silly as ever when I say it...but why, why didn't you marry me?

DOROTHY. Yes...I should have made a difference to this habitation, shouldn't I?

EDWARD. Would you have cared to come here then?

DOROTHY. Always...the spirit of me. And I do think you were a better match than the looking-glass.

EDWARD. I promise you should always have found yourself beautiful...in my eyes.

DOROTHY. But I'm widowed of my looking-glasses. Edward, have you noticed that for fifteen years there's not been one in my house...except three folding ones in the bathrooms.

EDWARD. I remember my wife remarking it.

DOROTHY. Some women did...and some men were puzzled without knowing why.

EDWARD. She wondered how you studied your parts.

DOROTHY. I could have told her how I learnt not to...and it's rather interesting.

EDWARD. Tell me.

DOROTHY. This is, perhaps, the little bit of truth I've found...my little scrap of gold. From its brightness shines back all the vision I have...and I add it proudly to the world's heap. Though it sounds the silliest thing...as silly as your loving me at fifty-seven, more babyishly than you did at seventeen.

EDWARD. Please heaven my clerks don't see me till...

DOROTHY. Till you're quite self-conscious again. Well...before the child in me died...such an actress you all thought as never was....

EDWARD. "O breath of Spring! Our wintry doubts have fled."

DOROTHY. But, remember, all children could be like that.

EDWARD. I deny it.

DOROTHY. And that's why they're not. Well, growing older as we say... and self-conscious, Edward...I found that the number of my looking-glasses grew. Till one day I counted them...and big and small there were forty-nine. That day I'd bought the forty-ninth...an old Venetian mirror...so popular I was in those days and felt so rich. Yes...then I used to work out my parts in front of every mirror in turn. One would make me prettier and one more dignified. One could give me pathos and one gave me power. Now there was a woman used to come and sew for me. You know! I charitably gave her jobs...took an interest in her "case"...encouraged her to talk her troubles out for comfort's sake. I wasn't interested...I didn't care one bit...it didn't comfort her. She talked to me because she thought I liked it...because she thought I thought she liked it. But, oddly...it was just sewing she liked, and she sewed well and sewing did her good...sewing for me. You remember my "Lily Prince" in "The Backwater"?

EDWARD. Yes.

DOROTHY. My first real failure.

EDWARD. I liked it.

DOROTHY. My first dead failure...dear Public. Do you know why? I hadn't found her in the mirrors, I'd found her in that woman as she sewed.

EDWARD. I didn't think it a failure,

DOROTHY. Well...the dear Public wouldn't pay to see it...and we've found no other word. But I knew...if that was failure..now I meant to fail. And I never looked in a mirror again. Except, of course, to do my hair and paint my poor face and comically comfort myself sometimes. To say..."Dorothy, as mugs go it's not such an ugly mug." I took the looking-glasses down...I turned their faces to the wall...for I had won free from that shadowed emptiness of self. But nobody understood. Do you?

EDWARD. If I can't...I'll never say that I love you again.

DOROTHY. What can we understand when we're all so prisoned in mirrors that whatever we see it's but ourselves...ourselves as heroes or slaves... suffering, triumphant...always ourselves. Truth lives where only other people are. That's the secret. Turn the mirror to the wall and there is no you...but the world of other people is a wonderful world.

EDWARD. We've called them your failures, have we...when we wouldn't follow you there?

DOROTHY. And I that have, proudly, never bargained was so tempted to bargain for success...by giving you what your appetites wanted...that mirrored mannequin slightly oversize that bolsters up your self-conceit.

EDWARD. But you had meant our youth to us, Dorothy....

DOROTHY. I'd given you that long since...the flower of me...had I grudged it?

EDWARD. I think we're frightened of that other world.

DOROTHY. Well you may be!

EDWARD. If we couldn't find ourselves there with our virtues and our vanity...the best and the worst of what we know.

DOROTHY. So you all failed me, you see...for I'd gien you all my life, and what other had I? And I failed...died...not to be born again. Oh, my poor theatre! Keep it for a while then to patronize and play with. But one day it shall break you all in pieces. And now my last curtsey's made....

The paper-knife she has been playing with snaps.

EDWARD. Dorothy...what an omen! Not your last visit here, too!

DOROTHY. A fine omen. I do not surrender my sword! But I shouldn't march off quite so proudly, Edward, if it weren't for a new voice from that somewhere in me where things are born saying...shall I tell you what it says?

EDWARD. Please.

DOROTHY. The scene is laid in Dorothy's soul. Characters...A voice... Dorothy. Dorothy discovered as the curtain rises in temper and tears. The Voice: "Thirty-five years finding out your mistake! But that's a very short time" Dorothy: "Boohoo!...but now I'm going to die" The Voice: "Who told you so?"

Dorothy: "Oh...aren't I?...or rather Am I not?" The Voice: "Dorothy, my dear... what led you that November day to your ruined Abbey...what voice was it called to you so loud to make it yours? Yours! What are you beside the wisdom of its years? You must go sit, Dorothy, sit very patiently in thc sunshine under the old wall...where marigolds grow...and there's one foxglove...(hsh, I planted it!). Did it trouble those builders...who built it not for themselves...nor for you...but to the glory of God they built it...did it trouble them that they were going to die?" Dorothy: "If they'd known that the likes of me would one day buy it with good hard cash they'd have had heart failure on the spot. Besides, they did die and their blessed Abbey's a ruin." Two thousand five hundred pounds it cost me to do it up.

EDWARD. Well?

DOROTHY. Well...if I say anything like that of course the voice is silent. But if I sit there after sunset when the world's all still...I often sit to watch the swallows, and if you keep quiet they'll swoop quite close...then I can hear the voice say: "They built the best they could...they built their hearts into the walls... they mixed the mortar with their own hearts' blood. They spoke the truth that was in them and then they were glad to die." "But was it true?" I ask. "And see how the wall is crumbling." And then the voice says: "What is Truth but the best that we can build?...and out of its crumbling other truth is built. Are you tired, Dorothy?" I answer: Yes, that I am very tired. But I sit there till the stars shine and there are friendly spirits around me. Not the dead...never...but the unborn waiting their heritage...my gift to them...mine, too. That's the true length of life... the finished picture of his being that the artist signs and sells...gives..loses! It was his very soul and it is gone. But then he is glad to go...to be dust again... nothingness...air...for then he knows most truly....

EDWARD. What?

DOROTHY. Why, I told you...that he was always nothingness called by some great name . . . that the world of other people is the only world there is. Edward, what's the time?

EDWARD. Past one.

DOROTHY. Well, I'm hungry. Take me out and give me lunch.

EDWARD. Bless you...I will.

With three fine gestures she puts on her hat again. Time was when one would sit through forty minutes of a dull play just to see Dorothy take off her hat and put it on again. Much less expressively he finds his and they go out together. The clerks all stare ecstatically as she passes.

THE END

The Madras House

1910

ACT I

The HUXTABLES live at Denmark Hill, for MR HUXTABLE is the surviving partner in the well-known Peckham drapery establishment of Roberts & Huxtable and the situation besides being salubrious is therefore convenient. It is a new house, MR HUXTABLE bought it half finished so that the interior might be to his liking; its exterior the builder said one might describe as of a Free Queen Anne Treatment; to which MR HUXTABLE rejoined, after blinking at the brick spotted with stone ornament, that After all it was inside they were going to live, you know.

Through the stained, grained front door, rattling with coloured glass, one reaches the hall, needlessly narrow, needlessly dark, but with its black and white tessellated pavement making for cleanliness. On the left is the stained and grained staircase with its Brussels carpet and twisted brass stair rods, on the right the drawing-room. The drawing-room can hardly be said to express the personality of MR HUXTABLE. The foundations of its furnishing are in the taste of MRS HUXTABLE. For fifteen years or so additions to this family museum have been disputed into their place by the six MISS HUXTABLES: LAURA (aged thirty-nine), MINNIE, CLARA, JULIA, EMMA, JANE (aged twenty-six). The rosewood cabinets, the picture from some academy of the early Seventies entitled In Ye Olden Time (this was a wedding present most likely), the gilt clock, which is a Shakespeare, narrowheaded, but with a masterly pair of legs, propped pensively against a dial and enshrined beneath a dome of glass, another wedding present. These were the treasures of MRS HUXTABLE'S first drawing-room, her solace in the dull post-honeymoon days. She was the daughter of a city merchant, wholesale as against her husband's retail; but even in the Seventies retail was lifting its head. It was considered though that KATHERINE TOMBS conferred some distinction upon young HARRY HUXTABLE by marrying him, and even now, as a portly lady nearing sixty, she figures by the rustle of her dress, the measure of her mellow voice with its carefully chosen phrases, for the dignity of the household.

The difference between one MISS HUXTABLE and another is to a casual eye the difference between one lead pencil and another, as these lie upon one's table after some weeks' use; a matter of length, of sharpening, of wear. LAURA's distinction lies in her being the housekeeper; it is a solid power, that of ordering the dinner. She is very silent. While her sisters are silent with strangers, she is silent with her sisters. She doesn't seem to read much either; one hopes she dreams, if only of wild adventures with a new carpet-sweeper. When there was some family bitterness as to whether the fireplace in summer should hold ferns or a Chinese umbrella, it was LAURA'S opinion that an umbrella gathers less dust, which carried the day. MINNIE and CLARA are inclined to religion; not sentimentally; works are a good second with them to faith. They have veered, though, lately, from district visiting to an interest in Missions - missions to Poplar or China (one is almost as far as the other); good works, the results of which they cannot see. Happily they forbear to ask why this proves the more soul-satisfying sort.

JULIA started life – that is to say, left school – as a genius. The head mistress had had two or three years of such dull girls that really she could not resist this excitement. Watercolour sketches were the medium. So JULIA was dressed in brown velveteen and sent to an art school, where they wouldn't let her do watercolour drawing at all. And in two years she learnt enough about the trade of an artist not ever to want to do those watercolour drawings again. JULIA is now over thirty and very unhappy. Three of her water-colours (early masterpieces) hang on the drawing-room wall. They shame her, but her mother won't have them taken down. On a holiday she'll be off now and then for a solitary day's sketching, and as she tears up the vain attempt to put on paper the things she has learnt to see, she sometimes cries. It was JULIA, EMMA and JANE who, some years ago, conspired to present their mother with that intensely conspicuous cosy corner. A cosy corner is apparently a device for making a corner just what the very nature of a corner should forbid it to be. They beggared themelves; but one wishes that MR HUXTABLE were more lavish with his dress allowances, then they might at least have afforded something not quite so hideous.

EMMA, having JULIA in mind, has run rather to coats and skirts and common sense. She would have been a success in an office and worth perhaps thirty shillings a week. But the HUXTABLES don't want another thirty shillings a week and this gift, such as it it is, has been wasted, so that EMMA runs also to a brusque temper.

JANE is meekly enough a little wild. MRS HUXTABLE'S power of applying the brake of good breeding, strong enough over five daughters, waned at the sixth attempt in twelve years, and JANE has actually got herself proposed to twice by not quite desirable young men. Now the fact that she was old enough to be proposed to at all came as something of a shock to the family. Birthdays pass, their celebration growing less emphatic. No one likes to believe that the years are passing; even the birthday's owner, least able to escape its significance, laughs and then changes the subject. So the MISS HUXTABLES never openly asked each other what the marriage of the youngest of them might imply; perhaps they never even asked themselves. Besides, JANE didn't marry. But if she does, unless perhaps she runs away to do it, there will be heart searchings at least. MR HUXTABLE asked though, and MRS HUXTABLE's answer – given early one morning before the hot water came scarcely satisfied him 'For,' said MR HUXTABLE 'if the girls don't marry some day what are they to do! It's not as if they had to go into the shop.'No, thank Heaven!' said MRS HUXTABLE.

Since his illness MR HUXTABLE has taken to asking questions – of anybody and about anything; of himself oftenest of all. But for that illness he would have been a conventional enough type of successful shop-keeper, coarsely fed, whiskered, podgy. But eighteen months' nursing and dieting and removal from the world seem to have brought a gentleness to his voice, a spark of humour to his eye, a childishness to his little bursts of temper – they have added, in fact, a wistfulness which makes him rather a lovable old buffer on the whole. This is a Sunday morning, a bright day in October. The family are still at church and the drawing-room is empty. The door opens and the parlourmaid – much becapped and aproned – shows in PHILIP MADRAS and his friend MAJOR

HIPPISLY THOMAS. THOMAS, long-legged and deliberate, moves across the room to the big French windows which open on to a balcony and look down on the garden and to many gardens beyond. THOMAS is a good fellow. PHILIP MADRAS is more complex than that. To begin with, it is obvious he is not wholly English. A certain litheness of figure, the keenness and colour of his voice, and a liking for metaphysical turns of speech show an Eastern origin perhaps. He is kind in manner but rather cold, capable of that least English of dispositions – intellectual passion. He is about thirty-five, a year or two younger than his friend. The parlour-maid has secured MAJOR THOMAS's hat and stands clutching it. As PHILIP passes her into the room he asks...

PHILIP. About how long ?

THE MAID. In just a few minutes now, I should say, sir. Oh, I beg pardon, does it appen to be the third Sunday in the month?

PHILIP. I don't know. Tommy, does it?

THOMAS *(from the window)*. Don't ask me. Well, I suppose I can tell you. *(And he vaguely fishes for his diary)*.

THE MAID. No, I don't think it does, sir. Because then some of them stop for the Oly Communion and that may make them late for dinner, but I don't think it is, sir.

She backs through the door, entangling the hat in the handle.

PHILIP. Is my mother still staying here?

THE MAID. Mrs Madras, sir. Yes, sir.

Then having disentangled the hat, the parlour-maid vanishes. PHILIP thereupon plunges swiftly into what must be an interrupted argument.

PHILIP. Well, my dear Tommy, what are the two most important things in a man's character? His attitude towards money and his attitude towards women.

THOMAS. *(ponderously slowing him up)*. Yes, you're full up with moral precepts. Why behave about money as if it didn't exist? I never said don't join the County Council.

PHILIP. *(deliberately, but in a breath)*. It is quite impossible for any decent man to walk with his eyes open from Waterloo to Denmark Hill on a Sunday morning without wishing me to stand for the County Council.

THOMAS *entrenches himself on a sofa.*

THOMAS. You've got what I call the Reformer's mind. I shouldn't cultivate it, Phil. It makes a man unhappy and discontented, not with himself, but with other people, mark you...so it makes him conceited and puts him out of condition both ways. Don't you get to imagine you can make this country better by tidying it up.

PHILIP. *(whimsically)*. But I'm very interested in England, Tommy.

THOMAS. *(not without some answering humour)*. We all are. But we don't all need to go about saying so. Even I can be interested in England, I suppose, though I have had to chuck the Army and take to business to earn bread and treacle for a wife and four children...and not a bad thing for me either. I tell you if every chap would look after himself and his family and lead a godly, righteous and sober life – I'm sorry, but it is Sunday – England would get on a damn sight better than it will with all your interference.

He leans back. PHILIP' s eyes fix themselves on some great distance.

PHILIP. It's a muddled country. One's first instinct is to be rhetorical about it...to write poetry and relieve one's feelings. I once thought I might be self-sacrificing - give my goods to the poor and go slumming - keeping my immortal soul superior still. There's something wrong with a world, Tommy, in which it takes a man like me all his time to find out that it's bread people want, and not either cake or crumbs.

THOMAS. There's something wrong with a man while he will think of other people as if they were ants on an ant heap.

PHILIP. *(relaxing to a smile)*. Tommy, that's perfectly true. I like having a good talk with you: sooner or later you always say one sensible thing.

THOMAS. Thank you; you're damn polite. And as usual, we've got right off the point.

PHILIP. The art of conversation!

THOMAS. *(shying at the easy epigram)*. Go on six County Councils if you like. But why chuck up seven hundred a year and a directorship if State wants you to keep 'em? And you could have double or more and manage the place if you'd ask for it.

PHILIP. *(almost venomously)*. Tommy, I loathe the Madras House. State may buy it and do what he likes with it.

JULIA and LAURA arrive. They are the first from Church. Sunday frocks, Sunday hats, best gloves, umbrellas and prayer books.

JULIA. Oh, what a surprise !

PHILIP. Yes, we walked down. Ah, you don't know...Let me introduce Major Hippisly Thomas...my cousin, Miss Julia Huxtable...and Miss Huxtable.

JULIA. How do you do?

THOMAS. How do you do?

LAURA. How do you do?

JULIA. Have you come to see Aunt Amy?

PHILIP. No, your father.

JULIA. He's walking back with her. They'll be last, I'm afraid.

LAURA. Will you stay to dinner?

PHILIP. No, I think not.

LAURA. I'd better tell them you won't. Perhaps they'll be laying for you.

LAURA goes out, decorously avoiding a collision with EMMA, who, panoplied as the others, comes in at the same moment.

PHILIP. Hullo, Emma !

EMMA. Well, what a surprise!

PHILIP. You don't know...Major Hippisly Thomas...Miss Emma Huxtable.

THOMAS. How do you do?

EMMA. How do you do? Will you stay to dinner?

PHILIP. No, we can't. *(That formula again completed, he varies his explanation.)* I've just brought Thomas a Sunday morning walk to help me tell Uncle Henry a bit of news. My father will be back in England tomorrow.

EMMA. *(with a round mouth).* Oh!

JULIA. It's a beautiful morning for a walk, isn't it?

THOMAS. Wonderful for October.

These two look first at each other, and then out of the window. EMMA gazes quizzically at PHILIP.

EMMA. I think he knows.

PHILIP. He sort of knows.

EMMA. Why are you being odd, Philip?

PHILIP is more hail-fellow-well-met with EMMA than with the others.

PHILIP. Emma...I have enticed a comparative stranger to be present so that your father and mother cannot in decency begin to fight the family battle over again with me. I know it's very cunning, but we did want a walk. Besides, there's a meeting tomorrow...

JANE peeps through the door.

JANE. You? Mother!

She has turned to the hall, and from the hall comes MRS HUXTABLE'S rotund voice, 'Yes, Jane!'

JANE. Cousin Philip !

MRS HUXTABLE sails in and superbly compresses every family greeting into one.

MRS HUXTABLE. What a surprise! Will you stay to dinner?

EMMA. *(alive to a certain redundancy).* No, Mother, they can't.

PHILIP. May I introduce my friend...Major Hippisly Thomas...my aunt, Mrs Huxtable.

MRS HUXTABLE. *(stately and gracious).* How do you do, Major Thomas?

PHILIP. Thomas is Mr Eustace State's London manager.

THOMAS. How do you do?

MRS HUXTABLE takes an armchair with the air of one mounting a throne, and from that vantage point begins polite conversation. Her daughters distribute themselves, so do PHILIP and HIPPISLY THOMAS.

MRS HUXTABLE. Not in the Army, then, Major Thomas?

THOMAS. I was in the Army.

EMMA. Jessica quite well, Philip?

PHILIP. Yes, thanks.

EMMA. And Mildred?

PHILIP. I think so. She's back at school.

MRS HUXTABLE. A wonderfully warm autumn, is it not?

THOMAS. Quite.

MRS HUXTABLE. Do you know Denmark Hill well?

THOMAS. Not well.

MRS HUXTABLE. We have always lived here. I consider it healthy. But London is a healthy place, I think. Oh, I beg your pardon...my daughter Jane.

JANE. How do you do?

They shake hands with ceremony. EMMA, in a mind to liven things up, goes to the window.

EMMA. We've quite a good garden, that's one thing.

THOMAS. *(not wholly innocent of an attempt to escape from his hostess, makes for the window, too).* I noticed it. I am keen on gardens.

MRS HUXTABLE. *(her attention distracted by JULIA'S making for the door).* Julia, where are you going?

JULIA. To take my things off, Mother.

JULIA departs. When they were quite little girls MRS HUXTABLE always did ask her daughters where they were going when they left the room and where they had been when they entered it and she has never dropped the habit. They resent it only by the extreme patience of their replies.

EMMA. *(entertainingly).* That's the Crystal Palace.

THOMAS. Is it?

They both peer appreciatively at that famous landmark. In the Crystal Palace and the sunset the inhabitants of Denmark Hill have acquired almost proprietary interest. Then MRS HUXTABLE speaks to her nephew with a sudden severity.

MRS HUXTABLE. Philip, I don't consider your mother's health is at all the thing !

PHILIP. *(amicably).* It never is, Aunt Kate.

MRS HUXTABLE. *(admitting the justice of the retort).* That's true.

PHILIP. Uncle Henry keeps better, I think.

MRS HUXTABLE. He's well enough now. I have had a slight cold. Is it true that your father may appear in England again?

PHILIP. Yes. he has only been on the Continent. He arrives tomorrow.

MRS HUXTABLE. I'm sorry.

JANE. Mother!

MRS HUXTABLE has launched this with such redoubled severity that JANE had to protest. However, at this moment arrives MR HUXTABLE himself; one glad smile.

MR HUXTABLE. Ah, Phil...I ad an idea you might come over. You'll stay to dinner. Jane, tell your aunt...she's taking er bonnet off.

JANE obeys. He sights on the balcony MAJOR THOMAS's back.

MR HUXTABLE. Who's that outside?

PHILIP. Hippisly Thomas. We wanted a walk; we can't stay.

MR HUXTABLE. Oh.

MRS HUXTABLE. Have you come on business?

PHILIP. Well...

MRS HUXTABLE. On Sunday?

PHILIP. Not exactly.

She shakes her head, gravely deprecating. THOMAS comes from the balcony.

MR HUXTABLE. Ow are you?

THOMAS. How are you?

MR HUXTABLE. Fine morning, isn't it? Nice prospect this...see the Crystal Palace?

While THOMAS turns with perfect politeness to view again this phenomenon, PHILIP pacifies his aunt.

PHILIP. You see, Aunt Katherine, tomorrow afternoon we have the first real conference with this Mr State about buying up the two firms, and my father is passing through England again to attend it.

MRS HUXTABLE. Of course, Philip, if it's business I know nothing about it. But is it suggested that your uncle should attend too?

Her voice has found a new gravity. PHILIP becomes very airy; so does MR HUXTABLE, who comes back to rejoin the conversation.

PHILIP. My dear, aunt, naturally.

MR HUXTABLE. What's this?

MRS HUXTABLE. *(the one word expressing volumes).* Constantine.

MR HUXTABLE. *(with elaborate innocence).* That's definite now, is it?

MRS HUXTABLE. You dropped a hint last night, Henry.

MR HUXTABLE. I dessay. I dessay I did. *(His eye shifts guiltily.)*

MRS HUXTABLE. Quite out of the question it seems to me.

JANE comes back.

JANE. Aunt Mary's coming.

MR HUXTABLE. *(genial again)* Oh.My daughter Jane...Major Thomas, Major Hippisly Thomas.

JANE. *(with discretion).* Yes, Father.

MRS HUXTABLE. *(tactfully).* You are naturally not aware, Major Thomas, that for family reasons into which we need not go, MR HUXTABLE has not spoken to his brother-in-law for a number of years.

PHILIP's eye meets THOMAS's in comic agony. But MR HUXTABLE too plunges delightedly into the forbidden subject.

MR HUXTABLE. Thirty years very near. Wonderful, isn't it? Interested in the same business. Wasn't easy to keep it up.

THOMAS. I had heard.

MR HUXTABLE. Oh yes, notorious.

MRS HUXTABLE. *(in reprobation).* And well it may be, Henry.*MRS MADRAS comes in. It is evident that PHILIP is his father's son. He would seem so wholly, but for that touch of 'self worship which is often self mistrust'; his mother's gift, appearing nowadays less lovably in her as a sort of querulous assertion of her rights and wrongs against the troubles which have been too strong for her. She is a pale old lady, shrunk a little, the life gone out of her.*

MRS HUXTABLE. *(some severity remaining)* Amy, your husband is in England again.

PHILIP presents a filial cheek. It is kissed.

PHILIP. How are you, Mother?

MR HUXTABLE. *(sotto voce).* Oh tact, Katherine, tact!

PHILIP. Perhaps you remember Reggie Thomas?

THOMAS. I was at Marlborough with Philip, Mrs Madras.

MRS MADRAS. Yes. Is he, Katherine?

Having given THOMAS a limp hand and her sister this coldest of responses, she finds her way to a sofa, where she sits silent, thinking to herself. MRS HUXTABLE keeps majestic hold upon her subject.

MRS HUXTABLE. I am utterly unable to see, Philip, why your uncle should break through this rule now.

MR HUXTABLE. There you are, Phil!

PHILIP. Of course it is quite for Uncle Henry to decide.

MR HUXTABLE. Naturally...naturally. *(still he has an appealing eye on PHILIP, who obliges him.)*

PHILIP. But since Mr State's offer may not be only for the Madras House but Roberts and Huxtable into the bargain...if the two principal proprietors can't meet him round a table to settle the matter...

THOMAS. *(ponderously diplomatic).* Yes...a little awkward...if I may say so...as Mr State's representative, MRS HUXTABLE.

MRS HUXTABLE. You don't think, do you, Major Thomas, that any amount of awkwardness should induce us to pass over wicked conduct?

This reduces the assembly to such a shamed silence that poor MR HUXTABLE can only add –

MR HUXTABLE. Oh, talk of something else...talk of something else.

After a moment MRS MADRAS'S pale voice steals in, as she turns to her son.

MRS MADRAS. When did you hear from your father?

PHILIP. A letter from Marienbad two or three days ago and a telegram yesterday morning.

MRS HUXTABLE, with a hostess's authority, now restores a polite and easy tone to the conversation.

MRS HUXTABLE. And have you left the Army long, Major Thomas?

THOMAS. Four years.

MRS HUXTABLE. Now what made you take to the Drapery Trade?

PHILIP. *(very explanatory).* Mr State is an American financier, Aunt Kitty, who has bought up Burrow's, the big mantle place in the city, and is about to buy us up too, perhaps.

MRS HUXTABLE. We are not in difficulties, I hope.

PHILIP. Oh, no.

MRS HUXTABLE. No. No doubt Henry would have told me if we had been.

As she thus gracefully dismisses the subject there appear up the steps and along the balcony the last arrivals from Church, MINNIE and CLARA. The male part of the company unsettles itself.

MR HUXTABLE. Ullo! Where have you been?

MINNIE. We went for a walk.

MRS HUXTABLE. *(in apparently deep surprise).* A walk, Minnie! Where to?

MINNIE. Just the long way home. We thought we'd have the time.

CLARA. Did you notice what a short sermon?

MR HUXTABLE. Oh, may I...My daughter Clara...Major Ippisly Thomas. My daughter Minnie...Major Thomas.

The conventional chant begins.

MINNIE. How d'you do?

THOMAS. How d'you do?

CLARA. How d'you do?

MINNIE. How d'you do, Philip?

PHILIP. How d'you do?

CLARA. How d'you do?

PHILIP. How d'you do?

The chant over, the company re-settles; MR HUXTABLE buttonholing PHILIP in the process with an air of some mystery.

MR HUXTABLE. By the way, Phil, remind me to ask you something before you go...rather important.

PHILIP. I shall be at your place in the morning. Thomas is coming to go through some figures.

MR HUXTABLE. *(with a regular snap).* Yes...I shan't.

PHILIP. The State meeting is in Bond Street, three o'clock.

MR HUXTABLE. I know, I know. *(Then, finding himself prominent, he captures the conversation).* I'm slacking off, Major Thomas, slacking off. Ever since I was ill I've been slacking off.

MRS HUXTABLE. You are perfectly well now, Henry.

MR HUXTABLE. Not the point. I want leisure, you know, leisure. Time for reading...time to think a bit.

MRS HUXTABLE. Nonsense! *(She adds, with correctness).* Major Thomas will excuse me.

MR HUXTABLE. ,*(on his hobby).* Oh, well...a man must...some portion of his life...

THOMAS. Quite. I got most of my reading done early.

MRS HUXTABLE. The natural time for it.

MR HUXTABLE. Ah lucky feller! Educated, I suppose. Well, I wasn't. I've been getting the books for years – good editions. I'd like you to see my library. But these geniuses want settling down to...if a man's to keep pace with the thought of the world, y'know. Macaulay, Erbert Spencer, Grote's Istory of Greece! I've got em all there.

He finds no further response, MRS HUXTABLE fills the gap.

MRS HUXTABLE. I thought the sermon dull this morning, Amy, didn't you?

MRS MADRAS. *(unexpectedly).* No, I didn't.

MINNIE. *(to do her share of the entertaining).* Mother, somebody ought to speak about those boys...it's disgraceful. Mr Vivian had actually to turn round from the organ at them during the last hymn.

JULIA, her things taken off, re-appears. MR HUXTABLE is on the spot.

MR HUXTABLE. Ah, my daughter Julia...Major –

JULIA. We've been introduced, Father.

She says this with a hauteur which really is pure nervousness, but MR HUXTABLE is sufficiently crushed.

MR HUXTABLE. Oh, I beg pardon.

But MRS HUXTABLE disapproves of any self-assertion and descends upon the culprit; who is for some obscure reason (or none) more often disapproved of than the others.

MRS HUXTABLE. Close the door, please, Julia.

JULIA. I'm sorry, Mother.

PHILIP closes the offending door. JULIA obliterates herself in a chair, and the conversation, hardly encouraged by this little affray, comes to an intolerable standstill. At last CLARA makes an effort.

CLARA. Is Jessica quite well, Philip?

PHILIP. Yes thank you, Clara.

MRS HUXTABLE. And dear little Mildred?

PHILIP. Yes thank you, Aunt Kate.

Further standstill. Then MINNIE contrives a remark.

MINNIE. Do you still like that school for her?

PHILIP. *(with finesse).* It seems to provide every accomplishment that money can buy.

MRS HUXTABLE discovers a sure opening.

MRS HUXTABLE. Have you been away for the summer, Major Thomas?

THOMAS. *(vaguely – he is getting sympathetically tongue-tied).* Oh...yes...

PHILIP. Tommy and Jessica and I took our holidays motoring around Munich and into it for the operas.

MRS HUXTABLE. Was that pleasant?

PHILIP. Very.

MRS HUXTABLE. And where was dear Mildred?

PHILIP. With her aunt most of the time...Jessica's sister-in-law, you know.

MINNIE. Lady Ames?

PHILIP. Yes.

MRS HUXTABLE. *(innocently, genuinely mobbish)*. Very nice for her.

MR HUXTABLE. We take a ouse at Weymouth as a rule.

MRS HUXTABLE. Do you know Weymouth, Major Thomas?

THOMAS. No, I don't.

MRS HUXTABLE. George III used to stay there, but that is a hotel now.

MR HUXTABLE. Keep your spare money in the country, y' know.

MRS HUXTABLE. Oh, and there is everything one wants at Weymouth.

But even this subject flags.

MRS HUXTABLE. You think more of Bognor, Amy, I know.

MRS MADRAS. Only to live in, Katherine.

They have made their last effort. The conversation is dead. MR HUXTABLE'S discomfort suddenly becomes physical.

MR HUXTABLE. I'm going to change my coat.

PHILIP. I think perhaps we ought to be off.

MR HUXTABLE. No, no, no, no, no, I shan't be a minute. Don't go, Phil; there's a good fellow.

And he has left them all to it. The HUXTABLE conversation, it will be noticed, consists mainly of asking questions. Visitors after a time fall into the habit too.

PHILIP. Do you like this house better than the old one, Clara?

CLARA. It has more rooms, you know.

MRS HUXTABLE. Do you live in London, Major Thomas?

THOMAS. No, I live at Woking. I come up and down every day. I think the country's better for the children.

MRS HUXTABLE. Not a cheerful place, is it?

THOMAS. Oh, very cheerful!

MRS HUXTABLE. I had thought not for some reason.

EMMA. The cemetery, Mother.

MRS HUXTABLE. *(accepting the suggestion with dignity)*. Perhaps.

CLARA. And of course there's a much larger garden. We have the garden of the next house as well.

JANE. Not all the garden of the next house.

CLARA. Well, most of it.

This stimulating difference of opinion takes them to the balcony. PHILIP follows. JULIA follows PHILIP. MINNIE departs to take her things off.

JULIA. Do you notice how near the Crystal Palace seems? That means rain.

PHILIP. Of course...you can see the Crystal Palace.

MRS HUXTABLE. Julia, do you think you won't catch cold on the balcony without a hat?

JULIA. *(meek, but before the visitor, determined).* I don't think so, Mother.

MRS HUXTABLE turns with added politeness, to MAJOR THOMAS.

MRS HUXTABLE. Yes, we used to live not so far along the hill; it certainly was a smaller house.

PHILIP is now on the balcony receiving more information.

PHILIP. That's Ruskin's house, is it? Yes, I see the chimney pots.

MRS HUXTABLE. I should not have moved, myself, but I was overruled.

EMMA. Mother, we had grown out of Hollybank.

MRS HUXTABLE. I was overruled. Things are done on a larger scale than they used to be. Not that I approve of that.

THOMAS. Of course one's family will grow up.

MRS HUXTABLE. People spend their money now-a-days. I remember my father's practice was to live on half his income. However, he lost the greater part of his money by unwise investments in lead, I think it was. I was at school at the time in Brighton. And he educated me above my station in life.

At this moment CLARA breaks out of the conservatory. Something has happened.

CLARA. Jane, the Agapanthus is out at last.

JANE. Oh!

They crowd in to see it. PHILIP crowds in, too. MRS HUXTABLE is unmoved.

MRS HUXTABLE. We are told that riches are a snare, Major Thomas.

THOMAS. It is one I have always found easy to avoid, Mrs Huxtable.

MRS HUXTABLE. *(oblivious of the joke, which indeed she would not have expected on such a subject).* And I have noticed that their acquisition seldom improves the character of people in my station of life. I am of course ignorant of my husband's affairs...that is to say, I keep myself as ignorant as possible...but it is my wish that the ordering of our household should remain as it was when we were first married.

THOMAS. *(forestalling a yawn).* Quite so. Quite so.

MRS HUXTABLE takes a breath.

MRS HUXTABLE. A family of daughters, Major Thomas...

EMMA. *(a little agonized).* Mother!

MRS HUXTABLE. What is it, Emma?

But EMMA thinks better of it and goes to join the Agapanthus party, saying -

EMMA. Nothing, Mother, I beg your pardon.

MRS HUXTABLE retakes her breath.

MRS HUXTABLE. What were we saying?

THOMAS. *(with resigned politeness).* A family of daughters.

MRS HUXTABLE. Yes. Were you in the war?

The inexplicable but characteristic suddenness of this rouses the MAJOR a little.

THOMAS. I was.

MRS HUXTABLE. I find that people look differently on family life to what they used. A man no longer seems prepared to marry and support a wife and family by his unaided exertions. I consider that a pity.

THOMAS. *(near another yawn).* Quite...quite so.

MRS HUXTABLE. I have always determined that my daughters should be sought after for themselves alone. That should ensure their happiness. Any eligible gentleman who visits here constantly is always given to understand, delicately, that nothing need be expected from Mr Huxtable beyond his approval. You are married, I think you said, Major Thomas.

This quite wakes him up, though MRS HUXTABLE is really innocent of her implication.

THOMAS. Yes, oh, dear me, yes.

MRS HUXTABLE. And a family?

THOMAS. Four children...the youngest is only three.

MRS HUXTABLE. Pretty dear!

THOMAS. No, ugly little beggar, but has character.

MRS HUXTABLE. I must take off my things before dinner. You'll excuse me. If one is not punctual oneself...

THOMAS. Quite.

MRS HUXTABLE. We cannot induce you to join us?

THOMAS. Many thanks, but we have to meet Mrs Phil for lunch in town at two.

MRS HUXTABLE. I am sorry.

THOMAS opens the door for her with his best bow and she graciously departs, conscious of having properly impressed him. CLARA, who has now her things to take off, crosses the room, saying to PHILIP, who follows her from the balcony –

CLARA. Yes, I'll tell father, Philip. I'm going upstairs.

THOMAS opens the door for her, but only with his second best bow, and then turns to PHILIP with a sigh.

THOMAS. Phil, we ought to be going.

PHILIP. Wait till you've seen my uncle again.

THOMAS. All right.

He heaves another sigh and sits down. All this time there has been MRS MADRAS upon her sofa, silent, as forgotten as any other piece of furniture for which there is no immediate use. PHILIP now goes to her. When she does speak it is unresponsively.

PHILIP. How long do you stay in town, Mother?

MRS MADRAS. I have been here a fortnight. I generally stay three weeks.

PHILIP. Jessica has been meaning to ask you to Phillimore Gardens again.

MRS MADRAS. Has she?

PHILIP. *(a little guiltily).* Her time's very much occupied...with one thing and another.

Suddenly MRS MADRAS rouses herself.

MRS MADRAS. I wish to see your father, Philip.

PHILIP. *(in doubt).* He won't be here long, Mother.

MRS MADRAS. No, I am sure he won't.

With three delicate strides THOMAS lands himself on to the balcony.

PHILIP. Tommy being tactful! Well, I'll say that you want to see him.

MRS MADRAS. No, please don't. Tell him that I think he ought to come and see me.

PHILIP. He won't come, Mother.

MRS MADRAS. No, I know he won't. He came to England in May, didn't he? He was here till July, wasn't he? Did he so much as send me a message?

PHILIP. *(with unkind patience).* No, Mother.

MRS MADRAS. What was he doing all the while, Philip?

PHILIP. I didn't see much of him. I really don't know what he came back for at all. We could have done this business without him, and anyway it hasn't materialized till now. This is why he's passing through England again. I don't think there's much to be gained by your seeing him, you know.

MRS MADRAS. You are a little heartless, Philip.

This being a little true, PHILIP a little resents it.

PHILIP. My dear mother, you and he have been separated for...how long is it?

MRS MADRAS. *(with withered force).* I am his wife still, I should hope. He went away from me when he was young. But I have never forgotten my duty. And now that he is an old man and past such sin and I am an old woman, I am still ready to be a comfort to his declining years, and it's right that I should be allowed to tell him so. And you should not let your wife put you against your own mother, Philip.

PHILIP. *(bewildered).* Really!

MRS MADRAS. I know what Jessica thinks of me. Jessica is very clever and has no patience with people who can do their best to be good...I understand that. Well, it isn't her duty to love me...at least it may not be her duty to love her husband's mother, or it may be, I don't say. But it is your duty. I sometimes think, Philip, you don't love me any longer, though you're afraid to say so.

The appeal ends so pathetically that PHILIP is very gently equivocal.

PHILIP. If I didn't love you, my dear mother, I should be afraid to say so.

MRS MADRAS. When are you to see your father?

PHILIP. We've asked him to dinner tomorrow night.

At this moment EMMA comes in with a briskness so jarring to poor MRS MADRAS's already wrought nerves, that she turns on her.

MRS MADRAS. Emma, why do you come bouncing in like that when I'm trying to get a private word with Philip ?

EMMA. Really, Aunt Amy, the drawing-room belongs to everyone.

MRS MADRAS. I'm sure I don't know why I come and stay here at all. I dislike your mother intensely.

EMMA. Then kindly don't tell me so. I've no wish not to be polite to you.

PHILIP *(pacifically).* Emma, I think Uncle Henry ought to attend this meeting tomorrow.

MRS MADRAS. *(beginning to cry).* Of course he ought. Who is he to go on like this about Constantine! My handkerchief's upstairs.

EMMA. *(contritely).* Shall I fetch it for you. Aunt Amy?

MRS MADRAS. No, I'll be a trouble to no one.

She retires, injured. PHILIP continues, purposely placid.

PHILIP. What's more, he really wants to attend it.

EMMA. I'm sorry I was rude...but she does get on our nerves, you know.

PHILIP. Why do you invite her ?

EMMA. *(quite jolly with him).* Oh, we're all very fond of Aunt Amy, and anyhow mother would think it our duty. I don't see how she can enjoy coming though. She never goes out anywhere...never joins in the conversation...just sits nursing herself.

PHILIP. *(quizzically).* You're all too good, Emma.

EMMA. Yes. I heard you making fun of Julia in the conservatory. But if one stopped doing one's duty how upside down the world would be! *(Her voice now takes that tone which is the well-bred substitute for a wink.)* I say...I suppose I oughtn't to tell you about Julia, but it is rather a joke. You know Julia gets hysterical sometimes when she has her headaches.

PHILIP. Does she?

EMMA. Well, a collar marked Lewis Waller came back from the wash in mistake for one of father's. I don't think he lives near here, but it's one of these big steam laundries. And Morgan the cook got it and she gave it to Julia...and Julia kept it. And when mother found out she cried for a whole day. She said it showed a wanton mind.

PHILIP's mocking face becomes grave.

PHILIP. I don't think that's at all amusing, Emma.

EMMA. *(in genuine surprise).* Don't you?

PHILIP. How old is Julia?

EMMA. She's thirty-four. *(Her face falls too).* No...it is rather dreadful, isn't it? *(Then wrinkling her forehead as at a puzzle).* It isn't exactly that one wants to get married. I daresay mother is right about that.

PHILIP. About what?

EMMA. Well, some time ago, a gentleman proposed to Jane. And mother said it would have been more honourable if he had spoken to father first, and that Jane was the youngest and too young to know her own mind. Well, you know, she's twenty-six. And then they heard of something he'd once done and it was put a stop to. And Jane was very rebellious and mother cried...

PHILIP. Does she always cry ?

EMMA. Yes, she does cry if she's upset about us. And I think she was right. One ought not to risk being unhappy for life, ought one?

PHILIP. Are you all happy now, then?

EMMA. Oh, deep down, I think we are. It would be so ungrateful not to be. When one has a good home and...! But of course living together and going away together and being together all the time, one does get a little irritable now and then. I suppose that's why we sit as mum as maggots when people are here, we're afraid of squabbling.

PHILIP. Do you squabble?

EMMA. Not like we used. You know till we moved into this house we had only two bedrooms between us, the nursery and the old night nursery. Now Laura and Minnie have one each and there's one we take by turns. There wasn't a bigger house to be got here or I suppose we could have had it. They hated the idea of moving far. And it's rather odd, you know, father seems afraid of spending money, though he must have got lots. He says if he gave us any more we shouldn't know what to do with it,...and of course that's true.

PHILIP. But what occupations have you girls?

EMMA. We're always busy. I mean there's lots to be done about the house and there's calling and classes and things. Julia used to sketch quite well. You mustn't think I'm grumbling, Philip. I know I talk too much. They tell me so.

PHILIP's comment is the question, half serious.

PHILIP. Why don't you go away, all six of you, or say five of you?

EMMA. *(wide-eyed).* Go away!

PHILIP. *(comprehensively).* Out of it.

EMMA. *(wider-eyed).* Where to?

PHILIP. *(with a sigh - for her).* Ah, that's just it.

EMMA. How could one! And it would upset them dreadfully. Father and Mother don't know that one feels like this at times...they'd be very grieved.

PHILIP turns to her with kindly irony.

PHILIP. Emma, people have been worrying your father at the shop lately about the drawbacks of the living-in system. Why don't you ask him to look at home for them?

MR HUXTABLE returns, at ease in a jacket. He puts his daughter kindly on the shoulder.

MR HUXTABLE. Now run along, Jane...I mean Emma...I want a word with your cousin.

EMMA. Yes, Father.

EMMA–JANE–obediently disappears. PHILIP then looks sideways at his uncle

PHILIP. I've come over, as you asked me to.

MR HUXTABLE. I didn't ask you.

PHILIP. You dropped a hint.

MR HUXTABLE. *(almost with a blush).* Did I? I dessay I did.

PHILIP. But you must hurry up and decide about the meeting tomorrow. Thomas and I have got to go.

MR HUXTABLE. Phil, I suppose you're set on selling.

PHILIP. Quite.

MR HUXTABLE. You young men! The Madras Ouse means nothing to you.

PHILIP. *(anti-sentimental).* Nothing unsaleable, Uncle.

MR HUXTABLE. Well, well, well! *(Then in a furtive fuss.)* Well just a minute, my boy, before your aunt comes down...she's going on at me upstairs, y'know ! Something you must do for me tomorrow, like a good feller, at the shop in the morning. *(He suddenly becomes portentous.)* Have you heard this yet about Miss Yates?

PHILIP. No.

MR HUXTABLE. Disgraceful ! Disgraceful ! !

PHILIP. She got on very well in Bond Street...learnt a good deal. She has only been back a few weeks.

MR HUXTABLE. *(snorting derisively).* Learnt a good deal! *(Then he sights THOMAS on the balcony and hails him.)* Oh, come in, Major Thomas. *(And dropping his voice again ominously.)* Shut the window if you don't mind; we don't want the ladies to hear this.

THOMAS shuts the window and MR HUXTABLE spreads himself to the awful enjoyment of imparting scandal.

MR HUXTABLE. I tell you, my boy, up at your place, got hold of she's been by some feller...some West End Club feller, I dessay...and he's put her in the...well, I tell you! ! Major Thomas will excuse me. Not a chit of a girl, mind you, but first hand in our Costume room. Buyer we were going to make her and all !

PHILIP frowns, both at the news and at his uncle's manner of giving it.

PHILIP. What do you want me to do?

MR HUXTABLE. *(more portentous than ever).* You wait, that's not what's the worst of it. You know Brigstock.

PHILIP. Do I?

MR HUXTABLE. Oh, yes, third man in the Osiery.

PHILIP. True.

MR HUXTABLE. Well...it seems that more than a week ago Miss Chancellor had caught them kissing.

PHILIP. *(his impatience of the display growing).* Caught who kissing?

MR HUXTABLE. I know it ain't clear. Let's go back to the beginning... Major Thomas will excuse me.

THOMAS *(showing the properest feeling).* Not at all.

MR HUXTABLE. Wednesday afternoon, Willoughby, that's our doctor, comes up as usual. Miss Yates goes in to see him. Miss Chancellor – that's our housekeeper, Major Thomas–over'ears, quite by accident, so she says, and afterwards taxes her with it.

PHILIP. Unwise.

MR HUXTABLE. No, no, her plain duty...she knows my principle about such things. But then she remembers about the kissing and that gets about among our young ladies. Somebody stupid there, I grant you, but you know what these things are. And then it gets about about Miss Yates...all over the shop. And then it turns out that Brigstock's a married man...been married two years...secret from us, you know, because he's living in and on promotion and all the rest. And yesterday morning his wife turns up in my office and has hysterics and says her husband's been slandered.

PHILIP. I don't see why Miss Yates should come to any particular harm at our place. A girl's only out of our sight at week ends and then we're supposed to know where she is.

MR HUXTABLE. (still instinctively spreading himself, but with that wistful look creeping on him now). Well...I had er up the day before. And I don't know what's coming over me. I scolded her well. I was in the right in all I said...but...! Have you ever suddenly eard your own voice saying a thing? Well, I did...and it sounded more like a dog barking than me. And I went funny all over. So I told her to leave the room. (He grows distressed and appealing.) And you must take it on, Phil...it ought to be settled tomorrow. Miss Yates must have the sack and I'm not sure Brigstock hadn't better have the sack. We don't want to lose Miss Chancellor, but really if she can't hold er tongue at her age...well, she'd better have...

PHILIP. (out of patience). Oh, nonsense, Uncle.

MR HUXTABLE. (his old unquestioning self asserted for a moment). No, I will not have these scandals in the shop. We've always been free of em...almost always. I don't want to be hard on the girl. If the man's in our employ and you can find im out...punish the guilty as well as the innocent...(That breath exhausted, he continues quite pathetically to THOMAS). But I do not know what's coming over me. Before I got ill I'd have tackled this business like winking. But when you're a long time in bed...I'd never been ill like that before...I dunno how it is...you get thinking...and things which used to be quite clear don't seem nearly so clear...and then after, when you start to do and say the things that used to come natural...they don't come so natural as they did and that puts you off something...

This is interrupted by the re-appearance of MRS HUXTABLE – lace-capped and ready for dinner. She is at the pitch to which the upstairs dispute with her husband evidently brought her. It would seem he bolted in the middle of it.

MRS HUXTABLE. Is it the fact, Philip, that if your uncle does not attend the meeting tomorrow that this business transaction with Mr – I forget his name

– the American gentleman...and which I of course know nothing about, will be seriously upset?

MR. HUXTABLE. *(joining battle).*Kitty, I don't see why I shouldn't go. If Constantine chooses to turn up...that is his business. I needn't speak directly to him...so to say.

MRS HUXTABLE. *(hurling this choice bolt from her vocabulary).* A quibble, Henry.

MR HUXTABLE. If he's leaving England now for good...

MRS HUXTABLE. But you do as you like, of course.

MR HUXTABLE. *(wistful again).* I should so like you to be convinced.

MRS HUXTABLE. Don't prevaricate, Henry. And your sister is just coming into the room. We had better drop the subject.

And in MRS MADRAS does come, but what with one thing and another MR HUXTABLE is now getting what he would call thoroughly put out.

MR HUXTABLE. Now if Amelia here was to propose seeing im –

MRS HUXTABLE. Henry...a little consideration!

MR HUXTABLE. *(goaded to the truth).* Well, I want to go, Kitty, and that's all about it. And I dropped a int, I did, to Phil to come over and help me through it with you. I thought he'd make it seem as if it was most pressing business...only he hasn't...so as to hurt your feelings less. Because I'd been bound to have told you afterwards or it might have slipped out somehow. Goodness gracious me, here's the Madras House, which I've sunk enough money in these last ten years to build a battleship very nearly...a small battleship, y'know...it's to be sold because Phil won't stand by me and his father don't care a button now. Not but what that's Constantine all over! Marries you, Amelia, behaves like a duke and an archangel mixed for eighteen months and then -

MRS HUXTABLE. *(scandalized 'Before visitors too!').* Henry!

MR HUXTABLE. All right, all right. And I'm not to attend this meeting, if you please!

The little storm subsides.

MRS MADRAS. It's to be sold, is it?

PHILIP. Yes, Mother.

MRS MADRAS. *(at her brother).* It was started with my money as well as yours.

MR HUXTABLE. is recovering and takes no notice.

PHILIP. Yes, Mother, we know.

MRS MADRAS. And if that's all you've lost by Constantine, I don't see you've a right to be so bitter against him.

She is still ignored. MR HUXTABLE quite cheery again, goes on affably.

MR HUXTABLE. D'you know, Major Thomas, that twenty year., ago when that shop began to be the talk of London, Duchesses have been known to go to all intents and purposes on their knees to him to design them a dress. Wouldn't do it unless he pleased – not unless he approved their figure. Ad Society under his thumb.

MRS HUXTABLE. *(from the height of respectability).* No doubt he knew his business.

MR HUXTABLE. *(in an ecstasy).* Knew his business! Knew his business ! ! My boy, in the old days...asked everywhere like one of themselves very nearly! First of his sort to break that barrier. D'you know, it's my belief that if Mrs Gladstone had been thirty years younger and a fashionable woman...he could have had a knighthood.

MRS HUXTABLE. *(explicitly).* He was untrue to his wife, Henry.

At this MR HUXTABLE is the moral man again. These sudden changes are so like him. They are genuine; he is just half conscious of their suddenness.

MR HUXTABLE. Yes, I know, and Amy did what she should have done. You see it wasn't an ordinary case, Major Thomas. It was girls in the shop. And even though he took em out of the shop...that's a slur on the whole trade. A man in his position...you can't overlook that.

MRS MADRAS. *(palely asserting herself).* I could have overlooked it if I had chosen.

PHILIP. *(to whom this is all so futile and foolish).* My dear mother, you were unhappy with my father and you left him...the matter is very simple.

MRS MADRAS. I beg your pardon, Philip...I was not unhappy with him.

MRS HUXTABLE. Amy, how could you be happy with a man who was unfaithful to you? What nonsense!

JANE and JULIA, from the balcony, finding the window locked, tap with their finger-nails upon the pane. The very sharpness of the sound begins to put out MR HUXTABLE again.

MR HUXTABLE. No, no, they can't come in. *(He mouths at them through the window).* You can't come in.

JANE mouths back.

MR HUXTABLE. What ? *(Then the sense of it coming to him he looks at his watch).* No, it isn't...two minutes yet.

And he turns away, having excluded the innocent mind from this unseemly discussion. But at the very moment LAURA comes in by the door. His patience flies.

MR HUXTABLE. Oh, damn! Well, I beg pardon. *(Then in desperate politeness)/.* Let me introduce...my daughter Laura...Major Thomas.

LAURA. *(collectedly).* We have met, Father.

MR HUXTABLE. *(giving it all up).* Well...how can I tell...there are so many of you !

MRS HUXTABLE. *(severely).* I think, Henry, you had better go to this meeting tomorrow.

MR HUXTABLE. *(wistful for a moment).* You thirlk I ought?

MRS HUXTABLE.. You know you ought not.

MR HUXTABLE. *(disputing it manfully)*. No...I don't know I ought not. It isn't so easy to know what ought and ought not to be done as you always make out, Kitty. And suppose I just do something wrong for once and see what happens.

MRS HUXTABLE. Henry, don't say such things.

MR HUXTABLE. *(very reasonably to MAJOR THOMAS)*. Well, since I've been ill –

But EMMA and MINNIE have come in now and JANE and, finding their exile a little unreasonable, rattle hard at the window. MR HUXTABLE gives it all up again.

MR HUXTABLE. Oh, let 'em in, Phil...there's a good feller.

THOMAS. Allow me. *(And he does so.)*

EMMA. *(crisply)*. Oh, what's it all been about?

MRS HUXTABLE. Never mind, Emma.

She says this to EMMA as she would have said it to her at the age of four. Meanwhile MR HUXTABLE has recovered.

MR HUXTABLE. You know, Major Thomas, Constantine could always get the better of me in little things.

JANE has sighted MINNIE and, callously, across the breadth of the room, imparts a tragedy.

JANE. Minnie, your frog's dead...in the conservatory.

MINNIE pales.

MINNIE. Oh, dear.

MR HUXTABLE....After the difterence I began to write to him as Dear Sir, to this day he'll send me business letters beginning Dear Arry.

MINNIE is hurrying to theglass house of death.

JANE. I buried it.

MR HUXTABLE.... Always at his ease, you know.

THOMAS escapes from him. PHILIP is bending over his mother a little kindlier.

PHILIP. I'll try to see you again before you go back to Bognor, Mother.

At this moment the gong rings. A tremendous gong, beloved of the English middle class, which makes any house seem small. A hollow sound: the dinner hour striking its own empty stomach. JANE, whose things are not taken off, gives a mitigated yelp and dashes for the door, dashes into the returning, tidy CLARA. MRS HUXTABLE shakes a finger.

MRS HUXTABLE. Late again, Jane.

PHILIP. We'll be off, Aunt Katherine.

MRS HUXTABLE. *(with a common humanity she has not shown before)*. Philip...never think I mean to be self-righteous about your father. But he made your mother most unhappy when you were too young to know of it...and there is the example to others, isn't there?

PHILIP. Yes...of course, Aunt Kate. I know just how you feel about it...I'm not fond of him either.

PHILIP must be a little mischievous with his aunt. She responds by returning at once to her own apparent self again.

MRS HUXTABLE. My dear boy...and your own father!

From the balcony one hears the tag of JULIA'S entertaining of MAJOR THOMAS. They have been peering at the horizon.

JULIA. Yes, it means rain...when you see it so clearly.

A general-post of leave-taking now begins.

PHILIP. Well, see you tomorrow, Uncle Henry.

MR HUXTABLE. Yes, I suppose so. Oh, and about that other matter ...

PHILIP. What can I do?

MR HUXTABLE. I'll telephone you in the morning.

PHILIP. Good-bye, Mother.

THOMAS. Good-bye Mrs Huxtable.

MRS HUXTABLE. *(with a final flourish of politeness).* You have excused this domestic discussion, I hope Major Thomas ... it will happen sometimes.

THOMAS. I've been most interested.

MINNIE comes back sadly from the frog's grave.

PHILIP. Good-bye Clara.

CLARA. Good-bye Philip.

MR HUXTABLE. You really won't stay to dinner?

PHILIP. Good-bye Laura.

THOMAS. Thanks, no. We meet tomorrow.

The general-post quickens, the chorus grows confused.

LAURA. Good-bye.

THOMAS. Good-bye.

JANE. Good-bye.

THOMAS. Good-bye.

PHILIP. Good-bye, Emma – oh, pardon.

There has been the confusion of crossed hands. Apologies, withdrawals, a treading on toes, more apologies.

EMMA. Good-bye Major Thomas.

PHILIP. Now good-bye, Emma.

THOMAS. Good-bye, Mrs Madras.

PHILIP. Good-bye.

THOMAS. Good-bye.

The chorus and the general-post continue, until at last PHILIP and THOMAS escape to a tram and a tube and their lunch, while the HUXTABLES sit down in all ceremony to Sunday dinner: roast beef, horse-radish, Yorkshire pudding, brown potatoes, Brussels sprouts, apple tart, custard and cream, Stilton cheese, dessert.

ACT II

The business offices of Roberts and Huxtable are tucked away upon the first floor somewhere at the back of that large drapery establishment. The waiting room – the one in which employee sits in shivering preparation for interviews with employer – besides thus having been the silent scene of more misery than most places on earth, is one of the very ugliest rooms that ever entered into the mind of a builder and decorator. Four plain walls of brick or plaster, with seats round them, would have left it a waiting room pure and simple. But the ugly hand of the money maker was upon it. In the person of a contractor he thrust upon the unfortunate room - as on all the others - everything that could excuse his price and disguise his profit. The walls, to start with, were distempered an unobjectionable green, but as that might seem too plain and cheap, a dado of a nice stone colour was added, topped with stencilling in dirty red of a pattern that once was Greek.

The fireplace is apparently designed to provide the maximum amount of work possible for the wretched boy who cleans it every morning, retiring from the contest well black-leaded himself. The mantelpiece above – only an expert in such abominations knows what it is made of; but it pretends, with the aid of worm-shaped dashes of paint, to be brown marble. It is too high for comfort, too low for dignity. It has to be dusted, and usually isn't.

The square lines of the two long windows, which look upon some sanitary brick airshaft, have been carefully spoilt by the ovaling of their top panes. The half glazed door, that opens from the passage, is of the wrong shape; the green baize door, that admits to MR PHILIP's room, is of the wrong colour.

And then the furnishing! Those yellow chairs upholstered in red cotton goose-flesh plush; that plush-seated, plush-backed bench, placed draughtily between the windows! There is a reasonable office table in the middle of the room. On the walls are, firstly, photographs of ROBERTS and HUXTABLE. ROBERTS was a Welshman and looks. No prosperous drapery business in London but has its Welshman. There is also a photograph of the premises – actual; and an advertisement sketch of them – ideal. There is a ten-year-old fashion plate: twenty faultless ladies engaged in ladylike occupations or serene in the lack of any. There is an insurance almanac, the one thing of beauty in the room. On the mantelpiece lies a London Directory, the one piece of true colour.

The hand of the money maker that has wrenched awry the Greek pattern on the wall has been laid also on all the four people who sit waiting for MR PHILIP at noon on this Monday; and to the warping more or less of them all.

MRS BRIGSTOCK, sitting stiffly on the plush bench, in brown quilled hat and coat and skirt, is, one would guess, a clerk of some sort. She lacks colour; she lacks repose; she lacks – one stops to consider that she might possibly be a beautiful woman were it not for the things she lacks. But she is the product of fifteen years or so of long hours and little lunch. Certainly at this moment she is not seen at her best. She sits twisting her gloved hands, pulling at a loose thread, now and then biting it. Otherwise she bites her lips; her face is drawn and she stares in front of *her with only a twist of the eye now and then towards her husband, who is uncomfortable upon a chair a few feet away.*

If one were asked to size up MR BRIGSTOCK, one would say: Nothing against him. The position of Third Man in the Hosiery does not require any special talents, and it doesn't get them; or if it does they don't stay there. And MR BRIGSTOCK stays there – just stays there. It sums him up – sums up millions of him – to say that in their youth they have energy enough to get into a position; afterwards in their terror – or sometimes only because their employers have not the heart to dismiss them – they stay there.

Sometimes, though, the employers have the heart and do. And then what happens? Considered as a man rather than a wage earner – not that it is usual for us so to consider him – he is one of those who happily for themselves get married by women whom apparently no other man much wants to marry. Subdued to what he works in, he is dressed as a Third Man in the Hosiery should be. He is, at the moment, as agitated as his wife and as he has no nervous force to be agitated with is in a state of greater wretchedness.

On the other side of the room sits MISS CHANCELLOR. Every large living-in draper's should have as housekeeper a lady of a certain age, who can embody in her own person the virtues she will expect in the young ladies under her. Decorum, sobriety of thought, tidiness, respect of persons - these are the qualities generally necessary to a shop-assistant's salvation. MISS CHANCELLOR radiates them. They are genuine in her, too. She is now planted squarely on her chair, as it might be in easy authority, but looking closely, one may see that it is a dignified resentment keeping her there unmovable.

In the middle of the room by the table sits MISS YATES. While they wait this long time the other three try hard to keep their eyes off her. It isn't easy; partly because she is in the middle of the room and they are not. But anyhow and anywhere MISS YATES is a person that you look at, though you may ignorantly wonder why. She is by no means pretty, nor does she try to attract you. But you look at her as you look at a fire or a light in an otherwise empty room. She is not a lady, nor is she well educated, and ten years' shop-assisting has left its marks on her. But there it is. To the seeing eye she glows in that room like a live coal. She has genius - she has life, to however low a use she – or the world for her – may put it. And commoner people are lustreless beside her.

They wait silently and the tension increases. At last it is slightly relieved by PHILIP'S arrival. He comes in briskly, his hat on, a number of unopened letters in his hand. They get up to receive him with varying degrees of respect and apprehension.

PHILIP. Good morning, Miss Chancellor. Good morning, Miss Yates. Good morning, Mr Brigstock.

MR BRIGSTOCK. *(introducing her).* Mrs Brigstock.

PHILIP nods pleasantly to MRS BRIGSTOCK, who purses her lips in a half-frightened, half-vengeful way, and sits down again. Then he puts his hat on the mantelpiece and settles himself in the master position at the table.

PHILIP. I'm afraid I've kept you waiting a little. Well, now –

There is a sharp knock at the door.

PHILIP. Come.

It is BELHAVEN. BELHAVEN is seventeen, perhaps, on the climb from office boy to clerk, of the usual pattern. PHILIP greets him pleasantly.

PHILIP. Oh, good morning, Bellhaven.

BELHAVEN. I've put Major Thomas in your room, sir, as the papers were there, but Mr Huxtable's is empty if you'd like...

PHILIP. No, this'll do.

BELHAVEN. Major Thomas said would you speak to him for a minute as soon as you came.

PHILIP. I'll go in now.

BELHAVEN. Thank you, sir.

PHILIP. *(to the waiting four).* Excuse me one minute, please.

BELHAVEN bolts back to his outer office by one door.– his way of opening and getting through it is a labour-saving invention; and PHILIP goes to find THOMAS through the other. There is silence again, held by these four at a greater tension than ever. At last MRS BRIGSTOCK, least able to bear it, gives one desperate wriggle-fidget. BRIGSTOCK looks at her deprecatingly and says...

MR BRIGSTOCK. Will you sit here, Freda, if you feel the draught?

MRS BRIGSTOCK. *(just trusting herself to answer).* No, thank you.

Silence again, but soon broken by PHILIP, who comes from the other room, throwing over his shoulder the last of his few words with THOMAS 'All right, Tommy.' TOMMY, even at the dullest business, always pleasantly amuses him. Then he settles himself at the table for the second time, conciliatory, kind.

PHILIP. Well, now...

MRS BRIGSTOCK, determined to be first heard, lets slip the torrent of her wrath.

MRS BRIGSTOCK. It's slander, Mr Madras, and I request that it shall be retracted immediately...before everybody...in the public press...by advertisement.

MR BRIGSTOCK. *(in an agonized whisper).* Oh, Freda...not so eadstrong.

PHILIP. is elaborately cool and good tempered.

PHILIP. Miss Chancellor.

MISS CHANCELLOR is even more elaborately cold and dignified.

MISS CHANCELLOR. Yes, sir.

PHILIP. I think we might inform Mrs Brigstock that we're sorry the accusation has become so public...it has naturally caused her some pain.

MRS BRIGSTOCK. *(ascending the scale)*. I don't believe it...I didn't believe it...if I'd have believed it -

MR BRIGSTOCK. *(interposing)*. Oh, Freda!

MISS CHANCELLOR. *(very definitely)*. I saw them kissing. I didn't know Mr Brigstock was a married man. And even if I had known it...I saw them kissing.

MISS YATES, opening her mouth for the first time, shows an easy impatience of their anger and their attitudes, too.

MISS YATES. Oh...what sort of a kiss?

MISS CHANCELLOR. Are there different sorts of kisses, Miss Yates?

MISS YATES. Well...aren't there?

MRS BRIGSTOCK *(growing shrill now)*. He owns he did that, and he knows he shouldn't have and he asked my pardon...and whose business is it, but mine...?

MR BRIGSTOCK *(vainly interposing this time)*. Oh, Freda!

MRS BRIGSTOCK *(climbing to hysterics)*. Hussy to let him...hussy...hussy!

PHILIP adds a little severity to his coolness.

PHILIP. Mrs Brigstock.

MISS YATES *(as pleasant as possible)*. All right...Mr Madras, I don't mind.

PHILIP. But I do. Mrs Brigstock, I shall not attempt to clear up this business unless we can all manage to keep our tempers.

(MISS YATES collectedly explains).

MISS YATES. I've been friends with Mr Brigstock these twelve years. We both came into the firm together...and I knew he was married...p'raps I'm the only one that did. And when I told him...all I chose to tell him as to what had happened to me...I asked him to kiss me just to show he didn't think so much the worse of me. And he gave me one kiss..here *(she dabs with one finger the left top corner of her forehead)* and that is the truth of that.

PHILIP. You might have given this explanation to Miss Chancellor.

MISS YATES. She wouldn't have believed it.

MISS CHANCELLOR. I don't believe it.

MRS BRIGSTOCK *(with gathering force)*. William! William!! William! ! !

BRIGSTOCK desperately musters a little authority.

MR BRIGSTOCK. Freda, be quiet...haven't I sworn it to you on the Bible?

MISS CHANCELLOR now puts her case.

MISS CHANCELLOR. I may say I have known other young ladies in trouble and whether they behaved properly or improperly under the circumstances...and I've known them behave both...they did not confide in their gentlemen friends...without the best of reasons.

PHILIP. There is no reason that they shouldn't, Miss Chancellor.

MISS CHANCELLOR. They didn't.

MISS YATES. Well...I did.

MISS CHANCELLOR. I had no wish for the scandal to get about. I don't know how it happened.

MISS YATES. Ask your little favourite, Miss Jordan, how it happened.

This shot tells. MISS CHANCELLOR's voice sharpens.

MISS CHANCELLOR. Mr Madras, if I am to be accused of favouritism -

PHILIP. Yes, yes...we'll keep to the point, I think.

MISS CHANCELLOR. If Mr Brigstock wasn't the man.–

MRS BRIGSTOCK *(the spring touched)*. William!

MISS CHANCELLOR. Why shouldn't she tell me who it was?

MISS YATES. Why should I?

MISS CHANCELLOR. Am I here to look after the morals of these young ladies or am I not?

MRS BRIGSTOCK. A set of hussies.

MR BRIGSTOCK. *(in agony)*. Freda, you'll get me the sack.

PHILIP. Brigstock, if I wished to give any one the sack, I should not be taking the trouble to discuss this with you all in - I hope – a reasonable way.

MRS BRIGSTOCK, much resenting reasonableness, stands up now to give battle.

MRS BRIGSTOCK. Oh, give him the sack, if you please, Mr Madras. It's time he had it for his own sake.

MR BRIGSTOCK. No, Freda!

MRS BRIGSTOCK. You've got your way to make in the world, haven't you? He's got to start on his own like other people, hasn't he?

MR BRIGSTOCK. *(feeling safety and his situations slipping)*. In time, Freda.

MRS BRIGSTOCK. Now's the time. If you're not sick-of the life you lead ... seeing me once a week for an hour or two...then I am. And this libel and slander makes about the last straw, I should think.

PHILIP. How long have you been married, Mrs Brigstock?

MRS BRIGSTOCK. Four years.

PHILIP. Four years!

MRS BRIGSTOCK *(a little quelled by his equable courtesy)*. Four years !

PHILIP *(in amazed impatience)*. My dear Brigstock, why not have come to the firm and told them? It could have been arranged for you to live out with your wife.

MR BRIGSTOCK. Well, I have been thinking of it lately, sir, but I never seem to happen on a really likely moment. I'm afraid I'm not a favourite in my department.

MRS BRIGSTOCK. No fault of his!

MR BRIGSTOCK. And its sometimes a very little thing makes the difference between a feller's going and staying...when all those that aren't wanted are cleared out after sale time, I mean, for instance. And of course, the thirty pound a year they allow you to live out on does not keep you...it's no use my saying it does. And when you're married...

MRS BRIGSTOCK *(who has gathered her grievances again)*. I agreed to it. I have my profession too. We've been saving quicker. It's three hundred pounds now, all but a bit...that's enough to start on. I've got my eye on the premises. It's near here, I don't mind telling you. Why shouldn't we do as well as others...and ride in our carriages when we're fifty !

MR BRIGSTOCK. *(deprecating such great optimism)*. Well, I've asked advice...

MRS BRIGSTOCK. You think too much of advice. If you'd value yourself higher ! Give him the sack, if you please, Mr Madras, and I'll say thank you.

She finishes, and suddenly MISS YATES takes up this part of the tale quite otherwise.

MISS YATES. He has asked my advice, and I've told him to stay where he is.

MRS BRIGSTOCK. *(her breath leaving her)*. Oh, indeed!

MISS YATES. He's as steady as can be. But his appearance is against him.

MRS BRIGSTOCK. *(hardly recovering it)*. Well, I never!

MR BRIGSTOCK. A feller does think of the future, Marion.

MISS YATES. I wouldn't if I were you. I don't know where we all get to when we're fifty and I've never met anyone who did. We're not in the shop any longer, most of us, are we? And we're not all in our carriages.

MR BRIGSTOCK. *(meekly)*. I suppose it can be done.

MISS YATES. Oh...premises near here and three hundred pounds. Perfect foolery and William ought to know it is. This firm'll undersell you and eat you up and a dozen more like you...and the place that's trusted you for your stock will sell up every stick and there you'll be in the gutter. I advised him to own up to you *(she nods at MRS BRIGSTOCK)* and live out and do the best he could.

MRS BRIGSTOCK. *(more drenched with the cold water than she'll own)*. I'm much obliged I'm sure...I've my own opinion...

PHILIP. *(who has been studying her rather anxiously)*. You've no children, Mrs Brigstock?

MRS BRIGSTOCK goes white.

MRS BRIGSTOCK. No, I've no children. How can you save when you have children? But if it was his child this hussy was going to have and I thought God wouldn't strike him dead on the spot, I'd do it myself, so I would...and he knows I would.

MR BRIGSTOCK. Haven't I taken my oath to you, Freda?

MRS BRIGSTOCK. How can I tell if he's speaking the truth...I ask you how can I tell? I lie awake at night away from him till I could scream with thinking about it. And I do scream as loud as I dare...not to wake the house. And if somebody don't open that window, I shall go off.

PHILIP. Open the window, please, Mr Brigstock.

PHILIP's voice is serious, though he says but a simple thing. MR BRIGSTOCK opens the window as a man may do in a sick room, helpless, a little dazed. Then he turns back to his wife, who is sitting, head tilted against the sharp back of the plush bench, eyes shut, mouth open. Only MISS YATES is ready with her bit of practical comfort.

MISS YATES. Look here, don't you worry. I could have married William if I'd wanted to. That ought to be proof enough.

MR BRIGSTOCK. There you are, Freda.

MISS YATES. Before he knew you.

MRS BRIGSTOCK. *(opening her eyes).* Did you ask her?

MISS YATES. No, he never asked me...but you know what I mean.

MISS YATES gives emphasis to this with what one fears must be described as a wink. MRS BRIGSTOCK looks at the acquiescent BRIGSTOCK and acknowledges the implication.

MRS BRIGSTOCK. Yes, I know. Oh, I don't believe it really.

Comforted, she discovers her handkerchief and blows her nose, after which MISS CHANCELLOR, who has been sitting all this while still, silent, and scornful, inquires in her politest voice.

MISS CHANCELLOR. Do you wish me still to remain, Mr Madras?

PHILIP. One moment.

MISS YATES. Oh, you'll excuse my back, sir *(and she turns to the table again).*

PHILIP. I don't think I need detain you any longer, Mr and Mrs Brigstock. Your character is now quite clear in the firm's eyes, Brigstock, and I shall see that arrangements are made for you to live out in the future. I apologise to you both for all this unpleasantness.

They have both risen at this and now BRIGSTOCK begins hesitatingly.

MR BRIGSTOCK. Well...thank you...sir...and...

MRS BRIGSTOCK. No, William.

MR BRIGSTOCK. All right, Freda! *(He struggles into his prepared speech).* We are very much obliged to you, sir, but I do not see how I can remain with the firm unless there has been, with regard to the accusation, some definite retractation.

PHILIP. *(near the end of his patience).* My good man, it is retracted.

MRS BRIGSTOCK. Publicly.

PHILIP. Nonsense, Mrs Brigstock.

MRS BRIGSTOCK. *(quite herself again).* Is it indeed...how would you like it? *(Then becoming self-conscious).* Well, I beg pardon. I'm sure we're very sorry for Miss Yates and I wish she were married.

MISS YATES. *(with some gusto).* So do I!

Suddenly MISS CHANCELLOR bursts out.

MISS CHANCELLOR. Then you wicked girl, why didn't you say so before...when I wished to be kind to you? And we shouldn't all be talking in this outrageous indecent way. I never did in all my life. I don't know how I manage to sit here. Didn't I try to be kind to you?

MISS YATES. *(unconquerable).* Yes, and you tried to cry over me. No, I don't wish I were married.

MR BRIGSTOCK. Of course it's not for me to say, Marion, but will the way you're going on now stop the other young ladies tattling?

The tone of the dispute now sharpens rather dangerously.

MRS BRIGSTOCK. How's Mr Brigstock to remain in the firm if Miss Chancellor does?

PHILIP. That is my business, Mrs Brigstock.

MISS CHANCELLOR. What...when I saw him kissing her...kissing her!

MRS BRIGSTOCK. William!

PHILIP. That has been explained.

MISS CHANCELLOR. No, Mr Madras, while I'm housekeeper here I will not countenance loose behaviour. I don't believe one word of these excuses.

PHILIP. This is just obstinacy, Miss Chancellor.

MISS CHANCELLOR. And personally I wish to reiterate every single thing I said.

And now it degenerates into a wrangle.

MRS BRIGSTOCK. Then the law shall deal with you.

MISS CHANCELLOR. You can dismiss me at once, if you like, Mr Madras.

MRS BRIGSTOCK. It's libellous...it's slander...!

MR BRIGSTOCK. Oh, Freda, don't.

MRS BRIGSTOCK. Yes, and she can be put in prison for it;

MISS CHANCELLOR. If Miss Yates and Mr Brigstock stay with this firm, I go.

MRS BRIGSTOCK. And she shall be put in prison...the cat.

MR BRIGSTOCK. Don't, Freda!

MRS BRIGSTOCK. The heartless cat ! Do you swear it isn't true, William?

PHILIP. Take your wife away, Brigstock.

PHILIP'S sudden vehemence causes MRS BRIGSTOCK to make straight for the edge of her self-control – and over it.

MRS BRIGSTOCK. Yes, and he takes himself away...leaves the firm, I should think so, and sorry enough you'll be before we've done. I'll see what the law will say to her...and they're not a hundred yards off...on the better side of the street too and a plate glass window as big as yours.

MR BRIGSTOCK. Do be quiet, Freda!

MRS BRIGSTOCK. *(in hysterics now).* Three hundred pounds and how much did Maple have when he started...or Whiteley...and damages what's more...And me putting up with the life I've led...!

They wait till the fit subsides – PHILIP with kindly impatience, BRIGSTOCK in mute apology – and MRS BRIGSTOCK is a mass of sobs. Then BRIGSTOCK edges her towards the door.

PHILIP. Wait...wait...wait. You can't go into the passage making that noise.

MR BRIGSTOCK. Oh, Freda, you don't mean it.

MRS BRIGSTOCK. *(relieved and contrite).* I'm sure I hope I've said nothing unbecoming a lady...I didn't mean to.

PHILIP. Not at all...it's natural you should be upset.

MRS BRIGSTOCK. And we're very much obliged for your kind intentions to us...

PHILIP. Wait till you're quite calm.

MRS BRIGSTOCK. Thank you.

Then with a final touch of injury, resentment, dignity, she shakes off BRIGSTOCK's timid hold .

MRS BRIGSTOCK. You needn't hold me, William.

WILLIAM follows her out to forget and make her forget it all as best he can. PHILIP comes back to his chair, still good humoured, but not altogether pleased with his own part in the business so far.

PHILIP. I'm afraid you've put yourself in the wrong, Miss Chancellor.

MISS CHANCELLOR. One often does, sir, in doing one's duty. *(Then her voice rises to a sort of swan song.)* Thirty years have I been with the firm...only thirty years. I will leave tomorrow.

PHILIP. I hope you recognize it will not be my fault if you have to.

MISS CHANCELLOR. Miss Yates can obviate it. She has only to speak the truth.

PHILIP now makes another effort to be frank and kindly.

PHILIP. Miss Chancellor, are we quite appreciating the situation from Miss Yates's point of view? Suppose she were married?

MISS YATES. I'm not married.

PHILIP. But if you told us you were, we should have to believe you.

MISS CHANCELLOR. Why, Mr Madras?

PHILIP. *(with a smile).* It would be good manners to believe her. We must believe so much of what we're told in this world.

MISS YATES. *(who has quite caught on).* Well, I did mean to stick that up on you...if anyone wants to know. I bought a wedding ring, and I had it on when I saw Dr Willoughby. But when she came in with her long face and her What can I do for you, my poor child?...well, I just couldn't...I suppose the Devil tempted me and I told her the truth.

PHILIP. That's as I thought, so far. Miss Yates, have you that wedding ring with you?

MISS YATES. Yes, I have...it's not real gold.

PHILIP. Put it on.

MISS YATES, having fished it out of a petticoat pocket, rather wonderingly does so, and PHILIP turns, maliciously humorous, to MISS CHANCELLOR.

PHILIP. Now where are we, Miss Chancellor?

MISS CHANCELLOR. I think we're mocking at a very sacred thing, Mr Madras.

MISS YATES. Yes...and I won't now.

With a sudden access of emotion she slams the ring upon the table. PHILIP meditates for a moment on the fact that there are some things in life Still inaccessible to his light-hearted logic.

PHILIP. True...true...I beg both your pardons. But suppose the affair had not got about, Miss Yates?

MISS YATES. Well...I should have had a nice long illness. It'd all depend on whether you wanted me enough to keep my place open.

PHILIP. You are an employee of some value to the firm.

MISS YATES. I reckoned you would. Miss McIntyre'd be pleased to stay on a bit now she's quarrelled with her fiance. Of course if I'd only been behind the counter . . .

MISS CHANCELLOR. *(who has drawn the longest of breaths at this calculated immodesty).* This is how she brazened it out to me, Mr Madras. This is just what she told Mr Huxtable...and you'll pardon my saying he took a very different view of the matter to what you seem to be taking.

MISS YATES. Oh, I've got to go now I'm found out...I'm not arguing about it.

MISS CHANCELLOR. *(severely).* Mr Madras, what sort of notions are you fostering in this wretched girl's mind?

PHILIP. *(gently enough).* I was trying for a moment to put myself in her place.

MISS CHANCELLOR. You will excuse me saying, sir, that you are a man...

PHILIP. Not at all!

A poor joke, but MISS CHANCELLOR remains unconscious of it.

MISS CHANCELLOR. Because a woman is independent and earning her living, she's not to think she can go on as one pleases. If she wishes to have children, Providence has provided a way in the institution of marriage. Miss Yates would have found little difficulty in getting married, I gather.

MISS YATES. Living in here for twelve years!

MISS CHANCELLOR. Have you been a prisoner, Miss Yates? Not to mention that there are two hundred and thiry-five gentlemen employed here.

MISS YATES. Supposing I don't like any of em.

MISS CHANCELLOR. My dear Miss Yates, if you are merely looking for a husband as such...well...we're all God's creatures, I suppose. Personally, I don't notice much difference in men, anyway.

MISS YATES. Nor did I.

MISS CHANCELLOR. Lack of self-control...

MISS YATES. Is it!

MISS CHANCELLOR....And self-respect. That's what the matter is. Are we beasts of the field, I should like to know? I simply do not understand this unlady-like attitude towards the facts of life. Is there nothing for a woman to do in the world but to run after men...or pretend to run away from them? I am fifty-eigh...and I have passed, thank God, a busy and a happy and I hope a useful life...and I have never thought any more or less of men than I have of any other human beings...or any differently. I look upon spinsterhood as an honourable state, as my Bible teaches me to. Men are different. But some women marry happily and well...and all women can't...and some can't marry at all. These facts have to be faced, I take it.

PHILIP. We may take it that Miss Yates has been facing them.

MISS CHANCELLOR. Yes sir, and in what spirit? I have always endeavoured to influence the young ladies under my control towards the virtues of modesty and decorum...so that they may regard either state with an indifferent mind. If I can no longer do that, I prefer to resign my charge. I will say before this young person that I regret the story should have got about. But when anyone has committed a fault, it seems to me immaterial who knows of it.

PHILIP. *(reduced to irony)*. Do you really think so?

MISS CHANCELLOR. Do you require me any more now?

PHILIP. I am glad to have had your explanation. We'll have a private talk tomorrow.

MISS CHANCELLOR. Thank you, sir. I think that will be more in order. Good morning.

PHILIP. Good morning.

MISS CHANCELLOR has expressed herself to her entire satisfaction and retires in good order. MISS YATES, conscientiously brazen until the enemy has quite disappeared, collapses pathetically. And PHILIP, at his ease at last, begins to scold her in a most brotherly manner.

MISS YATES. I'm sure she's quite right in all she says.

PHILIP. She may not be. But are you the sort of woman to have got yourself into a scrape of this kind, Miss Yates?

MISS YATES. I'm glad you think I'm not, sir.

PHILIP. Then what on earth did you go and do it for?

MISS YATES. I don't know. I didn't mean to.

PHILIP. Why aren't you married?

MISS YATES. That's my business. *(Then as if making amends for the sudden snap.)* Oh...I've thought of getting married any time these twelve years. But look what happens...look at the Brigstocks...

PHILIP. No, no no...that's not what I mean. Why aren't you to be married even now?

MISS YATES. I'd rather not say.

MISS YATES assumes an air of reticence natural enough; but there is something a little peculiar in the manner of it – so PHILIP thinks.

PHILIP. Very well.

MISS YATES. I'd rather not talk about that part of it, sir, with you, if you don't mind. *(Then she bursts out again).* I took the risk. I knew what I was about. I wanted to have my fling. And it was fun for a bit. That sounds horrid, I know, but it was.

PHILIP is watching her.

PHILIP. Miss Yates, I've been standing up for you, haven't I?

MISS YATES. Yes.

PHILIP. That's because I have unconventional opinions. But I don't do unconventional things.

MISS YATES. *(naïvely).* Why don't you?

PHILIP. I shouldn't do them well. Now you start on this adventure believing all that the other people say, so I'm not happy about you. As man to man, Miss Yates...were you in a position to run this risk?

MISS YATES honestly thinks before she speaks.

MISS YATES. Yes...I shall be getting a hundred and forty a year living out. I've planned it all *(she grows happily confidential).* There's a maisonette at Raynes Park and I can get a cheap girl to look after it and to take care of...I shall call him my nephew, like the Popes of Rome used to...or why can't I be a widow? I can bring him up and do him well on it. Insurance'll be a bit stiff in case anything happens to me. But I've got nearly two hundred saved in the bank to see me through till next summer.

PHILIP. Where are you going when you leave here? What relations have you?

MISS YATES. I have an aunt. I hate her.

PHILIP. Where are you going for the winter?

MISS YATES. Evercreech.

PHILIP. Where's that?

MISS YATES. I don't know. You get to it from Waterloo. I found it in the A.B.C.

PHILIP *(in protest).* But my dear girl...!

MISS YATES. Well, I want a place where nobody knows me, so I'd better go to one which I don't know, hadn't I? I always make friends. I'm not afraid of people. And I've never been in the country in the winter. I want to see what it's like.

PHILIP surrenders, on this point beaten; but takes up another more seriously.

PHILIP. Well...granted that you don't want a husband...it's your obvious duty to make the man help you support his child.

MISS YATES is ready for it; serious. too.

MISS YATES. I daresay. But I won't. I've known other girls in this sort of mess – one or two...with everybody being kind to them and sneering at them.

And there they sat and cried and were ashamed of themselves ! What's the good of that? And the fellows hating them. Well, I don't want him to hate me. He can forget all about it if he likes...and of course he will. I started by crying my eyes out. Then I thought that if I couldn't buck up and anyway pretend to be pleased and jolly well proud, I might as well die. And d'you know when I'd been pretending a bit, I found that I really was pleased and proud...And I am really proud and happy about it now sir...I am not pretending. I daresay I've done wrong...perhaps I ought to come to grief altogether, but -

At this moment a telephone in the table rings violently, and MISS YATES apologizes – to it apparently.

MISS YATES. Oh, I beg pardon.

PHILIP. Excuse me. *(Then, answering).* Yes. Who? No, no, no...State. Mr State. Put him through. *(He is evidently put through).* Morning! Who? My father...not yet. Yes, from Marienbad.

MISS YATES gets up, apparently to withdraw tactfully, but looking a little startled, too.

MISS YATES. Shall I...

PHILIP. No, no; it's all right.

BELHAVEN knocks, comes in and stands waiting by PHILIP, who telephones on.

PHILIP. Yes? Well?...Who...Mark who?...Aurelius. No. I've not been reading him lately...Certainly I will...Thomas is here doing figures...d'you want him ... I'll put you through.... No, wait. I'll call him here, if it's not private. *(Then calling out).* Tommy!

BELHAVEN. Major Thomas is in the counting house, sir.

PHILIP. Oh. *(Then through the telephone).* If you'll hold the line I can get him in a minute. Say Mr State's on the telephone for him, Belhaven.

BELHAVEN. Yes, sir...and Mrs Madras is below in a taxicab, sir, and would like to speak to you. Shall she come up or, if you're too busy to be interrupted, will you come down to her?

PHILIP. My mother?

BELHAVEN. No, not Mrs Madras...your Mrs Madras, sir.

PHILIP. Bring her up. And tell Major Thomas.

BELHAVEN. Yes, sir.

BELHAVEN achieves a greased departure and PHILIP turns back to MISS YATES.

PHILIP. Where were we?

MISS YATES. *(inconsequently).* It is hot in here, isn't it?

PHILIP. The window's open.

MISS YATES. Shall I shut it?

She turns and goes up to the window; one would say to run away from him. PHILIP watches her steadily.

PHILIP. What's the matter, Miss Yates?

She comes back more collectedly.

MISS YATES. Oh, I'm sure Miss Chancellor can't expect me to marry one like that now...can she?

PHILIP. Marry who?

MISS YATES. Not that I say anything against Mr Belhaven...a very nice young man. And, indeed, I rather think he did try to propose last Christmas. The fact is, y'know, it's only the very young men that ever do ask you to marry them here. When they get older they seem to lose heart...or they think it'll cost too much...or...but anyway, I'm sure it's not important...

This very out-of-place chatter dies away under PHILIP's sternly enquiring gaze.

PHILIP. There's one more thing I'm afraid I ought to ask you. This trouble hasn't come about in any way by our sending you up to Bond Street, has it?

MISS YATES *(diving into many words again)*. Oh, of course it was most kind of you to send me to Bond Street to get a polish on one's manners...but I tell you...I couldn't have stood it for long. Those ladies that you get coming in there...well, it does just break your nerve. What with following them about and the things they say you've got to hear, and the things they'll say...about you half the time...that you've got not to hear...and keep your voice low and sweet, and let your arms hang down straight. You may work more hours in this place, and I daresay it's commoner, but the customers are friendly with you.

PHILIP. Because, you see, Mr Huxtable and I would feel a little more responsible if it was anyone connected with us who...

MISS YATES *(quite desperately)*. No, you needn't...indeed you needn't...I will say there's something in that other place that does set your mind going about men. What he saw in me I never could think...honestly, I couldn't, though I think a good deal of myself, I can assure you. But it was my own fault, and so's all the rest of it going to be...my very own...

MAJOR THOMAS's arrival is to MISS YATES a very welcome interruption, as she seems, perhaps by the hypnotism of PHILIP's steady look, to be getting nearer and nearer to saying just what she means not to. He comes in at a good speed, glancing back along the passage, and saying...

THOMAS. Here's Jessica.

PHILIP. State on the telephone.

THOMAS. Thank you.

And he makes for it as JESSICA comes to the open door. PHILIP's wife is an epitome of all that aesthetic culture can do for a woman. More. she is the result - not of thirty-three years - but of three or four generations of cumulative refinement. She might be a race horse! Come to think of it, it is a very wonderful thing to have raised this crop of ladyhood. Creatures, dainty in mind and body, gentle in thought and word, charming, delicate, sensitive, graceful, chaste, credulous of all good, shaming the world's ugliness and strife by the very ease and delightsomeness of their existence; fastidious – fastidious – fastidious; also in these latter years with their attractions more generally saited by the addition of learning and humour. Is not the perfect lady perhaps the most wonderful achievement of civilisation, and worth the cost of her breeding, worth the toil and the helotage of – all the others? JESSICA MADRAS is even something more than a lady, for she is conscious of her ladyhood. She values her virtue and her charm: she is proud of her culture and fosters it. It is her weapon, it justifies her. As she floats now into the ugly room, exquisite from her eyelashes to her shoes, it is a great relief just the sight of her.

JESSICA. Am I interrupting?

PHILIP. No, come in, my dear.

THOMAS *(into the telephone)*. Hullo!

PHILIP. Well, Miss Yates, I want to see if I can that you are not more unfairly treated than people with the courage of their opinions always are.

THOMAS. Hullo!

PHILIP. Oh, you don't know my wife. Jessica, this is Miss Yates, who is in our costume room. You're not actually working in your department now, I suppose?

MISS YATES *(as defiant of all scandal)*. I am.

THOMAS (Still to the unresponsive telephone). Hullo! Hullo!

PHILIP *(finding MISS YATES beyond – possibly above him)*. Very well. That'll do now.

But MISS YATES~ by the presence of JESSICA, is now brought to her best costume department manner. She can assume at will, it seems, a new face, a new voice; can become, indeed, a black-silk being of another species.

MISS YATES. Thank you, sir. I'm sure I hope I've not talked too much. I always was a chatterbox, madam.

PHILIP. You had some important things to say, Miss Yates.

MISS YATES. Not at all, sir. Good morning, madam.

JESSICA. Good morning.

And there is an end of MISS YATES. Meanwhile the telephone is reducing THOMAS to impotent fury.

THOMAS. They've cut him off.

While he turns the handle fit to break it JESSICA produces an opened telegram, which she hands to PHILIP.

JESSICA. This...just after you left.

PHILIP. My dear, coming all this way with it! Why didn't you telephone?

THOMAS *(hearing something at last)*. Hullo...is that Mr State's office? No! Well...Counting house, are you still through to it?

JESSICA is watching zuith an amused smile.

JESSICA. I hate the telephone, especially the one here. Hark at you, Tommy, poor wretch! They put you through from office to office...six different clerks...all stupid and all with. hideous voices.

PHILIP has now read his telegram and is making a face.

PHILIP. Well, I suppose she must come if she wants to.

JESSICA. What'll your father say?

PHILIP. My dear girl...she has a right to see him if she insists...it's very foolish. Here, Tommy! (He ousts him from the telephone and deals expertly with it). I want a telegram sent. Get double three double O Central, and plug through to my room...not here...my room.

THOMAS. (fervently). Thank yer.

JESSICA. Got over your anger at the play last night?

THOMAS. Oh, sort of play you must expect if you go to the theatre on a Sunday. Scuse me.

Having admiringly sized up JESSICA and her costume, he bolts. PHILIP sits down to compose his telegram in reply.

JESSICA discovering that there is nothing attractive to sit on, hovers.

PHILIP. Can you put her up for the night?

JESSICA. Yes.

PHILIP. Shall I ask her to dinner?

JESSICA. She'll cry into the soup...but I suppose it doesn't matter.

PHILIP. Dinner at eight?

JESSICA. I sound inhospitable.

PHILIP. Well, I've only said we shall be delighted.

JESSICA. But your mother dislikes me so. It's difficult to see much of her.

PHILIP. You haven't much patience with her, have you, Jessica?

JESSICA. Have you?

PHILIP. *(whimsically)*. I've known her longer than you have.

JESSICA. *(with the nicest humour)*. I only wish she wouldn't write Mildred silly letters about God.

PHILIP. A grandmother's privilege.

JESSICA. The child sends me on another one this morning...did I tell you?

PHILIP. No.

JESSICA. Miss Gresham writes, too. She puts it quite nicely. But it's an awful thing for a school to get religion into it.

BELHAVEN slides in.

BELHAVEN. Yessir.

PHILIP. Send this at once, please.

BELHAVEN. Yessir.

BELHAVEN slides out. Then PHILIP starts attending to the little pile of letters he brought in with him. JESSICA, neglected, hovers more widely.

JESSICA. Will you come out to lunch, Phil?

PHILIP. Lord, is it lunch time !

JESSICA. It will be soon. I'm lunching with Margaret Inman and Watter Muirhead at the Dieudonne.

PHILIP. Then you won't be lonely.

JESSICA. *(mischievous).* Margaret may be if you don't come.

PHILIP. I can't, Jessica. I'm not nearly through.

She comes to rest by his table and starts to play with the things on it, finding at last a blotting roller that gives satisfaction.

JESSICA. Phil, you might come out with me a little more than you do.

PHILIP *(humorously final).* My dear, not at lunch time.

JESSICA. Ugly little woman you'd been scolding when I came in.

PHILIP. I didn't think so.

JESSICA. Are ugly women as attractive as ugly men?

PHILIP. D'you know...I don't find that women attract me.

JESSICA. What a husband!

PHILIP. D'you want them to?

JESSICA. Yes...in theory.

PHILIP. Why, Jessica?

JESSICA. *(with charming finesse).* For my own sake. Last day of Watter's pictures. He has sold all but about five...and there's one I wish you'd buy.

PHILIP. Can't afford it.

JESSICA. I suppose, Phil, you're not altogether sorry you married me.

Although PHILIP is used enough to her charming and reasoned inconsequence, he really jumps.

PHILIP. Good heavens, Jessica! Well, we've got through eleven years, haven't we?

JESSICA puts her head on one side and is quite half serious.

JESSICA. Are you in the least glad you married me?

PHILIP. My dear...I don't think about it. Jessica, I cannot keep up this game of repartee.

She floats away at once, half seriously snubbed and hurt.

JESSICA. I'm sorry, I know I'm interrupting.

PHILIP. *(remorseful at once, for she is so pretty).* No, no; I didn't mean that. These aren't important.

But he goes on with his letters and JESSICA stands looking at him, her face hardening just a little.

JESSICA. But there are times when I get tired of waiting for you to finish your letters.

PHILIP. I know...I never quite finish my letters now-a-days. You've got a fit of the idle-fidgets this morning...that's what brings you after me. Shall we hire a motor car for the week-end?

THOMAS bundles into the tete-a-tete, saying as he comes...

THOMAS. He'll make you an offer for the place here, Phil.

PHILIP. Good.

JESSICA stands there, looking her prettiest.

JESSICA. Tommy, come out and lunch...Phil won't.

THOMAS. I'm afraid I can't.

JESSICA. I've got to meet Maggie Inman and young Muirhead. He'll firt with her all the time. If there isn't a fourth I shall be fearfully in the cold.

PHILIP *(overcome by such tergiversation).* Oh, Jessica!

THOMAS is nervous, apparently; at least he is neither ready nor gallant.

THOMAS. Yes, of course you will. But I'm afraid I can't.

JESSICA. *(in cheerful despair).* Well, I won't drive to Peckham again of a morning. Wednesday, then, will you call for me?

THOMAS. Wednesday?

JESSICA. Symphony Concert.

THOMAS. *(with sudden seriousness).* D'you know I'm afraid I can't on Wednesday, either.

JESSICA. Why not?

THOMAS. *(though the pretence withers before a certain sharpness in her question).* Well...I'm afraid I can't.

It is evident that JESSICA has a temper bred to a point of control which makes it the nastier, perhaps. She now becomes very cold, very civil, very swift.

JESSICA. We settled it only last night. What's the time?

PHILIP. Five to one.

JESSICA. I must go. I shall be late.

THOMAS. (with great concern). Have you got a cab?

JESSICA. I think so.

THOMAS. We might do the next, perhaps.

JESSICA. All right, Tommy...don't be conscience-stricken. But when you change your mind about going out with me, it's pleasanter if you'll find some excuse. Good-bye, you two.

PHILIP. I shall be in by seven, my dear.

THOMAS. looks a little relieved, and then considerably worried; in fact, he frowns portentously. PHILIP disposes of his last letter.

PHILIP. We've so organised the world's work as to make companionship between men and women a very artificial thing.

THOMAS. (without interest). Have we?

PHILIP. I think so. What have we got to settle before this afternoon?

THOMAS. Nothing much. *(Then seeming to make up his mind to something.)* But I want three minutes' talk with you, old man.

PHILIP. Oh!

And he gets up and stretches.

THOMAS. D'you mind if I say something caddish?

PHILIP. No.

THOMAS. Put your foot down and don't have me asked to your house quite so much.

PHILIP looks at him for half a puzzled minute.

PHILIP. Why not?

THOMAS. I'm seeing too much of your wife.

He is so intensely solemn about it that PHILIP can hardly even pretend to be shocked.

PHILIP. My dear Tommy!

THOMAS. I don't mean one single word more than I say.

PHILIP. *(good-naturedly).* Tommy, you always have fiirted with Jessica.

THOMAS. I don't want you to think that I'm the least bit in love with her.

PHILIP. Naturally not...you've got a wife of your own.

THOMAS. *(in intense brotherly agreement).* Right. That's good horse sense.

PHILIP. And though, as her husband, I'm naturally obtuse in the matter...I really don't think that Jessica is in love with you.

THOMAS. *(most generously).* Not for a single minute.

PHILIP. Then what's the worry, you silly old ass?

THOMAS starts to explain, a little tortuously.

THOMAS. Well, Phil, this is such a damned subtle world. I don't pretend to understand it, but in my old age I have got a sort of rule of thumb experience to go by...which, mark you, I've paid for.

PHILIP. Well?

THOMAS. Phil, I don't like women and I never did...but I'm hardly exaggerating when I say I married simply to get out of the habit of finding myself once every six months in such a position with one of them that I was supposed to be making love to her.

PHILIP. is enjoying himself.

PHILIP. What do they see in you, Tommy?

THOMAS. God knows, old man...I don't. And the time it took up ! Of course I was as much in love with Mary as you like or I couldn't have asked her to marry me. And I wouldn't be without her and the children now for all I ever saw. But I don't believe I'd have gone out of my way to get them if I hadn't been driven to it, old man...driven to it. I'm not going to start the old game again now *(and he wags his head wisely).*

PHILIP. What's the accusation against Jessica? Let's have it in so many words.

THOMAS gathers himself up to launch the vindicating compliment effectively.

THOMAS. She's a very accomplished and a very charming and a very sweet-natured woman. I consider she's an ornament to society.

PHILIP *(with equal fervour).* You're quite right, Tommy...what are we to do with them?

THOMAS *(it's his favourite phrase).* What d'you mean?

PHILIP. Well...what's your trouble with her?

THOMAS *(tortuously still).* There ain't any yet...but...well...I've been dreading for the last three weeks that Jessica would begin to talk to me about you. That's why I'm talking to you about her. *(Then, with a certain enjoyment of his shocking looseness of behaviour).* I am a cad!

PHILIP. *(still amused - but now rather sub-acidly).* My standing for the County Council must be a most dangerous topic.

THOMAS. But that's just how it begins. Then there's hints...quite nice ones...about how you get on with each other. Last night in the cab she was talking about when she was a girl...

PHILIP. I walked home. Tactful husband!

THOMAS. Phil...don't you be French.

PHILIP suddenly serious, turns to him.

PHILIP. But, Tommy, do you imagine that she is unhappy with me?

THOMAS. No, I don't. But she thinks a lot...when she's bored with calling on people and her music and her pictures. And once you begin putting your feelings into words ... why, they grow.

PHILIP. But if she were I'd rather that she did confide in you.

THOMAS shakes his head vehemently.

THOMAS. What?

PHILIP. Your one sensible remark. Come along.

And he is gone. THOMAS follows, protesting.

THOMAS. Look here...what d'you mean by One Sensible Remark?. It's like your infernal...

He pulls the door to after him. The room is alone with its ugliness.

ACT III

In 1884 the Madras House was moved to its present premises in Bond Street. In those days decoration was mostly a matter of paint and wall-paper, but MR CONSTANTINE MADRAS, ever daring, proceeded to beautify the home of his professional triumphs. He could neither draw nor colour, but he designed and saw to it all himself, and being a man of great force of character, produced something which, though extraordinarily wrong, was yet, since it was sincere, in a way effective. It added to his reputation and to the attractiveness of the Madras House.

In twenty-six years there have been changes, but one room remains untouched from then till now. This is the rotunda, a large, lofty, skylighted place, done in the Moorish style. The walls are black marble to the height of a man, and from there to the ceiling the darkest red. The ceiling is of a cerulean blue, and in the middle of the skylight a golden sun, with spiked rays proceeding from its pleasant human countenance, takes credit for some of the light it intercepts. An archway with fretted top leads from the rest of the establishment. Another has behind it a platform, a few steps high, hung with black velvet. The necessary fireplace (were there hotwater pipes in 1884?) is disguised by a heavy multi-coloured canopy, whose fellow hangs over a small door opposite. On the floor is a Persian carpet of some real beauty. On the walls are gas brackets (1884 again!) the oriental touch achieved in their crescent shape. Round the wall are divans, many cushioned; in front of them little coffee-stools. It is all about as Moorish as Baker Street Station, but the general effect is humorous, pleasant, and even not undignified.

In the old, grand days of the Madras House the rotunda was the happy preserve of very special customers, those on whom the great man himself would keep an eye. if you had been there you spoke of it casually; indeed, to be free of the rotunda was to be a well-dressed woman and recognized by all society as such. Ichabod! Since MR CONSTANTINE MADRAS retired, the Madras House is on the way to becoming almost like any other shop; the special customers are nobody in particular, and the rotunda is where a degenerate management meet to consider the choice of ready-made models from Paris. A large oval table had to be imported and half a dozen Moorish chairs. It seemed, to the surprise of the gentleman who went innocently ordering such things, that there were only that number in existence. Scene of its former glories, this is now to be the scene, perhaps, of the passing of the Madras House into alien hands.

Three o'clock on the Monday afternoon is when the deal is to be put through, if possible, and it is now five minutes to. MAJOR THOMAS is there, sitting at the table; papers spread before him, racking his brains at a few final figures. PHILIP is there, in rather a school-boyish mood. He is sitting on the table, swinging his legs. MR HUXTABLE is there, too, dressed in his best, important and nervous, and he is talking to MR EUSTACE PERRIN STATE.

MR STATE is an American, and if American magazine literature is anything to go by, no American is altogether unlike him. He has a rugged, blood and iron sort of face, utterly belied by his soft, smiling eyes; rightly belied, too, for he has made his thirty or forty millions in the gentlest way – as far as he knows. You would not think of him as a money-maker. As a matter-of-fact, he has no love of money and little use for it, for his tastes are simple. But moneymaking is the honourable career in his own country, and he has the instinct for turning money over and the knack of doing so on a big scale. His shock of grey hair makes him look older than he probably is; his voice is almost childlike in its sweetness. He has the dignity and aptitude for command that power can give.

From the little canopied door comes MR WINDLESHAM, present manager of the establishment. He is a tailor-made man; and the tailor only left off for the wax modeller and wigmaker to begin. For his clothes are too perfect to be worn by anything but a dummy, and his hair and complexion are far from human. Not that he dyes or paints them; no, they were made like that. His voice is a little inhuman, too, and as he prefers the French language, with which he has a most unripe acquaintance, to his own, and so speaks English as much like French as his French is like English, his conversation seems as unreal as the rest of him. Impossible to think of him in any of the ordinary relations of life. He is a functionary. Nature, the great inventor, will evolve, however roughly, what is necessary for her uses. Millinery has evolved the man-milliner. As he comes in – and he has the gait of a water-wagtail – MR HUXTABLE is making conversation.

MR HUXTABLE. A perfect barometer, as you might say – when your eye gets used to it.

WINDLESHAM. *(to PHILIP; and with a wag of his head back to the other room).* They're just ready.

MR STATE. *(smiling benevolently at MR HUXTABLE).* Is it really? The Crystal Palace! But what a sound that has.

MR HUXTABLE. *(with modest pride).* And a very ealthy locality!

PHILIP. Come along and meet State. *(He jumps off the table, capturing WINDLESHAM's arm.)*

MR STATE. *(enthusiastic).* Denmark Hill. Compliment to Queen Alexandra.

MR HUXTABLE. *(struck by the information).* Was it now?

MR STATE. Herne Hill...Herne the Hunter! That's the charm of London to an American. Association. Every spot speaks.

PHILIP. *(as he joins them).* This is Mr Windlesham...our manager. He's going to show us some new models.

MR STATE impressively extends a hand and repeats the name.

MR STATE. Mr Windlesham.

WINDLESHAM. Most happy. I thought you'd like to see the very latest...brought them from Paris only yesterday.

MR STATE. Most opportune! *(Then with a sweeping gesture.)* Mr Philip, this room inspires me. Your father's design?

PHILIP. Yes.

MR STATE. I thought so.

PHILIP. That used to be his private office.

MR STATE. *(reverently).* Indeed! Where the Duchess went on her knees !
An historic spot. Interesting to me !

PHILIP. Something of a legend that.

*MR STATE, intensely solemn, seems now to ascend the pulpit of some philosophic
conventicle.*

MR STATE. I believe in legends, sir...they are the spiritual side of facts.
They go to form tradition. And it is not given to man to found his institutions in
securiy of mind except upon tradition. That is why our eye turn eastward to you
from America, Mr Huxtable.

MR HUXTABLE. *(in some awe).* Do they now?

MR STATE. Has it never struck you that while the progress of man has
been in the path of the sun, his thoughts continually go back to the place of its
rising? I have at times found it a very illuminating idea.

PHILIP. *(not indecently commonplace).* Well, have them in now,
Windlesham, while we're waiting.

WINDLESHAM. You might cast your eyes over these new girls, Mr
Phil...the very best I could find, I do assure you. Faces are hard enough to get,
but figures...well, there! *(Reaching the little door, he calls through.)* Allons
Mes'moiselles ! Non...non...par l'autre porte et à la gauche. *(Then back again.)*
You get the best effect through a big doorway. *(He further explains this by
sketching one in the air.)* One, two and four first.

*He exhibits some costume drawings he has been carrying, distributes one or two,
and then vanishes into the other room, from which his voice vibrates*

WINDLESHAM. En avant s'il vous plaît. Numéro un! Eh bien...numéro
trois. Non Ma'moiselle, ce n'est pas commode...regardez ce corsage-là...

MR HUXTABLE *(making a face).* What I'm always thinking is, why not
have a manly chap in charge of the place up here.

MR STATE *(with perfect justice).* Mr Windlesham may be said to strike a
note. Whether it is a right note...?

*Through the big doorway, WINDLESHAM ushers in a costume from Paris, the very
last word in discreet and costly finery, delicate in colour, fragile in texture; a
creation. This is hung upon a young lady of pleasing appearance, preoccupied with
its exhibition, which she achieves by slow and sinuous, never-ceasing movements.
She glides into the room. She wears a smile also.*

WINDLESHAM. One and two are both Larguillière, Mr Philip. He can't get
in the Soupçon Anglais, can he? Won't...I tell him. Promenez et sortez
Ma'moiselle.

*The young lady, Still smiling and sinuous, begins to circle the room. She seems to
be unconscious of its inhabitants, and they in return, rather dreadfully pretend not
to notice her, but only the costume.*

WINDLESHAM. Numéro Deux.

Another costume, rahshly inclined, with a hat deliberately hideous. The young lady contained in them is again slow and sinuous and vacantly smiling.

WINDLESHAM. But this is chic, isn't it? Promenez.

MR STATE. *(in grave enquiry).* What is the Soupçon Anglais?

PHILIP. A Frenchman will tell you that for England you must first make a design and then spoil it.

THOMAS. *(whose attention has been riveted).* Don't they speak English?

WINDLESHAM. Oh, pas un mot...I mean, not a word. Only came over with me yesterday... these three.

THOMAS. Because this frock's a bit thick, y'know.

WINDLESHAM. Numéro Trois!

A third costume, calculated to have an innocent effect. The accompanying young lady, with a sense of fitness, wears a pout instead of a smile.

PHILIP. What's this? *(His eye is on the surmounting hat of straw.)*

WINDLESHAM. *(with a little crow of delight).* That's the new hat. La belle Hélène again!

MR STATE. *(interested, still grave).* La belle Hélène. A Parisian firm?

WINDLESHAM *(turning this to waggish account).* Well...dear me...you can almost call her that, can't you? *(Suddenly he dashes at the costume and brings it to a standstill.)* Oh, mon Dieu, Ma'moiselle ! La gorgette...vous l'avez derangé.

He proceeds to arrange la gorgette to his satisfaction, also some other matters which seem to involve a partial evisceration of the underclothing. The young lady, passive, pouts perseveringly. He is quite unconscious of her separate existence. But THOMAS is considerably shocked and whispers violently to PHILIP.

THOMAS. I say, he shouldn't pull her about like that.

WINDLESHAM. *(skipping back to admire the result).* Là...comme ça.

The costume continues its round; the others are still circling, veering and tacking, while WINDLESHAM trips admiringly around and about them. It all looks like some dance of modish dervishes.

PHILIP. *(heartlessly).* La belle Hélène, Mr State, is a well known Parisian cocotte...who sets many of the fashions which our wives and daughters afterwards assume.

MR HUXTABLE. *(scandalised).* Don't say that, Phil; it's not nice.

PHILIP. Why?

MR HUXTABLE. I'm sure no ladies are aware of it.

PHILIP. But what can be more natural and right than for the professional charmer to set the pace for the amateur!

WINDLESHAM. *(pausing in the dance).* Quite la haute cocotterie, of course.

MR STATE. *(solemnly).* Do you infer, Mr Madras, a difference in degree, but not in kind?

PHILIP. *(courteously echoing his tone).* I do.

MR STATE. That is a very far-reaching observation, sir.

PHILIP. It is.

THOMAS. Do you know the lady personally, Mr. Windlesham?

WINDLESHAM turns, with some tag of a costume in his hand, thus unconsciously detaining the occupier.

WINDLESHAM. Oh, no...oh, dear me, no...quite the reverse, I do assure you. There's nothing gay in Paris to me. I was blasé long ago.

MR STATE. But touching that hat, Mr Windlesham.

WINDLESHAM. Oh, to be sure. Attendez, mademoiselle.

Tiptoeing, he dexterously tilts the straw hat from the elaborate head it is perched on.

WINDLESHAM. It's not a bad story. Sortez.

By this two costumes have glided out. The third follows. STATE, who has found it hard to keep his eyes off them, gives something of a sigh.

MR STATE. If they'd only just smile or wink I might get over the extraordinary feeling it gives me.

WINDLESHAM caressing the hat, takes up an attitude for his story.

WINDLESHAM. Well... it appears that a while ago out at the Pré Catalan...there was Hélène, taking her afternoon cup of buttermilk. What should she see but Madame Erlancourt one knows enough about that lady, of course...in a hat the very twin of hers...the very twin. Well...you can imagine! Someone had blundered.

MR STATE *(absorbed).* No, I don't follow.

PHILIP. Some spy in the service of that foreign power had procured and parted with the plans of the hat.

MR STATE. Madame What's-her-name might have seen it on before and copied it.

PHILIP. Mr State, Hélène doesn't wear a hat twice.

MR STATE. My mistake!

WINDLESHAM. So there was a terrible scene...

THOMAS. With madame...?

WINDLESHAM. (repudiating any such vulgarity). Oh, no. Hélène just let fly at her chaperone, she being at hand, so to speak.

MR STATE. *(dazzled).* Her what! *(Then with humorous awe.)* No, I beg your pardon...go on...go on.

WINDLESHAM. She took off her own hat...pinned it on the head of the ugliest little gamine she could find and sent the child walking along the grass in it. Then she sent to the kitchens for one of those baskets they bring the fish in...*(He twirls the hat)*...you see. Then she ripped a yard of lace off her underskirt and twisted it round. Then she took off both her...well...La Belle France, you know...there is something in the atmosphere ! It was her garters she took of...blue silk.

MR STATE. *(puritan)*. In public?

WINDLESHAM. *(professional)*. Oh,...it can be done. Hooked them together and fastened the bit of lace round the basket this way. Très simple! That's what she wore the rest of the afternoon and back to Paris. This is what's going to be the rage...

Having deftly pantomimed this creation of a fashion, he hands the hat with an air to MR STATE, who examines it. PHILIP is smilingly caustic.

PHILIP. La belle Hélène has imagination, Mr State. She is also, I am told, thrifty, inclined to religion, a vegetarian, Vichy water her only beverage; in fact, a credit to her profession and externally...to ours.

MR STATE hands back the hat, with the solemnest humour.

MR STATE. Mr Windlesham, I am much obliged to you for this illuminating anecdote.

WINDLESHAM. Not at all...Will you see the other three?

MR STATE. By all means.

WINDLESHAM. They won't be long in changing...but there's one I must just pin on.

MR STATE. No hurry.

He has acquired a new joy in WINDLESHAM, whom he watches dance away. Then a song is heard from the next room.

WINDLESHAM. Allons...numéro cinq...numéro sept...numéro dix. Ma'moiselle Ollivier...vous vous mettrez . . .

And the door closes. PHILIP looks at his watch.

PHILIP. But it's ten past three. We'd better not wait for my father.

They surround the table and sit down.

MR STATE. Major Thomas, have you my memoranda?

THOMAS. Here.

He hands them to STATE, who clears his throat, refrains from spitting, and begins the customary American oration.

MR STATE. The scheme, gentlemen, for which I desire to purchase the Madras House and add it to the interest of the Burrows enterprise, which I already control is – to put it shortly – this. The Burrows provincial scheme – you are aware of its purpose – goes well enough as far as the shareholding by the local drapery stores is concerned. It has been interesting to me to discover which aspects of the Burrows scheme suit which cities...and why. An absorbing problem in the psychology of local conditions! Now, we have eliminated from the mass a considerable number of cases where the local people will not join with us. And in your Leicesters and Norwiches and Plymouths and Coventrys...there the unknown name, the uninspiring name of Burrows, upon a fire-new establishment next door might anyhow be ineffective. But beyond that I have a reason...and I hope a not uninteresting reason to put before you gentlemen...why it is in these provincial centres that we should look to establish our Madras Houses...New Edition. Is that clear so far?

During this MR CONSTANTINE MADRAS has arrived. He turned aside for a moment to the door that the models came from, now he joins the group. A man of sixty, to whom sixty is the prime of life. Tall, quite dramatically dignified, suave, a little remote; he is one of those to whom life is an art of which they have determined to be master. It is a handsome face, Eastern in type, the long beard only streaked with grey. He does not dress like the ruck of men, because he is not of them. The velvet coat, brick-red tie, shepherd's-plaid trousers, white spats and patent boots, both suit him and express him subtly and well – the mixture of sensuous originality and tradition which is the man. PHILIP is purposely casual in greeting him; he has sighted him first. But MR STATE gets up, impressed. It is part of his creed to recognize greatness; he insists on recognizing it.

PHILIP. Hullo, Father !

MR STATE. Mr Madras! Proud to meet you again.

CONSTANTINE. *(graciously, without emotion).* How do you do, Mr State.

PHILIP. You know everyone, Father. Oh...Hippisly Thomas.

CONSTANTINE. *(just as graciously).* How do you do, sir. *(Then, with a mischievous smile, he pats HUXTABLE on the shoulder.)* How are you, my dear Harry?

MR HUXTABLE had heard him coming and felt himself turn purple. This was the great meeting after thirty years! He had let it come upon him unawares; purposely let it, for indeed he had not known what to say or do. He had dreaded having the inspiration to say or do anything. Now, alas, and thank goodness! It is too late. He is at a suitable disadvantage. He need only grunt out sulkily...

MR HUXTABLE. I'm quite well, thank you.

CONSTANTINE, with one more pat in pardon for the rudeness, goes to his chair.

MR STATE. A pleasant trip on the continent?

CONSTANTINE. Instructive. Don't let me interrupt business. I shall pick up the thread.

MR STATE. *(serving up a little re-warmed oration).* I was just proceeding to place on the table-cloth some preliminary details of the scheme that has been elaborating since our meeting in June last to consolidate your name and fame in some of the most important cities of England. We had not got far.

He consults his notes. CONSTANTINE produces from a case a slender cigarette holder of amber.

CONSTANTINE. You've some new models, Phil.

PHILIP. Yes.

CONSTANTINE. The tall girl looks well enough. May I smoke?

MR STATE. Allow me. *(Whipping out his cigar case.)*

CONSTANTINE. A cigarette, thank you, of my own.

He proceeds to make and light one. MR STATE offers cigars generally, and then places one to his own hand.

MR STATE. I occasionally derive some pleasure from a cold cigar. I was not for the moment entering upon the finance of the matter because I entertain no doubt that...possibly with a little adjustment of the proportion of shares and cash...that can be fixed.

MR HUXTABLE. *(in emulation of all this ease and grace).* I'll ave a cigarette, Phil...if you've got one.

PHILIP has one. And everyone makes themselves comfortable, while MR STATE continues enjoyably...

MR STATE. And I suspect that you are no more interested in money than I am, Mr Madras. Anyone can make money, if he has capital enough. The little that I have came from lumber and canned peaches. Now, there was poetry in lumber. The virgin forest...I'd go sit in it for weeks at a time. There was poetry in peaches...before they were canned. Do you wonder why I bought that mantle establishment in the city?

PHILIP. *(who is only sorry that sometime he must stop).* Why, Mr State?

MR STATE. Because, Mr Philip, I found myself a lonely man. I felt the need of getting into touch with what Goethe refers to as the woman spirit.. drawing us ever upward and on. That opportunity occurred and it seemed a businesslike way of doing the trick.

CONSTANTINE. (through a little cloud of smoke). And satisfying?

MR STATE. I beg your pardon?

CONSTANTINE. Has the ready-made skirt business satisfied your craving for the eternal feminine?

MR STATE. Mr Madras...that sarcasm is deserved...No, sir, it has not. The Burrows business, I discover, lacks all inner meaning...it has no soul. A business can no more exist without a soul than a human being can. I'm sure I have you with me there, Mr Huxtable.

Poor MR HUXTABLE quite chokes at the suddenness of this summons, but shines his best.

MR HUXTABLE. I should say so, quite.

MR STATE begins to glow.

MR STATE. There was fun, mind you...there still is...in making these provincial milliners hop...putting a pistol to their heads...saying Buy our Goods or be Froze Out. That keeps me lively and it wakes them up...does them good. But Burrows isn't in the Movement. The Woman's Movement. The Great Modern Woman's Movement. It has come home to me that the man, who has as much to do with Woman as manufacturing the bones of her corsets and yet is not consciously in that Movement is Outside History. Shovelling goods over a counter and adding up profits...that's no excuse for cumbering the earth...nothing personal, Mr Huxtable.

MR HUXTABLE is ready this time.

MR HUXTABLE. No, no...I'm listening to you. I'm not too old to learn.

MR STATE. Mind, I don't say I haven't taken pleasure in Burrows. We've had Notions...caused two Ideas to spring where one sprang before. There was Nottingham.

MR HUXTABLE. I know Nottingham...got a shop there?

MR STATE. (with wholesome pride). In two years the Burrows establishment in Nottingham has smashed competition. I've not visited the ciy myself. The notion was our local manager's. Simple. The Ladies' department served by gentlemen...the Gentlemen's by ladies. Always of course within the bounds of delicacy. Do you think there is nothing in that, Mr Huxtable.

MR HUXTABLE. (round-eyed and open-mouthed). Oh...well...

MR STATE. But are you the Mean Sensual Man?

MR HUXTABLE. (whose knowledge of the French language hardly assists him to this startling translation). No...I hope not.

MR STATE. Put yourself in his place. Surrounded by pretty girls...good girls, mind you...high class. Pay them well...let them live out...pay for their mothers and chaperones if necessary. Well...Surrounded by Gracious Womanhood, does the Sensual Man forget how much money he is spending or does he not? Does he come again? Is it a little Oasis in the desert of his business day? Is it a better attraction than Alcohol or is it not?

PHILIP. (bitingly). Is it ?

MR STATE. Then, sir...Audi Alteram Partem. I should like you to see our Ladies' Fancy Department at its best...just before the football season.

PHILIP. I think I do!

MR STATE. Athletes everyone of em...not a man under six foot...bronzed, noble fellows! And no flirting allowed...no making eyes...no pandering to anything Depraved. Just the Ordinary Courtesies of our Modern Civilization from Pure Clean-minded Gentlemen towards any of the Fair Sex who step in to buy a shilling sachet or the like. And pay, sir...The women come in flocks !

MR HUXTABLE. (bereft of breath). Is this how you mean to run your new Madras Houses ?

MR STATE. Patience, Mr Huxtable. It's but six months ago that I started to study the Woman Question from the point of view of Burrows and Co. I attended women's meetings in London, in Manchester and in one-horse places as well. Now Political Claims were but the narrowest, drabbest aspect of the matter as I saw it. The Woman's Movement is Woman expressing herself. Let us look at things as they are. What are a woman's chief means...how often her only means of expressing herself? Anyway...what is the first thing that she spends her money on? Clothes, gentlemen, clothes. Therefore, I say...though at Cannon Street we may palp with good ideas...the ready-made skirt is out of date...

WINDLESHAM, pins in his mouth, fashion plates under his arm and the fish-basket hat in his hand, shoots out of the other room.

WINDLESHAM. Will you have the others in now? *(Then back through the door.)* Allons, Mesmoiselles s'il vous plaît. Numéro cinq le premier. *(Then he turns the hat upside down on the table.)* I thought you'd like to see that they've actually left the handles on. But I don't think we can do that here, do you?

There comes in as before the most elaborate evening gown that ever was.

WINDLESHAM. *(as he searches for the design).* Numéro cinq...number five.

THOMAS is much struck.

THOMAS. I say...by Jove!

But the cold searching light seems to separate from the glittering pink affair the poor pretty smiling creature exhibiting it, until, indeed, she seems half naked. MR WINDLESHAM's aesthetic sense is outraged.

WINDLESHAM. Mais non, mais non...pas en plein jour. Mettez vous par là dans le...dans l'alcove...à côté du velours noir.

The costume undulates towards the black velvet platform. THOMAS is lost in admiration.

THOMAS. That gives her a chance, don't it? Damn pretty girl !

PHILIP. *(his eye twinkling).* She'll understand that, Tommy.

THOMAS. *(in good faith).* She won't mind.

MR STATE. *(who has been studying the undulations).* How they learn to walk like it...that's what beats me !

MR WINDLESHAM turns on the frame of lights which bear upon the velvet platform. The vision of female loveliness is now complete.

WINDLESHAM. There...that's the coup d'oeil.

The vision turns this way and that to show what curves of loveliness there may be. They watch, all but CONSTANTINE, who has sat silent and indifferent, rolling his second cigarette, which he now smokes serenely. At last PHILIP's voice breaks in, at its coolest, its most ironic.

PHILIP. And are we to assume, Mr State, that this piece of self-decoration really expresses the nature of any woman? Rather an awful thought!

THOMAS. *(in protest).* Why?

PHILIP. Or if it expresses a man's opinion of her...that's rather worse.

THOMAS. It's damned smart. Ain't it, Mr Huxtable?

MR HUXTABLE. *(who is examining closely).* No use to us, of course. We couldn't imitate that under fifteen guineas. Look at the...what d'you call it?

WINDLESHAM. *(loving the very word).* Diamanté.

THOMAS. *(with discretion).* Just for England of course you might have the shiny stuff marking a bit more definitely where the pink silk ends and she begins.

MR HUXTABLE. *(not to be sordid).* But it's a beautiful thing!

MR STATE. *(sweepingly).* Fitted to adorn the presiding genius of some intellectual and artistic salon. More artistic than intellectual perhaps...more likely to be the centre of Emotion than Thought!

WINDLESHAM. I could almost tell you who we shall sell that to. Mrs... Mrs...dear me...you'd all know the name. Assez, Mamoiselle...sortez.

He turns off the light. The vision becomes once more a ridiculously expensive dress, with a rather thin and shivering young person half inside it, who is thus unceremoniously got rid of.

WINDLESHAM. Numéro sept.

Another costume.

MR STATE. Now here again. Green velvet. Is it velvet?

WINDLESHAM. Panne velvet. Promenez, s'il vous plaît.

MR STATE. And ermine.

MR HUXTABLE. Good Lord...more buttons!

MR STATE. The very thing, no doubt, in which some Peeress might take the chair at a drawing-room meeting.

PHILIP. *(as he eyes the buttons and the ermine).* Either of the Humanitarian or of the Anti-Sweating League. Indeed, no peeress could dream of taking a chair without it.

MR STATE. *(in gentle reproof).* Sarcasm, Mr Philip.

PHILIP. *(won by such sweetness).* I really beg your pardon.

WINDLESHAM. Numéro dix.

A third costume.

PHILIP. What about this ?

MR STATE. Grey with a touch of pink...severely soft. An Anti-suffrage Platform.

PHILIP *(in tune with him).* No...it's cut square in the neck. Suffrage, I should say.

MR STATE. *(rubbing his hands).* Good! There is purpose in this persiflage, Major Thomas. Woman allures us along many paths. Be it ours to attend her, doing what service we may.

CONSTANTINE. You are a poet, Mr State.

MR STATE. I never wrote one in my life, sir.

CONSTANTINE. How many poets should cease scribbling and try to live such perfect epics as seems likely to be this purchase of yours of the Madras House.

MR STATE. *(much gratified).* I shall be proud to be your successor. *(Then he soars.)* But it is the Middle Class Woman of England that is waiting for me. The woman who still sits at the Parlour window of her Provincial Villa pensively gazing through the Laurel bushes. I have seen her on my Solitary Walks. She must have her chance to Dazzle and Conquer. That is every woman's Birthright...be she a Duchess in Mayfair or a doctor's wife in the suburbs of Leicester. And remember, gentlemen, that the Middle Class Women of England...think of them in bulk...they form one of the greatest Money Spending Machines the world has ever seen.

MR HUXTABLE. *(with a wag of the head; he is more at his ease now).* Yes...their husbands' money.

MR STATE. *(taking a long breath and a high tone).* All our most advanced thinkers are agreed that the economic independence of women is the next step in the march of civilization.

MR HUXTABLE. *(overwhelmed).* Oh...I beg pardon.

MR STATE. *(soaring now more than ever).* And now that the Seed of Freedom is sown in their Sweet Natures...what Mighty Forest...what a Luxuriant, Tropical, Scented growth of Womanhood may not spring up around us. For we live in an Ugly World. Look at my tie! Consider your vest, Major Thomas! *(His eye searches for those costumes, and finds one.)* This is all the Living Beauty that there is. We want more of it. I want to see that Poor Provincial Lady burst through the laurel bushes and dash down the road...Clad in Colours of the Rainbow.

WINDLESHAM has indeed detained the severely soft costume and its young lady and there she has stood for a while still smiling but wondering perhaps behind the smile into what peculiar company of milliners she has fallen. THOMAS, suddenly noticing that she is standing there, with the utmost politeness jumps up to hand his chair.

THOMAS. I say, though...allow me.

WINDLESHAM. Thank you...but she can't. Not in that corset.

MR STATE. Dear me, I had not meant to detain Mademoiselle. *(Then to amend his manners and rather as if it were an incantation warranted to achieve his purpose.)* Bon jour.

The young lady departs, a real smile quite shaming the unreal.

MR STATE. You clean forget they're there. We gave some time and money to elaborating a mechanical moving figure to take the place of...a real automaton, in fact. But sometimes it stuck and sometimes it ran away...

THOMAS. And the cost!

PHILIP. *(finely).* Flesh and blood is always cheaper.

MR STATE. You approve of corsets, Mr Windlesham?

WINDLESHAM. Oh, yes ... the figure is the woman, as we say.

MR STATE. Have you ever gone deeply into the Psychology of the question? A while ago I had a smart young Historian write Burrows a little Monograph on Corsets...price one shilling. Conservative, summing up in their favour. And we made up a little Museum of them...at Southampton, I think...but that was not a success. Major Thomas...we must send Mr Windlesham a copy of that Monograph. You will find it very interesting.

WINDLESHAM. I'm sure I shall. Can I do any more for you?

PHILIP. See me before I go, will you?

WINDLESHAM. Then it's au'voir.

And he flutters away.There is a pause as if they had to recollect where they were. It is broken by PHILIP saying meditatively.

PHILIP. I sometimes wonder if we realize what women's clothes are like...or our own, for that matter.

MR HUXTABLE. What's that?

PHILIP. Have you ever tried to describe a costume as it would appear to a strange eye? Can you think of this last? A hat as little like a hat as anything on a creature's head may be. Lace. Flowers of a colour it never pleases God to grow them. And a jewelled feather...a feather with stones in it. The rest might be called a conspiracy in three colours on the part of a dozen sewing women to persuade you that the creature they have clothed can neither walk, digest her food, nor bear children. Now...can that be beautiful?

MR STATE. *(To whom this is the real conversational thing).* Mr Philip, that notion is a lever thrust beneath the very foundations of society.

MR HUXTABLE. *(Showing off a little).* Oh...trying to upset people's ideas for the sake of doing it...silly.

THOMAS. *(with solid sense)* I think a crowd of well-dressed women is one of the most beautiful things in the world.

PHILIP. Have you ever seen an Eastern woman walk into a Bond Street tea shop?

THOMAS. No.

PHILIP. *(forcefully)* I have.

CONSTANTINE. Ah.

With one long meditative exhalation he sends a little column of smoke into the air. MR STATE turns to him deferentially.

MR STATE. We are boring you, Mr Madras, I'm afraid. You were Facile Princeps upon all these questions so long ago.

CONSTANTINE speaks in the smoothest of voices.

CONSTANTINE. No, I am not bored, Mr State...only a little horrified.

MR STATE. Why so?

CONSTANTINE. You see...I am a Mahommedan...and this attitude towards the other sex has become loathsome to me.

This bombshell, so delicately exploded, affects the company very variously. It will be some time before MR HUXTABLE grasps its meaning at all. THOMAS simply opens his mouth. MR STATE has evidently found a new joy in life. PHILIP, to whom it seems no news, merely says in light protest...

PHILIP. My dear Father!

MR STATE. *(as he beams round).* A real Mahommedan?

CONSTANTINE. I have become a Mahommedan. If you were not it would be inconvenient to live permanently at Hit...a village upon the borders of Southern Arabia...that is my home. Besides, I was converted.

THOMAS. *(having recovered enough breath).* I didn't know you could become a Mahommedan.

CONSTANTINE. *(with some severity)*. You can become a Christian, sir.

THOMAS. *(a little shocked)*. Ah...not quite the same sort of thing.

MR STATE. *(who feels that he really is re-discovering the old world)*. But how very interesting! Was it a sudden conversion?

CONSTANTINE. No...I had been searching for a religion...a common need in these times...and this is a very fine one, Mr State.

MR STATE. Is it?. I must look it up. The Koran! Yes, I've never read the Koran...an oversight.

He makes a mental note. And slowly, slowly, the full iniquity of it has sunk into MR HUXTABLE. His face has gome from red to white and back again to red. He becomes articulate and vehement. He thumps the table.

MR HUXTABLE. And what about Amelia?

MR STATE. *(with conciliatory calm)*. Who is Amelia?

PHILIP. Afterwards, Uncle.

MR HUXTABLE. *(thumping again)*. What about your wife? No, I won"t be quiet, Phil! It's illegal.

CONSTANTINE. *(with a half-cold, half-kindly eye on him)*. Harry...I dislike to see you make yourself ridiculous.

Only this was needed.

MR HUXTABLE. Who cares if I'm ridiculous. I've not spoken to you for thirty years...have I? That is...I've not taken more notice of you than I could help. And I come here today full of forgiveness...and curiosity...to see what your'e really like now...and whether I never really felt all that about you at all...and damned if you don't go and put up a fresh game on me ! What about Amelia? Religion this time! Mahommedan, indeed...at your age! Can't you ever settle down? I beg your pardon, Mr State. All right, Phil, afterwards! I've not done...but you're quite right...afterwards.

The gust over, MR STATE, who is a little beblown by it at such close quarters, says partly with a peace-making intention, partly in curiosity.

MR STATE. Do you indulge in a Harem?

MR HUXTABLE. If you insult my sister by answering that question...!

With a look and a gesture CONSTANTINE can silence him. Then with the coldest dignity he replies...

CONSTANTINE. My household, sir, is that of the ordinary Eastern gentleman of my position. We do not speak of our women in public.

MR STATE. I'm sure I beg your pardon.

CONSTANTINE. Not at all. It is five years since I definitely retired from business and decided to consummate my affection for the East by settling down there. This final visit to Europe...partly to see you, Mr State...was otherwise only to confirm my judgement on the question.

MR STATE. Has it?

CONSTANTINE. It has. I was always out of place amongst you. I was sometimes tempted to regret my scandalous conduct...*(a slight stir from MR HUXTABLE)*. Hush, Harry...hush! But I never could persude myself to amend it. It is some slight personal satisfaction to me to discover...with a stranger's eye...that Europe in its attitude towards women is mad.

MR STATE. Mad!

CONSTANTINE. Mad.

THOMAS. *(who is all ears)*. I say!

CONSTANTINE. You possibly agree with me, Major Thomas.

THOMAS. (much taken aback). No...I don't think so.

CONSTANTINE. Many men do but – poor fellows – they dare not say so. For instance, Mr State, what can be said of a community in which five men of some ability and dignity are met together to traffic in...what was the Numero of that aphrodisiac that so particularly attracted Major Thomas?

THOMAS is shocked even to violence.

THOMAS. No...really. I protest –

MR STATE. *(utterly calm)*. Easy, Major Thomas. Let us consider the accusation philosophically. *(Then with the sweetest smile)*. Surely that is a gross construction to put on the instinct of every beautiful woman to adorn herself.

CONSTANTINE. Why gross? I delight in pretty women prettily adorned. To come home after a day's work to the welcome of one's women folk...to find them unharassed by notions of business or politics...ready to refresh one's spirit by attuning it to the gentler, sweeter side of life...

THOMAS. *(making hearty atonement)*. Oh! Quite so...quite so.

CONSTANTINE. I thought you would agree with me, Major Thomas. That is the Mahommedan gentleman's domestic ideal.

THOMAS. *(brought up short)*. Is it?

CONSTANTINE. But you don't expect to find your wife dressed like that...the diamante and the...

THOMAS. *(mental discomfort growing on him)*. No...that was a going-out dress.

PHILIP. *(greatly enjoying this contest)*. Oh...Tommy! Tommy!

THOMAS. *(in tortuosity of mind - and conscience)*. But I tell you if my wife would...that is, if any chap's wife will...I mean...*(then he gets it out)* if a woman always kept herself smart and attractive at home then a man would have no excuse for gadding about after other women.

MR HUXTABLE joins the fray, suddenly, snappily.

MR HUXTABLE. She sits looking after his children...what more does he want of her?

CONSTANTINE. Harry is a born husband, Major Thomas.

MR HUXTABLE. I'm not a born libertine, I hope.

THOMAS. Libertine be damned!

MR STATE. *(pacifically)*. Gentlemen, gentlemen...these are abstract propositions.

MR HUXTABLE. Gadding after another man's wife, perhaps! Though I don't think you ever did that, Constantine...I'll do you justine...I don't think you ever did.

CONSTANTINE. I never did.

PHILIP. *(with intense mischief).* Oh, Tommy, Tommy...can you say the same?

THOMAS is really flabergasted at the indecency.

THOMAS. Phil, that ain't nice...that ain't gentlemanly. And I wasn't thinking of that and you know I wasn't. And...we ain't all so unattractive to women as you are.

MR STATE loses himself in the enjoyment of this repartee.

MR STATE. Ah,...sour grapes, Mr Philip. We mustn't be personal...but is it Sour Grapes?

PHILIP. *(very coolly on his defence).* Thank you, Tommy...I can attract just the sort of woman I want to attract. But as long as it's Numero Cinq, Six or Sept that attracts you...well...so long will Madras House be an excellent investment for Mr State.

That is the end of that little breeze and CONSTANTINE's voice completes the quieting.

CONSTANTINE. Phil is a cold-blooded egotist and if women like him that is their misfortune. I know his way with a woman...coax her onto the intellectual plane where he thinks he can better her. You have my sympathy, Major Thomas. I also am as susceptible as Nature means a man to be...as all women must wish him to be. And I referred to these going-out dresses because – candidly – I found myslef obliged to leave a country where wome are let loose with money to spend and time to waste. Encouraged to flaunt their charms on the very streets...proud if they see the busmen wink...

MR HUXTABLE. Not busmen *(He is only gently deprecating now).*

CONSTANTINE. Proud, my dear Harry, if they see a cabman smile.

MR HUXTABLE looks round and then nods solemnly and thoughtfully.

MR HUXTABLE. Yes, it's true. I'd deny it any other time, but I've been thinking a bit lately...and the things you think of once you start to think! And it's true. *(But with great chivalry)* Only they don't know they do it. *(Then a doubt occurring).* D'you think they know they do it, Phil?

PHILIP. Some of them suspect, Uncle.

MR HUXTABLE. *(his faith unspoiled).* No, what I say is it's Instinct...and we've just got to be as nice-minded about it as we can. There was Julia, this summer at Weymouth...that's one of my daughters. Bought herself a dress...not one of the Numero sort, of course...but very pretty...orange colour, it was...stripes. But you could see it a mile off on the parade...and her sisters all with their noses out of joint. I said to myself...Instinct...

Suddenly, MR STATE rescues the discussion.

MR STATE. Yes, sir...the noblest Instinct of all...the Instinct to Perpetuate our Race. Let us take High Ground in this matter, gentlemen.

CONSTANTINE. *(unstirred).* The very highest, Mr State. If you think that to turn Weymouth for a month a year into a cockpit of haphazard love-making with all the consequences that custom entails is the best way of perpetuating your race...well, I disagree with you...but it's a point of iew. What I ask is why Major Thomas and myself...already perhaps in a creditable state of marital perpetuation...should have our busy London lives obsessed by...What is this thing?

PHILIP. La belle Helene's new hat, father.

CONSTANTINE. Now, that may be ugly...I hope I never made anything quite so ugly myself ... but it's attractive.

PHILIP. *(with a wry face).* No, father

CONSTANTINE. Isn't it, Major Thomas?

THOMAS. *(honestly).* Well...it makes you look at 'em when you might not otherwise.

CONSTANTINE. Yes...it's provocative. Its intention is that none of the world's work shall be done while it's about. And when it's always about I honestly confess again that I cannot do my share. It's a terrible thing to be constantly conscious of women. They have their uses to the world...as you so happily phrased it, Mr State...their perpetual use...and the world's interest is best served by keeping them strictly to it. Are these provocative ladies *(he fingers the hat again)* remarkable for perpetuation nowadays?

Once more MR STATE bursts in – this time almost heart-brokenly.

MR STATE. I can't bear this, sir...I can't bear to take such a view of life...no man of feeling could. Besides, it's Reactionary...you're on the wrong track. You must come back to us, sir. You gave us Joy and Pleasure...can we do without them? When you find yourself once more among the Loveliness you helped us to Worship you'll change your mind. What was the end of that little story of the Duchess? How, on the appointed night, attired in her Madras Creation she swept into the Ballroom with a frou-frou of silk skirt wafting perfume as she came...while her younger rivals Pale before the Intoxication of her Beauty and every man in the room...young and old...struggles for a Glimpse...a Word...a Look *(Once again he starts to soar).* A Ballroom, sir...isn't it one of the sweetest sights in the World? When bright the lamps shine o'er Fair Women and Brave Men. Music arrises with its Voluptuous Swell. Soft eyes look Love to eyes which speak again. And all goes Merry as a Marriage Bell! Byron, gentlemen, taught me at my mother's knee. The poet of Love and Liberty...read every school in America.

At the end of this recitation, which MR HUXTABLE barely refrains from applauding, CONSTANTINE goes coolly on.

CONSTANTINE. Mr State, that is my case. The whole of our upper class life, which everyone with a say in the government of the country tries to lead...is now run as a ballroom is run. Men swaggering before women...the women ogling the men. Once a lad got some training in manliness. But now from the very start...! In your own progressive country...mixed education...oh, my dear sir...mixed education!

MR STATE. A softening influence.

CONSTANTINE. *(Unexpectedly)*. Of course it is. And what has it sunk to, moreover...all education nowadays? Book-learning. Because woman's a dab at that...though it's of quite secondary importance to a man.

THOMAS. *(feelingly)*. That's so.

CONSTANTINE. Yes. Read Nietzsche...as my friend Tarleton says. *(All one gathers from this cryptic allusion is that MR HUXTABLE at any rate reprobates Tarleton and inferentially Nietzsche)*. At Oxford and Cambridge it grows worse...married Professors...Newnham and Girton...sufffrage questions...purity questions.

MR HUXTABLE. Of course, some of the novels...

CONSTANTINE. From seventeen to thirty-four...the years which a man should consecrate to the acquiring of political virtue...wherever he turns he is distracted, provoked, tantalized by the barefaced presence of women. How's he to keep a clear brain for the larger issues of life? Why do you soldiers, Major Thomas, volunteer with such alacrity for foreign service?

THOMAS. *(with a jump)*. Good God...I never thought of that.

CONSTANTINE. What's the result? Every great public question...all politics, all religion, all economy is being brought down to the level of women's emotion. Admirable in its way...charming in its place. But softening, sentimentalizing, enervating...lapping the world, if you let it, in the nursery cotton wool of prettiness and pettiness. Men don't realize how far rotted by the process they are...that's what's so fatal. We're used to a whole Nation's anger being vented in scoldings...or rather we're getting used to the thought that it's naughty to be angry at all. Justice degenerates into kindness...that doesn't surprise us. Religion is a pretty hymn tune to keep us from fear of the dark. You four unfortunates might own the truth just for once...you needn't tell your wives.

MR STATE. I am not married.

CONSTANTINE. I might have known it.

MR STATE. *(a little astonished)*. But no matter.

CONSTANTINE. *(with full appreciation of what he says)*. Women haven't morals or intellect in our sense of the words. They have other incompatible qualities quite as important, no doubt. But shut them away from public life and public exhibition. It's degrading to compete for them. Perhaps we're too late already...but oh, my dear sentimental Sir *(he addresses the pained though admiring MR STATE)* if we could replant the laurel bushes thick enough we might yet rediscover the fine world we are losing.

Except PHILIP, who sits detached and attentive, they are all rather depressed by this judgement upon them. THOMAS recovers sufficiently to ask...

THOMAS. Are you advocating polygamy in England?

CONSTANTINE. That is what it should come to.

THOMAS. Well... I call that rather shocking. *(Then with some hopeful interest.)* And is it practical?

CONSTANTINE. I did not anticipate the reform in my lifetime...so I left for the East.

PHILIP. *(finely)* You did quite right, Father. I wish everyone of your way of thinking would do the same.

CONSTANTINE is ready for him.

CONSTANTINE. Are you prepared for so much depopulation? Think of the women who'd be off tomorrow.

MR HUXTABLE wakes from stupefaction to say with tremendous emphasis.

MR HUXTABLE. Never.

CONSTANTINE. Wrong, Harry.

MR HUXTABLE. No, I'm not wrong just because you say so! You ought to listen to me a bit sometimes. I always listened to you.

CONSTANTINE. Bless your quick temper.

Who could resist CONSTANTINE'S smile?...Well, not HUXTABLE.

MR HUXTABLE. Oh...go on...tell me why I'm wrong...I daresay I am.

CONSTANTINE. Even if you have liked bringing up six daughters and not getting them married...how have they liked it? You should have drowned them at birth, Harry...

MR HUXTABLE. You must have your joke, mustn't you?

CONSTANTINE. Therefore how much pleasanter for you...how much better for them...if you'd only to find one man ready for a small consideration to marry the lot.

MR HUXTABLE. *(with intense delight)*. Now if I was to tell my wife that she wouldn't see the umour of it.

CONSTANTINE. The woman emancipator's last ditch, Mr State, is the trust that women will side with him. Don't make any mistake. This is a serious question to them...of health and happiness...and sometimes of bread and butter. Quite apart from our customers here...kept women every one of them...

MR STATE. *(in some alarm)* You don't say.

CONSTANTINE. *(gently lifting him from the little trap)*. Economically. Kept by their husbands...or if they live on their dividends kept by Society.

PHILIP. What about men who live on their dividends?

MR STATE. No...now don't let us go on to politics.

CONSTANTINE....And apart from the parisoners in that chaste little fortress on Denmark Hill...we used to hundred free and independent women...making clothes for the others, the ladies. They are as free as you like...free to go...free to starve. How much do they rejoice in their freedom to earn their living by ruining their health and stifling their instincts? Answer me, Harry, you monster of good-natured wickedness.

MR HUXTABLE. What's that?

CONSTANTINE. What else is your Roberts and Huxtable but a harem of industry? Do you know that it would sicken with horror a good Mahommedan? You buy these girls in the open market...you keep them under lock and key...

MR HUXTABLE. I do?

CONSTANTINE. Quite right, Harry, no harm done. *(Then his voice sinks to the utmost seriousness).* But you coin your profits out of them by outting on exhibition for ten hours a day...their good looks, their good manners, their womanhood. Hired out it is to any stranger to hold as cheap for a few minutes as common decency allows. And when you've worn them out you turn them out...forget their very names...wouldn't know their faces if you met them selling matchess at your door. For such treatment of potential motherhood, my Prophet condemns a man to Hell.

MR HUXTABLE. *(breathless with amazement).* Well, I never did in all my born days! They can marry respectably, can't they? We like em to marry.

PHILIP. Yes, Uncle...I went into that question with Miss Yates and the Brigstocks this morning.

CONSTANTINE. *(completing his case)* I ask you all...what is to happen to you as a nation? Where are your future generations coming from? What with the well-kept women you flatter and aestheticize till they won't give you children and the free women you work at market rates till they can't give you children...

MR HUXTABLE. *(half humourously sulky).* Miss Yates has obliged us anyhow.

PHILIP. *(quickly copying him)* And we're going to dismiss her.

MR HUXTABLE flashes again into protestation.

MR HUXTABLE. What else can we do? But I said you weren't to be hard on the girl. And I won't be upset like this, I want to take things as I find em...that is as I used to find em...before there was any of these ideas going around...and I'm sure we were happier without em. Stifling their instincts...it's a horrid way to talk. And I don't believe it. I could send for every girl in the shop and not one of em would hint at it to me. *(He has triumphed with himself so far but his new-born intellectual conscience brings him down).* Not that that proves anything, does it? I'm a fool. It's a beastly world. But I don't make it so, do I?

PHILIP. Who does?

MR HUXTABLE. Other people *(PHILIP's eye is on him).* Oh, I see it coming. You're going to say we're all the other people or something. I'm getting up to you.

CONSTANTINE. (very carefully) What is this about a Miss Yates?

PHILIP. A little bother down at Peckham. I can tell you afterwards if you like.

CONSTANTINE. No...there is no need.

Something in the tone of this last makes PHILIP look up quickly. But MR STATE, with a sudden thought, has first dived for his watch and then at the sight of it gets up from the table.

MR STATE. Gentlemen, are you aware of the time? I may mention that I have a City appointment at four o'clock.

CONSTANTINE. *(polite but leisurely)*. Are we detaining you, Mr State? Not universal or compulsory polygamy, Major Thomas. That would be nonsense. The very distribution of the sexes forbids it. But its recognition is one of the logical outcomes of the aristocratic method of government. And that's the only ultimate method...all others are interim plans for sifting out various autocracies. The community of the future will specialize its functions. Women will find, I hope, some intellectual companions likes my son who will besides take a gentle interest in the County Council. There will be single-hearted men like Harry, content with old-fashioned domesticity. There will be poets like you, Mr State, to dream about women and to dress them...theeir bodies in silks and their virtues in phrases. But there must also be such men as Major Thomas and myself...

THOMAS rises, yet again, to this piece of chaff.

THOMAS. No, no, I'm not like that...not in the least. Because a fellow has been in the army! Don't drag me in.

MR STATE. As stimulating a conversation as I remember. A little hard to follow at times...but worth far more than the sacrifice of any mere business doings.

CONSTANTINE takes the hint graciously and is apt for business at once.

CONSTANTINE. My fault! Shall we agree, Mr State, to accept as much of your offer as you have no intention of altering? We are dealing both for the shops?

MR STATE. Yes. What are we proposing to knock off their valuation, Major Thomas?

THOMAS. Eight thousand six hundred.

CONSTANTINE. Phil, what were we prepared to come down.

PHILIP. Nine thousand.

CONSTANTINE. A very creditable margin. Your offer is accepted, Mr State.

MR STATE feels he must really play up to such magnificent conducting of business.

MR STATE. I should prefer to knock you down by only eight thousand.

CONSTANTINE. *(keeping the advantage)*. Isn't that merely romantic of you, Mr State...not in the best form of business art?

THOMAS. But the conditions you know?

CONSTANTINE. We accept your conditions. If they won't work you'll be only too anxious to alter them. So the business is done.

MR HUXTABLE'S eyes are wide.

MR HUXTABLE. But look here.

PHILIP. Uncle Harry has something to say...

MR HUXTABLE. *(assertively).* Yes.

CONSTANTINE. Something different to say, Harry?

MR HUXTABLE. *(after thinking it over).* No.

So CONSTANTINE returns happily to his subject.

CONSTANTINE. What interests me about this Woman Question...now that I've settled my personal share in it...is to wonder how Europe, hampered by such an unsolved problem, can hope to stand up to the Oriental revival.

THOMAS. What's that?

CONSTANTINE. You'll hear of it shortly. Up from the Persian Gulf to where I live we could grow enough wheat to feed the British Empire. Life there is simple and spacious...the air is not breathed out. All we want is a happy, hardy race of men under a decent government we shall soon beget it. But you Europeans! Is this the symbol you are marching to the future under. *(He has found again and lifts up la Belle Helenes new hat)* A cap of slavery! You are all idolators of women...and they are the slaves of your idolatry.

MR STATE. *(with undisguised admiration).* Mr Madras, I am proud to have met you again. If I say another word, I may be so interested in your reply that I shall miss my appointment. My coat? Thank you, Mr Philip. I have to meet a man about a new system of country house drainage that he wants me to finance. I can hardly hope for another Transcendental Discussion upon that.

CONSTANTINE. Why not?

MR STATE. If you were he! Good-bye sir. Good day, Mr Huxtable. Till tomorrow, Major Thomas. No, Mr Philip, don't you see me down.

He is off for his next deal. PHILIP civilly takes him past the door, saying.

PHILIP. Your car's at the Bond Street entrance, I expect.

And then comes back. CONSTANTINE is keeping half a friendly eye on HUXTABLE, who fidgets under it. THOMAS takes breath and expounds a grievance.

THOMAS. That's how he settles business. But leaves us all the papers to do. I shall take mine home. The four-thirty gets me indoors by a quarter to six. Time for a cup of tea! Phil, have you got China tea?

PHILIP. Downstairs.

MR HUXTABLE. I must be getting back, I think.

CONSTANTINE. Harry...your'e running away from me.

MR HUXTABLE. *(in frank, amused confession).* Yes...I was. Habit y'know...habit.

CONSTANTINE. *(with the most friendly condescension).* Suppose I go with you...part of the way. How do you go?

MR HUXTABLE. On a bus.

CONSTANTINE. Suppose we go together...on a bus.

MR HUXTABLE *(desperately cunning).* It's all right...they won't see me with you. We don't close till seven.

CONSTANTINE'S face sours.

CONSTANTINE. No, to be sure. Phil, I can't come to dinner I'm afraid.

PHILIP. Oh, I was going to tell you. Mother will be there. Tommy, you know the tea-room.

THOMAS. *(all tact).* Oh, quite!

PHILIP. Straight downstairs, first to the left and the second passage. I'll follow.

THOMAS departs. CONSTANTINE says indifferently...

CONSTANTINE. Then I'll come in after dinner.

PHILIP. You don't mind?

CONSTANTINE. No.

There stands MR HUXTABLE, first on one foot and then on the other, desperately nervous. CONSTANTINE smiling at him. PHILIP cannot resist it. He says...

PHILIP. It's afterwards now, Uncle. Fire away.

And is off. CONSTANTINE still smiles. Poor MR HUXTABLE makes a desperate effort to do the proper thing by this reprobate. He forms his face into a frozon. It's no use; an answering smile will come. He surrenders.

MR HUXTABLE. Look here...don't let's talk about Amelia.

CONSTANTINE. No...never rake up the past.

MR HUXTABLE. Lord! What else has a chap got to think of?

CONSTANTINE. That's why you look so old.

MR HUXTABLE. Do I now?

CONSTANTINE. What age are you?

MR HUXTABLE. Sixty.

The two sit dozvn together.

CONSTANTINE. You should come and stay with me at Hit...not far from Hillel...Hillel is Babylon, Harry.

MR HUXTABLE. *(curious).* What's it like there?

CONSTANTINE. The house is white and there are palm trees about it...and not far off flows the Euphrates.

MR HUXTABLE. Just like in the Bible. *(His face is wistful.)* Constantine.

CONSTANTINE. Yes, Harry.

MR HUXTABLE. You've said odder things this afternoon than I've ever heard you say before.

CONSTANTINE. Probably not.

MR HUXTABLE. *(wondering).* And I haven't really minded em. But I believe it's the first time I've ever understood you...and p'raps that's just as well for me.

CONSTANTINE. *(encouragingly).* Oh...why, Harry?

MR HUXTABLE. Because...d'you think it's only not being very clever keeps us...well behaved?

CONSTANTINE. Has it kept you happy?

MR HUXTABLE. *(impatient at the petty word).* Anyone can be happy. What worries me is having got to my age and only just beginning to understand anything at all. And you can't learn it out of books, old man. Books don't tell you the truth...at least not any that I can find. I wonder if I'd been a bit of a dog like you...? But there it is...you can't do things on purpose. And what's more, don't you go to think I'd have done them if I could...knowing them to be wrong. (Then comes a discovery). But I was always jealous of you, Constantine, for you seemed to get the best of everything...and I know people couldn't help being fond of you...for I was fond of you myself, whatever you did. That was odd to start with. And now here we are, both of us old chaps...

CONSTANTINE. *(as he throws back his head).* I am not old.

MR HUXTABLE. *(with sudden misgiving).* You don't repent, do you?

CONSTANTINE. What of?

MR HUXTABLE. Katherine said this morning that you might have...but I wasn't afraid of that. *(Now he wags his head wisely.)* You know...you evil-doers...you upset us all and you hurt our feelings and of course you ought to be ashamed of yourself. But...well...it's like the only time I went abroad. I was sick going...I was orribly uncomfortable...I ated the cooking...I was sick coming back. But I wouldn't have missed it...!

CONSTANTINE. *(in affectionate good fellowship).* Come to Arabia, Harry.

MR HUXTABLE. *(humorously pathetic about it).* Don't you make game of me. My time's over. What have I done with it now? Married. Brought up a family. Been master to a few hundred girls and fellows who never really cared a bit for me. I've been made a convenience of...that's my life. That's where I envy you. You've had your own way...and you don't look now as if you'd be damned for it either.

CONSTANTINE. *(in gentlemanly defiance).* I shan't be.

MR HUXTABLE *shakes a fist, somewhat, though unconsciously in the direction of the ceiling.*

MR HUXTABLE. It's not fair and I don't care who hears me say so.

CONSTANTINE. Suppose we shout it from the top of the bus.

As they start, MR HUXTABLE returns to his mundane, responsible self.

MR HUXTABLE. But you know, old man...you'll excuse me, I'm sure...and it's all very well having theories and being able to talk...still, you did treat Amelia very badly...and those other ones, too...say what you like! Let go my arm, will you!

CONSTANTINE. Why?

MR HUXTABLE. *(his scruples less strong than the soft touch of CONSTANTINE's hand).* Well...p'raps you needn't. *(A thought strikes him).* Are you really going away for good this time?

CONSTANTINE. Tomorrow.

MR HUXTABLE. *(beaming on him).* Then come home and see mother and the girls.

MAJOR THOMAS comes back, looking about him.

THOMAS. Excuse me...I left my hat.

CONSTANTINE. It will make them very uncomfortable.

MR HUXTABLE. *(his smile fading).* D'you think so? Won't it do em good...broaden their minds ?

PHILIP comes back, too.

MR HUXTABLE. Phil...shall I take your father ome to call?

PHILIP. *(after one gasp at the prospect says with great cheerfulness...)* Certainly.

CONSTANTINE. I'll be with you by nine, Phil.

MR HUXTABLE's dare-devil heart fails once more.

MR HUXTABLE. I say...better not be too friendly through the shop.

CONSTANTINE smiles still, but does not loose his arm. Off they go.

THOMAS. (still searching). Where the devil did I put it?

PHILIP. Pity you can't take father's place at dinner, Tommy.

THOMAS. stops and looks at him aggrievedly.

THOMAS. Are you chaffing me?

PHILIP. We might get some further light on the Woman Question. My mother's opinion and Jessica's upon such men as you and my father.

He picks up some papers and sits to them at the table.

THOMAS. Look here, Phil...don't you aggravate me into behaving rashly. Here it is. *(He has found his hat on a gasbracket - and he slams it on).*

PHILIP. With Jessica?

THOMAS. *(with ferocious gallantry).* Yes...a damned attractive woman.

PHILIP. After all...as an abstract proposition, Tommy...polyandry is just as simple a way...and as far as we know, as much Nature's way as the other. We ought to have put that point to the gentle Mahommedan.

THOMAS. *(after vainly considering this for a moment).* Phil, I should like to see you in love with a woman...It'd serve you right.

Suddenly PHILIP drops his mocking tone and his face grows gentle and grave.

PHILIP. Tommy...what's the purpose of it all? Apart from the sentimental wallowings of Mr Eustace Perrin State...and putting that Lord of Creation, my father, on one side for a moment...what do we slow-breeding, civilized people get out of love...and the beauty of women...and the artistic setting that beauty demands ? For which we do pay rather a big price, you know, Tommy. What do we get for it?

THOMAS. *(utterly at sea)*. I don't know.

PHILIP. It's an important question. Think it over in the train.

THOMAS. Old chap...I beg your pardon...the County Council is the best place for you. It'll stop your addling over these silly conundrums.

PHILIP. *(subtly)*. On the contrary.

THOMAS. *(his favourite phrase again)*. What do you mean?

PHILIP. Get out...you'll miss that four-thirty.

THOMAS gets out. PHILIP gets desperately to loathed business.

ACT IV

PHILIP, his mother, and JESSICA are sitting after dinner round the drawing-room fire in Phillimore Gardens. JESSICA rather, is away upon the bench of her long, black piano, sorting bound books of music, and the firelight hardly reaches her. But it flickers over MRS MADRAS, and though it marks more deeply the little bitter lines on her face, it leaves a glow there in recompense. She sits, poor anxious old lady, gazing not into the fire, but at the shining copper-fender, her hands on her lap as usual. Every now and then she lifts her head to listen. PHILIP is comfortable upon the sofa opposite; he is smoking and is deep besides in some weighty volume, the Longman Edition of the Minority Report of the Poor Law Commission, perhaps.

It is a charming room. The walls are grey, the paint is a darker grey. The curtains to the two long windows are of the gentlest pink brocade; the lights that hang on plain little brackets from the walls are a soft pink, too, and there is no other colour in the room, but the maziness of some Persian rugs on the floor and the mellowed brilliancy of the Arundel prints on the walls. There is no more furniture than there need be; there is no more light than there need be; yet it is not empty or dreary. There is just nothing to jar, nothing to prevent a sensitive soul finding rest there.

The parlour maid comes in; she is dressed in grey, too, capless, some black ribbons about her. (Really, JESSICA's home inclines to be a little precious!) She brings letters, one for JESSICA, two for PHILIP, and departs.

PHILIP. Last post.

JESSICA. Half-past nine. I suppose your father means to come?

PHILIP. He said so.

MRS MADRAS. Is your letter interesting, Jessica?

JESSICA. A receipt.

MRS MADRAS. Do you run bills?

JESSICA. Lots.

MRS MADRAS. Is that quite wise?

JESSICA. The tradesmen prefer it.

With that she walks to her writing-table. JESSICA'S manner to her mother-in-law is over-courteous, an unkind weapon against which the old lady, but half conscious of it, is quite defenceless. PHILIP has opened his second letter and whistles at its contents a bar of a tune that is in his head.

JESSICA. What's the matter, Phil? *(To emphasize his feelings he performs the second bar with variations.)* As bad as that?

For final comment he brings the matter to a firm close on one expressive note and puts the letter away. JESSICA flicks at him amusedly.

MRS MADRAS. How absurd! You can't tell in the least what he means.

JESSICA. No.

With forced patience she wanders back to her piano.

MRS MADRAS. You might play us something, Jessica...just to pass the time.

Unobserved, JESSICA casts her eyes up to the ceiling.

JESSICA. What will you have ?

MRS MADRAS. I am sure you play all the latest things.

JESSICA. I'm afraid you don't really like my playing.

MRS MADRAS. I do think it's a little professional. I prefer something softer.

PHILIP. Mother, what do you think parents gain by insisting on respect and affection from grown-up children?

MRS MADRAS. Isn't it their right?

PHILIP. But I asked what they gained.

JESSICA leaves the piano.

JESSICA. I'm afraid we are giving you a dull evening.

MRS MADRAS. *(with that suddenness which seems to characterize the HUXTABLE family).* Why do you never call me mother, Jessica?

JESSICA. Don't I?

MRS MADRAS. *(resenting prevarication).* You know you don't.

JESSICA. I suppose I don't think of you just like that.

MRS MADRAS. What has that to do with it?

JESSICA. *(more coldly courteous than ever).* Nothing...Mother.

MRS MADRAS. That's not a very nice manner of giving way, either, is it?

JESSICA. *(on the edge of an outburst).* It seemed to me sufficiently childish.

MRS MADRAS. *(parading a double injury).* I don't know what you mean. It's easy to be too clever for me, Jessica.

PHILIP mercifully intervenes.

MRS MADRAS. Isn't it natural? When an old woman has lost her husband or worse, if she's to lose her children, too, what has she left?

JESSICA. *(recovering a little kindness).* Her womanhood, Mother.

PHILIP. Her old-womanhood. You know, it may be a very beautiful possession.

The parlour maid announces 'MR CONSTANTINE MADRAS'. There stands Constantine in the bright light of the hall, more dramatically dignified than ever. As he comes in though, it seems as if there was the slightest strain in his charming manners. He has not changed his clothes for the evening. He goes straight to JESSICA, and it seems that he has a curious soft way of shaking hands with women.

CONSTANTINE. How do you do, Jessica? I find you looking beautiful.

JESSICA acknowledges the compliment with a little disdainful bend of the head and leaves him, then with a glance at PHILIP leaves the room. CONSTANTINE comes towards his wife. She does not look up, but her face wrinkles pathetically. So he speaks at last.

CONSTANTINE. Well, Amelia?

For MRS MADRAS it must be resentment or tears, or both. Resentment comes first.

MRS MADRAS. Is that the way to speak to me after thirty years?

CONSTANTINE. *(amicably).* Perhaps it isn't. But there's not much variety of choice in greetings, is there?

PHILIP, nodding to his father, has edged to the door and now edges out of it.

CONSTANTINE. They leave us alone. We might be an engaged couple.

She stays silent, distressfully avoiding his eye. He takes a chair and sits by her. He would say (as JESSICA no doubt would say of herself) that he speaks kindly to her.

CONSTANTINE. Well, Amelia? I beg your pardon. I repeat myself and you dislike the phrase. I hope, though, that you are quite well? Don't cry, dear Amelia...unless, of course, you want to cry. Well, then...cry. And, when you've finished crying...there's no hurry...you shall tell me why you wished to see me...and run the risk of upsetting yourself like this.

MRS MADRAS. *(dabbing her eyes).* I don't often cry. I don't often get a chance.

CONSTANTINE. I fear that is only one way of saying that you miss me.

The handkerchief is put away and she faces him.

MRS MADRAS. Are you really going back to that country tomorrow?

CONSTANTINE. Tomorrow morning.

MRS MADRAS. For good?

CONSTANTINE. *(with thanksgiving).* For ever.

MRS MADRAS. *(desperately resolute).* Will you take me with you?

It takes CONSTANTINE just a moment to recover.

CONSTANTINE. No, Amelia, I will not.

MRS MADRAS. *(reacting a little hysterically).* I'm sure I don't want to go and I'm sure I never meant to ask you. But you haven't changed a bit, Constantine...in spite of your beard. *(Then the voice saddens and almost dies away.)* I have.

CONSTANTINE. Only externally, I'm sure.

MRS MADRAS. Why did you ever marry me? You married me for my money.

CONSTANTINE. *(sighting boredom).* It is long ago.

MRS MADRAS. It isn't...it seems like yesterday. Didn't you marry me for my money?

CONSTANTINE. Partly, Amelia, partly. Why did you marry me?

MRS MADRAS. I wanted to. I was a fool.

CONSTANTINE. *(evenly still).* You were a fool, perhaps, to grumble at the consequence of getting what you wanted. It would have been kinder of me, no doubt, not to marry you. But I was more impetuous then and of course less experienced. I didn't realize you never could change your idea of what a good husband must be, nor how necessary it would become that you should.

MRS MADRAS. How dare you make excuses for the way you treated me?

CONSTANTINE. There were two excuses. I was the first. I'm afraid that you ultimately became the second.

MRS MADRAS. *(with spirit)*. I only stood up for my rights.

CONSTANTINE. You got them, too. We separated and there was an end of it.

MRS MADRAS. I've never been happy since.

CONSTANTINE. That is nothing to be proud of, my dear.

MRS MADRA.feels the strangeness between them wearing off.

MRS MADRAS. What happened to that woman and her son...that Flora?

CONSTANTINE. The son is an engineer...promises very well, his employers tell me. Flora lives at Hitchin...quite comfortably, I have reason to believe.

MRS MADRAS. She was older than me.

CONSTANTINE. About the same age, I think.

MRS MADRAS. You've given her money?

CONSTANTINE. *(his eyebrows up)*. Certainly...they were both provided for.

MRS MADRAS. Don't you expect me to be jealous?

CONSTANTINE. *(with a sigh)*. Still, Amelia?

MRS MADRAS. Do you ever see her now?

CONSTANTINE. I haven't seen her for years.

MRS MADRAS. It seems to me she has been just as well treated as I have...if not better.

CONSTANTINE. She expected less.

MRS MADRAS. And what about the others?

CONSTANTINE. *(his patience giving out)*. No, really, it's thirty years ago...I cannot fight my battles over again. Please tell me what I can do for you beyond taking you back with me.

MRS MADRAS. *(cowering to the least harshness)*. I didn't mean that. I don't know what made me say it. But it's dreadful seeing you once more and being alone with you.

CONSTANTINE. Now, Amelia, are you going to cry again?

MRS MADRAS. *(setting her teeth)*. No.

CONSTANTINE. That's right.

MRS MADRAS really does pull herself together and becomes intensely reasonable.

MRS MADRAS. What I really want you to do, if you please, Constantine, is not to go away. I don't expect us to live together...after the way you have behaved I could not consent to such a thing. But somebody must look after you when you are ill, and what's more, I don't think you ought to go and die out of your own country.

CONSTANTINE. *(meeting reason with reason)*. My dear...I have formed other ties.

MRS MADRAS. Will you please explain exactly what you mean by that?

CONSTANTINE. I am a Mahommedan.

MRS MADRAS. Nonsense.

CONSTANTINE. Possibly you are not acquainted with the Mahommedan marriage laws.

MRS MADRAS. D'you mean to say you're not married to me?

CONSTANTINE. No...though it was not considered necessary for me to take that into account in conforming to it...I did.

MRS MADRAS. Wel...I never thought you could behave any worse. Why weren't you satisfied in making me unhappy? If you've gone and committed blasphemy as well...I don't know what's to become of you, Constantine.

CONSTANTINE. Amelia, if I had been a Mahommedan from the beginning you might be living happily with me now.

MRS MADRAS. How can you say such a horrible thing? Suppose it were true?

CONSTANTINE. I came from the East.

MRS MADRAS. You didn't.

CONSTANTINE. Let us be quite accurate. My grandfather was a Smyrna Jew.

MRS MADRAS. You never knew him. Your mother brought you up a Baptist.

CONSTANTINE. I was an unworthy Baptist. As a Baptist I owe you apologies for my conduct. What does that excellent creed owe me for the little hells of temptation and shame and remorse that I passed through because of it?

MRS MADRAS. (in pathetic wonder). Did you, Constantine?

CONSTANTINE. I did.

MRS MADRAS. You never told me.

CONSTANTINE. (with manly pride). I should think not.

MRS MADRAS. But I was longing to have you say you were sorry and let me forgive you. Twice and three times I'd have forgiven you...and you knew it, Constantine.

CONSTANTINE recovers his humour, his cool courtesy, and his inhumanity, which he had momentarily lost.

CONSTANTINE. Yes, it wasn't so easy to escape your forgiveness. If it weren't for Mahomet, the Prophet of God, Amelia, I should hardly be escaping it now.

PHILIP comes delicately in.

PHILIP. I beg pardon...only my book. (Which he takes from the piano.)

CONSTANTINE. Don't go, Phil.

So PHILIP joins them and then, as silence supervenes, says with obvious cheerfulness.

PHILIP. How are you getting on?

MRS MADRAS (her tongue released). Philip, don't be flippant. It's just as your cousin Ernest said. Your father has gone and pretended to marry a lot of wretched women out in that country you showed me on the map, and I don't know what's to be done. My head's going round.

CONSTANTINE. Not a lot, Amelia.

MRS MADRAS. And if anybody had told me when I was a girl at school and learning about such things in History and Geography that I should ever find myself in such a situation as this, I wouldn't have believed them. *(She piles up the agony.)* Constantine, how are you going to face me Hereafter? Have you thought of that? Wasn't our marriage made in Heaven? I must know what is going to happen to us...I simply must. I have always prayed that you might come back to me and that I might close your eyes in death. You know I have, Philip, and I've asked you to tell him so. He has no right to go and do such wicked things. You're mine in the sight of God, Constantine, and you can't deny it.

Without warning, CONSTANTINE loses his temper, jumps up and thunders at her.

CONSTANTINE. Woman...be silent. *(Then, as in shame, he turns his back on her and says in the coldest voice.)* Philip, I have several things to talk over with you. Suggest to your mother that she should leave us alone.

PHILIP *(protesting against both temper and dignity).* I shall do nothing of the sort. While my father's in England and you're in our house, he can at least treat his wife with politeness.

MRS MADRAS *(with meek satisfaction).* I'd rather he didn't...it's only laughing at me. I'll go to bed. I'd much rather he lost his temper.

She gets up to go. CONSTANTINE's bitter voice stops her.

CONSTANTINE. Phil...when you were a boy...your mother and I once quarrelled in your presence.

PHILIP *(in bitterness, too).* I remember.

CONSTANTINE. I'm ashamed of it to this day.

MRS MADRAS *(quite pleasantly).* Well...I'm sure I don't remember it. What about?

CONSTANTINE. Oh...this terrible country. Every hour I stay in it seems to rob me of some atom of self-respect.

MRS MADRAS joins battle again at this.

MRS MADRAS. Then why did you come back? And why haven't you been to see me before...or written to me?

CONSTANTINE *(in humorous despair).* Amelia, don't aggravate me any more. Go to bed, if you're going.

MRS MADRAS. I wish I'd never seen you again.

PHILIP. Good night, Mother.

PHILIP gets her to the door and kisses her kindly. Then CONSTANTINE says with all the meaning possible...

CONSTANTINE. Good-bye, Amelia.

She turns, the bright hall light falling on her, looks at him hatefully, makes no other reply, goes. PHILIP comes back to the fire. All this is bitter to him, too. He eyes his father.

CONSTANTINE. I'm sorry. I'm upset. I was upset when came here.

PHILIP. What about? The visit to Denmark Hill?

CONSTANTINE *(who has apparently forgotten that)*. No...I didn't go there, after all.

PHILIP. Funked it?

CONSTANTINE *(accepting the gibe)*. I daresay. Once we were off the bus Harry began to mutter about hurting their feelings. I daresay I was funking it, too. I told him to tell them how unbendingly moral he had been with me. He shed three tears as we parted.

PHILIP. Yes...my mother was alone here. She's a disappointed woman...peevish with ill health. One has her at a disadvantage. But Aunt Kate...unveiled and confident with six corseted daughters to back her !

CONSTANTINE. You think, of course, that I've always treated your mother badly?

PHILIP. I can't help thinking so. Was it the only way to treat her?

CONSTANTINE. Was I meant to pass the rest of a lifetime making her forget that she was as unhappy as people who have outlived their purpose always are ?

PHILIP. Personally, I have this grudge against you both, my dear father. As the son of a quarrelsome marriage I have grown up inclined to dislike men and despise women. You're so full of this purpose of getting the next generation born. Suppose you thought a little more of its upbringing.

CONSTANTINE. What was wrong with yours?

PHILIP. I had no home.

CONSTANTINE. You spent a Sunday with me every month. You went to the manliest school I could find.

PHILIP. Never mind how I learnt Latin and Greek. Who taught me that every pretty, helpless woman was a man's prey...and how to order my wife out of the room?

CONSTANTINE *(with a shrug)*. My dear boy...they like it.

PHILIP. Do they?

CONSTANTINE. Well...how else are you to manage them?

PHILIP. Father, don't you realize that...in decadent England, at least, this manliness of yours is getting a little out of date...that you and your kind begin to look foolish at last?

CONSTANTINE *(voicing the discomfort that possesses him)*. I daresay. Thank God, I shall be quit of the country tomorrow! I got here late this evening because I travelled three stations too far in that Tube, sitting opposite, such a pretty little devil. She was so alive...so crying out for conquest...she had that curve of the instep and the little trick of swinging her foot that I never could resist. How does a man resist it? Yes. That's ridiculous and ignominious and degrading. I escaped from England to escape from it. Old age here...a loose lip and a furtive eye. I'd have asked you to shoot me first.

PHILIP. Was it that upset you?

CONSTANTINE. No. *(He frowns; his thoughts are much elsewhere. There is a moment's silence. PHILIP breaks it.)*

PHILIP. Father, what do you know about this Miss Yates affair?

CONSTANTINE gives him a sharp look; then carefully casual.

CONSTANTINE. What you've told me.

PHILIP. No more?

CONSTANTINE. Is there more to know?

PHILIP fishes out and hands across the letter over which he whistled.

PHILIP. This has just come from Miss Chancellor.

CONSTANTINE. Who's she?

PHILIP. The housekeeper at Peckham, who rashly accused Brigstock of being the other responsible party.

CONSTANTINE. Is he?

PHILIP. I think not. But she encloses a letter she has just had from Brigstock's solicitors to the effect that both an apology and compensation is due to him unless the slander is to come into court. Hers faithfully, Meyrick & Hodges.

CONSTANTINE. I don't know them.

PHILIP. We were all still making personal remarks at half-past twelve today...so by their expedition I should say they both are and are not a first-class firm. But suppose the whole thing is made public...then the question of the parentage must be cleared up. Miss Yates says its nobody's business but hers. That's an odd idea, in which, if she chooses to have it, the law seems to support her.

The steady eye and the steady voice have seemed to make the tension unbearable and Philip has meant them to. But he hardly expected this outburst. Constantine in his own dramatically dignified way has a fit of hysterics.

CONSTANTINE. Phil, I saw the little baggage when the shop closed. I insisted on her meeting me. You know how I've always behaved over these matters. No one could have been kinder. But she refused money.

PHILIP *(calling on the gods to witness this occasion)*. Well...I might have guessed. Oh...you incorrigible old man !

CONSTANTINE. She insulted me...said she'd done with me...denied me the right to my own child. I'd even have taken her away. But you're helpless. I never felt so degraded in my life...

PHILIP. Serve you right!

CONSTANTINE. But the girl's mad ! Think of my feelings. What does it make of me? Did she know what she was saying?

PHILIP *(framing his thoughts at last).* Possibly not...but I'm thankful some woman's been found at last to put you in your place.

These parental-filial passages have brought the two of them face to face, strung to shouting pitch. They become aware of it when JESSICA walks in very gently.

JESSICA. Your mother gone?

PHILIP. To bed.

JESSICA *(conscious of thunder).* Am I intruding? I sent Phil in for his book a while ago. He didn't return, so I judged that he was. Perhaps I'm not?

CONSTANTINE is master of himself again, though the hand holding the letter which PHILIP gave him does tremble a little still.

CONSTANTINE. Well...what does Miss Chancellor want ?

PHILIP. She asks my advice.

CONSTANTINE. Dismiss Baxter.

PHILIP. D'you mean Brigstock?

CONSTANTINE. Brigstock, then. Dismiss him.

PHILIP. What's he done to deserve it?

CONSTANTINE. He seems a nonentity of a fellow, and without grit enough to own up to his wife and risk his place. D'you want to protect a man from the consequences of what he is?

PHILIP. Society conspires to.

CONSTANTINE. Then pay him fifty pounds for the damage to his silly little reputation. That'll be a just consequence to you of sentimentalizing over him.

PHILIP. And stick to Miss Chancellor?

CONSTANTINE. Certainly. Thank her from the firm for nosing out such a scandal.

PHILIP. And what about Miss Yates?

JESSICA. The girl in your office this morning.

PHILIP. Yes.

JESSICA In the usual trouble?

PHILIP. How d'you know that?

JESSICA. By the tone of your voice.

CONSTANTINE *(more slowly, more carefully, a little resentfully).* Dismiss Miss Yates. Keep your eye on her...and in a year's time find her a better place and lover...if you can...in one of these new Madras Houses of State's. He seems to pay very well. *(Then with a breath of relief he becomes his old charming self again.)* Let us change the subject. How is Mildred, Jessica?

JESSICA. Growing.

CONSTANTINE. I've an appointment with my solicitor tonight...ten o'clock. There will be two or three thousand pounds to come to that young lady by my will. I mean to leave it as a dowry for her marriage...its interest to be paid to her if she's a spinster at thirty...which Heaven forbid.

PHILIP. What are you doing with the rest, Father?

CONSTANTINE. There are one or two...legacies of honour, shall I call them? What remains will come to you.

PHILIP. Yes...I don't want it, thank you.

CONSTANTINE. It isn't much.

PHILIP. Take it to Hit, that charming village on the borders of Southern Arabia. Stick it in the ground...let it breed more corn and oil for you. We've too much of it already...it breeds idleness here.

CONSTANTINE. Dear me!

They settle into a chat.

JESSICA. We're discussing a reduction of our income by a few hundreds a year.

PHILIP. I'm refusing State's directorship.

JESSICA. Though I'm waiting for Phil to tell me where the saving's to come in.

PHILIP. We ought to change that school of Mildred's, for one thing.

JESSICA. Nonsense, Phil.

PHILIP. My dear father, I spent a day there with the child, and upon my word the only thing she's being taught which will not be a mere idle accomplishment is gardening. And even in their gardens...No vegetables allowed !

JESSICA. Phil, I don't mean to have any nonsense with Mildred about earning her living. Accomplished women have a very good time in this world...serious women don't. I want my daughter to be happy.

PHILIP. If we've only enough life left to be happy with we must keep ourselves decently poor.

CONSTANTINE gets up.

CONSTANTINE. Could you get me a taxi, I wonder? It had started raining when I came.

PHILIP. There'll be one on the stand opposite.

CONSTANTINE. I mustn't be too late for Voysey.* He makes a favour of coming after hours.

JESSICA. I frankly cultivate expensive tastes. I like to have things beautiful around me. I don't know what else civilization means.

*Voysey is the solicitor in Barker's play, *The Voysey Inheritance*.

CONSTANTINE. I am sure that Philip can refuse you nothing.

PHILIP. If I do dismiss Miss Yates I wonder if I could do it brutally enough to induce her to accept some compensation.

JESSICA. What for?

PHILIP. She won't take money from this gentleman...whoever he is...that is, she won't be bribed into admitting her shame.

JESSICA. When a woman has gone wrong mayn't it be her duty to other women to own up to it?

CONSTANTINE *(who has stood still the while, stroking his beard).* If your auditors won't pass any decent sum, I should be happy to send you a cheque, Phil.

PHILIP *(with a wry smile).* That would be very generous of you, Father.

CONSTANTINE. Goodbye, Jessica.

JESSICA. Goodbye.

CONSTANTINE. Philip is fortunate in his marriage.

JESSICA. So good of you to remind him of that.

CONSTANTINE. You have a charming home. I wonder how much of your womanly civilization it would have needed to conquer me. Well...I leave you to your conversation. A pleasant life to you.

He bends over her hand as if to kiss it. She takes it as if fastidiously out of his soft grasp. So he bows again and leaves her.

CONSTANTINE. Victoria at eleven o'clock tomorrow, **PHILIP**.

PHILIP. Yes...I'll see you off.

CONSTANTINE. I have to do a little shopping quite early.

PHILIP. Shopping! What can the West send the East?

CONSTANTINE. I must take back a trinket or two.

PHILIP. To be sure! We do the same on our travels.

PHILIP sees him through the hall to the front door, hails a stray cab and is quit of him. JESSICA moves about as if to free the air of this visitation, and when PHILIP comes back ...

JESSICA. Does your father usually scatter cheques so generously and carelessly?

PHILIP. Jessica, while I have every respect for that young lady's independence...still two hundred pounds would be all to the good of the child's upbringing...and why shouldn't Miss Yates keep her secret?

JESSICA. Yes. I don't like your father. And I'm sometimes afraid that you're only an intellectual edition of him. It's very vital, of course, to go about seducing everybody to your own way of thinking. But really it's not quite civilized. You ought to learn to talk about the weather.

PHILIP. I cannot talk about what can't be helped.

He had settled to a chair and a cigarette, but on the impulse he abandons both and starts a lively argument instead. PHILIP's excited arguments are carried on in short dashes about the room and with queer un-English gestures.

PHILIP. And I wonder more and more what the devil you all mean by civilization. This room is civilization. Whose civilization? Not ours.

JESSICA *(in mock despair).* Oh dear!

PHILIP. Cheer up. Didn't you marry me because I thought more of Bach than Offenbach? Why shouldn't you share a fresh set of convictions? This sort of marriage is worthwhile, you know. Even one's quarrels have a certain dignity.

JESSICA. Go ahead...bless your heart.

PHILIP *(shaking his fist at the world in general)*. Whitechapel High Street's our civilization.

JESSICA. I don't know it.

PHILIP. Therefore you don't much matter, my dear...any more than my father did with his view of life as a sort of love-chase. *(He surveys the charming room that is his home.)* Persian carpet on the floor. Last supper by Ghirlandajo over the mantelpiece. The sofa you're sitting on was made in a forgotten France. This is a museum. And down at that precious school what are they cultivating Mildred's mind into but another museum...of good manners and good taste and ...*(He catches Jessica's half scornful, half kindly-quizzical look.)* Are we going to have a row about this?

JESSICA. If you Idealists want Mildred to live in the Whitechapel Road...make it a fit place for her.

PHILIP *(taking the thrust and enjoyably returning it)*. When she lives in it, it will become so. Why do I give up designing dresses and running a fashion shop to go on the County Council...if I can get on? And not to cut a fine figure there, either. But to be on a committee or committees. Not to talk finely even then...Lord keep me from the temptation...but to do dull, hard work over drains and disinfectants and...

JESSICA. Well...why, Phil? I may as well know.

PHILIP. To save my soul alive.

JESSICA. I'm sure I hope you may. But what is it we're to cultivate in poor Mildred's soul?

PHILIP stops in his walk and then . . .

PHILIP. Why not a sense of ugliness? Have you ever really looked at a London street...walked slowly up and down it three times...carefully testing it with every cultured sense?

JESSICA. Yes...it's loathsome.

PHILIP. Then what have you done?

JESSICA. What can one do?

PHILIP. Come home to play a sonata of Beethoven! Does that drown the sights and the sounds and the smell of it?

JESSICA. Yes...it does.

PHILIP *(in fierce revolt)*. Not to me...my God...not to me!

JESSICA *(gently bitter)*. For so many women, Phil, art has to make life possible.

PHILIP. Suppose we teach Mildred to look out of the window at the life outside. We want to make that impossible. Neither Art nor Religion nor good manners have made of the world a place I'll go on living in if I can help it. *(He throws himself into a chair.)* D'you remember in my young days when I used to spend part of a holiday lecturing on Shelley?

JESSICA. Yes.

PHILIP. I remember once travelling in the train with a poor wretch who lived...so he told me...on what margins of profit he could pick up by standing rather incompetently between the cornfield and the baker...or the coal mine and the fire...or the landowner and the tenant...I forget which. And he hated Jones...because Jones had done him out of a half per cent. on two hundred and fifty pounds...and if the sum had been bigger he'd have sued him, so he would. And the end of Prometheus was running in my head...This like thy glory Titan is to be Good, great and joyous, beautiful and free...and I thought him a mean fellow. And then he told me how he dreaded bankruptcy and how his uncle, who had been a clerk, had come to the workhouse...and what a disgrace that was. And I'm afraid he was a little drunk. And I wondered whether it would be possible to interest him in the question of Shelley's position as a prosodist...or whether even the beauties of Prometheus would comfort him at all. But when he asked me what I was going to Manchester for...do you know I was ashamed to tell him?

JESSICA. Yes...a terrible world...an ugly, stupid, wasteful world. A hateful world!

(There falls a little silence. Their voices hardly break it.)

PHILIP. And yet we have to teach Mildred what love of the world means, Jessica. Even if it's an uncomfortable business. Even if it means not adding her to that aristocracy of good feeling and good taste...the very latest of class distinctions. I tell you I haven't come by these doubts so easily. Beautiful sounds and sights and thoughts are all of the world's heritage I care about. Giving them up is like giving my carefully created soul out of my keeping before I die.I care about. Giving them up is like giving my carefully created soul out of my keeping before I die.

JESSICA (with a sudden fling of her hands). And into whose?

PHILIP (shaking his head at the fire). I'm afraid into the keeping of everybody we are at present tempted to dislike and despise. For that's Public Life. That's Democracy. But that's the Future. *(He looks across at his wife half curiously.)* I know it's even harder for you women. You put off your armour for a man you love. But otherwise you've your Honour and Dignity and Purity . . .

JESSICA. Do you want a world without that either?

PHILIP. I rather want to know just what the world gets by it. Those six thin girls at my uncle's...what do we get from them or they from the world? Little Miss Yates, now...her transgressions may be the most profitable thing about her . . .

JESSICA. Two wrongs don't make a right.

PHILIP *(quaintly)* They often do...properly mixed. Of course you women could serve yourselves up to such lords of creation as my father quite profitably, in one sense, if you would.

JESSICA *(her lip curling).* Tharnk you...we're not cattle.

PHILIP. No. Then there's a price to be paid for free womanhood, I think...and how many of you ladies are willing to pay it? Come out and be common women among us common men? *(He leans towards her and his voice deepens.)* Jessica, do you feel that it was you shot that poor devil six months ago?...that it's you who are to be hanged tomorrow?

JESSICA. I don't think I do.

PHILIP. That it's your body is being sold on some street this evening?

She gives a little most genuine shudder.

JESSICA. I hate to think about such things.

PHILIP *(summing up).* Then there's precious little hope for the Kingdom of Heaven upon earth. I know it sounds mere nonsense, but I'm sure it's true. If we can't love the bad as well as the beautiful...if we won't share it all out now...fresh air and art...and dirt and sin...then we good and clever people are costing the world too much. Our brains cost too much if we don't give them freely. Your beauty costs too much if I only admire it because of the uglier women I see...even your virtue may cost too much, my dear. Rags pay for finery and ugliness for beauty, and sin pays for virtue. Why can nothing keep for long more beauty in a good man's eyes than the ugliest thing on earth? Why need no man be wiser than the biggest fool on earth? Why does it profit neither man nor woman to be more righteous than the greatest sinner on earth? *(He clenches his hands.)* These are the riddles this Sphinx of a world is asking me. Your artists and scholars and preachers don't answer them...so I must turn my back for a bit on artist and scholar and preacher...all three.

JESSICA looks at him as he completes his apologia, sympathetic, if not understanding. Then she rallies him cheerfully.

JESSICA. Meanwhile, my dear Phil, I shall not stop subscribing to the London Symphony Concerts...and I shall expect you to take me occasionally.

PHILIP *(jumping back from his philosophic world).* Oh...that reminds me...I've a message for you from Tommy.

JESSICA. Have you? He was really irritating this morning.

PHILIP. We must take Tommy with a sense of humour. It wasn't so much a message as one of those little bursts of childlike confidence...he endears himself to one with them from time to time.

JESSICA. About me ?

PHILIP. Yes. What it comes to is this. Will you please not flirt with him any more because he hasn't the time, and he's too fond both of me and his wife to want to find himself seriously in love with you.

Now PHILIP has not said this unguardedly and JESSICA knows it. She'll walk into no little trap set for her vanity or the like. Still it is with hardly a steady voice that she says simply . . .

JESSICA. Thank you for the message.

PHILIP goes cheerfully on; he is turning the pages of his book.

PHILIP. He doesn't at all suppose you are in love with him...seriously or otherwise.

JESSICA *(steadily).* Do you?

PHILIP. No.

JESSICA *(her tone sharpening still).* And is this the first time you've discussed me with Tommy or anyone? Please let it be the last.

PHILIP. Are you angry, Jessica?

JESSICA. I'm more than angry.

PHILIP. I'm sorry.

Having kept her temper successfully, if not the sense of humour which PHILIP warned her he was appealing to, JESSICA now allows herself a deliberate outburst of indignation.

JESSICA. I despise men. I despised them when I was fifteen...the first year I was conscious of them. I've been through many opinions since...and I come back to despising them.

PHILIP. He was afraid you wouldn't be pleased with him. But he has my sympathies, Jessica.

JESSICA *(throwing back her head).* Has he!

PHILIP. Tommy is what the entertaining State called this afternoon the Mean Sensual Man.

JESSICA *(with utter contempt).* Yes. When we're alone, having a jolly talk about things in general, he's all the time thinking I want him to kiss me.

PHILIP. While what you really want is to have him wanting to kiss you but never to kiss you.

JESSICA *(in protest).* No.

PHILIP *(fixing her with a finger).* Oh yes, Jessica.

JESSICA's sense of humour returns for a moment.

JESSICA. Well...I can't help it if he does.

PHILIP. You can, of course. And the Mean Sensual Man calls it being made a fool of.

She puts a serious face on it again; not that she can keep one with PHILIP's twinkling at her.

JESSICA. I give you my word I've never tried to flirt with Tommy...except once or twice when he has been boring me. And perhaps once or twice when I was in the dumps...and there he was...and I was boring him. I know him too well to flirt with him...you can't fiirt with a man you know well. But he's been boring me lately and I suppose I've been a bit bored. But suppose I have been flirting with him...or thought he was safe enough. *(That attempt failing, there is a tack left, and on this she really manages to work herself back to indignation.)* And a caddish thing to go speaking to you about it.

PHILIP. So he said...so he said.

JESSICA. Worse than caddish...outrageous! I never heard of such a thing...you shouldn't have let him.

PHILIP. Should I have knocked him down when he mentioned your name?

JESSICA. Yes...I wish you had.

PHILIP. Little savage.

JESSICA. I can't laugh about this. I'm hurt.

PHILIP. My dear, if you have any sense at all you'll ask him to dinner and chaff him about it...before me.

JESSICA. Have you any understanding of what a woman feels when men treat her like this ? Degraded and cheapened.

But the high moral tone PHILIP will not stand. He drops chaff and tackles her.

PHILIP. I can tell you what the man feels. He'll be either my father or me. That's your choice. Tommy's my father when you've put on your best gown to attract him, or he's me when he honestly says that he'd rather you wouldn't. Do you want him to be me or my father? That's the first question for you.

JESSICA. I want a man to treat a woman with courtesy and respect.

PHILIP. And what does that come to? My dear, don't you know that the Mean Sensual Man...no, not Tommy for the moment, but say Dick or Harry...looks on you all as choice morsels...with your prettinesses, your dressings up, your music and art as so much sauce to his appetite. Which only a mysterious thing called your virtue prevents him from indulging...almost by force, if it weren't for the police, Jessica. Do you like that?

JESSICA. I don't believe it.

PHILIP. Do you really believe that most men's good manners towards most pretty women are anything else but good manners?

JESSICA. I prefer good manners to yours. *(Then, both fine taste and sense of humour to the rescue again.)* No...that's rude.

PHILIP *(with much more affection than the words convey).* I treat you as a man would treat another man...neither better nor worse. Is the compliment quite wasted?

JESSICA *(as amazed at this unreasonable world).* I want to be friends with men. I'd sooner be friends with them. It's they who flirt with me. Why?

PHILIP *(incurably mischievous).* Of course I've forgotten what you look like and I never notice what you have on...but I suspect it's because you're rather pretty and attractive.

JESSICA. Do you want women not to be?

PHILIP. No.

JESSICA. It's perfectly sickening. Of course, if I had dozens of children and grew an old woman with the last one, I should be quite out of danger. But we can't all be like that...you don't want us to be.

PHILIP. *(Purely negative),* No.

He leaves her free to justify herself.

JESSICA. I do my fair share of things, I make a home for you. I entertain your friends. It may cost your precious world too much...my civilisation...but you want all this done. *(Then with a certain womanly reserve)*. And Phil...suppose I'm not much nicer by nature than some of you men? When I was a baby, if I'd not been fastidious I should have been a sad glutton. My culture...my civilisation...mayn't be quite up to keeping the brilliant Tommy a decent friend to me. But it has its uses.

But PHILIP means to laugh this out of court too.

PHILIP. Look here, if it's only your culture keeps you from kissing Tommy...kiss him.

To be so driven from pillar to post really does exasperate her.

JESSICA. Phil...I sometimes think I'd sooner have been married to your father.

PHILIP. Why?

JESSICA. If you went on as he did instead of as you do...I should be sorry...I should despise you...but it would string me up and add to my self-respect enormously! *(Then a little appealingly.)* But it's when you're inhuman, Phil...that I'm ever so little tempted...

PHILIP *(contrite at once)*. I know I am. *(Then he gets up to stand looking into the fire, and what he says is heartfelt.)* But I do so hate that farmyard world of sex...men and women always treating each other in this unfriendly way...that I'm afraid it hardens me a bit.

JESSICA *(from her side, gently, with just a look at him)*. I hate it, too...but I happen to love you, Phil.

They smile to each other.

PHILIP. Yes, my dear. If you'd kindly come over here...I should like to kiss you.

JESSICA. I won't. You can come over to me.

PHILIP. Will you meet me half-way?

They meet half-way and kiss as husband and wife can. They stand together, looking into the fire.

PHILIP. Do you know the sort of world I want to live in?

JESSICA. Should I like it?

PHILIP. Hasn't Humanity come of age at last?

JESSICA. Has it?

PHILIP. Mayn't we hope so? Finery sits so well on children. And they strut and make love absurdly...even their quarrelling is in all good faith and innocence. But I don't see why we men and women should not find all happiness...and beauty, too,...in soberer purposes. And with each other...why not always some touch of the tranquil understanding which is yours and mine, dear, at the best of moments?

JESSICA *(happily)*. Do you mean when we sometimes suddenly want to shake hands ?

PHILIP *(happily, too).* That's it. And I want an art and a culture that shan't be just a veneer on savagery...but it must spring in good time from the happiness of a whole people.

JESSICA gives herself one little shake of womanly commonsense.

JESSICA. Well, what's to be done?

PHILIP *(nobody more practical than he).* I've been making suggestions. We must learn to live on a thousand a year...put Mildred to a sensible school...and I must go on the County Council. That's how these great spiritual revolutions work out in practice, to begin with.

JESSICA *(as one who demands a right).* Where's my share of the iob?

PHILIP *(conscious of some helplessness).* How is a man to tell you? There's enough to choose from.

JESSICA *(the burden of her sex's present fate upon her).* Ah, you're normal. Nobody sizes you up as a good man or a bad man...pretty or plain. There's a trade for bad women and several professions for plain ones. But I've been taught how to be charming and to like dainty clothes. And I dare say I'm excitable and emotional...but I can't help it. I'm well off, married to you, I know. You do make me forget I'm a female occasionally.

PHILIP. Male and female created He them...and left us to do the rest. Men and women are a long time in the making...aren't they?

JESSICA *(enviously).* Oh...you're all right.

PHILIP *(with some humble knowledge of himself).* Are we?

JESSICA. But I tell you, Phil, it isn't so easy for us. You don't always let us have the fairest of chances, do you?

PHILIP. No, I grant it's not easy. But it's got to be done.

JESSICA. Yes . . .

She doesn't finish, for really there is no end to the subject. But for a moment or two longer, happy together, they stand looking into the fire.

Appendix

Principal changes introduced by Granville Barker into the 1925 edition of The Madras House.

[Note:....indicates that some dialogue has been omitted whereas...represents the original pauses introduced by Granville Barker.]

ACT I

1910 text, p. 5 'PHILIP.....what are the two most important things in a man's character?' becomes, in 1925: 'what are the two master tests of a man's character?'

(1910 text, p. 6 'THOMAS. You've got what I call the Reformer's mind ?˘and got it badly, Phil. Not that you'll make this country any different by making it tidier, you know.

PHILIP. I'm very interested in England, Tommy.

THOMAS. So am I...even if I don't talk quite so much about it...even if I've had to chuck the army, to earn bread and treacle for a wife and a family...which ain't a bad thing for me either. What good will it do you, though, to chuck a thousand a year and a directorship if State wants you to keep'em?

PHILIP. The Madras House is Woman Incarnate and I loathe it. Your Mr State may buy the place and do whatever he likes with it.

THOMAS. You're sick of the dressmaking business. Right! But you'd think a lot dearer, Phil, if you didn't spell everything with a capital letter.

PHILIP. Tommy, that is a sound obsevation. I like a good talk with you. Sooner or later you always say one sensible thing.

THOMAS. Thank you.

(1910 p. 25 'sketch quite well.....You mustn't think')

1925: 'sketch quite well. D'you think novels and newspapers tell you the truth about things, Philip ?

PHILIP. Some novels may. Why?

EMMA. Because you'd think from them there wasn't anyone else in England like us. But I know lots.

(1910, p. 53 'I shouldn't do them well')

1925: 'Frankly...I prefer a quiet life.

MISS YATES: I expect you're right. It is safer.

(1910, p. 61 'Ugly little woman......I don't find that women attract me,)

1925: 'Attractive little woman you'd been scolding when I came in.

PHILIP. Is she?

JESSICA. Didn't you think so?

PHILIP. I'm afraid I don't often notice whether women are attractive or not...unless they mean me to. And then I don't find them so.'

(1910, p.78 'She took off her own hat..... . blue silk')

1925: 'Shen fetched in out of the Bois the ugliest little gamine she could find...put her own hat on its horrid little head...sat it at her table and stuffed it with cakes. Then she sent to the kitchens for one of those baskets they bring the fish in...

(He twirls the hat)...see ! Then she ripped a bit of ribbon and a couple of these (These being rosettes) off her pantalettes...'

(1910, p. 78 'Hooked them together.....the rage')

1925: 'Besides...la belle France, you know...there is something in the atmosphere! Twisted it round the basket...tres pratique! And that's what she wore the rest of the afternoon and back to Paris. And it's going to be all the rage.'

(1910, p. 80 'upon a fire-new establishment next door might anyhow be ineffective')

1925: 'upon an opposition establishment might cut no ice.'

(1910, p. 82 'derive some pleasure from a cold cigar')

1925: 'seek stimulus in a cold cigar.'

(1910 p. 82 'And I suspect that you are and satisfying?')

1925: 'And I know that you are no more the bond-slave of money than I am, Mr Madras. Anyone can make money, if he has capital enough. The little that I have came from lumber and canned peaches. Now there was poetry in lumber. The virgin forest! As a youth I was shy of society...but I could sit in contemplation of Nature for as much as an hour at a time. Rightly thought of there is poetry in peaches...even when they are canned. Do you ask then why I bought that mantle establishment in the city twelve years ago?

PHILIP *(who is only sorry that some time he must stop)*. I do, Mr State.

MR STATE. Because as the years rolled irresistibly on I came to realize that I had become a lonely man...and I felt the need of some communion with what Goethe calls, does he not, the Woman Spirit, which can draw us ever upward and on. Well, the Burrows business was in the market...and that seemed an appropriate path to the fulfilment of my desire.

CONSTANTINE. The fulfilment...?'

(1910, p. 83 'making these provincial milliners hop.....cumbering the earth')

1925: 'making these old back-country stores sit up and take notice...telling them: Gentlemen, come in, or be froze out. That's for their good...and for mine. But Burrows can't answer to the call of the Woman's Movement...the great Modern Woman's Movement...which is upon us...though as yet we may not measure its volume. But it is upon us...and our choice is to be in it, to do it glad service...or to have it flow over us. Let me assure you so. The old-time business of selling a reel of cotton and tinging on the cash machine...there's no salvation left in that.'

(1910, p. 83 'I don't say I haven't taken pleasure.....Notions...caused')

1925: 'Burrows has not been wholly barren soil. Here and there we have

sown a seed and made'
    (1910, p. 83 'I've not visited the city myself')
    1925: 'I visited the city last Fall.'
    (1910,p. 84 'just before the football season')
    1925: 'when Summer Time brings time for sport'
    (1910, p. 85 'The Woman's Movement is Woman expressing herself...out of date...')
    1925: 'What now, urbi et orbi, is the Modern Woman's Movement? It is woman expressing herself. How? Upon what roads is she marching? What is her goal? Is it for us to say? No. Nor as yet for her, it may be. Every morning I have placed upon my table not only the newspapers that affect her interests today...and they pile high...but also those of the same day and date of five and twenty years ago...no more than that. But the comparison is instructive. And one thing is certain. Burrows and the ready-made skirt belong to the dead past.'
    (1910, p. 85 'Mettez vous.....velours noir')
    1925: 'C'est pour un petit souper tres particulier, n'est-ce pas? Mettez-vous par la dans l'alcove...a cote du velours noir. They won't learn English; they simply won't. Lucky the lingo's like second nature to me.'
    (1910, p. 86 'a beautiful thing')
    1925 adds: '**MR STATE**. Yes, Mr Huxtable, and the question is: Do we accept the gospel of beauty, or do we not?'
    (1910, p.86 'MR STATE *(sweepingly)*. Fitted to adorn.....sortez')
    1925: '**WINDLESHAM**. But the trouble I'll have to prevent some old hag of seventy buying a thing like that...you'd never believe.'
    (1910, p. 87 'The very thing, no doubt.....I really beg your pardon')
    1925: 'And this for the adorning of some Queen ofthe Salons. You are doubtless acquainted with the novels of the Earl of Beaconsfield, Mr Philip?

    PHILIP. I have been.

    MR STATE. Now might not that costume step into or out of any one of them? A great man. A man of imagination. He brought your country to a viewpoint of Imperial...of Oriental splendour from which it has not receded. Yes...some one of your statesmen...some soldier of Empire will, we may hope, find repose from his cares and fresh ardour for his ambitions there !
    (1910, p. 87 '*A third costume*...doing what service we may')
    1925: The last mannequin, attired in dressing-gown and pyjamas, now appears.

    PHILIP. Or even here.

    MR STATE. Or even...! No...at this point my judgment stands disabled. Still...why not be attractive en intimite? Her household motions light and free...Wordsworth, I think. Our human nature's daily food...an unromantic simile. Why should it not be bright as well as good?'
    (1910, p. 88 '*(Then he soars.)* But')

1925: But you were for the Old Regime.

(1910, p. 88 'Middle Class Women.....think of them.....they form one of the greatest')

1925: 'middle-class woman..... think of her.....is potentially the greatest'

(1910, p. 88 'All our most advanced thinkers.....march of civilization')

1925: A sociologist will tell you, sir, that economic freedom is the inevitable sequel to the political freedom that women have now gained. And I suggest to you that any increased demand for spending power which will urge the middle-class husband to resist the financial encroachments of your proletariat...for something must be made to...may contribute largely to the salvation of your country.'

(1910, p. 89 'Thank you.....Not in that corset')

1925: 'D'you notice there hasn't been a mode you could sit in to advantage these fifteen years? But with a couch, y'know, we might get a sort of mermaid effect out of some ofthem.'

1910 p. 89 'WINDLESHAM. I'm sure.....any more for you')

1925: 'WINDLESHAM. Oh, thanks too awfully...I'm sure I shall. Send it to me to the farm, will you, Thomas? I do my serious reading there, week-ends.

MR STATE. You have a farm?

WINDLESHAM. Just a toy...but thank God for it! I'd be a nervous wreck with my mind on this all the time. Nature's my passion. Can I assist you any further?'

1910, p. 90 'Oh...trying to upset.....things in the world')

1925: 'Don't you be too clever, Phil.

MR STATE.....and recalls to me a project I once entertained for the founding at one of our more consenative universities of a chair of the Philosophy of Fashion. Major Thomas, will you remind me to consider that again?

MR HUXTABLE. Talk won't bring dividends...that's what I say.

MR STATE. A fallacy, Mr Huxtable, if I may so far correct you. Lift your head, broaden your horizon, and you will see, I think, that all human activities are one. And what we men of business should remember is that art, philosophy and religion can and should, in the widest sense of the term, be made to pay. And it's pay or perish, in this world.'

(1910, p. 93 'I was sometimes tempted to regret my scandalous conduct')

1925: 'I have been reproached with scandalous conduct.'

(1910, p.95 'Proud.....if they see a cabman smile')

1925: 'Let him but veil his leering, my dear Harry, and the lousiest beggar's tribute is but one more coin in the pocket of their shame.
To MR STATE this might be a physical flick in the face.'

(1910 pp. 98-99 'Every great public question.....fear of the dark')

1925: 'We view all our problems today...political, economic, religious, through the cloudy spectacles of womanly emotion...which has its place...but not, heaven help us, in the world of affairs. What wonder, then, that your labouring men, who can keep their womenkind to child-bearing and housework and gossip within doors...what wonder if they get the government from you? You, at your luncheon and dinner tables, the news in your newspapers dressed up as fiction, your statesmen and soldiers pursued at their work to fill picture pages, your weekends where women out-gamble you at cards, play up to you at sport, out-do you in the ribaldry of the smoking-room! An effete empire is yours, gentlemen...and the barbarian with his pick and shovel and his man's capacities is over its frontiers already. And what has been your defence against him? Soft talk and scoldings...coaxings and hysterics...and pretty dialectic trickery that your women have applauded. How they'll despise you soon for it!')

(1910, p. 99 'rediscover.....losing')

1925: 'recover strength to hold our place in the world'

(1910, p. 99 'That is what it should come to')

1925: 'That would be a part of the solution.'

(1910, p. 101 'PHILIP. What about men who live...Denmark Hill')

1925: 'MR STATE. Culture demands a leisure class, you know.'

(1910, p. 103 'besides, take a gentle interest in the County Council')

1925: 'be free to dedicate their emotions to municipal politics'

(1910, p. 105 'drainage.....If you were he!')

1925: 'sanitation I am about to finance. No poetry there, I fear.

CONSTANTINE. Sanitation? Your great American science...by which you foster your conglomerate millions in health...with folly enough in their heads to provide for the needful catastrophe when you become overcrowded.

MR STATE. Admirable! I dispute its truth. But how stimulating !'

(1910, p. 105 'Suppose we go together...on a bus')

1925: 'We'll go together...on a bus. D'you remember when the new shop opened how we loved to ride past and look at it...from the top of the bus ?'

(1910, p. 108 'You know.....hurt our feelings, and')

1925: 'But when I think how, ever since I've known you, you've had us all on the jump...and the games you've played, why'

(1910, p. 109 'It will make them very uncomfortable.....broaden their minds')

1925: 'Dare you, Harry, dare you?

MR HUXTABLE. Well...you must mind what you say, of course. But...I would like to have us all thinking a bit differently of you when you're gone.'

(1910, p.110 'I don't know.....miss that four-thirty'

1925: 'Damned if I know.

PHILIP. Trot along, then, or you will miss your train.'

(1910, p. 120 'I was upset when I came here.....daughters to back her')

1925: 'I was upset when I came.

PHILIP. The visit to Denmark Hill?

CONSTANTINE. No. I didn't go. I hadn't time.'
(1910,p. 121 'I can't help thinking so.....three stations too far in that Tube')
1925: 'Was she ever happy with you?

CONSTANTINE *(shrugging)*. For as long as she'd let herself be. And she could have had me back...more than once. I was fond of her...she was my wife. I've never found it hard to be kind to women. She could have had more children. Tell a woman in the East she might still bear children at forty...she'd ask nothing more of you. Rebellion against nature brings no happiness, Phil.

PHILIP. What else is civilization?

CONSTANTINE. And what better condemnation of about half of it?

PHILIP *(with his ironic smile)*. Well...I agree that this present stage of our moral progress is hardly suited to your simplicity of temperament, my dear father. A heart-breaking paradox...to find one's manliest virtues turned to mere weakness under temptation!

CONSTANTINE. You're a queer fellow, Phil. If I'd sat and turned all my vigour into phrases as you do...they'd have poisoned me.

PHILIP. That's a home thrust. Thoughts curdling into words...and into more thought and more words. Yes...it leaves one lifeless.

Exchanging ideas, merely, these two can keep quite friendly, it would seem.

CONSTANTINE. Well...you thrust home too. I couldn't get a cab from Blackheath. . . and vexed and worried as I was, I found I had travelled a station too far in the tube'
(1910, p. 121 'How does a man resist it? Yes. That's')
1925: 'And why should a man resist it? But in this civilization of yours...half-factory and half-hothouse...you're right...one's wholesomest instincts turn'
(1910, p. 123 'Phil, I saw the little baggage.....put you in your place)
1925: 'Phil...I've been battling with the little baggage these three hours...driving in a taxi round and round...I made her come and meet me...sitting till we were frozen in some asphalted dust-heap of a park at New Cross! ...

PHILIP *(apostrophizing all the gods at once)*. I might have guessed...I did guess! Oh, you incorrigible old man!

CONSTANTINE. How dared she not tell me about it!

PHILIP. The scandal ?

CONSTANTINE. About her baby. She knew...before I went to Marienbad.

PHILIP. Well...for an appropriate rounding off of your career! I came back in May to find you, didn't I...dignified and disdainful...in the office at Bond Street? *(Then, as in exasperated bewilderment.)* But why Miss Yates?

CONSTANTINE. Why not? (At which riposte even PHILIP's jaw must drop.) You have gathered together in Bond Street, these last three years, let me tell you, Phil, a most inappropriate personnel. These ladies with their social connections ought to be buying clothes there, not selling them. They've the wrong sort of manners too...and I should say their morals are doubtful. That's no matter in their own drawing-rooms. But with all the other young women imitating them...powder and paint and affectation...jazzing by night and smart chatter by day...I shouldn't have known the place. However, it's that American booby's business now. Little Yates seemed the only wholesome self-respecting creature in it.

PHILIP. I see.

CONSTANTINE *(man of the world, confiding comrade, and model employer once more)*. You'll have to help me, and make her take some money.

PHILIP. She was obstinate about that this morning.

CONSTANTINE. I'd not have believed that any young woman could have vexed me so. I made her every sort of proposal.

PHILIP *(the ironic smile lighting his face again)*. Even to a place in the household beneath the palm trees?

CONSTANTINE. No.

PHILIP. No, she'd be rather disruptive there.

CONSTANTINE. But of course she had the last word. The child is hers by law...and a scandalous law it is! I've had my troubles with women, heaven knows! But nothing like this has ever happened to me before.

PHILIP So...it has been left to little Yates to put you in your place !

CONSTANTINE *(darkly, resentfully)*. It seems funny to you, does it? Well, Phil, I trust no woman may ever make you feel that you've been made a mere convenience of.'

(1910, pp. 125–137 'PHILIP. If we've only enough life left.....*end of play*').

1925: CONSTANTINE. And he has forbidden me to leave her a ten thousand pound dowry. Did he tell you ?

Aesthetic, fastidious, detached as our charming JESSICA may be, there are some matters upon which she is common sense itself.

JESSICA. PHILIP...how dare you do such a thing?

PHILIP *(really a little guiltily)*. Well...I did mean to tell you.

JESSICA. Yes...when your father was safely away.

CONSTANTINE. Don't worry. Even the most ardent social reformers can't prevent people leaving them money. I've told Voysey to make it another five thousand. I very much approve of you, Jessica...and I hope dear Mildred will grow to be like you...pretty and witty and pleasantly extravagant. And I'm glad to see Phil so delightfully...you'll forgive me the phrase...so delightfully henpecked. For a man with his views about women should be. And he's luckier than he knows. I really believe, my dear, that your, charm and your art and your sense of beauty...your civilization...for so it is...all yours, all that's worthy to be called so...if I'd been broken to it in my young manhood it might even have conquered me. Goodnight...goodbye.

JESSICA. Goodbye, Father.

With which gracious peroration CONSTANTINE turns to the door and Philip follows him.

CONSTANTINE. And PHILIP...if you could give that Miss Yates her conge with sufficient brutality she might be stung, perhaps, into taking some compensation. If the auditors wouldn't pass it, I'd send you a cheque...as a private matter...with pleasure.

PHILIP *(appreciative, ironic)*. Yes, that's an idea! Victoria at eleven tomorrow? I shall see you off.

They pass out into the hall. After a moment PHILIP returns, to find JESSICA at her piano making a little casual music, soft-sounding passes over the keys.

JESSICA. I do dislike your father.

PHILIP. That's so much to the good.

JESSICA. But why poor Mildred should be disinherited! I owe you one for that, Phil.

PHILIP *(his thoughts on the past still)*. Did your parents squabble?

JESSICA. No indeed...they so seldom spoke.

PHILIP *(dismissing them to the past)*. Well...if only we cultivate our differences in candour and dignity...that may be, after all, the best service one generation does the next.

JESSICA. I'm up to an argument...say once a week.

PHILIP. Poor Jessica!

JESSICA *(speaking as she plays, playing punctuating speech)*. No...when you bore me I need only play a little louder. But don't become too much of an intellectual prototype of your dear papa...going round...seducing all and sundry, ..who've not the brains to resist you...to your own peculiar way of thinking. That I should find...socially tiresome...and rather vulgar of you. Is he, by the way, always so generous with his cheques to young ladies in trouble?

PHILIP barks out a contemptuous little laugh.

PHILIP. Vanity! To think that he couldn't resist dropping you that hint !

JESSICA turns from her piano, one is sorry to say, quite agreeably amused.

JESSICA. Has he really been up to mischief again...at his age!

PHILIP. If he hadn't been he'd love us to believe it! Vanity! His real spur, I do verily believe, to that fine and flamboyantly amorous career! Nature's energy must be slacking, you'd think, if she can find no other.

JESSICA *(with fine impatience)*. Let it slack! The way men allow Nature to befool them into swinging the pendulum...they've no other notion...between getting babies born and starting wars to destroy the surplus ! Let's have some leisure to enjoy our civilization.

PHILIP. But you don't. *(Then, with a sudden explosive vigour.)* Whitechapel High Street's our civilization.

JESSICA is familiarly alert to the challenge. With a goodnatured sigh she leaves her piano and, so to speak, daintily doubles her mental fists.

JESSICA. Ah! I've never been there.

PHILIP. Seconds out of the ring! A Manchester cotton mill, then...but you've never seen one. The Potteries...the Clyde...you've never been there. But the life we live! In this room for instance...a Persian carpet on the floor...Dutch tiles round the grate...and one fine piece of Ming on the mantelpiece. My dear, it's a museum! And I notice your taste in music has slipped back a century lately.

JESSICA. I cannot bear this Very modern noise.

PHILIP. Quite so! And Mildred's at that nice old-fashioned school having her mind made a museum lest she should grow into a horrid modern young lady.

JESSICA. Surely you say God forbid to that.

PHILIP. Oh, I'm a fogey! I'm forty-two next birthday. But the music, art, and manners young people batter us with today...what are they but an echo of the world we made...and a right revenge upon us for our blindness to it?

JESSICA. Well...are we to move to Manchester?

PHILIP. Don't get desperate! No, as a visionary I'm all for compromise. I'm going in for politics...the great art of compromise. Not for high-flying, speech-making politics...I'm too apt at speech-making, God forgive me...but for sordid, municipal politics, dull hard work over drains and dentistry in the schools and such like.

JESSICA. I've never been against public life for you...and I'll economize all that need be...but this passion to be on the London County Council is really morbid.

PHILIP. I want Whitechapel High Street made a fit place for Mildred to live in.

JESSICA. Only the people that live in it can make it so. Do they think it ugly?

PHILIP. I fear not.

JESSICA. Be careful you don't cease to.

PHILIP. I may cease to...I must risk that...I must save my soul alive. I've been a trafficker in beauty...I'm sick of it.

JESSICA. That is morbid.

PHILIP. It may be.

JESSICA. Let's go off to Italy for a month.

PHILIP. More art...more museums! Oh Jessica, Jessica! When things as they are drive us from sanctuary here...run away ! I'd have to run very far, now.

JESSICA. I don't need to run. And I'm not responsible for your ugly world. I've one of my own, thank heaven, to live in. You men have your work...whatever you choose. But art has to make life possible for some of us women, Phil.

PHILIP *(savagely almost)*. Give me the art and the artists that'll make most of the life we're content with impossible...I've no more use left for the other sort.

D'you remember when I was very young and used to salve my social conscience by lecturing on Shelley to select little audiences in the slums?

JESSICA. When we were engaged. And I nearly threw you over for throwing me over one evening for some wretched lecture.

PHILIP (his eyebrows up). Did you?

JESSICA (pleasantly). Very nearly.

PHILIP . Fancy that!

JESSICA. I did think marriage would cure you...but now you lecture me!

PHILIP. Well...I remember once travelling in the train with a poor wretch who lived...so he told me...on what margins of gain he could pick up by standing incompetently somewhere between the cornfield and the baker...or the coalmine and the fire...or the house and the tenant...I forget which. And he was weary and irritable and very unhealthy. And he hated Jones...because Jones had just done him out of a half per cent on two hundred and fify pounds...and if the sum had been bigger he'd have sued him, so he would ! And the end of Prometheus was running in my head: This like thy glory, Titan, is to be Good, great and joyous, beautiful and free...and I thought him a mean fellow. But on he maundered about his dread of bankruptcy. For his uncle, so it seemed, who had been in the insurance business, had come to the workhouse...and what a disgrace that was ! And I fear he was a little drunk. He'd have found no comfort in Shelley, I felt sure...and, with my lecture worrying me, my own well-springs of chariy were dry. But when he asked what was taking me to Canrling Town...somehow I was ashamed to tell him.

JESSICA (not untouched). Oh yes...it's a horrid world...an ugly, stupid, wasteful world.

PHILIP. He cured me, I believe, of lecturing on Shelley...which was a pity, in a way, for the lectures weren't so bad. But what is more, I've remembered that little swine through all these years with a sort of baulked affection. I would like to know how he is getting on.

JESSICA. You may meet him County Councilling.

PHILIP. Wangling some shifty contract. By Jove, I'll see he doesn't !

By now they are seated, one each side of the fire.

JESSICA. Don't turn your new leaf till after tomorrow, by the way. Take me to that concert. Tommy has chucked.

PHILIP. Tommy! That reminds me. Two words with you about Tommy. Is your sense of humour working? Tommy wants me to play the Turk and turn him out of the house before he finds himself fatally in love with you.

JESSICA, in every sense of the phrase, sits up.

JESSICA. What on earth do you mean?

PHILIP. That was the gist of a lunchtime talk today...across the roast beef and the roly-poly. Your coming to Peckham precipitated it.

JESSICA *(ominously)*. Are you serious, Phil?

PHILIP. Tommy was portentously serious.

JESSICA. How dared you discuss me...like that?

PHILIP *(deliberately at ease)*. I didn't...he got no change from me. No nice husband discusses his wife. Upon sound Mahommedan principles, he guards her in the harem of his heart. At worst you may catch him saying: Women, my boy, oh, I tell you...! And embedded in the nonsense that follows will be...

JESSICA. Stop trifling, Phil.

PHILIP. Well...I listened sympathetically. What else could I do?

JESSICA. You could have knocked him down.

PHILIP. Don't be histrionic, Jessica. He wants me to play the Turk. You fancy me as the noble savage. I couldn't have knocked him down...he'd have knocked me down. Then, if you hadn't despised me and flung yourself into his arms you'd have been no true woman.

JESSICA. You won't make me laugh.

PHILIP. What do you bet? And would it have solved the difficuly?

JESSICA. I'll solve that. This is all true, is it? Then I'll not have him inside my doors again nor speak to him again as long as I live. Nor to you...till you apologise. Goodnight.

And off she is going with extreme and icy dignity when his level voice stays her...not quite unwillingly.

PHILIP. My dear...flourishes apart...you are angry?

JESSICA. Much more than angry.

PHILIP. Hurt?

JESSICA. I should hope so.

PHILIP *(gently, reflectively; the soft answer that may turn away half-satisfied wrath)*. Tommy's a bit of a fool...but I'm fond of him...and I hoped you were. I don't want you to part us...for your own sake also. I do sympathize with him...just a bit.

JESSICA *(her exasperation wholesomely set free)*. Do you think, may I ask...and does he...that I've been falling in love with him?

PHILIP *(judiciously)*. No. So I sympathize with him the more.

JESSICA *(with tart response for this compliment)*. Thank you. That I've led him on?

PHILIP *(Still more judiciously)*. We now come to the making of very fine distinctions.

JESSICA. Oh, I despise men! I grew up despising them. You took me in for a bit. But I come back to despising you all.

PHILIP *(a grim twist to his voice)*. And you take good care to keep us contemptible, don't you?

JESSICA. How, pray?

PHILIP. I'm the child of a loveless marriage. I grew up disposed to dislike...and that's harder to cure than despising: despising will cure itself!...most men and all women. Thank heaven I managed to fall in love with you...and no questions asked. But I'm a cold-hearted brute. Tommy, now, is a simple sort...and what my entertaining friend MR STATE calls the Mean Sensual Man...

JESSICA *(finely contemptuous).* Yes! When we're alone, having an interesting talk, he's all the time thinking I want him to kiss me. Am I that sort of a woman? Answer me.

PHILIP *(a smile flickering).* Well...let me think. No, not quite. What you want is to have him wanting to kiss you but never to kiss you.

JESSICA. I do not.

PHILIP. I must take your word for it.

JESSICA. Can I help his wanting to kiss me?

PHILIP. I wonder, now, if you couldn't.

JESSICA. I'm a flirt, am I?

PHILIP. I believe that's what they are called.

JESSICA in the small breathing space after this pretty and swift exchange, shifts her ground.

JESSICA. I give you my word that I've never flirted with Tommy. He's not the sort of man I could fiirt with. And he's always talking of his children...and he takes me to help choose a hat for his wife ! And I like Mrs Tommy...though, of course, she's a goose and she doesn't make him any brighter. Heavens, I'd have to be pretty bored before I'd start flirting with him. But he has been boring me lately...and I suppose I've been trying to wake him up a little...I should never have called it flirting! If a man can't stand against the simplest sort of temptation, what is he worth? And how caddish to go talking to you about it !

PHILIP. So he said...so he said!

JESSICA *(in almost pitiful protest).* All my life I've wanted...and I've tried...to be friends with men...just friends. And one after the other they start fiirting with me! Why?

PHILIP *(the smile flickering again).* I've forgotten, of course, what you look like and I never notice what you have on...but I suspect it's because you're rather pretty and attractive.

JESSICA. And am I not to be? Am I to let you choose my hats?

PHILIP *(whimsically).* As a man-milliner, I might!

JESSICA. Am I to dress like those six thin girls of your uncle's?...though, goodness knows, poor dears, it makes little difference how you dress them !

PHILIP. No...I fear they don't profit the world.

JESSICA *(with most genuine impatience).* Oh, don't talk about our profiting the world...as if we were so many cattle.

The argument ceasing to be so very personal, PHILIP turns contemplative.

PHILIP. For this past thirty-six hours...now I come to consider...I have been perambulating the Woman Question. From the dowdy virginity of Denmark Hill I passed to Peckham and Miss Yates . . .

JESSICA. Those two wrongs don't make a right!

PHILIP. They must serve to...somehow. I wish you could have heard the far-flung nonsense of our business talk in Bond Street today.

JESSICA. You men parade in words just as fantastically as we do in our fashions.

PHILIP *(pleased at her happy hit).* That's not untrue. Anything to colour the dull work-a-day! And here I am now at my own fireside...and at the heart of the problem, Jessica.

JESSICA turns whimsical now, and oh~ so charming.

JESSICA. Sorry, I'm sure, if I don't suit! Oh, why don't you flirt with me, Phil?

PHILIP *(won to a quite brotherly good-humour).* I know...I know! Such a silly needless choice it seems to have to be making...poor you!...between me and my father. But that's more or less what it comes to, my dear.

JESSICA *(very genuinely indeed).* I detest and despise your father and all he stands for. But I did think that dear old blunt-headed Tommy was safe.

PHILIP turns on the charmer, and hits out nonetheless hard because he hits good-humouredly.

PHILIP. You unprincipled woman!

JESSICA *(genuinely amazed).* I ? I've not done a thing...that matters.

PHILIP. Quite so.

But JESSICA'S wits are about her.

JESSICA. Now don't let's be subtle and logical...that leads to trouble. By nature, perhaps, I'm not so very much nicer than some of you men. Mother tells me to this day that I was a glutton of a baby...thank God I grew up fastidious. My art and my culture, then, that you mock at, may have their uses, to start with, for me.

PHILIP *(giving her, of set purpose, the rough side of his tongue).* My good girl...if it's only your culture keeps you from kissing Tommy...and Dick and Harry..kiss them and have done.

JESSICA is really shocked.

JESSICA. PHILIP...how you can say such a brutal and disgusting thing to your own wife, I do not know.

PHILIP. But you do know that the Mean Sensual Man really looks on you all as choice morsels...with your charm and your pretty talk so much sauce to his appetite. Baulk it and he feels he's made a fool of.

JESSICA *(taking swift advantage).* So he is...and so he should be.

PHILIP *(honestly a little puzzled).* You don't feel the whole thing's degrading?

JESSICA. It's he that's degraded. A woman's either virtuous at heart or she isn't.

Poor PHILIP relaxes with a sigh.

PHILIP. One thing seems plain...the fireside problem doesn't yield to argument.

JESSICA. I'd hoped there couldn't be one...as long as I loved you, Phil.

Her sweetness and his love for her, he won't try to resist either.

PHILIP. Do you?

JESSICA. Deeply.

PHILIP. Come here, then...and kiss me.

JESSICA *(merrily enough)*. Nothing on earth should induce me to. You can come over to me.

PHILIP. I won't. I'll meet you halfway.

They meet, he takes her hand. Then she finds he is looking at the fire lost in thought.

JESSICA. And you forget to kiss me!

He kisses her hand, then, and smiles at her, though his eyes look beyond her still.

PHILIP. I have so come to fear the pleasant sounding word.

JESSICA. Even when it's mine?

PHILIP. Yes. Be a little patient with me, then, my dear, if loving you, which solved the simpler problem, opens a world of others to my restless mind.

JESSICA *(but as if she loved this strange thing too)*. Restless, ruthless, unsatisfied, mischievous mind! Well...after all, Phil, I did make my choice. I like being married to your sort...and, at times, when I don't like it, I feel it's very good for me.

PHILIP *(solidly)*. It is! And look here...don't be hard on old Tommy. He's a child. Let's ask him to dinner Friday...and we'll chaff his head of

JESSICA *(quite her assured self)*. No. Your pleasant brutalities I may have to endure...but I'll tackle Master Tommy in my own ladylike way...and heaven help him! He won't try to flirt with me again.

PHILIP. Then all will be well! But oh...but oh, the farmyard world of sex! Have we won nothing nobler from the jungle? Will mankind cease to be if we cease to strut in our finery?

JESSICA *(cheerily)*. You have ceased to strut in your finery. I shall strut in mine till it ceases to amuse me.

PHILIP. Till you find something better to do. We await your pleasure.

JESSICA. What do you mean by that?

PHILIP. Here's a whole world that waits to be made both beautiful and fine. We've done our best...and our worst.What are you going to do? You've got your freedom. Do you mean to pay the price of it? I love you...deeply. And I try to treat you now as I'd treat another man...neither better nor worse. What other compliment is there left to pay you? You'd be wise to value it...there's no higher code of honour. Our fireside problem is the world's in a sense...since male and female created He them, leaving us to do the rest: though men and women have been long enough in the making...for we two do sum up most of the differences in life between us. And we don't shirk them . . .

JESSICA. I do...often.

PHILIP. Then don't you dare to.

JESSICA *(with a little secret sigh)*. I always shall. It's easier for you to face things and not fear if the truth will hurt. You are free. You weren't brought up to think you must be either good or bad...and wondering whether you'd turn out pretty or plain. Yes...you let me forget I'm a female. And I see your vision, too...I think I do...when we've been frank and friendly with each other...when we feel we want to shake hands.....

PHILIP. Yes, that's the good moment.

JESSICA. But you can't be wise for us.

PHILIP. I know.

JESSICA. I suppose we've still to set ourselves free. *(Then, lest life should seem too tremendous, and too dull, she turns to him with her pretty smile).* So don't talk too much about things you don't understand.

PHILIP *(humorously meek)*. I'll try not.

JESSICA. Poor Phil!

She pats his cheek, then kisses it. 'Poor Phil' is but pretty irony, of course; such a charming home as he has such a charming wife! As long as he'll only see his visions in the domestic fire...!

THE END

His Majesty

1923–28

ACT I

W̶e are in the petit-salon of a large house near Zurich. Its architecture is a nineteenth-century echo of the eighteenth, and the furniture is the usual Louis Seize sort of thing. Some business-like-looking letter files and a typewriter on its table have crept in, though; and what must be a rolled-up map hangs between the two long windows which give towards the garden and the lake. The big bronze-featured writing-table in front of this is tidily covered with papers and despatch-boxes. On either side are double doors.

MR. HENRY DWIGHT OSGOOD an American gentleman, aged forty or so, correctly dressed in a recently pressed suit, stands waiting, hat and gloves in hand. To him there enters COLONEL GUASTALLA, a younger man, in spirit if not in years; ready of speech but discreet, quick, but ever at his ease. He is dressed in a plain uniform which faintly recalls that of the old Austrian Empire.

GUASTALLA. Yes Mr. Osgood, if you can give us two minutes more his Majesty will be delighted to see you himself. Do sit down. And then you can bear witness too that he is still safe here in Switzerland.

OSGOOD. Does not the published assurance of the president of the Federation suffice? By the way Colonel... if I'm to submit you my copy....

GUASTALLA. If he talks freely you'd better. I've been discreet, I hope.

OSGOOD. Excessively.

GUASTALLA. But we pay the right sort of compliment, I've been taught, to you gentlemen of the Press when we flavour all we do want published with an occasional something we don't.

OSGOOD. Why, Colonel...the Press-man is human. Some of us you can trust and some you can't. This is the royal sanctum?

GUASTALLA. It should be! We're cramped. I've only the little cubby-hole you were kept waiting in. There's the large salon, of course. But her Majesty had a whole wing turned into nurseries.

OSGOOD. Is that so?

The cadence of MR. OSGOOD'S response is in itself a cradle song.

GUASTALLA. I worked in the garden-house all the summer. Things are quiet enough as a rule. People of no importance I can see at my hotel. Were you followed, did you notice, coming here?

OSGOOD. I certainly was. Some brand of policeman...by the look of his boots. Are you much troubled that way?

GUASTALLA. Not by the Swiss. The concierge will keep them posted. Quite right! If he didn't I should have to see someone did.

OSGOOD. Spies in a man's very home . . .!

GUASTALLA. Agents...they prefer to be called. Oh...kings in exile look for these, little attentions. When two of the Great Powers withdrew their ambassadors a year ago...I was vexed...I feared our importance was waning. But we found it was only post-war economy. They were sharing the head-housemaid with Paris. Our own people at home are apt to be rather a nuisance. They're anxious...and upstart governments always overdo the thing . . .! His Majesty.

KING HENRY comes in; a man in his forties. He wears a simple uniform. He is not a very handsome man, nor probably a very clever man; but he is shrewd. His courtesy is innate and he has an ironic, a mischievous sense of humour. He has charm. There are depths in him too; for at times, one may notice, he withdraws into himself, seems to withdraw altogether else~where. He gives his hand now to MR. OSGOOD with cordial simplicity.

He has been followed into the room by COUNT ZAPOLYA, whose appearance proclaims him to be a distinguished diplomat and statesman of the old school. And this—it sometimes happens so—is what he is.

THE KING. How do you do, Mr. Osgood? Always glad to see any citizen of your great Republic.

OSGOOD. Your Majesty.

THE KING.... that views the affairs of our old world with such disinterested benevolence...and has contributed so generously to its restoration. Seventy-three million dollars and more, I think, sent to my poor starving Carpathia. It would have paid half the war indemnity. What a good thing we didn't get it sooner! Do you know Count Zapolya?

Nothing could be more characteristic of his Majesty than this blend of formality and irony and simplicity. Only very dull men do not find themselues at ease with him.

OSGOOD. I have had the honour.

THE KING. Are you straight from Karlsburg now?

OSGOOD. I left there day before yesterday, Sir.

THE KING. Bringing the newspapers that tell me I left here for Carpathia a week ago travelling under the name of Fischer. Facts inaccurate...but the size of the head-lines most gratifying! You prefer to get your information first hand. Quite right! Zapolya, won't you join her Majesty? Five o'clock. She'll give you tea in the schoolroom with the children...English fashion. I shan't have to keep you long.

COUNT ZAPOLYA bows acquiescently to the kind command; then, as he turns to go, asks MR. OSGOOD very courteously....

ZAPOLYA. When did we meet, Sir?

OSGOOD. Paris...1919. And...if his Majesty will allow me...I have wanted ever since to tell you, Count, that we all thought when they presented you with the treaty you played them off the stage. You had our sympathy.

ZAPOLYA. Thank you. It was a melancholy occasion. But...like a true tragedian...I ate a good lunch afterwards.

Bowing once more, he departs. His Majesty seats himself.

THE KING. Now, Mr. Osgood. Won't you sit down? Sit down, Guastalla. Now?

OSGOOD. With your Majesty's permission I will go in off the deep end. Do you...or not...expect to be restored to the Carpathian throne in the near future?

THE KING. You have just come from Karlsburg . . .!

OSGOOD. Not direct, Sir. I have been spending a day at Eisenthal.

THE KING. *(To GUASTALLA.)* You didn't tell me that. I think, then, I must interview you, Mr. Osgood.

OSGOOD. Any news I have that is news is at your Majesty's disposal.

THE KING. No...I'd rather not hear it.

The curtness of this brings MR. OSGOOD deferentially to his feet.

OSGOOD. If your Majesty regrets receiving me...why, I have not been received.

THE KING. Never mind! Sit down again. What does it matter? Now listen to me. Do you want to take notes?

OSGOOD. No, Sir.

THE KING. Do you never take notes?

OSGOOD. I am not that incompetent.

THE KING. You'll carry away all I say in your head?

OSGOOD. Yes, Sir.

THE KING. Dear me! I couldn't do that.

OSGOOD. You'd learn, Sir...if you had to.

THE KING. I hope I should. I doubt it. Well! Carpathia was broken in the War...and I did not shirk the peace that was offered me...that you saw Count Zapolya sign. I made no complaint and no excuses to my people. What thanks had I? You connived at my exile. I was the scapegoat. What followed for Carpathia? Red revolution, bankruptcy and famine...with Europe's pawnbrokers and stockjobbers to the rescue...and a Jew's peace now that the Philistines have done. For I know what Karlsburg's like to-day, Mr. Osgood. Police in the streets again...trams running...shops open. But rotten with intrigue in politics and finance...a moral chaos. Yes, I'd be glad to restore some dignity and decency to my country if I could. But I want no more bloodshed. And this young madcap at Eisenthal...! You saw Stephen Czernyak?

OSGOOD. I had an hour's talk with Count Czernyak.

THE KING. He doesn't pretend I've encouraged him?

MR. OSGOOD. He most respectfully complains that you haven't.

THE KING. What sort of men has he got there?

OSGOOD. Youngsters...the mass of them...that weren't in the War.

THE KING. Quite so. Any guns to count? No...don't tell me...I'd rather not hear. I'm fond of Stephen Czernyak...I've known him from a child. His mother was the first friend her Majesty made in Carpathia. The cutting-up of that Eisenthal province was a scandal. The Neustrians are treating their slice of it abominably...and this government in Karlsburg hasn't treated what's left us much better. But I will not win back my kingdom by bloodshed. I inherited one war. One's enough.

OSGOOD. Then you do not propose, Sir...may I say?...to drop out of the skies to lead these mountaineers down to Karlsburg...to kick Madrassy and his government and the Assembly and the British Mission and the French Mission and the Jews and the lawyers all into the Danube with one kick.

THE KING. You may say that I shall not re-enter Carpathia like a thief or as a conqueror...however attractive the rest of the programme may be.

This seems to bring the conversation to such a full stop that MR. OSGOOD gets up again; but this time a more satisfied man.

OSGOOD. Then I will now thank your Majesty for a very challenging talk. With that Colonel Guastalla has told me besides I am confident of making a dignified story of it.

THE KING rises too, and begins a kindly cross-examination. This habit, bred by countless inspections of regiments, factories, schools, model dwellings and the like, has become second nature with him.

THE KING. Going straight back to Karlsburg?

OSGOOD. No, Sir. Now I know there's nothing doing, I sail on Saturday.

THE KING. Taking a holiday?

OSGOOD. Going home.

THE KING. For good?

OSGOOD. I hope so.

THE KING. I've always wanted to see America.

OSGOOD. Your Majesty may count on a welcome.

THE KING. No Ellis Island? We wretched kings, though...prisoners of custom...when we're not exiles! You're from New York?

OSGOOD. Not to begin with, Sir.

THE KING. Where from, then?

OSGOOD. Iowa City, Iowa.

THE KING. Iowa City, Iowa! You can have found nothing more romantic in Europe, Mr. Osgood, than I find that. But you've liked my country, I hope.

OSGOOD. A most beautiful country, Sir.

THE KING. Do you speak the language?

OSGOOD. For railroad, hotel and eating-house purposes only.

THE KING. That's been a drawback. You'd have liked my people too. Farmers and peasants...steady and sensible...if you only leave them alone. Don't judge by Karlsburg and its mob. Comic operas and stock-exchange scandals are the chief crops there. Interested in farming?

OSGOOD. Mrs. Osgood and I, Sir, operate a small farm in New Jersey. She does, I should say.

THE KING. Jersey? Cows!

OSGOOD. Chickens with us, mostly.

THE KING. But I breed poultry!

OSGOOD. I have that in mind, Sir.

THE KING. What's your fancy, now?

OSGOOD. Mrs. Osgood's for Rhode Island Reds. I've stood by Wyandottes. We consider utility.

THE KING. But prize birds pay. The soil's wrong here. I've not done badly, though. *(He takes from his writing-table a triple photograph frame.)* My Bourbourgs. Mark me now...they've a future as a dominant. Louis Quatorze...Louis Quinze...Louis Seize! A family joke...not for publication.

They really do call to mind the state portraits of these gentlemen, though the birds are the more majestic. MR. OSGOOD conscientiously plays the connoisseur; and the KING finds this a far more cheerful subject than Carpathian politics.

OSGOOD. Magnificent lobes!

THE KING. Aren't they? Try cod-liver oil. Do my people want me back, d'you think?

He replaces the frame. With the question his voice has shifted to a minor key. MR. OSGOOD looks a trifle uncomfortable.

OSGOOD. Is it for me to say, Sir?

THE KING. Come...to a mere exile...not yet so used to the truth that I don't sometimes prefer it!

The frank charm of this would be hard to resist indeed. And, button after button undone, MR. OSGOOD'S studied reserve at last slips off him.

OSGOOD. Your Majesty...what an opening! And how I'd have jumped for it once on a time! Ten years ago my considered opinion upon the whole European problem should have been placed at your disposal. My God, Sir...you couldn't have found a more rusé young fellow than me...shipped eastward, nineteen eighteen.

THE KING. In your army?

OSGOOD. Attached Political Intelligence. I have flat feet...which disqualified me from tramping to the trenches with the rest and being shot like a man. Not that I felt quarrelsome! I came full of pity for you all....

THE KING. That is apt to turn to dislike.

OSGOOD. Sir...my first sight here was a hospital and my second a battlefield two days old...and my first clear thought that there were men here...statesmen, so-called...who'd had such things in mind all along.

THE KING. They hadn't, I assure you.

OSGOOD. Well...I could better forgive them that than some of their jobbery since. I know lots less than I did. But I've sat in my machine by roadsides and had the common country-folk stand round me with distrustful eyes. If their talk's been strange their meaning's been plain...and your Majesty put it pat. For the dear Lord's sake leave us in peace. I don't know now which rile me more...the men that fool their fellow-men and call it government or the fellows behind that they let fool them...that stir the mud and fish their dirty profit from it. But if for five short minutes I could be God Almighty I'd make a handful of the lot and drop them in the cold Atlantic...and we'd hear the joy-bells ring. Me, Sir...in my intellectual shirtsleeves...with my New York culture shed! What's wrong with an axe and a spade and a bit of land to clear, said my grand-dad when he went West...and I'll pity the government that had tried monkeying with him. And what's wrong with exile from a world like this? That's the question...man to man...I'd like to have been asking you. Colonel, I fear you should never have presented me.

With which apology MR. OSGOOD buttons on his perfect manners again. But the KING is undisturbed, is much refreshed, indeed, by this Western breeze.

THE KING. Not at all, Mr Osgood, not at all! What you say is most interesting....

At this moment the QUEEN appears; and they all three turn, as people do turn, and even instinctively stand to attention at the sight of her. She is a woman old enough to have a son of sixteen, robust enough to have borne six children besides and to feel the better for it. Whether she is beautiful or not one would never stop to ask: there is a natural magnificence about her that puts aside such questioning. She is utterly unself-conscious. Her manner is usually gracious, for graciousness has been bred into her as one of the attributes of a queen. When she does not wish to be gracious—how should she ever suppose she is being rude? She is showing people what she thinks of them; and the sooner they know it the better. She is never — in any sense — slow to move; and she now comes into the room quickly, as if she thought to find her husband alone. She certainly shows no pleasure at finding MR. OSGOOD there; and the temperature of Switzerland seems to fall a degree or two. But the KING with his charming smile, sets things right again.

THE KING. My dear...this is Mr. Osgood of the United Press and of Oyua City, Oyua, North America. He has been ten years in Europe finding out all about it...but he doesn't like it and he's going home.

If there should be any irony in this MR. OSGOOD does not perceive it; he is fully occupied in bowing to the QUEEN, who inclines her head, eyeing him steadily.

OSGOOD. *Your Majesty.*

Once more the KING proffers a cordial hand.

THE KING. Good-bye then. You did choose a bad time for a first visit. After a war things are always in a bit of a tangle. But think kindly of us. There's a lot in what you say. Even in the old days one wished now and then one wasn't a king. But being a king...one had to do one's best to be a king, you know.

OSGOOD. Your Majesties.

MR. OSGOOD has evidently studied the old Carpathian Court etiquette; for he bows once where he stands, three paces back bows again, and yet again at the open door where he finds GUASTALLA waiting for him. The QUEEN, her eyebrows lifting slightly, is not unpleased by this.

GUASTALLA. I'll come down with you.

THE KING. Bon voyage! Oh...Guastalla!

MR. OSGOOD has departed.

THE KING. D'you know his hotel? We might send him...send his wife...a couple of cockerels and a pullet or so, if he'd care to take them. From the number five pen, will you say? Friendly fellow!

GUASTALLA follows MR. OSGOOD. The KING and QUEEN are alone.

THE QUEEN. Why do you waste time with such people?

THE KING. My dear Rosamund! The Press! Besides...one must be extra civil to America.

THE QUEEN. Why?

His blandness takes on a whimsical tinge.

THE KING. That is a searching question. We always are. I don't know why. Where's Zapolya?

THE QUEEN. He never takes tea.

THE KING. No...but I do. And I thought he'd like to see the children.

THE QUEEN. He's looking old.

THE KING. He's growing old. Time passes.

THE QUEEN. It does indeed! You've not finished your talk with him. Do you want me here?

THE KING. Yes...I'd only have to tell you all about it after. We'd not got beyond his asthma when this American man arrived. I always begin with his asthma. He's just come from Eisenthal.

THE QUEEN. The American?

THE KING. Yes.

THE QUEEN. Did you tell him you'd never countenance Stephen Czernyak?

THE KING. What else could I tell him?

THE QUEEN. Henry...if you'd listened to me...if Cyril and Margaret hadn't had chicken-pox and I'd not been nursing them...you'd have been in Karlsburg weeks ago. What came of all the bargaining with Madrassy? Nothing...and I said nothing would. This talking to journalists...it's so undignified! And now Zapolya's to tell us what Paris thinks! Who cares? I wish you'd not sent for him...he's a pessimist. And who is Madrassy that he should presume to bargain with you?

THE KING. He's the head of the present Carpathian government, my dear.

THE QUEEN. Nonsense! Carpathia is yours, Henry. Go and take it. Go to Eisenthal. Ride into Karlsburg at the head of your army....

THE KING. Dear Rosamund...you're romantic. The problem's not so simple.

THE QUEEN. When you know what you want all problems are simple.

THE KING. Well...I want my tea at the moment. And I hope you've not eaten all the muffins between you.

He has been locking away a paper or two taken from his pocket. He slips his arm in hers and walks her off to the nursery.

The falling of the dusk tells us that an hour or more has passed. The talk with COUNT ZAPOLYA has reached that stage when its pendulum is slowing but will not stop, when a half-hearted shove at intervals does not suffice to set it at full swing again; a recognisable moment in all such talks. The QUEEN sits enthroned; COUNT ZAPOLYA is in a small chair, in respectful discomfort; the KING paces the room, at times drifts to the windows, then comes back to his table looking idly for nothing in particular.

THE KING. No...Madrassy won't fight if he can help it. Fighting's not his line.

ZAPOLYA. With Czernyak one step nearer Karlsburg he may have to give place, then, to those that will.

THE KING. I don't see this Opposition taking office. There's nothing they agree upon.

ZAPOLYA. They'll manage to agree upon taking office if they get the chance. They could govern for a little if the Activists would join.

THE KING. Who's the best man in that gang?

ZAPOLYA. New men...all of them.

THE KING. I get their paper...a readable rag! Up and be doing's their motto...no matter much what apparently! Does the wily Madrassy count on my stopping Czernyak, then?

ZAPOLYA. He must think you set him on to start with.

THE KING. Takes me for a fool as well as a liar!

ZAPOLYA. And he spun out his parley with you to make you hold him back.

THE QUEEN. Of course he did!

ZAPOLYA. For Czernyak has a fighting chance, Sir.

The KING's attention is fixed.

THE KING. With five thousand men...armed anyhow? The Treaty leaves us ten thousand.

The QUEEN sits up very straight.

THE QUEEN. Us!

THE KING. Carpathia. Madrassy.

THE QUEEN. Carpathia's not Madrassy...not yet!

THE KING. *(smoothly)*...leaves the government in Karlsburg ten thousand troops.

ZAPOLYA. Mostly boys...going stale in barracks.

THE KING. The militia besides.

ZAPOLYA. Villagers mainly. Will they march against you?

THE QUEEN. No.

ZAPOLYA...or at all, if they can help it!

THE KING...and ten batteries. Nothing heavy, of course.

ZAPOLYA. He has a fighting chance.

THE KING. I want no bloodshed.

ZAPOLYA. That is another matter, Sir.

What is it that is really vexing his Majesty?

THE KING. Why didn't Madrassy move troops up there three months ago?

ZAPOLYA. He was raising his American loan! New York bankers have all your Majesty's objections to bloodshed.

THE KING....before Stephen had men enough to make any sort of fight for it?

ZAPOLYA. I see Stephen Czernyak with two men and a boy making some sort of fight for it.

THE KING. Why didn't he make a fuss at Geneva about these Neustrian guns?

ZAPOLYA. He did, Sir.

THE KING. No, no...a real fuss!

ZAPOLYA. The mischief was done. Neustria apologised. The culprit is being tried. Everything's correct. Besides...while Madrassy was wondering whether he wouldn't want you back, your flag hoisted in the mountains was an asset to him . . with his own Opposition.

THE KING. He was always too subtle, was Madrassy.

THE QUEEN. A time-server!

ZAPOLYA. If a politician can serve his moment of time to any purpose, Ma'am...that may not be a reproach. Why didn't your Majesties go back when he gave you the half-chance?

THE QUEEN. He made conditions. He had no right to.

ZAPOLYA. I should have gone.

THE QUEEN. To put ourselves in his power?

ZAPOLYA. He was evidently afraid you wouldn't be.

THE QUEEN. He never meant us to accept them.

ZAPOLYA. What better reason could you want, Ma'am, for doing so?

THE KING. He was my tutor in classics, you know, when I was a small boy. He has got on...since. I made him Minister of Education. I've never quite outgrown the feeling that if I don't please him he'll give me fifty lines of Virgil to learn.

THE QUEEN. He took an oath of allegiance to you, Henry. He has broken it and he'll be damned everlastingly. I hope he remembers that, sometimes.

THE KING. He has enough else to worry him now. The country's in a devil of a mess.

THE QUEEN. And deserves to be!

His Majesty's mind returns to its vexations.

THE KING. Why were these Neustrian banks allowed to find Czernyak money? Why wasn't that stopped at once?

ZAPOLYA. Geneva can't touch them, Sir.

THE KING. Their own government could.

ZAPOLYA. Yes...but Neustria has a first-class political scandal of her own blowing up...and civil war in Carpathia will leave her looking comparitively virtuous.

THE KING. A nice neighbour! But now they've stopped supplies!

ZAPOLYA. Yes.

THE KING. Finally?

ZAPOLYA. I think they want to see if your Majesty will make a move...and the effect of it. I think the rumour you'd gone back may have been of their spreading.

THE KING. The effect of that was that Carpathian securities went down with a bump.

THE QUEEN. Madrassy would see they did!

THE KING. But I'll make a move now if this new Paris group will find the money for it.

ZAPOLYA. Yes.

THE KING. Unconditionally?

ZAPOLYA. They've made no conditions.

THE KING. Would you risk your money like that?

ZAPOLYA. I am not an expert, Sir, in this post-war warfare. And like the old crossbowman I can't help chuckling when sometimes the guns do more hurt to the gunners than the enemy. But I grasp its principles...so called. You look for trouble...or discreetly foster it. Securities go down and you buy. When the trouble's over they go up and you sell. And there's a profit.

THE KING. They may not go up. Then you're ruined.

ZAPOLYA. Not if you've been reckless enough...for then your rivals step in to save you. High finance has its altruism. It desires not the bankruptcy of a sinner...of a sufficiently spectacular sinner. Bankruptcy is catching. I think the Crédit Ponthyon...to do it justice...wants a settled Carpathia. That is why they want your Majesty back there. Monsieur Ferdinand...a-straddle on the hearthrug, his morning cigar in his mouth...took a high moral tone with me. Oh...the international Jew with his gospel may sell the poor world salvation yet, at a price...make us members one of another...since the Christian church cannot. Mere prejudice, no doubt, to balk at the price...as I do.

The QUEEN rises impatiently.

THE QUEEN. Nothing's being settled! Things are at a crisis. We must be practical. How does this map let down?

THE KING. Pull the red string. No, my dear...that's blue! The red string.

For her Majesty is not so practical as all that; few of us are. COUNT ZAPOLYA goes to her rescue . . .

ZAPOLYA. Allow me, Ma'am.

...and the map is lowered. It shows us Carpathia, all belittled as she now is, powerful neighbours elbowing round her. Karlsburg stands out as a knot of roads and railways in the centre; Eisenthal and its mountains are over to the north, near the Neustrian border. The QUEEN turns business-like.

THE QUEEN. Where's Eisenthal? And railhead? It's not a hundred miles from Karlsburg.

ZAPOLYA. A hundred and twenty, Ma'am.

THE KING. Surely the railway's cut. Their War Office can't be all that incompetent.

THE QUEEN. It's a week's marching.

ZAPOLYA. Nine days, Ma'am.

THE QUEEN. Go to Eisenthal, Henry...and the whole country will rise. Ride into Karlsburg at the head of your army . . .

The KING'S voice strikes calmly, coldly through her enthusiasm.

THE KING. London may be for recognising me, you think, if the recall's constitutional?

ZAPOLYA. Constitutional is music in London's ears. But popular clamour ...enough of it...might do.

THE KING. Paris?

ZAPOLYA. ...is against you.

THE KING. Then why is the Crédit Ponthyon ready to back me?

ZAPOLYA. Once the Crédit Ponthyon is backing you Paris may change its mind.

THE KING. If I borrow the money first...they'll see I can pay it back!

ZAPOLYA. That puts it crudely, Sir.

At this moment COLONEL GUASTALLA comes in, and rather hurriedly. He is now in civilian clothes.

GUASTALLA. You've not needed me, I hope, Sir. I was called away to my hotel.

The QUEEN disapproves, first, of GUASTALLA'S bouncing into the room like this; secondly, of his bouncing in without his uniform; thirdly, of his speaking before he is spoken to. It is, therefore, in her iciest tones that she points out even a fourth offence....

THE QUEEN. And you have now left the door open, Colonel Guastalla.

He has not only done this, but he crosses to open the other door as he says . . .

GUASTALLA. Yes, Ma am...I have something private to say...if his Majesty will allow me.

and he looks carefully into the room beyond.

THE KING. Frederika Bozen's there, isn't she?

THE QUEEN. Yes.

GUASTALLA. No, Sir.

They are all now in a thorough draught.

THE KING. The colds we catch talking secrets in this house!

THE QUEEN. Tiresome woman! I told her to sit there.

THE KING. And the money spent spying on us! Piles of reports...can't you see them? If I hatch out a dozen chickens every Foreign Office in Europe rings with it. Well?

GUASTALLA. Captain Dod, Sir, sent to say that if the weather does break flying mayn't be too safe for some weeks...and the authorities have dropped him a strong hint that the repairs to his engine are taking too long.

THE KING. I thought he'd been sent about his business.

GUASTALLA. You gave no positive orders, Sir.

There is something a little disingenuous in the tone; a very sharp eye might detect that GUASTALLA avoids looking at the QUEEN. The KING's eye is sharp enough; nevertheless his voice is quite casual as he explains to ZAPOLYA....

THE KING. Dod is the Englishman that...is he English or American, Guastalla?

GUASTALLA. English, Sir.

THE KING.... that was to have flown us... home. Very well. We can have the doors shut now.

THE QUEEN. And you would like to resume your uniform, Colonel Guastalla.

She sounds slightly mollified. GUASTALLA shuts one set of doors; and, departing, the other, with a cheerfully deferential....

GUASTALLA. Certainly, Ma'am.

THE KING. Poor Guastalla! In and out twenty times a day...and has to change each time.

THE QUEEN. To pander to a Swiss Government and its dignity! They'd make us dress like grocers within doors if they could.

Poor GUASTALLA gone, the KING quietly re-links the broken chain of their talk.

THE KING. But if I make no move...and these Neustrian banks have stopped supplies...what is Czernyak to do? He can't live on the country. He'll have to disband.

THE QUEEN. Henry!

THE KING. It's hard on him, I know. If I write him a letter...Will that help?...telling him to disband....

Before COUNT ZAPOLYA she really should not! But the QUEEN can endure this no longer.

THE QUEEN. Henry...you'll break my heart! You bargain with that scoundrel Madrassy for weeks...though it's plain as daylight that he's tricking you. You talk to journalists and give them chickens. But when ten thousand men want to lay down their lives for you...all you'll do is to tell them not to.

THE KING. Six thousand at most.

THE QUEEN. What's the difference?

THE KING. If it comes to fighting there's some difference. Can you see that a letter gets to him?

ZAPOLYA. I'll try, Sir.

THE KING. I've no right to countenance such folly.

ZAPOLYA. But, sooner than disband, he may choose to fight...while he still can.

THE KING. D'you think he will?

ZAPOLYA. Don't you?

THE KING.— *as he can when needs must — looks facts in the face.*

THE KING. Yes, I do. Do these Neustrian gentlemen think so too?

ZAPOLYA. They're tired of waiting. I fancy their game is to force him to.

THE KING. Knowing he can't win?

ZAPOLYA. What do they care for that, Sir? They want three months' anarchy in Carpathia...and they'll get it. Whatever happens they won't lose.

At which conclusion his Majesty looks pretty grim; and for all comment....

THE KING. I hope there's a Hell.

He walks up to the map and stands studying it. The QUEEN, a little wide-eyed at this new prospect, turns to COUNT ZAPOLYA in almost childish appeal....

THE QUEEN. Can't he win?

ZAPOLYA. Not by all the rules, Ma'am. Miracles happen.

THE QUEEN. I think he might.

The KING is intent on the map still.

THE KING. Eisenthal! Ever there?

ZAPOLYA. I was born twenty miles away...across the present frontier, Sir.

THE KING. Of course! Stupid of me!

THE QUEEN. Why do you use that map, Henry?

The symbolic sight of poor despoiled Carpathia is more than she can bear.

THE KING. It's the latest. I keep it rolled up.

THE QUEEN. Did they know, Count Zapolya, when they handed you that infamous treaty, that they were asking you to sign away the very house you were born in?

ZAPOLYA. So long ago, Ma'am, that no doubt they thought I'd forgotten.

The KING has begun to pace the room.

THE KING. How could Stephen let himself be tricked like this?

ZAPOLYA. Has he been tricked, Sir? He always meant to fight. He has had their money. They leave him in the lurch. He's free of them...and so would you be.

THE KING. He can't think he'll win.

THE QUEEN. I think he'll win.

THE KING. If he did...I can't go back on such terms. I've said I won't.

ZAPOLYA. How could you refuse to...if he really won?

THE KING. I'll have no bloodshed.

THE QUEEN. Dear Henry...don't keep saying what you won't have. What will you?

Lashed by her vehemence, HENRY comes to a standstill, facing the facts again.

THE KING. The plain truth is, I suppose, that I don't much want to go back...upon any terms. With things as they are! Would you? Would you take office again? He appeals to ZAPOLYA, who responds smilingly, sadly; for indeed he is both looking old and growing old.

ZAPOLYA. I, Sir? Oh, yes! The old horse dies happier in the shafts.

THE QUEEN. I trust we shall see you in office again, Count Zapolya.

But this is for the KING's benefit and encouragement rather than his, and he knows it.

ZAPOLYA. Thank you, Ma'am...but I could not advise his Majesty to recall me. True...I am one of the few Elder Statesmen that did not make the War. But worse...I made the Peace. This new democracy has no faith in God...but it still needs a Devil to believe in...to cast the burden of its follies and sins upon. Leave me in exile to play that harmless part. Find some respectable demagogue...when the time comes...to make a fresh start with . .; who'll give the mob its stomachful of flattery and sensation. Fed fat, the beast will be less trouble to you.

Her Majesty dislikes irony.

THE QUEEN. You are not serious, I think, Count Zapolya.

The KING is pacing the room again, half attentive, half wrapt in his thoughts.

THE KING. Back to that puppet-show! Poultry farming's a man's job beside it! But I used to have some quite good ideas about being a king.

ZAPOLYA. Government is a strange art, Sir. An expert calling at which the expert fails...and the wise man when he is too wise!

THE KING. You'll stay and dine?

ZAPOLYA. Your Majesty is most kind.

THE KING. I shall write to Stephen to disband.

ZAPOLYA. Yes...I should, Sir.

TIIE KING. But you think he'll disobey me.

THE QUEEN. I hope he'll disobey you.

THE KING. I know you do, Rosamund...but you really mustn't say so.

ZAPOLYA. I venture to hope he'll disobey you, Sir. But write the letter. Five thousand men facing such odds for you...shows you are still to be counted with. The letter will free you from blame for the folly of it. And if by chance he should win...success never needs much explaining away.

The KING gives him a sidelong look.

THE KING. There's even the chance that he might obey me. Not that anyone ever has yet!

ZAPOLYA. The letter will take some days to reach him.

THE KING. True! Dinner's at half-past eight.

His reputation for subtlety thus sustained, COUNT ZAPOLYA, bowing, departs. The QUEEN bends her head in punctilious acknowledgment, but then gives an erasperated little sigh.

THE QUEEN. Why can't he bow properly? Even he!

THE KING. He did bow.

THE QUEEN. Once! Who told that American what to do?

THE KING. They know all these things.

THE QUEEN. Our own people think they can treat us as they please now. Guastalla bounces into this room...as if it were any room. While we're living like this, be more strict about such things...not less! And you leave all the scolding to me.

THE KING. I do wish, by the way, you wouldn't seduce Guastalla from his duty.

THE QUEEN. Henry...what a thing to say.

THE KING. He knew perfectly well that I meant Dod and his machine to be sent about their business. But you're his goddess...you've only to lift your finger! You and he think, I suppose, that you've only to say Go Back or Go to Eisenthal often enough for it to end in my going!

THE QUEEN. Not at all.

THE KING. Well...that is how most people are persuaded to do things. Czernyak has been a fool. No man is safe from his supporters...that's the first lesson every leader has to learn.

THE QUEEN. Don't be paradoxical.

The KING, having coasted the room again, looked out of the window, glanced again at the map, now comes to a standstill, flings himself into a chair and lets his thoughts drift away.

THE KING. If you could begin again, Rosamund, would you choose to be a queen?

THE QUEEN. Yes, of course.

THE KING. *(with his whimsical smile)* Even mine?

THE QUEEN. But I am a queen.

THE KING. This place is cramped, I know. And it's very Swiss...naturally! But it's not uncomfortable. You'd never come to think of it as home?

THE QUEEN. How can you ask?

THE KING. What made my grandfather build that great stucco barrack of a palace? Dreary and draughty! Put less than twenty at table and the private dining room's a desert. And one winter when I was a boy...and the city electricians had struck and it was foggy...I lay in bed there by candlelight and I could not see the ceiling! That's a fact. You've never stayed at the Castle. Charming! But its drains are wrong.

THE QUEEN. Your grandfather thought of what was due to the greatness of his country.

THE KING. He did! And look at it! But he was a nice old man when you knew him. Do you carry in your mind, I wonder, any constant picture of me? What is it?

THE QUEEN. Whenever I'm angry with you...then I try to think of you standing that day before the altar...crowned, with your sword stretched out, taking your oath to save Carpathia in her need.

THE KING. Or die.

THE QUEEN. Or die. And riding back with the crowd cheering you!

THE KING. It didn't.

THE QUEEN. Henry...I heard it!

THE KING. It yelled at me. I might have been a circus. But they weren't very cheerful yells. The war was going badly. Was there much to choose between that noise and the shouting in the square the night they bombed Grandpapa's statue...the night we ran away?

THE QUEEN. And I wish we'd died rather!

THE KING. It seemed the sensible thing to do...to give the Democrats their chance.

THE QUEEN. Much they made of it!

THE KING. But it may have been my chance...to be a king and not a puppet for five minutes...and to die. It so seldom occurs to the well-meaning man that sometimes the best service he can do the world may be to get out of it.

THE QUEEN. Cyril would have revenged us when he grew up.

THE KING. The silly sort of thing he'd have found expected of him! *(She is sitting by him now, and he puts a friendly hand on hers)* But as we did very sensibly make a bolt of it, I wish it amused you more now to think of us togged up as chauffeur and lady's maid...though anything less like one than you looked! The man at the barrier was a fool not to spot you.

THE QUEEN. *(miserably)* I believe he did. Why else did he grin?

THE KING. I never thought of it! Yes...they were all glad to be rid of us.

THE QUEEN. I try not to let little things humiliate me.

THE KING. I drove the two hundred and thirty-five miles in nine hours and forty minutes...and we stopped once for petrol. There's nothing humiliating in that.

In sudden surrender to Fate she breaks out....

THE QUEEN. Henry...why don't you abdicate? Send to Madrassy and tell him you'll abdicate. I'll never say another word about it to vex you. You can run the farm and enjoy yourself. And we're still fit to bring up the children, I suppose.

THE KING. No...while they're all supposed to be squabbling about me I can't abdicate. No...if that flying man can be ready I shall go back to-morrow.

The QUEEN'S spirits leap from misery to hope, to ecstasy almost.

THE QUEEN. To Eisenthal?

THE KING. No, Rosamund! My dear...I've said No to that so many times. Please don't suggest it again.

THE QUEEN. But you can't go to Karlsburg...as things are.

THE KING. Not very well.

THE QUEEN. Where will you go, then?

THE KING. I'm considering.

He rings the little telephone on his table.

THE QUEEN. But why?

THE KING. Zapolya's an old fox! I won't have civil war started. Stephen must come to heel. And I must have a good talk with Madrassy.

THE QUEEN. He'll have you murdered...if he gets the chance.

THE KING. I don't think so.

THE QUEEN. Of course he'll have you murdered.

THE KING. No...it wouldn t do.

THE QUEEN. He could hang the man that did it.

THE KING. Rosamund...don't be so tortuous.

THE QUEEN. He's a traitor! He s a Republican! He's a trickster and a Socialist! Why shouldn't he have you murdered?

THE KING.... or so passionate! You set me defending people I disapprove of...and it warps my judgment.

THE QUEEN accepts the situation—whatever it puzzlingly is.

THE QUEEN. Very well! I think you ought to fight...and I think it's wicked to stop men fighting in a good cause. But we'll go.

THE KING's eyebrows lift.

THE KING. You can't go.

THE QUEEN. I shall certainly go.

THE KING. I'll take Guastalla. It'll be a risky journey...whatever happens when I get there.

THE QUEEN. Do you expect me to sit here and wait? I'm your wife, Henry...even if I might be a better one.

THE KING. My dear...if we both came to grief the children would be left pretty helpless.

THE QUEEN. I' m sorry...I' m not that sort of a mother.

THE KING. Well, perhaps they're not that sort of children...as they're yours.

They are now standing affectionately together. Her eyes, he sees, are filling with tears.

THE QUEEN. You think if I come I'll upset everything. I know I'm unpleasant to people. I wasn't always. It's this life here. I know I worry you! I try not to! You're so patient! I wish you weren't. You think me a fool!

THE KING. Far from it. I think you talk nonsense now and then. But we all do that. And you're often right by instinct when my judgment's wrong. I only wish you didn't want me to be something I'm not.

The QUEEN dries her eyes and breaks out in humorous desperation.

THE QUEEN. You're so good, Henry!

THE KING. *(whimsically.)* That's against me I admit.

THE QUEEN. And I want you to be great...and I mean you to be. But I never forget, I hope, that I'm only your wife and the mother of your children.

THE KING. You're a bit of a child yourself, you know.

THE QUEEN. so are you!

And GUASTALLA comes in, answering the bell, to find them laughing happily at each other. He has put on his uniform, and his manner is now, surely, all that could be desired.

GUASTALLA. Your Majesty rang?

The KING is dismayedly apologetic as he says....

THE KING. Oh...have you changed! You'll have to run down to your hotel again to get in touch with Dod. I'm so sorry. And I must send a couple of messages through our friend in Karlsburg. We'll do that first. Bring your cipher. We shall want some money. That means a letter to Paris.

GUASTALLA. They're opened now, Sir, whichever way I send them.

THE KING. It won't matter much.

No bustle so pleasant as that which ends in decision, wisely or no. GUSTALLA vanishes. The KING is at his table, business-like. The QUEEN surveys him with such puzzled affection.

THE QUEEN. Oh...I wish I understood you! You're not a coward...and you won't fight. You argue like a lawyer...and let anyone get the better of you. You ask everyone's advice and agree with all they say...and now you do this foolhardy thing.

THE KING. It's the right thing to do. You can come if you like.

She might be a child promised a treat; sedate, though, in her pleasure.

THE QUEEN. Thank you, Henry. I must go and kiss Teresa good-night.

THE KING. Don't tuck her up for five minutes. I'll be there when I've sent these telegrams.

He has a note-block and pencil in hand; and he turns now to consult the map again. She comes up and gives him a shy little kiss on the cheek before she leaves him.

ACT II

A salon in an eighteenth-century Carpathian chateau, built under French influence, of course. It is a beautiful room; but it is now incongruously furnished with a kitchen table, five or six old wooden chairs and a grand piano, and there are no curtains to the long windows that give upon the terrace. One can tell that pictures have been taken from the walls; and the glass chandelier has been badly smashed. The place has in fact been looted; only the grand piano was too cumbrous to be carried off. At right angles to the windows, a double door opens into one of the other salons; at right angles to this a small doorway in the panelling leads along the corridor.

It is late afternoon.

At the kitchen table, where they have evidently been having some sort of a rough meal, sit COUNTESS CZERNYAK and her daughter DOMINICA. COUNTESS CZERNYAK is fifty or over; and, by her face, one may tell her for a woman who has come, through whatever storms, into an autumn calm that is very beautiful, who is content now to be a sensitive, tolerant, humorous observer of the world. DOMINICA is young and has spirit, the livelier for its being under control. Both she and her mother are dressed for a journey.

DOMINICA.... so if you don t want that grey silk, Mamma, I could dye the stuff and it would do for a dinner dress.

COUNTESS CZERNYAK. There might be other things in those old trunks.

ELLA, COUNTESS CZERNYAK's maid, comes in; a buxom young woman in her twenties. She also is dressed for a journey. This can hardly account, though, for her present excitement, which good manners hardly suppress.

DOMINICA. Well, next time we come . . .! Ready to start, Ella?

ELLA. If you please, my lady, there are three strange people in the garden. Yes, just ready! And the Colonel has got his gun...so I thought I'd better warn you. I hope the coffee wasn't very nasty. He says he gives them while he counts ten to say who they are and then he shoots. It's the only way now he is alone here, he says.

DOMINICA. What are they like?

ELLA. One's dressed as a woman. Oh . . .!

COUNTESS CZERNYAK. God be good to us...it's the Queen.

It is indeed the QUEEN who, weary and dusty as from tramping the roads, has appeared at one of the windows.

THE QUEEN. Oh, my dear Ja-ja...at last!

JA-JA, we find, is COUNTESS CZERNYAK (it is a nursery name the children gave her; she was their "official governess" in the old Court days); and the QUEEN is ready to fall on her neck in relief.

COUNTESS CZERNYAK. We'd given you up, Ma'am. We've been here since the day before yesterday.

THE QUEEN. The King and Guastalla have gone round the back way....

With a gasp, and as if moved by the same spring, DOMINICA and the buxom ELLA vanish down the corridor.

THE QUEEN. What's the matter?

COUNTESS CZERNYAK. Nothing, I hope.

But for her fatigue, the QUEEN'S nerves might be still more on edge. COUNTESS CZERNYAK is calm, but her lips are pressed tight – and tighter as, in the near distance, a shot is heard.

THE QUEEN. What's that? What has happened?

COUNTESS CZERNYAK. We'd better wait here now...till we know.

But the QUEEN realises – what it might mean.

THE QUEEN. Oh, Ja-ja...that couldn't happen! Yes...it could!

COUNTESS CZERNYAK. Here's somebody.

We hear steps down the echoing corridor and, to the COUNTESS'S unspeakable relief, the KING comes in. The QUEEN shuts her eyes, crosses herself, and, to our knowledge, says nothing. The KING's uniform is as dusty and travelstained, even more; but he is in high spirits. He has been followed into the room by DOMINICA, who now grasps a kitchen poker.

THE KING. It's all right. No one's hurt. How are you, Countess? He had me covered. Guastalla let fly at him from the back of the dust-bin...missed him by an inch! And were you coming for us with the poker?

DOMINICA. I broke the window, Sir. I saw he couldn't hear me . . .!

THE QUEEN. Who was it? Who did it?

THE KING. I don't know. He apologised. Nice old man! There's no harm done. Took us for brigands! Well, we look it.

COUNTESS CZERNYAK. I'm so sorry, Sir.

And, as far as his Majesty is concerned, that ends that.

THE KING. Sit down, my dear...you're dead tired. But here we are...safe and sound...at last!

COUNTESS CZERNYAK. We'd given up hope of you...we were just leaving.

THE QUEEN. How long since we left?

THE KING. It's twenty past five now by Swiss time. We got up from the aerodrome at a quarter to six yesterday morning. Thirty-six...thirty-five hours and a half. Not so bad...considering!

THE QUEEN. We had to come down in a fog...and sleep by a haystack...and wait all this morning while Guastalla and the Englishman went trying to find oil. And now we've walked ten miles.

COUNTESS CZERNYAK. You've had no dinner! There's nothing in the house, Ma'am, but scraps. But the car can go to the village.

THE QUEEN. Give me some coffee.

THE KING. I'm not hungry. We've been eating Sausage and cheese and raw onion all day. Most sustaining!

COLONEL GUASTALLA now arrives, laden with three ruck-sacks; the contents of two of them he empties on the table. COUNTESS CZERNYAK is managing to wash out a coffee-cup for the QUEEN. She and GUASTALLA greet each other with friendly formality.

COUNTESS CZERNYAK. Sugar, Ma'am?

THE QUEEN. Please.

GUASTALLA. Countess!

COUNTESS CZERNYAK. Colonel!

THE KING. Well, Countess...where's Madrassy?

COUNTESS CZERNYAK. He was here by midday yesterday. He has been gone two hours.

THE KING. Can't be helped! He came, anyhow . . and came quick. And where's your belligerent son?

COUNTESS CZERNYAK. Was Stephen to come here too, Sir?

THE KING. If he got my message.

DOMINICA hands the QUEEN her coffee.

THE QUEEN. Thank you, Dominica. You're looking very pretty. When did I last see you?

DOMINICA. Two years ago, your Majesty.

THE QUEEN. Long years, my dear!

COUNTESS CZERNYAK. Did Dr. Madrassy know?

THE KING. Yes.

COUNTESS CZERNYAK. He said nothing. There's been no word from Stephen. I've had not a word from him since he went to Eisenthal four months ago.

THE QUEEN. How's that, Ja-ja?

COUNTESS CZERNYAK. Letters would be stopped, Ma'am, in any case. There's a price on his head. It's placarded all over Karlsburg. They pasted one up in front of my window.

THE QUEEN. Time we were back, indeed!

THE KING. He could get here safely enough. Madrassy came alone?

COUNTESS CZERNYAK. With a secretary...and another car full of detectives.

THE QUEEN. *(scornfully.)* Detectives!

COUNTESS CZERNYAK. Nobody seems to know hereabouts...or to care much...who's governing the country.

THE KING. It all looked so peaceful from the air. I know now just what it feels like to be Providence...and preside calmly over everyone's troubles. A pity we had that breakdown...but we could not keep our bearings.

THE QUEEN. Captain Dod did wonders, I'm sure...but I do think he found it all much too amusing.

THE KING. I've enjoyed the jaunt thoroughly so far. And you were splendid. Now the dull part begins. What's this, Guastalla?

He is at the table surveying the packages.

GUASTALLA. The Paris code, Sir. I couldn't manage much but money and papers. But I could drive back for the bigger things now. Dod must stand by his machine.

For the first time the QUEEN becomes aware of the strangeness of her surroundings.

THE QUEEN. What has happened to this room, Ja-ja?

THE KING. Are you on the telephone?

COUNTESS CZERNYAK manages to answer both questioners at a time.

COUNTESS CZERNYAK. It hasn't been put back, Sir. Well, we saved the big Velasquez, Ma'am...it's rolled up and hidden in the laundry...and some of the Sevres. But of course there was a lot of looting. They took the telephone wire and the posts to make fences.

GUASTALLA. There'll be one in the village, Sir. It's probably working.

DOMINICA. The detectives were using it yesterday. Mamma...why not take the Velasquez back with us?

COUNTESS CZERNYAK. My dear...what should we do with it?

DOMINICA. Sell it to the Jews. We could now.

DOMINICA should not, first, talk to her mother, except very indirectly, in the QUEEN'S presence; secondly, she should not be so flippant. The discipline that follows, though kindly, is cold.

THE QUEEN. Dominica.

DOMINICA. Yes, Ma'am.

THE QUEEN. Put my cup down. You've grown a little wild.

The KING is now bending over a map.

THE KING. If he only left two hours ago he can't be back in Karlsburg yet.

COUNTESS CZERNYAK. He was to stop and dine at Gratz, I think, with the Cardinal Archbishop.

This is altogether too much for her Majesty.

THE QUEEN. With the Archbishop!

THE KING. Good! He can wait for me there. No! His car will be faster than yours, Countess.

THE COUNTESS. Much.

THE KING. He'd better come back here to me, then...detectives and all! Be off, Guastalla! If you miss him at Gratz...well, we'll see.

COUNTESS CZERNYAK. Let Dominica drive you down, Colonel. The car knows her!

GUASTALLA. Thank you.

DOMINICA, curtseying to the QUEEN departs. GUASTALLA follows her.

THE KING. Her Majesty will sleep here, in any case, Countess.

COUNTESS CZERNYAK. It'll be a harder bed than the haystack, I fear, Ma'am.

THE KING. A troublesome house-party for you. Sorry! I didn't know you'd be so put to it to entertain us.

Her Majesty's indignation now boils over.

THE QUEEN. Madrassy! You made him a Minister and he betrayed you. He betrayed his fellow-traitors. He has been leagued with murderers...and he left them to their fate. And he's dining with the Archbishop!

The KING is busy over his map; and philosophical.

THE KING. Yes...the world's like that. I must get hold of Stephen somehow...and quickly. I must have a light on this map.

COUNTESS CZERNYAK. We've a big table in there, Sir.

THE KING. Any note-paper?

COUNTESS CZERNYAK. They were writing all day yesterday....

THE KING. Don't trouble.

He carries his map into the other room. With a certain formality – which does not in the least traverse her gentle affection for the QUEEN – COUNTESS CZERNYAK asks....

COUNTESS CZERNYAK. What can I do for your Majesty?

THE QUEEN. Nothing, dear Ja-ja. But it's like old times to hear you ask that. Sit down. Shut the door first...we mustn't disturb the King. Now tell me all your news. Letters and newspapers only tantalise one. The children are nearly well again. I thought for three days Sophia would catch chicken-pox too. So hard to isolate them in that wretched villa. A sensible little doctor...did everything I told him, But, oh, what a country! Crevices between rocks! What a climate...and what people! I got bronchitis in June. But I'm quite strong now.

If COUNTESS CZERNYAK smiles at this sequel to "Tell me all your news" it is inwardly.

COUNTESS CZERNYAK. I've heard every now and then from Frederika Bozen....

THE QUEEN. A good creature. Clever with her needle. A little selfish! Do you think I ought to have let Margaret cut her hair?

COUNTESS CZERNYAK. She sent begging me to beg you to let her.

THE QUEEN. They all think Ja-ja has still only to say the word! She'd set her heart on it. But it looks so...up-to-date.

Dusk is falling; and in the dimmer light the room looks yet more stark and bare. The KING returns.

THE KING. Better not leave this money lying about!

THE QUEEN. How much did you bring?

THE KING. A million marks...a hundred thousand francs' worth. And a hundred thousand francs...which may be two million marks more by to-morrow morning.

THE QUEEN. I don't understand that.

THE KING. If the mark slumped six weeks ago at the rumour that Madrassy was parleying with me...what will it do when it hears I'm back? May I have that candlle?

It stands on the piano, stuck in a wine-bottle. COUNTESS CZERNYAK lights it for him.

THE QUEEN. It ought to go up!

THE KING. Yes...that's what a loyal mark would do! You've not seen this morning's paper?

COUNTESS CZERNYAK. No, Sir.

THE KING. Our leaving must have leaked out by now. Thank you.

COUNTESS CZERNYAK. Forgive the candlestick.

THE KING. They'll censor the news here, I suppose.

He goes out, his hand protecting the faint candleflame. COUNTESS CZERNYAK sits by the QUEEN again.

THE QUEEN. I'm sorry you had to receive Madrassy here. But the King thought it best.

COUNTESS CZERNYAK. I had some interesting talks with him, Ma'am.

THE QUEEN. Really! You couldn't have found much to agree upon.

COUNTESS CZERNYAK. That made them the more interesting.

The QUEEN gives her a sidelong glance—and changes the subject.

THE QUEEN. You must be very proud of Stephen.

COUNTESS CZERNYAK. Yes. When he was a naughty boy...and very naughty...one was proud of him somehow, Still.

The QUEEN is not too pleased with her friend's tone. She puts a plump question.

THE QUEEN. And you're glad to see us back?

COUNTESS CZERNYAK. It's like old times, Ma'am.

THE QUEEN. Then why don't you seem glad? Ja-ja...things must have changed if you've changed!

COUNTESS CZERNYAK. No, Ma'am...I'm too old to change. You can count on me.

THE QUEEN. I'd no idea your home had been so wrecked. Why did you never tell me? The Russians are savages...and always were...though one can't say that now.

COUNTESS CZERNYAK. They were only here a day. Our troops began it.

THE QUEEN. Are you sure? Who says so?

COUNTESS CZERNYAK. They were retreating...they'd been beaten. And when you're beaten...if you've any strength left...it's a relief to smash something. I daresay they thought that if they didn't do it the Russians would.

THE QUEEN. I begged the King to punish all that propaganda in the army.

COUNTESS CZERNYAK. I came back as soon as I heard...and by then our own people from the farms were looting. When they knew I was packing what was left here they came in a crowd. And I stood in this room, Ma'am, and saw it wrecked round me by men and women I'd known, some of them, as children...and I'd tried, I did think, to be kind to them. One or two wanted to stop it...and one of them snatched back a little silver Madonna they'd taken...I suppose he thought I valued it. They killed him...there by that window. His own brother helped to kill him. *(There is a moment's empty silence.)* I walked through the village yesterday...I'd not been here since. They smiled at me...they were kindly. I believe they've forgotten. Better so.

The QUEEN is really fond of her.

THE QUEEN. Poor Ja-ja! We'll build it all up again.

COUNTESS CZERNYAK. No, Ma'am...I mean to leave it like this while I live. I shan't be coming back often...Dominica's so busy in Karlsburg...and we've a comfortable, ugly, little flat there. But I find myself here among the wreckage. For my life's like this, Ma'am.

The QUEEN almost shakes a finger.

THE QUEEN. That's morbid.

COUNTESS CZERNYAK. One mustn't complain. We lucky ones have been borrowing prosperity for these few hundred years. But the older the debt the less one likes paying.

THE QUEEN. And that's Dr. Madrassy talking, I think.

COUNTESS CZERNYAK. Oh no, Ma'am!...it s not at all the sort of thing I say to him. We were arguing about French poetry most of the time. He'll have none of these new young Catholics...but I think there's a lot in them.

The QUEEN hardly hears this; she too is finding something of herself in the wrecked room.

THE QUEEN. I dreamt last night...I woke with such a jump and the moon was shining on me...about that last Birthday ball...d'you remember it?...before the War. I think of it so often...the men in their uniforms and all those pretty girls kissing my hand. Oh...surely that wasn't just show! It meant something, didn't it? What has happened to them that they've done nothing to set the world right again? Not a thing...till Stephen shames them! What has happened to them all, Jaja?

COUNTESS CZERNYAK. Some are living on what they ve got left...and some are in Paris. Some are earning their living.

THE QUEEN. Well...as things are...we mustn't blame them for that.

COUNTESS CZERNYAK. Here and there they haven't done badly. Andrew Palffy's a partner in the Bibiena Bank. He says he blackmailed the Levinskys into making him one...though what worse he could tell about them than everyone knows, I can't imagine. He gives his friends work. My sister Kate does typing there.

THE QUEEN. *(kindly.)* She was always so practical.

COUNTESS CZERNYAK. Little Countess Sarkotic runs a teashop. You remember, Ma'am...she used to fancy herself in a cap and apron handing cups round at bazaars. Oh, sometimes it has made no real difference. Hilda Lenygon's professionally disreputable now...all but!...and I begin to respect her.

Her Majesty is not amused.

THE QUEEN. And you still cut your jokes...which I always appreciate. Will you have my rooms made ready now, please? I may be able to lie down for an hour.

COUNTESS CZERNYAK. Very good, Ma'am.

It does indeed seem like old times. COUNTESS CZERNYAK rises, curtsies and goes. Left alone, the QUEEN lights a cigarette. The KING comes from the inner room. He has a written sheet of notepaper in his hand and is waving it about to dry it.

THE KING. You didn't bring your fountain pen?

THE QUEEN. No.

THE KING. This ink's atrocious. Cigarette to spare? I've smoked all mine. And there's no blotting paper.

She gives him – and he achieves the lighting of – a cigarette, the letter still in his hand.

THE QUEEN. Time we were back indeed! I wish we were going on to Gratz. I'd like to tell the Cardinal Archbishop what I think of him.

THE KING. Cardinals, alas, care less than most people what one thinks of them...unless, of course, one's the Pope!

THE QUEEN. This money you've brought...it's not the kind without your head on it, I hope.

THE KING. My dear...there's no other kind now.

THE QUEEN. Your money is the real money, surely.

THE KING. There's a Karlsburg restaurant has its walls papered with hundred mark notes with my head on them.

THE QUEEN. You've told me that before. I don't think it amusing.

THE KING. Do you want to hear my letter to Stephen?

THE QUEEN. Now that you're back every other sort of bank-note should be burned.

THE KING. The banks would be much obliged to us.

THE QUEEN. Why?

THE KING. Aha! You should have read that little book on Currency I sent up to you when you were ill. A bank-note is a note of the bank's debt to its holder. Therefore if you burn it....

No; after thirty-six hours of aeroplane, haystack and cross-country tramp, she really cannot!

THE QUEEN. Never mind! I'm sure there's trickery somewhere.

THE KING. Well...there often is!

He has waved the letter dry, and now starts to read it....

My dear Stephen....

THE QUEEN. Don't you write a letter of this sort in the third person?

But he too is weary enough to be shorter of patience than usual.

THE KING. No, I don't! I've known him from a baby...and after three sentences my grammar goes all to pieces. Do let us be sensible.

THE QUEEN. Henry...here we are...dropped out of the air...helpless...ridiculous! Look at you...and I've not had my hair done since yesterday. But you're God's anointed and I'll die with you if need be. We should think of that, and not try to be...sensible.

He puts a gentle hand on her rumpled hair.

THE KING. Dear heart...you're worn out.

THE QUEEN. I'm not...I'm not! I'll sit with my eyes shut for ten minutes. At least we've a roof to cover us.

On his way back the KING notices, among the others on the table, a little packet tied up with pink ribbon.

THE KING. What on earth's this?

THE QUEEN. Two Grand Crosses of St. Anne and five Second Class St. Andrews. They were in the cupboard in your bedroom. I thought they might be useful.

This most happily restores him his sense of humour.

THE KING. I daresay they will be.

He goes to finish his letter. It is almost dark now, and the flickering candlelight casts, through the half-open doors, queer shadows about the bare room. The QUEEN sits motionless; her eyes closed. After a moment COLONEL HADIK appears at the little door. He is old, and more than old; the life of the body has lost its meaning for him. He is dressed in rough country clothes. But, whatever his birth and breeding, he is an aristocrat, and would look it whatever he wore. Silently though he comes, the QUEEN senses his presence and opens her eyes.

THE QUEEN. What is it?

HADIK. I beg your Majesty's pardon...I thought Countess Czernyak was here.

THE QUEEN. No.

He bows and is going, when....

THE QUEEN. Are you the caretaker?

HADIK. Yes, Ma'am.

THE QUEEN. Was it you that fired at his Majesty?

HADIK. No...I recognised him in time, Ma'am.

The QUEEN has now become fully aware of him.

THE QUEEN. Were you always a caretaker?

HADIK. No, Ma'am. My name is Hadik. I was Colonel and chief instructor in Ballistics at the Military Academy. The Peace Treaty closed it.

THE QUEEN. I know. Are you related to Countess Czernyak?

HADIK. Her cousin, Ma'am.

THE QUEEN. What are Ballistics?

HADIK. The mathematics of gunnery, Ma'am.

THE QUEEN. But have you no pension?

HADIK. There are...so I'm told...to be old-age pensions for all when the Budget is balanced. But I am not counting on that. May I look for Countess Czernyak now, Ma'am?

THE QUEEN. She is giving orders about my rooms. Who else is here in the house?

HADIK. No one, Ma'am...except, for the moment, her maid. They will be moving your Majesty's bed into the State Apartments...and I had better help. It is only my camp-bed, I fear. But it is not uncomfortable.

THE QUEEN. Thank you, Colonel. I disapprove of your being in this menial position. I shall tell Countess Czernyak so. And those responsible for your neglect will be punished.

HADIK. I am content, Ma'am. I want no one punished.

THE QUEEN. But how can you manage? What do you do?

HADIK. I study mathematics still. In the higher mathematics lies knowledge that has hardly yet been cursed by man's use of it. I can still work in the garden. I need only bread besides...and a little wine. I'll kill a man in self-defence if I must. I do not justify that. But such is the nakedness of our nature...of which I am no longer ashamed. May I go now and help move that bed, Ma'am?

As she does not answer – for indeed she is at a loss for further comment and she is not accustomed to reiterating her wishes – he bows and goes. After a moment the QUEEN calls....

THE QUEEN. Henry!...

and the KING appears in the door-way.

THE KING. Yes, my dear.

THE QUEEN. The man that shot at you is Ja-ja's cousin and a Colonel of Ballistics at the Military Academy...and he's the caretaker here...and he's quite mad. What has come to this country?

THE KING. But he didn't. Guastalla shot at him.

THE QUEEN. Dear Henry...don't be so literal!

The QUEEN leans back again and closes her eyes; the KING disappears.

The room is now sufficiently lit by a new and very brassy oil lamp, bought in the village evidently. In the QUEEN'S chair – the only fairly comfortable one – sits COUNTESS CZERNYAK asleep, and settled to sleep, if we may judge by the rug she spread over her knees that has now slipped down. There is light in the other room too, as we see when COLONEL GUASTALLA, coming out, quietly opens the half-door. And from it – between this opening and a closing as quiet – comes the sound of voices, high in argument. Two we know; the third is a strange one. It is DR. MADRASSY'S. So he is back from Gratz and his dinner with the Cardinal Archbishop, and some hours must have passed.

THE KING'S VOICE. But my good Madrassy...here we are... two men with wills of our own....

MADRASSY'S VOICE. Helpless, Sir, I assure you!

THE KING'S VOICE. Nonsense!

THE QUEEN'S VOICE. And very wicked nonsense!

GUASTALLA is crossing the room to the little door in the panelling; but he sees that the rug has fallen to the floor, and he comes back to pick it up. As he puts it over the Countess' knees she opens her eyes.

GUASTALLA. It grows chilly about now.

COUNTESS CZERNYAK. What is the time?

GUASTALLA. Twenty-five past four.

COUNTESS CZERNYAK. Will they never have done?

GUASTALLA. Nothing harder, is there, than to agree to disagree!

COUNTESS CZERNYAK. We might all have been in our beds...if we had any...hours ago.

GUASTALIA. Who's for the top of the piano?

COUNTESS CZERNYAK. You can toss for it with Dr. Madrassy.

GUASTALLA gives – one cannot think why – a grim little smile.

GUASTALLA. He shall have it if he'll stay.

COUNTESS CZERNYAK. Why do you keep fidgeting in and out like this?

GUASTALLA. Come now...I didn't wake you the last time. We want an evening paper. The enemy's chauffeur may have one.

Once more the half-door opens and again MADRASSY'S voice is heard, more emphatically this time; the interview is evidently coming to a full close. GUASTALLA slips quietly away.

MADRASSY'S VOICE. Very well, Sir...we've said all the sensible things we can say. We'll part...and do the least foolish possible.

With which rather calculated farewell, he takes leave of their Majesties and joins COUNTESS CZERNYAK. DR. MADRASSY is a man of sixty, the scholar turned politician. His exact, fastidious mind makes the brutalities of politics seem more brutal by its clear recognition of them, and offers itself as a sacrifice to their brutality. Not a happy man, therefore! Only a sense of the need for going on sustains him; only the salt of a bitter humour lets him palate life for the time at all. He closes the door and stands looking at COUNTESS CZERNYAK as in mute appeal for understanding, though not sympathy. All her response is . . .

COUNTESS CZERNYAK. What made you suppose they'd go back without more ado...looking ridiculous...feeling ridiculous?

MADRASSY. I didn't! But I had to give them the chance to. I haven't spared them. I always liked him. Broken loyalties lie heavy on a man.

From the inner room come the KING and QUEEN. The dispute is taken up as if it had never been interrupted.

THE KING. You won't force me to fight you, Madrassy, and don't think it.

MADRASSY. It won't be my policy to begin, Sir.

THE KING. I am not a puppet in Czernyak's hands...and you've no right to doubt my word.

MADRASSY. You can sensibly do one of two things, Sir. Be off back again. Or head this rabble from Eisenthal...blaze your way to Karlsburg...and try me as a traitor when you get there...if you catch me.

THE QUEEN. You are a traitor, Dr. Madrassy...and if his Majesty had you taken out and shot here and now you'd have no right to complain.

THE KING. Nonsense! If we're to come to that Madrassy could better have me shot. He has a dozen men here.

MADRASSY. I shan't, Sir. I've my reputation as a moderate man to keep up. But after this most compromising talk to you I'll be getting back to Karlsburg, if you please, to reconstruct my Cabinet...while I still can.

THE QUEEN. By bringing men into it who've boasted they'd have us killed like vermin if we dared set foot in our own country again!

MADRASSY. Yes! The only way left me, Ma'am...now you've done so...to stop them doing it.

COLONEL GUASTALLA *has returned, a newspaper in his hand.*

GUASTALLA. A three o'clock edition, Sir. Racing tips mainly. But the mark has started sliding.

MADRASSY. And now I'll be told that I held back the news while I speculated. Czernyak's advance leaking out has done it, I suppose.

THE KING wheels round.

THE KING. Has he advanced? When?

MADRASSY. Early this morning. He'll be in Zimony by to-morrow.

There are times when his Majesty can lose his temper; and, for a moment, this looks like being one of them.

THE KING. We've been talking for two hours...and you never tell me that.

MADRASSY smiles his wryest smile.

MADRASSY. I thought you knew, Sir...and didn't know, perhaps, that I did.

THE KING. Then he has never had my message. I sent him strict orders not to move a man.

MADRASSY. He got it. A little late...but in time to obey you. We tapped it...but I had it

THE KING. Zimony! How far from here, Guastalla?

GUASTALLA. Sixty miles.

THE KING. And where's Czernyak himself at the moment? Perhaps you can tell me that.

MADRASSY. On his way here with a dozen cars and fifty men to try and capture me. And if I wait much longer he will.

THE KING. He will not. I am responsible for your safety.

MADRASSY. Thank you, Sir...I won't risk it.

THE KING. D'you think I knew such a trick was being played on you?

MADRASSY. No need you should. But Colonel Guastalla was in and out a good deal while we were talking, I noticed.

THE KING. Did you know of this, Guastalla?

GUASTALLA owns up – and with confident rectitude.

GUASTALLA. Count Czernyak passed Pfalz with eight motor cars an hour ago, Sir.

His Majesty is speechless; MADRASSY is very cool.

MADRASSY. Pfalz? The road's trenched and wired ten miles on.

GUASTALLA. Yes...I'm waiting to hear if he's through.

He faces DR. MADRASSY squarely. Hostilities are evidently commencing, while the KING looks on. But now they are all conscious that COLONEL HADIK is on the threshold, pausing there as if he had not expected such a roomful.

HADIK. I beg your Majesty's pardon.

THE KING. No...come in.

He says this amicably enough; how has poor COLONEL HADIK offended? – who now does his errand, speaking more to COUNTESS CZERNYAK than to anyone, yet, somehow, not exclusively to her.

HADIK. Dominica would like to know whether she shall bring in some hot malted milk and biscuits. The kitchen stove is lit.

MADRASSY. Which means perhaps that he is!

THE KING. Does it, Guastalla?

GUASTALLA. Yes, Sir.

THE KING. How perfectly childish!

MADRASSY. But I congratulate your Majesty upon so efficient an Intelligence Service! How have you worked it, colonel? Are my fellows asleep? They ought to have warned me.

GUASTALLA. They're at the telephone in the village. Czernyak's headquarters has wireless. We've been picking up Morse with our aeroplane set. The air's buzzing with news. It doesn't need much de-coding.

MADRASSY. He's two hours away still.

GUASTALLA. About that.

THE KING. Then have some malted milk before you go...as the stove is lit.

COLONEL HADIK gravely departs; and after this flash of sarcasm the KING himself turns grave.

You have done your duty, Guastalla, no doubt . . .but in future let me know what you're doing, please. I came back to stop this sort of folly...not to profit by it. When I've stopped it I'll be off again...I give you my word...if there's no more use I can be. Run your Republic...who cares?...if you've turned republican...why not? But if I were the fool or the trickster you seem to take me for, I'd surrender my sword to the first soldier you could send against me with honour enough to .

. .! By the bye, Guastalla, I must have a sword. Why was mine left behind?

He speaks of it as John Citizen speaks of his umbrella.

GUASTALLA. In the hurry, Sir. I' m sorry.

THE KING. Well...find me one somehow. Rosamund, do sit down...then we all can. I'm dead tired.

The QUEEN does not know whether she is standing or sitting; her body is weary, but her spirit is afire. She sits down, however; and the rest dispose themselves, GUASTALLA near the KING, COUNTESS CZERNYAK discreetly apart.

THE QUEEN. Dr. Madrassy...was there ever a moment when you meant to give us back our own?

THE KING. Better have been frank with me!

MADRASSY. Old habit clings, Sir. We never were very frank with you. If Czernyak hadn't played the fool...or if you'd been content to let him . . .! If you'd been patient till these new people with money to spend had begun crying out for a King and a Court again . . .! They're a vulgar lot, though...you wouldn't have liked them. But remember...it's little more than a year yet since the red flag was flying over Karlsburg.

THE QUEEN. And you were saluting it.

MADRASSY. As it happens, Ma'am, I never did...I never had to. While the Red Terror raged I was down with rheumatic fever...and through the White Terror that followed I had shingles.

THE QUEEN. How lucky for you!

MADRASSY. Yes...I used to lie awake at night with the shingles and think so.

THE QUEEN. Were you in the Revolutionary Government or not?

MADRASSY. To this day, Ma'am, I don't know. I was Minister of Education...and nobody bothered about such amenities...or about me. They were shooting and hanging people and in far too much terror themselves to think of anything else.

THE QUEEN. You could have resigned...on principle.

MADRASSY. No. On principle...it's the only one I've clung to...I never resign. Perhaps I was dismissed. Perhaps someone reappointed me when the tumult was over. I had a bed in my office and telephones by the bed. And if anyone came to talk politics my secretary said that whatever I'd got was undoubtedly catching. My staff stuck to me...a sound lot...and the work went on somehow. And through Red Terror and White Terror not a school in the country was closed.

The KING smiles gravely.

THE KING. You're proud of that?

MADRASSY. Yes. I'm proud of that. I don't suppose the children were taught much. But we fed them a little and kept them off the streets...street sights weren't pretty just then. When I did get out of bed I found my dear countrymen weary of Red Terrors and White Terrors too. Reconstruction was the cry...which meant that we all sat round trying to guess what would happen next.

DOMINICA CZERNYAK has now brought in the malted milk in cups on a tray and is handing one to the QUEEN. COLONEL HADIK follows with a tin of biscuits.

THE QUEEN. Thank you , my dear. Aren't you very sleepy?

DOMINICA. Oh no, Ma'am...it's all been much too exciting.

MADRASSY. And I guessed right.

The KING gets his cupful.

DOMINICA. The one with the spoon is your Majesty's. It has sugar in.

THE KING. Thank you.

MADRASSY. So I found myself my country's saviour. And really...considering...I've not done so badly.

THE QUEEN. You're an opportunist, Dr. Madrassy.

MADRASSY. That is the word, Ma'am.

THE QUEEN. You were a defeatist in the War, I think.

MADRASSY. History had taught me the use men make of victory.

THE QUEEN. Are we much better off for being beaten?

MADRASSY. We've saved our souls alive. Little else, I know. But when your conquerors overreach themselves...as conquerors will...urge them to the extreme of their folly. You get your revenge...if that's what you want...the sooner. No biscuits, thank you.

HADIK. Your car is waiting.

MADRASSY. Thank you. High time too! My fellows will be furious you've been too clever for them. Furious with me! They wanted to come half a regiment strong...with machine guns and searchlights and heaven knows what else.

He is gulping down his malted milk as he stands ready to go. The KING rises too.

THE KING. So you must put me in the wrong.

MADRASSY. If I can, Sir.

THE KING. You're not jealous of my coming back to make peace? I apologise for asking.

MADRASSY. A little jealous. I'm human.

THE KING. Nor afraid for your job?

MADRASSY. I've a wife and children to keep.

THE KING. Is there nothing reasonable we can agree to do?

MADRASSY. Much, Sir. But by to-morrow you'll have borrowed a sword...and if I've a good word for you I'll be out of office the day after.

THE KING. Who are these gentlemen that want to hang me that you want for colleagues?

MADRASSY. Brisgau, Bruckner...and probably Medrano.

THE KING. Activists all?

MADRASSY. I must hook them if I can. I must keep them quiet somehow.

THE KING. Is this the Bruckner that shot the President of the Assembly?

MADRASSY. No...that was Bruckner the Christian Democrat. He has given up politics.

THE KING. He was acquitted.

MADRASSY. Yes...but he can't get on with his party. Too thorough-going! This one's a silent fellow. May I wish your Majesties good-night?

THE KING. If you make me fight you I give you leave to hang me.

MADRASSY. My work'll be cut out to stop my hotheads making me attack you, Sir. I shall isolate you at Zimony and cut off supplies. With six thousand men to feed you'll be looting the town in a day or so.

THE KING. I shall pay for every loaf.

MADRASSY. A starving town won't sell food. So you'll have to surrender...or attack. I'm told, though, those Neustrian guns are no good. They need calibrating.

THE KING. They'll not fire a shot...unless you fire the first.

MADRASSY. I'm the slippery politician, Sir.... I don't fight. I hope you won't. But it may be your task to fight...if not to fight and win to fight and fail. To fight...knowing you'll fail...hating to fight and with no faith in fighting.

THE KING. Pretty damnable doctrine!

MADRASSY. Is it? We must not be egoists...even in virtue. And if a few months' more ignorant war are needed in this war-rotted country to prove that such well-meaning people as you and I, Sir, are none of us any use here...the price must be paid. What has our credit with our fellows or ourselves or with history to do with it? Good-night, Countess.

A little quiet mischief is in COUNTESS CZERNYAK'S response, mischievous friendliness almost.

COUNTESS CZERNYAK. I hope Stephen won't catch you.

MADRASSY. I hope...after your kindness...that I shan't catch him. May I have back...if you've done with it...that little pamphlet on Rickets which you thought might keep you awake? I must thank the author for sending it to me.

She finds it for him.

THE KING. Rickets?

MADRASSY. Rachitis, Sir...a very common child's disease...due to under-feeding. It came as I was leaving...I read it on the journey...with a letter from its eminent author thanking me for the chance I gave him to examine our Karlsburg school children while the Peace Treaty was in the making...when they were dying like flies. Well...we know all about Rickets now...so he tells me. I only hope it's true. That much reality made sure of! We do wring a little knowledge from the God above our warring gods. A bitter fruit...but sound. Good-night, Sir.

DR. MADRASSY departs, GUASTALLA accompanying him but almost immediately returning. The QUEEN rises, relieved of the burden of such a presence.

THE QUEEN. A perverse mind! You've given him his chance. He's a beaten man...and knows it!

The KING is at his map again; it still lies on the table.

THE KING. Plucky of him to come back though, and risk being caught! Pfalz...sixty miles. Stephen should be here by seven. Zimony...fifty...fifty-five. Guastalla...take notes, please.

THE QUEEN. Colonel Hadik...what is calibrating?

HADIK. The adjustment of the bore of a gun, Ma'am.

THE QUEEN. Is it hard to do?

HADIK. Given the machinery...no, Ma'am.

THE QUEEN. We must make the machinery.

THE KING. We shall want more money. Can we keep in touch with Paris? Yes...we've our backs to the frontier.

GUASTALLA. Paris will keep in touch with us, Sir...as long as they want to provide it.

The QUEEN has seated herself at the piano, and she begins to strike resoundingly magnificent chords, which after a little resolve themselves into the last dance of Borodine's Prince Igor ballet. The KING, concentrating his tired mind, is moved – even he! – to protest.

THE KING. Oh, my dear Rosamund...at this time of night!

THE QUEEN. I feel alive again.

THE KING. Is Zimony friendly, I wonder. We must have a proclamation out before Czernyak's troops arrive.

GUASTALLA. I could start now...if you'll draft it...and knock up a printer early.

THE KING. You must have some sleep.

GUASTALLA. I shall manage. You'll send Dod there with his aeroplane? He's keen as mustard.

THE KING. He knows there'll be no fighting?

GUASTALIA. He can drop propaganda...and there'll be reconnaissance...and he'll look dangerous up aloft. It'll all help.

THE KING. Very well. Now then! To my people....

The QUEEN has relapsed to the slow movement.

THE QUEEN. D'you remember this, Henry...at the Opera in Zurich...on my birthday? And I cried...we felt so lonely...with that crowd of Swiss staring at us.

THE KING. I remember. To my people....

THE QUEEN. Dominica...this piano's out of tune.

DOMINICA. Yes...it must be, Ma'am.

THE QUEEN. Very bad for it. Have it seen to.

DOMINICA. Yes, Ma'am.

GUASTALLA has brought the lamp to the table to concentrate its light on the map and his notes. We hear her Majesty at the piano plainly enough. The rest of the assemblage are discreetly in the shade.

THE KING. To my people....

THE QUEEN. And did you know, Henry, that your state charger is in the farm stables here?

This really does interest the KING.

THE KING. Snowjacket!

THE QUEEN. Ja-ja bought him from the dealer they sold him to. Colonel Hadik gives him exercise.

THE KING. How does he go, Colonel? He was always doped when I got on him.

THE QUEEN. Henry!

THE KING. My dear...if you'd ever been drifted sideways down the street...saluting and saluting...with brass bands blaring at you! Thank you, Ja-ja...it was like you.

HADIK. He needs corn, Sir.

GUASTALLA is intent on the map now, and the soldier in him speaks.

GUASTALLA. Suppose Madrassy does attack us, Colonel?

HADIK. Occupy the station and the bridge.

THE KING. Surely they could shell us out of that.

HADIK. They've no big guns, Sir. Their seventy-five's a pretty thing...six batteries of them! And it carries my range-finder...which your Majesty was once good enough to praise. I have the letter you wrote me.

THE KING. Did I? Have you? That's right! You must come along too...and give us good advice.

THE QUEEN. And will you please see, Colonel Guastalla, that Snowjacket goes to Brantomy?

GUASTALLA. I'll do my best, Ma'am.

THE KING. My dear Rosamund!

THE QUEEN. Do trust my judgment...in some things.

The KING makes another try at the proclamation. The QUEEN plays on.

THE KING. To my people. Relying only upon the justice of my cause.... His inspiration flags.

COUNTESS CZERNYAK. Won't you go to bed, Ma'am? It's nearly five.

THE QUEEN. In a minute. I'm not tired.

Having said so, however, she discovers that she is – and indeed has some right to be – simply extenuate with fatigue. It is creeping on them all. And now the KING looks up to find COLONEL HADIK at his side, trembling a little, anxious to speak.

HADIK. Would your Majesty perhaps give me some less responsible appointment? I was proud of my guns once...but I am not very wise now. I could still fight...but you never know who guns kill...and I think now it may not be right to....

The old man trembles more and more. COUNTESS CZERNYAK comes to give him a reassuring touch on the arm.

COUNTESS CZERNYAK. Basil....

HADIK. If I might wait upon your Majesties...as a servant....

THE KING. You shall do whatever you like best to do, my dear Colonel.

The kind voice steadies him. The QUEEN has stopped playing now.

THE QUEEN. How still!

THE KING. Well, these will be the main points. Peace at home and abroad...due observance of Treaties with hope of readjustment....

GUASTALLA. I have your draft of a year ago, Sir, if that'll help.

THE QUEEN. Your poor beautiful home, Ja-ja! But we'll build it up.

THE KING. I'd like to say something different if I could. Adherence to League of Nations...good government under Constitution...union of all classes and parties....

He goes on trying to find something different to say, while the QUEEN strikes a few last, desolate, single notes before she betakes herself to the camp-bed in the state apartments upstairs.

ACT III

*T*he KING *did establish his headquarters at Zimony railway station. Though all the engines were got away when orders came from Karlsburg to cut the line, one or two coaches were left; and these, drawn up to the platform, serve their Majesties to live in. Cramped accommodation certainly; but by putting up two rough wooden hoardings between the coaches and the platform wall, a spacious, though rather draughty, ante-room is made. One of the waiting-rooms has contributed a large table and some chairs; so it serves its purpose well enough.*

Sitting round the table, at the moment, we find the KING, COLONEL GUASTALLA and DR. MADRASSY. Besides these there are GENERAL HORVATH and his aide-de-camp; COUNT STEPHEN CZERNYAK and MR. BRUCKNER.

The table is ranged with papers and pens and ink; a conference is evidently in progress, over which the KING is presiding.

GENERAL HORVATH is an old soldier, upon whose more military virtues good living and an easy good nature have told, by the look of him, pretty severely. A gentleman withal. His aide-de-camp is remarkable for nothing but the extreme correctness of his uniform. STEPHEN CZERNYAK is a man in the early thirties; handsome, not merely nor necessarily in feature, but in vzrtue of a certain nobility of spirit that informs him; there is something of the panther about him, his strength seems a coiled-up spring; he is a born leader of men, though where he will lead them is another matter. MR. BRUCKNER, who (with DR. MADRASSY) is the only man not in uniform, might be passed over by a casual observer, and might for a while defeat the curious, so closely can he wrap himself in dull taciturnity. He can sit at such a meeting as this immobile and apparently indifferent, till his presence is forgotten. He prefers to have a paper or a book to rest his eyes upon, for when he looks at you there is a brooding strength in them that you do not forget. He is plebeian, but not vulgar; the temptations of the flesh pass him by. We are at a pause in the proceedings. GUASTALLA is busy writing and the others sit silent. But there is an unrelaxed tension to be felt, a sign that all is not over.

After a moment the KING speaks, a touch of suppressed impatience in his tone.

THE KING. Finished, Guastalla?

GUASTALLA. Just about, Sir! "...and except for the matters here set down, either party..." Receives?

MADRASSY. Reserves. I write a shocking hand, I fear.

GUASTALLA. *(as he copies on.)* "...reserves full liberty of action." Finished, Sir. Shall I read it over?

THE KING. Yes.

GUASTALLA. Protocol of armistice concluded at Zimony railway station November 11,1923. Present: His Majesty King Henry, Count.... "

CZERNYAK. His Majesty the King of Carpathia.

GUASTALLA pauses. No one takes up the challenge. After a moment the KING, catching GUASTALLA'S eye, says quietly....

THE KING. Go on.

GUASTALLA. ...Count Stephen Czernyak, commanding his Majesty's forces; Guastalla, aide. On behalf of the Government established at Karlsburg, General Horvath, Dr. Madrassy, Mr. Bruckner..." *(to the aide-de-camp)* I fear I haven't your name.

The aide-de-camp confides it to him voicelessly.

THE AIDE-DE-CAMP. Papp.

GUASTALLA. *(noting his badges.)* A Captain.

THE AIDE-DE-CAMP. Yes.

THE KING. I think we can take it as read. I'll sign. Guastalla and Captain....

GUASTALLA. Papp.

THE KING.... can certify copies while you and the General mark your maps, Czernyak, and make your dispositions. Here?

The document is before him.

GUASTALLA. Yes, Sir.

THE KING. Give me a pen that will write.

DR. MADRASSY hands his own fountain pen to GUASTALLA, who gives it to the KING, who signs.

THE KING. Now, General.

The document passes in turn to GENERAL HORVATH, to STEPHEN CZERNYAK, DR. MADRASSY, MR. BRUCKNER; and they sign it. Meanwhile the KING has himself handed the pen back with a courteous....

Thank you, Dr. Madrassy.

And the signing over, he rises abruptly with a....

Good afternoon, gentlemen.

As he passes towards the railway carriage they also rise, respectfully and silently; MR. BRUCKNER is a bit behindhand in this tribute. As the KING mounts the steps, however, GENERAL HORVATH breaks forth in a voice that has echoed over many a barrack-yard, mellowed now by time and five courses for dinner.

HORVATH. Your Majesty!

THE KING. Yes?

HORVATH. Will your Majesty now permit me to express the most profound regret that circumstances should have brought me into apparent conflict with your Majesty? I have endeavoured to combine duty to my country with all possible respect for your Majesty personally. And I pray that from this moment the spectres of discord and anarchy....

THE KING. I make no complaint, General...nor need you feel self-conscious. I hope your wife is quite well, by the way.

HORVATH. I thank your Majesty...she is pretty well.

THE KING. My compliments to her, please.

He goes into the carriage. His tone has been – and for the first time since we knew him – slightly acid. But GENERAL HORVATH vas too deeply moved by his own

oratory to notice that. He turns to find STEPHEN CZERNYAK looking at him with
the politest contempt. But he does not notice this either.

CZERNYAK. Will you come to my office, General? Our maps agree, I
expect. I can show you the doubtful place from the top of the signal-box if your
glasses are good enough. I've broken mine.

HORVATH. At your service! What I said to his Majesty surprised you,
Count Czernyak...vexed you, Madrassy.

MADRASSY. Not at all!

HORVATH. It came from my heart. This is an honourable armistice for all
concerned. (*To CZERNYAK again.*) You'd have liked a little fighting first. I
understand that. You're young. But what is the object of war? The making of
peace. You tell me we've been Europe's laughing-stock, sitting facing each other
these three weeks...and not a shot fired. No, Czernyak! Between fellow-
countrymen...a bloodless campaign, brought to a creditable conclusion...rightly
thought of, what can be more glorious? Where is your office?

CZERNYAK. Fourth door down the platform. The Ladies' Waiting Room!
Briskly and imressively the GENERAL departs. His intellectual diet, one fears, has
also been rather debilitating. He must have fed full upon stories of iron-handed
soldiers with the hearts of children, upon praise of the soldier as the true enemy of
war and the like. The ghastly fiasco of the Great War being over, he now prefers to
see himself in this light; a very fine light too! GUASTALLA finds that CAPTAIN
PAPP is waiting with perfect politeness, in the most correct of attitudes. He
responds with....

GUASTALLA. I'll follow you, Captain Papp.
So CAPTAIN PAPP follows his chief. He out of hearing, CZERNYAK allows himself
the slight relief of....

CZERNYAK. I thought you and your colleague had come to do the
necessary twaddling, Dr. Madrassy.
And he follows. GUASTALLA meanwhile has opened the door in the opposite
hoarding: he now calls through. . ..

GUASTALLA. Dod!

DOD S VOICE. Hullo!

GUASTALLA. Conference over! (*Then, returning, to MADRASSY.*) Captain
Papp is a fair specimen, is he, of your new army officer?

MADRASSY. Very.

GUASTALLA. What relation...forgive me!...to the General's tailor?

MADRASSY. A good guess. He's his son.

GUASTALLA. Old Horvath never did pay his bills!

CAPTAIN ROGER DOD appears: an Englishman in his thirties. Good health, good
temper, unselfconsciousness and tolerance, and a cheerful ability to turn his hand
to anything and do it well enough – and to enjoy doing it – are his passport all over
the world.

This is Mr. Roger Dod...who flew us from Zurich...commands our air force...edits our official gazette...distributes our propaganda. Dr. Madrassy is anxious to meet you.

DR. MADRASSY'S manner is cool in the extreme; but if he thinks DOD cares a rap for that he is much mistaken.

MADRASSY. We are flattered, Mr. Dod...just to say to you personally what I said to the British Minister about you some days ago...by the interest you take in our country's affairs.

DOD. Don't mention it, Sir. I'm enjoying myself.

MADRASSY. I don't doubt that. You've been dropping on us nothing deadlier than pamphlets and newspapers so far.

DOD. They've done a bit of damage, I hope.

MADRASSY. Are you author-in-chief as well?

DOD. Bless you, no! I only run the team. All the bright young spirits we could comb out who've a turn for literature. Quite a few! And it keeps them out of mischief.

A young officer comes in and salutes.

GUASTALLA. What is it?

THE YOUNG OFFICER. Lieutenant Vida, Sir...asking for Count Czernyak.

GUASTALLA. In his office.

THE YOUNG OFFICER. And would his Majesty see Mr. Nagy?

GUASTALLA. The Mayor?

THE YOUNG OFFICER. Yes, Sir. He has been waiting about since twelve o'clock. And the old farmer wants to know if his Majesty means to take his evening walk round the farm.

GUASTALLA. He can wait.

THE YOUNG OFFICER. He won't wait, Sir. It's milking time.

GUASTALLA. Ask Colonel Hadik then. He's inside.

The YOUNG OFFICER passes on into the railway carriage. GUASTALLA turns to go.

MADRASSY. I must telephone the text, please, to Karlsburg as soon as it's verified.

GUASTALLA. I've nowhere less draughty to ask you to wait, I fear.

MADRASSY. You can't be very comfortably installed.

GUASTALLA. There were houses in the town for the asking. But her Majesty won't leave headquarters.

MADRASSY. A train without an engine. Symbolic! Is the famous Snowjacket still in his horse-box?

GUASTALLA. He was kicking it to bits. Too much corn. He's out at grass.

MADRASSY. Symbolic indeed!

The YOUNG OFFICER comes from the railway carriage and speaks to GUASTALLA.

THE YOUNG OFFICER. Will you please see the Mayor, Sir?

GUASTALLA. Curse the Mayor! I'm busy.

So whether he will or won't is not quite clear. He departs, however, and the YOUNG OFFICER follows him. DOD takes up the thread of his own discourse, as if it has not been interrupted.

DOD. No...politics aren't my pigeon. I don't really know what all this row's about. Nor is journalism.

MADRASSY. You have a gift for it. You have added appreciably to the confusion of the public mind.

Why waste these delicacies of sarcasm?

DOD. But your King's a good fellow...and I'm for him. And the country's for him, my belief is...if you'd give it the chance to say so. We've fought clean at least. Couldn't you have censored that caricature of the two of them...riding bareback into Karlsburg?

MADRASSY. It was vulgar.

DOD. It was vile. If at any time you care to introduce me to the fellow that did it I'll have pleasure in horsewhipping him.

MADRASSY. The world looks like that to him...and I find the groups of people round the kiosks grinning at his grossness begin to look like that to me. Your view of life is a prettier one, I'm sure. But is it any truer?

DOD. I don't see what that has to do with it. Good afternoon.

With which most British remark DOD leaves them. Not one sign of interest has MR. BRUCKNER shown so far in the proceedings; and there is a shade of irony in MADRASSY'S tone as he turns to him now – for, really, such silence seems almost a pose.

MADRASSY. Well, Bruckner?

BRUCKNER looks up to ask in his turn with matter-of-fact readiness.

BRUCKNER. Back to Karlsburg to-night?

MADRASSY. Or finish the business while we're at it?

BRUCKNER. You and his Majesty seem to get along famously.

MADRASSY. What do you make of him?

BRUCKNER. We'd better have forced him to fight.

MADRASSY. Suppose he had beaten us?

BRUCKNER. How sorry would you be?

MADRASSY. When I do go over to the enemy...I shall hope to take you with me.

BRUCKNER. That's a bargain.

This little duel of edged humour is brought to an end by the KING'S return, cap on head, stick in hand, on his way for a walk evidently. DR. MADRASSY rises to ask....

MADRASSY. What time will it suit you, Sir, to renew our discussion?

The KING turns, most amiably.

THE KING. Now, if you like. I was only going for my walk. I want some tobacco...and I've a few serious words to say to my bootmaker. Why don't you come too...both of you? Or would it compromise you to be seen with me? What have we to discuss?

MADRASSY. The week's none too long to turn round in. There are various questions. We shall demobilise when your Majesty has disbanded...not before. You'll need transport.

THE KING. Come...you can find us transport. Back to railhead, at any rate! The men must be got home comfortably.

MADRASSY. Then there are your personal plans.

THE KING. True.

MADRASSY. What are they?

The KING is frankness and simplicity incarnate; and surely, they think, there must be something behind this. Is there?

THE KING. Well...I gave you my word I'd be off again once this trouble was ended...if I found I wasn't wanted. Thanks for your help...and yours, Mr. Bruckner...in ending it so harmlessly.

MADRASSY. You're content to be off?

THE KING. No...I'm not. I've had a happy time here...playing at soldiers...and at being a king again. And I don't want to boast...but we've been quite popular. You're not...so I gather...in Karlsburg, for the moment. Money market hectic...trade upset...strikes to be settled! And you're to blame...because you're there to be blamed. A soulless city! But here it has been all quite simple and human...and I've felt at home. For, indeed, I am! However...if you're sure I'm not wanted...I gave you my word.

BRUCKNER. Who wants you, Sir...and what for? That's the question. Can you answer it? We'd have to...if we weren't to get rid of you once and for all now while we can.

His Majesty seems to become simpler and franker still.

THE KING. I suppose we've all lain awake a night or two at some time hoping the morning might bring us an answer to that. Well...the power and the glory are yours nowadays, Mr. Bruckner...and I hope you'll enjoy them! I get on with my fellow-man. I'm afraid that's my only gift. But I really like the creature...Homo sapiens, you know...even when he isn't...and he usually isn't...I like him!

From his place at the head of the table he picks up the blotting pad; and on it....

Here we have him complete...head, body, two arms, two legs! Sitting in Council and listening by the hour...I used to find myself drawing him again and again...like this...and wondering what he'd say to it all. For you gentlemen that govern him...and there are so many of you nowadays...despise him, don't you? He knows that. You flatter him...because you're afraid of him...and you come at last to hate him. He knows! He can't do without you for the moment. But it's a sort of comfort to him...tussling with life...to feel that there's one fellow-creature, at least, free enough from the tussle to want nothing from him...not even his vote...who'll wish him well now and then with a word or two, if that's all there's the chance to do...and no questions asked. A most unpretentious job! But...strip it of its flummery...it might be a real job still. However...I gave you my word.

Being answered, MR. BRUCKNER makes no further remark. But he keeps his eyes on the KING for a little.

MADRASSY. Switzerland won't receive you again, Sir.

THE KING. That complicates matters.

MADRASSY. And we've our conditions to make now for letting you go.

The KING looks from one to the other before he asks, with a smile....

THE KING. Abdication?

BRUCKNER. Yes.

THE KING. Is this wise of you? It wasn't in the bargain. You won't let me go unless I formally abdicate. But if I don't want to go...suppose I say No?

MADRASSY. How can you? In a week's time...with your men dispersed...you'll be helpless.

THE KING. While I've breath in my body I can still say No.

MADRASSY. The answer to that, Sir, is one I don't want to make...even in words. Nor does Mr. Bruckner, I feel sure.

But the KING will have none of " It hurts me more than it does you."

THE KING. But why not? You could retire again...with whooping-cough, perhaps, this time...to your Ministry of Education, while they tried me and shot me. Your views upon regicide, Mr. Bruckner, are very practical, I understand. There's no surer way, of course, to bring back my son in my place able to make a clean sweep of the lot of you. But you'll have thought of that.

MADRASSY. Does it follow, Sir, because nothing could be sillier than to make a martyr of you...that we shan't do it...shan't have to do it whether we like it or not?

THE KING. Madrassy, you won't frighten me...and I'm sorry you think you can. But you'd depress anyone...friend or foe! Are you really so helpless? Is this what democracy has come to? Are you sure I'm not wanted here...are you quite sure?

Through the door in the hoarding there approaches somewhat diffidently MR. GEORGE PETER NAGY, the MAYOR OF ZIMONY. A plump little robin redbreast of a man, all that a Mayor should be.

THE MAYOR. Most humbly begging your Majesty's pardon.

THE KING. Not at all! Come along, Mr. Mayor. Sorry you've been kept about. Seen Colonel Guastalla?

THE MAYOR. The Colonel was too busy.

THE KING. He is busy for the moment. Quite right to come to me, then. What can I do for you? Do you three know each other? Dr. Madrassy...Mr.

Bruckner...Mr. George Peter Nagy, Mayor of Zimony.

THE MAYOR. Perhaps your Majesty will be good enough to tell me...since no one else takes the trouble to...if everything has been settled...what is settled about us?

THE KING. Why....

Before he can get further STEPHEN CZERNYAK returns, enough of angry import about him for the KING to ask quickly....

What's wrong, Stephen?

CZERNYAK'S eyes fall on the MAYOR; a pleasing civilian object for any soldier in a rage.

CZERNYAK. Oh...you've sneaked in, have you? Just as well! Horvath insists he may occupy the town, Sir. I object. You support me, may I take it?

THE KING. After four hours' talk...aren't we clear about that?

CZERNYAK. I think so. He's not to advance his troops.

MADRASSY. The town's on our flank, does he say?

CZERNYAK. A trick, was it?

MADRASSY. We settled in Council before we left that whatever happens we were to occupy. I told Horvath to be precise. He said he hated to hurt your Majesty's feelings.

If the KING did not scent trouble ahead he might laugh outright at this. CZERNYAK, meanwhile, rounds furiously on the MAYOR.

CZERNYAK. And you told General Horvath this morning, did you, that you'd welcome his troops?

THE MAYOR. I did.

CZERNYAK. *(To the KING.)* The thanks you get, Sir, for not billeting and requisitioning. The town has been in bounds, Dr. Madrassy, for five hundred men a day...and only side arms carried...so that this fellow's tradesmen could rob them at leisure...while we've been lying out in barns and pigsties.

MADRASSY. And you've been running my blockade, Mr. Mayor.

THE MAYOR. We have. I couldn't let the town starve...and hungry soldiers wouldn't have sat quiet here very long. They'd have been at our throats first and at yours next. But it has been a pretty poor blockade. I've not been so certain you didn't mean us to run it.

MADRASSY. You must not accuse me of duplicity, if you please.

THE MAYOR. Everything has cost more in consequence, of course!

The KING cannot let this pass unappreciated.

THE KING. I take off my hat to you, Madrassy. But why did you say you would welcome the troops, Mr. Mayor?

THE MAYOR. Because he told me he meant to march in on me whether I liked it or not. So what better could I say?

CZERNYAK. Can you and your kind never think of anyone's interests but your own?

THE MAYOR. It's not for me to indulge in fine feelings at this town's expense. I'm not made Mayor for that. Give me my own choice...I'm for his Majesty.

THE KING. Thank you, Mr. Mayor.

THE MAYOR. It stands to reason! I look up to your Majesty...and that makes it easier for others to look up to me. And your Majesty...and her Majesty, I must say...have been most affable. A good deal affabler than ever the Mayoress and I can afford to be. And here's real history going on. I could wave a flag with the best. But then again...what's all this to-ing and fro-ing for? To do us plain folk good...if what we're told is true. We thank you. Zimony was fought over in the War...you won't expect us to forget that, will you? We've built it up again...not so different to what it was. Leave us the good we've got...that's all we ask. This country's a bit sick of these squabblings and manœuvrings...if I may say so...and we did hope your Majesty's coming back meant that you'd just say the word....

THE KING. What word, Mr. Mayor?

THE MAYOR. Ah...well...there! People come quarrelling to me...I listen...I've got to. I let them talk till they're tired...there's not much else I can do...and as often as not they don't seem to know what they're quarrelling about. And I say to myself: Now, there ought to be some word...! But if your Majesty doesn't know it...I'm sure there's nobody does. Well...if it's still not settled what's to happen to us, I must wait till it is. Honoured and obliged by this interview, your Majesty, General and gentlemen, I'm sure.

The MAYOR departs, carrying off, we must agree, the honours of the discussion.

THE KING. He has done his best for everybody, has the Mayor. You must see he doesn't suffer, Madrassy.

CZERNYAK. Meanwhile, Sir...is Horvath to put his troops in the town? With his guns over the river...when the armistice ends he could tell us to surrender or shoot us to bits.

MADRASSY. Shall we have Horvath back and discuss the point, Sir?

THE KING. Certainly not. We settled and signed. Tell General Horvath from me that as a soldier and a gentleman I expect him to behave like one.

MADRASSY. We shall have to override him, then.

THE KING. You may. You won't override me.

MADRASSY. If we'd brought up the point, Sir, you'd have yielded it.

THE KING. How do you know?

MADRASSY. Now that you're beaten....

CZERNYAK. We're not beaten.

MADRASSY.... your troops may get out of hand.

THE KING. Nonsense! I give you my word to keep order in the town.

MADRASSY. If we'd chosen to fight....

CZERNYAK. Well...you didn't.

MADRASSY. But if you mean to disband when the week's over, Sir...what difference does it make? Be reasonable!

THE KING. Here are men ready to give their lives for me. And you ask me to put them to shame before you? They shall go home as honourably as they came.

MADRASSY. I can't give way now. And I don't go back to Karlsburg, Sir, without your word that you'll abdicate.

THE KING. Or your loyal colleagues will be saying that I've bribed or cajoled you. Mr. Bruckner's a witness I don't try to. Isn't that what he's here for? Or will he be suspect now? I condole with you both. I'd sooner sweep a crossing than make one with such a crew.

MADRASSY. Do you mean to make us fight you...after all?

THE KING. Give me choice of weapons...yes, I'll fight you and beat you! And you'd thank me.

MADRASSY. Well, Bruckner?

MR. BRUCKNER takes a second or so to consider.

BRUCKNER. We'd better go and talk to Horvath.

MADRASSY. Can we load the blame on him? I'll try if you will. There's his professional pride to reckon with. Ours...as you say, Sir...is to save our skins.

These scholastic ironies do not interest MR. BRUCKNER, and he has gone. DR. MADRASSY follows. He can hardly be out of hearing before CZERNYAK lets loose vith....

CZERNYAK. Sir...Sir...break off with them! They've given us the chance. Send them packing. Give me my head now and I'll have you in Karlsburg in a week. I can do it! Horvath's been blabbing. His command's at sixes and sevens...rotted with politics. It may be a bloody business with the regiment on our flank here. But mop that up...the rest won't fight. They might come over...be thankful to have gentlemen to officer them again. Bruckner thinks so...you can see. He's had a quiet look round and he's for backing down. And what the devil do you want?

This last is to LIEUTENANT VIDA, who has appeared, saluting.

VIDA. Sorry, Sir. Didn't know you were with his Majesty.

THE KING. Never mind!

VIDA. Bakay's here, Sir.

CZERNYAK. I can t bother with him now.

VIDA. Very well, Sir. His sentence was read to his battalion. They didn't take it well.

CZERNYAK. What do I care? Keep him locked up till to-morrow.

VIDA. Very good, Sir. Have you ordered the goods siding guns to be shifted?

CZERNYAK. No.

VIDA. I thought perhaps you didu't want these gentlemen from Karlsburg to get too close a look at them.

CZERNYAK. Massimo has done it on his own accouut. Quite right.

THE KING. Who's Bakay? What's he sentenced for?

CZERNYAK. Our crack sergeant-major. Six months' cells, isn't it?

VIDA. Yes, sir...for spreading disaffection.

CZERNYAK. I'll have to let him off. We've no place left to put him. How many in the sheds now, Vida?

VIDA. Thirty-four I think.

CZERNYAK. Keep the fellow about. I may find time for him.

LIEUTENANT VIDA salutes—smartness itself; discipline seems good under STEPHEN CZERNYAK—and goes. CZERNYAK turns to the KING again, as if there'd been no interruption.

CZERNYAK. For God's sake, Sir! Before they give in and send back to tell me! It's our last chance. Take it...for God's sake!

The KING is looking at him affectionately; but he shakes his head.

THE KING. We must wage a war for you some day...against the heathen.

CZERNYAK. Very well. Since you came I've obeyed orders...I can do that. But I don't understand you, Sir. Every chance we've given you...you've thrown away. It's wicked! I'll say it...if it's no use to say it. You don't want to win.

THE KING. I want to do more than that now.

CZERNYAK. But disband us...you ve nothing left even to bargain with.

THE KING. I can't bargain. You think I'll never get to Karlsburg unless I fight my way there. You're a soldier...you must think so. But men, remember, are held prisoners of their success...they walk ever after in the way of it. These two...Bruckner...Madrassy! They're in power...and helpless...prisoners of the men that keep them there. Helpless, we may find soon, not to bring their guns up and start blowing us to bits...though they don't want to...they know what comes of that in the end. If I let you start blowing them to bits, dear Stephen...I may ride Snowjacket into Karlsburg in triumph...but I should be a prisoner of that power.

CZERNYAK. It seems to me, Sir...once you win...no matter how you win...you can have your own way after.

THE KING. Do you believe that? I recommend you not to believe it. When I'm rid of you all, I'm not sure I shan't walk to Karlsburg. It's only sixty miles...and a straight road. Who could stop me? The people would be friendly. And when next I open Parliament I shall walk down the hill from the Castle...frock coat, top hat, with an umbrella if it's raining. That's half a mile, no more. The police could keep the street clear. Will it be very unkingly?

CZERNYAK. Not if you do it, Sir.

THE KING. Worth trying...d'you think?

CZERNYAK. I don't believe in miracles, I fear.

THE KING. Nor I. And I don't know the Mayor's magic word. It would be the natural thing to do. You don't believe in my divine right, Stephen. But the fact is...if I haven't that, I've no other. Nor has any man. This time I must put it to the proof. I'll be off for my walk round the farm now. If they don't knuckle under...those three...you can send for me. But I fancy they will.

And the KING departs, leaving CZERNYAK to set his teeth to the worst. He rouses himself as one does to carry on routine, and calls....

CZERNYAK. Orderly!

The door in the hoarding through which all the main traffic has been passing (the one opposite that of the KING'S departure) opens. Almost before the orderly can appear....

Have that prisoner sent in.

The door closes. CZERNYAK drops into a chair and sits brooding. Meanwhile his mother has appeared at the railway-carriage door.

COUNTESS CZERNYAK. She wants news, Stephen.

CZERNYAK. We've signed...but there's a hitch.

COUNTESS CZERNYAK. She won't stir out till they've gone.

CZERNYAK. I'm to offer her Horvath's profoundest homage.

COUNTESS CZERNYAK. For heaven's sake, don't! She's up, at any rate! Cousin Basil's playing chess with her. But I've a mind to pack Ella home and sprain my ankle and take to my own bed. Then she'd have her clothes to brush, at least. This is a bitter business for you, my dear.

A few years ago – for he is still young enough – the last words would have broken him down; a few years hence he might soften to them. Now he only sets his teeth the harder.

CZERNYAK. I'd not have asked him to thank me, even! I wish she were the man.

COUNTESS CZERNYAK. She's not very wise.

CZERNYAK. What does that matter?

LIEUTENANT VIDA now returns with his prisoner under guard, and COUNTESS CZERNYAK discreetly stands aloof. SERGEANT-MAJOR BAKAY, the prisoner, is a hard-bitten soldier with all the marks of long service on him. He fought through the Great War, evidently. He is disciplined to the last inch of self control and can conduct himself with dignity even under these circumstances, though one can tell that he takes them very badly indeed. VIDA hands CZERNYAK the paper with the man's sentence on it, and everyone stands to attention. CZERNYAK glances through the paper and then scowls at its victim.

CZERNYAK. Three days' field-punishment . . .! Pleasant for his regiment...won't it be...to see their senior sergeant-major chained to a gun-carriage! And six months' cells...as and when possible.

BAKAY. I'd rather be shot, General.

CZERNYAK. Who asked you what you'd rather be? Am I to waste good bullets on you?

BAKAY. We've not spent many of'em so far.

CZERNYAK. Hold your impertinent tongue when I'm talking to you! Why isn't the fellow's face washed before he's brought to me? Can't you be shut in a coal-shed for a few hours without messing yourself up like this? What sort of a soldier are you?

At this juncture ROGER DOD strolls back; but, finding a row on, he also discreetly stands aloof.

BAKAY. Try me and see! Put me to fight, I say...which I came for. Bring a bull out of those fields and I'll fight it.

CZERNYAK. You'll fight or not as you're ordered. And you won't ask why. You're fed...you get your pay.

BAKAY. And let's earn it honest...was all I ever meant...for that swine of a corporal to go peaching on me. He's for it...front or back...the first scrap that sees me alongside him. This whole countryside's making game of us. Push through then, I say...and show 'em. Let us loose a day or two in Karlsburg...and we'll show 'em. And let the cowards go home again...whoever they are!

The last three words show us well enough what SERGEANT-MAJOR BAKAY's real offences of the tongue were. CZERNYAK now "plays the game" with a vengeance – a vengeance on himself and the prisoner and all the world for having to play it.

CZERNYAK. Listen you to me. His Majesty is graciously pleased on the happy occasion of this armistice to remit your sentence. And I reduce you to the ranks. Cut off his stripes. Cut them off with that pen-knife here and now. Give him double fatigues. Set him digging latrines for a week. And I trust you're grateful.

As an experienced sergeant-major, BAKAY can at least admire the artistry of abuse.

BAKAY. His Majesty's a kind gentleman, I don't doubt. And I'd follow you to hell, General...which I set out to...and you know it!

CZERNYAK. Much obliged! See I'm told, Vida, when they want me in the office. Take him away. Wash his face!

BAKAY is removed. In the succeeding calm DOD strolls forward, and COUNTESS CZERNYAK leaves the lobby of the carriage too.

DOD. Feel better? Nothing like a bout of slanging for expelling poisons from the system. Discipline's been amazing good though...considering. I give you full marks. A little sport might have helped. Or even theatricals! When bad blood's brewing set fellows to making fools of themselves!

CZERNYAK. We've managed to give you a sporting enough time, I hope.

DOD. Thank you.

CZERNYAK. The whole business ordained by Providence, no doubt, to that end.

DOD. Providence can beat you...and the rest of us...when it comes to irony, General.

CZERNYAK surrenders to this impervious Englishman at discretion; he has a liking for him and some respect, too.

CZERNYAK. Have you settled on your next adventure?

DOD. Yes. Air surveying in South Siam. Come along and learn to click the camera. You'll need a change. I must see this through, though.

COUNTESS CZERNYAK. How will it end, Captain Dod? As you don't care...perhaps you know.

GUASTALLA arrives, in a bit of a hurry.

GUASTALLA. You're wanted.

CZERNYAK gives him a glance; then, without a word, gets up and goes. A glum silence falls.

DOD. Has the enemy given in?

GUASTALLA. Oh, yes!

DOD. Poor Czernyak! Cheer up...lots of queer things may happen yet.

COUNTESS CZERNYAK. They should never have come back. It was hopeless. That world has vanished. Why did you let them come, Colonel?

GUASTALLA. How could I stop them? They had to try. I didn't think it was hopeless.

COUNTESS CZERNYAK. Then you didn't think.

The worries of the affair – and they all fall on him, the bigger ones at second hand, the smaller quite his own – are beginning to try GUASTALLA'S perfect temper.

GUASTALLA. I'm not asked to think. I'm a shorthand typist with good table manners, warranted to look well in uniform.

COUNTESS CZERNYAK. He must abdicate now.

GUASTALLA. She'd sooner die.

COLONEL HADIK has appeared in the doorway of the railway carriage, and he stands there as if listening – not to the now desultory conversation below him, however.

DOD. Of course I may be wrong in thinking I could settle the whole business in ten minutes if everyone concerned would only show a little common-sense. But in my dear country we do learn to settle things. We're always scrapping...no harm in that! But no good in it unless you make friends after....

HADIK. Did you hear gunfire?

They all turn at the sudden question—and stare; but COLONEL HADIK is an odd old gentleman.

GUASTALLA. No.

DOD. No.

GUASTALLA. The armistice is signed, Colonel.

HADIK. So I'm told.

COUNTESS CZERNYAK. How goes the game, Cousin Basil?

HADIK. I now give her Majesty a rook and a knight only. With patience she might make a player.

He does not move from where he stands, but listens still. The rest take up the train of their thoughts again; and DOD'S talk flows sententiously on.

DOD. Frontiers are your trouble. Frontiers make for xenophobia....

GUASTALLA. For what?

DOD. A pet of a word, ain't it?...and I know what it means! There's a lot to be said for landing in a country from the sea...especially if you've been sick on it...makes you feel friendlier to the foreign devil.

COUNTESS CZERNYAK. I see anarchy ahead here.

GUASTALLA. The Powers might interfere then. I wish they would.

DOD. That's when they won't. There's prestige in a little peaceful Occupation. But when bombs go off...and soldiers get nerves...and someone says Shoot...and you hit the wrong people...and the Pacifists at home make a fuss . . .! I say, Colonel...your ears are good.

For now they have all heard it.

HADIK. Our twenty-pounder with the faulty primer, that time, I should say.

GUASTALLA. But nobody can be firing now!

DOD. Whose car can I steal?

HADIK. It's a mile away and more...coming into the wind.

DOD. It's towards the town.

DOD is already off and away. GUASTALLA calls after him.

GUASTALLA. Send word!

DOD. Right!

Into the doorway of the other carriage comes the QUEEN. She is pale and excited. She looks a tragic figure as she stands there, a long wrap thrown round her.

THE QUEEN. There's fighting!

GUASTALLA. Something's wrong, Ma'am.

THE QUEEN. They've attacked us?

GUASTALLA. Our guns are firing.

THE QUEEN. Thank God!

GUASTALLA. But we signed the Armistice...not half an hour ago.

She does not hear this...or heed.

THE QUEEN. Ja-ja...we're fighting...we're not disgraced.

GUASTALLA. Where's his Majesty?

COUNTESS CZERNYAK. He went for his walk.

THE QUEEN. There's another!

GUASTALLA. Ours?

HADIK. I couldn't tell.

GUASTALLA. Will he hear them? Please don't stir from this spot, Ma'am.

GUASTALLA goes after the KING.

THE QUEEN. That last was closer, wasn't it?

HADIK. The wind.

COLONEL HADIK has come down from the carriage doorway and in it there appears ELLA, COUNTESS CZERNYAK'S maid, looking a little startled.

THE QUEEN. They've tried to trick us...I prayed God they might...and we're paying them out. I thought first: Henry kept it as a surprise for me. Dear Colonel...did you think you'd never hear your guns again? And I'd taken your Bishop...the one on the left. I was wondering where you'd gone.

HADIK. You should not have taken that Bishop, Ma'am.

More firing, evidently; and the QUEEN'S spirits rise higher still.

THE QUEEN. Two together!

COUNTESS CZERNYAK. Get her Majesty's fur cloak, Ella. You mustn't catch cold.

THE QUEEN. I want my field-glasses...quick. We'll climb the signal-box...we can see lots from there. And another!

HADIK. That makes the full battery.

ELLA having gone for the cloak, COUNTESS CZERNYAK must needs go herself for the glasses. The QUEEN turns to COLONEL HADIK again in childish joy.

THE QUEEN. This waiting here...I don't know how I've borne it! We won't stop so long at the next station...will we?

HADIK. Very undisciplined practice! I hope they won't fire Number Four again too soon...or they'll hurt themselves.

THE QUEEN. What's that queer buzzing?

HADIK. Machine guns, Ma'am.

THE QUEEN. Let's get as close as we can.

She can wait no more, but is off just as ELLA appears with the cloak, which COLONEL HADIK takes from her with....

HADIK. Give it to me, Ella. Stay you here.

And he follows the QUEEN with it as COUNTESS CZERNYAK comes out with the field-glasses and speeds after her too. ELLA is left with eyes staring wide.

Some little time must have passed, for though the dusk was gathering as the firing started, it would be quite dark now if the platform were not lit by the steel glare of the high-swinging arc lamps. The QUEEN, glad enough (if she thought about it) of her fur cloak, is waiting, still and tense. COUNTESS CZERNYAK is watching at one of the hoarding doors. ELLA comes to the door of the railway carriage.

ELLA. There's another motor car come back, please.

COUNTESS CZERNYAK. Who's?

COLONEL GUASTALLA arrives in all haste, and her Majesty pounces on him.

GUASTALLA. Here s the King, Ma'am.

THE QUEEN. You're to tell him they're not to blame. You're to praise them...you're to praise them!

GUASTALLA. Ma'am...it's a terrible business...and a very difficult business. I beg you to be careful what you say.

The KING comes quickly in; and there is a look on his face that we have not seen before.

THE QUEEN. Henry....

THE KING. Fetch me my sword, somebody! Don't talk to me now, please. Where's General Horvath? Guastalla...find Czernyak. He's to come here to me.

GUASTALLA. General Horvath has just driven up, Sir!

THE KING. Will somebody fetch me that sword?

They are all staring at the KING; and, no one else moving, with a half-articulate " Yes, y' Majesty" ELLA vanishes into the carriage.

GUASTALLA. I've not seen Count Czernyak, Sir. I'll send to find him.

GUASTALLA departs. That word "sword" has been music to the QUEEN.

THE QUEEN. Henry...you're going to lead them! Oh, at last! You'll draw your sword and lead them!

The KING stares at her in blank angry amazement.

THE KING. Do you know what has happened?

She meets him with defiance.

THE QUEEN. Yes, I do.

THE KING. Blackguards and brigands!

THE QUEEN. But not if you lead them! God's giving you another chance...to draw your sword and lead them. On your horse too...your white horse!

He rasps out a very harsh....

THE KING. Nonsense!

THE QUEEN. I could!

And harshness turning cold....

THE KING. Please try not to make a fool of yourself.

The QUEEN cries out in despair.

THE QUEEN. What does that matter!

STEPHEN CZERNYAK'S here now; wrought to a desperate pitch, and controlled. He salutes and stands to attention as might any subaltern.

CZERNYAK. Sir?

THE KING. What section began it?

CZERNYAK. Battery A took their guns across the bridge about two o'clock.

THE KING. Without orders!

CZERNYAK. The men themselves.

THE KING. No officers?

CZERNYAK. Two went later, Sir. They didn't know the armistice was signed. It's fair to say that. Nor was it.

THE KING. It was when the Kathy battalion went in.

CZERNYAK. Yes, Sir.

THE KING. Officers too.

CZERNYAK. Seven, Sir.

THE KING. They knew by then?

CZERNYAK. I can't say, Sir.

THE KING. You're their chief. You've no excuse?

CZERNYAK. I don't make any.

Suddenly the KING'S wrath blazes.

THE KING. Mother of God! Couldn't they at least find armed men to shoot at? None of Horvath's troops in the town?

CZERNYAK. No, Sir.

THE KING. Did you know that, Rosamund?

He is met again with an obstinately defiant....

THE QUEEN. Yes.

CZERNYAK. They went for the Town Hall. They didn't shoot at first. They warned all the women to stand clear. These tradesmen have been cheating them for weeks. They'd thought when we did advance... .

THE KING. There'd be looting.

CZERNYAK. They're human. They want their own back. So did you, Sir.

THE KING. Finish your report.

CZERNYAK. They're barricaded now in the big square...where the White Hart Inn is...fifteen hundred of them. I kept Horvath with me...and the telephone's cut, so his staff has had no orders yet...unless those politicians have chipped in....

THE KING. And we gave him our word to protect the town if he'd keep his troops out of it?

CZERNYAK. Yes. I sent for my own Eisenthalers to come and round the fools up....

He stops. This is, to him, the worst of all.

THE KING. Well?

CZERNYAK can only make a helpless gesture.

They won't stir!

CZERNYIAK. They're paraded. I've been talking to them.

THE KING. Where?

Does his Majesty mean to see what he can do? CZERNYAK checks him with the bitter chivalry of....

CZERNYAK. No...don't, Sir...They've been talking to me...some of them! I'd no answer. Give me my orders, please.

THE KING. I've no orders.

For the first time STEPHEN CZERNYAK loses self control.

CZERNYAK. I wish to God I were with them, then...waiting to be shot! You've broken me, Sir...you've broken me!

By this ELLA has returned with the sword. She has indeed been standing with it at the KING'S side for several moments before he perceives her.

THE KING. What is it?

ELLA. Please, your Majesty...the sword.

THE KING. Thank you, Ella.

Though he thanks her vith his customary courtesy and takes the trouble to remember her name, ELLA is glad enough to be off. A silence falls. The KING stands there, sword in hand, motionless. At last the QUEEN asks (though by the tone of her voice we may guess she knows the answer)....

THE QUEEN. What are we waiting for, Hemy?

THE KING. For General Horvath. Won't you go in?

THE QUEEN. No.

THE KING. Very well.

Silence again. Then comes GUASTALLA, ushering in GENERAL HORVATH, who is followed, shadow-like, by the correct CAPTAIN PAPP. HORVATH is in a state of empurpled distraction.

GUASTALLA. General Horvath, Sir.

THE KING. General...my troops have mutinied and disgraced me. I surrender my sword to you.

While HORVATH is recovering from the shock of this, we can just hear the QUEEN'S low, bitter....

THE QUEEN. God forgive us!

HORVATH, when he does recover, all but bursts into tears. Anything – anything sooner than take this sword that the KING is holding out to him!

HORVATH. Oh...please don't! No...I do beg your Majesty not to! Anyone else, of course, that's mixed up in it...if they'd like to surrender I'd be only too pleased...and to see they come to no harm. But not your Majesty. No...I really couldn't!

THE KING. I am offering you my sword, Sir.

HORVATH. But I only took command...I told them...because I was devoted to your Majesty's true interests...and feeling in a sense I was still in your Majesty's service...for your Majesty's dear grandfather gave me my commission with his own hands...fortysix years ago in April. And how can I....

The KING'S black rage has abated; but he is now very rapidly losing his temper.

THE KING. How much longer am I to hold this sword?

HORVATH. And everything can be settled quite simply. There are four inns in that square...and the silly fellows will all be drunk by to-night. And I've talked to the Mayor and he's most amenable. And if Count Czernyak will be good enough to help me I can arrest the lot without any trouble. And Madrassy will keep the worst out of the papers....

The KING can stand no more of it; he throws the sword on the ground with a great clatter and vanishes into the railway carriage. While this parley has been on, DOD and, a little later, BRUCKNER have arrived on the scene. Needless to say they do not obtrude themselves. DOD, one notices, has been in the wars. The KING departed, that emblematic sword draws all looks to it, till the looker can break the spell. Then the QUEEN'S voice again ends the silence—though she is speaking half to herself.

THE QUEEN. Common men do the brave thing. Why isn't it the right thing? I'm sorry they fired on the town. Why should they surrender? What happens if they won't? I hope they won't.

By this she has turned to HORVATH with something of her old defiant fire. He puffs protestingly.

HORVATH. But they must! It's most irregular! We must have order. My own men may go next. The whole country's in such a state! But you're not to distress yourself, Ma'am. Gount Czernyak snd I will settle it all in the friendliest way.

He turns, and is most surprised to find the correct CAPTAIN PAPP at his heels.

Where's Doctor Madrassy? Didn't you find him? Don't follow me about. Don't stand there like a tailor's dummy. Tongue-tied fool!

Poor CAPTAIN PAPP, at this cruelly appropriate placarding, turns and flees. HORVATH feels a little better for his outburst.

Your Majesty will excuse me...if I leave you.

As if they were back in the Palace and the old days had come again, he makes the ceremonial triple bow of leave-taking before he goes. No one else moves.

They have their eyes on the QUEEN. She must speak, she feels.

THE QUEEN. Is there nothing left to do?

Then, suddenly, she begins to shake all over. COUNTESS CZERNYAK, who has not been far from her, comes up and touches her arm.

COUNTESS CZERNYAK. My dear...how cold you are! Come in.

THE QUEEN. No...I'm not cold.

With a great effort she steadies herself.

Has much damage been done? Some to you, Captain Dod, I fear. How was that?

DOD. It's nothing, Ma'am. I was helping put out a fire. An enraged old lady threw a chopper at me. The men had a gaudy hour of it. Not so many casualties...no one dead yet, I think.

THE QUEEN. Countess Czernyak will bandage you properly if you'll go in with her. We had everything ready...in case.

This, in all its courtesy, is a command; and without a word COUNTESS CZERNYAK and he go into the carriage. Once more she must speak.

THE QUEEN. Are we prisoners?

CZERNYAK. If Mr. Bruckner will be good enough to pick up that sword.

No one so far has noticed MR. BRUCKNER, common-place and obscure in the background. The QUEEN looks at him now as she might at the incarnation of some dangerous disease that had just declared itself. He shakes his head, with what passes, on his countenance, for a smile, as who should say "It's none of my business." GUASTALLA interposes with....

GUASTALLA. May I present Mr. Bruckner, Ma'am?

MR. BRUCKNER, being presented, and becoming the centre of attention, proceeds deliberately and very forcibly and rather more elaborately to present himself.

BRUCKNER. Haven't we had enough of this foolery? If we've anything to fight about we ought to be fighting. If you still want to win you've a chance left. A long chance! But if it's your last...better than none!

THE QUEEN. What chance?

BRUCKNER. As you have started in...why not keep Horvath chatting a while and dash for the best of our guns? If you get them you might beat us. Not a pretty trick! But if you win you'll be whitewashed. And if you're not...you'll have won.

GUASTALLA. His Majesty has surrendered.

BRUCKNER. What does that matter? Lock him in...before we lock you in. Haven't you been itching to? Why didn't you...weeks ago? You might have been in Karlsburg by this. Now it won't be so easy. You can let him loose and stick a crown on him once you've landed him there.

All this leaves them dumbfounded a moment – well it may! Then, for all comment, comes CZERNYAK'S cold....

CZERNYAK. You had better find somebody, Sir, to pick up that sword.

BRUCKNER. Very well.

He turns on his heel. But suddenly the QUEEN's voice stops him.

THE QUEEN. Mr. Bruckner.

BRUCKNER. Madam.

THE QUEEN. Are you laughing at us? Is this a trap?

BRUCKNER. No.

THE QUEEN. I'm stupid, then. If it s good advice...why do you give it us? Suppose we take it?

GUASTALLA gasps with horror.

GUASTALLA. How could we take it, Ma'am?

She appeals to STEPHEN CZERNYAK, who responds like a man half hypnotised.

THE QUEEN. Count Czernyak?

CZERNYAK. It wouldn't be a very pretty trick.

THE QUEEN. Do you want us to win, Mr. Bruckner?

BRUCKNER. There are things I want less.

GUASTALLA. Shall I fetch his Majesty, Ma'am?

THE QUEEN. No.

CZERNYAK. General Horvath is waiting for me, Ma'am.

THE QUEEN. He can wait.

We could detect then a slight tremor in CZERNYAK'S voice; in hers, none.

BRUCKNER. Here's what I'm after...it's simple enough. That starved pedant Madrassy has tangled me up in his politics too. I want him sent back to his school books. So do you.

CZERNYAK. And further.

BRUCKNER. Very well. I've been for fighting and making you fight. Let's know who's to be master. This wretched country needs to know...for it needs one. I mean to be its master if I can be...and there are men that will back me. Yes...tell my colleagues in the Ladies' Waiting Room that, Colonel Guastalla...if you think it's news to them. If I can't be...I'd as soon have you rattling your sabre. Or you, Madam! You seem to believe in yourself. That's the first thing. People with nothing better to believe in will believe in you.

Her Majesty stiffens against such familiarity.

THE QUEEN. Possibly! What can you do for us...what can you do? Don't interfere, please. Don't speak! I need no advice.

For to GUASTALLA'S – and even CZERNYAK'S – horror, though to MR. BRUCKNER'S grim amusement, she is unfastening from her neck the pearls she always wears; and it is obvious what she means to do with them.

BRUCKNER. Do you want to bribe me?

THE QUEEN. Yes. If this isn't enough...tell me how.

And BRUCKNER finds the necklace in his hands. He smiles very grimly indeed.

BRUCKNER. What's it worth?

THE QUEEN. I'm afraid I don't know. Quite a lot. I could sign something as well.

But he hands it back, with what is very nearly a bow.

BRUCKNER. I respect you, Madam, for the attempt. I am not above bribes. But you haven't my price in your pocket for the moment...and I shouldn't like to cheat you. Besides...once a man has taken his bribe he's no longer worth it, remember! No...I must fight you for a bit...and beat you if I can. Thank me for that, at least.

CZERNYAK has taken his decision.

CZERNYAK. Tell your colleagues in the Waiting Room, Mr. Bruckner, that I'm taking your advice. But if I beat you and have my way...I'll skin you alive.

BRUCKNER. You'll be quite right to.

CZERNYAK. I don't ask your Majesty's approval.

THE QUEEN. You have it.

GUASTALLA. For God's sake don't say that, Ma'am.

THE QUEEN. You have it.

CZERNYAK, with her clarion note to hearten him, has gone. She says swiftly to GUASTALLA.

I'll tell the King.

GUASTALLA. Very well, Ma'am.

BRUCKNER notes this.

BRUCKNER. There's nothing more then, I fancy, that I can do for your Majesty.

THE QUEEN. You'll do what best pays you...I understand that. If you find a little later it might pay you better to be beaten...I'll see that you're paid.

She says it with such contempt that he cannot resist a masked retort.

BRUCKNER. Your Majesty is too kind. A post at Court, perhaps...in uniform.

CAPTAIN DOD, at this moment, comes from the carriage, his arm beautifully bandaged. The QUEEN, having turned her back upon the unspeakable BRUCKNER, greets him graciously.

THE QUEEN. That's right, Captain Dod. Come and have it dressed again, please...to-morrow morning.

And she enters the carriage. BRUCKNER finds that GUASTALLA is staring at him in no friendly way. So he says with a certain briskness....

BRUCKNER. We'd better be getting back to our lines before trouble starts. Or will you make us prisoners? Etiquette apart, I don't recommend it. Horvath in command is worth ten thousand men to the other side, any day.

He departs, jauntily for him. DOD is a little puzzled.

DOD. What's up now?

GUASTALLA. God knows!

DOD. Light me a cigarette...there's a good chap.

For his bandaged arm makes this a hard job.

I wonder if they looted the printer's. We could get in first with this mutiny story. If I give it a twist our way it might even do us a bit of good. Better copy than an armistice, anyhow! That's old Hadik's, isn't it?

His eye has caught the sword still lying where the KING flung it.

GUASTALLA. Yes...I had to borrow one.

DOD. Don't leave it lying about, then. Besides...it looks so silly.

GUASTALLA stiffens with correctitude.

GUASTALLA. I can't touch it.

DOD. Can't you? I can.

And he picks it up without more ado.

ACT IV

A railway carriage is cramped quarters for a three weeks' stay; but, by dint of removing some of the fixed furniture, this twenty-year-old saloon has been turned into a tolerable sitting-room for the KING and QUEEN. A table with inkstand and papers on it, set against one of the line of windows that look out, drearily enough, to the farther side of the station, shows that he conducts his business there. Another little table in the corner may be GUASTALLA's; another, by the odds and ends on it, is the QUEEN's. It is afternoon, and a cold grey autumnal afternoon at that.

The place is empty. But COLONEL HADIK opens one of the narrow doors to usher in SIR CHARLES CRUWYS, saying as he does so....

HADIK. Colonel Guastalla, Sir, is not yet back from the funeral.

SIR CHARLES. The funeral?

HADIK. But I was to tell his Majesty at once of your arrival. The British Minister?

SIR CHARLES. Yes.

COLONEL HADIK passes across to the other narrow door and passes through it to find the KING. We notice that he is carrying a large official-looking letter. He has become, by sheer devotion to his simple duties, the perfect butler.

SIR CHARLES CRUWYS is no more than fifty, one supposes, but he has already acquired the silvery hair and silky benevolence of the distinguished diplomat. He is due for promotion as soon as these Carpathian troubles are settled – though when will that be? He would not, in fact, have been left here these four years but for the need of a good man at such a post. He is, you discover after a little, a very "good man" indeed. Do not be deceived by that air of taking everything more seriously than his business, with which the diplomatist learns to avoid the risk of indiscreet talk about it. (Sometimes, of course, appearances are not deceptive.)

SIR CHARLES, awaiting his Majesty, gives a glance round; then, apparently, he finds the place remarkably cold, for he starts to put on the motoring coat, carried over his arm. While he is doing so COLONEL GUASTALLA arrives, hurriedly, as if he knew he was late. SIR CHARLES, caught with one arm in the coat and one out, asks politely . . .

SIR CHARLES. May I?

GUASTALLA. Please! It is chilly. The heating won't work without the engine...and the oil-stoves I asked for smell. You've not been kept waiting, I hope.

GUASTALLA, oddly enough, is carrying a bunch of flowers; red and yellow chrysanthemums. He puts this down on the table in the corner.

SIR CHARLES. I've been having a brisk half-hour with the Commandant...your head gaoler here. He has been treating you civilly...has he?

GUASTALLA. He thinks so, I m sure.

SIR CHARLES. Not quite the sort of fellow they should let represent them.

GUASTALLA. But suppose he does?

SIR CHARLES appreciates this riposte, and the disdain that inspires it. But his talk to the Commandant has worried him a little.

SIR CHARLES. That opens up unpleasant vistas.

GUASTALLA. We're cut off from news, of course. I gave my parole before they passed me through the wire not to ask for any. We've to thank you, Sir Charles, for my little outing, I think.

SIR CHARLES. I shan't be sorry to be back in Karlsburg before dark. My government escort, even, does not inspire confidence.

The QUEEN'S entry interrupts him. She is paler than she was, visibly strained by this ordeal; graver and quieter too, her old unquestioning confidence abashed. She has a smile for SIR CHARLES, though, as she gives him her hand.

THE QUEEN. Sir Charles Cruwys. We met long ago...at Stuttgart.

SIR CHARLES. Good of your Majesty to remember.

THE QUEEN. The King wishes me to be present. Do you play tennis still?

SIR CHARLES. Oh yes, Ma'am.

THE QUEEN. Can you still jump the net standing?

SIR CHARLES postures comic despair.

SIR CHARLES. No, Ma'am. Ah...no!

GUASTALLA has retrieved his flowers from the table.

GUASTALLA. A woman ran out of a shop and asked me to bring your Majesty these.

THE QUEEN. Oh! Did you thank her for me? I hope you thanked her.

The break in her voice tells us much. We should not have heard it but that she was taken by surprise. The KING comes in. He is as cool and cheerful as ever; rather brusquer perhaps. He shakes hands with SIR CHARLES in a business-like way. In his other hand is that official-looking letter delivered to him by COLONEL HADIK.

THE KING. How-do-you-do, Sir Charles? You've had a cold drive. Please sit down. What can I do for you?

For all this easy civility, there is a certain ring of challenge in the KING'S voice. SIR CHARLES and he face each other, as they sit, duellist-wise. The QUEEN has turned away and seated herself apart; her pale face is outlined against the pallor of the windows; she holds that simple gift of the flowers as if it were a friend's hand. As to the challenge, SIR CHARLES neither accepts nor declines it. He measures his words.

SIR CHARLES. Upon your Majesty's abdicating I am authorised by my government to offer you a suitable asylum.

THE KING. That's very civil of them. And this that you've brought me...is the form I fill up?

He gives an almost jaunty twirl to the official-looking letter.

SIR CHARLES. I believe so, Sir. I did not bring it. It came with me.

THE KING. A nice distinction.

SIR CHARLES'S reply has its edge too.

SIR CHARLES. One clings to the correct thing...as long as may be.

THE KING. I expected it sooner.

SIR CHARLES. This has been a troublesomely uncertain week.

THE KING. So I gather from what reaches me of our cook's conversation with her favourite sentry. Who may I ask...if anyone...is now governing the country?

SIR CHARLES. You may well ask, Sir! Dr. Madrassy is still in office. He'll come to-morrow, I presume, to ask that back from you...if he's still in office.

The QUEEN turns her head.

THE QUEEN. I think, Sir Charles, that, whatever else happens, you'll find Dr. Madrassy in office...till we put him out once and for all.

This last phrase draws a quick glance from the KING; while SIR CHARLES, still courteous, grows stern.

SIR CHARLES. Will your Majesties please face the facts of the situation? You're prisoners here...and helpless. Madrassy and his mongrel government are at such odds that they're as helpless...all but! In the country the bottom's dropping out of things. The mark's going to glory...the towns can't buy food...the peasants are digging up their guns again. And here's winter suddenly...to make all worse!

THE KING. And where is Count Czernyak, if you please?

SIR CHARLES vents a little hiss of exasperation.

SIR CHARLES. I told them it was childish not to tell you! Czernyak and his mutineers are fifteen miles from Karlsburg.

THE KING. Thank you. So the cook and her sentry were right. There's been fighting?

SIR CHARLES. Gunfire...and a casualty or two, I suppose. Enough to give the newspapers headlines.

The soldier in the KING says to GUASTALLA with a certain satisfaction....

THE KING. That's fifteen miles a day, Guastalla.

GUASTALLA. Rather more, Sir.

SIR CHARLES. Horvath had orders to keep out of range. But he can't get back any further.

THE KING. How many mutineers?

SIR CHARLES. A couple of thousand still.

THE KING. And what happens next?

SIR CHARLES. That's the question. They won't surrender.

THE QUEEN. Surrender!

High indignation is in the word. The KING explains.

THE KING. Her Majesty approves of their conduct. I, of course, cannot.

THE QUEEN. Why should they surrender?

SIR CHARLES. They can be surrounded and shot to pieces at any moment,

Ma'am. My wonder is the order's not been given. Before I get back it may be. But Madrassy won't court-martial more than a dozen of them...Czernyak apart, of course...I've his word for that...if they'll surrender.

THE KING.... and I abdicate.

THE QUEEN. Do you really think, Sir Charles, that we're to be tricked like this?

It is an unpleasant moment, which the KING has to redeem by asking good-humouredly....

THE KING. Are you tricking us?

Her Majesty is implacable.

THE QUEEN. Or being tricked himself!

SIR CHARLES. The diplomat finds that still less complimentary, Ma'am.

THE QUEEN. Madrassy daren't fight...he never has dared. And here's his last chance to cheat us...and then tell men that will fight for us that there's nothing left to fight for. Isn't that the trick? Hurry back, Sir Charles...or you may find Count Czernyak in Karlsburg before you...and his Majesty proclaimed.

SIR CHARLES. Good God, Ma'am...you can't think that's possible! Two thousand men...all but starving...and not much more than their bare fists left them to fight with! D'you want them massacred? Do you, Sir?

A moment's silence before the KING answers.

THE KING. They know they can't win. They must know that. But they'd sooner be killed to a man than give in. Foolish of them...and I must abdicate to save their skins. Will they thank me? What if they've the right of it? Is the battle that's worth losing...and the cause...the one battle we must fight...and the cause that can't be lost? Thank Madrassy for holding his hand. It has been hard to, I'm sure. But I almost wish I had my sword again...and that he'd put me among them...so that I could be foolish too.

Another moment of silence before SIR CHARLES returns to practical politics.

SIR CHARLES. By to-morrow, Sir, I'm promised two boats' crews from the Firefly. She was within reach, thank goodness! They'll go on guard here...and if I don't like the look of things I shall pack you across the frontier whether you abdicate or not.

"The impudence!" is probably what springs to his Majesty's lips at this; but he translates it into....

THE KING. You can't do that! No government worth its salt will let you.

SIR CHARLES. I can, Sir...and I shall.

THE KING. I shall formally protest.

SIR CHARLES. That will make no difference.

THE KING. Really, Sir Charles...what business is this of yours?

SIR CHARLES. Sir...Carpathia may shoot her Ministers and Generals or her Bankers and Editors if she finds them a nuisance...by the dozen...and welcome! It's a method of government like any other...and there's a lot to be said for it. But we can't have your throat cut. There may not be much belief left in kings nowadays...but there's still a lot of sentiment about them...pleasant, wholesome sentiment. We don't want that churned up into passion...and other passions churned up to clash with it. We can't afford to have this affair of yours turn tragedy. Europe's nerves aren't braced to it for the moment. You'll be ready to leave, please, to-morrow.

The KING gives a bitter little shrug.

THE KING. Lock the doors. Start the train. What can I do?

SIR CHARLES. We kept our fingers out of the pie as long as we could. I don't say we'd not have welcomed your success. But what less could you expect us to welcome?

THE KING. However I'd come by it? Whatever I'd done with it?

SIR CHARLES. This mess won't clear up yet awhile...and you're well out of it, Sir, believe me.

The KING seems to speak from far away.

THE KING. There are two ways of looking at this world, aren't there? As a chaos that you fish in for your profit...you can always pull something up. Then there's the world of your idea...and some of us would sooner go on to the end, hoping that may come true. Have you ever been possessed by an idea, Sir Charles?

SIR CHARLES can afford now to return to the amenities of conversation, and most readily he does.

SIR CHARLES. In my youth I believed I was a poet.

THE KING. And were you?

SIR CHARLES. My friends thought the evidence insufficient.

THE KING. They may have been wrong.

SIR CHARLES. I still feel sometimes that they were.

THE KING. And the further the reality slips from you...the better you know the idea was true. I came back set not to fight...and with nothing I wanted to win. But I did come to think for a little that there was something for me to do here. I shall never do it. Who wants it done? Yet I've never felt so much a king as I do now. As a poet...you'll understand that. I'll walk to the gate with you...I'm glad of the exercise. If I'd still faith enough in my idea...would the barbed wire be down when we reached it?

But SIR CHARLES cannot let these pretty metaphysics fog the business that's in hand.

SIR CHARLES. What's your answer to Madrassy, Sir?

THE KING. Poor Madrassy! Finessing for my skin all week with Bruckner and his catastrophic friends! And now that your Firefly's over the horizon...here's his reward. *(Once more he twirls that official envelope.)* He's to flourish it signed and sealed in their faces tomorrow. A respectable Republic in being! Stocks and shares mounting again! And their only excuse for letting hell loose spirited away!

Yes...I think you'll have dished the new revolutionaries very nicely, between you.

SIR CHARLES. Your Majesty has it pat.

He says this with genuine admiration; the KING would be a master at the game, that's clear. They have all risen. SIR CHARLES is moving towards the door, when suddenly, with a side glance at the QUEEN.

THE KING. Shall I sign now, Rosamund...or wait till to-morrow?

She does not look at him.

THE QUEEN. Why ask me?

To this, very noticeably, he does not reply.

THE KING. Have we made the best bargain we can? Once I started bargaining I'd be a very Jew. Can't I have my mutineers amnestied...Czernyak and all?

SIR CHARLES. He'd let off the lot if he dared, Sir. But Bruckner's nominee took over Horvath's command this morning.

The KING watches the QUEEN still. She makes no move.

THE KING. It s a close game.

Suddenly she turns, to ask lightly....

THE QUEEN. Sir Charles...will you take a note for me to Karlsburg? And could Dominica come out to see her mother, Henry?

THE KING. *(interpreting.)* Countess Czernyak.

SIR CHARLES. I'm sure she can.

THE QUEEN. I'll fetch it.

She goes out, with unexpected swiftness. They begin the casual talk of men kept waiting.

THE KING. How's Captain Dod, by the way?

SIR CHARLES. In hospital...and I mean to keep him there. They'll save his arm...but it's badly poisoned.

THE KING. I'm sorry...I'm glad! *(His mind does not seem to be on the subject.)* And what happened at the funeral, Guastalla?

GUASTALLA. I walked behind the bier. Your Majesty's wreath was a very pretty one.

THE KING. In the country here, did you know, a child's body's carried by children. There's no coffin...they cover it with flowers.

SIR CHARLES. I didn't know, Sir.

THE KING. This happened the day of the mutiny...our one casualty, I'd hoped! Her father kept the tollgate. She used to sit on his shoulder to take the pennies. When she heard the firing she ran out to see the soldiers....

He stops. He pretends to no sentimental grief. But still...! SIR CHARLES is tactful.

SIR CHARLES. No one holds your Majesty responsible for that sorry affair.

THE KING. That is sound constitutional doctrine, I know. Karlsburg's cursing me pretty roundly, I suppose, though. Martial law?

SIR CHARLES. No...everyone's enjoying the crisis, I think. Spending money! Why not...when it may be worthless to-morrow? The opera's crowded. I dropped in last night...to show I'd nothing on my mind.

THE KING. What were they giving?

SIR CHARLES. Tosca.

THE KING. Terrible stuff. Cats on the tiles! What's this new woman like?

SIR CHARLES. She can do everything but sing. Mozart would put her in her place. No...Madrassy has been very sensible. Even the Stock Exchange panic has gone on long enough now for as many people to be doing well out of it as badly. And the knowing ones must have done very well indeed.

THE KING. Will my backers in Paris go bankrupt?

SIR CHARLES. Not, Sir, if for this last week they've been backing you to lose...as I should suppose they have.

THE KING. I hope they have.

The QUEEN returns with the letter.

THE QUEEN. Here it is. Thank you.

SIR CHARLES. I'll seal it.

THE QUEEN. No need. It's to ask her to bring me some stockings.

SIR CHARLES. To-morrow, Ma'am.

He turns towards the door again, the KING with him.

THE KING. Suppose you do find Czernyak in Karlsburg, Garibaldi worked just such a miracle...and gave a nation faith in itself for fifty years.

SIR CHARLES. Then Madrassy would need no answer, Sir.

THE KING. But Carpathia would be asking for another sort of king. We'd like news of the children....

They all go out together. Left alone, her Majesty and GUASTALLA turn to each other, like conspirators, glad of each other's support but none too pleased that they need it, nor with each other.

THE QUEEN. Why did he make me listen? I couldn't bear it another minute. How much does he know?

GUASTALLA. You've not told me yet how much you've told him, Ma'am.

THE QUEEN. If he guesses why doesn't he say so! He has hardly spoken to me these three days.

GUASTALLA. I've a message from Czernyak. It was in the flowers. I've burnt it.

THE QUEEN. Weren't they sent to me?

She pulls them aside a moment later, as if they had won a little gentleness from her on false pretences.

He's in touch with Bruckner. Did he get the money?

GUASTALLA. I suppose so.

THE QUEEN. I'm beginning not to care.

GUASTALLA. Will you please warn me, Ma'am, when you mean to tell his

Majesty?

THE QUEEN. Why?

GUASTALLA. I'll ask for my dismissal. I won't wait for it.

THE QUEEN. Why should he dismiss you?

GUASTALLA. I'm deceiving him, Ma'am.

The QUEEN looks him up and down.

THE QUEEN. If I can deceive him...surely you can.

GUASTALLA. There's a difference.

Her Majesty grows colder still.

THE QUEEN. You should not be doing what you think it wrong to do, Colonel Guastalla.

GUASTALLA. I am glad to be of service...to your Majesty.

As she looks at him standing there, his eyes averted, most shocking thoughts surge in her mind, recollections of the KING's mild chaff about his adoring her. Surely he cannot imagine that . . .!

THE QUEEN. You will please not think of it in that way.

GUASTALLA. Very well, Ma'am. Was that letter about stockings?

As a fellow-conspirator he has every right to know. But he is frozen with a....

THE QUEEN. You heard me say so. You should not ask such a question.

And, to their mutual relief, the conspirators part. She leaves him standing there.

The carriage is empty. The window-blinds are drawn, and the grey light of morning filters through them. ELLA, the maid, bustles in and begins snapping them up in great haste. COUNTESS CZERNYAK follows her, hastily too.

COUNTESS CZERNYAK. Who is it, Ella?

ELLA. I don't know, my lady.

By the other door in comes COLONEL HADIK.

COUNTESS CZERNYAK. Who is it, Basil?

HADIK. Bruckner.

COUNTESS CZERNYAK. At this hour! They're not out of bed.

By the door way from which COUNTESS CZERNYAK came comes COLONEL GUASTALLA.

HADIK. Mr. Bruckner to see his Majesty.

GUASTALLA. I know. I've told him.

COUNTESS CZERNYAK. He must wait.

GUASTALLA. He's to come in.

At which moment MR. BRUCKNER, who has not waited, even for this, does come in. He stands there, glum and bodeful. After a moment COUNTESS CZERNYAK says....

COUNTESS CZERNYAK. Run along now, Ella. You can tidy later.

ELLA runs along. COUNTESS CZERNYAK follows her.

BRUCKNER. Was that Countess Czernyak?

GUASTALLA. Yes.

BRUCKNER. I thought so.

The KING enters, shaved and spruce, but still in his dressing-gown. He greets his visitor with very cool politeness.

THE KING. Good morning, Mr. Bruckner. Your business is pressing?

BRUCKNER. Can I speak to your Majesty alone?

THE KING. Certainly. Will you have some coffee?

BRUCKNER. No, thank you.

THE KING. Please do. Then I can finish mine with a better grace.

BRUCKNER. Very well.

THE KING. Let Ella bring it in, please, Colonel Hadik. Get your own, Guastalla. It's a headache for me if I start work first.

COLONEL HADIK has left the room. GUASTALLA follows him. But MR. BRUCKNER is not to be disconcerted by these civilities. He is of very set purpose indeed. So the KING, still studying him, changes tactics with a more familiar....

THE KING. Out with it!

MR. BRUCKNER comes out with it; purpose in every word.

BRUCKNER. If you'll do as I tell you I'll have you in Karlsburg within the week.

The KING duly digests every word; then queries with the politest irony...

THE KING. In my coffin?

BRUCKNER. As king. On your white horse...with your crown on...in a week or two!

THE KING. Really! This is a familiar promise. Count Czernyak made it me last. I'll own I didn't think I'd next hear it from you.

BRUCKNER. Czernyak's dead.

Then something has happened at last. The KING shows neither surprise nor grief, but brings all his wits to bear.

THE KING. Killed?

BRUCKNER. Yes.

THE KING. When?

BRUCKNER. About two o'clock this morning. He d been with me till past one. I had him brought back to my quarters. Here's all I found in the pockets.

He takes from his own pocket a carefully wrapped up little packet.

THE KING. Who killed him?

Before BRUCKNER can answer COLONEL HADIK comes in with the tray of coffee, which he puts down upon a convenient table.

HADIK. If your Majesty will forgive me...Ella is not yet properly dressed.

He departs; the perfect butler! BRUCKNER, put out by the interruption, says rather sourly....

BRUCKNER. Does he like carrying trays?

THE KING. I daresay.

He says it with the ghost of a smile; but his eyes are sternly questioning still, and it is to them MR. BRUCKNER half replies with . . .

BRUCKNER. He came in to make terms.

THE KING. Not with my knowledge.

BRUCKNER. Granted.

THE KING. And rashly...it seems!

BRUCKNER. D'you think I had him killed?

THE KING. Did you come to terms?

BRUCKNER. I thought his offer too good to be true.

THE KING. As yours, Mr. Bruckner, seems to me.

BRUCKNER. You've come pretty near beating us, though. D'you know how near?

THE KING. I think I know.

This may have a meaning for him, which escapes MR. BRUCKNER.

BRUCKNER. I've been wondering all this week if the very legend of you locked up here mightn't beat us! Why didn't Madrassy make terms with you? He has missed his chance. Czernyak has missed his...once and for all. I see mine now. That's frank.

THE KING. Admirably!

The KING hands him his coffee; he is surprised to find how glad he is of it.

BRUCKNER. You'll have to trust me a bit. But if I fail I'm done for.

THE KING. That's a fair pledge. But what use can I be to you?

BRUCKNER. The two of us can stop things here stampeding to perdition. If we don't...and pretty quickly...I don't know now what else can.

THE KING. We make...politically...an odd pair, Mr. Bruckner.

BRUCKNER. Does that matter?

To which the KING makes frank and respectful response.

THE KING. No. But I thought things were going so well with you.

BRUCKNER. Yes. I've the troops in hand. I can wipe out these men Czernyak has left stranded. I've purged my own party and I can turn out Madrassy if I want to. Yes...everything's going well with me, thank you! But where am I going? When I'm where I want to be...what next? That's the one question most men won't ask in time, isn't it? What has brought me here? I'll tell you. Count Czernyak wasn't over civil...he meant me no good...I don't blame him. He didn't like talking terms...but he knew I meant fighting...so his game was up...though he'd have had a last fling at me, I suppose, with any men that would have followed him. I sent two young hopefuls of mine to see him through the lines. They picked a quarrel with him and shot him. I was planning to-day's work with the Staff when the news came back. It took me ten minutes to find out I daren't punish them for it. Daren't! I've not pushed my way and other men out of it without knowing what that means! I lay down an hour to think things over...then I started here to you. I won't be hustled to the devil if I can help it.

Can we shake free and make a fresh start and do the sensible thing between us? That's the question. I must be back by midday to carry on.

All this gulping his coffee. Now he puts the cup down, and waits response. What the KING is thinking of it all who can say? Not MR. BRUCKNER, for the moment.

THE KING. Have you a practical plan?

BRUCKNER. I think so. I'll bring you to Karlsburg. There's clamour enough to put you on trial and make a martyr of you. I shall let things go hang for a week till everyone's pretty frightened...for that'd mean stiff reprisals. Then I'll march in the troops for a day's shooting. Then I'll risk it...I'll proclaim you. And you'll proclaim peace and the union of parties and the rest. Your own manifesto! That Englishman dropped twenty on my head one day.

THE KING. And what next?

BRUCKNER. We'll work a plebiscite to take the wind from Madrassy's sails. Then we must govern and stand no nonsense.

THE KING. That will be for you to do.

BRUCKNER. Yes. By what right? Because I can. If I can't...I'll take the consequences.

THE KING. I should find myself sharing those with you, at least. Who is to support us?

BRUCKNER. The men that are sick of this neverending muddle called politics.

THE KING. Quite a large following!

BRUCKNER.... that'll do a hand's turn or so to put an end to it.

THE KING. Ah...not quite so large!

BRUCKNER.... if we make it worth their while. Not with money. Stuff men with money when they're no more use. I want young men...kept on the stretch. Bully them a bit...and let them do a bit of bullying.

THE KING. Your two young murderers may still be useful.

BRUCKNER. I'll bring them to book for you...once things are safe.

THE KING. Would that be quite fair? Yes...it all sounds most practical.

MR. BRUCKNER is not over-susceptible to irony; but he becomes conscious of the fact that he has, at least, not stirred his Majesty to any enthusiasm. His brows twist into a frown and he begins to undo the little packet of the things found in CZERNYAK'S pockets.

BRUCKNER. I'll hand you these, I think.

As he bends over, loosening the string, the KING studies him curiously.

THE KING. Did we ever meet in the old days, Mr. Bruckner?

BRUCKNER. Remember the top of my head, do you? I was boot-black at the Vigado Club when you were Crown Prince and used to come there. I've blacked your boots many a time.

For the first time the KING feels a little drawn towards him.

THE KING. So you were! You were famous as a boot-black. And always reading!

BRUCKNER. It was dull between-times.

THE KING. I used to bring you books. You kept a little stack of them under a duster in the corner. Didn't you go up to some university later? We all subscribed.

BRUCKNER. Yes...and a bit later, when the war came, to prison. And when peace came...into exile.

THE KING. Were we fellow-exiles?

BRUCKNER. I came back when you left.

THE KING. What did you go to prison for?

BRUCKNER. Optimism. Belief in the millennium in the brotherhood of man and the rest of it. I'm quite cured.

He has the contents of the parcel spread out now: a paper or so, two bundles of bank-notes, and a little something twisted up in tissue paper.

Czernyak tried to bribe me with silly promises. But here's his list...and a pretty full one...of my underlings. These *(the bank-notes)*, I daresay, were for paying a couple of them to cut my throat. And these, I think, are her Majesty's.

The tissuepaper, untwisted, shows the QUEEN'S pearls. Were it a mislaid umbrella brought back, his Majesty could not say more casually....

THE KING. I believe so.

BRUCKNER. The letter she wrote sending them...isn't a very discreet letter.

He hands it to the KING, who glances it over.

THE KING. Not very.

BRUCKNER. No one else has read it...as far as I know.

The KING hands it back.

THE KING. Thank you. I doubt if I can pay your price for it.

BRUCKNER. Take it! Take the lot! I'm not driving a bargain. I want no hold on you. I'll take these if you like and write a receipt for them. Then you'll have bought me and paid for me.

He swings the pearls in his hand.

THE KING. That would give you a very tight hold on me.

These finessing scruples are more than MR. BRUCKNER can bear.

BRUCKNER. What is it you want, then? Here s all you've been asking for...if you'll trust me to give it you. You wouldn't think the better of me if I'd come to you talking loyalty and patriotism.

THE KING. The worse!

BRUCKNER. I'm not gentleman enough? It can't be that...in these days.

THE KING. No. You are a man of some talent, Mr. Bruckner...and I, at least, am a king. We can both afford not to be snobs.

BRUCKNER. If you'd brought back your old gang...if you took on Madrassy's nondescripts...how long would that last? There's more to be done now, I tell you, than look wise and say smooth things while the old machine clanks round. There's one way to govern a country...just one. Find where its real power is...and give that play. It's in me for the moment...and the men of my mind. When I've done all I can...when I lose grip...the next good man may scrap me. I give him leave.

THE KING. But what is your need of me?

What can MR. BRUCKNER do but answer such a candid question?

BRUCKNER. I shouldn't count myself clever if it weren't for the fools around...but I do try to see things as they are and not as I'd fancy them. Once I get to work...I shan't be very popular.

THE KING. Oh...why not?

BRUCKNER. With the middle-class mob that never wakes up to anything till the virtue's going out of it? But keep the shops open and the trains running on time...and they'll think all's well with the world! Not with your friends. Not with my horny-handed kith and kin, I promise you! For we've to get this country to work again...and to fight again, maybe. Men are children, mostly, and...give them a chance...wicked children...and as lazy as they're let be. Put tools and guns in their hands...you must! But take care the ideas in their heads aren't dangerous toys to play with.

THE KING. The sight of me with a crown on occasionally would keep them amused, you think.

BRUCKNER. It all counts. You're impressing me now, you know...even in your dressing-gown.

At this his Majesty laughs outright.

THE KING. I'm so glad.

BRUCKNER. But there's more to you than that. You like people...I can't!...and they like you, That counts. They believe in you. And that counts...doesn't it?

The KING weighs this in his mind for a moment. Then....

THE KING. Mr. Bruckner...when you sent your two young friends off with Count Czernyak did you think...or didn't you...they might murder him? Will you answer me that?

MR. BRUCKNER wonders if he shall, then decides that he will.

BRUCKNER. Yes...I did.

THE KING. Thank you.

He is sitting at his table. He rings a little bell on it. Then he takes from a despatch-case that long official envelope we have already seen, and from it the document.

BRUCKNER. Is that what's troubling you? He's as well out of the way. He'd done his best for you. What more was he doing but mischief...flinging his men to their death?

THE KING. And he might have beaten you.

BRUCKNER. Yes...and then where should I have been? I'm sorry. But half measures were no use with him. It was the best thing to do...and the best way to do it.

COLONEL GUASTALLA comes in. The KING is now signing the document.

THE KING. Will you witness this please, Guastalla? It's my abdication.

MR. BRUCKNER – though he was beginning to expect this – is at loss for a juster comment than....

BRUCKNER. That's useful!

But, indeed, what comment could be juster? The KING yields his place to GUASTALLA, who sits and signs. He turns to MR. BRUCKNER again.

THE KING. I shall watch your career with interest, Mr. Bruckner, This body-politic's corrupt enough, perhaps, to need your medicine. When you're cured of your modesty...I think you may be very popular indeed. But you'll do well enough without me for a puppet. And I shall find poultry-farming pleasanter...and far more dignified. How much belief in me was to be left when we'd shaken hands over Czernyak's dead body? Enough for your purpose! I could serve that well enough, no doubt...as the dumb sign of a faith made tame and ridiculous...its loyalties turned to the breeding of snobs. No, I'll betray my cause in my own way.

GUASTALLA is at his side with the document of abdication. He takes it and hands it to MR. BRUCKNER.

Will you give this to Madrassy? He's still your chief, isn't he? But you'll be fighting him in the open soon.

BRUCKNER. I hope so.

THE KING. You may beat him. With the best intentions he betrays his beliefs. But the belief that has been betrayed may then beat you. I'll give it a chance to. Czernyak has been killed, Guastalla.

GUASTALLA. Yes, Sir.

BRUCKNER. I trust the news won't upset her Majesty very much.

The KING is surprised – though really he should not be – at this little touch of common humanity.

THE KING. Thank you.

MR. BRUCKNER weighs the abdication in his hand.

BRUCKNER. You've missed your chance.

THE KING. Do you think so? I could hardly tell you, Mr. Bruckner, how fantastically unreal all you've been saying has seemed to me. If ill-luck ever sends you abroad again...look me up. I'd much like to know if it doesn't come to seem so to you. Good-bye.

BRUCKNER. I wish your Majesty a pleasant journey.

As MR. BRUCKNER nears the door which GUASTALLA is holding open for him, the KING, turning to the table where the debris from CZERNYAK'S pockets is still lying, asks....

THE KING. You're sure you've no use for these...spoils of war?

BRUCKNER. None.

And so, with some dignity, he departs, GUASTALLA following him. The KING goes to the other door and calls...

THE KING. Rosamund!

When the QUEEN comes in he is standing again by the table.

These are yours, I think. I should burn the letter. Stephen Czernyak has been killed.

THE QUEEN. Fighting?

THE KING. No. Did you send him the money as well?

THE QUEEN. All I had.

THE KING. He went in with it to bargain and they shot him in cold blood. You're not to blame for that.

THE QUEEN. I'll take the blame. I'm very sorry.

THE KING. Shall I tell his mother...or will you?

THE QUEEN. I must.

The QUEEN has the necklace in her hand and the letter. The KING, half-automatically, has opened one of the packets of notes.

THE KING. But what was he to do with these?

THE QUEEN. Bribe people. He gives an exasperated sigh.

THE BING. How many more times am I to tell you that this old note with my head on it is worthless?

THE QUEEN. Not if we'd won! And if the people he bribed cheated us and we didn't...I wanted them to be cheated too. Don't always think me a fool, Henry.

At this moment – fortunately perhaps – GUASTALLA reappears; and the QUEEN before she turns to go (she is glad to go) says....

Colonel Guastalla has been in no way to blame.

And she leaves them. The KING is a little brusque with GUASTALLA, who is evidently preparing, metaphorically, to surrender his sword.

THE KING. Now, Guastalla...don't apologise. I knew you were up to something. You can't keep a secret to save your life. And don't try and resign. That does no good. We must clear up these papers. They may pack us off at any moment now.

So they set to work. It is dusk, and the arc lamps of the station, already lighted, flare through the windows. Near one of them stands the QUEEN, tense and still. She is gazing out; but she has just turned away from DOMINICA CZERNYAK, who, by the door, and in some distress, drops a departing curtsey.

DOMINICA. Then may I please take my leave of your Majesty?

The QUEEN turns back, remorse quenching anger.

THE QUEEN. No...don't go like that, child. I didn't mean to hurt you. But if your mind's made up...why ask me to approve...when you must know I don't? Don't stand there tongue-tied as if you were afraid of me. I've had you about me since you were a baby. There's nothing to make me very terrifying now!

DOMINICA. I've never been afraid of your Majesty. But of course I don't talk to you as I would to any one else.

She does not mean her candour to cut so deep. But it does; though a while ago her Majesty might have thought this was just as it should be.

THE QUEEN. I see. Well...your mother thinks it her duty to go with us...and you don't think it your duty to be with her.

DOMINICA. She doesn't think it, Ma'am.

THE QUEEN. She thinks you'd better stay, perhaps, and keep a few friends here. Then here's a retreat for her. And if I approve...then our friends can't blame you. Yes...a very good plan! Why do you humiliate me by making me say bitter things to you?

Under the sudden storm of anger and pride and pain with which this ends, poor DOMINICA, who is, after all, very young, bursts into tears.

DOMINICA. I didn't mean to...I didn't! I'm so Sorry for your Majesty...but I thought it would make you angry if I said so. And Mamma's going with you because she loves you...more than anyone in the world except Stephen and me. And Stephen's dead!

The QUEEN, remorseful again, even, perhaps, shamed a little, sinks into a chair.

THE QUEEN. Come and sit by me a minute. Forgive me. Stephen's death has been a great shock...to the King...and to me. I've been trying all day to break it to your mother. I never thought I could be such a coward. I'll tell her now...before you go. Or will you tell her?

DOMINICA. But she knows, Ma'am. She has known since this morning.

THE QUEEN. Are you sure?

DOMINICA. She said when she kissed me: You've heard Stephen's dead. I said: Yes. There wasn't time for more. She had to announce me to you.

THE QUEEN. She has been with me all day. I ought to have known she knew!

DOMINICA. I think she'd rather not talk about it...if you don't mind, Ma'am.

THE QUEEN. He died for his country...and for us...just as truly as if he'd died fighting. You can always remember that. See that Masses are said for him. Your mother's so busy packing she mayn't think of it. I'll send you the money.

Then with simple affection for the girl she adds....

But come with us...won't you? There's still time.

DOMINICA shakes her head.

DOMINICA. No, Ma'am...I can't.

THE QUEEN. You re behaving very foolishly. You don't know what may happen here. We're leaving the country to its fate...and it deserves no better...to Socialism...and Communism...or even worse. You may find yourself a waitress in a tea-shop...or anything. What good can you do by staying?

DOMINICA. The worse things were, I think, the more I should have to stay.

THE QUEEN. Dominica...you're not in love with anyone undesirable, are you?

DOMINICA. No, Ma'am, not with anyone at all. But....

THE QUEEN. Well? Tell me the truth.

DOMINICA tells it.

DOMINICA. It's my country, you see.

The QUEEN has no more to say. COLONEL HADIK appears. He carries some bundles of newspapers.

THE QUEEN. What are those, Colonel?

HADIK. The newspapers his Majesty asked for. Sir Charles Cruwys has just come. He brought them in his car. He will wait upon your Majesty whenever it is convenient. The engine is now being attached. But there may be a little delay...for something, it seems, is broken. And his Majesty asks you to allow Jakab to take leave of you also.

THE QUEEN. Who? I remember. Yes.

HADIK. The farmer. And could your Majesty perhaps find a good-bye present for him?

THE QUEEN. I'll try.

COLONEL HADIK goes out again. He is a little excited and upset by the bustle of departure, a little shaky.

THE QUEEN. What's to become of him?

DOMINICA. He'll go back, Ma'am, to his garden and his gun...and do his sums. He was quite happy.

The QUEEN sighs rather enviously.

THE QUEEN. Once you're old, nothing matters much. You've *(she pats the girl's hand)* all sorts of things to hope for. I'm not afraid for you, my dear. You're good. Yes...be gallant...be gay! And never let anyone pity you. Pray for us sometimes, won't you? We shall be so far away. Give me a kiss. Go to your mother now. Stay with her till we start.

She looks up to see JAKAB standing in the doorway. He is an old farmer; of the earth earthy, and it is hard caked earth at that. He is in his working clothes, for it is a week-day; but they have been brushed to rights very strenuously by somebody. DOMINICA has obediently risen, dropped her curtsey and gone. What the QUEEN is to do with the mute old man, who stands rigidly staring at her from the doorway, she cannot think. She is nearing the end of her resources of tact. At last she says helplessly....

THE QUEEN. Good-bye.

Then the image finds a slow tongue.

JAKAB. This is your Majesty?

THE QUEEN. Yes.

JAKAB. Happy to have a look at your Majesty...as my wife...and his Majesty...said I ought...it being the last chance there'll be. And his Majesty's been a lot about the farm...very friendly.

This gives the QUEEN her cue.

THE QUEEN. Thank you for the butter and the eggs...such good eggs...and the milk you've sent us.

JAKAB. *(encouragingly.)* They've been paid for...I'll say that.

The KING comes in. He is brisk and lively. The one great change in him is that he no longer wears his uniform. He had instead to send into Zimony for a reach-me-down, and, frankly, the cut and the pattern of Zimony clothes leave a little to be desired. But he carries them with ease and dignity. He could be dignified and easy in a bathing-dress, it seems.

THE KING. Just seen Sir Charles! Bermuda's where they're sending us. And our Naval escort's parading on the platform. He wants me to inspect it. Very civil of him!

THE QUEEN. Henry! You can't!

THE KING. Why not?

THE QUEEN. Dressed like that!

The horrors of war pale before the scene she imagines.

THE KING. Oh, nonsense! Good-bye, Jakab. Six months here with you...and I'd know something of farming. He tells me I've an eye for a calf. Poultry I'm not to be flattered about...but who'd have thought I'd an eye for a calf.

The KING'S good spirits and the familiar topic bring the old farmer to life a little, and he winks portentously at the QUEEN.

JAKAB. I said it to please him. But you've not a bad eye for a calf.

THE KING. And he's going to keep Snowjacket.

COUNTESS CZERNYAK has come in and is waiting in silence. The QUEEN turns to her with an affection that she tries to keep from seeming remorseful.

THE QUEEN. Yes...dear Ja-ja?

COUNTESS CZERNYAK. We're starting at once, Ma'am. Your hat-box hasn't come from the town. Shall I ask if we may send for it?

THE QUEEN. No...we'll manage.

COUNTESS CZERNYAK. Very well, Ma'am.

Her face calm and unchanging, she goes. The QUEEN says swiftly to the KING...

THE QUEEN. Henry, she knows.

He is amazed; rather shocked.

THE KING. Who told her?

THE QUEEN. I can't think. Say nothing to her to-night.

THE KING. Very well.

JAKAB has been waiting to pursue the only subject that interests him; but he never cares how long he waits.

JAKAB. Not that he'll earn his keep!

The KING is jovial but firm.

THE KING. Now...not one penny do you bluff out of me for that tale!

JAKAB. He's no use for ploughing. He'll go in the small muck-waggon. But how often do I have it out?

THE KING. You'll ride him to market every Friday.

JAKAB. I won't. My son's got a motor car.

THE QUEEN. Snowjacket should be shot, Henry.

But this JAKAB takes very badly.

JAKAB. Oh...I'll shoot him...and thank you! He'd fetch a bit as horseflesh.

COLONEL GUASTALLA comes swiftly in with...

GUASTALLA. The escort's paraded, Sir.

THE KING. Jakab, don't be surly. Very well...I'll come.

JAKAB. Surly!

The QUEEN makes a last, almost tearful appeal.

THE QUEEN. Henry...won't you...please...?

THE KING. What, my dear?

THE QUEEN. Put on your uniform?

JAKAB. Me surly!

THE KING. Certainly not. I've abdicated. It would be most improper.

JAKAB. And well I might be surly with all these carryings-on! My barns made barracks of! Sentries and pickets...!

THE KING. You've coined money out of us.

JAKAB. But you're going now.

THE KING. You farmers talk as if you were the only people on earth that mattered.

JAKAB. So we are. Governments! I've seen 'em come and I've seen 'em go. Red...white...all colours! There's nothing I ask of 'em but to let me alone. Politics! My son's for politics...and my wife'd be if she got about. He sneaks into Zimony to see your Majesties. Your Majesty gives him a pretty smile...well, he thought so!...so he's for politics. God help the land when I'm gone! Will politics grow corn...or raise beef? Jacks-in-office come round badgering me! Will I plant this...will I sow that? Why won't I pay no taxes. I'll feed you or starve you...take your choice...according as you worrit me or let me alone. But no politics! My work's cut out watching the weather. That's chancy enough for me.

He now finds that the KING has missed the greater part of htis discourse, having gone to inspect the parade. He wags a head at the door.

Is he coming back?

GUASTALLA. Not till we start, probably.

JAKAB. Oh!

Even GUASTALLA'S tact seems exhausted; the QUEEN'S endurance is ebbing, and there JAKAB still stands. At last she says, helplessly...

THE QUEEN. Guastalla...I've nothing to give him.

JAKAB. Yes...I did understand there was something might be given me.

THE QUEEN. I'm sorry.

JAKAB. I'd thought of an order.

Her Majesty's mind weakens.

THE QUEEN. But what more can we order?

JAKAB. To wear. Lots used to have 'em. And his Majesty being so friendly...my wife says: You ask for an order.

She can bear no more.

THE QUEEN. Please go away.

JAKAB turns on her grimly, yet with no intended unkindness.

JAKAB. It's not me that's going away.

GUASTALLA comes to the rescue.

GUASTALLA. His Majesty has abdicated, Mr. Jakab...and cannot confer decorations. They would not be valid.

JAKAB. When did he?

GUASTALLA. This morning.

JAKAB. Oh! I ought to have asked sooner . . .when my wife told me. Well... I wish your Majesty a good journey.

He makes a rough bow and is going. But the QUEEN rallies. Life shall not outmock her. She goes to her little table, finds there a small morocco case, opens it and presents it to him, saying... .

THE QUEEN. Mr. Jakab! Yesterday you would have been a knight of St. Andrew.

JAKAB is delighted.

JAKAB. Now that's most lady-like of your Majesty...and I'm much obliged...and so'll my wife be. Of course if it's not valid it don't do you any good. But you mean it kindly. Much obliged to your Majesty, I'm sure.

GUASTALLA manœuvres him out; for the QUEEN is near a breakdown, might break down now did not COUNTESS CZERNYAK return. A little courage is due to her.

THE QUEEN. Yes...dear Ja-ja?

Before an answer can be given JAKAB and GUASTALLA are back again. This is unendurable.

GUASTALLA. Forgive me, Ma'am...the inspection...I forgot! May we go the other way?

JAKAB. Cold weather for the time of year! And your Majesty feels it...boxed up like this. To be sure you must!

They are gone again – thank God! – by the other door.

COUNTESS CZERNYAK. The hat-box has come, Ma'am. I've not money enough to pay for it, I'm afraid.

THE QUEEN. I've none. Ask Guastalla.

COUNTESS CZERNYAK hurries after him. And now the QUEEN does utterly and irretrievably break donvn, collapses, shaken with weeping, into the nearest chair, where, unluckily, SIR CHARLES CRUWYS finds her.

She looks up to discover him standing there.

SIR CHARLES. I most humbly beg your pardon, Ma'am.

THE QUEEN. It's the first time...it is indeed! I've stood up to the worst. But little things happen you're not ready for...silly things. Did they laugh?

SIR CHARLES is puzzled.

SIR CHARLES. Who, Ma'am?

THE QUEEN. The escort. He shouldn't have inspected them in that suit, should he? It doesn't fit him...it was ready-made. They didn't laugh?

SIR CHARLES. No, indeed!

THE QUEEN. Sailors are so kind.

SIR CHARLES. He's talking to my French and Italian colleagues. I've left them to have their say...there's been a little feeling! I ought to have given them more of a show. I brought you these, Ma'mn.

He hands her a few letters.

THE QUEEN. From the children? Oh...thank you!

SIR CHARLES. They're to join you at Toulon...with both governesses and the head nurse. It's the shortest train journey.

THE QUEEN. Where is Bermuda?

SIR CHARLES. It's an island...a small island...near America. An excellent climate. No mosquitoes.

THE QUEEN. I've never been across the sea...not even to England. We don't travel like other people, you know...and I was married so young. It's a very small island, I expect. Do sit down, Sir Charles...please. One of my bad dreams when I was a child was that I was left on a piece of land no bigger than a dinner plate...for the lesson-books never said it need be any bigger...surrounded entirely by sea. And I'd wake up screaming.

She has dried her tears; but, they being dry, pain and anger flush through her again.

Oh this wicked country! Thank God it's not mine...not really mine! Better have none! But why do they let us go...why haven't they killed us? I want to stop hating them...it poisons you to have to sit still and hate people.

And again pain and anger have exhausted her.

We've been putting petrol on the ponds here because of the mosquitoes. They don't all give you malaria...you tell them by their legs. I can't die fighting...but they could have found some way to kill me. Tell me more about Bermuda.

SIR CHARLES is about to, when the KING enters, alert and cheerful.

THE KING. Honoured, my dear Sir Charles, by such an escort. A very smart body of men! A little pale, some of them. These modern ships do coop them up. What's that young officer's name again?

SIR CHARLES. Anstruther.

THE KING. Say it once more.

SIR CHARLES. Anstruther.

THE KING. Thank you...I shall remember it now. He knows Bermuda, Rosamund. Charming place! Houses built of coral. Not much rain. American tourists. British Atlantic Fleet. No mosquitoes to speak of.

SIR CHARLES. I must bid your Majesties good-bye.

The KING shakes hands warmly.

THE KING. You ve been most kind!

THE QUEEN. Most kind!

THE KING. Next year...if we've behaved ourselves...you might let us run over to America for a week or so.

SIR CHARLES. It's possible, Sir.

THE KING. Incognito.

SIR CHARLES. That would not be so easy.

THE KING. I've to think of the future. We've seven children to marry. And I expect I'm a pauper.

THE QUEEN. Henry...don't joke about such things.

THE KING. I'm serious. Europe must face democracy...and America's problem is to leaven the social lump.

SIR CHARLES. Our policy, Sir, has long been to bring in the New World to redress the bank-balances of the Old. The War brought the process to some confusion.

THE KING. And we may yet see the South American states weary of revolution and dictatorship and demand constitutional kings. Good-bye.

SIR CHARLES. But there's to be no confiscating your private funds.

THE KING. The farm at Zurich will take some winding up. I put a pile of money into it. What about Bermuda for poultry now?

Can the QUEEN bear it one moment more?

THE QUEEN. Why don't we start? Why don't we go?

SIR CHARLES. They're waiting, I fear, for me to get out. Something comes from Bermuda. Potatoes! I'll ask about poultry. We shall be in touch with you till you leave Toulon. Your Majesty.

He bows to the QUEEN, who gives him her hand to kiss.

THE KING. Good-bye, again.

He gives SIR CHARLES'S hand another cordial shake.

SIR CHARLES. Good-bye, Sir.

He departs. The KING and QUEEN are alone. All's over. Nothing more to do. After a blank incomprehensible moment they sit down and turn to the letters and newspapers that have been brought for them.

THE KING. Pleasant fellow!

THE QUEEN. Yes. What does he care?

THE KING. We're off!

For the train has given a jerk, which nearly upsets them.

THE QUEEN. No.

For it jerks no more.

THE KING. Something went wrong with the connecting rod. Funny if they couldn't start the train!

THE QUEEN. At least they might give us a good engine. The state this country's in!

THE KING. If it were the best engine in the world I couldn't drive it.

THE QUEEN. Henry...don't be sententious. Hildegarde sends you her love...she has pulled out three teeth...and you owe her fifteen francs.

THE KING. She shall have it.

How quickly letters and newspapers can make life commonplace again! But yet another spasm of wrath shakes the QUEEN.

THE QUEEN. Carted away like cattle!

THE KING. You should have come the round with me just now. Everyone friendly and cheerful!

THE QUEEN. Thankful to be rid of us!

THE KING. I suppose they are.

THE QUEEN. And you're glad to go.

THE KING. I suppose I am. Bermuda may be interesting. There'll be lots of things to do....

The door bursts open and in comes COLONEL HADIK, in great distress.

THE KING. Why don't we start?

HADIK. You're starting, Sir. I must bid your Majesties good-bye.

THE KING. You're coming to the frontier.

HADIK. That's countermanded. God keep your Majesties!

KING and QUEEN are on their feet in a minute.

THE KING. My dear Colonel! I'd so much more to say to you. You've been goodness itself...ever since you wanted to shoot me! God bless you.

The QUEEN catches both his hands.

THE QUEEN. Dear Colonel Hadik...dear, dear Colonel Hadik! You knew we'd fail...you never minded. Oh, such a strength to me!

THE KING. And we won't forget our chess.

HADIK. Out of my grave, Ma'am...to be your servant! Back to it! But your Majesty's most humble servant...to the end...to the end!

And even in the haste of his departure, the old man manages, totteringly, to make that triple bow Court etiquette prescribes. But the effect of it on the QUEEN, when he has vanished...!

THE QUEEN. No...he did that to mock me! He did! God forgive me...I'm wicked. But I think my heart's broken.

The KING puts a comforting arm round her.

THE KING. My dear...my dear! You're always so plucky. We've our lives to live.

She pulls herself together. They are alone; and now surely all is over, for the train gives a more purposeful jerk. And the KING says....

There! We're off now!

THE QUEEN. Read your papers.

He settles himself comfortably and opens the first one to hand.

THE KING. It has been a tiring day.

THE QUEEN. You never thought we'd win. I think I've believed we should...till this very minute.

THE KING. But, my dear...I came back to stop civil war. I've stopped it...and there won't be another. All the men are to be sent home. No reprisals...no court-martialling! I've done what I came to do. I have won.

THE QUEEN. Don't be paradoxical, Henry.

The KING puts his hand out to one of the radiators, and says with some satisfaction....

THE KING. The heat's coming on.

THE QUEEN. The whole world's laughing at us!

THE KING. It'll all be forgotten in a month or so.

THE QUEEN. That's comforting!

He has found something of import in his newspaper.

THE KING. Do you remember my seeing some journalist the day we left?

THE QUEEN. But I'd do it again. I'm not sorry for anything but the failure...not for Czernyak being killed...nor anything. Misfortune doesn't soften us. I did tell myself: If we're beaten I'll at least be a better woman. But I'm not that either. I haven't changed a bit.

He is deeper still in the newspaper.

THE KING. Did I tell him I wasn't going back to Carpathia? Well...I wasn't. So perhaps I did.

THE QUEEN. I could have done my duty here. You're either a queen or you're not. I'm no use as anything else.

THE KING. I must write and apologise.

THE QUEEN. If we're to live like common people I shall nag at you, Henry...I know it...and be horrid to the children! Apologise? What for?

For her ear has belatedly caught the objectionable word.

THE KING. I misled him.

THE QUEEN. Apologise to a journalist!

He reads, with a half-enjoyable dismay....

THE KING. But spite of the smooth démenti his Majesty's eye flashed, I thought, towards the map of Carpathia behind the rococo writing-table and he fingered the hilt of his sword.

THE QUEEN. How vulgar!

THE KING. It isn't rococo...and I wasn't wearing one.

THE QUEEN. The table's rococo.

THE KING. Louis Seize furniture is not rococo. Clever of him to guess at the map though! I never had it down before strangers.

Suddenly they are shaken in their chairs: almost out of them.

THE QUEEN. Are we stopping?

THE KING. No...this is where the line was cut. Bumpy, isn't it?

He reads on.

At which moment her Majesty swept into the room. A stately blonde, a woman in whom mothercraft goes hand in hand with high political intelligence....

THE QUEEN. Show me!

She takes the paper and is soon deep in it herself. The train moves on through the night towards the frontier.

THE END

The Secret Life

1919-22

ACT I

SCENE I

A house that faces the sea; the salted turf runs up to its white, rough-cast walls. This one is cut through in the middle by steps that lead up by five feet or so to a loggia which opens on one side to the sitting room, on the other to the dining room. On the grass, at each side of the steps, a seat stands against the wall. But as it is a warm summer night, and as the rooms are small, the loggia, which is itself as large as a room, is being used as one. A piano has even been run out of a window; and around it are gathered four or five people. They cannot be seen unless they stand up, the parapet that bounds the loggia prevents this. But their voices can be plainly heard, and one of the party—a man—is coming to the end of a curious, half-sung, half-spoken performance of 'Tristan and Isolde'. He accompanies himself on the piano. He proceeds in English when it happens to fit the music, when it doesn't he relapses incongruously into the German. On the white steps sits a solitary figure in white; Joan Westbury.

STEPHEN SEROCOLD'S VOICE.....weherndern all! And sinking...be drinking...unbewusst...hochte Lust! Uplifted, transfigured, Isolde sinks into Brangaene's arms. Hush! Her spirit is passing. The faithful Brangaene relaxes her hold of the lifeless body....

THE VOICE OF SIR GEOFFREY SALOMONS. Always an awkward moment!

SEROCOLD. Shut up! Awestruck in death's presence the rough soldiers stand motionless.

EVAN STROWDE'S VOICE. Their hard eyes fill with tears.

SEROCOLD (*protesting violently through the harmonies*). No!

STROWDE. You used to fill them with tears.

SEROCOLD. Never! King Mark, stern and noble, calm without though inwardly shaken...

STROWDE. Wagner always must be flattering that sort of man.

SALOMONS. Every one does.

SEROCOLD (drowning them with voice and piano both)....raises his hand as if in benediction of the tragic lovers. The twilight deepens. The curtain falls. He closes with some elaboration. There is, however, no applause; an ironic silence rather. After a moment, Miss Eleanor Strowde's voice is heard, saying...

ELEANOR. Thank you.

SEROCOLD. Well...not so bad, considering! May I have a drink?

ELEANOR. They'll be in the dining-room, Evan.

STROWDE unhurriedly walks across to the dining-room and turns on the light there.

SEROCOLD. Sir Geoffrey Salomons, K.C.B., your performance of King Mark...for all that I thumped the notes for you...was rotten.

SALOMONS. Time has, I fear, added a patine to my voice.

SEROCOLD. Patina, Sir, et praeterea nihil. And in future I shall address your envelopes K.C.B. flat.

STROWDE *(calling back)*. What about my Kurwenal?

SEROCOLD. What, indeed!

SALOMONS. You have been shamelessly practising, Serocold.

SEROCOLD. Certainly...I gave half a morning to it. Well...Tristan, Isolde, chorus, and orchestra...I ask you! Odd...Eleanor's note telling me you'd be dining...and that very day I'd happened on my old score.

SALOMONS. Which I notice has my name on it.

SEROCOLD. Horrid habit it was of yours...writing your name in other people's books. *(He forces a sigh, the mocking sigh of reminiscent middle-age.)* Well, I shall never make that noise again!

STROWDE. Whisky, Stephen?

SEROCOLD. Not much.

SALOMONS. I've been trying to recall our last bout.

SEROCOLD. I came back to Balliol in the spring after Evan got his fellowship.

SALOMONS. I was down by then.

SEROCOLD. You were there.

STROWDE. Soda?

SEROCOLD. Tap.

STROWDE. Same for you, Geoffrey?

SALOMONS. Soda. No whisky.

ELEANOR. The water looks worse than it tastes. But we have to bring every drinkable drop from the village.

SEROCOLD. I suppose one can't sink a well so near the sea.

SALOMONS *(with the slightest touch of orientalism)*. But it's a charming place, Miss Strowde.

ELEANOR. For a summer six weeks. Evan likes the bathing. We're getting too old for our long walks.

SALOMONS. And with such weather.

SEROCOLD. It will start to rain next Friday...as I change trains at Fayet St. Gervais.

SALOMONS. It will start to pour on Wednesday morning as I leave Perth.

SEROCOLD. You deserve no better...keeping us sitting through August over your wretched Tied Industries Bill.

SALOMONS. You should have put your trust in the Permanent Official, and passed the thing in May.

STROWDE returning with the drinks, notices the still figure on the steps. He is a man of fifty. Lady Westbury is rather younger. A woman that, in her youth, must have been very flowerlike; the fragility, and a sense of fragrance about her, remains.

STROWDE. Is that you, Joan?

JOAN. Yes .

STROWDE. Couldn't you endure it?

JOAN. I could hear perfectly. Look at the moon.

STROWDE. It might be a ship on fire.

JOAN. Burnt out.

ELEANOR'S VOICE. My dear...I thought you'd stolen to bed. Don't sit there without something round your shoulders. You're not in Egypt now.

JOAN. The desert's far colder.

ELEANOR. I shall get you a shawl.

JOAN. No Eleanor.

ELEANOR. And an ugly one...as a punishment.

STEPHEN SEROCOLD now leans over the loggia; a middle-aged man, who has kept his youth.

SEROCOLD. I fear we made a horrid noise.

JOAN. I always come home hungry for music.

SALOMONS. A horrid sight, Serocold!

SEROCOLD. What is?

SIR GEOFFREY SALOMONS joins him. You would know Sir Geoffrey was a Jew; but mainly because he seems a little conscious of the racial difference himself. Irony is his main conversational key.

SALOMONS. Romantic youth...dragged from its grave and gibbeted. The three of us used to meet in rooms at Oxford, Lady Westbury...I had the piano, that's why they put up with me...to find food for our undergraduate souls. We didn't want to listen to music...we wanted to make it. And Tristan was the great dish...served as it has just been served to you. And I've known us sit silent for an hour after...gorged with emotion.

STROWDE, having given Serocold his whisky, asks Joan...

STROWDE. Whisky, lemonade, or Eleanor's butter-milk?

JOAN. Nothing, thank you.

SALOMONS. Think...if you had but stuck to art and your ideals, my good Serocold, you might now be worth three pounds a week as pianist in a cinema.

SEROCOLD. And a steadier, better-paid job on the balance, it'd be, than my present one.

SALOMONS. You surprise me. I thought you were a venal politician. I have always envied you.

SEROCOLD. No one will bribe me, Salomons...no one, at least, has ever tried. Whether that is a compliment to my character, or an estimate of my unimportance...! No, my beauty has faded in my country's service...late hours in the House are ruinous to the complexion...and I've nothing to live on but the money that ought to be spent keeping up the family estate.

ELEANOR STROWDE comes back with the shawl for Joan. She is grey-haired; a few years older than her brother.

ELEANOR. Put this on.

She wraps it round her with a certain austere tenderness.

JOAN. It's not ugly.

ELEANOR. Not on you.

JOAN *(with finesse).* Thank you...and thank you, kind Eleanor.

Sir GEOFFREY SALOMONS grows playfully portentous.

SALOMONS. I take leave, Miss Strowde, to look upon this as a significant occasion. We sit here and celebrate with due mockery our emancipation from the toils of the wanton art that seduced our youth. Consider us. Serocold is the most popular man in London.

SEROCOLD *(with a flourish).* Shall I deny it? No.

SALOMONS. Why, they tell me that if you didn't light up the lobby with your smile, your poor party couldn't sometimes muster ten votes. I govern England.

JOAN *(repaying him a little irony, in her turn).* All of it, Sir Geoffrey?

SALOMONS. To be accurate, there are about a dozen such sitting in offices, signing papers. We're all the real government England has. She won't stand more. And she'd get rid of us...if she knew who we were.

JOAN. And what about you, Evan?

STROWDE. I have left the market-place.

SALOMONS. Truly..and the dust your feet shook has been laid with our tears.

SEROCOLD. Vexing fellow. Well...you're fifty.

STROWDE. I know it. Look at the moon rising. Time on the move! Can you bear the sight of it?

SEROCOLD. Just...if I keep busy.

JOAN. And she's dead, poor thing.

STROWDE. A shining nonentity...still going on her ordered way.

SEROCOLD. The moral's as plain as the moon is, thank you.

STROWDE. I'm not mocking, Stephen. I envy you your restlessness. My youthful ambition was to do some one thing just as perfectly...before I died.

SALOMONS. Did you assume a Lunar life to do it in?

STROWDE. Now, it is not for one of your race, Geoffrey, to gibe at our religious fallacies.

SEROCOLD *(with calculated despair).* Evan, that was a fatal reply. Salomons will now come the Old Testament over us. At Oxford he couldn't open his mouth without boasting he was a Jew. All the evening his ageless almond eye has been silently reminding me that beneath my clothes I am still stained with woad. Salomons, you may lend me money if you like . But if you patronise me...I'll have your teeth drawn...I will publish a pamphlet proving you to be in a world-conspiracy with Mr. Judas Abramovitch of Moscow...I will cut your throat on the Stock Exchange.

STROWDE. Have you really a sense, Geoffrey, that we ultra-Europeans are so different?

SALOMONS. Yes...very deep down I feel a stranger among you. But my mentality is now a little like the money you let me learn to master...it's a currency. By nature you're all for absolute values, for rooted virtues...flourish or perish! You're capable of suicide and murder...how seldom a Jew commits either!...and of all extremes. I'm for what's marketable.

STROWDE. And no Christian paradoxes!

SALOMONS. But don't you want to see heroism and patriotism and altruism...all the kingdom of heaven that's within you...turned to some practical account? The marketing of ideals is the trade that matters...and there is a world-conspiracy of the people who know it. Join us, Miss Strowde.

ELEANOR. I! Why?

SALOMONS. Then...for one thing...you wouldn't be so down as you were at dinner on poor Serocold's political morality.

SEROCOLD. My political immorality.

SALOMONS. She will no longer...forgive me!...stand helplessly confused between the two.

SEROCOLD. Oh, Evan and Eleanor are like the man with the million pound bank note who starved.

SALOMONS. My dear Serocold, that's not how to deal with idealists. Then they protest that they'll die with dignity. Persuade them it's we who are poor without them.

ELEANOR. We must all cash in our principles, must we?

SALOMONS. Not for mere cash. Don't misunderstand me. My race and its pupils have mastered a larger technique. I'm not a money-lender nowadays...I'm a Civil Servant...a damned bureaucrat. If I weren't I'd be a philanthropist. I work with a finer currency than gold.

STROWDE. Stephen wants to buy me back. But I protest there's nothing left of me to sell.

SEROCOLD. Nonsense!

STROWDE. Not one principle.

SEROCOLD. Buy you!

STROWDE. You and I got into Parliament, Stephen, in nineteen hundred and...peace time. War time got me out of it. Why?

SEROCOLD. Why indeed! I could have patched up the row with Bellingham in ten minutes if I'd been on he spot.

STROWDE. My beliefs proved unworkable. I have no new ones. Geoffrey thinks he knows a lot...that suffices him. You strike attitudes. When I hear you talk politics nowadays, Stephen, it's like hearing you sing Tristan.

SEROCOLD. As bad as that.

STROWDE. As incredible. Scratch off our clothes, O survivor of wrecked civilisations, and instead of the savage it's likelier you'll find nothing at all.

SALOMONS. But, my dear good heroic fellow...why not be content with appearances? Why risk disillusion? Cultivate morality...but not religion. Elaborate your politics. And exalt good manners. The achievement in a hundred thousand years or so of the gentleman, the lady, and the leisure class with appetites turned to taste, is a most important one. Don't let democratic cant belittle that. Indulge yourselves, incidentally, in a little art...a few good tunes, a picture or so, a scene full of pretty girls. Provide such things...for now that the human brute is well fed, his passions need distracting...

STROWDE. And a little alcohol.

SALOMONS. Yes, if you can't be sentimental without it. But never be carried off on crusades you can't finance...don't overdraw on your moral credit. Don't, for one moment, let art and religion and patriotism persuade you that you mean more than you do. Stand by Jerusalem when it comes to stoning the prophets. I must be off.

ELEANOR. Before you're answered.

SALOMONS. Answers are echoes.

ELEANOR. What does that mean?

SEROCOLD. It means that we all talk the same nonsense and all have to do the next thing there is to be done.

SALOMONS. But thank you for a charming evening.

ELEANOR. Till October.

SALOMONS. The Committee is to meet on the fifteenth. But you'll get your summons.

ELEANOR. My first full-fledged official committee. I feel cock-a-hoop.

A skittish phrase for ELEANOR. SEROCOLD goes back to the piano to strum delicately and sing little snatches. ' Tristan,' ' Isolde.'

SALOMONS. Good-bye, Lady Westbury. Once more, my condolences upon the catastrophe. But I must not agree that insurance is a mockery.

ELEANOR. Be thankful you weren't burnt in your bed.

JOAN. My first fire! It's inspiriting to have to start life again in one's dressing-gown and the gardener's boots.

STROWDE. Your car's round here, Geoffrey.

SALOMONS. Good-night, Serocold.

SEROCOLD sings to the melody of the Liebestod . . .

SEROCOLD. Good-night, Sir Geoffrey...Salomons K.C.B. flat...hidden handed bureaucrat...Beast in Revelations...your number will shortly be up.

SALOMONS. Not going abroad?

STROWDE. I've no impulse to. Europe still reproaches one. Perhaps...in the winter.

SALOMONS. If Serocold don't recapture you.

They have gone down the steps and away round the house, STROWDE kindling a pocket torch. The two women lean together on the parapet.

JOAN. You've never been to Karnak, Eleanor?

ELEANOR. No.

JOAN. We break our journey at Luxor whenever there's time. You should stand on the great gate and watch the moon rising over the Nile...and then think of all the armies that have marched...

ELEANOR *(touching her hand).* My child, you're as cold as a toad. Cheer up! Mark'll be home for good next year...and think of the fun you'll have rebuilding.

JOAN *(with a rather wan smile).* Energetic Eleanor! But as if he hadn't enough to worry him in Cairo at this moment.

ELEANOR *(the kindly scold).* You go to bed now.

SEROCOLD *(as he softly strums).* How many more volumes to this infernal history that Evan has found refuge in?

ELEANOR. One to publish...one to write.

SEROCOLD. How long'll that take you?

ELEANOR. I don't know.

SEROCOLD. Can't you finish it for him, Eleanor?

ELEANOR. Hardly.

SEROCOLD *(pleasantly ironic).* Books must be written, I admit...but there are lots of men fit for nothing else. We philistine politicians may be a poor lot...but we do get things done.

JOAN *(half to herself, as she leans on the parapet).* I must pray now to the moon...as one burnt-out lady to another...to teach me to order my ways.

SEROCOLD breaks into song again; from the second act this time.

SEROCOLD. Oh rest upon us...night du Liebe.

JOAN. Burnt out inside...the moon is. Gutted...such an ugly word!

SEROCOLD *(singing away).* Give forgetting...that I live. Take me out...in deinen schoss....

ELEANOR has gone into the sitting-room. Joan stares out to sea.

SCENE II

It is morning, and the sun is shining. Eleanor, wrapped in a fur coat, is sitting in the loggia, writing. SEROCOLD, dressed for his journey, comes out of the house and stands by the head of the steps talking to her.

SEROCOLD. Good morning, ma'am.

ELEANOR. Has the car come?

SEROCOLD. Not yet, I think.

ELEANOR. There's ample time. It's to pick up Joan at the Cottage Hospital.

SEROCOLD. I'm interrupting?

ELEANOR. No, I've just finished.

SEROCOLD. Proofs?

ELEANOR. Pages one to sixty...volume four...of the infernal history.

SEROCOLD. We've been in for a swim. I left Evan basking. Are you cold?

ELEANOR. No. I work in a fur coat all the year round. Thin blood...old age!

SEROCOLD. Inteuectual passion, Eleanor...chilling but admirable. Am I to post these in London?

ELEANOR. I'm coming up with you...for the day.

SEROCOLD. My dear! Eighty miles up and eighty miles down at eighty in the shade.

ELEANOR. I'm going to lunch at Kate Gosset's to meet Lord Clumbermere.

SEROCOLD *(with much meaning in the exclamation)*. Oh! And what does Kate want with him?

ELEANOR. I want fifty thousand pounds out of him for the Institute of Social Service,

SEROCOLD. Well...I daresay you'll get it.

ELEANOR. I'm told he's a good little man.

SEROCOLD. He's good for that much.

ELEANOR *(pointedly)*. You should know.

SEROCOLD *(bland)*. I assure you, we got nothing for his peerage. Reward of merit! I did hope he'd be substantially grateful. But divil a threepenny bit!

ELEANOR. He bought his baronetcy surely.

SEROCOLD (bitter-sweet). Ah...Egerton gave him that. *(He looks back towards the house, and lifts his voice a little.)* Good morning, fair lady!

ELEANOR. I hope the taxi-man didn t hurry you. How's Lester?

JOAN, to whom this has been spoken, comes from the sitting-room, and speaks first to ELEANOR, then to STEPHEN SEROCOLD.

JOAN. She had a good night. My heroic maid who went back for my pearls.

SEROCOLD. Her point of honour.

ELEANOR. She didn t get them.

JOAN. I'm almost glad she didn't. Pearls at that price! *(To Eleanor)* You saw her arm.

ELEANOR. Rather perverse of you!

JOAN. Is it? Yes, Lester would think so. We discuss now what we'll do with the insurance money. She's to decide!

She goes back into the house; a moment later comes out again with a parasol, goes down the steps and sits on one of the benches there silently. Eleanor being now quite free of her writing table, SEROCOLD fixes her.

SEROCOLD. You may take it from me, Eleanor, that the pro-Leaguers will vote against Egerton on the Japanese question...and he'll resign...and Bellingham must be sent for. He can form a government even without dissolving. And I'll lay you five to two that it all comes off before Christmas.

She lets him finish; then she shakes her head with a half smile.

ELEANOR. I'm not interested, Stephen.

SEROCOLD. You definitely refuse to help shepherd Evan back to the fold.

ELEANOR. Yes. I'm sorry your week-end has been wasted.

SEROCOLD. I've enjoyed myself! Don't be nasty.

ELEANOR. If Evan chooses to go back into politics he will, whatever I say.

SEROCOLD. And of course he will...it's the obvious thing to do. But why drift back?

ELEANOR. If he ever serves under Mr. Bellingham again...I shall be surprised.

SEROCOLD. You must serve under the man who's there! Bellingham has his failings...and his wife's a disaster.

ELEANOR. I don't call Mrs Bellingham a disaster.

SEROCOLD. She's so dull.

ELEANOR *(beyond indignation even)*. My objection to your respected chief is simply that he's a liar.

SEROCOLD. I shouldn't call him a liar.

ELEANOR...that he's a trickster.

SEROCOLD. He can be tricky when he's driven to it.

ELEANOR. He has no principles.

SEROCOLD *(cheerily)*. I tell him that. But he says that his answer is Emerson's...

ELEANOR. It would be!

SEROCOLD. That a foolish consistency is the bugbear of little minds.

ELEANOR. Well...he is consistently disloyal to his friends.

SEROCOLD *(with just a little heat added to the lightness)*. No, Eleanor, there you're wrong. And it hurts him when they say the sort of things about him that you're saying. But how can he go on working with them afterwards?

ELEANOR *(very directly)*. Would you tolerate a tithe of his dishonesty in your own lawyer?

SEROCOLD *(changing ground with the utmost grace)*. Ah . . that opens a wide question. I want an honest lawyer. I've got one, I think...and I do my best to deserve him. But isn't Bellingham the sort of Prime Minister that our dear public want?

ELEANOR. Then let the people of England cultivate political intelligence.

SEROCOLD. And what's to happen meanwhile? After all, we're responsible.

ELEANOR. Who are we?

SEROCOLD. The governing classes.

ELEANOR. Who are they?

SEROCOLD *(with a candour that quite obliterates irony, should there by chance be any at the very bottom of his mind)*. Nowadays...the people of goodwill and energy...wherever they spring from...who'll trouble to learn the tricks of the trade. I'm a good democrat. I'll work with any one who'll work with me. And I say that the great thing is to keep things going...to make for righteousness somehow...by the line of least resistance.

ELEANOR *(the moralist)*. You've all deteriorated since the war.

SEROCOLD. And what sort of a morality's yours, may I ask...truckling to Clumbermere for money? Travelling up to London to do it, too!

ELEANOR *(the realist)*. I offer Lord Clumbermere social salvation...cheap at the price. I've nothing else to sell him. We must start. Have I got a hat on? Joan, dear, forgive my deserting you. Be nice to Evan. I'll be back to dinner . . .

SEROCOLD. With fifty thousand honest sovereigns jingling in your pocket!

ELEANOR. You'll find me in the car...in two minutes.

ELEANOR goes into the house. SEROCOLD comes down a few steps and leans against the wall within a good range of JOAN.

SEROCOLD. We physicians of the body politic, you'll observe...of whatever school...are at one in our firm faith in bleeding.

JOAN. Who is Lord Clumbermere...ought I to know?

SEROCOLD. Tanner's Inks he was. God knows what else now...now that he himself is appropriately de-personalised into Clumbermere. An able devil.

JOAN. You want Evan back.

SEROCOLD. Bellingham wants to make it up with him. But he must hold out a hand.

JOAN. Was he trying to work with?

SEROCOLD. Infinitely.

JOAN. But you keep on trying!

SEROCOLD. It's my job. And the party's so loaded up nowadays with axe-grinders of all sorts...

JOAN. D'you think Eleanor's is the right woman's way into politics?

SEROCOLD. I don't like women in public affairs, I'm afraid...though it's too unpopular a thing to say. They make bad worse...not better.

JOAN. Her Institute and her Guilds.

SEROCOLD. They're nice new toys.

JOAN. And Sir Geoffrey's Committee! She thinks you'll soon be left chattering in your clubs.

SEROCOLD. She has been devilling for Evan all her life. She's sick of it...that's all.

JOAN. You miss Mary.

SEROCOLD. Damnably.

JOAN. I'm so glad I was home that summer and saw her before she died.

SEROCOLD. She was very fond of you.

JOAN. Life's eddies are so strange. Evan and Eleanor take this cottage for August...I'm burnt out of house and home, and cast on their mercy.

SEROCOLD. And do you remember our first meeting?

JOAN. Shamelessly...no.

SEROCOLD. Evan and Eleanor, Mary and I, you and your husband...emptied together from various trains on the platform at Verona.

JOAN. Oh yes...I was on my honeymoon.

SEROCOLD. I had a vision of it this morning...as I floated on the sea. and of the man with the guitar who offered to pass the time for us by singing 'Rigoletto' right through for three lire. My Tristan fooleries must have reminded me. And our last meeting?

JOAN. Such is the blank I call my mind...!

SEROCOLD. Tea at the Military Tournament...nineteen thirteen. Your boy was with you.

JOAN. Which?

SEROCOLD. The one that was killed.

JOAN. They were both killed.

SEROCOLD. Both!

JOAN. Within a month.

SEROCOLD (there being nothing better to say). I forgot. I won't blunder further by saying sympathetic things. I fear I used sometimes, rather meanly, to thank God Mary had no children. Then I lost her.

JOAN (detaching her mind). I was once taken through Vickers's to see the armour-plate making...and the big steam hammer cracked a nut for my benefit. They gave me the nut, and told me just where to place it. Mighty goings on leave us, don't you think, almost too dazed to complain? Won't Eleanor be waiting for you?

SEROCOLD. Heavens...yes. Good-bye.

JOAN. Good-bye.

SEROCOLD. Come and see Braxted again some day?

JOAN. I'd like to.

He goes into the house and so away. JOAN sits looking out to sea. After a moment STROWDE, in a bathing-suit covered by a voluminous dressing gown, comes as if *from the beach. JOAN, motionless, is aware of him.*

JOAN. Good morning.

STROWDE. Did you sleep?

JOAN. Yes.

STROWDE. The night through?

JOAN. Oh no!

STROWDE. For how long?

JOAN. Three hours. Don't give me away.

STROWDE. I'll give you till Wednesday to get a night's rest. Then I'll tell on you.

JOAN. I don't want to be doctored. I'm having such a peaceful time.

STROWDE. Eleanor gone?

JOAN. With Stephen Serocold.

STROWDE *(his tone changing just a little)* We've a day together.

JOAN *(not indifferently).* Yes.

STROWDE. Our first for a while.

JOAN. For a long while. You're to go back into Parliament, please, Evan, and into the Cabinet...at once.

STROWDE. The voice of Stephen!

JOAN. Why don't you?

STROWDE. I must dress. Then I'll tell you.

JOAN. Don't you believe in yourself any longer?

STROWDE. Is that enough of a faith?

JOAN. Its revenges are simple.

STROWDE. I've been clearing out the wardrobe of my mind lately. I used to have quite a fashionable mind. I find worn-out stuff and stuff I 've never worn. And one can't get rid of it. It mocks me from the rubbish heap.

JOAN. Better be burnt out.

STROWDE. Yes...you're lucky.

JOAN. I do feel, though, that one cannot start in collecting again. Let God's eye behold me still in my dressing-gown and the gardener's boots.

STROWDE. Shall we lunch out here? It won't be too hot. The parlourmaid's eye not being as God's, I will shift to a less symbolical attire. I want to talk to you, Joan.

JOAN. Well...We'll talk.

He goes in to dress. She does not move. She is, indeed, of a very still habit.

SCENE III

It is nearly midnight, and the moon is shining. Joan, wrapped from the chill in a
white cloak, is sitting on the steps as before. Strowde comes out of the house.

JOAN. What had happened? Is she very tired?

STROWDE. She hasn't come. He drove here to tell me.

JOAN. But it's the last train.

STROWDE. No...I've sent him to the Junction now. There's a nine-thirty
express she might have caught.

JOAN. And if not?

STROWDE. She could motor forty miles and get here about three in the
morning.

JOAN. Couldn't she have telegraphed?

STROWDE. Yes...up to seven.

JOAN. Not like Eleanor.

STROWDE. I'm sorry. Will you wait up?

JOAN. I think so...a little longer.

STROWDE. She'll come.

JOAN. Is she still rifling Lord What's his name's pockets...while Kate
Gossett holds him down? The silly man must have been struggling.

STROWDE. Clumbermere's his name...if you ever want to thank him for
our day together.

By this they have settled themselves to wait.

JOAN. A long day, Evan.

STROWDE. Has it seemed so?

JOAN. Eighteen years long. *(A silence; then she says, as if released from the*
spell of time) How easy to talk to you, though...surprisingly!

STROWDE *(wholesomely matter-of-fact)*. No...we've had something to
say...and haven't had to repeat ourselves...as we'd have done talking day in and
day out....

JOAN *(yielding again for a moment to the spell)*. For eighteen years. *(Then*
again shaking free) I believe I've told you everything. You've not told me much.

STROWDE. Several anecdotes. Do you want more? I've a good memory.
Sometimes I exercise it to see if the anecdotes strung together have any
meaning.

JOAN. Ought I to be ashamed to have so little to tell? No spiritual
adventures. Housekeeping in odd corners of the world...a husband and two
children.

STROWDE. Dutiful happiness.

JOAN. Yes .

STROWDE. As we agreed then...all for the best.

JOAN. I've never doubted it.

STROWDE *(his tone sharpening a little; the edge towards himself, though).* But when people say that, they're apt to mean...all for the second best, aren't they?

JOAN *(countering with irony).* And that's not worth clinging to...in these hard times?

STROWDE. It has also been said, Joan, that Second Best is what the Devil relies on to keep this world his own.

There is a silence before she asks, as of things long past . . .

JOAN. Was it God tempted us then?

STROWDE. God's the great tempter. But...even as you now understand what you then were...you did love me?

JOAN. Yes.

STROWDE. And you've never doubted that either?

JOAN. Never.

STROWDE. Though the love for Mark survived. And you had your boys.

JOAN *(as making final confession).* I couldn't have lived my love for you, Evan...it would have killed me.

STROWDE. Did I understand that? (He is disposed to laugh.) It's always hard to believe that a little human happiness will hurt one.

JOAN. I think some power in me would always have kept me from you...some innermost power.

STROWDE. I'd have put up a fight with it. I can be less of an altruist...than I was then.

JOAN. But what would you have brought to surrender? Nothing you loved. Nothing that loved you. *(Now she joins him in protective mockery.)* It's shocking for a woman to discover that wifehood and motherhood are really best carried through as matters of business...but if she loves a man she can only make him miserable.

STROWDE. I'd be glad enough to be made unhappy once again.

JOAN *(with a touch of mischief).* Has no one managed it in these eighteen years? No, no...I'm not curious.

STROWDE faces her, and asks very seriously, but almost disinterestedly...

STROWDE. Then, in the sense that you've always loved me...do you love me still?

JOAN. Yes.

STROWDE. Oh...why not!

JOAN. I keep it a secret from my everyday self. But...I love you.

STROWDE. Well, it's a word of all work, isn't it?..and we wear out its meanings one by one, as we fulfil and prove them...or as we fail to.

JOAN. Perhaps, Evan...for a last meaning..to love is to love the unattainable.

He breaks the tension.

STROWDE. Still, you've not much to complain of. Mark's a first-rate fellow.

JOAN'S voice is never hard, nor ever dry, but sometimes it empties of all tone; as now.

JOAN. My boys are gone.

STROWDE. Yes...I won't pretend to understand what that means.

JOAN. One's capable, you know, of uncomprehended suffering. I watched women making a sort of emotional profit out of their loss. People called me stoical...but it was only that I didn't understand...or want to. Why ask what an earthquake's for? My bitterest moment was when I came home to find their kit sent back from France. Burnt up with everything else now, I'm glad to think. The emptyings, poor dears, of their pockets...of a dead boy's pockets!

STROWDE *(setting his teeth to this)*. Death leaves us that...and life breeds in us fantastic hopes.

JOAN. The night the second news had come we lay awake holding hands... and Mark said suddenly: "I'm sorry, my dear...I'm sorry." And I said: " Oh, Mark, don't apologise." We didn't feel very sane.

STROWDE *(his brows knit, but his eyes lifted a little)*. Nature wastes life...for she can afford to. And our human nature spends loving-kindness...and we must afford to. You and he have each other. I'm sure he needs you.

She comes back with relief to practical things.

JOAN. I wish I'd not left him just now...but the doctor won't let me stay out the summer there. His work's a failure, he says...so they thought they must send him red ribbons and things. When his K.C.B. badge came he threw it into the corner and cursed. It has been a bad three years. We used to fear that you and your party would come in to theorise us out of existence. I remember the evening when he brought the paper to Gizeh with the news of your bye-election majority. "Evan will take three steps into the F.O.," he said...." and I shall resign." *(A little grimly)* It's his friends have let him down.

STROWDE. Did he really picture me astraddle before the official mantel-piece with my chest puffed out and: Gentlemen, now I'm in power...?

JOAN. But why aren't you, Evan?

He looks at her in silence for a moment.

STROWDE. If I say: Thanks to you...don't misunderstand.

JOAN *(puzzled and ready to be hurt for his sake all the same)*. Oh, my dear!

STROWDE. But understand I do thank you that I am not a popular political figure to-day...putting on all the airs of wisdom.

JOAN. Was your history writing the better choice?

STROWDE. Well, the Industrial History is honestly laboured stuff. You've not read it?

JOAN. Horrid confession...no. I began to.

STROWDE. Shamefuller still!

JOAN. Three volumes.

STROWDE. And a fourth to come.

JOAN. And a fifth.

STROWDE. Perhaps. A job almost any one could have done, and nobody did. Shall I tell you why I took it on...even before the other job failed me?

JOAN. Why?

STROWDE. This sounds unselfish...it wasn't. I really had to find something more than housekeeping for Eleanor to do. My marriage!

JOAN. It's been a happy one?

STROWDE. Quite.

JOAN. Dear Eleanor.

STROWDE. The best of women. And she brings some meaning to that banal praise.

JOAN. What's to happen when the history is finished?

STROWDE (businesslike). Eleanor's goodness begins to be accounted wisdom of the current sort. Committees are seeking her out. Even Salomon's, you see, that shrewd appraiser of what's worth while...

JOAN. I meant what's to happen to you?

STROWDE. (with just a touch of irony, not an unkind one, though). Eleanor, grown a power in the land and backed by much Clumbermere money, may find me employment.

JOAN. Nonsense. When will the last volume be done?

STROWDE. Ah, that's a question. (He turns his head suddenly) I hear the car changing gear on Pewsey Hill.

JOAN. He has been very quick.

STROWDE. Impossibly. She'll have found a taxi at the Junction, and they've met half-way.

JOAN. (her voice taking on more colour). Evan...stir yourself out of the hopelessness and disbelief.

STROWDE. (grimly). When the donkey's at the end of his tether and has eaten his patch bare, he's to cut capers and kick up a dust, is he?

JOAN. Have you no purpose left in you?

STROWDE. (grimly indeed). None. Have you?

JOAN. Second Best has exploited me, you may say, and left me for dead. But I was firmly minded that you'd make for yourself a great career.

STROWDE. How shamefully romantic of you!

JOAN. Don't you want to be a power in the world?

STROWDE. Save me from the illusion of power! I once had a glimpse...and I thank you for it, my dear...of a power that is in me. But that won't answer to any call.

JOAN. Not to the call of a good cause?

STROWDE. (as one who shakes himself free from the temptations of *unreality).* Excellent causes abound. They are served...as they are!...by eminent prigs making a fine parade, by little minds watching for what's to happen next. Track such men down...past picture-paper privacy, and their servants' knowledge of them. Oh, never mind if they drink a little, if they're foolish over women or sordid about money...we won't damn them for their weaknesses. But search for their strength..which is not to be borrowed or bargained for...it must spring from the secret life...

JOAN. Yes...I know.

STROWDE....and what is it, as a rule, but the old ignorant savagery? Nothing to be ashamed of...but why deck it with new names? Women should know, even if we forget, what savages men still are. But you and I climbed together to a chilly height. Was it illusion...the truth we found there?

JOAN. Who am I to say...that never put it to the proof?

STROWDE. Well...if we loved the unattainable in each other...and if all we could easily have taken mattered so little besides that we let it go with hardly a murmur...why, I've learnt to believe, I suppose, in what's unattainable from life and nothing else can content me or stir me now.

JOAN. *(steadily).* It would have been better than if we had never met...and never loved.

STROWDE. No...that's blasphemy. At least don't join the unbelieving mob who cry: Do something, anything, no matter what...do your devilmost...all's well while the wheels go round...while something's being done!...Lord, give us increase...if we stop to question, barbarous poverty will overwhelm us again. Are we so few steps upward from the beast that gluts and starves?

JOAN *(with an irony that is irony of the soul).* But seek first the kingdom of God...and the desire of all things else shall be taken from you?

STROWDE *(very simply).* It has been taken from me. I don't complain...and I don't make a virtue of it. I'm not the first man who has found beliefs that he can't put in his pocket like so much small change. But am I to deny them for that?

JOAN. No...one can't.

STROWDE *(choosing his words).* If I could be...call it in love again...then, perhaps I'd dare stretch out my hand for power.

JOAN. Don't waste time...next time...over a woman.

STROWDE. I promise you.

She breaks the tension now, and lightens her distress with something like a laugh.

JOAN. I never put such fantastic value on myself. If we'd kissed and parted...as we couldn't marry and settle...!

STROWDE *(grimly responsive to her tone).* And we never even kissed.

For a little now, they survey this eighteen-year span, detachedly enough; puzzled, acquiescent, interested.

JOAN. Is life meant to be so serious?

STROWDE. Tell me how to forget you...and the meaning of you.

JOAN. I'm changed.

STROWDE. How many times have we met since that cold and desperate parting?

JOAN. A dozen perhaps.

STROWDE *(with a lover's courtesy)*. You outface the years very beautifully.

JOAN. Thank you...says my vanity.

STROWDE. But such things are tokens for strangers to know you by. What shines for me is the vision of the truth of you which you gave me when you said...weighing the words, but not sadly, I remember...when you said that you loved me. And that, you see, whatever it may mean, has not changed.

JOAN *(firmly)*. I can wish it had never come to your cutting the commonplace earth from under us, Evan, by asking the question. But that was, and it is the truth of me. I'd unsay it if I could.

STROWDE. Yes. We live another life from the beasts only in this tiresome belief that beyond the tokens of our living something we call truth exists. Yet there's nothing near to truth that we learn, but when we've felt the burden we'd cast it away...we'd unsay it if we could.

JOAN *(desperately, even with some impatience showing)*. But if I'm to stand to you for ever as a symbol of denial...of uselessness...of a sort of death in life! Evan, Evan...no recording angel will consent to write: He could not be a conquering hero all for thinking of a love affair.

STROWDE. It sounds absurd, doesn't it?

Her tone changes; there is pain in it now.

JOAN. Has it been...oh, but it can't have been this wintertime with you ever since? We did wisely.

STROWDE. We did right.

JOAN *(fearlessly probing, for that may help)*. No, I don't say so. I did what I felt then I could be sure of doing well.

STROWDE *(putting it to the inscrutable gods)*. And we must always try to do more...even knowing that we'll fail! A grim burden for the fledgling soul. Why not make the best of things?

JOAN *(echoing)*. The devil's own second best of things. *(She turns to him again with pain in her voice and eyes.)* You've suffered.

STROWDE *(shrugging)*. Why...I've had my losses as you have. When the war came my beliefs about men and things were an enemy the more. I fought against them and beat them...and they're dead. And what remains? I'm rather sullen-minded.

JOAN. Is it right to leave present fighting to ignobler minds?

STROWDE. How can one go in again without purpose or conviction...without even ambition or vanity as an excuse...remount the merry-go-round?

JOAN. Yes...Mark says the most pitiful thing he meets is the well-meaning man who daren't stop. He sees him, he says, poor dear, in the mirror of a morning.

STROWDE (*with a savage shake of the head*). I'd be an ill-meaning man pretty soon.

JOAN. Why?

STROWDE. Can you think of a greater driving force for evil than the man who has seen a better way and accepts the worse...who knows there's a wisdom that escapes him and must deny it? I'd sooner trust things to fools, if the fools would take heart, than to disillusioned men.

JOAN. And there's always Eleanor!

STROWDE. Yes, let the busy women have a try at tidying up. But, frankly, I fear they'll make a commonplace world of it.

JOAN. Here she is.

STROWDE. Weary, but cheerful.

JOAN. Bless her!

STROWDE goes quickly into the house. After a moment ELEANOR comes out. Weary she may be, but she does not show it much. She is subduedly, and a little strangely, cheerful.

ELEANOR. Dear Joan...forgive me.

JOAN. Good hunting?

ELEANOR. Good enough. Has Evan looked after you?

JOAN. Perfectly.

STROWDE returns.

ELEANOR. You didn't get my message. But I missed even that train.

JOAN. (*merrily*) You have a callous brother. I said you might be lying cold and stiff. He said it was unlikely.

STROWDE. No one is ever anxious about Eleanor. There are sandwiches and barley-water for you.

ELEANOR. Go to bed, Joan. I didn't dream you'd sit up.

JOAN. Naughty of me. Good-night.

ELEANOR kisses her, more tenderly than, one would say, the occasion demanded.

ELEANOR. My dear...!

JOAN. I'm sure you've most intriguing things to tell Evan about Lord Bumble-bee...or whatever his silly name is. Good-night, Evan.

STROWDE. Good-night, Joan.

She goes. There is a little pause, as if they were waiting for her to get out of earshot.

STROWDE. Well, what's wrong?

ELEANOR. Mark Westbury fell down dead in his office in Cairo this morning.

STROWDE. Good God!

ELEANOR. By pure chance I met Neville Hamerton at the corner of

Whitehall, and he told me. So I went back with him to the F.O. to stop them sending her a telegram. That's what kept me, of course. Shall I tell her tonight or not?

STROWDE. Yes, I should.

ELEANOR. Would she take it better from you?

STROWDE *(almost sharply)*. Why should she?

ELEANOR *(with a hint of evasion)*. You knew Mark very well.

STROWDE *(concluding this small excursion)*. Not better than you know her.

ELEANOR. It'll seem like the end of the world. Both her boys...the house burnt down...and now this.

STROWDE *(taking to abstractions, as his wont is)* Mark is an immeasurable loss. But all losses are...till one measures them by forgetting them.

ELEANOR. They only had each other.

STROWDE. The breaking of a last link brings relief with it too.

ELEANOR *(her brows knitting)*. Evan, don't be so callous.

STROWDE *(reasonably)*. I am not. It will be a great shock...and a great grief...till Nature rebels and says: Die of it, or get over it.

ELEANOR. Is this how I'm to talk to Joan?

STROWDE. Don't start talking at all. Tell her Mark's

dead, kiss her, and come away the moment she loosens your hand.

ELEANOR faces her mission with misgiving, as well she may.

ELEANOR. Well...I'll go up now. Lord Clumbermere was very sound. I think he'll give us thirty thousand.

This last inappropriate remark by no means shows an unsympathetic mind. The thought was there, and she found some support in it. STROWDE, though, is not unconscious of the effect of its simple utterance.

STROWDE. Good. Shall I take the sandwiches to your room?

ELEANOR. No, thank you...I'm not hungry.

ELEANOR goes into the house. He now has but to put out the lights below, lock up and go to bed.

ACT II

SCENE I

Braxted Abbey, Stephen Serocold's home, is a Tudor house, built on monastic foundations. It has, on the first floor above ground, a long panelled gallery with six high embrasured windows, which overlook the broad terrace. Here is the end of the gallery, and we face the last of these windows, through which we can see the cypresses that border the terrace, and the sky. Set out from the blank wall on our left is a writing table; sitting at it one can command the gallery's length. A small door in the panelling cuts off the corner, it opens to a small turret staircase which descends but does not ascend. The window is open, for it is a summer afternoon. On the window seat are SEROCOLD and LADY PECKHAM. She is a woman over fifty, of pronounced vitality, if somewhat insensitive. By the way she is dressed she has just arrived. She is chattering.

LADY PECKHAM...He never forgave me for ruffling his hair once at a supper party at Frankie Turnour's. I told that silly scared girl he married that she'd better learn to. But I think she prefers him pompous. He has gone very bald, though, lately.

SEROCOLD. He works hard. Bellingham gets on with him. He ballasts the Cabinet. God knows we need that.

LADY PECKHAM *(nodding towards the garden)*. Where did Joan Westbury spring from? I've not met her for an age.

SEROCOLD. She's been about.

LADY PECKHAM. You brought Evan and Eleanor down with you?

SEROCOLD. Yesterday.

LADY PECKHAM. Who else is coming?

SEROCOLD. The Kittredges.

LADY PECKHAM. I've seen them.

SEROCOLD. We only hold eight these days.

LADY PECKHAM. Lunching to-morrow?

SEROCOLD. Bellingham.

LADY PECKHAM *(cocking her head)*. You stick to your point, don't you?

SEROCOLD. No, never...but I keep on coming back to it.

LADY PECKHAM. He hates Evan.

SEROCOLD *(cheerfully)*. Evan despises him. But I'll make it a match.

LADY PECKHAM *(her gaze on the garden again)*. And are those two going to?

SEROCOLD. I haven't heard so. But they're walking nicely in step. It looks connubial.

LADY PECKHAM. How long has Mark Westbury been dead?

SEROCOLD. He died in August. This is only June.

LADY PECKHAM. They'd better hurry up. They're not getting any younger. She'll want more children. And why not?

SEROCOLD. *(with mild idealism).* My dear Mildred...there are other objects in marrying.

LADY PECKHAM. That's an obvious one. Why do you ask these Kittredges?

SEROCOLD. I like them...and it's as well to be civil to Americans.

LADY PECKHAM. Are they rich?

SEROCOLD. I'm sure they'd hate to be thought so.

LADY PECKHAM. That's very morbid. Who is it with Evan and Joan.

SEROCOLD. Why, Oliver!

LADY PECKHAM. Heavens...I must get new spectacles. You've no right to look so young, you know, Stephen. I wasn't out of the nursery when you were born.

SEROCOLD. Mildred, I believe I may live to be a hundred. It's terrible...
From some way along the terrace below, OLIVER GAUNTLETT's voice is heard calling " Hullo, darling Mother!" Lady Peckham waves a hand to him.

LADY PECKHAM. Bless you, my son.

SEROCOLD. Things bore me and never tire me. I'm no real good to this government...but, honestly, I don't think Bellingham could get on without me. I'm happy down here. All the years Mary was ill I got into the habit of leaving myself with her on the Monday morning and she'd hand it me back well cared for on the Friday night.

LADY PECKHAM. Poor Stephen!

SEROCOLD. You never could stand a sick-bed, could you?

LADY PECKHAM. Stand by one, d'you mean? Not for long.

SEROCOLD. We had more of a married life, though, than most people.

LADY PECKHAM. You're good right through, Stephen.

SEROCOLD. I'm harmless. *(Now he broaches something which it would seem has been on his mind)* I'm pretty vexed, Mildred, about this escapade of Oliver's.

LADY PECKHAM. Nothing in it.

SEROCOLD. Why go to an Anarchist meeting? And if you must go, why in God's name get arrested there!

LADY PECKHAM. They didn't charge him with anything.

SEROCOLD. Every paper had a paragraph.

LADY PECKHAM. A fortnight ago...all forgotten. The tradition of the English gentleman, Stephen, is that he may go where he pleases and do what he likes.

SEROCOLD. No doubt. But England's so full of gentlemen now...competition has abolished these privileges. Talk to him seriously.

LADY PECKHAM. Try it yourself.

SEROCOLD. I have.

LADY PECKHAM. Well?

SEROCOLD. He says Anarchy interests him.

LADY PECKHAM. Why shouldn t it?

SEROCOLD. My dear Mildred, I'm in the Cabinet, and I'm his uncle.

LADY PECKHAM. That's not his fault.

SEROCOLD. That's what he said. I think it most courageous and forgiving of me to ask him down here.

LADY PECKHAM. It is.

By this it is evident that JOAN, STROWDE and OLIVER GAUNTLETT have arrived under the window; and one can talk from the gallery to the terrace with perfect ease.

LADY PECKHAM. How are you, Joan?

JOAN'S VOICE. Do you want to know?

LADY PECKHAM. I ask.

JOAN. I feel like flying.

SEROCOLD. Door's locked inside. I'll open it.

He goes down the turret stair. The exchange of compliments proceeds.

LADY PECKHAM. Hot?

JOAN. No.

LADY PECKHAM. Pretty frock.

JOAN. One I had dyed.

LADY PECKHAM. You're losing a comb.

JOAN. Thank you. When did you get here?

LADY PECKHAM. About six.

JOAN. How's London?

LADY PECKHAM. Horrid.

OLIVER GAUNTLETT comes in by the turret door. He is a young man, and he has lost an arm. STROWDE follows him. He carries a printed paper that has an official look about it. This he opens in a minute, and sets himself to at the writing-table. OLIVER kisses his mother with real affection.

OLIVER. Where's Dolly?

LADY PECKHAM. Went down to the lake with Miss Susan Kittredge. Well, Evan?

STROWDE. Well, Mildred?

No greeting could be friendlier.

OLIVER. You look very handsome, Mother.

LADY PECKHAM. Thank you kindly. How are you?

OLIVER. Kicking. Evan won't take me on.

LADY PECKHAM. Why should he?

SEROCOLD'S VOICE. Mildred, come and see the Alderney bull.

LADY PECKHAM. Now?

SEROCOLD. Yes.

LADY PECKHAM. All right.

OLIVER *(hailing).* Uncle Stephen!

SEROCOLD'S VOICE. Hullo.

OLIVER. I positively was not drunk.

SEROCOLD. I wish you had been.

STROWDE *(looking up from his reading).* Distressing to the nice-minded historian...to note how aggressively moral revolutionaries become.

OLIVER. New Year before last at Blair I tried to get drunk and couldn't. Nor wine nor spirits has passed my lips since. I think I'll try again.

LADY PECKHAM. Do you feel you really must?

OLIVER. Why did you give me such a queer head?

LADY PECKHAM *(as she kisses the top of it in farewell).* I sometimes wish it had been an even thicker one.

OLIVER. But what about my future?

STROWDE. Did the worthy Sir Charles Phillips positively throw you down the office steps?

OLIVER. He wept over me. I resigned.

LADY PECKHAM. I shall shortly have the pleasure of telling that gentleman publicly that he's a liar.

OLIVER. For saying I was frolicsomely drunk! Dear Mother, he meant that kindly.

LADY PECKHAM. Still, I shall not deny myself the pleasure.

LADY PECKHAM passes down the gallery.

OLIVER. Grin through a mask and explode an idea on them...and your Phillipses show the white scuts of their minds like rabbits.

STROWDE. What precise shade of red are you? Anarchy's black, by the way.

OLIVER. Evan, I will tell you a secret. I was down there searching for a Chinese debating society...and I got into the wrong meeting.

STROWDE. Did the Bobbies frog-march you?

OLIVER. Well, I'm glad they didn't give me a chance of going back on the poor scared devils. But I had to get quit of old Phillips. So I worked up Bakunin, and had a fine set-to with him.

STROWDE. What s wrong with the City?

OLIVER. What's wrong with a mine that's on a map and a cotton-field on a balance-sheet?

STROWDE. Not primitive enough?

OLIVER. Maybe. Digging potatoes might sweat all the nonsense out of me, d'you think? But I can't.

STROWDE. You play an amazing game of tennis, though.

OLIVER. I write a better hand than I did. It's harder to.

STROWDE. I don't see what use I can be. If politics are your game...won't you do better attacking the citadel of the constitution from within..as you happen to have the entree?

OLIVER. Yes...the Right Honourable Brooke Bellingham's lunching to-morrow. I might wag my tail at him and be a Cabinet Minister in no time.

STROWDE. Why not?

OLIVER. There's a longer lease for the old gang in letting the youngsters in than in keeping them out, isn't there? I'm not for bombs. There's not enough difference between a dead Bellingham and a live one.

STROWDE. And there's something to be said, you know, for simple and vulgar ambition.

OLIVER. They're all twitteringly afraid of you, Evan. If your name comes up at a dinner-table, Uncle Stephen gets that genial...!

STROWDE. They flatter me.

OLIVER. You're going to stand again at the Election?

STROWDE. I may.

OLIVER. They think you mean to give them hell.

STROWDE. I must manage to keep up the impression.

OLIVER. I want to learn what's what. I've chucked a success in the City.

STROWDE. You could have given them hell there. A spectacular bankruptcy. You've a name to discredit. That's real revolution.

OLIVER. You're spoiling for a fight, you know..for all you sit there writing niggling notes on that report of Eleanor's damned Committee.

STROWDE. I'd be setting you to type them.

OLIVER. I will...till the time comes

STROWDE. And if the time never comes?

OLIVER. How long have you believed that?

STROWDE. It is my firm disbelief.

OLIVER. Then why don't you shoot yourself?

STROWDE. I must finish these notes.

OLIVER. I must dress.

STROWDE. Dinner at eight?

OLIVER. It takes me half an hour. But you might think me over.

STROWDE.Yes, I will.

OLIVER. Thank you.

OLIVER goes down the gallery, leaving STROWDE to his note-making.

LADY PECKHAM. Have you any feeling for Oliver?

STROWDE. Honestly?

LADY PECKHAM. Of course.

STROWDE. Well...it's hard to define....

LADY PECKHAM. Then you haven't.

STROWDE. I can't contradict you.

LADY PECKHAM. Why expect it? You were pretty young. We were happy for a bit.

STROWDE. And you threw me over just as suddenly, Mildred.

LADY PECKHAM. You didn't complain.

STROWDE. I had no right to.

LADY PECKHAM. I took a sort of pride, Evan, in sending you off whistling. *(She relaxes to reminiscence)* I remember my father, when I was fifteen, setting forth great-aunt Charlotte to me...which had to be done as she's in the history books...and took some doing! He said: She was a bad lot, but a good fellow.

STROWDE. You have a genius, Mildred, for making things seem simple.

LADY PECKHAM *(summarily)*. Well...I've more energy than brains. And I never could fuss about my immortal soul. I'm not sure that I have one. I used to think I might grow one. But if you can only get it by fussing about it...I don't want that sort. So when I die there'll be an end of me. I don't mind. I've done all I can for Oliver. He has lost the need for me. And the same sort of thing's to be gone through with Dolly... though she's no concern of yours...nor of anyone else's now.

STROWDE *(measuring his mind to the matter)*. I don't of course, refuse responsibility,...if you really think I can do something for the boy that no one else can.

LADY PECKHAM *(grimacing, and dragging out the accusing word)*. You're so dry, Evan.

STROWDE *(undisturbed)*. But he's twenty-six...

LADY PECKHAM. Twenty-five.

STROWDE. And he is what he is. He's looking ahead. Why should he thank us for tying this corpse of a story round his neck?

LADY PECKHAM *(as business-like as he)*. He doesn't get on with the Gauntletts. And he can hardly inherit...what with Victor's two sons...and it's a third on the way, I daresay. He was dutifully fond of Peckham, and Peckham liked him...died when he was twelve, though...so that's all theyknew of each other. Peckham was no fool.

STROWDE *(half-humorously)*. I never thought so.

LADY PECKHAM. Except over women. But a sensible husband to me...and I was no end of a nuisance of a tomboy when he married me. It's my money Oliver gets. I saw to that.

STROWDE. But surely he'd hate me if he knew...whatever I might learn to feel for him.

LADY PECKHAM. And you'd sit down under it?

STROWDE. What else could I do?

LADY PECKHAM. What a question!

STROWDE. Give me the answer.

LADY PECKHAM (*with a sudden blaze of feeling*). I'm angry with you.

STROWDE. I retain great respect for your anger.

LADY PECKHAM. Even in those days you always seemed to be looking for something over my shoulder.

STROWDE. Most ungallant of me!

LADY PECKHAM. No...I hoped you'd find it.

STROWDE. I never did.

LADY PECKHAM. Are you going to marry Joan Westbury?

Though this is fired at him without warning his answer is perfectly balanced.

STROWDE. I hope so.

LADY PECKHAM (*quickly*). You'd mind her knowing?

STROWDE (*countering effectively*). Would you?

LADY PECKHAM. Oliver's very fond of her.

STROWDE. Is he?

LADY PECKHAM (*her voice dropping a tone or two*). When I saw you three in the garden together just now..

STROWDE. Well?

LADY PECKHAM. I got ready to give him up. It's far likelier, when he's told, that he'll learn to hate me.

STROWDE (*a little askew*). And it's also possible, isn't it, that Joan might turn her back on the three of us.

LADY PECKHAM (*simply*). I hadn't thought of that.

For the first and only time he permits himself something of a score.

STROWDE. Hadn't you? I'm afraid I had.

LADY PECKHAM (*most genuinely shocked*). Good God, Evan...you used not to think me a cad. And you'd let her?

STROWDE. You credit me with the queerest powers.

LADY PECKHAM. I've no patience with people that only seem able to live in a mix-up of the past and the future....

STROWDE. The present!

LADY PECKHAM. If Joan finds she's jealous of me, let her take Oliver from me...and from you too. I could. That ought to satisfy her.

STROWDE. I doubt if you understand Joan.

LADY PECKHAM. Well enough!

STROWDE....even though you understand me.

LADY PECKHAM. You'd have puzzled me once if I'd let you. But we took things for granted. Well...you bear me no grudge, do you?

STROWDE. On the contrary, I apologise.

LADY PECKHAM *(robust, to his subtlety)*. What for?

STROWDE. For looking over your shoulder.

LADY PECKHAM. I can tell you this, Evan...whatever it was you set out to be when I sent you packing, you ought to be six times the size of it by now. I've played the fool pretty blindly, no doubt...but I'm wise where I need to be..

STROWDE *(seriously)*. That's a great boast.

LADY PECKHAM. Even if I'm not very wise. And you can't put me in the wrong over my children...for they've had the best of me...and I don't have to ask questions about them...I know.

STROWDE. Adopting him as my secretary or what not would prompt some people's memories...that was one good reason, I thought, for snubbing the boy.

LADY PECKHAM. Thank you.

STROWDE *(his eyes travelling to the gallery's end)* Here come the What's-his-names...American people...Kittredges.

LADY PECKHAM *(without turning)*. Can they hear us?

STROWDE. Not yet...they're stopping to look at a picture.

But their talk seems at an end. LADY PECKHAM adds a postscript.

LADY PECKHAM. I've wondered what the second housemaid felt like when she swore her baby on the footman.

STROWDE. And the footman was adjured to have the feelings of a man! I'm sorry.

LADY PECKHAM. You'd better dress for dinner. *(Then she smiles wryly)* I once gave you a dog. Did you get fond of it?

STROWDE. Very. I'm afraid you can't shame me, quite so easily.

LADY PECKHAM. Well, Oliver's going wrong...and it's breaking my heart.

STROWDE. You'd cut bits out of yourself for him.

LADY PECKHAM. He is a bit cut out of me.

STROWDE *(gravely)*. We must tell him if you think it right.

LADY PECKHAM. No. No use.

STROWDE. I wish that I didn't agree.

LADY PECKHAM *(with all her sincerity, and of this, at least, she has much)*. But if you can't take what's your own when it's offered you, my friend, I don't know what else is to do you good.

STROWDE *(neither lifting nor lowering his voice)*. Look out!

MR KITTREDGE's *voice is heard saying as he approaches,* "Is it my ignorance to suppose that a Hobbema?

LADY PECKHAM *(brightly, as she turns)*. We'll hope not, Mr. Kittredge, as it is ear-marked for income-tax.

MR KITTREDGE and SUSAN appear, ready for dinner. He is an old man; of the aristocracy of New England, and of a higher aristocracy too. Susan is his

SCENE II

Half an hour later. STROWDE has nearly reached the end of the Report and of his notes on it. LADY PECKHAM comes down the gallery.

LADY PECKHAM. You'll be late for dinner.

STROWDE. No.

LADY PECKHAM. You will. Because I want to talk to you.

And she sits on the other side of the writing table.

STROWDE. What about?

LADY PECKHAM. Oliver.

STROWDE *(with more than a casual acquiescence)*. Yes. What do you want me to do?

LADY PECKHAM. Queer his turning to you...so instinctively.

STROWDE. How long since he turned fantastically minded? I've hardly seen him since he grew up.

LADY PECKHAM. He has been very mum with me this last year or two.

STROWDE. Is it the strain of the war still?

LADY PECKHAM. I don't see why it should be. He was only three months out...got smashed..came home.

STROWDE. He had three years among the stay-at-homes...growing up to it. His mind is jangled at the moment. It mayn't last.

LADY PECKHAM. He's very unhappy. I've always wondered whether sometime he ought not to be told.

STROWDE *(looking at her, so to speak, from under his brows)*. D'you think that would cheer him?

LADY PECKHAM. D'you think it's possible he knows?

STROWDE. Haldly possible. What gossip there was...

LADY PECKHAM. How should we know what gossip there was?

STROWDE. Then why should very stale echoes of it drift his way? Still, it's possible.

LADY PECKHAM. Don't think I'd mind telling him he's your son.

This plain fact--which she has purposely put so plainly - lies, one may say, for consideration on the table between them.

STROWDE. My dear Mildred...surely it would be a piece of wanton cruelty.

LADY PECKHAM. I consider you've a right to forbid me to.

STROWDE. You've been seriously thinking of telling him?

LADY PECKHAM. Yes.

STROWDE. Tell me why.

She turns her eyes on herself for a moment, a comparatively infrequent habit.

LADY PECKHAM. I'm a tough old heathen...and I'm a sentimental fool. The two things go together, I suppose.

STROWDE. Often.

granddaughter; a girl of a grave simplicity, of which she is only a little conscious and not at all ashamed.

MR. KITTREDGE *(with his light touch)*. Very unfair, I agree, for any mere nobody to paint such a picture.

LADY PECKHAM *(as one bullies one's oldest friend)*. Evan, will you go and get dressed?

STROWDE. Dear me...you're my hostess, aren't you?

LADY PECKHAM. I wait dinner twenty minutes and no more. British punctuality, Miss Susan.

STROWDE *(with admirable vigour)*. You count a hundred and walk to the hall and pick up the others, and you'll find me waiting by the soup tureen. And I'll trust to your honour for a measured hundred, Miss Kittredge....
By which time he is down the gallery and away.

MR. KITTREDGE *(in his musical tone)*. This was your home, Lady Peckham?

LADY PECKHAM. Mamma started married life by being restless. I got born in Venice. But I grew here.

MR. KITTREDGE. I know better than to be enthusiastic in England..; so I won't remind you how beautiful it is.

LADY PECKHAM *(with British politeness)*. You needn't. I know. Though it's ramshackle, all but the kitchens. They're Norman. You must see them. A bit of a nuisance to Stephen now he can't keep it up. He could sell it to a Trade Union for a Convalescent Home. But we've a cousin who's gone into oil, and won't break the entail.

MR. KITTREDGE. I picture a sick bricklayer meditating in the cloister upon his spiritual affinity to the men who built it...as a refuge from the anarchy of mind without.

LADY PECKHAM. I can picture him asleep over the Sunday paper.

MR. KITTREDGE. They were Hospitallers, weren t they?

LADY PECKHAM. Order of St. John...and I'm a something or other of that now too.

SUSAN has been standing reposefully where she paused by the window. She now announces as a matter of course, though much to Lady Peckham's astonishment...

SUSAN. One hundred.

LADY PECKHAM. What? Oh, thank you.

MR. KITTREDGE. I ask your approval of Susan's up-bringing. She does what she is told without comment.

Lady Peckham, once she gets what she'd call the hang of a talk, has a shrewd humour of her own.

LADY PECKHAM. Then she's both a very good girl and a very deceitful one.

The young woman in question now unobtrusively takes part.

MR. KITTREDGE. She smiles. I always think that I know what she means when she smiles...but perhaps it's only because I'm fond of her. However, in that at least I'm not deceived.

LADY PECKHAM *(briskly)*. Come along. *(But she has to collect the half-dozen etceteras that women, dressed for dinner, carry round in a country house.)* You're writing a book about us, aren't you, Mr. Kittredge...somebody told me!

MR. KITTREDGE. No, indeed...the warfare of my works is accomplished. They repose in the half-calf of a definitive edition upon the shelves of those gentlemanly libraries which, the advertisements inform me, cannot be considered complete without them. In my hey-day I was read, apparently, but not bought. Now I am bought but not read. Heaven forbid, though, that I should quarrel with the bread and butter I still need to consume.

LADY PECKHAM. But you're a professor?

MR. KITTREDGE. Emeritus .

LADY PECKHAM. Does that mean you don't earn any money by it?

MR. KITTREDGE. That also is implied.

SUSAN *(close at his side)*. Your books are read, Grandfather.

MR. KITTREDGE *(his voice caressing her)*. Family pride...pray pardon it, madam. *(They now make vague starts on their way to dinner.)* From sheer force of habit, though, I am collecting materials for a book I shall never write now...and England is rich in them at the moment.

LADY PECKHAM *(seeking a foothold amid the rising waters of intellect)*. What's it called?

MR. KITTREDGE. The Selection of an Aristocracy might serve for a title.

LADY PECKHAM. What does that mean?

MR. KITTREDGE. You must not indulge my garrulity. I believe...the idea is not a new one, of course...that a community can only be kept self-respecting and powerful by courage in the continuing selection of an aristocracy.

LADY PECKHAM. Aren't they born?

MR. KITTREDGE. In that case, circumstances will call for their being bred and born unconventionally at times.

LADY PECKHAM *(turning a sharp eye on his unconscious serenity)*. Oh! Yes...I never thought of that.

Now they move slowly down the gallery.

MR. KITTREDGE. In the United States, unfortunately, for the last eighty years...my lifetime!...the methods of our material advancement have been too crudely selective for anything one can call an aristocracy to adhere in the social structure. But you are somewhat luckier. Barriers break, but new classes form. The art of social sympathy flourishes just a little more easily in England....

LADY PECKHAM *(reduced to politeness)*. Ah! Yes...very interesting, I'm sure....

By this they have disappeared.

SCENE III

It is Sunday, near lunch time. ELEANOR is alone in the gallery with her letters and papers. On the terrace a very noisy game is in progress. DOLLY GAUNTLETT's fresh young voice is heard, crying, "Run, Joan! No, not a straighter...she'll get you. Stop at Apollo. Oh, I knew she would! That's three games to them. Why didn't you stop at Apollo?" And then Joan's, cheerful but distracted: "But I have to do it in five, haven't I?"

DOLLY. Well you'd two to spare.

JOAN. No, I took three up.

OLIVER'S VOICE. Yes, she did...one to the Faun...and one to Diana...

DOLLY. Susan, you're no end of a shot. Let's play women against men... and Evan may run twice.

STROWDE'S VOICE. Miss Dorothy Gauntlett...do you know my age?

DOLLY. Fiddledeedee! Look how Joan runs.

JOAN. Tactful child!

ELEANOR walks to the window with a letter which she waves.

ELEANOR. Evan!

STROWDE. What s that? I'll come up.

DOLLY *(raising loud protest).* No, no, no! We can't play four.

ELEANOR. I won't keep him long.

DOLLY. Why do you desecrate the Sabbath by reading reports? Come down and play Straighters.

ELEANOR. I believe I last played Straighters, Dolly, the year before you were born.

DOLLY. Mother's a dab at it still.

The game thus checked, the players seem to be resting beneath the window.

SUSAN. Does that drawing in the library date its being invented?

DOLLY. It's older...because of the counting by chases. The tennis court was pulled down in seventeen-fifty...

STROWDE, a little the worse for his bout of Straighters, comes in by the turret door, and ELEANOR hands him the letter. The voices from below form a curious counterpoint to their talk.

OLIVER. It's only Rounders played straight up the Terrace.

ELEANOR. From Sir Curtis Henry.

STROWDE. What's he plaguing you for?

ELEANOR. Duddington's been at him.

STROWDE. He's been at me.

DOLLY. The paving makes your feet so hot... that's the worst.

ELEANOR. Why Sir Curtis should suppose that I could or would persuade you to stand as the Party nominee, I can't imagine.

SUSAN. Was this how Apollo and Diana got their arms broken?

STROWDE finishes the letter and gives it back.

STROWDE. Stockton-on-Crouch is growing agitated, evidently.

DOLLY. There used to be a rule in my young days not to touch the statues.

ELEANOR. But Duddington thinks you could carry it as an Independent, doesn't he?

STROWDE. Duddington's job as an election agent is to find the greatest common measure of agreement...

DOLLY. Oliver, fetch us a towel.

OLIVER. What for?

STROWDE....and to collar votes from Anarchists, Christadelphians, Anti-vivisectionists, members of the Flat Earth Society and old Uncle Tom Cobley and all.

DOLLY. We three females will then go dabble our six hot feet in the fountain.

STROWDE puts his head sharply out of the window.

STROWDE. Dolly, don't be a fool...you'll give yourselves frightful colds.

DOLLY. Silence, Methusaleh.

ELEANOR. Well, what shall I say to the valiantly tactful Sir Curtis?

DOLLY. Come along!

JOAN. No!

DOLLY. Joan Westbury...do you want me to carry you there like a sack of potatoes or a Sabine lady?

STROWDE. Give him a taste of your quality. You'll be a candidate yourself yet.

JOAN. I shall ask your mother to put you on a lowering diet, Dolly.

STROWDE. My part in the answer is that I'm still considering whether I'll stand at all.

DOLLY. I'd tuck Susan under my arm too for tuppence. Come along. Come along! If you stick to me you can't go wrong!

And DOLLY can be heard whooping triumphantly along the terrace. The other two follow her, their voices tell us.

SUSAN. Are you so hot?

JOAN. Only breathless...a little.

ELEANOR. Very well. I'll say that.

STROWDE turns to go, but turns again.

STROWDE. Have you read my notes on your report?

ELEANOR. I was just about to. You haven't told me what you make of it as a whole.

STROWDE. It's dull.

ELEANOR. The Industrial Birth-rate is not a lively subject. Perhaps Part Two upon Wages of Young Persons will amuse you more.

STROWDE. When is that to be ready?

ELEANOR. We still have the West Riding evidence to take.

STROWDE. Shall I do a draft in rhyme for you?

 Equal work for equal wages,

Boys and girls who read these pages!

Men and women through the ages!

Twelve disinterested sages

Have arrived by easy stages

At the...gages...cages....

But I fear my nonsense doesn't ring like Dolly's.

ELEANOR (*who has been looking at him very steadily for the last fen-moments*). Evan...since we passed the last of those proofs in September you haven't, as far as I know, done a stroke of work. You make a mock bow now and then to this Committee drudgery of mine . . .

STROWDE. It must be. But you enjoy it.

ELEANOR. As long as I'm busy I'm happy, I fear.

STROWDE. Don't be ashamed of that.

ELEANOR. Are we ever to begin our last volume?

STROWDE. Probably never. I'm sorry.

Her face does not change, magnanimity does not fail her.

ELEANOR. Well...give me good reason why, and we'll say no more about it.

His face does change. It softens; but the softening seems to age it rather. His eyes seek distances.

STROWDE. Do you remember the book's very first plan?

ELEANOR. Yes...if you confided it to me.

STROWDE. When it was to be called...long ago...The Philosophy of Machinery. A towering title!

ELEANOR. I was looking at your discarded chapters only the other day.

STROWDE. Any good?

ELEANOR. Very well written.

STROWDE (*with a touch of the schoolboy*). And a poser of a problem. I can quote my first sentence: How is the spirit of man to be given power over his prosperity? Most conscientiously we set to and rounded up the prosperous facts and counted the cost of them in four fat volumes. Only the problem remains.

ELEANOR. Quite so.

STROWDE (*in a tone that might almost be thought compassionate*). You still face the future, Eleanor?

ELEANOR (*with some humour*). It's coming.

STROWDE (*promptly responsive*). The prospects of the break-up of the atom don't alarm you.

ELEANOR. If we can break it up we can teach it how to behave...if we choose.

STROWDE. I ought to respect your confident sanity. It has been as a strong wall about my more domestic self these forty years. Father bequeathed it to you.

ELEANOR. I think so.

STROWDE. I'm not a bit like him?

ELEANOR. Not very.

STROWDE *(whimsically)*. Poor Mother!

ELEANOR *(gravely)*. No, I believe she was a very happy woman.

STROWDE *(remorseful)*. My dear...we've been happy...and thank you. Forgive the gibe.

ELEANOR. Is there anything I could have done you, Evan, that I have not?

STROWDE *(chivalrously candid)*. No indeed. You were fully yourself at sixteen. You have been unwearied in welldoing. And I'm still a naughty boy. But why is it, Eleanor, that for all your goodness and my cleverness, for all the assembled virtues of this jolly houseparty, and the good-will that's going begging throughout the world...how is it that we shan't establish the Kingdom of Heaven on earth by Tuesday week?

ELEANOR. We could be content with less.

STROWDE *(finely)*. I used to think that was one reason we failed.

ELEANOR. Yes. I have some sense, even some sense of humour...of my own. But I am still simple enough to wonder why.

STROWDE. For you have never found that the whole world's turmoil is but a reflection of the anarchy in your own heart?

ELEANOR. No.

STROWDE. That's where we differ, then.

She looks rather sadly across the gulf between them.

ELEANOR. I fear you have always kept up appearances a little with me.

STROWDE. I fear you have always believed in them.

ELEANOR. And I'm to end by confessing I know nothing about you.

STROWDE. Do you want to know more than what I mean to be up to next? This time, as it happens, I can't tell you...for the best of reasons. Mischief, perhaps.

ELEANOR. Yes...you're a naughty boy at heart.

STROWDE *(with a dash of impatience)*. Where the devil else can one be anything at all? Have you never gone adventuring...dear good Eleanor...in your secret heart?

ELEANOR *(her curbed resentment just evident)*. I notice you call me good in the tone you might tell your wife...if you had one...that she was pretty.

STROWDE. And then I escape to where there is neither prettiness nor goodness.

ELEANOR. I let you. Would she?

STROWDE. Is that why I haven't married?

ELEANOR. I have never enquired into your relations with women...

STROWDE (*brotherly in the extreme*). My dear...don't talk like a Scottish divine addressing King Charles the Second!

ELEANOR. I have supposed that as a rule they weren't very civilised.

STROWDE. Possibly not...though possibly not in your sense of the word. For civilisation formulates vice as it formulates virtue, doesn't it...and I'm not interested in formulas.

ELEANOR (*dismissing sophistry*). Our work together is to end then. Well... if you're going into Bellingham's government...if you're going to marry Joan Westbury...

STROWDE (*not quite to be treated so, but wielding his own weapons*). And civilise the relation.

ELEANOR. I hadn't Joan in mind...and please don't pretend to think it.

STROWDE. But the angels in heaven, you know, are not what we should call civilised.

ELEANOR. When these trifles are settled, no doubt you'll tell me.

LADY PECKHAM, as from Church, and, as usual, in the best of spirits, comes in by the turret door. She is followed by MR KITTREDGE.

LADY PECKHAM. Morning, Evan.

STROWDE. Been to Church?

LADY PECKHAM. Sitting among the tombs of the Serocolds. I believe I wrecked my youthful eyesight sight reading those epitaphs in sermon-time.

MR. KITTREDGE. I was whisperingly commanded to translate the Latin ones.

LADY PECKHAM. I accept your translations, Mr Kittredge.

MR. KITTREDGE. There are more ways than one of reading most epitaphs.

LADY PECKHAM. I'd better write my own.

MR. KITTREDGE. The work of a lifetime!

STROWDE. Stephen go with you?

LADY PECKHAM. Haven't seen him.

STROWDE. In your absence the effigies are left, I fear, to set a rather chilly example.

LADY PECKHAM. Stephen ought to go to Church when he's here. It's not fair to the Rector. I like going. I much prefer saying my prayers in public...and it's the only place where they'll let me sing.

From the other end of the gallery comes DOLLY's voice, strepitant, with " Evan... stand still...you're the winning post...stick your arms out." STROWDE does as he is bid, and the rest gaze. MR KITTREDGE obligingly clears a chair from the course. We hear a skurrying. DOLLY and JOAN are racing down the gallery neck and neck. The winning post reached, JOAN flings herself in a chair, with an "Ay de mi!". DOLLY is barefoot; a strapping young lady of twenty, abounding in healthy, thoughtless vigour.

DOLLY. Did I win?

STROWDE. Not you!

DOLLY. Oh...I lose a pound...and I wanted one badly. You're nowhere!

This last is addressed to SUSAN KITTREDGE who comes in conscientiously, a bad third. MR KITTREDGE shakes a humorously solemn head at her.

MR. KITTREDGE. Susan, if you mean to invest your small capital in racing you must do better.

DOLLY *(the sport!).* No...she wasn't to pay if she lost...because she thinks betting's wrong.

SUSAN. I don't. I only said I didn't bet.

DOLLY. What about bare feet over the gravel for a handicap anyway?

SUSAN. I caught my dress on the big door.

ELEANOR. Joan...ought you to run like that?

JOAN *(sunnily triumphant).* But I won!

ELEANOR, after this grave and spectacled remonstrance, returns to reading her report. The rest of the company settle themselves at ease, DOLLY in the window seat, oblivious to chills. MR. KITTREDGE sets the talk to a smooth flow again.

MR. KITTREDGE. A granddaughter is a terrifying responsibility for an ignorant old man whose business it has been to theorise about life. But I think it a subtle form of cruelty to children to educate them in ideals that the world they will emerge into never means to abide by. So I try to fix Susan's attention upon the simple arithmetic of things. Is that wise?

LADY PECKHAM. Mr Kittredge, you're a most accomplished flirt, and I only wish I were up to your form. Bait Eleanor for a bit...she's intellectual. I'll look on..

MR. KITTREDGE. Miss Strowde is entrenched against frivolity.

ELEANOR *(over the edge of the report).* No.

MR. KITTREDGE. But it's true. As my spirit outwears its fleshly trammels I feel in it the stirrings of a quite reckless youth.

Here a towel comes flying through the window. DOLLY, with ready skill, catches it.

DOLLY. Thank you, Oliver.

STROWDE. Did you feel an older man at fifty, sir?

MR. KITTREDGE. Much .

STROWDE. That's cheering.

DOLLY *(as a matter of general interest).* Mother...I've cut my great toe.

LADY PECKHAM. Wash it with Condy.

DOLLY *(and with some pride).* It's bleeding.

LADY PECKHAM. I don't believe I've ever felt any particular age. I sleep like a log...I don't dream...and every morning at half-past seven I wake up wide and say to myself: Hullo, here I am again.

STROWDE. Good for you, Mildred. Be grateful.

MR. KITTREDGE. What do you find fifty's worse symptom, Mr. Strowde?

STROWDE. That it's easy to stop and hard to begin.

MR. KITTREDGE. Yes...if one stops to think. Doing defeats itself. In disgust of mere doing men turn to destroy.

STROWDE. I'd enlist under Oliver for red revolution...but I don't think there'll be one if I enlist.

DOLLY *(her head out of the window)*. Do you hear that, Oliver?

OLIVER'S VOICE. No.

STROWDE. Or I might apply for his leavings in the City. Mildred...do you see me as a financier-philanthropist and a secret menace to the peace of Europe?

LADY PECKHAM. You talk worse nonsense than he does.

MR. KITTREDGE. We're all driven to talk nonsense at times...when no other weapon is left us against the masters of the world...who have made language and logic, you see, to suit their own purposes.

DOLLY. Got a handkerchief, Oliver?

OLIVER'S VOICE. Dash it, I fetched you a towel. Wipe your nose on the corner.

DOLLY *(as one who speaks the tongue that Milton spoke)*. I wish to blow my nose.

LADY PECKHAM. Really, Dolly!

DOLLY. Don't you want me to be clean?

LADY PECKHAM. Very, very clean, my darling...you'll never be godly.

DOLLY. Thank God!

SEROCOLD comes down the gallery.

SEROCOLD. Good morning, guests.

LADY PECKHAM. Just up?

SEROCOLD. Mildred...I was milking a cow on behalf of your breakfast at six-thirty.

STROWDE. No one believes that, Stephen.

SEROCOLD. It is very nearly true.

DOLLY. Uncle Stephen, will you lend me a pound?

SEROCOLD *(with ceremonially avuncular politeness)*. For how long is the accommodation required?

DOLLY. Till I can take you on at tennis.

SEROCOLD. I do not play tennis for money.

DOLLY. But how mean of you when you've got some!

SEROCOLD. No Bellingham for lunch.

LADY PECKHAM. Oh?

DOLLY. Well, he'd have been a bit tough...would Broken Bellows. That is a joke.

The joke, however, is ignored.

SEROCOLD. Telephones he has toothache. Not even neuralgia!

LADY PECKHAM. Evan, who told him you were here?

STROWDE. Stephen, I trust.

SEROCOLD. He invited himself...he told me he wanted to meet you by accident.

STROWDE. You are an incorrigible intriguer.

DOLLY. It's Oliver! The silly old snob won't lunch with a gaol-bird. Hurrah!

JOAN. Perhaps he has toothache.

SEROCOLD. You've not yet met our Prime Minister, Mr. Kittredge?

MR. KITTREDGE. Not for thirty years. I shall hope for another chance.

STROWDE. Don't. Well...I'm unfair to the creature, I suppose. I retain a perverse affection for him. But the worst of democracy, don't you find, sir, is that it tends to breed these low forms of political life. You could slice bits out of Bellingham and each bit would wriggle off...and he'd find them all seats in Parliament and make them under-secretaries.

DOLLY. Vote for Brooke Bellingham...our only bulwark against Bolshevism.

SEROCOLD. Dolly...I'll send you electioneering.

STROWDE. Think of it. A line of alliteration between us and the abyss.

OLIVER'S VOICE. A bas Belinjam! Conspuez Brooke.

LADY PECKHAM (*as one who is really anxious for the information*). D'you think it's coming?

MR. KITTREDGE. Why, we are living already, you may say, under a dictation of the intellectual proletariat...and how few of us complain! Yes, I think we must finally be ruled by the people who provide us with what we want most in the world. Comforts, power, or wisdom. Artisan, king, or philosopher. Which will you exalt?

STROWDE. Not the philosopher, Mildred.

LADY PECKHAM. Think not? Why not?

STROWDE. He'll always be finding fresh things for you to do without. That makes his job easy for him.

LADY PECKHAM (*cheerily*). I wouldn't mind a revolution...if Oliver and you and Stephen would run it.

SEROCOLD. I will not. I'm tired.

LADY PECKHAM. But save us from cads.

MR. KITTREDGE. Amen.

STROWDE. Yes, when we consider what the gentlemen have been capable of occasionally, God knows what the cads may do.

ELEANOR (*to give - for Mr. Kittredge's benefit - the conversation a seemlier turn*). You're a Conservative, I fancy, Mr. Kittredge...like most Americans I meet.

MR. KITTREDGE. You may call me a re-actionary, Miss Strowde. Me...as they say in my expressive country...for the divine right of kings, rather than the divine rights of property.

SEROCOLD *(the harassed farmer)*. Well, any one may have this property who likes....if they'll pay me five hundred a year to manage it for them.

LADY PECKHAM. Twenty years back, if we'd known it, was our time for a good revolution.

DOLLY. It's never too late to smash.

LADY PECKHAM. I don't want any more killing.

DOLLY *(radiant in the sunshine by the window)*. I tell you though..women are going to fight in the next war. And if we hurry up I can be in the Air Force. Susan, I'll come and bomb your little head off, first thing.

SUSAN *(with ' New England ' seriousness - as it is called elsewhere)*. Please do.

From now the talk flags and loosens a little.

SEROCOLD. How long do you stay in England, Mr. Kittredge?

MR. KITTREDGE. Will you promise me a General Election by November? Susan is studying politics, and she wants to see one.

LADY PECKHAM *(stupent)*. What on earth is she doing that for?

SEROCOLD. I can't promise.

ELEANOR *(with one of her rare smiles for the girl)*. I can provide you with more profitable study meanwhile.

SUSAN. Thank you, indeed. Lady Westbury says that she'll come back to Countesbury with us, Grand father.

JOAN. May I leave it at perhaps, for a little? But I've travelled Eastwards so much that it's time I went...West, isn't it?

DOLLY. D'you mean die?

JOAN. I didn't.

SEROCOLD. My dear Dolly!

DOLLY. That's what that means.

MR. KITTREDGE. Please do come and see us, Lady Westbury, sitting in blankets before our wigwams.

JOAN. What must I bring to trade with?

MR. KITTREDGE. Your heart.

SUSAN. Our woods are beautiful in the autumn.

JOAN. I thought you called it the Fall.

MR. KITTREDGE. That sounds too sad, don't you think? But by November we're tucked up in snow very often.

JOAN. I may go on to Japan. Eva Currie wants me to...to be there by Christmas.

LADY PECKHAM. Dolly, go and make yourself half way decent for lunch.

DOLLY *(who knows an order when she hears it)*. Mother.

STROWDE. Die...how we hate the word! and we none of us really believe we're going to.

LADY PECKHAM. I believe it.

STROWDE. Oh, we're ready to surrender what we've done with and don't value...

ELEANOR. The work of our minds lives on.

STROWDE. By taking thought to? Show me a living faith, and I'll show it you careless of life. Dolly there, in her pride of body...

DOLLY. I say!

STROWDE...would jump out of that window for sixpence.

DOLLY. I'll do it for a pound. Oliver's underneath.

STROWDE. But this world of the mind we've made for ourselves is cumbered with things that we won't let die. Ask Oliver...if I yield to temptation and go back to trying to help govern this ungrateful country whether he'll promise to see me decently assassinated when I've done my devilmost?

DOLLY (her head out of the window). Oliver, will you please see Evan decently assassinated?

OLIVER'S VOICE. It hasn't been settled yet who's to be let off living...but he may choose his lamp-post on the chance.

STROWDE. You'll be content, Mildred, if a little of you lives on in that child?

LADY PECKHAM. Heaven forbid I should worry her!

DOLLY. What a disgusting thought!

SEROCOLD. Then don't you think it.

DOLLY. I won't!

And, every bit herself, she sets out down the gallery.

STROWDE. Dolly, I'll toss you for a pound.

DOLLY (at this gleam of great hope). Oo! Suppose I lose.

STROWDE. A month's credit.

DOLLY. Oo!

But, too fearful of the risk, DOLLY disappears.

STROWDE. The life of the mind is a prison in which we go melancholy mad. Better turn dangerous...and be done away with.

DOLLY's voice is heard from the end of the gallery.

DOLLY. Evan.

STROWDE. Hullo!

DOLLY. I'll risk it. Heads!

STROWDE takes out a coin and tosses it.

MR. KITTREDGE. There is, of course, that faculty we call the soul by which we may escape into uncharted regions.

STROWDE. Heads it is!

DOLLY (her voice is fervent). Thank God!

MR. KITTREDGE. But the rulers of men seldom seek them. Very naturally!

JOAN. Why?

MR. KITTREDGE. A confusing place, the world where the soul wanders ...made of mud and light...and the mud sticks and the light dazzles. Lonely...yet in it we can keep nothing of our own. For entering we abandon everything but hope...and hope is a lure.

JOAN. Towards what?

MR KITTREDGE. This is a secret.

JOAN. They can overhear.

MR. KITTREDGE.....well known, and disbelieved. It's so discouraging. The soul of man is in the making still...we are experiments to be tried again and yet again...and the light lures us to extinction. Can you rule a country prosperously on such a creed? No...have a comfortable kingdom of Heaven just round the corner...or who will take a step towards it?

STROWDE. Besides, Stephen, you don't want this country governed.

SEROCOLD. Truthfully, I think we want it kept amused at the moment...till we see what's going to happen next.

The three men begin to move down the gallery. SUSAN, attentive, has already been standing fora moment or two by the turret door. Some moments ago too, ELEANOR came to the end of her report and her brother's notes on it, and she has been sitting - her face unchanging, but particularly still.

STROWDE. So I'm not your man.

ELEANOR. Evan.

STROWDE *(pausing)*. Yes.

ELEANOR *(a little cryptically)*. Are these notes for vulgar reading?

STROWDE *(even more so)*. My legacy to you.

MR. KITTREDGE *(casually, to his host)*. I don't quite understand why Mr. Bellingham hasn't dissolved before this.

SEROCOLD. We can't get defeated in the House on any likely issue.

STROWDE. Prisoned minds, Mr. Kittredge...and a world of power to be wielded that might stagger the purpose of a Caesar. What the deuce will happen next? For all that I don't much care, I shake in my shoes.

The three men have disappeared.

LADY PECKHAM. What notes, Eleanor?

ELEANOR. Evan poking fun at my report.

SUSAN goes out by the turret door. The three women, without looking, are conscious of her disappearance.

LADY PECKHAM. That's a strange, still girl. Is she stone cold inside, or just on the boil?

JOAN. I see great beauty in her.

LADY PECKHAM *(her eyebrows up)*. Do you!

JOAN. It'll shine out in time.

LADY PECKHAM. I don't understand Americans. They're so solemn.

JOAN, light of foot, moves slowly down the gallery.

    ELEANOR. They take things seriously.

    LADY PECKHAM. And so devilish gay when they' re gay.

    ELEANOR. I don't find them hard to understand.

A moment's silence, now that the two are alone; then LADY PECKHAM cocks her head with what,unkindly, might be called a grin.

    LADY PECKHAM. We two old harridans, Eleanor!

    ELEANOR *(mustering enough humour)*. Thank you.

    LADY PECKHAM. Between us, I expect, we've tasted most of the fat and the lean of life. Well...nothing tastes like it.

    ELEANOR. You're worried about Oliver.

    LADY PECKHAM. Not a bit.

    ELEANOR. What took him to that meeting? Who encourages him in this foolishness?

    LADY PECKHAM. I think he spins it out of his own inside.

    ELEANOR. Well, as long as he behaves himself!...

    LADY PECKHAM. I hope he'll do more than that.

    ELEANOR *(with a will-not-be-exasperated sigh)*. We're at odds, I'm afraid, Mildred.

    LADY PECKHAM *(plumply)*. We always were.

The distant lunch gong is heard.

    LADY PECKHAM . I should get Evan married to Joan Westbury if I were you. That might settle him. Or are you too jealous of her?

    ELEANOR. What an amazing question!

    LADY PECKHAM. You're so consistent, Eleanor...that's what's the matter with you.

    ELEANOR. There's little I could do...in any case.

    LADY PECKHAM. Were you ever in love?

ELEANOR, for a second, does not mean to answer.
Then - why shouldn't she ?

    ELEANOR. Once.

    LADY PECKHAM. What happened?

    ELEANOR *(after a moment's appropriate emptiness)*. Nothing.

    LADY PECKHAM. I believe you. *(She doesn't in the least mean this to be brutal; commiserative rather. Then she goes on)* If you hate Joan, try putting a little poison in her soup...and then getting on your knees to ask God to forgive you for it. That'd teach you something.

They have collected their belongings, and make a move now for lunch.

    ELEANOR. A little hard on her!

    LADY PECKHAM. Well, considering everybody in this world means considering nobody, you know....

They pass down the gallery.

SCENE IV

It is Sunday evening about ten o'clock (summer time). Joan is sitting alone by the open window; the clear sky still glows a little. She has turned out the light near her, but those farther down the gallery are apparent. After a moment OLIVER's voice is heard from below.

OLIVER. Lady Westbury.

JOAN. Yes.

OLIVER. May I come up?

JOAN. You may. *(When his way of coming up is apparent she calls out)* Oliver! You'll kill yourself!!

His head and shoulders appear at the window. He stops, a little breathless. This is something of a feat for a one-armed man, though a creeper may be helping him a little.

OLIVER. That wasn't so bad. Now comes the pull. If you take hold we'll both tumble. Hold your breath and think hard. Now!

With a great effort he flings himself over the window-sill into the room, and rolls on the floor. But he picks himself up lightly enough.

OLIVER. And I'm not drunk, am I?

JOAN. You shouldn't run such risks.

OLIVER. I was last night...on one half glass of claret. Nobody noticed. To-night I've had a bottle of port to my own whack...and I'm so sober that it hurts. May I sit and talk to you?

JOAN. Yes.

He sits on the window-seat facing her, not very close.

OLIVER. Shall I try not to talk about myself?

JOAN. No, I'd like you to.

But not many people would find her easy to talk to at all, she is so still and so aloof. There is a little silence.

OLIVER. Why won't Evan take me on?

JOAN. He hasn't told me.

OLIVER. They say you're going to marry him.

JOAN *(her eyebrows lifting)*. Do they? *(Then whimsically)* Well...shall I?

OLIVER. Don't ask me. I'm in love with you too.

She lets the simple speech find its full value in her ears, then says as simply...

JOAN. Thank you, Oliver.

OLIVER *(in a happy, quite childish surprise)*. D'you mean it?

JOAN. Didn't you expect so much as a thank you?

OLIVER. May I say just once...I love you..like that? The echoes won't be troublesome.

They have not moved, either of them. She is listening in the stillness to other boys' voices

JOAN. I live among echoes, my dear. But you mustn't.

OLIVER. I won't. *(His voice hardens to a perversely obstinate tone)* What am I to do, please, if Evan won't take me on?

JOAN. Is he your only hope?

OLIVER *(With deliberation)*. He's in my way.

JOAN. What does that mean?

OLIVER. Sounds like a plot to blow him sky high one day as he walks into Downing Street. I think I did make Uncle Stephen believe at dinner that I'd been sworn into at least one secret society...for all he pretended not to.

JOAN. It's Mr. Serocold's business, I suppose, to take such things seriously.

OLIVER. Yes, it is. So why doesn't he? Tell them the truth and they don't believe you!

JOAN. I will.

OLIVER. The men with the secrets that count will know each other when the time comes, won't they?

JOAN. Yes, that sounds more dangerous.

OLIVER. There'll be nothing doing else.

JOAN. Why is Evan in your way?

OLIVER *(launched on the full youthful enjoyment of a talk about oneself)*. I wonder what it is in one that picks out a man or a woman. Evan was picked out for me, you may say. Mother has always been fond of him. My father was fond of him. I remember saying once, when I was eight, that I meant to grow up to be like him.

JOAN. And you're not fond of many people.

OLIVER. I hate most people...when I come to think of it.

JOAN. Is that why it hurts you to be sober?

OLIVER. I shall swear off drink again, though...it just doesn't do not to know what a glass of claret's going to cost you.

One half of her disposition towards him is as simple (though by no means the same) as his towards her. But the other half is - in involuntary defence perhaps coloured by the ironic superiority of forty something to twenty something.

JOAN. But tell me how one soberly hates people. I don't think I know.

OLIVER. Well, you can't love the mob, surely to goodness! Because that's to be one of them...chattering and scolding and snivelling and cheering...maudlin drunk, if you like! I learned to be soldier enough to hate a mob. There's discipline in Heaven. If I can't love a thing I must hate it.

JOAN. How long have you been so unhappy?

OLIVER. Don't think I'm out after happiness, please.

JOAN *(gravely)*. Do you ever pray, Oliver?

OLIVER *(prompt)*. All the time. Whenever I'd a hard job on in the City I'd walk there in the morning praying like fun. If I hadn't prayed my way in at this window I'd have broken my neck. I pray all the time.

JOAN. How old are you? I forget. His face takes on a deeper shade than any and all the fantastic flourish goes out of speech.

OLIVER. I believe I'm still eighteen.

JOAN. How's that?

OLIVER. Years don't count for much, do they as against memory, say? Parts of me seem to forget all about the war...but there's some part of me doesn't. A shell missed me outside Albert and did for my watch. I could shake it and it would tick for a bit...but the spring was gone. I've an idea I don't grow any older now...and when I come to die it'll seem an odd out-of-date sort of catastrophe. I'm furious that I'm still alive at all. Perhaps it's that makes me hate people. I used to pray night after night at school that I'd be killed when I got to France.

JOAN (moved, but more deeply by memories). That was perverse of you...to be fighting against our prayers.

OLIVER. Oh, once I was there I didn't mind saving my skin. But I tell you...this is a beast of a world to have left on one's hands.

A little silence; then Joan rallies to the commonplace.

JOAN. Well, what are you going to do about it?

OLIVER. Destroy.

JOAN. What?

OLIVER. All I can learn to.

JOAN. Didn't you see enough destruction?

OLIVER. A futile sort. My firm bought a lot of shares, and we thought we had a mine in Eastern Galicia...so I was sent out two years ago to see. The town was a rubbish heap. Typhus had done well too. But there they were breeding children to build it all up again...that being the cheapest way. So if we can't do some better destroying than that who'll ever be able to make a fresh start? Save me from weary people with their No More War. What we want is a real one.

JOAN. And where's the enemy?

OLIVER. If I knew where I shouldn't be sitting here, helpless. I'm looking for him. But we're tricked so easily...on from the time that we're tricked into getting born! This world's all tricks, isn't it? Well, it's something to feel free from the greedy instinct to, live.

JOAN (puzzled, kindly, and as curious as it is in her to be). And what has Evan to teach you?

OLIVER. I want to find out how it is he has failed.

JOAN. Has he failed, then?

OLIVER (a trifle savagely). Yes...and you'll have to comfort him for it if you marry him.

JOAN (provokingly, rather). But wise men like your uncle say that if he'll take office again, now the bunglers have had a chance...there's his career still. And he wasn't a failure in office before.

OLIVER. He'll need more comfort than that, if I'm right about him. Nothing's much easier, is it, than to make that sort of success if you've the appetite for it. Find a few ready-made notions to exploit. But Evan set out to get, past all tricks, to the heart of things...didn't he? Don't you know? Don't you love him? Are you weary of the puzzle too?

JOAN. The very tallest of us ask for comfort sometimes.

OLIVER. Is it a stone dead heart of things...and, dare no one say so when he finds out?

JOAN. I suppose one would never dare.

OLIVER. Evan won't take me on because he's afraid of me.

JOAN (the one-time mother in her sharply asserting itself) Nonsense!

OLIVER. I can tell he's afraid of me. Why? Because he knows that I know he has failed. And he knows that I hate him for it.

JOAN. Very wicked nonsense, Oliver!

OLIVER (flinging out harshly). Oh, do him in with comfort if you like. Trick him. Do your best, dear Evan, and no man can do more in this worst-of-all possible worlds! If he had any self-respect left in him he'd thank you to hate him rather.

JOAN (with a flash of inspiration). You're very like him.

OLIVER (struck, though he could not say why). Am I?

JOAN. Oh...not in any ordinary sense.

OLIVER. We're all like mother to look at...more or less.

A short silence, while they turn back from this blind alley.

JOAN (lightly enough). And how is it...with all else to be thrown on the rubbish heap...that you love me?

OLIVER. You're out of reach.

JOAN (as if she did indeed, and better than ever he could...). Yes...I understand.

OLIVER. So I'm not jealous of the fellow. But I rather wish I hadn't told you.

JOAN. Why?

OLIVER (boyhood having its way). Or that you'd laughed...that would set me free again. Please set me free.

JOAN. Am I to ask Evan to take you on?

OLIVER (obsessed). Yes...for I want to be free of him too. Somehow he's right athwart my understanding of things, though I can't tell why. And I won't take a step that I can't see clear. Then I shan't take many...is the answer. I've been told that before.

JOAN. If you came to understand him you might learn not to hate him.

OLIVER. Yes, there's that danger!

Joan surveys him for a moment, then says with evident intent...

JOAN. Oliver...you never laugh now, I've noticed.

OLIVER. At myself?

JOAN. Well, that's a simple form of destruction. You might try it to begin with.

He stands up, stung, as she meant he should be.

OLIVER. Good night.

JOAN. I've made you angry.

OLIVER *(pride quite forbidding response)*. No. I was off on my walk when I saw you at the window.

JOAN. Every night...wet or fine...how many miles?

OLIVER. Seven or eight...till I'm too tired to think.

JOAN *(more sorrowful for him than she can say, or he could understand)*. The night is all one's own, isn't it...if only the inconsiderate sun wouldn't rise.

OLIVER *(taking refuge in bravado)*. Is this how you comfort me? There's no need, thank you. I've not failed yet. *(Then, for a last shot, as with charming impudence)* Good night, Joan.

JOAN. But mind your prayers, Oliver. *(He turns, rather amazed.)* For innermost prayers are answered...they must be...and in mockery sometimes.

OLIVER. Something in me was killed, d'you think?

JOAN Not stone dead, we'll hope.

OLIVER. No, Joan...we won't hope, whatever else we do.

He opens the door into the turret.

JOAN. Not by the window again?

OLIVER. Too easy.

JOAN *(in the same soft clear voice that welcomed him)*. Good night, then, my dear.

He goes away.

SCENE V

It is Monday morning, a little after nine. SIR LESLIE HERIOT, in motoring things, comes striding along as if looking for some one. He is an ebullient, middle-aged man, pleasant, coarse-grained, and always a little louder than, we'll hope, he means to be. If anything is written quite unmistakably upon him, it is success and an intense enjoyment of it. He glances out of the window; then faces down the gallery again just as STROWDE's voice is heard from the other end .

STROWDE. Hullo, Heriot.

HERIOT. Hullo, Strowde.

STROWDE. What are you doing here?

HERIOT. Came to run Stephen up to town. Good morning, Miss Strowde.

ELEANOR'S VOICE. Good morning, Sir Leslie.

STROWDE appears. ELEANOR must be lagging behind.

STROWDE. You must have left early.

HERIOT. Seven o'clock. I've not been at home...week-ending at Eckersley...it's sixty miles..; the road must be better through Basingstoke. How are you?

STROWDE. I'm alive.

SIR LESLIE takes up an habitual "I-never-beat-about-the-bush" attitude.

HERIOT. Get any talk with Bellingham yesterday?

STROWDE. He didn't come.

HERIOT *(flavourishly)*. I knew he wouldn't.

STROWDE. How's your job nowadays?

HERIOT *(who, oddly enough, is really a modest soul)*. There's enough to do without making more. But I'm up to the trick of it this time. Let your office fellows pull the cart while you drive.

STROWDE. That is undoubtedly the whole art of government.

HERIOT *(as one who reverences the process)*. And take time to think. I used to keep my nose buried in papers eight hours a day. Now I send for the men who write them...there's a new lot of quite good young men...and size them up instead. *(Turning his head)* How is my Women's Industry committee getting on, Miss Strowde?

ELEANOR now appears.

ELEANOR. We're making the interim report you asked for.

HERIOT *(with entire honesty)*. Did I?

ELEANOR. Though I think it's a pity to mangle the subject.

HERIOT. Oh no...no, no! Be practical...that's the great thing. *(He just does not smack STROWDE on the back)* Does this fellow help you out at all?

ELEANOR, who how surprising! has not come to talk to SIR LESLIE, is searching the writing-table.

ELEANOR. Surely I did leave my spectacles....

STROWDE *(answering HERIOT)*. Not at all.

HERIOT. And the great history's finished?

ELEANOR. No.

HERIOT. I hear you're coming out into politics.

ELEANOR. I think not.

HERIOT. But do...it's great fun. No, perhaps you're right. We need intellectual spade-work...

STROWDE *(having found the spectacles)*. Here they are.

ELEANOR. Thank you.

HERIOT *(magnanimously overriding the neglect of him for a pair of spectacles)*. And I take off my hat...I do indeed...to this steady self-sacrifice of all personal ambition by which public men profit...or should profit. *(Then in his never-beat-about-the-bush attitude again)* Strowde...have we got to fight you at the election?

STROWDE. Who said I was going to stand?

HERIOT *(omniscient)*. But you are.

ELEANOR has now passed out of sight.

STROWDE. I ve been asked to.

HERIOT. I know all about it.

STROWDE. When is it to be...secrets apart?

HERIOT *(as colleague to colleague)*. I doubt if the old man has started to make up his mind. November...February. We could drop the Insurance Bill if the Chinese business would straighten out.

STROWDE. You think you'll come back?

HERIOT. Who else can? *(As brother to brother)* Look here...is it only Bellingham stands in the way?

STROWDE. Of...?

HERIOT....your coming back to us?

STROWDE *(blandly)*. Oh, dear, no.

HERIOT. What else?

STROWDE. Why do you want me?

HERIOT *(benevolent, warm, but, one fears, patronising)*. My dear fellow...am I to flatter you?

STROWDE *(a shade subtly!)* If you think it advisable.

HERIOT. Well, I won't. I'll come straight to the point. I came here this morning to come to the point with you.

STROWDE *(as he would encourage a child)*. Good.

HERIOT now speaks, as he would tell you, with a due sense of the subject's importance.

HERIOT. It's two years since I told Bellingham how vital I felt it to be for the Party to get you back. I've given him till now to make it up with you. Well, now I'm ready to say that sine qua non...sine qua non me!...We must find you a seat again, and a seat in the Cabinet, after the election.

STROWDE *(easily).* I've found the seat, Heriot.

HERIOT. Even if we fight you there?

STROWDE. Do your damnedest.

HERIOT. I don't want to.

STROWDE now takes the rudder.

STROWDE. Bellingham's getting a bit feeble, is he?

HERIOT *(innocently pricking an ear).* D'you hear people say that?

STROWDE. If he'll take me at your dictation it'll show the Gang, won't it, that you've got a strangle hold on him? And it'll show you that he feels you've got the Party behind you.

HERIOT *(playfully disapproving).* That's very tortuous.

STROWDE. Tortuous...but not very tortuous.

HERIOT *(the statesman again).* Bellingham is a leader to whom I have been consistently loyal...and to whom I shall be as consistently loyal as long as he is my leader. Does that imply that I am to sacrifice the interests of the Party rather than...put pressure on him?

STROWDE *(aggravatingly unimpressed).* How soon do you think you'll be strong enough to kick him out?

HERIOT *(with true dignity).* Strowde...I cannot humour your brutality. I am a realist, I hope...but matters of this magnitude do surely demand a certain amenity of mind for their discussion.

STROWDE *(all unmoved).* As a detached observer, I've been giving you a couple of years.

HERIOT *(nearing exasperation).* If you think this intellectual ruthlessness of yours is a strength, you're wrong...it's a weakness. People don't answer to it...and political facts most certainly never answer to it.

STROWDE *(tart).* What the devil, my dear Heriot, is a political fact?

HERIOT *(placable).* Now, now, don't let's begin generalising. We're men of affairs. As an under-secretary the old man declares he never knew what you'd say next. No wonder he thinks that in the Cabinet you'll be the death of him.

STROWDE. I daresay I should be.

HERIOT *(ignoring that point).* But I tell him we must consider your essential value. You certainly will find him feebler. But after a year or two of the old hard grind I'm pretty confident you'd find yourself...subdued to what you work in.

STROWDE. And with?

HERIOT. Or with. The potter's hand! Statesmanship...so I phrase it...*(and he enjoys phrasing it)*...is the art of dealing with men as they most illogically are, and with the time as it nearly always most unfortunately is. We hope for a better...we strive for a better. Never let us cease to proclaim that.

But the day's work must be done.

Upon which wise maxim he comes to a full close.

STROWDE *(casually).* You're making a fool of yourself over the Trusts.

HERIOT *(who is a keen picker-up of good ideas).* D'you think so? Why do you think so?

STROWDE. Your figures are wrong.

HERIOT. They're official figures.

STROWDE. They'll mean nothing two years hence. If the Act makes the business attractive its finance will be swamped...and if it doesn't the big companies won't work it...then the little ones can't.

HERIOT swallows this, somewhat wryly. But, confound it, Strowde is worth having to work with.

HERIOT. Destructive criticism...not to be ignored on that account ...Salomons said something of the sort to me six months ago. But we are faced with the demand for a bill.

STROWDE. It being the business of the legislature to legislate.

HERIOT. God knows I'd be glad to drop it. But that'd only make room for the emergence of several most awkward questions...just as the election's coming on. Well, if nobody works the damned act at least it can't do any harm *(and he throws the business where he so safely throws all business, upon the stream of time).* Where were we?

STROWDE *(casually).* Do you miud my sister joining the discussion?

HERIOT. Not at all. *(and glad to re-assert some superiority)* I never make mysteries.

STROWDE *(lifting his voice a trifle).* Eleanor...spare us a minute.

HERIOT. And I'm sure Miss Strowde is the soul of discretion.

ELEANOR appears again.

ELEANOR. Yes.

STROWDE *(an enigmatic eye on Eleanor).* We two have worked in unison for so long.

HERIOT, with a second person and a woman! to deal with, becomes very oracular.

HERIOT. Well...to write history or to make it ...that is the question.

ELEANOR *(dryly, finely).* The writing should warn one to be rather more particular in the making, Sir Leslie.

STROWDE *(the unkindness pleasantly masked).* The practical question is... could Heriot and I between us get rid of Bellingham the sooner? I might put that problem to the old gentleman if he sends for me.

HERIOT *(with a gape).* Thank you.

STROWDE. Adding, of course, that you scouted very idea when I so much as hinted it...as you do.

HERIOT. I naturally do.

STROWDE *(hitting clean).* That's your method. It isn't mine. In some things perhaps I'm even less of a mystery-maker than you. Bellingham's sixty-seven. He has poor health. He has been twice Prime Minister. He ought to be able to measure by now the amount of annoyance he can endure. And you don't suppose that when you were putting your sine qua non this idea didn't occur to him.

HERIOT *(brought to something very like sulkiness).* I can't help his suspicious nature.

STROWDE. But if we didn't get rid of him the sooner the intermediate friction would not, on the balance, be profitable to the country. *(Then, venturing rather far in irony)* And we must think of our country, Heriot.

HERIOT. Your humour eludes me.

STROWDE *(infinitely business-like and cheerful).* Then there's a further possible question...how long would it take me after to get rid of you?

To this, however, HERIOT rises, happily, like a man.

HERIOT. I bet you a thousand pounds you don't.

STROWDE. I'll bet you a set of my history in half calf to the Premiership that I do.

HERIOT. Let's be serious. Serocold's waiting for me.

STROWDE. You repeat your offer?

HERIOT. What's your alternative?

STROWDE. Shall I sit below the gangway and snipe at you?

HERIOT. You've been getting your eye in lately, I've noticed.

STROWDE. The Chinese meeting? You deserved that.

Recovering his vantage. He is, after all, a Minister of State, and Strowde-!

HERIOT. Excellent speech. Personally, I'd be grateful to you. Fighting keeps me up to the mark...and with a timid public opinion it's the man in office who scores. Look at this present opposition...sitting like a row of turnips...

STROWDE *(finely).* Or shall I stick to intellectual spade-work?

HERIOT *(who, within his range, be it noted, is anything but a fool).* You won't. You're restless. You'll get back to the House and you won't have enough to do there. You'll grow depressed and dyspeptic and you'll take to making acid interruptions inaudible in the press gallery. You'll find yourself chief of a little group of righteous high-brows in passionate agreement upon abstract principles, without an interest in common and considering themselves insulted if you ask them to vote solid.

STROWDE *(with some genuine admiration).* Now here is a wise man, Eleanor...a disillusioned man.

HERIOT *(genuinely pleased with the compliment).* Don't look at me so sternly, Miss Strowde.

ELEANOR. It's an effect of the sunlight on my spectacles, Sir Leslie. Please forgive them!

HERIOT'S glance goes by chance down the gallery.

HERIOT. Who's this?

STROWDE. Lady Westbury.

HERIOT. Do I know her?

STROWDE. You must have known Mark Westbury.

HERIOT. Oh yes...useful fellow...Egypt did for him.

So much for Mark. STROWDE sticks to his hard jesting.

STROWDE. If you really want to ease matters with Bellingham I should tell him of our bet. The prospect of a fight over the inheritance would amuse him. He wouldn't think the worse of you...and he'd like me the better for it.

HERIOT *(ruefully appreciative)*. So he would...the old scoundrel!

JOAN appears.

JOAN. Good morning.

SIR LESLIE beamingly descends on her.

HERIOT. How d'you do, Lady Westbury? I fear you don't remember me...Leslie Heriot.

JOAN *(with shadowless courtesy)*. Yes, indeed. You once gave me tea in your big room in Whitehall after my husband had been waiting for you three hours and a half.

HERIOT *(to encourage her)*. Strong Indian tea...and you hated it.

JOAN *(poising the words)*. Not the tea, I'm sure.

HERIOT. The cake, then...office cake!

JOAN *(not having a mallet and chisel handy)*. Perhaps it was the cake.

Having made this success, SIR LESLIE turns the light of his assurance on STROWDE.

HERIOT. When are you coming to town, Strowde?

STROWDE. Wednesday morning.

HERIOT. Lunch with me.

STROWDE. All right.

HERIOT *(benevolent)*. Good-bye, Miss Strowde. Forgive me. You'll thank me. Don't think me a cynic. I respect ideals. But I test them...as life tests them.

STROWDE *(with a mischievous smile)*. My sister really thinks of us both as being about ten years old. I've been a trouble to her, Heriot...and her fear is now that I may corrupt your happy faith in life.

HERIOT *(infinitely robust)*. Try.

ELEANOR. Nothing would, Sir Leslie, I'm sure.

HERIOT *(in bright innocence)*. I do feel young...and look at the work I get through.

SEROCOLD'S VOICE is heard from the end of the gallery.

SEROCOLD. Heriot, are you ready?

HERIOT. Coming.

SEROCOLD. I must be at the office by eleven.

But STROWDE grapples him with a voice that has, indeed, more than a little steel in it.

STROWDE. But if we're to be fellow-conspirators, we must agree on a creed.

HERIOT. A programme?

STROWDE. The father and mother of a programme.

HERIOT. Well?

STROWDE *(adding, for re-assurance, a touch of humour)* I believe, for instance...Heriot, when I've won that bet I'll open Cabinet meetings by having this repeated, all standing...I believe that men cease to be fools to become knaves, and that we must govern them by fear and with lies. They will work under threat of starvation. Greed makes them cunning...

SEROCOLD'S VOICE. Evan...I shall be late back.

STROWDE. Wait a minute!...but desire makes them dangerous. If they rightly remembered yesterday, they wouldn't get out of their beds to-morrow. Sleep's the great ally of the rulers of this world...for it rounds each day with oblivion.

HERIOT never does quite knows when this fellow is serious.

HERIOT. That's a creed I should keep to myself.

STROWDE. That, I know, is the rule. But...as between souls of discretion ...don't you agree?

HERIOT. Seriously, I do not. And I take these things seriously, Strowde ...or I shouldn't be where I am. I am a democrat...with certain reservations. *(He interrupts himself for a benevolent...)* Good-bye, Lady Westbury.

JOAN. Good-bye.

HERIOT now takes STROWDE'S arm and starts down the gallery as a ship might leave a bay, with such swelling sails.

HERIOT. I have an almost unbounded faith in the ultimate perfectibility of man. I think that the political, the social, the ethical progress of the centuries are evidence of it. But mind you...the freer the democracy the firmer must be the guiding hands. Use force when necessary. And do not cxpect to find in the masses a grasp of the principles upon which we base our actions. Appeal rather to the heart of the people...

The two men disappear. The two women wait, smiles suppressed for a decent thirty seconds.

ELEANOR. Well?

JOAN *(evenly)*. I remember Mark saying after that interview...Deliver us from clean-shaven young Ministers, with busts of Napoleon on the mantelpiece. And he has grown vulgar.

ELEANOR. He caricatures himself now. Men of that crude and abounding vitality of mind seldom mature...fortunately. When they do they're dangerous. Evan shouldn't poke fun at him so resklessly.

JOAN. Oh...by the time the sting penetrates he's thinking of something else.

STROWDE returns.

STROWDE. One can't help liking him.

ELEANOR *(very definitely)*. I can.

STROWDE. You prefer people all of a moral piece. Our Heriots are stitchings from the rag-bag. There are sound bits in him. After all, we British have had the cutting up of some good minds for this last generation or so. He's not one of God's elect. However, he offers to represent us. The puzzled human elector finds a bit of his favourite stuff in the patchwork, and says...Ah, this is my man. Heriot has courage and good health...and he's a success.

ELEANOR. What is his offer worth?

STROWDE *(unexpectedly)*. It was worth while manoeuvring him into making it. The next move is Bellingham's. No hurry for mine.

And this seems, in a flash, to release ELEANOR from some inhibition. For she speaks as she has not yet spoken.

ELEANOR. Thank you for letting me hear your tallk, Evan. I see I can be no more use to you. You're my brother...I thought I knew you...you've become a stranger to me. I fear there's only one thing I believe in...choosing a cause to serve it singlemindedly. When you first took ofiice, after six months you rode open-eyed for a fall. I saw that, if no one else did. I worked at your book with you. Your brains went into it, no doubt. My life went into it. What does it mean to me to feel that if I burned every copy now, you'd hardly shrug your shoulders...and to find this task of mine...which you've taught me, and thank you...this report spattered with your mockeries! I sat up last night crying over it like a child over a copy-book. From to-day, please, let's pretend to be like-minded no more. Turn in your tracks and be the thing you despise. Does it matter? The curse is on you, it seems, of coming at last to despise whatever you do and are. I'm sorry...but I must save myself...my soul, if you like...from despair.

A silence follows, noticeable, though her voice was never lifted. Then STROWDE says, as quietly...

STROWDE. That's clearly put...and quite indisputable.

ELEANOR. Perhaps I shouldn't have said so much before you, Joan. Perhaps I've been right to.

STROWDE. I shall now have to advertise...Wanted, a political hostess.

He pauses, his sentence unfinished. In the silence ELEANOR, unhurriedly, but with neither another word nor a look, gets up and goes out by the turret door.

JOAN. Upright, downright Eleanor!

STROWDE *(as if following out his uninterrupted thought)*. Or will you save me a sovereign's worth of Agony column, Joan, and take the job?

She does not answer at once, and when she does, it is as if some other woman, far away, were speaking.

JOAN. No, I can t.

STROWDE looks at her; then refuses the words' meaning.

STROWDE. Am I to tell Bellingham and his gang, then, to go to the devil without me? By all means.

JOAN. That's another matter.

STROWDE. Do you mean you won't marry me, Joan?

JOAN. I can't.

Now he must take the meaning, and he does. He allows himself a moment to recover reasonableness.

STROWDE. How long since you made up your mind to say this? You could have given me some sign. I've been taking things too much for granted.

JOAN *(rather helplessly)*. I did, too.

STROWDE *(keeping control at the cost of a loosening rein)*. What has happened? What have I done? What has changed you?

JOAN *(dully, almost)*. I love you still.

STROWDE. Don't say that.

JOAN *(as if she would get to that far-away woman if she could)*. But...let me be.

STROWDE *(fiercely, even brutally)*. So I did!...

JOAN. Like a fool? You leave that unspoken. *(Then pitifully.)* Do I seem to be cheating you now?

STROWDE *(recovering reasonableness, kindliness too)*. Let's say no more for the moment. I see what's wrong. We mustn't try to live out the fag-end of a difficult past. We must start fresh.

JOAN *(with a little smile)*. When the war was at its worst, they say you were at your hopefullest. I see why they want you to work with...You'll lose little in losing the last of me.

He sits close by her, friendly, brotherly; but more.

STROWDE. I want you.

She turns and looks at him, eyes to eyes. But her look is fearful.

JOAN. How did you find your way into the dream that my true life is? I wish you never had. The selfish soul of me might have died the sooner, left lonely...and who'd have been the wiser then? I could have done my duty to the end...married again, even...headed a dinner-table...not yours, though!

She does her best to make light of the strange trouble; and he helps her.

STROWDE. Why not mine as well as another?

JOAN. Should I have liked you if I'd never loved you, I wonder?

STROWDE. The answer is that you did, you know.

JOAN. And we couldn't let well alone. But you're free of me now...I set you free. Oh, this has been a jealous devil, like all barren things.

STROWDE. Barren?

JOAN *(her voice non-echoing all the meaning of the dreadful word)*. Ask your heart...and your own life ever since...God forgive us! It isn't that one sits idle. I've known how to be kind...I've hated evil...when I've suffered loss I've suffered indeed. But none of it has truly mattered. My boys...yes, a bad blow. And when

Eleanor came tip-toeing with the news from Cairo I let grief have its will of me...I knew I so safely could...and I slipped the more easily out of its clutches back into my dream. And we agreed to be glad, you remember, that I could still care for Mark.

STROWDE. Yes. I said I understood that. I fear I lied to you. I never did.

JOAN. He was very good to me. So would you be. One must live honourably. But all the while I was half ashamed to be giving him what I valued so little. And you want what's left!

STROWDE. My dear, don't despise me for that. I won't lose your love in winning you.

JOAN. But you would.

STROWDE. Why? Why ever?

JOAN. We chose to dream. The empty beauty would vanish at a touch.

He sees defeat. But he tries to outflank it.

STROWDE. This is merely morbid, Joan.

JOAN *(responding readily enough to his common sense. This, truly, is what is so hopeless).* Isn't it? Try beating me. I've laughed at myself. I've prayed...these past weeks with your eyes on me...for some miracle to give birth in me to anything wholly human that I could bring you. *(With a sudden change of front, though.)* I do think that if I could once go quite obliviously to sleep I might wake up different.

STROWDE. I didn't know you weren't sleeping well again.

She turns a little desperate for a moment.

JOAN. Evan, has one to die to sleep? Well, surely then there'll be an end to this terrible constant consciousness of being...of purposeless being.

STROWDE. You're not, in your doctor's sense, ailing, are you, except for this? You've seemed so well and so gay.

JOAN. He can't make me sleep...and he can't keep me still. I'm one of Nature's pranks, I tell him...body and mind, quite conscienceless now, quite irresponsible.

He makes now a new and different effort.

STROWDE. You'd better marry me, Joan. I'll find you lots to do...work you to death by midnight. You shall sleep like a log and wake every morning a different woman. I'll be a perfectly selfish husband, I promise you. Think how a bride will deck my election platform! And you must flatter me, please, with constant affection...for my brainwork's too apt to be dry and cruel. And we shall need to go soft a little...to be genial. *(But the helpful irony breaks down quite)* Oh, my dear love! Oh, my dear...my dear!

She is helpless to sustain him.

JOAN. I'd so like to make you happy, too. And Oliver told me last night that he loved me.

STROWDE *(struck).* Why do you suddenly tell me that?

JOAN *(with no further intention)*. It's interesting and a propos. He was standing just where you're standing now. Do what you can for the boy. He finds life hard at the moment. Give him a hand.

STROWDE *(gravely deferent)*. If you say so.

JOAN. Thank you.

STROWDE. Give me yours.

With an amused smile she lifts it and looks at it ; rather disparagingly.

JOAN. This?

STROWDE *(as a friend)*. Marry me.

JOAN *(taking the privilege offered)*. Some other time! Oh, can't we pretend that there'll be some other possible time?

STROWDE. No other but the time one wastes and comes to want.

With baffling swiftness she has changed.

JOAN. And the eternity in which we met.

STROWDE. In which I won you.

JOAN. Yes, Evan...truly, utterly.

STROWDE *(violently breaking out)*. Don't mock me. There's nothing to separate us...and here we stand apart. *(He has not moved her, he has not even recalled her to this their battleground .)* Where are you, Joan...where are you?

She shakes her head sadly.

JOAN. Go to work and forget me.

STROWDE *(viciously)*. I'd better. Indeed, it has been a barren business...you're right.

JOAN. With everything real made bitter to you?

STROWDE. Worse, my dear...tasteless. And I've sampled much. Would it help to find things to forgive me?

JOAN *(with a half-smile)*. Oh, I've tried that.

STROWDE. Well, well...let nothing about me be a reproach to you. If I've only cared to believe the unbelievable and attempt the impossible...if that only ends in damnable impotence, what wonder! I lose you.

She is, by this, you would say, a little surprised at her own coldness.

JOAN. Yes, I won't keep you waiting for the miracle.

STROWDE. What sort of creatures are we to set up as spiritual ladies and gentlemen? Strength's in the mud that we're made of. Housekeeping and my career...but I'm not clever enough to get you safely tangled in that. I feel like a boy crossed in his first love affair. When we were out on the hill there yesterday, watching that rainbow, I was shaking standing beside you...you were so beautiful.

JOAN. The first double-rainbow I'd ever seen...except one in a book.

STROWDE. But even that didn't help!

She brings herself back to the world of passing things, but—ironically—it only prompts her to ask...

JOAN. What's the time, Evan?

STROWDE. Twenty to ten.

JOAN. I must go and say good-bye to Susan.

He is utterly defeated.

STROWDE. So our lives can't be made to fit...and here's an end. We two are evidently not the centre of a divinely appointed system of things.

JOAN. But you don't believe it is.

STROWDE. I've never found worse to say of it! Though if we're to keep some patient pity for our fellow-men, perhaps it's the best faith to hold. What do you mean to do, by the way, if you don't marry me?

JOAN *(frank to herself)*. I'm done.

STROWDE. I've energy left. Let's hope that I find, nothing new to believe in.

She is by the window, and she draws a long breath as if that might bring her new life; and, in a sense, it seems to.

JOAN. There's a chill in the air. Summer's over..its burden's lifting. I'm deeply unhappy to be failing you...but I could start off light-heartedly round the world this morning. Would you follow me if I beckoned you...a day's march behind?

STROWDE. Yes.

JOAN. No...we'll go for a walk down to the lake before lunch...and talk politics. I've set you free.

STROWDE. Have you? That may be beyond your power too.

JOAN *(facing him)*. But, deep deep down in your heart...you never did picture us married and settled did you?

STROWDE. No...I'll confess it.

JOAN. Nor I...ever. That is what's so strange...and so wrong, I suppose. Forgive me.

STROWDE *(with a smile)*. I shall never forgive you...for that would be to lose the very last of you, Joan.

JOAN. Twelve o'clock?

STROWDE. Earlier if you like. I've only these letters to see to.

JOAN. I'll try.

She goes down the gallery, lightly, not happily; rather as if happiness were as nothing to her. He sits to his letters. After a moment he finds himself saying...

STROWDE. Most merciful God...who makest thy creatures to suffer without understanding..

But he leaves the prayer unfinished and goes on with his letters.

ACT III

SCENE I

At the Strowdes' house in Bedford Square. EVAN works habitually in the front room downstairs. It is lined with books. His big writing-table is between the windows; he sits—and is sitting at the moment—with his back to them. On his left, and facing the door, is a smaller table, its chair backing on to the book-cases.
It is a morning in March, and foggy without. OLIVER comes in, carrying a time-table and some opened letters. He does not speak, and has time to go to the smaller table and put them down, as well as to glance at a few others left there for him, before EVAN says, habitually, and hardly looking up from his own writing...

STROWDE. Morning.

OLIVER. Morning, sir.

STROWDE. I thought you'd be late in this fog.

OLIVER. I walked. Will you make up the diary now?

STROWDE. Yes.

OLIVER deals with diary and letters and time-table with a chief-of-staff air.

OLIVER. Unless you motor half the night I don't see that you can speak for Hughes at Neath on the twenty-first and at Dover the next afternoon.

STROWDE. Cut Dover. Philpot will lose the seat anyhow.

OLIVER. I'm keeping four free days for emergencies in that fortnight.

STROWDE. Get me the Bible, will you? I want to verify...I think it's First Kings, nineteen. I must go to Nottingham. There's a letter....

OLIVER. Yes...for the Saturday. And a solid four at Stockton, Tuesday to polling day...will that be right?

STROWDE. Ask Duddington.

OLIVER. He has rung up to say he may take the twelve-forty down to-day, and not wait for us.

OLIVER with the Bible taken from its place, walks over to STROWDE and at the same time puts a press cutting on his table.

OLIVER. Did you see this?

STROWDE *(giving it half a glance).* The Guardian?

OLIVER. Yes. They're all ducking and dodging over the Trust question.

STROWDE *(without contempt).* Naturally.

OLIVER *(with his chapter found).* What's the quotation?

STROWDE. Now, O Lord, take away my life, for I am not better than my fathers. Very modern and progressive and disillusioned of Elijah! Why ever should he expect to be?

OLIVER. Verse four.

STROWDE. Thank you.

OLIVER. And these to go back in the History file?

"These" are some MSS. piled a few inches high on the table. They might be, and

are, the chapters of a book.

    STROWDE. Please.

    OLIVER. Clumbermere's coming at three, you know.

    STROWDE. Yes.

OLIVER has noted the wrong entry on the appointment tablet; he now puts down the lump of MS. he has taken up, to alter it. At this moment the PARLOURMAID enters.

    MAID. Did you ring, sir?

    STROWDE. What time must we leave, Oliver?

    OLIVER. The train's four-fifty.

    STROWDE. Pack my bag for one night, please. No dress clothes. Tea at four-fifteen. Miss Strowde gone out yet?

    MAID. No, sir. She's expecting Miss Kittredge to call for her at eleven.

    STROWDE. Will you lunch?

    OLIVER. Thank you.

    STROWDE. Mr. Gauntlett will lunch.

    MAID. Yes, sir.

The MAID goes. STROWDE has now finished his writing and leans back. OLIVER stands beside him.

    STROWDE. I doubt if it'll be such a walk over.

    OLIVER. For you...at Stockton?

    STROWDE. The whole election.

    OLIVER. Well...you like a good fight.

    STROWDE (*genially*). You want us whacked. Traitor!

    OLIVER. Not more than enough to hurt.

    STROWDE. If we were, Bellingham'd throw up the leadership.

    OLIVER. Then a year or two's opposition would pay you.

    STROWDE. Personally...yes...with anything worth opposing. How much longer do you mean stay with me, Oliver?

    OLIVER (*guardedly*). That's still for you to say.

The relation between the two is obuiously an easy one as long as it relates to the work they are busy about. STROWDE himself, his mind on immediate things, has lost much of his brooding air. But OLIVER, it ould almost seem, has acquired it.

    STROWDE. We must see that the sweets of office don't quite spoil your old appetite for revolution. (*He hands over the sheets of paper he has been busy on*) Put this straight...it's the speech for Thursday...and type that bit of it in triplicate.

OLIVER still has a part of the History MS. in his hand. He holds it and looks at it as if it were something more than typed paper.

    OLIVER. Why do you get all this stuff out night after night?

The question and the action draw them beyond business bounds, and their tone to each other, changes. STROWDE, one would say, turns restrainedly affectionate, and OLIVER seems to grow sensitive and very watchful.

STROWDE. My derelict past. I've been looking for what I could steal from it. Live stuff...almost! You've read it?

OLIVER. You said I might.

STROWDE. I wanted you to.

OLIVER. Who else ever has?

STROWDE. No one. Yes...Eleanor typed those three chapters you're holding. The rest...no one.

OLIVER *(nodding towards the bookcase where they are).* Why did none of it find a way into the four upstanding volumes?

STROWDE *(with a smile for the past).* First it was to be for the first, you know...and then for the last.

OLIVER. And now there's to be no last.

STROWDE. Do you feel like writing one?

OLIVER. Whenever a thought was precious to you...you hid it away here.

STROWDE. Whenever it was not current coin...I laid it by. A queer task ...bestowing the love of one's mind *(he fngers the lifeless paper at his side).* Scraps of me, too unsure for utterance. As if this flimsiness itself could cohere and live! Well, I bequeath it to you, Oliver...this much of the failure you were so keen to track down. Burn it. It's just worth destroying.

OLIVER, however, seems to fnd more in the matter than this.

OLIVER. But better inherit a failure, I suppose...for there's something to be done with it...than a success.

STROWDE *(with his kindly smile).* That sounds quite wise. Are you growing patient?

OLIVER *(a bitter tang in his voice).* I'm turning coward, perhaps.

STROWDE. I doubt it. What has happened?

OLIVER. I'm lonely.

STROWDE *(with a head-shake).* Why, of course!

OLIVER *(something from deeper down ousting the bitterness).* I meant to live with the dead. I felt I must never forget them. But they're dead to me now. I used to find courage by mustering in the dark that regiment of fellows....I've marched miles with them night after night. One crack regiment, I thought, temptation proof, could make an end of the muddle you've made. And you'd be glad enough when the time came. But the time never comes, you told me. Damnable of you!

STROWDE (and he means it). I'm sorry.

But OLIVER has evidently learnt how to indulge in the self-destruction of laughter.

OLIVER. Never mind. I'm busy. I'm growing hopeful and helpless and almost good-natured. Don't give me away, though.

STROWDE *(merrily).* Have we begun to impress even you...the gang of us...with our statesmanlike airs? Do you thrill at the sight of the red-leather despatch-box with First Lord of the Treasury on it and an Urgent slip sticking out? You must take a cold chisel to the lock of it the first time it comes to me.

OLIVER now does put the papers away, and out of his mind too; and tackles the forthcoming subject in lively earnest.

OLIVER. But I can't see what's to stop you, Evan, from being thrust to the top of this muddle of minds.

STROWDE. No...quite immodestly...nor can I.

OLIVER. I watch them sizing you up. They don't like you.

STROWDE. Why should they?

OLIVER. Why do they trust you, then?

STROWDE. I'm not altogether one of them...and they've lost the habit of trusting each other.

OLIVER. Heriot thought he was making a smart move when he had you handed the hardest job going...this Clumbermere business.

STROWDE. Do you think he wants me to fail at it?

OLIVER *(answering acutely to this test)*. No...I think he hopes that some sorry moment will give him a chance to wring your hand and say: Well, never mind, old man!

STROWDE *(appreciatively)*. Yes, I can hear him.

OLIVER. Mulready wants to quarrel with you.

STROWDE. I can't oblige Mulready.

OLIVER. What, not with one little row, and then kiss and be friends...instead of flattering him till he feels a perfect fool?

STROWDE. He is...and if he wasn't kept in mind of it he'd become a nuisance.

OLIVER. You do treat Uncle Stephen as a fellow creature.

STROWDE. One's fond of Stephen.

OLIVER now drops the liveliness a little and puts STROWDE on the defensive.

OLIVER. But I sit and watch you thresh out a scheme with some man...who's honest and capable at least. How is it he doesn't see that you're mocking him?

STROWDE *(deprecatory)*. No...I assure you.

OLIVER. Every letter I write for you...it's like laying a snare.

STROWDE *(ironic)*. Why...am I not theirs very faithfully, their most obedient humble servant? If the schemes will come to nothing in the end, is the mockery mine? What do you expect of me, Oliver?

OLIVER. Poor devils! Each one of them believes in something. If it's not in what he's doing it's in what he hopes to be...even if it's only in what he has failed to be. I suppose he expects you to beieve a little in him.

STROWDE *(sarcastic)*. That's unreasonable. *(But now, in coldest sincerity..)* Are you still out to destroy? I'm showing you the sure way. It's to fulfil. The reddest revolutionary is but a part of what he turns against. It's the destiny of a spiritual generation to destroy itself by fulfilling its faith and completing its work...and we dignify our passions to this end! Not so pleasant, I grant you, to be doing one's share of the job cold-heartedly and open-eyed. But disbelief's a power...and power is satisfying. I lived half my life in the happiness...and unhappiness...of a vision. One fine day I find that the world I'm living in is nothing like the idea of the world I've been living by. It comes quite casually...conversion to disbelief. But you know it's the truth you've found by finding you've always known it...known all along that your vision was a vision and no more.

OLIVER. And you leave happiness and unhappiness behind?

STROWDE. You cease to suffer...you cease to hope. You have no will to be other than you are. You are, therefore, extraordinarily efficient. Be something ruthlessly...what else counts?...and let life become what it will. Watch me succeed, Oliver. That will teach you how to down me in turn. It's the best service I can do you.

OLIVER finds but one comment.

OLIVER. Wouldn't you sooner I killed you now where you sit?

STROWDE. That would be rash and well-meaning of you...and hardly worth while.

OLIVER (drawn on now irresistibly). I came to get what I could from you...though you told me to go my own way...and I've tried to since. But I've never been able to get free of you, Evan. When I was small you were jolly to me...and I liked that. Then I turned against you and wondered why. Odd, how one ignorantly stores up scraps of knowledge about people and things till one can put them together and make out what they mean. Three times, I think, Mother has started to try and tell me about...us three. I've managed to stop her...for where was the need...when, in every sense that counts, I believe I've always known.

STROWDE has nothing to say but...

STROWDE. Have you? Oh, my dear boy!

OLIVER. Don't...don't. We can't begin to be fond of each other.

STROWDE (half humbly). No...I could never find any way to begin. But lately...I've learnt to be rather fond of you. I hope nothing I ever said seemed to give your mother away.

OLIVER (in a way, the more confident now of the two). Oh no! Dear Mother and all the other facts of Nature...one accepts them and has done with it. There was one fellow at school...I never knew of his saying a word...but he had some damned story about her inside him, I could see. So I made a row with him...though scrapping wasn't the thing...and as near killed him as was decent. One can't be her son for nothing.

STROWDE. What makes you tell me now that you know?

OLIVER. I...had a feeling you'd like me to.

At this moment the MAID comes in, announcing " Mr. Serocold." He is close on her heels.

SEROCOLD. Sorry I'm late.

STROWDE. You'll be later at Number Ten.

SEROCOLD. The P.M. always keeps me waiting. Slack's the word!

STROWDE. Here's what I'm going to say on Thursday. Oliver'll type you a copy.

SEROCOLD, with a nod to his nephew, takes the few sheets of paper.

SEROCOLD. You're seeing Clumbermere?

STROWDE. Three o clock.

SEROCOLD *(having hit on the passage marked for typing; as he reads)*. His people won't like this, will they?

STROWDE *(with a pleasant curtness)*. They're not meant to.

SEROCOLD *(as he pulls a face)*. I'm very sure Bellingham won't.

STROWDE. He need not, either.

SEROCOLD *(pulling it even longer)*. But, my dear fellow, this is a pledge.

STROWDE. Well...I'm nobody. I'm not in the government...I'm not even in the House yet. If I choose to stake my small reputation that the Trust question will have to be squared inside those lines, what does it matter?

SEROCOLD hands the damned thing back, saying...

SEROCOLD. How long will this take you, Oliver?

OLIVER. Three minutes.

OLIVER goes off with it.

SEROCOLD *(in deprecatory protest)*. Evan...you are difficult.

STROWDE *(as one skilled in hitting nails on the head)*. I've gruelled at this business, my dear Stephen, till I know its necessities...and we'll have to come to their heel.

SEROCOLD *(the ever-comforting phrase)*. In time.

STROWDE. And I know Clumbermere. He has got his Bellinghams and Heriots and Stephen Serocolds to deal with too. So I give him a pistol, you see, to put at their heads, and he gives me one to put at yours.

SEROCOLD *(rueful)*. Quite so. Set the strong men face to face, and they're back to back before you know where you are.

STROWDE. Thank you!

SEROCOLD. But surely if we must offend our own people we might at least get some support out of Clumbermere's lot for doing so.

STROWDE. Good Lord...we don't want their support! Then Clumbermere would have to start bargaining with us for a great deal more than it's good to give him. He knows that, too.

SEROCOLD. But I've to persuade Number Ten.

STROWDE *(with finality)*. Tell Number Ten that if I'm right it's all right...and if I'm wrong they'll be rid of me.

The door opens and ELEANOR looks in.

    ELEANOR. Evan, are you busy?

    STROWDE. Yes...come in.

    ELEANOR. Come in, my dear.

This is to SUSAN KITTREDGE who then follows her.
ELEANOR shakes hands silently with Stephen.

    STROWDE. Good morning, Miss Susan.

    ELEANOR. Bad news.

It is indeed written on their faces.

    STROWDE. What?

    ELEANOR. Joan's very ill.

    SEROCOLD. Joan Westbury?

    SUSAN. A letter from my grandfather this morning.

    SEROCOLD. Is she still out there?

    SUSAN. Since Christmas.

    ELEANOR. May Evan read it?

    SUSAN. Of course.

SUSAN has the letter in her hand. STROWDE takes it without a word.

    SEROCOLD. What's the matter with her?

    ELEANOR. It's a tumour on the brain.

    SEROCOLD. Good God!

    SUSAN. Grandfather didn't know for a while that she wasn't sleeping at all.
Now she's had a doctor from Boston that he says he can trust. *(Then to
STROWDE, Who is silently intent on the letter)* I'm afraid it's dreadfully illegible
...he never types.

    SEROCOLD. Aren't they operating?

    ELEANOR. They won't. They give her a few weeks.

    SEROCOLD. When was that written?

    ELEANOR. Ten days ago.

    SEROCOLD. Does she know?

    ELEANOR. He doesn't say.

    SEROCOLD. Poor Joan! I suppose they dose her with morphia.

    ELEANOR. Surely!

    SEROCOLD. I must go.

*After all, what can be done, and what more can be said? Glancing at STROWDE,
he goes out. ELEANOR and SUSAN talk on in lower tones.*

    ELEANOR. You've been crying.

    SUSAN *(who has been, indeed).* I do all the usual things, I'm afraid.

    ELEANOR. Never be afraid, my dear, of doing the usual things.

    SUSAN. And she's three thousand miles away.

    ELEANOR. What a worry for your grandfather!He's being most kind.

Suddenly STROWDE speaks, and they both turn.

STROWDE. This is from Countesbury?

SUSAN. Yes.

He goes back to his reading.

ELEANOR. I thought she was ill in the summer. Why...she had planned to go on to Japan, hadn't she, Evan?

SUSAN. Yes. He thinks that the illness...her mind...they say it makes one very restless.

SEROCOLD looks in again with the paper that Oliver has typed in his hand. He says softly, not so softly as to make sympathy mawkish....

SEROCOLD. Good-bye, Eleanor. Let me know when you hear again, please.

ELEANOR. You're dining to-morrow.

SEROCOLD.Oh...yes. *(To Susan)* Good-bye.

SUSAN. Good-bye.

He disappears. STROWDE's intent stillness - for the letter is long and not easily read - sets up a strain. It is half to relieve it that Susan says . . .

SUSAN. I'll write to-day...but it'll miss the mail.

ELEANOR. To Joan?

SUSAN. I'm sure grandfather would have cabled if she were...worse.

ELEANOR. She's dying, my dear.

SUSAN. I know...though I don't understand it really.

ELEANOR. That is as it should be.

SUSAN. Why?

ELEANOR. If we thought often of dying we should soon think of nothing else. Time enough, then, for you.

SUSAN. But...

STROWDE has finished the letter, has risen, and with a curt "Thank you" he hands it her back and goes out. ELEANOR comments on the slight strangeness of this...

ELEANOR. Evan had hoped to marry her, you know.

SUSAN. Yes.

ELEANOR. The Election won't leave him much time to be unhappy.

SUSAN. No.

ELEANOR's business-like mind will work.

ELEANOR. Twenty-past ten, is it?

SUSAN. Just.

ELEANOR. When did you last hear from Joan herself?

SUSAN. Two weeks ago.

ELEANOR. Was she ill then, when she wrote...did she say?

SUSAN. No. But that may have been because...we were playing a childish game...I did once start to tell you...pretending we'd changed places. She has my rooms at home...they're in a wing by themselves built over the gardo she used to write me...such good letters...and sign them Susan. I was no use at answering.

I've kept them all.

OLIVER comes in.

OLIVER. Morning. Morning, Susan.

SUSAN. Good Morning, Oliver.

He picks up the railway guide from his table and turns the leaves. Later he sits and unlocks a drawer for some money. This seems to break the spell that still held ELEANOR slightly, and she says to the girl...

ELEANOR. If you wouldn't mind waiting at the ministry while I see Mr Pemberton... then we could go straight on to Poplar. They'll give us lunch at the factory. I must be back and at Grosvenor Road by two-thirty. I'll get my papers.

SUSAN. Very well.

ELEANOR. This is shocking news, Oliver.

OLIVER. Very.

ELEANOR goes. SUSAN looks across, with a distinct frown, at the taciturn young man.

SUSAN. Don't you care?

OLIVER. Yes. What good will that do?

SUSAN. Some good to you.

OLIVER. I wasn't thinking of my own moral improvement for the moment.

SUSAN. Must we quarrel...even about this?

OLIVER *(bitter-sweet)*. It's how I show affection for you, Susan.

SUSAN. Thank you. *(But she cannot play up to this sort of thing now, and she bursts out)* I'd give anything to be with her. Oh...how horribly casual you all are! I bring you such news...you all say that you loved her...you go about your business....

OLIVER. Sentimental Susan!

SUSAN. How is one to learn to like you? I've tried not to seem a sightseer ...simply curious about everything. I've tried to forget myself among you and find out what I really cared for. I knew how to love her without wasting time about it, thank goodness. *(and then—common sense catching up with emotion)* Selfish brute...that won't save her! You're right.

ELEANOR'S voice is heard from the hall, "Ready, Susan"

SUSAN *(repentant for what she thinks is her harsh unreason)*. I'm sorry, Oliver.

OLIVER *(armoured and cool)*. Why should you like us, my dear Susan?

SUSAN, honestly a little hurt, goes without another word. OLIVER goes about his business, whatever it is, with an almost suspicious steadiness. After a moment STROWDE comes back.

STROWDE. As it happens the boat doesn't sail till three.

OLIVER. The eleven-twenty train will do you, then.

STROWDE. They're keeping me a cabin.

OLIVER. You've four hundred odd in current.

STROWDE. I'll write to Manning for an overdraft. You can cable another five to New York.

Then, with no more emotion than he'd give to the boat or the train or the bank-account . . .

OLIVER. Do you expect to see her alive?

STROWDE. Hardly. I'll give you a line for Duddington.

OLIVER. You might just be back for the polling.

STROWDE. If he thinks he can get my photograph and the gramophone records elected, he's welcome to try. Or you'd make an excellent member. Say to Stephen I'm sorry.

By now STROWDE is as busy at his table. The two talk while they work.

OLIVER. Eleanor's just gone out.

STROWDE. Yes.

OLIVER. You won't come back.

STROWDE. That's always possible.

OLIVER. To this conspiracy you won't.

STROWDE. No...I don't see yet another welcome from the gang.

OLIVER. Why ever are you going? What's the use?

STROWDE. None.

OLIVER gibes. Why does it - but it does - seem to make the whole thing a bit more bearable?

OLIVER. I,ve been wondering what could happen to save you. You a success! Why...the first temptation trips you up.

STROWDE. *(suddenly, straight at him).* You'd go.

OLIVER. I can't tell. I'd forgotten her lately. Yes, I'd start swimming there.

STROWDE. Here's the cheque.

OLIVER *(as he takes it).* What about your packing?

STROWDE. Tell them to fill another bag.

OLIVER. Will you cable you're starting?

STROWDE. (after playing with hope for a second). No.

OLIVER. I'll be back in ten minutes.

He gets to the door, when his father's voice stops him.

STROWDE. Oliver. I'm dumb with you...but something that I am you must be too. Forgive me the forgetting it.

To just this much Oliver can and will respond, simply and honestly.

OLIVER. I'm glad I've found you.

STROWDE. I claim no rights in you. But I'm glad.

OLIVER. It's something to go on with.

As he goes, STROWDE echoes him as if the words were - they are! - the very last he wanted to feel the meaning of.

STROWDE. To go on with!

SCENE II

We see the corner by the window in Susan's little sitting-room at Countesbury, Massachusetts. It is a white room; and now the snow outside makes it seem whiter still. And the snow brings with it a silence too. JOAN, wrapped in shawls, is tucked into an armchair. MR. KITTREDGE is sitting by her. Her eyes are closed, she might be dead. When she speaks she does not open them at first. And she never moves, at most a hand reaches out; while he - for he sits by her long hours like this - has fallen almost motionless too.

JOAN. So white! And white now even when I shut my eyes.

MR. KITTREDGE. No pain then?

JOAN. None since this morning, thank you.

MR. KITTREDGE. We are wise children when we fear the dark.

JOAN. Yes...now that I don't sleep much at night time, I'm learning how to lose myself in light. What more has dear Susan to say?

MR. KITTREDGE. I had finished the letter.

JOAN. Stupid of me!

MR. KITTREDGE. Did you doze?

JOAN. I slipped out through the window...into the snow.

MR. KITTREDGE. Why...a step or two further would have taken you into your famous London fog that Susan finds so beautiful.

JOAN *(a flicker of light in her eyes).* I was in London this morning...there was no fog...it was full of cheerful noise. And yesterday I was in camp again beyond Khartoum...watching the little black babies crawl about the sand. I can remember one that died and didn't want to die...most of them, you know, come and go as easily...and he fought the air with his fists.

MR. KITTREDGE. If memory's a measure of affection, we have given bits of our hearts to the unlikeliest things.

JOAN *(with a smile for him).* Have you ever given your heart...all of a piece?

MR. KITTREDGE *(responsive; fostering the smile's life, as one might blow, ever so gently, upon a spark).* One tries to. It's the taking coming short is the trouble. Study the money market. That's what sends the values down.

JOAN. Oh, I have let myself be loved...most generously. I'm glad that's to my credit.

MR. KITTREDGE. But never given your heart?

JOAN. One tries to...desperately. Probably it's a mistake to try.

MR. KITTREDGE. We can't help trying.

Her thoughts pass like clouds, the light and shade changing in her face.

JOAN. I wonder if I've been a very wicked woman.

MR. KITTREDGE. Probably not...if you wonder.

JOAN. I'd have been so content to be nothing but a wife and a mother...a link in the chain. In our pedigree book at home there's an Edward Marshall, knight, not so far back, that married...two little dashes...Eliza. Plain, simple Eliza! Who was she? Scandalous mystery...no one wanted to remember! But I've always felt tenderly and dutifully towards my great, great, great...and then, after all, one loses count...great grandmother Eliza.

For a moment or two they do not speak. Her face turns to the window, and in the white light seems lifeless, quite.

JOAN. Such a bright, silent land! Do you love it as we love England? Not yet. It's harder. It doesn't look back yet and seem to love you...as England does.

MR. KITTREDGE. It must take more toll of us first, perhaps.

JOAN. So many generations of the souls and bodies of men to be given to this earth to breed it a soul of its own.

MR. KITTREDGE *(puzzled a little).* Of their souls too?

JOAN. It may have mine and welcome. My old world has a kindly soul...with a farm and a church and a house with its garden to show for it. I don't think I want to believe, though, that your quiet spirit must pass into the clatter of cities...or is that a music to you with a meaning?

MR. KITTREDGE. With no clear meaning. That's why I've fallen silent in these last years...while I watch the new generations giving themselves to strange tremendous forces to breed...what sort of a monster world.

JOAN *(with just one nod of the head).* Yes, I was very scared sailing up the harbour to New York and driving to the station. Those blasphemous towers of Babel weren't a bit like you. But I think you'll come out on top. Yes...I have a vision of the sublimer you, conscious, persistent, wise...coming out truly on top.

MR. KITTREDGE. Well...it may be that a consciousness of purpose is still the greatest power.

Silence falls again. JOAN breaks it to a livelier tune. She is happy now, always, when she speaks of her boys.

JOAN. Harry, till he was ten, poor infant, had dreadful headaches...and he asked me once, Mother, am I good? So I said he was. Then he asked, need he pray for eternal life? For if it's going to hurt like this, he said, I don't see how I could bear it.

MR. KITTREDGE. I wish I'd known Harry.

JOAN. I wish he'd known you in time. Some of those boys, under the shadow of death, came suddenly to a maturity of mind.

MR. KITTREDGE. This world at least was theirs. What a gift to them!

JOAN *(reproachfully).* You're seldom bitter.

MR. KITTREDGE. Too seldom...I dread the vapid benevolence of old age.

JOAN. Better the pain of anger?

MR. KITTREDGE. Life keeps us capable of pain.

JOAN. So uselessly!

MR. KITTREDGE. Not quite. And I think the rough and cunning God of

Nature abets our honest passions of love and hate...because they never quite cancel out...and he profits on the balance. Even as our worldly virtue thrives upon alien sin...let us most humbly remember.

JOAN *(her heart bowed)*. But barren righteousness there is no god to pardon.

MR. KITTREDGE. None...though men have made many.

She looks at him appealingly now.

JOAN. I have that shamefullest sin to confess...a sin of being. I have treasured a secret self...oh, an ego, if ever there was one.

MR. KITTREDGE *(humouring her thought)*. A tyrant?

JOAN. Too aloof and alone for tyranny.

MR. KITTREDGE. Lonely?

JOAN. Never so human.

MR. KITTREDGE. Dear me! What can be done about it?

JOAN *(a strain of torture showing)*. It doesn't age, it doesn't suffer...and now I've lain awake with it so much I doubt if it ever sleeps. So I have this dread that it's undying.

MR. KITTREDGE *(with a certain dispersive briskness)*. I once knew a promising young man possessed of the same devil. He fell in love, had his heart broken...broken into. Ego came out to fight and could never quite get back again.

JOAN *(responding with a gleam of merriment)*. How vulgar...says my secret self, and sniffs. No, I could never flatter it into being a heart-breaker. It was never half so human. May I confess?

MR. KITTREDGE. Will my absolution serve?

JOAN. Give it me of your wisdom and your kindness if you can. *(And there follows her soul's confession.)* Once, in the sheer place of my self's refuge, I found that I was not alone. I turned back to life for safety. We loved the unattainable in each other, so we said...and were content to part. When there was no more need for parting we found that it was true. A faith was born to us...a dead faith...to my shame. And I left him to bear its burden. The world he worked for had much hope of him...and need of him.

MR. KITTREDGE. And he failed it?

JOAN. He let life go. He worked on...lifelessly. Better if we had disbelieved.

MR. KITTREDGE. There's no doing that.

JOAN. Rash uplifted souls! Too proud to pray to the god of the godlike in us to dull our sense and dim our eyes.

MR. KITTREDGE. I do not believe in any such high god.

JOAN *(her mind struggling)*. Then why had I no power to bring the faith that kindled to a living birth...to set it free...that we might serve it? Nor any will to give it being? For I hadn't...that was the worst. This sacred self that cannot yield to life...what is it worth? Let's only hope the soul's as mortal as the body is.

And now brutal, physical ill takes its advantage of the tortured mind.

MR. KITTREDGE. Your head is hurting you again.

JOAN *(gasping)*. Beginning to. Will you please talk to me very sternly?

MR. KITTREDGE. Take my hand.

JOAN. Thank you...that's comforting.

She grips his hand tightly. He talks to steady her, to gie her moral foothold, if he can.

MR. KITTREDGE. We must be patient...with headaches and in the wintertime of our souls. The first discovery, do you know, of my imaginative life was to find a story coming to an unhappy end and to hide the book away with its last chapter still unread. But suddenly that small boy thought: No story ever ends. A very moral anecdote. *(Joan cannot help another gasp.)* Grip my hand hard...and I'll grip yours harder.

JOAN. Please.

MR. KITTREDGE. My dear, my dear...are there to be no honest failures in this world? Is man's salvation from the brute so small a business that we should each expect a rounded share in it? I've written a book or two on ethics.. unfinished stories in their kind...not so bad though. But maybe what I've best learned how to do by that is to sit here so cleverly...confound the pain, we've had three weeks of it...and hold your hand.

JOAN. Be stern with me...or I can't bear it, I'm afraid.

MR. KITTREDGE. I m afraid you can. Headache or heartache or a harder thing...those that can suffer them must suffer them, it seems. You are the stuff, Joan, that forges well.

There comes into her voice a touch of conquering strength.

JOAN. I am learning a way, I think, through the dark and clamour of this pain. Will you tell him, please, that as the light grows there's always a moment when he's with me...till it grows too dazzling.

MR. KITTREDGE. I'll tell him. Ah...the grip's loosening. Not such a long bout.

She comes, almost as suddenly, out of the agony. Taking her hand back, she finds it stained.

JOAN. Oh...I've cut your hand with my ring.

MR. KITTREDGE *(gallantly)*. Good...I have shed my blood for you.

JOAN *(with a lady's smile for her knight)*. Thank you.

MR. KITTREDGE. Keep the head still now. Set your mind free.

Again a silence falls.

JOAN *(her eyes closed, and, as it would seem, exhaustedly at ease)*. Yesterday you told me that three times in your life you had been near to...it was a deserter's phrase...falling out from the tyrannous procession of the years.

MR. KITTREDGE. Yes...three times...no more. Good friends, clean enemies, and hard work have kept me happy mostly.

JOAN. What held you in place?

MR. KITTREDGE. Inconsequent things. Once, it was the thought of an unfinished book that had been paid for. Once, a night's sleep made all the difference. But once my self-respect did seriously protest against a premature indulgence in the ignorance of death.

JOAN. Did the troubles pass?

MR. KITTREDGE. No. They were unsolved problems. I face them still.

JOAN. To be so hustled in our chains down this road we call time. Then to be hustled off it...crippled still...into an eternity of empty freedom...a mocking threat! I've taken every happening so easily...and I'm at peace about the past. A little tired now, by this pain, and memory plays tricks...with real and unreal. That's most immoral, I'm sure.

MR. KITTREDGE. There is an Eastern prayer...for those that would leave life behind...begins: From the need to know by name or by form...deliver me.

JOAN *(with quite a laugh; a child's laugh)*. Oh, I like that! Anyway, though, my geese were always swans...weren't yours?

MR. KITTREDGE. Are there any fairer swans?

JOAN *(as if she prayed)*. For all denial of what I had to give...forgive me. From the soul's empty freedom...deliver me. If death cannot make fruitful may it break and end what life could not break nor use.

MR. KITTREDGE *(his voice very hushed)*. But we must be patient in understanding too. What gospel is it for the flesh that dies to know it serves a greater end than its own? Joy of life is its heritage. But man's soul is of man's making. He stumbles and halts in his chosen ways. In the way of vision...we see and find small reason to believe. The way of thought brings power...but it is power to bind...it is law. Whence comes our newer being and its freedom...how has life been gained for the soul? I do not know. What is to come of it? We're conscious mostly yet of the good life's failure. A bitter business!

JOAN. I've tried to be bitter. So have you. And that's a failure.

Now comes the comfort of his faith. And she listens, as to the absolution she had asked.

MR. KITTREDGE. This I can believe. The generation of the spirit is not as the generation of the flesh...for its virtue is diffused like light, generously, unpriced. Doing and suffering and the work of thought must take its toll of us. And all that life corrupts death can destroy. Then we may cease to know. But, freed from self's claim upon it, scattered, dissolved, transformed, that inmost thing we were so impotently may but begin, new breathed, the better to be. For comfort's sake we lead our busy lives. Who wouldn't want to forget sometimes this strange, new, useless burden of the soul? Left comfortless, we must bear it for a while as bravely as we may. *(He is conscious of a change in her. He looks keenly, for perhaps the great change has begun.)* Joan...where are you?

JOAN. Not so far.

For a passing moment her face is alert.

MR. KITTREDGE. Why...what can you hear now that my chattering ceases? But impalpably it is veiled.

JOAN. Nothing any more. There's silence now. There's light and silence.

He hardly thinks that she will open her eyes again.

SCENE III

Strowde's study again. LORD CLUMBERMERE is sitting Waiting; an old gentleman (though his birth did not formally confer the title) of an ungainly FIgure and an originally insignificant face, which the sheer practice of life has made characteristic and interesting. He is reading a little leather-bound pocket volume. The MAID opens the door.

THE MAID. Beg pardon, my lord...I wasn't sure that neither of them had come in.

LORD CLUMBERMERE. No.

THE MAID *(speaking back to the hall)*. Will you wait upstairs, Miss?

SUSAN'S VOICE. I can leave this on the desk...or I'll write Mr. Strowde a note.

Whereupon THE MAID holds the door wide, and LORD CLUMBERMERE rises with cumbrous politeness as SUSAN comes in, a cablegram in her hand.

SUSAN. Here? Excuse me.

She goes to Oliver's desk and sits there. THE MAID goes. LORD CLUMBERMERE sits down again. SUSAN, having taken a sheet of paper, decides not to write. Instead, she puts the cablegram itself into an envelope, which she addresses. Then, looking up, she finds Lord Clumbermere is looking at her.

LORD CLUMBERMERE *(in his soft, slow way)*. You came with Miss Strowde to see round our Garden City. I showed you round. My name is Clumbermere.

SUSAN *(colourlessly)*. Yes. I didn't think you'd remember me.

LORD CLUMBERMERE. You're Miss Susan Kittredge. You come from America

SUSAN. Yes.

LORD CLUMBERMERE. That cablegram's bad news. I'm sorry...

OLIVER comes in hurriedly, and as if directly from the street.

OLIVER. You never got my message, my lord! Your City office said they could find you...I rang up Grosvenor Square as well...and you've been here since three.

LORD CLUMBERMERE *(charitably unreproachful)*. I have.

OLIVER. I'm very sorry. The message was that Mr. Strowde couldn't keep the appointment with you..he is sailing this afternoon on the ' Aquitania.'

LORD CLUMBERMERE. Sudden.

OLIVER takes, for the frst time, a good look at SUSAN and sees in her face..

OLIVER. Susan...what's the matter?

In silence she hands him the envelope.

OLIVER. She's dead?

SUSAN. Yes.

He says, automatically, as he opens it . . .

OLIVER. Please excuse me. *(He reads it, and then for all comment...)* This has come through quickly. *(Then turning again to the sympathetically attentive old gentleman)* My uncle thought...I've just left him...you might like to make some suggestion to avoid bringing your business with Mr. Strowde to a standstill.

LORD CLUMBERMERE. I know no more than you tell me, of course...but if you now want to telephone to Southampton to stop him, there's a line in my office that can be relied on...and it's at your service.

OLIVER *(with a frown)*. Thank you. The boat sailed at three.

SUSAN *(striking, involuntarily, almost an eager note)*. That might mean four.

OLIVER *(coldly masking some surprise)*. It might.

LORD CLUMBERMERE *(accommodatingly)*. Then the Admiralty wireless will do as well. He could land at Cherbourg.

OLIVER *(bringing all this to a full stop)*. Yes. You'd rather not see my uncle, of course. His point was that...whenever Mr. Strowde did come back the Government's relations to him might have altered.

LORD CLUMBERMERE is pleasantly amused at the senatorial tone; but he keeps his secret.

LORD CLUMBERMERE. I catch that point.

OLIVER. And if you think the business pressing...?

LORD CLUMBERMERE. I think we had now better let things happen for a little...will you tell your good uncle with my compliments? But say I'm always pleased to talk to a man that has a mind of his own and knows it...when they find another.

OLIVER. I'll say so. And I'm sure Mr. Strowde would have wished me to say that he was sorry to leave things in the lurch.

LORD CLUMBERMERE *(expanding a little, now that Oliver has, apparently, finished patronising him)*. Well, you know, from one cause and another...accidents and such like...that's always occurring. We just can't help thinking this world won't go on without us...the evidence is that it will. A little differently? Perhaps. Any worse? That's more doubtful. *(Then rolling round a smile on Susan)* Not that you should feel this way.

SUSAN. Why not?

LORD CLUMBERMERE *(making it into quite a little song)*. You're young. I'm old.

SUSAN. If it's all to make so little difference, why do you work fourteen hours a day, Lord Clumbermere?

LORD CLUMBERMERE *(naughtily)*. The newspapers say that of me. I don't do more than six hours' real work.

SUSAN *(with friendly persistence)*. Why do any?

LORD CLUMBERMERE. It's a habit I've got into. It passes the time...keeps me happy...and I don't know what else would.

SUSAN now hesitates a moment; but then, keenly...

SUSAN. It isn't my business to ask, I know, but...do you want Mr. Strowde to come back?

LORD CLUMBERMERE. In a friendly sense?

SUSAN *(putting it very straight).* Do you think he ought to come back?

LORD CLUMBERMERE *(rather like a benevolent old bear whom a rash cub has defied).* Dear young lady, that pistol is not loaded. It is not my business to say.

SUSAN *(contrite).* I beg your pardon.

LORD CLUMBERMERE now takes account of the silent OLIVER.

LORD CLUMBERMERE. Am I keeping you and Miss Kittredge from private conversation?

OLIVER. No, I think not.

LORD CLUMBERMERE. For my next appointment is not till four, and I have only a mile and a quarter to walk to it. This is my day for meeting men on their own ground. If I meet them on mine more than four days a week, I find I grow too obstinate.

OLIVER, wrought as he is today with suppressed emotions and a tortured mind, can really hardly bear this sententious old gentleman.

OLIVER. Is that a bad business quality?

LORD CLUMBERMERE. It is an unpleasing human quality.

OLIVER. I thought that the set jaw and the thump on the table were the only sure signs of a strong man.

To this juvenile outrage LORD CLUMBERMERE unexpectedly responds with a pathetic and disarming smile.

LORD CLUMBERMERE. Don't you like me?

OLIVER *(shamed).* I'm sorry, sir...if that sounded rude.

LORD CLUMBERMERE. I judged you didn't like me when you came to bring papers to that Amalgamated Plantations meeting last November year...which was the first time I saw you.

OLIVER *(recovering superiority).* It must please people amazingly to find out how well you remember them.

LORD CLUMBERMERE *(with meek benevolence).* I hope it does. I mean it to. Will you be out of a job now?

OLIVER *(much taken aback).* Well, I've hardly had time to consider. Possibly.

LORD CLUMBERMERE. I can offer you one.

OLIVER. A firm offer?

LORD CLUMBERMERE. I make no other kind.

What prouder moment for a young man than when—with studied courtesy—he can refuse an offer!

OLIVER. No, thank you, my lord. I've tried the City. I am against you, I fear.

LORD CLUMBERMERE. Is that so? And what are you for?

OLIVER. It's not an easy question to answer, you think?

But OLIVER is not a pretentious fool; for all that he is sometimes tempted to behave like one.

LORD CLUMBERMERE. I think there's only one way to answer it, Mr. Gauntlett...and I doubt if you've had time to find that. Miss Kittredge has her eye on this little volume that I carry in my pocket to occupy odd moments. No, it's not a Testament...though I carry a Testament sometimes. Nor a Ready Reckoner. Allow me.

He hands it to SUSAN with a bow.

OLIVER *(who is being won to friendliness)*. What is it, Susan?

SUSAN. Everybody's Book of Short Poems.

LORD CLUMBERMERE. They're poor poems mostly, I should suppose. It was the Everybody's caught my fancy just about forty years ago, at Bletchley station, when I was travelling in ink.

OLIVER. Ink for everybody!

LORD CLUMBERMERE. That s what I had to make it if I could.

OLIVER. You did.

LORD CLUMBERMERE *(warming comfortably to reminiscence)*. Then bottles, pens, paper, typewriters, rubber, lead mines, and a line of steamships. I have prospered you may say, by giving people what they want...and then a little more of what they want...and sometimes, maybe, by persuading them to take rather more than they did want. Are you against that?

OLIVER *(with some severity)*. What do you want, my lord?

LORD CLUMBERMERE. Ah...that's the riddle...and there's a catch in it. There's always a catch in the riddles Life sets us to guess, Mr. Gauntlett. I have had to live to find the answer...and I don't say I've found it even yet. Now the poem I happened to be reading when Miss Kittredge came in...page sixty two, I have no literary memory, but I retain numbers...is entitled, "I know that my own will come to me." A helpful thought...but an awful thought. I never supposed I wanted lots of money...but I've got it. I despise titles...I'm a lord. I was bred to the Baptist ministry, and I still think I'm a spiritually minded man. And perhaps if I'd been blessed with three children instead of seven, I might be running a chapel now. You'd say I've sunk my soul...not to mention other people's...all in money and money's worth. Well, money's a hard master...so is success. You think you're all for truth and justice. Right. Come and run my pen factory and find out if that is so.

OLIVER sees that this does need an answer.

OLIVER. If I ran your pen factory, I'd be for the pen, the whole pen, and nothing but the pen.

LORD CLUMBERMERE. Then you d be little use to me. If we want a good gold nib, it's religion we must make it with.

OLIVER. I'm sure that sentiment has been applauded on many a Pleasant Sunday Afternoon.

LORD CLUMBERMERE. It has.

OLIVER *(making his attack)*. But are you a devil, then, my lord, that you want to beat the souls of men into pen nibs?

LORD CLUMBERMERE. I hope not. But if I am, Mr. Gauntlett, please show me the way out of the pit. For I've tried to uplift my fellows...gratis; that was a failure...at five per cent; that wasn't quite such a failure...but it was all a failure really. Odd now! My last turn to with Mr. Strowde was on this very subject, when we crossed with a party on the 'Caronia' to a conference upon the scientific management of Industry in Chicago. *(TO SUSAN)* You're not from Chicago?

SUSAN *(who is very attracted by Lord Clumbermere, though much of her mind is elsewhere)*. No, I've never been there. I don't know much of America, I fear.

LORD CLUMBERMERE *(with a bow that a duke might envy)*. You are America...you don't need to be too self-conscious. I must have done a hundred miles round the decks coming and going, arguing with him. A fine mind. That's eighteen years ago. I was interested in his future.

OLIVER. Did you offer him the pen factory?

LORD CLUMBERMERE *(quite unable to resist this)*. Why, Mr. Gauntlett, I wish to make no comparisons...but I offered him the rubber and the steamships. And I will again if he wants a job.

SUSAN. One for you, Oliver.

OLIVER *(gallantly)*. Yes.

LORD CLUMBERMERE. But he said he had enough to think about.

OLIVER *(joining battle again)*. You don't despise sheer thinking.

LORD CLUMBERMERE. Why, no. My factories are run by thought.

OLIVER. As well as by faith and honour.

LORD CLUMBERMERE grows a little graver; and he speaks to himself now, as much as to his hearers.

LORD CLUMBERMERE. Yes, I'm greedy of all three. And I get greedier. I sometimes wish I didn't...but I do. Why should the immortal part of man be all used up making him safe and comfortable? It's humiliating. And even the demand for simple goodness is greater than the supply. My business swallows a lot...it could swallow a lot more.

OLIVER *(bitterly)*. Then do you wonder there are people that want to blow you and your factories to smithereens?

LORD CLUMBERMERE. No, I sympathise. But it isn t practical of them ...and it wouldn't be popular...for where should we all be then? Subtracting evil doesn't leave good...not as I was taught to do sums. So I must seek salvation the other way.

OLIVER. What is that?

LORD CLUMBERMERE meditatively looks at his watch; he gets up, and as he speaks, recaptures his little volume.

LORD CLUMBERMERE. On page one hundred and twelve...thank you, I wasn't forgetting it...there is a poem entitled "It's the little bit extra that counts for God." A good thought. Righteousness is profit, Mr. Gauntlett...and before we can have honest profit we must pay our way. I know that is only the creed of a business man. It's half-past three...and I'm a slow walker. *(TO SUSAN).* Good afternoon.

SUSAN *(thanks in her eyes).* Could you give me a job?

LORD CLUMBERMERE. I might.

SUSAN. I may come and ask for one.

LORD CLUMBERMERE. Do. My coat's outside. *(He pauses, to add a little shyly)* I liked to think when I was beginning to do well that my business was, as you might say, the practical side of literature. Great poems must have been written in my ink...and treaties have been signed with my pens. So's my hat. *(As he goes out he is saying to OLIVER)* Will you tell your uncle then that I think things must be let happen for a little now...till we see a chance to interfere again . . .

The door closes on the two of them. But in a moment OLIVER returns - to find SUSAN very ready for him.

SUSAN. Oliver, why wouldn't you telephone? I thought he'd stay talking for ever! Don't you mean to send the wireless?

OLIVER. I don't think so.

SUSAN. Why not? Don't they want him back now?

OLIVER can let himself go at last; andn what's more, he can take it out of Susan.

OLIVER. Did they ever want him here? They hated him, they were afraid of him, they're thankful to be rid of him and they're furious he's gone! Poor Uncle Stephen...I caught him at Downing Street...and his temper for once did run out like a line with a fish at the end of it. You should have heard Henry Chartres over the telephone. Stop and see Eleanor's face when I tell her. Then there's Duddington, his election agent...he'll be here soon.

SUSAN *(piercing all this).* But why don't you want him back?

OLIVER *(scornfully).* He threw away a seat in the Cabinet, did he, just to go and cry at her bedside? But now it's too late he's to dodge back thanking God she didn't wait to die till he was well out on the Atlantic. Don't be so materially minded, my dear, even if you are a sentimentalist.

She is stubborn to her point, spiritedly gentle in her insistence on it. He lashes at her from any vantage he can find .

SUSAN. I didn't say I thought it right his going at all. I hadn't an idea he'd gone.

OLIVER. What a wife you'll make some day, Susan, for a successful man!

SUSAN. What's the precise point of that, please?

OLIVER. Spartan but accommodating! Ever ready to indicate the practical ideal.

SUSAN. What's to happen to this world if people won't choose their duty and stick to it though their hearts break?

OLIVER. Yes, you've the patter quite pat. Good girl...trailing with your notebook at Eleanor's heels too...giving Clumbermere and Co. marks for their interest in Social Welfare. And she's not been looking so glum lately at the wicked party politicians round the lunch table.

SUSAN. She's been glad to see him busy again...and happy.

OLIVER. Busy and happy...oh, what more is there to be! *(He even takes a turn at what he thinks is a most American phrase)* And isn't it just too wonderful to have the great men that govern the great British Empire feeding off the very next plate!

SUSAN *(who has a temper)*. Will you send that wireless?

OLIVER *(his heart speaking at last)*. No...let him go...he was glad to go.

SUSAN. Do you mean to torture him for a week with the doubt if he'll find her alive?

She pressed her advantage quite legitimately, and OLIVER owns up.

OLIVER. Ah...you have me there. Smart Susan!

SUSAN. Isn't it for him to say now whether he'll come back or not?

OLIVER. Yes. He won't.

SUSAN. I'm sure he will.

He considers this dispassionately, and with a touch of weariness, for he has been at some strain.

OLIVER. There's time enough then. If I go down to the Admiralty I can actually talk to him. I'll take you. You can tell him in a hushed voice...not too hushed, and it'll be a bit broken by the buzzing...that Joan has...passed over, is the pretty phrase, isn't it...and will he please come back and forget her.

But, now that she has made her point, SUSAN may have a fling too.

SUSAN. Oh...it's been nothing but an afternoon's delight to you...the destruction of his going. Oliver...what has maimed you so! I'm sorry...I'm very sorry. I forgot your arm.

OLIVER. Maimed in my mind, you mean?

SUSAN *(remorsefully)*. Yes.

OLIVER. I daresay.

SUSAN. It's wrong of me to be impatient just because I can't understand you...or any of you. But this talk about everything, and nothing said about anything! I think that silly old man was quite right about you, Oliver...and you don't know what you want.

OLIVER. There's a worse mischief with most of us, Susan. What we do want doesn't count. We want money and we want peace...and we want our own way. Some of us want things to look beautiful, and some want to be good. And Clumbermere gets rich without knowing why...and we statesmen sit puzzling how best to pick his pocket. And you want Evan to come back to the muddle of it all.

SUSAN *(with strait vision)*. He belongs here.

OLIVER. If he'd come back...he or another...and make short work of the lifeless lot of us!

SUSAN. Is there such a thing?

OLIVER. As what?

SUSAN. Short work.

OLIVER *(feeling, all the same, that she is getting the better of him)*. Clever child!

SUSAN. Why didn't Joan marry him? They'd have had some happiness at least...and that would have helped.

OLIVER *(a last effort)*. Why doesn't life plan out into pretty patterns and happy endings? Why isn't it all made easy for you to understand?

SUSAN. Don't mock at me any more, Oliver.

OLIVER. I'm sorry. *(Then, knowing it is truth indeed as he says it)* I only do it because I'm afraid of you.

SUSAN. Nonsense.

He looks at her, half enviously, a little fearfully.

OLIVER. You're so alive.

SUSAN *(fearlessly commonplace)*. If she loved him she should have married him.

OLIVER shakes his head.

OLIVER. Love isn't all of that sort. Sometimes it brings Judgment Day.

SUSAN. But that's when the dead awake...isn't it?

OLIVER Yes...to find this world's done with.

SUSAN is ready enough to believe there are things involved that she doesn't understand. But she means to understand them. After all, with good will, what can't be understood! OLIVER watches her, questioning himself about her, spokes the wheel of her thought occasionally.

SUSAN. I see that he had to go.

OLIVER. He didn't stop to argue it.

SUSAN. But he'll come bac...

OLIVER. If he does!

SUSAN. When he does...different.

OLIVER. Why?

SUSAN does her best to say; knows, as she says it, how flat and inadequate it must sound.

SUSAN. Loving her so to the last...and being cheated...is like dying for love.

He'll be born again...in a way.

OLIVER. You believe in miracles. You would believe in miracles. Simple Susan!

SUSAN *(simply indeed)*. Of that sort. Don't you?

OLIVER. No. *(And that ends it. SUSAN looks dashed, but recovers as quickly. He gets up saying . . .)* I'll go to the Admiralty now.

SUSAN. I'll wait for Eleanor.

OLIVER. Then you'll tell her?

SUSAN *(a smile dawning)*. That he's coming back...and that she won't know him again?

OLIVER *(grimacing for her benefit)*. Poor Evan!

SUSAN. Wouldn't you want to be raised from the dead?

OLIVER. No, indeed.

SUSAN. You'll have to be...somehow.

He stops at the door and considers her as she sits there, modest, confident— confident, it would seem merely in an honest mind and her unclouded youth. Then he says...

OLIVER. Do you wonder I'm afraid of you, Susan?

And goes out.

THE END

The Marrying of Ann Leete

1899

ACT I

The first three acts of the comedy pass in the garden at Markswayde, MR.
CARNABY LEETE'S house near Reading, during a summer day towards the close
of the eighteenth century: the first act at four in the morning, the second shortly
after mid-day, the third near to sunset. The fourth act takes place one day in the
following winter; the first scene in the hall at Markswayde, the second scene in a
cottage some ten miles off: part of the Markswayde garden looks to have been laid
out during the seventeenth century. In the middle a fountain; the centrepiece the
figure of a nymph, now somewhat cracked, and pouring nothing from the
amphora; the rim of the fountain is high enough and broad enough to be a
comfortable seat. The close turf around is in parts worn bare. This plot of ground is
surrounded by a terrace three feet higher. Three sides of it are seen. From two
corners broad steps lead down; stone urns stand at the bottom and are rounded
convexly into broad stone seats.
Along the edges of the terrace are growing rose trees, close together; behind these,
paths; behind those, shrubs and trees. No landscape is to be seen. A big copper
beech overshadows the seat on the left. A silver birch droops over the seat on the
right. The trees far to the left indicate an orchard, the few to the right are more of
the garden sort. It is the height of summer, and after a long drought the rose trees
are dilapidated .

   It is very dark in the garden. Though there may be by now a faint morning
light in the sky it has not penetrated yet among these trees. It is very still, too. Now
and then the leaves of a tree are stirred, as if in its sleep; that is all. Suddenly a
shrill, frightened, but not tragical scream is heard. After a moment ANN LEETE
runs quickly down the steps and on to the fountain, where she stops, panting.
LORD JOHN CARP follows her, but only to the top of the steps, evidently not
knowing his way. ANN is a girl of twenty: he an English gentleman, nearer forty
than thirty.

   LORD JOHN. I apologise.

   ANN. Why is it so dark?

   LORD JOHN. Can you hear what I'm saying?

   ANN. Yes.

   LORD JOHN. I apologise for having kissed you...almost unintentionally.

   ANN. Thank you. Mind the steps down.

   LORD JOHN. I hope I'm sober, but the air...

   ANN. Shall we sit for a minute? There are several seats to sit on somewhere.

   LORD JOHN. This is a very dark garden.

There is a slight pause.

   ANN. You've won your bet.

   LORD JOHN. So you did scream!

   ANN. But it wasn't fair.

   LORD JOHN. Don't reproach me.

ANN. Somebody's coming.

LORD JOHN. How d'you know?

ANN. I can hear somebody coming.

LORD JOHN. We're not sitting down.

ANN'S brother, GEORGE LEETE comes to the top of the steps, and afterwards down them. Rather an old young nan.

GEORGE. Ann!

ANN. Yes.

GEORGE. My lord!

LORD JOHN. Here.

GEORGE. I can't see you. I'm sent to say we're all anxious to know what ghost or other bird of night or beast has frightened Ann to screaming point, and won you...the best in Tatton's stables—so he says now. He's quite annoyed.

LORD JOHN. The mare is a very good mare.

ANN. He betted it because he wanted to bet; I didn't want him to bet it.

GEORGE. What frightened her?

ANN. I had rather, Lord John, that you did not tell my brother why I screamed.

LORD JOHN. I kissed her.

GEORGE. Did you?

ANN. I had rather, Lord John, that you had not told my brother why I screamed.

LORD JOHN. I misunderstood you.

GEORGE. I've broke up the whist party. Ann, shall we return?

LORD JOHN. She's not here.

GEORGE. Ann.

LADY COTTESHAM, ANN's sister and ten years older, and MR. DANIEL TATTON, a well-living, middle-aged country gentleman, arrive together. TATTON carries a double candlestick...the lights out.

MR. TATTON. Three steps?

SARAH. No...four.

LORD JOHN. Miss Leete.

TATTON in the darkness finds himself close to GEORGE.

MR. TATTON. I am in a rage with you, my lord.

GEORGE. He lives next door.

TATTON. My mistake. (*He passes on*). Confess that she did it to please you.

LORD JOHN. Screamed!

MR. TATTON. Lost my bet. We'll say...won your bet...to please you. Was skeered at the dark...oh, fie!

LORD JOHN. Miss Leete trod on a toad.

MR. TATTON. I barred toads...here.

LORD JOHN. I don't think it.

MR. TATTON. I barred toads. Did I forget to? Well...it's better to be a sportsman.

SARAH. And whereabout is she?

ANN. (*From the corner she has slunk to*.) Here I am, Sally.

MR. TATTON. Miss Ann, I forgive you. I'm smiling, I assure you, I'm smiling.

SARAH. We all laughed when we heard you.

MR. TATTON. Which reminds me, young George Leete, had you the ace?

GEORGE. King...knave...here are the cards, but I can't see.

MR. TATTON. I had the king.

ANN. (*Quietly to her sister.*) He kissed me.

SARAH. A man would.

GEORGE. What were trumps?

MR. TATTON. What were we playing...cricket?

ANN. (*As quietly again.*) D'you think I'm blushing?

SARAH. It s probable.

ANN. I am by the feel of me.

SARAH. George, we left Papa sitting quite still.

LORD JOHN. Didn't he approve of the bet?

MR. TATTON. He said nothing.

SARAH. Why, who doesn't love sport!

MR. TATTON. I'm the man to grumble. Back a woman's pluck again... never. My lord...you weren't the one to go with her as umpire.

GEORGE. No...to be sure.

TATTON. How was it I let that pass? Playing two games at once. Haven't I cause of complaint? But a man must give and take.

The master of the house, father of GEORGE and SARAH COTTESHAM and ANN, MR. CARNABY LEETE, comes slowly down the steps, unnoticed by the others. A man over fifty—à la Lord Chesterfield.

GEORGE. (*To Lord John.*) Are you sure you're quite comfortable there?

LORD JOHN. Whatever I'm sitting on hasn't given way yet.

MR. TATTON. Don't forget that you're riding to Brighton with me.

LORD JOHN. Tomorrow.

GEORGE. To-day. Well...the hour before sunrise is no time at all.

MR. TATTON. Sixty-five miles.

LORD JOHN. What are we all sitting here for?

MR. TATTON. I say people ought to be in bed and asleep.

CARNABY. But the morning air is delightful.

MR TATTON.. (*Jumping at the new voice.*) Leete! Now, had you the ace?

CARNABY. Of course.

MR. TATTON. We should have lost that too, Lady Charlie.

SARAH. Bear up, Mr. Tat.

MR. TATTON. Come, a game of whist is a game of whist.

CARNABY. And so I strolled out after you all.

MR. TATTON. She trod on a toad.

CARNABY. (*Carelessly.*) Does she say so?

MR. TATTON. (*With mock roguishness.*) Ah!

GEORGE is on the terrace, looking to the left through the trees. TATTON is sitting on the edge of the fountain.

GEORGE. Here's the sun...to show us ourselves.

MR. TATTON. Leete, this pond is full of water!

CARNABY. Ann, if you are there...

ANN. Yes, Papa.

CARNABY. Apologise profusely; it's your garden.

ANN. Oh...

CARNABY. Coat-tails,Tatton...or worse?

MR. TATTON. (*Ruefully discovering damp spots about him.*) Nothing vastly to matter.

LORD JOHN. Hardy, well-preserved, country gentleman!

MR. TATTON. I bet I'm a younger man than you, my lord.

ANN. (*Suddenly to the company generally.*) I didn't tread upon any toad...I was kissed.

There is a pause of some discomfort.

SARAH. Ann, come here to me.

LORD JOHN. I apologised.

GEORGE. (*from the terrace.*) Are we to be insulted?

CARNABY. My dear Carp, say no more.

There is another short pause. By this it is twilight, faces can be plainly seen.

SARAH. Listen...the first bird.

MR. TATTON. Oh, dear no, they begin to sing long before this.

CARNABY. What is it now...a lark?

MR. TATTON. I don't know.

ANN. (*Quietly to SARAH.*) That's a thrush.

SARAH. (*Capping her.*) A thrush.

CARNABY. Charming!

MR. TATTON. (*To LORD JOHN.*) I don't see why you couldn't have told me how it was that she screamed.

CARNABY. Our dear Tatton! (*Sotto voce to his son.*) Hold your tongue, George.

MR. TATTON. I did bar toads and you said I didn't, and anyway I had a sort of right to know.

LORD JOHN. You know now.

SARAH. I wonder if this seat is dry.

LORD JOHN. There's been no rain for weeks.

SARAH. The roads will be dusty for you, Mr. Tat.

MR. TATTON. Just one moment. You don't mind me, Miss Ann, do you?

ANN. I don't mind much.

MR. TATTON. We said distinctly...To the orchard end of the garden and back and if frightened—that's the word—so much as to scream...! Now, what I want to know is...

LORD JOHN. Consider the bet off.

MR. TATTON. Certainly not. And we should have added... Alone.

CARNABY. Tatton has persistence.

SARAH. Mr. Tat, do you know where people go who take things seriously?

MR. TATTON. Miss Leete, were you frightened when Lord John kissed you?

GEORGE. Damnation!

CARNABY. My excellent Tatton, much as I admire your searchings after truth I must here parentally intervene, regretting, my dear Tatton, that my own carelessness of duennahood has permitted this—this...to occur.

After this, there is silence for a minute.

LORD JOHN. Can I borrow a horse of you, Mr. Leete?

CARNABY. My entire stable; and your Ronald shall be physicked.

SARAH. Spartans that you are to be riding!

LORD JOHN. I prefer it to a jolting chaise.

MR. TATTON. You will have my mare.

LORD JOHN. (*Ignoring him.*) This has been a most enjoyable three weeks.

CARNABY. Four.

LORD JOHN. Is it four?

CARNABY. We bow to the compliment. Our duty to his grace.

LORD JOHN. When I see him.

GEORGE. To our dear cousin.

MR. TATTON. (*To LADY COTTESHAM.*) Sir Charles at Brighton?

SARAH. (*Not answering.*) To be sure...we did discover...our mother was second cousin...once removed to you.

CARNABY. If the prince will be there...he is in waiting.

LORD JOHN. Any message, Lady Cottesham?...since we speak out of session.

SARAH. I won't trust you.

CABNABY. Or trouble you while I still may frank a letter. But my son-in-law is a wretched correspondent. Do you admire men of small vices? They make admirable husbands though their wives will be grumbling— Silence, Sarah—but that's a good sign.

SARAH. Papa is a connoisseur of humanity.

ANN. (*To the company as before.*) No, Mr. Tatton, I wasn't frightened when Lord John...kissed me. I screamed because I was surprised, and I'm sorry I screamed.

SARAH. (*Quietly to ANN.*) My dear Ann, you re a fool.

ANN. (*Quietly to SARAH.*) I will speak sometimes.

SARAH. Sit down again.

Again an uncomfortable silence, a ludicrous air about it this time.

MR. TATTON. Now, we'll say no more about that bet, but I was right.

LORD JOHN. Do you know, Mr. Tatton, that I have a temper to lose?

MR. TATTON. What the devil does that matter to me, sir...my lord?

LORD JOHN. I owe you a saddle and bridle.

MR. TATTON. You'll oblige me by taking the mare.

LORD JOHN. We'll discuss it to-morrow.

MR. TATTON. I've said all I have to say.

GEORGE. The whole matter's ridiculous!

MR. TATTON. I see the joke. Good-night, Lady Cottesham, and I kiss your hand.

SARAH. Good morning, Mr. Tat.

MR. TATTON. Good morning, Miss Ann, I...

SARAH. (*Shielding her sister.*) Good morrow is appropriate.

MR. TATTON. I'll go by the fields. (*To CARNABY.*) Thank you for a pleasant evening. Good morrow, George. Do we start at mid-day, my lord?

LORD JOHN. Any time you please.

MR. TATTON. Not at all. (*He hands the candlestick—of which he has never before left go—to GEORGE.*) I brought this for a link. Thank you.

CARNABY. Mid-day will be midnight if you sleep at all now; make it two or later.

MR. TATTON. We put up at Guildford. I've done so before. I haven't my hat. It's a day and a half's ride.

TATTON goes quickly up the other steps and away. It is now quite light. GEORGE stands by the steps, LORD JOHN is on one of the seats, CARNABY strolls round, now and then touching the rose trees, SARAH and ANN are on the other seat.

GEORGE. Morning! These candles still smell.

SARAH. How lively one feels and isn't.

CARNABY. The flowers are opening.

ANN. (*In a whisper.*) Couldn't we go in?

SARAH. Never run away.

ANN. Everything looks so odd.

SARAH. What's o' clock...my lord?

LORD JOHN. Half after four.

ANN. (*To SARAH.*) My eyes are hot behind.

GEORGE. What ghosts we seem!

SARAH. What has made us spend such a night?

CARNABY. Ann incited me to it. (*He takes snuff*)

SARAH. In a spirit of rebellion against good country habits...

ANN. (*To her sister again.*) Don't talk about me.

SARAH. They can see that you're whispering.

CARNABY..... Informing me now she was a woman and wanted excitement.

GEORGE. There's a curse.

CARNABY. How else d'ye conceive life for women?

SARAH. George is naturally cruel. Excitement's our education. Please vary it, though.

CARNABY. I have always held that to colour in the world-picture is the greatest privilege of the husband. Sarah.

SARAH. (*Not leaving ANN'S side.*) Yes, Papa.

CARNABY. Sarah, when Sir Charles leaves Brighton...

SARAH rises but will not move further.

CARNABY. (*Sweetly threatening.*) Shall I come to you?

But she goes to him, now.

CARNABY. By a gossip letter from town...

SARAH. (*Tensely.*) What is it?

CARNABY. You mentioned to me something of his visiting Naples.

SARAH. Very well. I detest Italy.

CARNABY. Let's have George's opinion.

He leads her towards GEORGE.

GEORGE. Yes?

CARNABY. Upon Naples.

GEORGE. I remember Naples.

CARNABY. Sarah, admire those roses.

SARAH. (*Cynically echoing her father.*) Let's have George's opinion.

Now CARNABY has drawn them both away, upon the terrace, and, the coast being clear, LORD JOHN walks towards ANN, who looks at him very scaredly.

CARNABY. Emblem of secrecy among the ancients.

SARAH. Look at this heavy head, won't it snap off?

The three move out of sight.

LORD JOHN. I'm sober now.

ANN. I'm not.

LORD JOHN. Uncompromising young lady.

ANN. And, excuse me, I don't want to...play.

LORD JOHN. Don't you wish me to apologise quietly, to you?

ANN. Good manners are all mockery, I'm sure.

LORD JOHN. I'm very much afraid you're a cynic.

ANN. I'm not trying to be clever.

LORD JOHN. Do I tease you?

ANN. Do I amuse you?

LORD JOHN. How dare I say so!

ANN. (*After a moment.*) I was not frightened.

LORD JOHN. You kissed me back.

ANN. Not on purpose. What do two people mean by behaving so...in the dark ?

LORD JOHN. I am exceedingly sorry that I hurt your feelings.

ANN. Thank you, I like to feel.

LORD JOHN. And you must forgive me.

ANN. Tell me, why did you do it?

LORD JOHN. Honestly I don't know. I should do it again.

ANN. That's not quite true, is it?

LORD JOHN. I think so.

ANN. What does it matter at all!

LORD JOHN. Nothing.

GEORGE, SARAH and then CARNABY move into sight and along the terrace, LORD JOHN turns to them.

LORD JOHN. Has this place been long in your family, Mr. Leete?

CARNABY. Markswayde my wife brought us, through the Peters's...old Chiltern people...connections of yours, of course. There is no entail.

LORD JOHN walks back to ANN.

SARAH. George, you assume this republicanism as you would—no, would not—a coat of latest cut.

CARNABY. Never argue with him...persist.

SARAH. So does he.

The three pass along the terrace.

ANN. (*To LORD JOHN.*) Will you sit down?

LORD JOHN. It's not worth while. Do you know I must be quite twice your age?

ANN. A doubled responsibility, my lord.

LORD JOHN. I suppose it is.

ANN. I don't say so. That's a phrase from a book...sounded well.

LORD JOHN. My dear Miss Ann...(*He stops.*)

ANN. Go on being polite.

LORD JOHN. If you'll keep your head turned away.

ANN. Why must I?

LORD JOHN. There's lightning in the glances of your eye.

ANN. Do use vulgar words to me.

LORD JOHN. (*With a sudden fatherly kindness.*) Go to bed...you're dead tired. And good-bye...I'll be gone before you wake.

ANN. Good-bye.

She shakes hands with him, then, walks towards her father who is coming down the steps.

ANN. Papa, don't my roses want looking to?

CARNABY. (*Pats her cheek.*) These?

ANN. Those.

CARNABY. Abud is under your thumb, horticulturally speaking.

ANN. Where's Sally?

She goes on to SARAH, who is standing with GEORGE at the top of the steps. CARNABY looks LORD JOHN up and down.

LORD JOHN. (*Dusting his shoulder.*) This cursed powder!

CARNABY. Do we respect innocence enough...any of us?

GEORGE comes down the steps and joins them.

GEORGE. Respectable politics will henceforth be useless to me.

CARNABY. My lord, was his grace satisfied with the young man's work abroad or was he not?

LORD JOHN. My father used to curse everyone.

CARNABY. That's a mere Downing Street custom.

LORD JOHN. And I seem to remember that a letter of yours from....where were you in those days?

GEORGE. Paris...Naples...Vienna.

LORD JOHN. One place...once lightened a fit of gout.

CARNABY. George, you have in you the makings of a minister.

GEORGE. No.

CARNABY. Remember the Age tends to the disreputable.

GEORGE moves away, SARAH moves towards them.

CARNABY. George is something of a genius, stuffed with theories and possessed of a curious conscience. But I am fortunate in my children.

LORD JOHN. All the world knows it.

CARNABY. (*To SARAH.*) It's lucky that yours was a love match, too. I admire you. Ann is 'to come,' so to speak.

SARAH. (*To LORD JOHN.*) Were you discussing affairs?

LORD JOHN. Not I.

GEORGE. Ann.

ANN. Yes, George.

She goes to him; they stroll together up the steps and along the terrace.

SARAH. I'm desperately fagged.

LORD JOHN. (*Politely.*) A seat.

SARAH. Also tired of sitting.

CARNABY. Let's have the Brighton news, Carp.

LORD JOHN. If there's any.

CARNABY. Probably I still command abuse. Even my son-in-law must, by courtesy, join in the cry...ah, poor duty-torn Sarah! You can spread abroad that I am as a green bay tree.

CARNABY paces slowly away from them.

LORD JOHN. Your father's making a mistake.

SARAH. D'you think so?

LORD JOHN. He's played the game once.

SARAH. I was not then in the knowledge of things when he left you.

LORD JOHN. We remember it.

SARAH. I should like to hear it.

LORD JOHN. I have avoided this subject.

SARAH. With him, yes.

LORD JOHN. Oh!...why did I desert the army for politics ?

SARAH. Better fighting.

LORD JOHN. It sat so nobly upon him...the leaving us for conscience sake when we were strongly in power. Strange that six months later we should be turned out.

SARAH. Papa was lucky.

LORD JOHN. But this second time...?

SARAH. Listen. This is very much a private quarrel with Mr. Pitt, who hates Papa...gets rid of him.

LORD JOHN. Shall I betray a confidence?

SARAH. Better not

LORD JOHN. My father advised me to this visit.

SARAH. Your useful visit. More than kind of his grace.

LORD JOHN. Yes...there's been a paragraph in the *Morning Chronicle*. 'The Whigs woo Mr. Carnaby Leete'.

SARAH. We saw to it.

LORD JOHN. My poor father seems anxious to discover whether the Leete episode will repeat itself entirely. He is chronically unhappy in opposition. Are your husband and his colleagues trembling in their seats?

SARAH. I can't say.

LORD JOHN. Politics is a game for clever children, and women, and fools. Will you take a word of warning from a soldier? Your father is past his prime.

CARNABY *paces back towards them.*

CARNABY. I'm getting to be old for these all-night sittings. I must be writing to your busy brother.

LORD JOHN. Arthur?...is at his home.

SARAH. Pleasantly sounding phrase.

CARNABY. His grace deserted?

SARAH. Quite secretaryless!

LORD JOHN. Lady Arthur lately has been brought to bed. I heard yesterday.

SARAH. The seventh, is it not? Children require living up to. My congratulations.

LORD JOHN. Won't you write them?

SARAH. We are not intimate.

CARNABY is sitting on the fountain rim; he dips handkerchief in the water, and wrings it; then takes off his wig and binds the damp handkerchief round his head.

CARNABY. Wigs are most comfortable and old fashioned...unless you choose to be a cropped republican like my son.

GEORGE. Nature!

CARNABY. Nature grows a beard, sir.

LORD JOHN. I've seen Turks.

CARNABY. Horrible...horrible! Sit down, Carp.

LORD JOHN sits on the fountain rim, GEORGE begins to pace restlessly; he has been nursing the candlestick ever since TATTON handed it to him.

CARNABY. George, you look damned ridiculous strutting arm-in-arm with that candlestick.

GEORGE. I am ridiculous.

CARNABY. If you're cogitating over your wife and her expectations...

GEORGE paces up the steps and away. There is a pause.

CARNABY. D'ye tell stories...good ones?

LORD JOHN. Sometimes.

CARNABY. There'll be this.

LORD JOHN. I shan't.

CARNABY. Say no more. If I may so express myself, Carp, you have been taking us for granted.

LORD JOHN. How wide awake you are! I'm not.

CARNABY. My head's cool. Shall I describe your conduct as an unpremeditated insult?

LORD JOHN. Don't think anything of the sort.

CARNABY. There speaks your kind heart.

LORD JOHN. Are you trying to pick a quarrel with me?

CARNABY. As may be.

LORD JOHN. Why?

CARNABY. For the sake of appearances.

LORD JOHN. Damn all appearances.

CARNABY. Now I'll lose my temper. Sir, you have compromised my daughter.

LORD JOHN. Nonsense!

CARNABY. Villain! What's your next move?

For a moment LORD JOHN sits with knit brows.

LORD JOHN. (*brutally.*) Mr. Leete, your name stinks.

CARNABY. My point of dis-ad-vantage!

LORD JOHN. (*Apologising.*) Please say what you like. I might have put my remark better.

CARNABY. I think not; the homely Saxon phrase is our literary dagger. Princelike, you ride away from Markswayde. Can I trust you not to stab a socially sick man? Why it's a duty you owe to society...to weed out...us.

LORD JOHN. I'm not a coward. How?

CARNABY. A little laughter...in your exuberance of health.

LORD JOHN. You may trust me not to tell tales.

CARNABY. Of what...of whom?

LORD JOHN. Of here.

CARNABY. And what is there to tell of here?

LORD JOHN. Nothing.

CARNABY. But how your promise betrays a capacity for good-natured invention!

LORD JOHN. If I lie call me out.

CARNABY. I don't deal in sentiment. I can't afford to be talked about otherwise than as I choose to be. Already the Aunt Sally of the hour; having under pressure of circumstances resigned my office; dating my letters from the borders of the Chiltern Hundreds...I am a poor politician, sir, and I must live.

LORD JOHN. I can't see that your family's infected...affected.

CARNABY. With a penniless girl you really should have been more circumspect.

LORD JOHN. I might ask to marry her.

CARNABY. My lord!

In the pause that ensues he takes up the twist of bass to play with.

LORD JOHN. What should you say to that?

CARNABY. The silly child supposed she loved you.

LORD JOHN. Yes.

CARNABY. Is it a match?

LORD JOHN. (*Full in the other's face.*) What about the appearances of black-mail?

CARNABY. (*Compressing his thin lips.*) Do you care for my daughter?

LORD JOHN. I could...at a pinch.

CARNABY. Now, my lord, you are insolent.

LORD JOHN. Is this when we quarrel?

CARNABY. I think I'll challenge you.

LORD JOHN. That will look well.

CARNABY. You'll value that kiss when you've paid for it. Kindly choose Tatton as your second. I want his tongue to wag both ways.

LORD JOHN. I was forgetting how it all began.

CARNABY. George will serve me...protesting. His principles are vile, but he has the education of a gentleman. Swords or...? Swords. And at noon shall we say? There's shade behind a certain barn, midway between this and Tatton's.

LORD JOHN. (*Not taking him seriously yet.*) What if we both die horridly?

CARNABY. You are at liberty to make me a written apology.

LORD JOHN. A joke's a joke.

CARNABY deliberately strikes him in the face with the twist of bass.

    LORD JOHN. That's enough.

    CARNABY. (*In explanatory apology.*) My friend, you are so obtuse. Abud!

    LORD JOHN. Mr. Leete, are you serious ?

    CARNABY. Perfectly serious. Let's go to bed. Abud, you can get to your work.

Wig in hand, MR. LEETE courteously conducts his guest towards the house. ABUD returns to his tools and his morning's work.

ACT II

LORD JOHN. A good woman.

SARAH. Evidently. Where's Ann? We'll go in.

LORD JOHN. You're a mother to your sister.

SARAH. Not I.

CARNABY. My wife went her ways into the next world; Sarah hers into this; and our little Ann was left with a most admirable governess. One must never reproach circumstances. Man educates woman in his own good time.

LORD JOHN. I suppose she, or any young girl, is all heart.

CARNABY. What is it that you call heart...sentimentally speaking?

SARAH. Any bud in the morning.

LORD JOHN. That man Tatton's jokes are in shocking taste.

CARNABY. Tatton is honest.

LORD JOHN. I'm much to blame for having won that bet.

CARNABY. Say no more.

LORD JOHN. What can Miss Ann think of me?

SARAH. Don't ask her.

CARNABY. Innocency's opinions are invariably entertaining.

LORD JOHN. Am I the first...? I really beg your pardon.

GEORGE and ANN come down the steps together.

CARNABY. Ann, what do you think...that is to say—and answer me truthfully...what at this moment is your inclination of mind towards my lord here?

ANN. I suppose I love him.

LORD JOHN. I hope not.

ANN. I suppose I love you.

CARNABY. No..no..no..no..no..no..no.

SARAH. Hush, dear.

ANN. I'm afraid, papa, there's something very ill-bred in me.

Down the steps and into the midst of them comes JOHN ABUD, carrying his tools, among other things a twist of bass. A young gardener, honest, clean and common.

ABUD. (To CARNABY.) I ask pardon, sir.

CARNABY. So early, Abud!...this is your territory. So late...Bed.

ANN starts away up the steps, SARAH is following her.

LORD JOHN. Good-bye, Lady Cottesham.

At this ANN stops for a moment, but then goes straight on.

SARAH. A pleasant journey.

SARAH departs too.

GEORGE. (Stretching himself.) I'm roused.

CARNABY. (TO ABUD.) Leave your tools here for a few moments.

ABUD. I will, sir.

ABUD leaves them, going along the terrace and out of sight.

CARNABY. My head is hot. Pardon me.

Shortly after mid-day, while the sun beats strongly upon the terrace, ABUD is working dexterously at the rose trees. DR. REMNANT comes down the steps, hatted, and carrying a stick and a book. He is an elderly man with a kind manner; type of the eighteenth century casuistical parson. On his way he stops to say a word to the gardener.

DR. REMNANT. Will it rain before nightfall?

ABUD. About then, sir, I should say.

Down the other steps comes MRS. OPIE, a prim, decorous, but well bred and unobjectionable woman. She is followed by ANN.

MRS. OPIE. A good morning to you, Parson.

DR. REMNANT. And to you, Mrs. Opie, and to Miss Ann.

ANN. Good morning, Dr. Remnant. (*To ABUD.*) Have you been here ever since...?

ABUD. I've had dinner, Miss.

ABUD'S work takes him gradually out of sight.

MRS. OPIE. We are but just breakfasted.

DR. REMNANT. I surmise dissipation.

ANN. (*To MRS. OPIE.*) Thank you for waiting five hours.

MRS. OPIE. It is my rule to breakfast with you.

DR. REMNANT. (*Exhibiting the book.*) I am come to return, and to borrow.

ANN. Show me.

DR. REMNANT. Ballads by Robert Burns.

ANN. (*Taking it.*) I'll put it back.

MRS. OPIE. (*Taking it from her.*) I've never heard of him.

DR. REMNANT. Oh, ma'am, a very vulgar poet!

GEORGE LEETE comes quickly down the steps.

GEORGE. (*To REMNANT.*) How are you?

DR. REMNANT. Yours, sir.

GEORGE. Ann.

ANN. Good morning, George.

GEORGE. Did you sleep well?

ANN. I always do...but I dreamt.

GEORGE. I must sit down for a minute. (*Nodding.*) Mrs. Opie.

MRS. OPIE. I wish you a good morning, sir.

GEORGE. (*To ANN.*) Don't look so solemn.

LADY COTTESHAM comes quickly to the top of the steps.

SARAH. Is Papa badly hurt?

ANN. (*Jumping up.*) Oh, what has happened?

GEORGE. Not badly.

SARAH. He won't see me.

His three chidren look at each other.

DR. REMNANT. (*Tactfully.*) May I go my ways to the library?

SARAH. Please do, Doctor Remnant.

DR. REMNANT. I flatly contradicted all that was being said in the village.

SARAH. Thoughtful of you.

DR. REMNANT. But tell me nothing.

DR. REMNANT bows formally and goes. GEORGE is about to speak when SARAH with a look at MRS. OPIE says...

SARAH. George, hold your tongue.

MRS. OPIE. (*With much hauteur.*) I am in the way.

At this moment DIMMUCK, an old but unbenevolent-looking butler, comes to the top of the steps.

DIMMUCK. The master wants Mrs. Opie.

MRS. OPIE. Thank you.

GEORGE. Your triumph!

MRS. OPIE is departing radiant.

DIMMUCK. How was I to know you was in the garden?

MRS. OPIE. I am sorry to have put you to the trouble of search, Mr. Dimmuck.

DIMMUCK. He's in his room.

And he follows her towards the house.

GEORGE. Carp fought with him at twelve o' clock.

The other two cannot speak from amazement.

SARAH. No!

GEORGE. Why, they didn't tell me and I didn't ask. Carp was laughing. Tatton chuckled...afterwards.

SARAH. What had he to do?

GEORGE. Carp's second.

SARAH. Unaccountable children!

GEORGE. Feather parade...throw in...parry quarte: over the arm...put by: feint...flanconade and through his arm...damned easy. The father didn't wince or say a word. I bound it up...the sight of blood makes me sick.

After a moment, SARAH turns to ANN.

SARAH. Yes, and you've been a silly child.

GEORGE. Ah, give me a woman's guess and the most unlikely reason to account for anything!

ANN. I hate that man. I'm glad Papa's not hurt. What about a surgeon?

GEORGE. No, you shall kiss the place well, and there'll be poetic justice done.

SARAH. How did you all part?

GEORGE. With bows and without a word.

SARAH. Coming home with him?

GEORGE. Not a word.

SARAH. Papa's very clever; but I'm puzzled.

GEORGE. Something will happen next, no doubt.

ANN. Isn't this done with?

SARAH. So it seems.

ANN. I should like to be told just what the game has been.

GEORGE. Bravo, Ann.

ANN. Tell me the rules...for next time.

SARAH. It would have been most advantageous for us to have formed an alliance with Lord John Carp, who stood here for his father and his father's party...now in opposition.

GEORGE. Look upon yourself—not too seriously—Ann, as the instrument of political destiny.

ANN. I'm afraid I take in fresh ideas very slowly. Why has Papa given up the Stamp Office?

SARAH. His colleagues wouldn't support him.

ANN. Why was that?

SARAH. They disapproved of what he did.

ANN. Did he do right...giving it up?

SARAH. Yes.

GEORGE. We hope so. Time will tell. An irreverent quipster once named him Carnaby Leech.

SARAH. I know.

GEORGE. I wonder if his true enemies think him wise to have dropped off the Stamp Office?

ANN. Has he quarrelled with Sir Charles?

SARAH. Politically.

ANN. Isn't that awkward for you?

SARAH. Not a bit.

GEORGE. Hear a statement that includes our lives. Markswayde goes at his death...see reversionary mortgage. The income's an annuity now. The cash in the house will be ours. The debts are paid...at last.

ANN. And there remains me.

GEORGE. Bad grammar. Meanwhile our father is a tongue, which is worth buying; but I don't think he ought to go over to the enemy...for the second time.

SARAH. One party is as good as another; each works for the same end, I should hope.

GEORGE. I won't argue about it.

ANN. I suppose that a woman's profession is marriage.

GEORGE. My lord has departed.

ANN. There'll be others to come. I'm not afraid of being married.

SARAH. What did Papa want Mrs. Opie for?

ANN. There'll be a great many things I shall want to know about men now.

GEORGE. Wisdom cometh with sorrow...oh, my sister.

SARAH. I believe you two are both about as selfish as you can be.

GEORGE. I am an egotist...with attachments.

ANN. Make use of me.

GEORGE. Ann, you marry—when you marry—to please yourself.

ANN. There's much in life that I don't like, Sally.

SARAH. There's much more that you will.

GEORGE. I think we three have never talked together before.

ABUD, who has been in sight on the terrace for a few moments, now comes down the steps.

ABUD. May I make so bold, sir, as to ask how is Mrs. George Leete?

GEORGE. She was well when I last heard.

ABUD. Thank you, sir.

And he returns to his work.

ANN. I wonder will it be a boy or a girl.

GEORGE. Poor weak woman.

SARAH. Be grateful to her.

ANN. A baby is a wonderful thing.

SARAH. Babyhood in the abstract...beautiful.

ANN. Even kittens...

She stops, and then in rather childish embarrassment, moves away from them.

SARAH. Don't shudder, George.

GEORGE. I have no wish to be a father. Why?

SARAH. It's a vulgar responsibility.

GEORGE. My wayside flower!

SARAH. Why pick it?

GEORGE. Sarah, I love my wife.

SARAH. That's easily said.

GEORGE. She should be here.

SARAH. George, you married to please yourself.

GEORGE. By custom her rank is my own.

SARAH. Does she still drop her aitches?

GEORGE. Dolly...

SARAH. Pretty name.

GEORGE. Dolly aspires to be one of us.

SARAH. Child-bearing makes these women blowzy.

GEORGE. Oh heaven!

ANN. (*Calling to ABUD on the terrace.*) Finish to-day, Abud. If it rains...

She stops, seeing MR. TETGEEN standing at the top of the steps leading from the house. This is an intensely respectable, selfcontained-looking lawyer, but a man of the world too.

MR. TETGEEN. Lady Cottesham.

SARAH. Sir?

MR. TETGEEN. My name is Tetgeen.

SARAH. Mr. Tetgeen. How do you do?

MR. TETGEEN. The household appeared to be in some confusion and I took the liberty to be my own messenger. I am anxious to speak with you.

SARAH. Ann, dear, ask if Papa will see you now.

DIMMUCK appears.

DIMMUCK. The master wants you, Miss Ann.

SARAH. Ask papa if he'll see me soon.

ANN goes towards the house.

SARAH. Dimmuck, Mr. Tetgeen has been left to find his own way here.

DIMMUCK. I couldn't help it, my lady.

And he follows ANN.

SARAH. Our father is confined to his room.

GEORGE. By your leave.

Then GEORGE takes himself off up the steps, and out of sight. The old lawyer bows to LADY COTTESHAM, who regards him steadily.

MR. TETGEEN. From Sir Charles...a talking machine.

SARAH. Please sit.

He sits carefully upon the rim of the fountain, she upon the seat opposite.

SARAH. (*Glancing over her shoulder.*) Will you talk nonsense until the gardener is out of hearing? He is on his way away. You have had a tiring journey?

MR. TETGEEN. Thank you, no...by the night coach to Reading and thence I have walked.

SARAH. The country is pretty, is it not?

MR. TETGEEN. It compares favourably with other parts.

SARAH. Do you travel much, Mr. Tetgeen? He has gone.

MR. TETGEEN. (*Deliberately and sharpening his tone ever so little.*) Sir Charles does not wish to petition for a divorce.

SARAH. (*Controlling even her sense of humour.*) I have no desire to jump over the moon.

MR. TETGEEN. His scruples are religious. The case would be weak upon some important points, and there has been no public scandal...at the worst, very little.

SARAH. My good manners are, I trust, irreproachable, and you may tell Sir Charles that my conscience is my own.

MR. TETGEEN. Your husband's in the matter of...

SARAH. Please say the word.

MR. TETGEEN. Pardon me...not upon mere suspicion.

SARAH. Now, is it good policy to suspect what is incapable of proof?

MR. TETGEEN. I advise Sir Charles, that, should you come to an open fight, he can afford to lose.

SARAH. And have I no right to suspicions?

MR. TETGEEN. Certainly. Are they of use to you?

SARAH. I have been a tolerant wife, expecting toleration.

MR. TETGEEN. Sir Charles is anxious to take into consideration any complaints you may have to make against him.

SARAH. I complain if he complains of me.

MR. TETGEEN. For the first time, I think...formally.

SARAH. Why not have come to me?

MR. TETGEEN. Sir Charles is busy.

SARAH. (*Disguising a little spasm of pain.*) Shall we get to business?

MR. TETGEEN now takes a moment to find his phrase.

MR. TETGEEN. I don't know the man's name.

SARAH. This, surely, is how you might address a seduced housemaid.

MR. TETGEEN. But Sir Charles and he, I understand, have talked the matter over.

The shock of this brings SARAH to her feet, white with anger.

SARAH. Divorce me.

MR. TETGEEN. (*Sharply.*) Is there ground for it?

SARAH. (*With a magnificent recovery of self control.*) I won't tell you that.

MR. TETGEEN. I have said we have no case...that is to say, we don't want one; but any information is a weapon in store.

SARAH. You did quite right to insult me.

MR. TETGEEN. As a rule I despise such methods.

SARAH. It's a lie that they met...those two men?

MR. TETGEEN. It may be.

SARAH. It must be.

MR. TETGEEN. I have Sir Charles's word.

Now he takes from his pocket some notes, putting on his spectacles to read them.

SARAH. What's this...a written lecture?

MR. TETGEEN. We propose...first: that the present complete severance of conjugal relations shall continue. Secondly: that Lady Cottesham shall be at liberty to remove from South Audley Street and Ringham Castle all personal and private effects, excepting those family jewels which have merely been considered her property. Thirdly: Lady Cottesham shall undertake, formally and in writing not to molest—a legal term—Sir Charles Cottesham. (*Her handkerchief has dropped, here he picks it up and hands it to her.*) Allow me, my lady.

SARAH. I thank you.

MR. TETGEEN. (*Continuing.*) Fourthly: Lady Cottesham shall undertake ...etc...not to inhabit or frequent the city and towns of London, Brighthelmstone, Bath, The Tunbridge Wells, and York. Fifthly: Sir Charles Cottesham will, in acknowledgement of the maintenance of this agreement, allow Lady C. the sum of two hundred and fifty pounds per annum, which sum he considers sufficient for the upkeep of a small genteel establishment; use of the house known as Pater House, situate some seventeen miles from the Manor of Barton-le-Street, Yorkshire; coals from the mine adjoining; and from the home farm, milk, butter and eggs. (*Then he finds a further note.*) Lady Cottesham is not to play cards.

SARAH. I am a little fond of play.

MR. TETGEEN. There is no question of jointure.

SARAH. None. Mr. Tetgeen...I love my husband.

MR. TETGEEN. My lady...I will mention it.

SARAH. Such a humorous answer to this. No...don't. What is important? Bread and butter...and eggs. Do I take this?

MR. TETGEEN. (*Handing her the paper.*) Please.

SARAH. (*With the ghost of a smile.*) I take it badly.

MR. TETGEEN. (*Courteously capping her jest.*) I take my leave.

SARAH. This doesn't call for serious notice? I've done nothing legal by accepting it?

MR. TETGEEN. There's no law in the matter; it's one of policy.

SARAH. I might bargain for a bigger income. (*MR. TETGEEN bows.*) On the whole I'd rather be divorced.

MR. TETGEEN. Sir Charles detests scandal.

SARAH. Besides there's no case...is there?

MR. TETGEEN. Sir Charles congratulates himself.

SARAH. Sir Charles had best not bully me so politely...tell him.

MR. TETGEEN. My lady!

SARAH. I will not discuss this impertinence. Did those two men meet and talk...chat together? What d'you think of that?

MR. TETGEEN. 'Twas very practical. I know that the woman is somehow the outcast.

SARAH. A bad woman...an idle woman! But I've tried to do so much that lay to my hands without ever questioning...! Thank you, I don't want this retailed to my husband. You'll take a glass of wine before you go?

MR. TETGEEN. Port is grateful.

She takes from her dress two sealed letters.

SARAH. Will you give that to Sir Charles...a letter he wrote me which I did not open. This, my answer which I did not send.

He takes the one letter courteously, the other she puts back.

SARAH. I'm such a coward, Mr. Tetgeen.

MR. TETGEEN. May I say how sorry...?

SARAH. Thank you.

MR. TETGEEN. And let me apologise for having expressed one opinion of my own.

SARAH. He wants to get rid of me. He's a bit afraid of me, you know, because I fight...and my weapons are all my own. This'll blow over.

MR. TETGEEN. (*With a shake of the head.*) You are to take this offer as final.

SARAH. Beyond this?

MR. TETGEEN. As I hinted, I am prepared to advise legal measures.

SARAH. I could blow it over...but I won't perhaps. I must smile at my husband's name. Butter and eggs...and milk. I should grow fat.

ANN appears suddenly.

ANN. We go to Brighton to-morrow! (*and she comes excitedly to her sister.*)

SARAH. Was that duel a stroke of genius?

ANN. All sorts of things are to happen.

SARAH. (*Turning from her to MR. TETGEEN.*) And you'll walk as far as Reading?

MR. TETGEEN. Dear me, yes.

SARAH. (*To ANN.*) I'll come back.

SARAH takes MR. TETGEEN towards the house. ANN seats herself. After a moment LORD JOHN CARP, his clothes dusty with some riding, appears from the other quarter. She looks up to find him gazing at her.

LORD JOHN. Ann, I've ridden back to see you.

ANN. (*After a moment.*) We're coming to Brighton tomorrow.

LORD JOHN. Good.

ANN. Papa's not dead.

LORD JOHN. (*With equal cheerfulness.*) That's good.

ANN. And he said we should be seeing more of you.

LORD JOHN. Here I am. I love you, Ann. (*He goes on his knees.*)

ANN. D'you want to marry me?

LORD JOHN. Yes.

ANN. Thank you very much; it'll be very convenient for us all. Won't you get up?

LORD JOHN. At your feet.

ANN. I like it.

LORD JOHN. Give me your hand.

ANN. No.

LORD JOHN. You're beautiful.

ANN. I don't think so. You don't think so.

LORD JOHN. I do think so.

ANN. I should like to say I don't love you.

LORD JOHN. Last night you kissed me.

ANN. Do get up, please.

LORD JOHN. As you wish.

Now he sits by her.

ANN. Last night you were nobody in particular...to me.

LORD JOHN. I love you.

ANN. Please don't; I can't think clearly.

LORD JOHN. Look at me.

ANN. I'm sure I don't love you because you're making me feel very uncomfortable and that wouldn't be so.

LORD JOHN. Then we'll think.

ANN. Papa...perhaps you'd rather not talk about Papa.

LORD JOHN. Give yourself to me.

ANN. (*Drawing away from him.*) Four words! There ought to be more in such a sentence...it's ridiculous. I want a year to think about its meaning. Don't speak.

LORD JOHN. Papa joins our party.

ANN. That's what we're after...thank you.

LORD JOHN. I loathe politics.

ANN. Tell me something against them.

LORD JOHN. In my opinion your father's not a much bigger blackguard—I beg your pardon—than the rest of us.

ANN.... Miserable sinners.

LORD JOHN. Your father turns his coat. Well...?

ANN. I see nothing at all in that.

LORD JOHN. What's right and what's wrong?

ANN. Papa's right...for the present.

ANN. When shall we be married?

LORD JOHN. Tomorrow?

ANN. (*Startled.*) If you knew that it isn't easy for me to be practical you wouldn't make fun.

LORD JOHN. Why not tomorrow?

ANN. Papa—

LORD JOHN. Papa says yes..suppose.

ANN. I'm very young..not to speak of clothes. I nust have lots of new dresses.

LORD JOHN. Ask me for them.

ANN. Why do you want to marry me?

LORD JOHN. I love you.

ANN. It suddenly occurs to me that sounds unpleasant.

LORD JOHN. I love you.

ANN. Out of place.

LORD JOHN. I love you.

ANN. What if Papa were to die?

LORD JOHN. I want you.

ANN. I'm nothing..I'm nobody..I'm part of my family.

LORD JOHN. I want you.

ANN. Won't you please forget last night ?

LORD JOHN. I want you. Look straight at me.

She looks, and stays fascinated.

LORD JOHN. If I say now that I love you—

ANN. I know it.

LORD JOHN. And love me?

ANN. I suppose so.

LORD JOHN. Make sure.

ANN. But I hate you too...I know that.

LORD JOHN. Shall I kiss you?

ANN. (*Helplessly.*) Yes.

He kisses her full on the lips.

ANN. I can't hate you enough.

LORD JOHN. (*Triumphantly.*) Speak the truth now.

ANN. I feel very degraded.

LORD JOHN. Nonsense.

ANN. (*Wretchedly.*) This is one of the things which don't matter.

LORD JOHN. Ain't you to be mine?

ANN. You want the right to behave like that as well as the power.

LORD JOHN. You shall command me.

ANN. (*With a poor laugh.*) I rather like this in a way.

LORD JOHN. Little coquette!

ANN. It does tickle my vanity.

For a moment he sits looking at her, then shakes himself to his feet.

LORD JOHN. Now I must go.

ANN. Yes..I want to think.

LORD JOHN. For Heaven's sake..no!

ANN. I came this morning straight to where we were last night.

LORD JOHN. As I hung about the garden my heart was beating.

ANN. I shall like you better when you're not here.

LORD JOHN. We're to meet in Brighton?

ANN. I'm afraid so.

LORD JOHN. Good-bye.

ANN. There's just a silly sort of attraction between certain people, I believe.

LORD JOHN. Can you look me in the eyes and say you don't love me?

ANN. If I looked you in the eyes you'd frighten me again. I can say anything.

LORD JOHN. You're a deep child.

GEORGE LEETE appears on the terrace.

GEORGE. My lord!

LORD JOHN. (*Cordially.*) My dear Leete.

GEORGE. No..I am not surprised to see you.

ANN. George, things are happening.

LORD JOHN. Shake hands.

GEORGE. I will not.

ANN. Lord John asks me to be married to him. Shake hands.

GEORGE. Why did you fight?

ANN. Why did you fight?

LORD JOHN. (*Shrugging.*) Your father struck me.

ANN. Now you've hurt him..that's fair.

Then the two men do shake hands, not heartily.

GEORGE. We've trapped you, my lord.

LORD JOHN. I know what I want. I love your sister.

ANN. I don't like you..but if you're good and I'm good we shall get on.

GEORGE. Why shouldn't one marry politically?

LORD JOHN. (*In Ann's ear.*) I love you.

ANN. No..no..no..no..no..(*discovering in this an echo of her father, she stops short.*)

GEORGE. We're a cold-blooded family.

LORD JOHN. I don't think so.

GEORGE. I married for love.

LORD JOHN. Who doesn't? But, of course there should be other reasons.

GEORGE. You won't receive my wife.

LORD JOHN. Here's your sister.

LADY COTTESHAM comes from the direction of the house.

SARAH. Back again?

LORD JOHN. You see.

From the other side appears MR. TATTON.

MR. TATTON. As you all seem to be here I don't mind interrupting.

GEORGE. (*Hailing him.*) Well...neighbour?

MR. TATTON. Come..come..what's a little fighting more or less!

GEORGE. Bravo, English sentiment..relieves a deal of awkwardness.

The two shake hands.

SARAH. (*Who by this has reached LORD JOHN.*)..And back so soon?

ANN. Lord John asks to marry me.

LORD JOHN. Yes.

MR. TATTON. I guessed so..give me a bit of romance!

SARAH. (*Suavely.*) This is perhaps a little sudden, my dear Lord John. Papa may naturally be a little shocked.

GEORGE. Not at all, Sarah.

MR. TATTON. How's the wound?

GEORGE. Not serious..nothing's serious.

SARAH. You are very masterful, wooing sword in hand.

ANN. George and I have explained to Lord John that we are all most anxious to marry me to him and he doesn't mind—

LORD JOHN. Being made a fool of. I love—

ANN. I will like you.

MR. TATTON. Oh, Lord!

ANN. (*To her affianced.*) Good-bye now.

LORD JOHN. When do I see you?

ANN. Papa says soon.

LORD JOHN. Very soon, please. Tatton, my friend, Brighton's no nearer.

MR. TATTON. Lady Cottesham..Miss Leete..I kiss your hands.

LORD JOHN. (*Ebulliently clapping GEORGE on the back.*)Look more pleased. (*Then he bends over LADY COTTESHAM'S hand.*) Lady Charlie..my service to you..all. Ann. (*And he takes ANN'S hand to kiss.*)

ANN. If I can think better of all this, I shall. Good-bye.

She turns away from him. He stands for a moment considering her, but follows TATTON away through the orchard. GEORGE and SARAH are watching their sister, who then comments on her little affair with life.

ANN. I'm growing up. (*Then with a sudden tremor.*) Sally, don't let me be forced to marry.

GEORGE. Force of circumstances, my dear Ann.

ANN. Outside things. Why couldn't I run away from this garden and over the hills..I suppose there's something on the other side of the hills.

SARAH. You'd find yourself there..and circumstances.

ANN. So I'm trapped as well as that Lord John.

SARAH. What's the injury?

ANN. I'm taken by surprise and I know I'm ignorant and I think I'm learning things backwards.

GEORGE. You must cheer up and say: John's not a bad sort.

SARAH. A man of his age is a young man.

ANN. I wish you wouldn't recommend him to me.

SARAH. Let's think of Brighton. What about your gowns?

ANN. I've nothing to wear.

SARAH. We'll talk to Papa.

GEORGE. The war-purse is always a long one.

SARAH. George..be one of us for a minute.

GEORGE. But I want to look on too, and laugh.

SARAH. (*Caustically.*) Yes..that's your privilege..except occasionally. (*Then to her sister.*) I wish you all the happiness of courtship days.

GEORGE. Arcadian expression!

ANN. I believe it means being kissed..often.

SARAH. Have you not a touch of romance in you, little girl?

ANN. Am I not like Mr. Dan Tatton? He kisses dairy-maids and servants and all the farmer's daughters..I beg your pardon, George.

GEORGE. (*Nettled.*) I'll say to you, Ann, that—in all essentials—one woman is as good as another.

SARAH. That is not so in the polite world.

GEORGE. When you consider it no one lives in the polite world.

ANN. Do they come outside for air sooner or later?

SARAH. (*Briskly.*) Three best dresses you must have and something very gay if you're to go near the Pavilion.

ANN. You're coming to Brighton, Sally?

SARAH. No.

ANN. Why not?

SARAH. I don't wish to meet my husband.

GEORGE. That man was his lawyer.

ANN. The political difference, Sally?

SARAH. Just that. (*Then with a deft turn of the subject.*) I don't say that yours is a pretty face, but I should think you would have charm.

GEORGE. For fashion's sake cultivate sweetness.

SARAH. You dance as well as they know how in Reading.

ANN. Yes..I can twiddle my feet.

SARAH. Do you like dancing?

ANN. I'd sooner walk.

GEORGE. What..and get somewhere!

ANN. Here's George laughing.

SARAH. He's out of it.

ANN. Are you happy, George?

GEORGE. Alas..Dolly's disgraceful ignorance of etiquette damns us both from the beautiful drawing-room.

SARAH. That laugh is forced. But how can you...look on?

There is a slight pause in their talk. Then...

ANN. He'll bully me with love.

SARAH. Your husband will give you just what you ask for.

ANN. I hate myself too. I want to take people mentally.

GEORGE. You want a new world..you new woman.

ANN. And I'm a good bit frightened of myself.

SARAH. We have our places to fill in this. My dear child, leave futile questions alone.

GEORGE. Neither have I any good advice to give you.

ANN. I think happiness is a thing one talks too much about.

DIMMUCK appears. And by now ABUD'S work has brought him back to the terrace.

DIMMUCK. The master would like to see your Ladyship now.

SARAH. I'll say we've had a visitor...Guess.

GEORGE. And you've had a visitor, Sarah.

ANN. Papa will know.

SARAH. Is he in a questioning mood?

ANN. I always tell everything.

SARAH. It saves time.

She departs towards the house.

DIMMUCK. Mr. George.

GEORGE. What is it?

DIMMUCK. He said No to a doctor when I haven't even mentioned the matter. Had I better send..?

GEORGE. Do..if you care to waste the doctor's time.

DIMMUCK gives an offended sniff and follows LADY COTTESHAM.

ANN. I could sit here for days. George, I don't think I quite believe in anything I've been told yet.

GEORGE. What's that man's name?

ANN. John—John is a common name—John Abud.

GEORGE. Abud!

ABUD. Sir?

GEORGE. Come here.

ABUD obediently walks towards his young master and stands before him.

GEORGE. Why did you ask after the health of Mrs. George Leete?

ABUD. We courted once.

GEORGE. (*After a moment.*) Listen, Ann. Do you hate me, John Abud?

ABUD. No, sir.

GEORGE. You're a fine looking fellow. How old are you?

ABUD. Twenty-seven, sir.

GEORGE. Is Once long ago?

ABUD. Two years gone.

GEORGE. Did Mrs. Leete quarrel with you?

ABUD. No, sir.

GEORGE. Pray tell me more.

ABUD. I was beneath her.

GEORGE. But you're a fine-looking fellow.

ABUD. Farmer Crowe wouldn't risk his daughter being unhappy.

GEORGE. But she was beneath me.

ABUD. That was another matter, sir.

GEORGE. I don't think you intend to be sarcastic.

ABUD. And..being near her time for the first time, sir..I wanted to know if she is in danger of dying yet.

GEORGE. Every precaution has been taken..a nurse..there is a physician near. I need not tell you..but I do tell you.

ABUD. Thank you, sir.

GEORGE. I take great interest in my wife.

ABUD. We all do, sir.

GEORGE. Was it ambition that you courted her?

ABUD. I thought to start housekeeping.

GEORGE. Did you aspire to rise socially?

ABUD. I wanted a wife to keep house, sir.

GEORGE. Are you content?

ABUD. I think so, sir.

GEORGE. With your humble position?

ABUD. I'm a gardener, and there'll always be gardens.

GEORGE. Frustrated affections..I beg your pardon...To have been crossed in love should make you bitter and ambitious.

ABUD. My father was a gardener and my son will be a gardener if he's no worse a man than I and no better.

GEORGE. Are you married?

ABUD. No, sir.

GEORGE. Are you going to be married?

ABUD. Not especially, sir.

GEORGE. Yes..you must marry..some decent woman; we want gardeners.

ABUD. Do you want me any more now, sir?

GEORGE. You have interested me. You can go back to your work.

ABUD obeys.

GEORGE. (*Almost to himself*) I am hardly human.

He slowly moves away and out of sight.

ANN. John Abud.

He comes back and stands before her too.

ANN. I am very sorry for you.

ABUD. I am very much obliged to you, Miss.

ANN. Both those sayings are quite meaningless. Say something true about yourself.

ABUD. I'm not sorry for myself.

ANN. I won't tell. It's very clear you ought to be in a despairing state. Don't stand in the sun with your hat off.

ABUD. (*Putting on his hat.*) Thank you, Miss.

ANN. Have you nearly finished the rose-trees?

ABUD. I must work till late this evening.

ANN. Weren't you ambitious for Dolly's sake?

ABUD. She thought me good enough.

ANN. I'd have married her.

ABUD. She was ambitious for me.

ANN. And are you frightened of the big world?

ABUD. Fine things dazzle me sometimes.

ANN. But gardening is all that you're fit for?

ABUD. I'm afraid so, Miss.

ANN. But it's great to be a gardener..to sow seeds and to watch flowers grow and to cut away dead things

ABUD. Yes, Miss.

ANN. And you're in the fresh air all day.

ABUD. That's very healthy.

ANN. Are you very poor?

ABUD. I get my meals in the house.

ANN. Rough clothes last a long time.

ABUD. I've saved money.

ANN. Where do you sleep?

ABUD. At Mrs. Hart's..at a cottage..it's a mile off.

ANN. And you want no more than food and clothes and a bed and you earn all that with your hands.

ABUD. The less a man wants, Miss, the better.

ANN. But you mean to marry ?

ABUD. Yes..I've saved money.

ANN. Whom will you marry? Would you rather not say? Perhaps you don't know yet?

ABUD. It's all luck what sort of a maid a man gets fond of. It won't be a widow.

ANN. Be careful, John Abud.

ABUD. No..I shan't be careful.

ANN. You'll do very wrong to be made a fool of.

ABUD. I'm safe, Miss; I've no eye for a pretty face.

DIMMUCK arrives asthmatically at the top of the steps.

DIMMUCK. Where's Mr. George? Here's a messenger come post.

ANN. Find him, Abud.

ABUD. (To DIMMUCK.) From Dolly?

DIMMUCK. Speak respectful.

ABUD. Is it from his wife?

DIMMUCK. Go find him.

ANN. (As ABUD is immovable.) Dimmuck...tell me about Mrs. George.

DIMMUCK. She's doing well, Miss.

ABUD. (Shouting joyfully now.) Mr. George! Mr. George!

ANN. A boy or a girl, Dimmuck?

DIMMUCK. Yes, Miss.

ABUD. Mr. George! Mr. George!

DIMMUCK. Ecod . . is he somewhere else ?

DIMMUCK somewhat excited himself, returns to the house.

ANN. George!

ABUD. Mr. George! Mr. George!

GEORGE comes slowly along the terrace, in his hand an open book, which some *people might suppose he was reading. He speaks with studied calm.*

GEORGE. You are very excited, my good man.

ABUD. She's brought you a child, sir.

ANN. Your child!

GEORGE. Certainly.

ABUD. Thank God, Sir!

GEORGE. I will if I please.

ANN. And she's doing well.

ABUD. There's a messenger come post.

GEORGE. To be sure..it might have been bad news.

And slowly he crosses the garden towards the house.

ABUD. (*Suddenly, beyond all patience.*) Run..damn you!

GEORGE makes one supreme effort to maintain his dignity, but fails utterly. He gasps out...

GEORGE. Yes, I will. (*And runs off as hard as he can.*)

ABUD. (*In an ecstasy.*) This is good. Oh, Dolly and God..this is good!

ANN. (*Round eyed.*) I wonder that you can be pleased.

ABUD. (*Apologising..without apology.*) It's life.

ANN. (*Struck.*) Yes, it is.

And she goes towards the house, thinking this over.

ACT III

It is near to sunset. The garden is shadier than before. ABUD is still working. CARNABY LEETE comes from the house followed by DR. REMNANT. He wears his right arm in a sling. His face is flushed, his speech rapid.

CARNABY. Parson, you didn't drink enough wine...damme, the wine was good.

DR. REMNANT. I am very grateful for an excellent dinner.

CARNABY. A good dinner, sir, is the crown to a good day's work.

DR. REMNANT. It may also be a comfort in affliction. Our philosophy does ill, Mr. Leete, when it despises the more simple means of contentment.

CARNABY. And which will be the better lover of a woman, a hungry or a well-fed man?

DR. REMNANT. A good meal digests love with it; for what is love but a food to live by..but a hungry love will ofttimes devour its owner.

CARNABY. Admirable! Give me a man in love to deal with. Vous l'avez vu?

DR. REMNANT. Speak Latin, Greek or Hebrew to me, Mr. Leete.

CARNABY. French is the language of little things. My poor France! Ours is a little world, Parson...a man may hold it here. (*His open hand.*) Lord John Carp's a fine fellow.

DR. REMNANT. Son of a Duke.

CARNABY. And I commend to you the originality of his return. At twelve we fight...at one-thirty he proposes marriage to my daughter. D'ye see him humbly on his knees? Will there be rain, I wonder?

DR. REMNANT. We need rain...Abud?

ABUD. Badly, sir.

CARNABY. Do we want a wet journey tomorrow! Where's Sarah?

DR. REMNANT. Lady Cottesham's taking tea.

CARNABY. (*To ABUD with a sudden start.*) And why the devil didn't you marry my daughter-in-law..my own gardener?

GEORGE appears dressed for riding.

GEORGE. Good-bye, sir, for the present.

CARNABY. Boots and breeches!

GEORGE. You shouldn't be about in the evening air with a green wound in your arm. You drank wine at dinner. Be careful, sir.

CARNABY. Off to your wife and the expected?

GEORGE. Yes, sir.

CARNABY. Riding to Watford?

GEORGE. From there alongside the North Coach, if I'm in time.

CARNABY. Don't founder my horse. Will ye leave the glorious news with your grandfather at Wycombe?

GEORGE. I won't fail to. (*Then to ABUD.*) We've been speaking of you.

ABUD. It was never any secret, sir.

GEORGE. Don't apologise.

Soon after this ABUD passes out of sight.

CARNABY. Nature's an encumbrance to us, Parson.

DR. REMNANT. One disapproves of flesh uninspired.

CARNABY. She allows you no amusing hobbies...always takes you seriously.

GEORGE. Good-bye, Parson.

DR. REMNANT. (*As he bows.*) Your most obedient.

CARNABY. And you trifie with damnable democracy, with pretty theories
of the respect due to womanhood and now the result...hark to it squalling.

DR. REMNANT. Being fifty miles off might not one say: The cry of the
new-born?

CARNABY. Ill-bred babies squall. There's no poetic glamour in the world
will beautify an undesired infant...George says so.

GEORGE. I did say so.

CARNABY. I feel the whole matter deeply.

GEORGE half laughs.

CARNABY. George, after days of irritability, brought to bed of a smile.
That's a home thrust of a metaphor.

GEORGE laughs again.

CARNABY. Twins!

GEORGE. Yes, a boy and a girl...I'm the father of a boy and a girl.

CARNABY. (*In dignifed, indignant horror.*) No one of you dared tell me that
much!

SARAH and ANN come from the house.

GEORGE. You could have asked me for news of your grandchildren.

CARNABY. Twins is an insult.

SARAH. But you look very cheerful, George.

GEORGE. I am content.

SARAH. I'm surprised.

GEORGE. I am surprised.

SARAH. Now what names for them?

CARNABY. No family names, please.

GEORGE. We'll wait for a dozen years or so and let them choose their
own.

DR. REMNANT. But, sir, christening will demand—

CARNABY. Your son should have had my name, sir.

GEORGE. I know the rule..as I have my grandfather's which I take no
pride in.

SARAH. George!

GEORGE. Not to say that it sounds his, not mine.

CARNABY. Our hopes of you were high once.

GEORGE. Sarah, may I kiss you? (*He kisses her cheek.*) Let me hear what you decide to do.

CARNABY. The begetting you, sir, was a waste of time.

GEORGE. (*Quite pleasantly.*) Don't say that.

At the top of the steps ANN is waiting for him.

ANN. I'll see you into the saddle.

GEORGE. Thank you, sister Ann.

ANN. Why didn't you leave us weeks ago?

GEORGE. Why!

They pace away, arm-in-arm.

CARNABY. (*Bitterly.*) Glad to go! Brighton, Sarah.

SARAH. No, I shall not come, Papa.

CARNABY. Coward. (*Then to REMNANT.*) Good-night.

DR. REMNANT. (*Covering the insolent dismissal.*) With your kind permission I will take my leave. (*Then he bows to SARAH.*) Lady Cottesham.

SARAH. (*Curtseying.*) Doctor Remnant, I am yours.

CARNABY. (*Sitting by the fountain, stamping his foot.*) Oh, this cracked earth! Will it rain..will it rain?

DR. REMNANT. I doubt now. That cloud has passed.

CARNABY. Soft, pellucid rain! There's a good word and I'm not at all sure what it means.

DR. REMNANT. Per.. lucere...letting light through.

REMNANT leaves them.

CARNABY. Soft, pellucid rain!...thank you. Brighton, Sarah.

SARAH. Ann needs new clothes.

CABNABY. See to it.

SARAH. I shall not be there.

She turns from him.

CARNABY. Pretty climax to a quarrel!

SARAH. Not a quarrel.

CARNABY. A political difference.

SARAH. Don't look so ferocious.

CARNABY. My arm is in great pain and the wine's in my head.

SARAH. Won't you go to bed?

CARNABY. I'm well enough..to travel. This marriage makes us safe, Sarah ..an anchor in each camp..There's a mixed metaphor.

SARAH. If you'll have my advice, Papa, you'll keep those plans clear from Ann's mind.

CARNABY. John Carp is so much clay..a man of forty ignorant of himself.

SARAH. But if the Duke will not.

CARNABY. The Duke hates a scandal.

SARAH. Does he detest scandal!

CARNABY. The girl is well-bred and harmless..why publicly quarrel with

John and incense her old brute of a father? There's the Duke in a score of words. He'll take a little time to think it out so.

SARAH. And I say: Do you get on the right side of the Duke once again, - that's what we've worked for—and leave these two alone.

CARNABY. Am I to lose my daughter?

SARAH. Papa..your food's intrigue.

CARNABY. Scold at Society..and what's the use?

SARAH. We're over-civilized.

ANN rejoins them now. The twilight is gathering.

CARNABY. My mother's very old...your grandfather's younger and seventy-nine...he swears I'll never come into the title. There's little else.

SARAH. You're feverish..why are you saying this?

CARNABY. Ann..George..George via Wycombe..Wycombe Court..Sir George Leete baronet, Justice of the Peace, Deputy Lieutenant..the thought's tumbled. Ann, I first saw your mother in this garden..there.

ANN. Was she like me?

SARAH. My age when she married.

CARNABY. She was not beautiful..then she died.

ANN. Mr. Tatton thinks it a romantic garden.

CARNABY. (*Pause.*) D'ye hear the wind sighing through that tree?

ANN. The air's quite still.

CARNABY. I hear myself sighing..when I first saw your mother in this garden...that's how it was done.

SARAH. For a woman must marry.

CARNABY. (*Rises.*) You all take to it as ducks to water..but apple sauce is quite correct..I must not mix metaphors.

MRS. OPIE comes from the house.

SARAH. Your supper done, Mrs. Opie?

MRS. OPIE. I eat little in the evening.

SARAH. I believe that saves digestion.

MRS. OPIE. Ann, do you need me more to-night?

ANN. Not any more.

MRS. OPIE. Ann, there is gossip among the servants about a wager...

ANN. Mrs. Opie, that was...yesterday.

MRS. OPIE. Ann, I should be glad to be able to contradict a reported.. embrace.

ANN. I was kissed.

MRS. OPIE. I am shocked.

CARNABY. Mrs. Opie, is it possible that all these years I have been nourish- ing a prude in my..back drawingroom?

MRS. OPIE. I presume I am discharged of Ann's education; but as the salaried mistress of your household. Mr. Leete, I am grieved not to be able to deny such a rumour to your servants.

She sails back, righteously indignant.

CARNABY. Call out that you're marrying the wicked man..comfort her.

SARAH. Mrs Opie!

CARNABY. Consider that existence. An old maid..so far as we know. Brevet rank..missis. Not pleasant.

ANN. She wants nothing better..at her age.

SARAH. How forgetful!

CARNABY. (*The force of the phrase growing.*) Brighton, Sarah.

SARAH. Now you've both read the love-letter which Tetgeen brought me.

CARNABY. Come to Brighton.

ANN. Come to Brighton, Sally.

SARAH. No. I have been thinking. I think I will accept the income, the house, coals, butter and eggs.

CARNABY. I give you a fortnight to bring your husband to his knees..to your feet.

SARAH. I'm not sure that I could. My marriage has come naturally to an end.

CARNABY. Sarah, don't annoy me.

SARAH. Papa, you joined my bridegroom's political party..now you see fit to leave it.

She glances at ANN, who gives no sign, however.

CARNABY. What have you been doing in ten years?

SARAH. Waiting for this to happen..now I come to think.

CARNABY. Have ye the impudence to tell me that ye've never cared for your husband?

SARAH. I was caught by the first few kisses; but he...

CARNABY. Has he ever been unkind to you?

SARAH. Never. He's a gentleman through and through...quite charming to live with.

CARNABY. I see what more you expect. And he neither drinks nor..nor.. no one even could suppose your leaving him.

SARAH. No. I'm disgraced.

CARNABY. Fight for your honour.

SARAH. You surprise me sometimes by breaking out into cant phrases.

CARNABY. What is more useful in the world than honour?

SARAH. I think we never had any..we!

CARNABY. Give me more details. Tell me, who is this man?

SARAH. I'm innocent..if that were all.

ANN. Sally, what do they say you've done?

SARAH. I cry out like any poor girl.

CARNABY. There must be no doubt that you're innocent. Why not go for to force Charles into court?

SARAH. My innocence is not of the sort which shows up well.

CARNABY. Hold publicity in reserve. No fear of the two men arranging to meet, is there?

SARAH. They've met..and they chatted about me.

CARNABY. (*After a moment.*) There's sound humour in that.

SARAH. I shall feel able to laugh at them both from Yorkshire.

CARNABY. God forbid! Come to Brighton..we'll rally Charles no end.

SARAH. Papa, I know there's nothing to be done.

CARNABY. Coward!

SARAH. Besides I don't think I want to go back to my happiness.

They are silent for a little.

CARNABY. How still! Look..leaves falling already. Can that man hear what we're saying?

SARAH. (*To ANN.*) Can Abud overhear?

ANN. I've never talked secrets in the garden before to-day. (*Raising her voice but a very little.*) Can you hear me, Abud?

No reply comes.

CARNABY. Evidently not. There's brains shown in a trifle.

SARAH. Does your arm pain you so much?

ANN. Sarah, this man that you're fond of and that's not your husband is not by any chance Lord John Carp?

SARAH. No.

ANN. Nothing would surprise me.

SARAH. You are witty..but a little young to be so hard.

CARNABY. Keep to your innocent thoughts.

ANN. I must study politics.

SARAH. We 'll stop talking of this.

ANN. No..let me listen..quite quietly.

CARNABY. Let her listen..she's going to be married.

SARAH. Good luck, Ann.

CARNABY. I have great hopes of Ann.

SARAH. I hope she may be heartless. To be heartless is to be quite safe.

CARNABY. Now we detect a taste of sour grapes in your mouth.

SARAH. Butter and eggs.

CARNABY. We must all start early in the morning. Sarah will take you, Ann, round the Brighton shops..fine shops. You shall have the money...

SARAH. I will not come with you.

CARNABY. (*Vexedly.*) How absurd..how ridiculous..to persist in your silly sentiment.

SARAH. (*Her voice rising.*) I'm tired of that world..which goes on and on, and there's no dying..one grows into a ghost..visible..then invisible. I'm glad paint has gone out of fashion..the painted ghosts were very ill to see.

CARNABY. D'ye scoff at civilisation?

SARAH. Look ahead for me.

CARNABY. Banished to a hole in the damned provinces! But you're young yet, you're charming..you're the wife..and the honest wife of one of the country's best men. My head aches. D'ye despise good fortune's gifts? Keep as straight in your place in the world as you can. A monthly packet of books to Yorkshire..no.. you never were fond of reading. Ye'd play patience..cultivate chess problems.. kill yourself!

SARAH. When one world fails take another.

CARNABY. You have no more right to commit suicide than to desert the society you were born into. My head aches.

SARAH. George is happy.

CARNABY. D'ye dare to think so?

SARAH. No..it's a horrible marriage.

CARNABY. He's losing refinement..mark me..he no longer polishes his nails.

SARAH. But there are the children now.

CARNABY. You never have wanted children.

SARAH. I don't want a little child.

CARNABY. She to be Lady Leete..some day..soon! What has he done for his family?

SARAH. I'll come with you. You are clever, Papa. And I know just what to say to Charles.

CARNABY. (*With a curious change of tone.*) If you study anatomy you'll find that the brain, as it works, pressing forward the eyes..thought is painful. Never be defeated. Chapter the latest ..the tickling of the Carp. And my throat is dry..shall I drink that water?

SARAH. No, I wouldn't.

CARNABY. Not out of my hand?

ANN. (*Speaking in a strange quiet voice, after her long silence.*) I will not come to Brighton with you.

CARNABY. Very dry!

ANN. You must go back, Sally.

CARNABY. (*As he looks at her, standing stiffly.*) Now what is Ann's height.. five feet ..?

ANN. Sally must go back, for she belongs to it..but I'll stay here where I belong.

CARNABY. You've spoken three times and the words are jumbling in at my ears meaninglessly. I certainly took too much wine at dinner..or else....Yes.. Sally goes back..and you'll go forward. Who stays here? Don't burlesque your sister. What's in the air..what disease is this?

ANN. I mean to disobey you.. to stay here..never to be unhappy.

CARNABY. So pleased!

ANN. I want to be an ordinary woman..not clever..not fortunate.

CARNABY. I can't hear.

ANN. Not clever. I don't believe in you, Papa.

CARNABY. I exist..I'm very sorry.

ANN. I won't be married to any man. I refuse to be tempted..I won't see him again.

CARNABY. Yes. It's raining.

SARAH. Raining!

CARNABY. Don't you stop it raining.

ANN. (*In the same level tones, to her sister now, who otherwise would turn, alarmed, to their father.*) And I curse you..because, we being sisters, I suppose I am much what you were, about to be married; and I think, Sally, you'd have cursed your present self. I could become all that you are and more..but I don't choose.

SARAH. Ann, what is to become of you?

CARNABY. Big drops..big drops!

At this moment ABUD is passing towards the house, his work finished.

ANN. John Abud..you mean to marry. When you marry..will you marry me?

A blank silence, into which breaks CARNABY'S sick voice.

CARNABY. Take me indoors. I heard you ask the gardener to marry you.

ANN. I asked him.

CARNABY. I heard you say that you asked him. Take me in..but not out of the rain.

ANN. Look..he's straight-limbed and clear eyed..and I'm a woman.

SARAH. Ann, are you mad?

ANN. If we two were alone here in this garden and everyone else in the world were dead..what would you answer?

ABUD. (*Still amazed*) Why..yes.

CARNABY. Then that's settled..pellucid.

He attempts to rise, but staggers backwards and forwards. SARAH goes to him alarmed.

SARAH. Papa!..there's no rain yet.

CARNABY. Hush, I'm dead.

ANN. (*Her nerves failing her.*) Oh..oh..oh..!

SARAH. Abud, don't ever speak of this.

ABUD. No, my lady.

ANN. (*With a final effort.*) I mean it all. Wait three months.

CARNABY. Help me up steps...son-in-law.

CARNABY has started to grope his way indoors. But he reels and falls helpless.

ABUD. I'll carry him.

Throwing down his tools ABUD lifts the frail sick man and carries him towards the house. SARAH follows.

ANN. (*Sobbing a little, and weary.*) Such a long day it has been..now ending.
She follows too.

ACT IV

The hall at Markswayde is square; in decoration strictly eighteenth century. The floor polished. Then comes six feet of soberly painted wainscot and above the greenish blue and yellowish green wall painted into panels. At intervals are low relief pilasters; the capitals of these are gilded. The ceiling is white and in the centre of it there is a frosted glass dome through which a dull light struggles. Two sides only of the hall are seen.

In the corner is a hat stand and on it are many cloaks and hats and beneath it several pairs of very muddy boots.

In the middle of the left hand wall are the double doors of the dining-room led up to by three or four stairs with balusters, and on either side standing against the wall long, formal, straight backed sofas.

In the middle of the right hand wall is the front door; glass double doors can be seen and there is evidently a porch beyond. On the left of the front door a small window. On the right a large fireplace, in which a large fire is roaring. Over the front door, a clock (the hands pointing to half-past one.) Over the fireplace a family portrait (temp. Queen Anne), below this a blunderbuss and several horse-pistols. Above the sofa full-length family portraits (temp. George I). Before the front door a wooden screen, of lighter wood than the wainscot, and in the middle of it a small glass panel. Before this a heavy square table on which are whips and sticks, a hat or two and brushes; by the table a wooden chair. On either side the fire stand tall closed-in armchairs, and between the fireplace and the door a smaller red-baize screen.

When the dining-room doors are thrown open another wooden screen is to be seen. There are a few rugs on the floor, formally arranged.

MRS. OPIE stands in the middle of the hall, holding out a woman's brown cloak: she drops one side to fetch out her handkerchief and apply it to her eye. DIMMUCK comes in by the front door, which he carefully closes behind him. He is wrapped in a hooded cloak and carries a pair of boots and a newspaper. The boots he arranges to warm before the fire. Then he spreads the Chronicle newspaper upon the arm of a chair, then takes off his cloak and hangs it upon a peg close to the door.

DIMMUCK. Mrs. Opie.. will you look to its not scorching?

MRS. OPIE still mops her eyes. DIMMUCK goes towards the dining-room door, but turns.

DIMMUCK. Will you kindly see that the *Chronicle* newspaper does not burn?

MRS. OPIE. I was crying.

DIMMUCK. I leave this tomorrow sennight..thankful, ma'am, to have given notice in a dignified manner.

MRS. OPIE. I understand..Those persons at table..

DIMMUCK. You give notice.

MRS. OPIE. Mr. Dimmuck, this is my home.

LORD ARTHUR CARP comes out of the dining-room. He is a thinner and more earnest-looking edition of his brother. MRS. OPIE turns a chair and hangs the cloak to warm before the fire, and then goes into the dining-room.

LORD ARTHUR. My chaise round?

DIMMUCK. I've but just ordered it, my lord. Your lordship's man has give me your boots.

LORD ARTHUR. Does it snow?

DIMMUCK. Rather rain than snow.

LORD ARTHUR takes up the newspaper.

DIMMUCK. Yesterday's, my lord.

LORD ARTHUR. I've seen it. The mails don't hurry hereabouts. Can I be in London by the morning?

DIMMUCK. I should say you might be, my lord.

LORD ARTHUR sits by the fire, while DIMMUCK takes off his pumps and starts to put on his boots.

LORD ARTHUR. Is this a horse called "Ronald?"

DIMMUCK. Which horse, my lord?

LORD ARTHUR. Which I'm to take back with me..my brother left here. I brought the mare he borrowed.

DIMMUCK. I remember, my lord. I'll enquire.

LORD ARTHUR. Tell Parker..

DIMMUCK. Your lordship's man?

LORD ARTHUR. ..he'd better ride the beast.

SARAH comes out of the dining-room. He stands up; one boot, one shoe.

SARAH. Please put on the other.

LORD ARTHUR. Thank you..I am in haste.

SARAH. To depart before the bride's departure.

LORD ARTHUR. Does the bride go with the bridegroom?

SARAH. She goes away.

LORD ARTHUR. I shall never see such a thing again.

SARAH. I think this entertainment is unique.

LORD ARTHUR. Any commissions in town?

SARAH. Why can't you stay to travel with us tomorrow and talk business to Papa by the way?

DIMMUCK carrying the pumps and after putting on his cloak goes out through the front door. When it is closed, her voice changes.

SARAH. Why..Arthur?

He does not answer. Then MRS. OPIE comes out of the dining-room to fetch the cloak. The two, with an effort, reconstruct their casual disjointed conversation.

SARAH..Before the bride's departure?

LORD ARTHUR. Does the bride go away with the bridegroom?

SARAH. She goes.

LORD ARTHUR. I shall never see such an entertainment again.

SARAH. We are quite unique.

LORD ARTHUR. Any commissions in town?

SARAH. Is she to go soon too, Mrs. Opie?

MRS. OPIE. It is arranged they are to walk..in this weather..ten miles..to the house.

SARAH. Cottage.

MRS. OPIE. Hut.

MRS. OPIE takes the cloak into the dining-room. Then SARAH comes a little towards LORD ARTHUR, but waits for him to speak.

LORD ARTHUR. (*A little awkwardly.*) You are not looking well.

SARAH. To our memory..and beyond your little chat with my husband about me..I want to speak an epitaph.

LORD ARTHUR. Charlie Cottesham behaved most honourably.

SARAH. And I think you did. Why have you not let me tell you so in your ear till now, to-day?

LORD ARTHUR. Sarah..we had a narrow escape from...

SARAH. How's your wife?

LORD ARTHUR. Well..thank you.

SARAH. Nervous, surely, at your travelling in winter?

LORD ARTHUR. I was so glad to receive a casual invitation from you and to come..casually.

SARAH. Fifty miles.

LORD ARTHUR. Your father has been ill?

SARAH. Very ill through the autumn.

LORD ARTHUR. Do you think he suspects us?

SARAH. I shouldn't care to peep into Papa's innermost mind. You are to be very useful to him.

LORD ARTHUR. No.

SARAH. Then he'll go back to the government.

LORD ARTHUR. If he pleases..if they please..if you please.

SARAH. I am not going back to my husband. Arthur...be useful to him.

LORD ARTHUR. No..you are not coming to me. Always your father! (*After a moment.*) It was my little home in the country somehow said aloud you didn't care for me.

SARAH. I fooled you to small purpose.

LORD ARTHUR. I wish you had once made friends with my wife.

SARAH. If we..this house I'm speaking of..had made friends where we've only made tools and fools we shouldn't now be cursed as we are..all. George, who is a cork, trying to sink socially. Ann is mad..and a runaway.

LORD ARTHUR. Sarah, I've been devilish fond of you.

SARAH. Be useful to Papa. (*He shakes his head, obstinately.*) Praise me a little. Haven't I worked my best for my family?

LORD ARTHUR. Suppose I could be useful to him now, would you, in spite of all, come to me..no half measures?

SARAH. Arthur..(*He makes a little passionate movement towards her, but she is cold* .) It's time for me to vanish from this world, because I've nothing left to sell.

LORD ARTHUR. I can't help him. I don't want you.

He turns away.

SARAH. I feel I've done my best.

LORD ARTHUR. Keep your father quiet.

SARAH. I mean to leave him.

LORD ARTHUR. What does he say to that?

SARAH. I've not yet told him.

LORD ARTHUR. What happens?

SARAH. To sell my jewels..spoils of a ten years' war. Three thousand pound..how much a year?

LORD ARTHUR. I'll buy them.

SARAH. And return them? You have almost the right to make such a suggestion.

LORD ARTHUR. Stick to your father. He'll care for you?

SARAH. No..we all pride ourselves on our lack of sentiment.

LORD ARTHUR. You must take money from your husband.

SARAH. I have earned that and spent it.

LORD ARTHUR. (*Yielding once again to temptation.*) I'm devilish fond of you...

At that moment ABUD comes out of the dining-room. He is dressed in his best. SARAH responds readily to the interruption.

SARAH. And you must give my kindest compliments to Lady Arthur and my..affectionately..to the children and I'll let Papa know that you're going.

LORD ARTHUR. Letters under cover to your father?

SARAH. Papa will stay in town through the session of course..but they all tell me that seventy-five pounds a year is a comfortable income in..Timbuctoo.

She goes into the dining-room. ABUD has selected his boots from the corner and now stands with them in his hand looking rather helpless. After a moment—

LORD ARTHUR. I congratulate you, Mr. Abud.

ABUD. My lord..I can't speak of myself.

CARNABY comes out of the dining-room. He is evidently by no means recovered from his illness. He stands for a moment with an ironical eye on JOHN ABUD.

CARNABY. Son-in-law.

ABUD. I'm told to get on my boots, sir.

CARNABY. Allow me to assist you?

ABUD. I couldn't, sir.

CARNABY. Désolé!

Then he passes on. ABUD sits on the sofa, furtively puts on his boots and afterwards puts his shoes in his pockets.

LORD ARTHUR. You were so busy drinking health to the two fat farmers that I wouldn't interrupt you.

CARNABY. Good-bye. Describe all this to your brother John.

LORD ARTHUR. So confirmed a bachelor!

CARNABY. Please say that we missed him.

LORD ARTHUR hands him the newspaper.

LORD ARTHUR. I've out-raced your *Chronicle* from London by some hours. There's a paragraph..second column..near the bottom.

CARNABY. (*Looking at it blindly.*) They print villainously now-a-days.

LORD ARTHUR. Inspired.

CARNABY. I trust his grace is well?

LORD ARTHUR. Gouty.

CARNABY. Now doesn't the social aspect of this case interest you?

LORD ARTHUR. I object to feeding with the lower classes.

CARNABY. There's pride! How useful to note their simple manners! From the meeting of extremes new ideas spring..new life.

LORD ARTHUR. Take that for a new social-political creed, Mr. Leete.

CARNABY. Do I lack one?

LORD ARTHUR. Please make my adieux to the bride.

CARNABY. Appropriate...'à Dieu'...she enters Nature's cloister. My epigram.

LORD ARTHUR. But..good heavens..are we to choose to be toiling animals?

CARNABY. To be such is my daughter's ambition.

LORD ARTHUR. You have not read that.

CARNABY. (*Giving back the paper, vexedly.*) I can't see.

LORD ARTHUR. "The Right Honourable Carnaby Leete is, we are glad to hear, completely recovered and will return to town for the opening of Session."

CARNABY. I mentioned it.

LORD ARTHUR. "We understand that although there has been no reconciliation with the Government it is quite untrue that this gentleman will in any way resume his connection with the Opposition."

CARNABY. Inspired?

LORD ARTHUR. I am here from my father to answer any questions.

CARNABY. (*With some dignity and the touch of a threat.*) Not now, my lord.

DIMMUCK comes in at the front door.

DIMMUCK. The chaise, my lord.

CARNABY. I will conduct you.

LORD ARTHUR. Please don't risk exposure.

CARNABY. Nay, I insist.

LORD ARTHUR. Health and happiness to you both, Mr. Abud.

LORD ARTHUR goes out, followed by CARNABY, followed by DIMMUCK. At that moment MR. SMALLPEICE skips excitedly out of the dining-room. A ferret-like little lawyer.

MR. SMALLPEICE. Oh..where is Mr. Leete?

Not seeing him MR. SMALLPEICE skips as excitedly back into the dining-room. DIMMUCK returns and hangs up his cloak then goes towards ABUD, whom he surveys.

DIMMUCK. Sir!

With which insult he starts for the dining-room reaching the door just in time to hold it open for SIR GEORGE LEETE who comes out. He surveys ABUD for a moment, then explodes.

SIR GEORGE LEETE. Damn you..stand in the presence of your grand-father-in-law.

ABUD stands up. CARNABY returns coughing, and SIR GEORGE looks him up and down.

SIR GEORGE LEETE. I shall attend your funeral.

CARNABY. My daughter Sarah still needs me.

SIR GEORGE LEETE. I wonder at you, my son.

CARNABY. Have you any money to spare?

SIR GEORGE LEETE. No.

CARNABY. For Sarah, my housekeeper; I foresee a busy session.

ABUD is now gingerly walking up the stairs.

SIR GEORGE LEETE. Carnaby..look at that.

CARNABY. Sound in wind and limb. Tread boldly, son-in-law.

ABUD turns, stands awkwardly for a moment and then goes into the dining-room.

SIR GEORGE LEETE. (*Relapsing into a pinch of snuff*) I'm calm.

CARNABY. Regard this marriage with a wise eye..as an amusing little episode.

SIR GEORGE LEETE. Do you?

CARNABY. And forget its oddity. Now that the humiliation is irrevocable, is it a personal grievance to you?

SIR GEORGE LEETE. Give me a dinner a day for the rest of my life and I'll be content.

CARNABY. Lately, one by one, opinions and desires have been failing me... a flicker and then extinction. I shall shortly attain to being a most able critic upon life.

SIR GEORGE LEETE. Shall I tell you again? You came into this world without a conscience. That explains you and it's all that does. That such a damnable coupling as this should be permitted by God Almighty..or that the law shouldn't interfere! I've said my say.

MR. SMALLPEICE again comes out of the dining-room.

MR. SMALLPEICE. Mr Leete.

CARNABY. (*Ironically polite.*) Mr. Smallpeice.

MR. SMALLPEICE. Mr. Crowe is proposing your health.

MR. CROWE comes out. A crop-headed beefy-looking farmer of sixty.

MR. CROWE. Was.

CARNABY. There's a good enemy!

MR. CROWE. Get out of my road..lawyer Smallpeice.

CARNABY. Leave enough of him living to attend to my business.

MR. SMALLPEICE. (*wriggling a bow at CARNABY.*) Oh..dear sir!

SIR GEORGE LEETE. (*Disgustedly to MR. SMALLPIECE.*) You!

MR. SMALLPEICE. Employed in a small matter..as yet.

CARNABY. (*To CROWE.*) I hope you spoke your mind of me.

MR.CROWE. Not behind your back, sir.

MRS. GEORGE LEETE leads LADY LEETE from the dining-room. LADY LEETE is a very old, blind and decrepit woman. DOLLY is a buxom young mother; whose attire borders on the gaudy.

CARNABY. (*With some tenderness.*) Well...Mother...dear?

MR. CROWE. (*Bumptiously to SIR GEORGE LEETE.*) Did my speech offend you, my lord?

SIR GEORGE LEETE. (*Sulkily.*) I'm a baronet.

LADY LEETE. Who's this here?

CARNABY. Carnaby.

DOLLY. Step down..grandmother.

LADY LEETE. Who did ye say you were?

DOLLY. Mrs. George Leete.

LADY LEETE. Take me to the fire-side.

So CARNABY and DOLLY lead her slowly to a chair by the fire where they carefully bestow her.

MR. SMALLPEICE. (*To FARMER CROWE.*) He's leaving Markswayde, you know...and me agent.

LADY LEETE. (*Suddenly bethinking her.*) Grace was not said. Fetch my chaplain..at once.

MR. SMALLPEICE. I will run,

He runs into the dining-room.

DOLLY. (*Calling after with her country accent.*) Not parson Remnant.. t'other one.

LADY LEETE. (*Demanding.*) Snuff.

CARNABY. (*To his father.*) Sir..my hand is a little unsteady.

SIR GEORGE and CARNABY between them give LADY LEETE her snuff.

MR. CROWE. Dolly...ought those children to be left so long?

DOLLY. All right, father..I have a maid.

LADY LEETE sneezes.

SIR GEORGE LEETE. She'll do that once too often altogether.

LADY LEETE. I'm cold.

DOLLY. I'm cold..I lack my shawl.

CROWE. Call out to your man for it.

DOLLY. (*Going to the dining-room door.*) Will a gentleman please ask Mr. George Leete for my Cachey-mire shawl?

MR. CROWE. (*To CARNABY.*) And I drank to the health of our grandson.

CARNABY. Now suppose George were to assume your name, Mr. Crowe?

MR. TOZER comes out of the dining-room. Of the worst type of eighteenth century parson, for which one may see Hogarth's 'Harlot's Progress.' He is very drunk.

SIR GEORGE LEETE. (*In his wife's ear.*) Tozer!

LADY LEETE. When..why!

SIR GEORGE LEETE. To say grace.

LADY LEETE folds her withered hands.

MR. TOZER. (*through his hiccoughs.*) Damn you all.

LADY LEETE. (*Reverently, thinking it is said .*) Amen.

MR. TOZER. Only my joke.

CARNABY. (*Rising to the height of the occasion.*) Mr. Tozer, I am indeed glad to see you, upon this occasion so delightfully drunk.

MR. TOZER. Always a gen'elman..by nature.

SIR GEORGE LEETE. Lie down..you dog.

GEORGE comes out carrying the cashmere shawl.

GEORGE. (*To his father.*) Dolly wants her father to rent Markswayde, sir.

MR. CROWE. Not me, my son. You're to be a farmer-baronet.

SIR GEORGE. Curse your impudence!

CARNABY. My one regret in dying would be to miss seeing him so.

GEORGE goes back into the dining room.

MR. CROWE. I am tickled to think that the man marrying your daughter wasn't good enough for mine.

CARNABY. And yet at fisticuffs, I'd back John Abud against our son George.

DR. REMNANT has come out of the dining-room.

TOZER has stumbled towards him and is wagging an argumentative finger.

MR. TOZER... Marriage means enjoyment!

DR. REMNANT. (*Controlling his indignation.*) I repeat that I have found in my own copy of the prayer book no insistence upon a romantic passion.

MR. TOZER. My 'terpretation of God's word is 'bove criticism.

MR. TOZER reaches the door and falls into the dining-room.

CARNABY. (*Weakly to DR. REMNANT.*) Give me your arm for a moment.

DR. REMNANT. I think Lady Cottesham has Mrs. John Abud prepared to start, sir.

CARNABY. I trust Ann will take no chill walking through the mud.

DR. REMNANT. Won't you sit down, sir?

CARNABY. No.

For some moments CROWE has been staring indignantly at SIR GEORGE. Now he breaks out.

MR. CROWE. The front door of this mansion is opened to a common gardener and only then to me and mine!

SIR GEORGE LEETE. (*Virulently.*) Damn you and yours and damn them...and damn you again for the worse disgrace.

MR. CROWE. Damn you, sir..have you paid him to marry the girl?

He turns away, purple faced and SIR GEORGE chokes impotently. ABUD and MR. PRESTIGE come out talking. He is younger and less assertive than FARMER CROWE.

MR. PRESTIGE. (*Pathetically.*) All our family always has got drunk at weddings.

ABUD. (*In remonstrance.*) Please, uncle.

CARNABY. Mr. Crowe..I have been much to blame for not seeking you sooner.

MR. CROWE. (*Mollified.*) Shake hands.

CARNABY. (*Offering his with some difficulty.*) My arm is stiff..from an accident. This is a maid's marriage, I assure you.

MR. PRESTIGE. (*Open mouthed to DR. REMNANT.*) One could hang bacon here!

DOLLY. (*Very high and mighty.*) The family don't.

CARNABY. (*To his father.*) And won't you apologise for your remarks to Mr. Crowe, sir?

LADY LEETE. (*Demanding.*) Snuff!

CARNABY. And your box to my mother, sir.

SIR GEORGE attends to his wife.

DOLLY. (*Anxiously to DR. REMNANT.*) Can a gentleman change his name?

MR. CROWE. Parson..once noble always noble, I take it.

DR. REMNANT. Certainly..but I hope you have money to leave them, Mr. Crowe.

DOLLY. (*To ABUD.*) John.

ABUD. Dorothy

DOLLY. You've not seen my babies yet.

LADY LEETE sneezes.

SIR GEORGE LEETE. Carnaby..d'ye intend to murder that Crowe fellow...or must I?

MR. SMALLPEICE skips from the dining-room.

MR. SMALLPEICE. Mr. John Abud..

MR. CROWE. (*To DR. REMNANT as he nods towards CARNABY.*) Don't tell me he's got over that fever yet.

MR. SMALLPEICE...The ladies say..are you ready or are you not?

MR. PRESTIGE. I'll get thy cloak, John.

MR. PRESTIGE goes for the cloak. CARNABY has taken a pistol from the mantel-piece and now points it at ABUD.

CARNABY. He's fit for heaven!

GEORGE LEETE comes from the dining-room and noticing his father's action says sharply..

GEORGE. I suppose you know that pistol's loaded. *Which calls everyone's attention. DOLLY shrieks.*

CARNABY. What if there had been an accident!

And he puts back the pistol. ABUD takes his cloak from PRESTIGE.

ABUD. Thank you, uncle.

MR. PRESTIGE. I'm a proud man. Mr. Crowe..

CARNABY. Pride!

GEORGE. (*Has a sudden inspiration and strides up to ABUD.*) Here ends the joke, my good fellow. Be off without your wife.

ABUD stares, as do the others. Only CARNABY suddenly catches REMNANT'S arm.

MR. PRESTIGE. (*Solemnly.*) But it's illegal to separate them.

GEORGE. (*Giving up*). Mr. Prestige..you are the backbone of England.

CARNABY. (*To REMNANT.*) Where are your miracles?

MRS. PRESTIGE comes out. A motherly farmer's wife, a mountain of a woman.

MRS. PRESTIGE. John..kiss your aunt.

ABUD goes to her, and she obliterates him in an embrace.

GEORGE. (*To his father.*) Sense of humour..Sense of humour!

LADY LEETE. Snuff.

But no one heeds her this time.

CARNABY. It doesn't matter.

GEORGE. Smile. Let's be helpless gracefully.

CARNABY. There are moments when I'm not sure—

GEORGE. It's her own life.

TOZER staggers from the dining-room drunker than ever. He falls against the baluster and waves his arms.

MR. TOZER. Silence there for the corpse!

MR. CROWE. You beast!

MR. TOZER. Respect my cloth..Mr. Prestige.

MR. CROWE. That's not my name.

MR. TOZER. I'll have you to know that I'm Sir George Leete's baronet's most boon companion and her la'ship never goes nowhere without me. (*He subsides into a chair.*

LADY LEETE. (*Tearfully.*) Snuff.

From the dining-room comes ANN; her head bent. She is crossing the hall when SARAH follows, calling her.

SARAH. Ann!

ANN turns back to kiss her. The rest of the company stand gazing. SIR GEORGE gives snuff to LADY LEETE.

ANN. Good-bye, Sally.

SARAH. (*In a whisper.*) Forget us.

GEORGE. (*Relieving his feelings.*) Good-bye, everybody..good-bye, everything.

ABUD goes to the front door and opening it stands waiting for her. She goes coldly, but timidly to her father, to whom she puts her face up to be kissed.

ANN. Good-bye, Papa.

CARNABY. (*Quietly, as he kisses her cheek.*) I can do without you.

SIR GEORGE LEETE. (*Raging at the draught.*) Shut that door.

ANN. I'm gone.

She goes with her husband. MRS. OPIE comes hurriedly out of the dining-room, too late.

MRS. OPIE. Oh!

DR. REMNANT. Run..Mrs. Opie.

CARNABY. There has started the new century!

MRS. OPIE opens the front door to look after them.

SIR GEORGE LEETE. (*With double energy*) Shut that door.

LADY LEETE sneezes and then chokes. There is much commotion in her neighbourhood.

SIR GEORGE. Now she's hurt again.

DOLLY. Water!

MR. CROWE. Brandy!

SARAH. (*Going.*) I'll fetch both.

GEORGE. We must all die..some day.

MR. TOZER. (*Who has struggled up to see what is the matter.*) And go to—

DR. REMNANT. Hell. You do believe in that, Mr. Toper.

MRS. OPIE. (*Fanning the poor old lady.*) She's better.

CARNABY. (*To his guests.*) Gentlemen..punch.

PRESTIGE and SMALLPEICE; MRS. PRESTIGE, GEORGE and DOLLY move towards the dining-room.

MR. PRESTIGE. (*To SMALLPEICE.*) You owe all this to me.

MR. CROWE. Dolly..I'm going.

MRS. PRESTIGE. (*To her husband as she nods towards CARNABY.*) Nathaniel..look at 'im.

GEORGE. (*To his father-in-law.*) Must we come too?

MRS. PRESTIGE. (*As before.*) I can't help it..a sneerin' carpin' cavillin' devil!

MRS. OPIE. Markswayde is to let..as I hear..Mr. Leete?

CARNABY. Markswayde is to let.

He goes on his way to the dining-room meeting SARAH who comes out carrying a glass of water and a decanter of brandy. SIR GEORGE LEETE is comfortably warming himself at the fire.

* * * * * * * * * * * *

The living room of JOHN ABUD'S new cottage has bare plaster walls and its ceilings and floor are of red brick; all fresh looking but not new. In the middle of the middle wall there is a latticed window, dimity curtained; upon the plain shelf in front are several flower-pots. To the right of this, a door, cross beamed and with a large lock to it besides the latch. Against the right hand wall is a dresser, furnished with dishes and plates: below it is a common looking grandfather clock; below this a small door which when opened shows winding stairs leading to the the room above. In the left hand wall there is a door which is almost hidden by the fireplace which juts out below it. In the fireplace a wood fire is laid but not lit. At right angles to this stands a heavy oak settle opposite a plain deal table; just beyond which is a little bench. On either side of the window is a Windsor armchair. Between the window and the door hangs a framed sampler.

In the darkness the sound of the unlocking of a door and of ABUD entering is heard. He walks to the table, strikes a light upon a tinder-box and lights a candle which he finds there. ANN is standing in the doorway. ABUD is in stocking feet.

ABUD. Don't come further. Here are your slippers.

He places one of the Windsor chairs for her on which she sits while he takes off her wet shoes and puts on her slippers which he found on the table. Then he takes her wet shoes to the fireplace. She sits still. Then he goes to the door and brings in his own boots from the little porch and puts them in the fireplace too. Then he locks the door and hangs up the key beside it. Then he stands looking at her; but she does not speak so he takes the candle, lifts it above his head and walks to the dresser.

ABUD. (*Encouragingly.*) Our dresser..Thomas Jupp made that. Plates and dishes. Here's Uncle Prestige's clock.

ANN. Past seven.

ABUD. That's upstairs. Table and bench, deal. Oak settle..solid.

ANN. Charming.

ABUD. Windsor chairs..Mother's sampler.

ANN. Home.

ABUD. Is it as you wish? I have been glad at your not seeing it until to-night.

ANN. I'm sinking into the strangeness of the place.

ABUD. Very weary? It's been a long nine miles.

She does not answer. He goes and considers the flower-pots in the window.

ANN. I still have on my cloak.

ABUD. Hang it behind the door there..no matter if the wet drips....I can wipe up the puddle.

She hangs up her cloak. He selects a flower-pot and brings it to her.

ABUD. Hyacinth bulbs for the spring.

ANN. (*After a glance.*) I don't want to hold them.

He puts back the pot, a little disappointed.

ABUD. Out there's the scullery.

ANN. It's very cold.

ABUD. If we light the fire now that means more trouble in the morning.

She sits on the settle.

ANN. Yes, I am very weary.

ABUD. Go to bed.

ANN. Not yet. (*After a moment.*) How much light one candle gives! Sit where I may see you.

He sits on the bench. She studies him curiously.

ANN. Well..this is an experiment.

ABUD. (*With reverence.*) God help us both.

ANN. Amen. Some people are so careful of their lives. If we fail miserably we'll hold our tongues..won't we?

ABUD. I don't know..I can't speak of this.

ANN. These impossible things which are done mustn't be talked of..that spoils them. We don't want to boast of this, do we?

ABUD. I fancy nobody quite believes that we are married.

ANN. Here's my ring..real gold.

ABUD. (*With a sudden fierce throw up of his head.*) Never you remind me of the difference between us.

ANN. Don't speak to me so.

ABUD. Now I'm your better.

ANN. My master..The door's locked.

ABUD. (*Nodding.*) I know that I must be..or be a fool.

ANN (*After a moment.*) Be kind to me.

ABUD (*With remorse.*) Always I will.

ANN. You are master here.

ABUD. And I've angered you?

ANN. And if I fail..I'll never tell you..to make a fool of you. And you're trembling. (*She sees his hand, which is on the table, shake*)

ABUD. Look at that now.

ANN. (*Lifting her own.*) My white hands must redden. No more dainty appetite..no more pretty books.

ABUD. Have you learned to scrub?

ANN. Not this floor.

ABUD. Mother always did bricks with a mop. Tomorrow I go to work.

You'll be left for all day.

ANN. I must make friends with the other women around.

ABUD. My friends are very curious about you.

ANN. I'll wait to begin till I'm seasoned.

ABUD. Four o'clock's the hour for getting up.

ANN. Early rising always was a vice of mine.

ABUD. Breakfast quickly...and I take my dinner with me.

ANN. In a handkerchief.

ABUD. Hot supper, please.

ANN. It shall be ready for you.

There is silence between them for a little. Then he says timidly.

ABUD. May I come near to you?

ANN. (*In a low voice.*) Come. He sits beside her, gazing.

ABUD. Wife...I never have kissed you.

ANN. Shut your eyes.

ABUD. Are you afraid of me?

ANN. We're not to play such games at love.

ABUD. I can't help wanting to feel very tender towards you.

ANN. Think of me..not as a wife..but as a mother of your children..if it's to be so. Treat me so.

ABUD. You are a part of me.

ANN. We must try and understand it..as a simple thing.

ABUD. But shall I kiss you?

ANN. (*Lowering her head.*) Kiss me.

But when he puts his arms round her she shrinks.

ANN. No.

ABUD. But I will. It's my right.

Almost by force he kisses her. Afterwards she clenches her hands and seems to suffer.

ABUD. Have I hurt you?

She gives him her hand with a strange little smile.

ANN. I forgive you.

ABUD. (*Encouraged.*) Ann..we're beginning life together.

ANN. Remember..work's enough..no stopping to tallk.

ABUD. I'll work for you.

ANN. I'll do my part..something will come of it.

For a moment they sit together hand in hand. Then she leaves him and paces across the room.

There is a slight pause.

ANN. Papa..I said..we've all been in too great a hurry getting civilised. False dawn. I mean to go back.

ABUD. He laughed.

ANN. So he saw I was of no use to him and he's penniless and he let me go. When my father dies what will he take with him?...for you do take your works with you into Heaven or Hell, I believe. Much wit. Sally is afraid to die. Don't you aspire like George's wife. I was afraid to live..and now..I am content.

She walks slowly to the window and from there to the door against which she places her ear. Then she looks round at her husband.

ANN. I can hear them chattering.

Then she goes to the little door and opens it. ABUD takes up the candle.

ABUD. I'll hold the light . . the stairs are steep.

He lights her up the stairs.

THE END